# INTERNATIONAL
# LAW REPORTS

Volume

## 25

(1958–I)

# INTERNATIONAL LAW REPORTS

VOLUME 25

(1958–I)

*Edited by*

E. LAUTERPACHT, CBE QC

*Fellow of Trinity College, Cambridge;*
*of Gray's Inn, Barrister-at-Law*

GROTIUS PUBLICATIONS

CAMBRIDGE
UNIVERSITY PRESS

# CAMBRIDGE
## UNIVERSITY PRESS

University Printing House, Cambridge CB2 8BS, United Kingdom

Cambridge University Press is part of the University of Cambridge.

It furthers the University's mission by disseminating knowledge in the pursuit of education, learning and research at the highest international levels of excellence.

www.cambridge.org
Information on this title: www.cambridge.org/9780521463706

First published by Butterworths 1963
Reprinted by Cambridge University Press 1994
Reprinted 2017

Printed in Singapore by Markono Print Media Pte Ltd

A catalog record for this publication is available from the British Library

ISBN 978-0-521-46370-6 Hardback

# PREFACE

THE earliest volumes of the *Annual Digest of Public International Law Cases* covered decisions given in two, three or even, in one case, four calendar years. The volume for 1946 was the first to be restricted to the judgments given in a single year. Now the quantity of material available is so great that, for the first time, it has been necessary to divide the cases for a single year into two parts—the present one, which contains the decisions of international tribunals, and Part II which contains the decisions of municipal courts.

The presentation of the annual material in two volumes will not remain a feature of the *International Law Reports*. Instead, the present system of volumes identified by calendar years will be replaced with one in which volumes of approximately uniform size appear as and when the appropriate amount of material reaches the Editor, without reference to the date of the cases. These volumes will be numbered consecutively. For convenience of reference in the future, the first volume in the series will be the volume of the *Annual Digest* containing decisions given in 1919–1922, which should henceforth be cited as *Annual Digest*, 1 (1919–1922). In anticipation of the new system, the volumes for 1958 carry the numbers 25 and 26 respectively. The present part should be cited as *International Law Reports*, 25 (1958–I), and Part II as *International Law Reports*, 26 (1958–II). Future volumes should be referred to by their serial numbers only.

When the new system becomes effective, it will no longer be necessary to delay the publication of decisions rendered in the courts of any one country in any particular year until all the cases decided in all countries in that year have become available. Instead, it should in due course become possible to print material in the *International Law Reports* within a relatively short time after it becomes public. The qualification involved in the use of the phrase " in due course " is required because obviously it will not be possible simply to follow the present volume, which contains cases decided in 1958, with one which contains exclusively decisions for 1961 or 1962. Unavoidably, the next few volumes of the *Reports* will be heavily weighted with cases for the years 1959, 1960 and 1961.

To help the reader to find cases, particularly during the transitional period, cumulative tables of cases will be produced more frequently. A volume containing a consolidated index, tables of cases and table of treaties for volumes 1–26 of the *Annual Digest* and *International Law Reports* series is now in preparation.

The present volumes contain two other innovations which are, however, intended to form a permanent feature of the *Reports*. In the first place, page references have been added to the Classification

v

(which has been moved to a position immediately after the Table of Contents) so that the reader may at a glance not only see in detail the topics of international law upon which the cases reported in the volume have some bearing, but also ascertain immediately where in the volume the cases may be found. Second, each volume includes a detailed Table of Treaties cited and considered. The frequency with which the decisions of international and municipal courts involve points of treaty interpretation is increasing; and it has been felt, therefore, that it would be helpful to incorporate in the volume this piece of technical apparatus which will enable the reader readily to ascertain whether any particular section of a treaty has been the subject of judicial consideration or mention. An attempt has been made to supply for each treaty at least one reference to an English text.

One other change may be mentioned. The Table of Cases Cited will no longer be included in the *Reports*. Enquiry indicates that the use made of this table does not really justify its preparation and publication.

As stated above, the present volume contains only the decisions of international tribunals. Some of these tribunals have already been fully represented in the *Reports, e.g.,* the International Court of Justice and the European Commission of Human Rights. The printing of the available decisions of the United Nations Tribunal for Libya is completed in this volume. I am grateful to the officials of the United Nations who made the texts available for publication. The opportunity has also been taken of introducing into this volume all those decisions, not previously printed in the *Reports*, of the Court of Justice of the European Coal and Steel Community given from the time of its establishment up to the end of 1958. Mr. D. G. Valentine has continued with his customary felicity the arduous task of translating these decisions into English.

Among the international tribunals which have not previously been represented in these volumes is the Arbitral Commission on Property, Rights and Interests in Germany. Dr. K. Skubiszewski has prepared twenty-eight decisions of this Commission—which is one of the busiest international courts sitting to-day—covering the period since its inception to the end of 1958. Dr. P. Merlin, Registrar of the Commission, has been very helpful in providing copies of the judgments. I should like to take this opportunity of expressing my appreciation to them. In addition, valuable decisions are included for the first time from each of the following tribunals: the Arbitral Tribunal for the Agreement on German External Debts; the Mixed Commission for the Agreement on German External Debts; and the Italian-Swiss Permanent Conciliation Commission. This last body, as a true conciliation commission, is not strictly speaking a " judicial body ". But this is an observation which from time to time could be validly made of other sources of the decisions printed in these

*Reports*; and, having regard to the content of the decision (as well as the composition of the Commission), it would seem wrong to omit material of such value. I would like to thank Dr. E. Diez, the Legal Adviser of the Swiss Federal Political Department, for bringing the decision to my attention and for supplying me with a copy of the text.

It has not been possible to include in the present volume the decisions given in 1958 either by the administrative tribunals of the various international organizations or by Professor Sauser-Hall in the arbitration between Saudi Arabia and the Arabian American Oil Company. They will be printed in volume 27 of these *Reports*.

I must record with deep regret the death of Professor Edwin D. Dickinson, the distinguished American international lawyer, who had been a member of the Advisory Committee of these *Reports* since 1932. Professor Richard R. Baxter, who has discharged with great skill and devotion the most exacting task of contributing the decisions of the United States courts, has accepted an invitation to join the Advisory Committee; and I need hardly say how glad I am that the reliance which I place upon his advice can thus be formally acknowledged.

Once again, I wish to express my gratitude, and that, I can imagine, of other users of these *Reports*, to the Ford Foundation for the continuance of its generous support.

I owe a particular debt of gratitude to Mrs. A. B. Lyons, B.Sc. (Econ.), and Miss Gillian White, Ph.D. (Lond.), from whom I have received continuous and essential help. In addition to the assistance which Miss White has given me in editing the material for the press, she has also prepared the Tables of Treaties and the Index. I also wish to thank both Mrs. E. E. Jansen, who has again prepared the Tables of Cases, and Mrs. S. Rainbow, who has provided much able secretarial help.

Lastly, I would like to express my appreciation to Messrs. Butterworth & Co. and their printers and compositors for their customary helpfulness and patience in the face of unexpected difficulties.

E. LAUTERPACHT

TRINITY COLLEGE,
CAMBRIDGE.
*November 1962.*

# ADVISORY COMMITTEE

# CONTRIBUTORS

# TABLE OF CONTENTS

[See also CLASSIFICATION]

# CLASSIFICATION

## PART I

## INTERNATIONAL LAW IN GENERAL

## PART II

## STATES AS INTERNATIONAL PERSONS

### A. IN GENERAL

### B. COMPOSITE AND DEPENDENT STATES AND TERRITORIES

# PART III

# STATE TERRITORY

# PART V
# STATE RESPONSIBILITY

## PART VI

# THE INDIVIDUAL IN INTERNATIONAL LAW

## PART VII
## DIPLOMATIC AND CONSULAR INTERCOURSE AND PRIVILEGES

## PART VIII

## TREATIES

## PART XI
## WAR AND NEUTRALITY

# TABLE OF CASES

[ALPHABETICAL]

(The figures in heavier type indicate the page numbers of the actual reports. The
ordinary type indicates pages containing notes or relevant cross-references.)

# TABLE OF CASES

## European Commission of Human Rights

## Franco-Italian Conciliation Commission

## International Court of Justice

## Italian-Swiss Permanent Conciliation Commission

## Italian-United States Conciliation Commission

## Mixed Commission for the Agreement on German External Debts

## United Nations Tribunal for Libya

# TABLE OF TREATIES

[This table contains a list, in chronological order according to the date of signature, of the treaties referred to in the decisions printed in the present volume. It has not been possible to draw a helpful distinction between treaties judicially considered and treaties which are merely cited.

In the case of bilateral treaties, the names of the parties are given in alphabetical order. Multilateral treaties are referred to by the name by which they are believed commonly to be known, *e.g.*, Hague Convention No. I of 1899; Treaty of Versailles, 1919. References to the texts of the treaties have been supplied, including wherever possible at least one reference to a text in the English language. The full titles of the abbreviated references will be found in the List of Abbreviations.]

# LIST OF ABBREVIATIONS

OF TITLES OF COLLECTIONS OF DECISIONS, LAW
REPORTS, PERIODICALS, COLLECTIONS OF TREATIES,
ETC., MENTIONED IN THE TEXT

| | |
|---|---|
| ABGB | = Allgemeines Bürgerliches Gesetzbuch (Austrian Civil Code) |
| *Actes* | = Actes [et Documents] de la Ie–IVe Conférence de la Haye chargée de réglémenter diverses matières de droit international privé (The Hague, 1893–1894, 7 vols.) |
| ADHGB | = Allgemeines Deutsche Handelsgesetzbuch (German Commercial Code) |
| ADWO | = Allgemeines Deutsche Wechselordnung (German Bills of Exchange Law) |
| A.J. (or A.J.I.L., or Am. J. Int.) | = American Journal of International Law |
| Annual Digest | = Annual Digest and Reports of Public International Law Cases |
| B.F.S.P. | = British and Foreign State Papers |
| BGB | = Bürgerliches Gesetzbuch (German Civil Code) |
| BGBl | = Bundesgerichtsblatt (Germany) |
| B.G.E. | = Entscheidungen des Bundesgerichts (Switzerland) |
| BGHZ | = Entscheidungen des Bundesgerichtshofes in Zivilsachen (Germany) |
| B.W. | = Burgerlijk Wetboek (Netherlands Civil Code) |
| Cass. | = [Decision of the] Cour de Cassation (France) |
| D.P. (or Dalloz) | = Recueil périodique et critique de Jurisprudence, de Législation et de Doctrine (founded by Dalloz; merged with Sirey, 1955) |
| EGBGB | = Einführungsgesetz zum Bürgerliches Gesetzbuch (Introductory Law of the [German] Civil Code) |
| F. (or Fed.) | = Federal Reporter (United States) |
| F.2d | = Federal Reporter, Second Series (United States) |
| HGB (or ADHGB) | = Handelsgesetzbuch (German Commercial Code) |
| Hudson | = Manley O. Hudson, International Legislation (Washington, 1931–1950) 9 vols., covering treaties from 1919–1945. |

| | | |
|---|---|---|
| I.C.J. Reports | = | International Court of Justice: Reports of Judgments, Advisory Opinions and Orders |
| Ky. | = | Kentucky Reports |
| L.N.T.S. | = | League of Nations Treaty Series |
| L.R.C.P. | = | Law Reports Common Pleas Cases (England, cases in the Common Pleas Division of the High Court, 1865–1875) |
| Martens | = | G. F. Martens, Recueil de Traités. The various series are referred to as follows: |
| Martens, R.; Martens R.2 | = | Recueil, 1st and 2nd editions respectively |
| Martens, N.R. | = | Nouveau Recueil. |
| Martens, N.R.G. | = | Nouveau Recueil Général. |
| Martens, N.R.G., 2nd ser.; Martens, N.R.G., 3rd ser. | = | Nouveau Recueil Général, 2nd and 3rd series |
| Moore, *Arb.* | = | J. B. Moore, History and Digest of the International Arbitrations to which the United States has been a Party (Washington, 1898, 6 vols.) |
| N.E. | = | Northeastern Reporter (United States) |
| N.Y. | = | New York Reports |
| Op. Attys. Gen. | = | Opinions of the Attorney General (United States) |
| OR | = | Obligationenrecht (Code des Obligations) (Swiss Law of Obligations) |
| Pas. | = | Pasicrisie Belge |
| P.C.I.J. | = | Publications of the Permanent Court of International Justice: Reports of Judgments, Advisory Opinions, Orders, and other Acts and Documents |
| Rec. des Cours | = | Recueil des Cours de l'Académie de Droit International de la Haye |
| Recueil des Décisions | = | Recueil des Décisions de la Commission Franco-Italienne (under Article 83 of the Peace Treaty with Italy, 1947) |
| Reichsanzeiger | = | Deutscher Reichsanzeiger und Preussischer Staatsanzeiger (Gazette of the German Empire and the Prussian State, 1871–1945) |
| Reports of Decisions and Advisory Opinions | = | Reports of Decisions and Advisory Opinions of the Arbitral Tribunal and Mixed Commission on German External Debts |
| R.G. | = | Rapports du Conseil fédéral à l'Assemblée fédérale sur sa gestion (Switzerland) |
| RGBl | = | Reichsgesetzblatt (Germany) |

RGR Kommentar   = Reichs gerichtsräte-Kommentar, Bürger-
BGB                    liches Gesetzbuch (Das Bürgerliche Gesetz-
buch mit besonderer Berücksichtigung des Reichsgerichts und des Bundesgerichtschofes. German Civil Code with commentary relating to the Reich Supreme Court and the Federal Supreme Court)

R.G.Z.           = Entscheidungen des Reichsgerichts in Zivilsachen (Germany)

R.O.            = Recueil officiel des lois et ordonnances de la Confédération suisse

Stat.           = United States Statutes at Large

T.A.M.         = Recueil des Décisions des Tribunaux Arbitraux Mixtes

T.I.A.S.       = Treaties and other International Acts Series (United States)

Traités        = Recueil des Traités de la France (Paris, 1880–1917) 23 vols. covering treaties from 1713–1906

U.K.T.S.      = United Kingdom Treaty Series

U.N.R.I.A.A.  = United Nations Report of International Arbitral Awards

U.N.T.S.      = United Nations Treaty Series

U.S.            = United States Reports (Supreme Court)

U.S.T.          = United States Treaties and Other International Agreements (Washington, published on a calendar year basis, covering treaties from January 1, 1950)

U.S.T.S.      = United States Treaty Series

U.S. Treaties  = Treaties, Conventions, International Acts, Protocols and Agreements between the United States of America and Other Powers, 1776–1937, compiled under the direction of the Committee on Foreign Relations of the United States Senate by Malloy (vols. 1 and 2), Redmond (vol. 3), and Trenwith (vol. 4)

Z. f. ausländ. u.  = Zeitschrift für ausländisches und internationales Privatrecht
internat.
Privatrecht

ZGB          = Zivilgesetzbuch (Swiss Civil Code)

ZR           = Unpublished decisions of the German Federal Supreme Court in civil cases.

# PART I

# INTERNATIONAL LAW
# IN GENERAL

## II.—Sources

[*See also* PART X, DISPUTES: A, I, ii, Arbitration; The Law Applied by Arbitral Tribunals.]

International law—Sources of—General principles of law— " Public policy " as a general principle—Relevance to interpretation of treaties—Hague Convention of 1902 on Guardianship of Infants.

See p. 242 (*Case concerning the Application of the Convention of 1902 Governing the Guardianship of Infants*), at p. 269.

International law—Sources of—General principles of law— Principles of private international law—Use of comparative law —Absence of uniformity of laws—Effect of.

See p. 33 (*Swiss Confederation* v. *German Federal Republic (No. 1)*).

International law—Sources of—General principles of law— Generally recognized principle—Application by Arbitral Commission.

See p. 544 (*Greek Powder & Cartridge Co.* v. *German Federal Republic*).

International law—Sources of—General principles of international law, of justice, and of equity—Application by Arbitral Commission.

See p. 527 (*Scheidt* v. *German Federal Republic (Jurisdiction)*).

## IV.—Relation to Municipal Law

[*See also* PART VIII, TREATIES: B, VII, Operation and Enforcement of Treaties, Necessity for Municipal Legislation; *and* PART VI, THE INDIVIDUAL IN INTERNATIONAL LAW: A, In General.]

International Law—Relation to municipal law—Municipal law enacted subsequent to treaty—Supremacy of international law —Provisions of Peace Treaty as *lex fori* for Conciliation Commission.

See p. 91 (*Flegenheimer Claim*), at pp. 107, 127.

# PART II

# STATES AS INTERNATIONAL PERSONS

## E—STATE SUCCESSION

## I.—Succession to Rights

**State succession—Succession to rights—Succession to State lands and buildings—Distinction between public and private State property—Succession of Libya to Italian State property in Libya —United Nations General Assembly Resolution 388 (V) of December 15, 1950, on " Economic and Financial Provisions Relating to Libya "—Interpretation of.**

ITALY *v.* UNITED KINGDOM OF GREAT BRITAIN AND NORTHERN IRELAND AND UNITED KINGDOM OF LIBYA.

GENERAL LIST NO. 1 (MERITS).

*United Nations Tribunal for Libya.*[1]  *January 31, 1953.*

(Yörükóglu, President; Wickström, Sanchez-Gavito JJ.)

THE FACTS.—This was a claim for the restoration to Italy of the administration of certain properties of the State in Libya.  The claim was based on and involved the interpretation and application of certain provisions of United Nations General Assembly Resolution 388 (V) entitled " Economic and Financial Provisions Relating to Libya ".[2]  The Preamble and paragraphs 1, 2, 3 (*a*) and 5 of Article I of the Resolution provide:

"*Whereas*, in accordance with the provisions of Article 23 and paragraph 3 of Annex XI of the Treaty of Peace with Italy, the question of the disposal of the former Italian colonies was submitted on September 15, 1948 to the General Assembly by the Governments of France, the Union of Soviet Socialist Republics, the United Kingdom of Great Britain and Northern Ireland and the United States of America,

"*Whereas*, by virtue of the above-mentioned provisions, the four Powers have agreed to accept the recommendation of the General Assembly and to take appropriate measures for giving effect to it,

"*Whereas* the General Assembly, by its resolutions of November 21, 1949, and of November 17, 1950, recommend that the independence of

---

[1] An account of the establishment of this Tribunal is given at the beginning of the report of the proceedings on the *Request for Interim Measures* in this case: see below, p. 517.

[2] *Official Records*, Fifth Session, Supplement No. 20 (A/1775).

Libya should become effective as soon as possible, and in any case not later than January 1, 1952,

"*Whereas* paragraph 19 of Annex XIV of the Treaty of Peace with Italy, which contains the economic and financial provisions relating to ceded territories, states that ' The provisions of this Annex shall not apply to the former Italian colonies. The economic and financial provisions to be applied therein will form part of the arrangements for the final disposal of these territories pursuant to Article 23 of the present Treaty ',

"*Whereas* it is desirable that the economic and financial provisions relating to Libya should be determined before the transfer of power in that territory takes place, in order that they may be applied as soon as possible,

> *The General Assembly*
>
> *Approves* the following articles:
>
> *Article I*

" 1. Libya shall receive, without payment, the movable and immovable property located in Libya owned by the Italian State, either in its own name or in the name of the Italian administration of Libya.

" 2. The following property shall be transferred immediately:

> (a) The public property of the State (*demanio pubblico*) and the inalienable property of the State (*patrimonio indisponibile*) in Libya, as well as the relevant archives and documents of an administrative character or technical value concerning Libya or relating to property the transfer of which is provided for by the present resolution;
>
> (b) The property in Libya of the Fascist Party and its organizations.

" 3. In addition, the following shall be transferred on conditions to be established by special agreement between Italy and Libya:

> (a) The alienable property (*patrimonio disponibile*) of the State in Libya and the property in Libya belonging to the autonomous agencies (*aziende autonome*) of the State.

" 5. Italy shall retain the ownership of immovable property necessary for the functioning of its diplomatic and consular services and, when the conditions so require, of the schools necessary for the present Italian community whether such property is owned by the Italian State in its own name or in the name of the Italian administration of Libya. Such immovable property shall be determined by special agreements concluded between Italy and Libya.

Article X, paragraph 1, is also relevant, and it provides:

" 1. A United Nations Tribunal shall be set up, composed of three persons selected by the Secretary-General for their legal qualifications from the nationals of three different States not directly interested. The Tribunal, whose decisions shall be based on law, shall have the following two functions:

(a) It shall give to the administering Powers, the Libyan Government after its establishment, and the Italian Government, on request by any of those authorities, such instructions as may be required for the purpose of giving effect to the present resolution;

(b) It shall decide all disputes arising between the said authorities concerning the interpretation and application of the present resolution. The Tribunal shall be seised of any such dispute on the unilateral request of one of those authorities."

The facts of the case were stated by the Tribunal as follows:

" The Memorial instituting these proceedings was presented by the Agent of the Italian Government on December 22, 1951. In it the said Agent names the British Government as the defendant and makes the following submissions:

'(a) the return to the Italian Government of the administration of its *patrimonio disponibile* in Tripolitania and Cyrenaica, of which the said Government still has the right of ownership;

(b) the restitution of the administration of the buildings listed in Annexes 3 and 4, over which the Italian Government, pending the conclusion of agreements with the Libyan Government, intends to claim ownership for the requirements of its diplomatic and consular services and of the schools in Tripolitania.'

" Libya came into being as an independent state two days after the presentation of the aforesaid Memorial, and the Tribunal, as it has declared in its decision of February 18, 1952,[1] delivered in the [*Case of the Request for*] *Interim Measures*, considered the Government of Libya as a co-defendant and communicated the Memorial to both the British and the Libyan Governments. In the same decision, the Tribunal rejected the Libyan Government Agent's exception of lack of jurisdiction, having ruled that the instant action has been properly brought before the Tribunal, its subject-matter being the transfer of the administration of properties comprised in the categories specified in Article I, paragraphs 3 (a) and 5 of the United Nations General Assembly Resolution 388 (V), dated December 15, 1950, and the said action being based as it is on Article X, paragraph 1 (b), of said Resolution 388 (V).

" In its Counter-Memorial, submitted on January 31, 1952, the British Government contends that by Article 23 (1) of the Italian Peace Treaty,[2] Italy renounced all rights and title to the Italian territorial possessions in Africa, Libya *inter alia*, and that ' the continued ownership of the property in question by Italy is incon-

[1 Reported below, p. 517.]
[2 *U.N.T.S.*, vol. 49, p. 3. Article 23 provides:
" 1. Italy renounces all right and title to the Italian territorial possessions in Africa, *i.e.* Libya, Eritrea and Italian Somaliland.
" 2. Pending their final disposal, the said possessions shall continue under their present administration.
" 3. The final disposal of these possessions shall be determined jointly by the Governments of the Soviet Union, of the United Kingdom, of the United States of America, and of France within one year from the coming into force of the present Treaty, in the manner laid down in the joint declaration of February 10, 1947, issued by the said Governments, which is reproduced in Annex I."]

sistent with such renunciation.' It is further contended in the said Counter-Memorial that Resolution 388 (V) does not convey any title to the property in question and that 'no inference as to the ownership thereof can be drawn therefrom.'

" With these two contentions as its legal basis, and after referring to the compliance by the British Government with the United Nations General Assembly Resolution of November 17, 1950, the said Counter-Memorial submits (a) that the British Government acted in a proper fashion when it handed over the property in question ' to the custody of the Government of the United Kingdom of Libya, pending a final settlement ', and (b) that the present proceedings against it are misconceived.

" With regard to the factual chapter of the Libyan Agent's Counter-Memorial, mention should be made of the statements contained therein with respect to the properties listed in Annexes 3 and 4 of the Italian Agent's Memorial, *i.e.* those properties whose administration Italy wants restituted to it in order to meet the requirements of its diplomatic and consular services in Libya and of the schools serving the Italian community in Tripolitania. The said statements read as follows:

' 3. Under arrangements made with the Italian Government, the whole of the properties listed in Annex 4 to the Memorial of the Italian Government have, for some time, been in the possession of the Italian Government for use as schools.

' 4. The Libyan Government has undertaken to give up to the Italian Government two buildings in Tripoli (included in Annex 1 to the Italian Government's Memorial) for use as diplomatic and/or consular premises. Negotiations are in progress for handing over these buildings, which are acceptable to the Italian Government.

' 5. A building in Benghazi, formerly the Tribunale Militare, has been handed over to the Italian Government for use as diplomatic and/or consular premises.'

" This same chapter of the Libyan Agent's Counter-Memorial contains the following statement with regard to the Italian Government's claim to the administration of the properties which constituted its *patrimonio disponibile* in Tripolitania and Cyrenaica, namely:

' 6. In addition to the buildings mentioned in paragraphs 3 to 5 above the Italian Government in its Memorandum claims the administration of some 500 buildings or other properties. Out of all these properties the Italian Government can, under the terms of United Nations Resolution of December 15, 1950, expect to obtain the transfer of a building in Tripoli for a hospital and one or two more buildings in Libya for diplomatic and/or consular use. In other words the Italian Government claims that because it has legitimate aspirations towards obtaining perhaps three or more buildings out of 500 properties, it ought to administer all the 500 until the three are decided upon.'

" In the chapter of the said Counter-Memorial on the law applicable to the case, the Libyan Agent reiterates the British Agent's allegations and expounds an additional thesis, namely, that even if, contrary to the contention of the respondent Governments, the Tribunal were to rule that the Italian State retains the 'technical ownership' of the properties in question, it has without a doubt surrendered its claim to the 'beneficial ownership, use and enjoyment of all the properties with the exception of the few required for diplomatic and/or consular use, and use as schools and hospitals, as provided by the United Nations Resolution of December 15, 1950.'

" In this respect, the said Agent contends that 'the terms of the United Nations Resolution itself, apart from the Italian renunciation, clearly indicate that the beneficial enjoyment of the properties is to go to Libya with the exceptions just stated.'

" Lastly, the said Counter-Memorial states that the Libyan Government 'will preserve the property in accordance with its obligations and will not deal with it otherwise than in accordance with the United Nations Resolution of December 15, 1950 ', and concludes with the allegation that 'it is incompatible with the sovereign status of the Libyan Government that the properties should be placed under the control of any other Government.'

" In the Reply and Rejoinders, the Italian Agent, on the one hand, and the British and Libyan Agents, on the other, sustained their positions, the Italian Agent having added in the said Reply that his Government reserves 'for a later date the request for reparation of the damage' caused to it by the transfer which the British Government made to the Libyan Government of the administration of the *patrimonio disponibile* and of the 'immovable property mentioned in paragraph 5, Article I, of the Resolution ' [Reply, paragraphs XVIII (a) and (f)]."

*Held:* (1) that the claim of the Italian Government for the return to it of the administration of the properties constituting the *patrimonio disponibile* in Tripolitania and Cyrenaica must be rejected.

However, in the absence of the agreement called for by Article 1, paragraph 3 (*a*), of Resolution 388 (V), the Libyan Government (a) should abstain from disposing of any of the said properties without obtaining either a statement on the part of the Italian Government that it had no objection to the specific act of disposal or the express authorization of the Tribunal to perform the said act of disposal, and (b) should maintain the present administrative agency entrusted with the custodianship of those properties.

(2) The claim of the Italian Government for the restitution to it of the administration of the properties listed in Annex 3 of the Memorial must be rejected without prejudice.

(3) The Italian Government was entitled to administer the properties listed in Annex 4 of the Memorial until the conclusion of the

agreement called for by Article 1, paragraph 5, of Resolution 388 (V).

The Tribunal said: " The Tribunal will deal, in the first place, with the Italian Agent's claim that the administration of the properties constituting the *patrimonio disponibile* in Tripolitania and Cyrenaica be returned to his Government. The administration of these properties was transferred to the Libyan Government by the British Government when, on December 24, 1951, Libya achieved its independence.

" With regard to the said claim, the Agents for the respondent Governments contend that the continued ownership by Italy of the properties in question is inconsistent with the renunciation made by the Italian Government in Article 23 of the Peace Treaty, signed in Paris on February 10, 1947, which reads as follows: [The Tribunal here stated the provisions of Article 23,[1] and continued:]

" The Italian Agent in his Reply contests this allegation of the said Agents and refers to United Nations Document A/AC.38/SC.1/R.1/Add.1 which contains the following excerpts from Fauchille's *Traité de droit international public*, namely:

' When a dismembered State cedes a portion of its territory, property which constitutes *public* property, namely property which by its nature is used for a public service, existing on the annexed territory, passes with its inherent characteristics and legal status to the annexing State; being devoted to the public service of the ceded province, it should belong to the sovereign power which is henceforward responsible for it . . .

'As regards *private* State property, *i.e.* property which the State possesses in the same manner as a private person, in order to derive income from it, it must be noted that failing any special provisions it does not become part of the property of the annexing State. In spite of the loss the dismembered State has suffered, it remains the same person as before and does not, any more than a private person, cease to be the owner of the things it possesses in the annexed territory and there is no principle preventing it from having the ownership of immovable property in that territory.'

" The Tribunal is of the opinion that the principles set forth in the above quotation constitute a generally accepted rule of international law. Private state property does not become part of the property of the successor state unless there is a ' special provision ' to that effect.

" The Tribunal considers that this rule is followed in the Italian Peace Treaty wherein the loss of sovereignty by Italy over the ceded territories is established in Part I, entitled ' Territorial Clauses ', and the transfer of privately-owned state property within the said ceded territories is regulated by means of Annex XIV (' Economic and Financial Provisions Relating to Ceded Territories '), paragraph 1, which reads as follows:

' 1. The Successor State shall receive, without payment, Italian State and para-statal property within territory ceded to it under the present Treaty, as well as all relevant archives and documents of an

[1 See above, p. 4, n. 2.]

administrative character or historical value concerning the territory in question, or relating to property transferred under this paragraph.

' The following are considered as State or para-statal property for the purposes of this Annex: movable and immovable property of the Italian State, of local authorities and of public institutions and publicly owned companies and associations, as well as movable and immovable property formerly belonging to the Fascist Party or its auxiliary organizations.'

" Annex XIV, paragraph 1, constitutes, as far as the territories ceded by Italy by means of the Territorial Clauses of the Peace Treaty are concerned, the ' special provision ' which is necessary in order that the private state property in the ceded territories be transferred to the annexing state.

" However, Annex XIV expressly excluded the former Italian Colonies from its scope. The terms of paragraph 19 of the said Annex XIV are the following:

' 19. The provisions of this Annex shall not apply to the former Italian Colonies. The economic and financial provisions to be applied therein will form part of the arrangements for the final disposal of these territories pursuant to Article 23 of the present Treaty.'

" The procedure established in the above-quoted paragraph 19 led to the adoption by the United Nations General Assembly of Resolution 388 (V), which bears the title ' Economic and Financial Provisions Relating to Libya '. The said Resolution 388 (V), consequently, occupies the place, as far as the regulation of the economic and financial issues in Libya is concerned, that Annex XIV does with regard to the issues of identical nature posed by the cession of territory effected by means of the Territorial Clauses of the Peace Treaty.

" The process whereby Resolution 388 (V) was adopted is succinctly and clearly expressed in its preamble, which is transcribed in its entirety together with Article I, paragraphs 1, 2 and 3 (a) thereof, the latter provisions being the next subject which the Tribunal intends to analyse. [The Tribunal here quoted the provisions of the Resolution, which are reproduced at pp. 2–4 above.]

" It appears clear to the Tribunal that the above-quoted Article I, paragraph 1, sets forth the general objective to be attained in the matter of state property in Libya, namely, that title to all such property shall be vested in the Libyan Government; that paragraph 2, in line with the generally accepted rule of international law to which the Tribunal has referred above, establishes, through the use of the formula ' shall be transferred immediately ', Libya's right to full and immediate ownership of its *demanio pubblico* and *patrimonio indisponibile*; and that paragraph 3 (a) makes the transfer to the Libyan Government of the *patrimonio disponibile* dependent on the special agreement between Italy and Libya which is to determine certain conditions of the said transfer.

" The factors mentioned in the preceding paragraphs have led the Tribunal to conclude that the renunciation made by Italy in Article 23 of the Peace Treaty encompassed the *demanio pubblico* and the *patrimonio indisponibile* but had no effect on its title to the properties constituting its *patrimonio disponibile* in this country, and that, in the absence of the special agreement between Italy and Libya called for by Resolution 388 (V), Article I, paragraph 3 (a), the said title to the *patrimonio disponibile* remains vested in the Government of Italy.

" The nature of the transfer which the said paragraph 3 determines shall take place on some future date will be examined in the following paragraphs.

" In this respect, the Tribunal has taken into account, firstly, the fact that when the *Ad Hoc* Political Committee of the United Nations General Assembly was discussing the terms of the ' Economic and Financial Provisions Relating to Libya ', the Italian Representative to the said organ announced that his Government desired to transfer its *patrimonio disponibile* in Libya to the Libyan Government, without compensation, as Italy's contribution to the economic reconstruction of Libya.

" The controlling factor of the State property provisions of Resolution 388 (V) certainly is the desire to be of assistance to the new Libyan State and to ensure it the means which will make possible its future existence. The return to Italy of the administration of the *patrimonio disponibile* would run counter to this spirit.

" The circumstance that Italy renounced the properties which it owned as a private person in Albania (Article 29 of the Peace Treaty), as well as within the territories it ceded to France, Greece and Yugoslavia (Annex XIV),[1] is also worthy of note.

" Reference should also be made to the fact that Italy gave its full co-operation to the United Nations General Assembly in the drafting of Resolution 530 (VI), dated January 29, 1952, entitled ' Economic and Financial Provisions Relating to Eritrea ', and that in the said resolution provision is made for the transfer without compensation to the successor state of the *patrimonio disponibile* and for the said transfer to be contemporaneous to the final transfer of powers to the successor state by the Administering Power.

" Also, as Libya is to receive the properties in question without

[1 Article 29 provides:
" Italy formally renounces in favour of Albania all property (apart from normal diplomatic or consular premises), rights, concessions, interests and advantages of all kinds in Albania, belonging to the Italian State or Italian para-statal institutions. Italy likewise renounces all claims to special interests or influence in Albania, acquired as a result of the aggression of April 7, 1939, or under treaties or agreements concluded before that date.

" The economic clauses of the present Treaty, applicable to the Allied and Associated Powers, shall apply to other Italian property and other economic relations between Albania and Italy."

For the provisions of paragraph 1 of Annex XIV, see above, p. 7.]

compensation, it seems clear to the Tribunal that the conditions to be established by the agreement envisaged by Resolution 388 (V), Article I, paragraph 3, can only concern the practical details of the formal transfer of title and the protection of the interests of third parties.

" Consequently, the Tribunal finds that, in so far as the properties constituting the *patrimonio disponibile* in Libya are concerned, all that has yet to be transferred to Libya by means of the agreement called for by Resolution 388 (V), Article I, paragraph 3 (a), is title to the said properties.

" The soundness of the above interpretation is borne out by considering what the situation would be if it were supposed that the object of the future transfer envisaged by Resolution 388 (V), Article I, paragraph 3 (a), is not only that of the formal title to the properties concerned but also the right to administer the said properties. In such a hypothetical case, the administration of the *patrimonio disponibile* would have been turned over to the Italian Government in order that, after a short period of time, this Government would transfer the said administration to the Libyan Government. In the Tribunal's opinion, it is not permissible to conclude that the General Assembly of the United Nations had in mind a procedure of this nature when it adopted Resolution 388 (V).

" It seems opportune to state at this juncture that, in modern practice, the exercise by a foreign state of the rights of full ownership to large portions of land is not considered as an encroachment on the sovereignty of the territorial state. In the present case, in which title to the properties in question is still vested in Italy but the other attributes of ownership are properly being exercised by the Libyan Government, it is evident that the juridical status of the said properties can have no effect whatever on the latter's sovereignty.

" In view of the aforesaid reasons, the Tribunal rejects the Italian Agent's first claim. In doing so, the Tribunal establishes that, as title to the properties in question is yet to be vested in the Libyan Government, the said Government shall abstain from disposing of any of the said properties and shall maintain the present-day administrative agency entrusted with the custodianship of the said properties. It is in this manner that the Tribunal interprets the Libyan Agent's commitment to the effect that his Government ' will preserve the property in accordance with its obligations and will not deal with it otherwise than in accordance with the United Nations Resolution of December 15, 1950 ', as well as the statement the said Agent made in the [*Case of the Request for*] *Interim Measures* with respect to the administrative measures that the said Libyan Government has taken with respect to the custodianship of the properties in question.[1]

[1 Reported below, p. 517.]

" The Italian Agent's second claim—*i.e.* the restitution of the administration of the properties listed in Annex 3 (buildings for the Italian diplomatic and consular services) and Annex 4 (schools for the Italian community) to the Memorial—will be examined in the following paragraphs.

" This subject is governed by Resolution 388 (V), Article I, paragraph 5. [The Tribunal here stated the provisions of Article I, paragraph 5 (see above, p. 3), and continued:]

" It will be recalled that the Libyan Agent, in his Counter-Memorial, informs the Tribunal that the Italian Government has for some time been in possession of all of the properties listed in Annex 4 (schools); that the Libyan Government ' has undertaken to give up ' to the Italian Government two buildings in Tripoli for use as diplomatic and consular premises; and that, with the same object in mind, a building in Benghazi ' has been handed over to the Italian Government.'

" Chapter V of the Italian Agent's Reply makes it clear that the Government of Italy is not satisfied with the present-day situation because (a) it is not based on the special agreements called for by Resolution 388 (V), Article I, paragraph 5; (b) ' to grant the use of a property is quite a different thing from granting the ownership of the property, use being considered as only one of the elements of ownership (*godimento*), there lacking the other element (*disponibilità*)'; (c) the building being used for its diplomatic establishment in Benghazi has been leased to it; and (d) it has yet to receive all the buildings required by its diplomatic and consular services in Libya.

" The Tribunal agrees with the opinion that the said paragraph 5 calls for the vesting in the Italian Government of title to the properties specified therein, but this is a matter which does not fall within the purview of the Italian Agent's second claim.

" The Tribunal will examine separately the Italian Agent's petitions that his Government be reinstated in the administration of (A) the properties listed in Annex 3 of the Memorial (buildings for the Italian diplomatic and consular services in Libya) and (B) the properties listed in Annex 4 of the Memorial (schools for the Italian community in Tripolitania).

" (A) The circumstance that the Italian Government heretofore did not have diplomatic and consular establishments in Libya underlines the need for an agreement between the Governments concerned, specifying the buildings that are to be used for the said establishments. The pleadings in the present case seem to indicate that such an agreement has only partially been reached.

" Moreover, the said pleadings do not afford the Tribunal with precise information as to the Italian Government's present-day desires on the subject. For example, although Annex 3 of the Memorial lists nine properties, three of which are located in Tripoli, the Italian Agent in his Reply [Chapter V (b)] states that while the

Libyan Government has designated two buildings to be handed over to the Italian Government for the latter's diplomatic and consular services in Tripoli, ' there is lacking . . . a third building in Tripoli, a building at Misurata, and one in Benghazi.'

" With respect to the said two buildings in Tripoli, the pleadings indicate solely that they are not among those listed in Annex 3 but are included in Annex 1 of the Memorial.   The arrangements in Benghazi are also obscure, for in respect thereto the Italian Agent states that a building in that city, known as the ex-Tribunale Militare, has been leased to his Government and it is impossible to determine whether or not the final part of the above quotation from the Reply refers to that property or to some other.

" In view of this lack of precision and that the pleadings in the present case indicate that the negotiation between the Libyan and the Italian Governments of the relative agreement envisaged by Resolution 388 (V), Article I, paragraph 5, is still proceeding, the Tribunal rejects without prejudice the petition of the Italian Agent under reference.

" (B) With respect to the properties listed in Annex 4, the Italian Agent insists in having a decision of the Tribunal even though, as stated above, the Libyan Agent states that the Italian Government has for some time been in possession of all of the said properties. Given these circumstances, the Tribunal rules that until the conclusion of the agreement called for by Resolution 388 (V), Article I, paragraph 5, relative to the schools for the Italian community, the Italian Government is entitled to administer the properties listed in the said Annex 4 of the Italian Agent's Memorial."

" For these reasons, the Tribunal decides:
" I. The Italian Government's claim, that the administration of the properties constituting the *patrimonio disponibile* in Tripolitania and Cyrenaica be returned to it, is rejected.   However, in the absence of the agreement called for by Resolution 388 (V), Article I, paragraph 3 (a), the Libyan Government (a) shall abstain from disposing of any of the properties constituting the said *patrimonio disponibile* without obtaining either a statement on the part of the Italian Government to the effect that it has no objection to the specific act of disposal or the express authorization of the Tribunal to perform the said act of disposal, and (b) shall maintain the present administrative agency entrusted with the custodianship of those properties;
" II. The Italian Government's claim, that the administration of the properties listed in Annex 3 of the Memorial be now restituted to it, is rejected without prejudice;
" III. The Italian Government is entitled to administer the properties listed in Annex 4 of the Memorial until the relative agreement called for by Resolution 388 (V), Article I, paragraph 5, is concluded.

" The present sentence has been drawn up in the English and French languages, the English text being authoritative."

[Report: Unpublished.]

**State succession—Succession to rights—Succession to properties and institutions—Whether State-owned or State-controlled—General Assembly Resolution 388 (V), Article I—Property of Italian State.**

ITALY v. LIBYA.

GENERAL LIST NO. 2.

*United Nations Tribunal for Libya.*[1] *July 3, 1954.*

(Sanchez-Gavito, President; Wickström and Yörükóglu JJ.)

THE FACTS.—This was a claim by the Italian Government for a declaration under Article X, paragraph 1 (a), of the United Nations General Assembly Resolution 388 (V) of December 15, 1950, entitled " Economic and Financial Provisions Relating to Libya ", that the terms of an Agreement dated June 28, 1951, made between it and the Government of the United Kingdom[2] were in accordance with the provisions of the said Resolution. The provisions of Resolution 388 (V) relevant to the case are as follows:—

*Article I, paragraphs 3 and 4:*

" 3. In addition, the following shall be transferred on conditions to be established by special agreement between Italy and Libya:

(*a*) The alienable property (*patrimonio disponibile*) of the State in Libya and the property in Libya belonging to the autonomous agencies (*aziende autonome*) of the State;

(*b*) The rights of the State in the capital and the property of institutions, companies and associations of a public character located in Libya.

" 4. Where the operations of such institutions, companies and associations extend to Italy or to countries other than Libya, Libya shall receive only those rights of the Italian State or the Italian administration of Libya which appertain to the operations in Libya. In cases where the Italian State or the Italian administration of Libya exercised only managerial control over such institutions, companies and associations, Libya shall have no claim to any rights in those institutions, companies and associations."

*Article II:*

" Italy and Libya shall determine by special agreements the conditions under which the obligations of Italian public or private social insurance organizations towards the inhabitants of Libya and a proportionate part of the reserves accumulated by the said organizations shall be transferred to similar organizations in Libya. That

---

[1] An account of the establishment of this Tribunal is given below, at p. 517.

[2] Exchange of Notes between the Government of the United Kingdom and the Italian Government concerning the Disposal of Italian Private Property in Cyrenaica and Tripolitania (U.N.T.S., vol. 118, p. 115; U.K.T.S., No. 62 (1951), Cmd. 8312).

part of the reserves shall preferably be taken from the real property and fixed assets in Libya of the said organizations."

*Article VI, paragraph 1:*

" 1. The property, rights and interests of Italian nationals, including Italian juridical persons, in Libya, shall, provided they have been lawfully acquired, be respected."

*Article VII:*

" Property, rights and interests in Libya which, as the result of the war, are still subject to measures of seizure, compulsory administration or sequestration, shall be restored to their owners, and, in cases submitted to the Tribunal referred to in Article X of the present resolution, following decisions of that Tribunal."

*Article IX:*

" The following special provisions shall apply to concessions:

1. Concessions granted within the territory of Libya by the Italian State or by the Italian administration of Libya, and concession contracts (*patti colonici*) existing between the *Ente per la Colonizzazione della Libia* or the *Istituto della Previdenza Sociale* and the concessionaires of land to which each contract related shall be respected, unless it is established that the concessionaire has not complied with the essential conditions of the concession.

2. Land placed at the disposal of the *Ente per la Colonizzazione della Libia* and the colonization department of the Italian State or the Italian administration of Libya and which has not been the object of a concession shall be transferred immediately to Libya.

3. Land, buildings and their appurtenances referred to in subparagraph (*d*) of paragraph 4 below shall be transferred to Libya in accordance with the arrangements to be made under that subparagraph.

4. Special agreements between Italy and Libya shall provide for:

(*a*) The liquidation of the *Ente per la Colonizzazione della Libia* and of the colonization department of the *Istituto della Previdenza Sociale*, the interim status of those institutions for the purpose of enabling them to fulfil their obligations towards concessionaires whose contracts are still in operation, and, if necessary, the taking over of their functions by new organizations;

(*b*) The repayment by those institutions to financial concerns of the quotas subscribed by the latter in the establishment of the *Ente per la Colonizzazione della Libia*, and, in the case of the *Istituto della Previdenza Sociale*, the reconstitution of that part of its reserves invested by that constitution in its colonization department;

(*c*) The transfer to Libya of the residual asssets of the institutions to be liquidated;

(*d*) Arrangements relating to land placed at the disposal of these institutions and to the buildings on and appurtenances to that land, in which, after their abandonment by the concessionaires, no further investment could be made by the institutions.

(*e*) Payments in amortization of the debts of concessionaires owed to the institutions.

5. In consideration of the renunciation by the Italian Government

of its claims against those institutions, the latter shall cancel the debts of the concessionaires and the mortgages securing those debts."

*Article X, paragraph 1:*

" 1. A United Nations Tribunal shall be set up, composed of three persons selected by the Secretary General for their legal qualifications from the nationals of three different States not directly interested. The Tribunal, whose decisions shall be based on law, shall have the following two functions:

(*a*) It shall give to the administering Powers, the Libyan Government after its establishment, and the Italian Government, on request by any of those authorities, such instructions as may be required for the purpose of giving effect to the present resolution;

(*b*) It shall decide all disputes arising between the said authorities concerning the interpretation and application of the present resolution. The Tribunal shall be seised of any such dispute on the unilateral request of one of those authorities."

The facts of the case were stated by the Tribunal as follows:

" On June 28, 1951, an Agreement was concluded by an exchange of notes between the British and Italian Governments regarding the Italian property in Libya which had been in the custody of the British Military Occupation Administration.

" Article 5 of this Agreement contains the special provisions regarding twenty-five institutions, companies and associations, hereinafter called establishments, listed in paragraph 1.

" Under paragraph 2, the British Government undertook to release the property of the establishments on receipt of a full discharge and indemnity as provided in Article 2 of the Agreement.

" Paragraph 5 provides that the property of:

Sezione Autonoma per le Case Popolari in Libia (S.C.A.P.L.I.); Ente Autonomo Fiera Campionaria di Tripoli (E.A.F.C.); Ente Turistico ed Alberghiero della Libia (E.T.A.L.)

would be released to duly appointed liquidators and that the liquidation would be undertaken in accordance with the laws in force in the territory, including the statutes governing the operations of the said establishments.

" Paragraph 6 provides that in the course of the liquidation of these three establishments any capital or property or share in any capital or property which would normally have passed to the Italian State should pass to Libya in accordance with Article I, paragraph 3, of the United Nations Resolution of December 15, 1950.

" Paragraph 7 provides that the property of:

Società Coloniale Italiana (S.C.I.); Istituto Nazionale della Previdenza Sociale (Ramo Assicurazione) (I.N.P.S.); Istituto Nazionale per l'Assicurazione contro gli Infortuni sul Lavoro (I.N.A.I.L.); Istituto per l'Assistenza Sociale nell'Africa Italiana (I.A.S.A.I.); Istituto Nazionale per le Case degli Impiegati dello Stato (I.N.C.I.S.); Reale Automobile Club d'Italia (R.A.C.I.);

Banco di Napoli; Istituto Nazionale delle Assicurazioni (I.N.A.); Società Anonima Petroli Libia (Petrolibia); Banco di Sicilia; Ente Italiano Audizioni Radiofoniche (E.I.A.R.); Società Anonima Azienda Tabacchi Italiani (A.T.I.); Società Anonima Trasporti Africa (S.A.T.A.); Magazzini Generali di Tripoli (M.G.); Società Italo-Americana del Petrolio (S.I.A.P.); Società Emulsione Bitumi Italiana Colas (S.E.B.I.C.); Nafta Società Italiana pel Petrolio ed Affini (N.A.F.T.A.); Società Anonima Vacuum Prodotti Petroliferi; Ala Littoria S.A.; [and] Società Agricola Coloniale della Stampa Emilio de Bono

would be handed over to their duly appointed representatives.

" Paragraph 8 provides that the property of:

Istituto Nazionale della Previdenza Sociale (Ramo Assicurazione); Istituto Nazionale per l'Assicurazione contro gli Infortuni sul Lavoro; [and] Istituto per l'Assistenza Sociale nell'Africa Italiana

would be released without prejudice to Article II of the Resolution.

" Lastly, paragraph 9 provides that the final arrangements for dealing with the property of:

Ente per la Colonizzazione della Libia [and] Istituto Nazionale della Previdenza Sociale (Ramo Colonizzazione)

would be made in due course in accordance with the terms of Article IX of the Resolution.

" It should also be mentioned that the British and Italian Governments expressly recognized the right of the Libyan Government to refer to the Tribunal any question whatsoever regarding the establishments under reference.

" In his Memorial submitted on March 7, 1953, the Agent of the Italian Government addressed a request to the Tribunal, which the said Agent qualifies as a request for instructions under the terms of Article X, paragraph 1 (a), of United Nations Resolution No. 388 (V) dated December 15, 1950.[1]   In the aforesaid Memorial the said Agent stated:

" ' that following the adoption of the aforesaid Resolution by the United Nations General Assembly, the British Government found itself obliged to re-examine the status of the establishments placed under custody with the purpose of transferring to the new Libyan State those properties comprised in the categories assigned to the said State by the Resolution and, furthermore, of restoring to their legitimate owners, in conformity with Article VII of the Resolution, the properties found to belong to persons other than the Italian State or the Italian Administration of Libya;

' that during the course of negotiations which led to the Agreement under consideration, the Italian Government presented the documentation necessary to define the juridical and patrimonial status of each one of the establishments concerned;

' and that he requested the Tribunal, under the terms of Article X, paragraph 1 (a), of the Resolution, to declare that the stipulations of the

[1 The terms of para. 1 of Article X are set out at p. 3 above.]

Agreement are in conformity with the provisions contained in Article I, paragraphs 3 (b) and 4, and Articles II, VI, VII and IX of the Resolution.'

" It is pertinent to recall at this juncture that Article IX of the Resolution contains the special provisions applying to concessions, and to transcribe paragraphs 3 and 4 of Article I, Articles II and VII as well as the first sentence of paragraph 1 of Article VI, the said sentence being the only one in the said Article that seems to have a bearing on the present request. [The Tribunal here stated the provisions of these Articles and continued:]

" In his Counter-Memorial, the Agent of the Libyan Government set forth:

" ' that in the discussions which led to the Agreement, neither the provisional Government of Libya nor the Governments of Cyrenaica or Tripolitania were represented, and that when the British Government made known to them the terms of the proposed Agreement, they objected to it and reserved their right to exercise in due course before the Tribunal their rights to the properties referred to in the Agreement, and requested the British Government to make this clear to the Italian Government;

' that this Agreement could not settle the question of which were the rights of the Italian State in the capital and property of establishments of a public character which were to be transferred to Libya and that only an agreement between Italy and Libya, as provided by paragraph 3 of Article I of the Resolution, could settle this question;

' that, furthermore, the said Agreement could not have settled whether the property of the said establishments had been lawfully acquired within the meaning of Article VI of the Resolution; and

' that if the claim of the Italian Government was that, whether by reason of the Agreement or otherwise, no rights in the capital or property of the establishments dealt with by the said Agreement ought to be transferred to Libya under paragraph 3 of Article I of the Resolution, otherwise than as provided in the Agreement, and that the property of those establishments was all lawfully acquired within the meaning of paragraph 1 of Article VI of the Resolution, the Agent of the Libyan Government submitted " that the Italian Government should furnish full particulars in support of such a claim ".'

" In his Reply, the Agent of the Italian Government presented certain arguments in support of his request which will be examined hereinbelow."

[It is convenient to summarize these arguments at this point: (1) The Italian Government contended that the Libyan Government was bound by the Agreement of June 28, 1951, because the British Government, in concluding it, exercised their powers of Administering Power. (2) It was further contended that the Agreement of 1951 could not mention the matter of the lawful acquisition of properties, since that question had no connection with the problems dealt with by the Agreement. (3) The Italian Government admitted that the property of the establishments mentioned in paragraph 5 of Article 5 of the

Agreement was released to liquidators because the Italian State had ownership rights in the property which should be transferred to Libya. They further admitted that the property of the establishments listed in paragraph 7 of the Agreement was handed over to their own representatives because the Italian Government did not have any ownership rights in regard to any of these establishments.]

" In his Rejoinder, the Agent of the Libyan Government, firstly, raised the question that the request should not be entertained; and, secondly, maintained that the Agreement was contrary to the provisions of the Resolution and claimed that a large number of the establishments under consideration were statal or para-statal institutions dealt with by Article I, paragraph 3 (*b*), of the Resolution, and that much more than appears from the Agreement should be transferred to Libya."

*Held: As regards the Preliminary Exception.*—(1) that the exception that the request should not be entertained must be rejected and that the Tribunal would entertain the request as introducing a dispute, in accordance with Article X, paragraph 1 (*b*), of the Resolution.

The Tribunal said: " The exception to the effect that the request should not be entertained, raised by the Agent of the Libyan Government, is based on the following grounds: that the instructions of the Tribunal provided for in Article X, paragraph 1 (*a*), of the Resolution should precede the action in relation to which the Tribunal's opinion is requested, for such instructions can never be *ex post facto*; and that after the Agreement had been concluded and put into force, the questions raised with regard thereto became the proper subject-matter for a dispute in the nature of those contemplated by Article X, paragraph 1 (*b*), of the Resolution.

" In accordance with the terms of Article X, paragraph 1 (*a*), the Tribunal shall, on request by any of the parties, give such instructions as ' may be required for the purpose of giving effect to the Resolution ', and it appears from this very text that such instructions can only be requested from the Tribunal before the action in relation to which the opinion of the Tribunal is sought. In view of the fact that the Agreement has been concluded and executed, controversies in regard thereto are disputes falling within the terms of Article X, paragraph 1 (*b*), of the Resolution.

" But this does not lead necessarily to the conclusion that the request cannot be entertained, for, according to the Tribunal's Rules of Procedure, the procedure is the same in the case of requests for instructions as in the case of disputes. It is true that the Agent of the Libyan Government has, in his Rejoinder, referred to certain conditions which have not been met in the present case and which, in his opinion, are required for the request to be considered as posing a dispute. Nevertheless, he has not even tried to explain which are such conditions. Moreover, this attitude contradicts the final part of his Counter-Memorial which contains a formal invitation to the Italian Government to plead the merits of the case.

" Given these circumstances, the Tribunal rejects the exception to the effect that the request should not be entertained and decides to entertain the request as posing a dispute in the terms of Article X, paragraph 1 (b), of the Resolution.

*As regards the Merits.*—(2) that the release of the property of specified owners to their liquidators was in conformity with Article 1, paragraph 3 (b), of the Resolution, reserving the right of the parties to come before the Tribunal in case of disagreement with regard to the conditions on which the liquidation was based.

(3) that the release of the property of specified establishments to the representatives of those establishments, without prejudice to Article II of the Resolution, was in conformity with the provisions of that Article and of Article I, paragraph 3 (b), of the Resolution.

(4) that the provisions of the Agreement of 1951 relating to certain specified establishments were in conformity with Article I, paragraph 3 (b), of the Resolution.

(5) that the parties should submit supplementary conclusions with regard to the other establishments, containing explanations on the points indicated as well as additional evidence.

(6) that the time-limits for depositing these conclusions and evidence be fixed by order of the President.

The Tribunal said: " This request is not formulated clearly, and in order to understand it, the precise meaning of the alleged conformity of the Agreement with the different Articles of the Resolution, quoted in the Memorial, must be established.

" Firstly, the Tribunal notes that the conformity of the Agreement with Article VI cannot be examined, for the Agent of the Italian Government himself has declared in his Reply, and rightly so, that the Agreement could not mention the matter of the lawful acquisition of properties since this question has no connection with the problems dealt with by the Agreement.

" Furthermore, the Tribunal notes that the Agreement did not deal directly with the subject-matter of the provisions of Articles II and IX, and that Article VII contains the general provisions which led to the conclusion of the Agreement. The comparison, nevertheless, should be made between Article VII, Article I, paragraphs 3 (b) and 4, as well as Articles II and IX of the Resolution on the one hand, and paragraphs 2, 5, 7, 8 and 9 of Article 5 of the Agreement, on the other. Moreover, it should be taken into consideration that the Agent of the Italian Government has admitted that the property of the establishments mentioned in paragraph 5 was released to liquidators because the Italian State had ownership rights thereto which should be transferred to Libya while the property of the establishments listed in paragraph 7 was handed over to their own representatives because the Italian Government did not have any such rights in regard to any of the said establishments.

" It appears from this comparison that under the terms of the Agreement the twenty-five establishments have been classified in four categories, each of which has been dealt with in a different way, and that the two categories established by paragraphs 5 and 7 are related to Article I, paragraph 3 (*b*), in that the establishments listed in paragraph 5 have been considered as falling within paragraph 3 (*b*) and those listed in paragraph 7 as not falling within the said paragraph 3 (*b*), whereas the category established by paragraph 8 is related to Article II, and the category established by paragraph 9 is related to Article IX. It should be observed that the establishments mentioned in paragraph 8 are also listed in paragraph 7.

" Consequently, there are reasons to believe that the request seeks to obtain a decision confirming that this division of the twenty-five establishments into four categories and the different treatment accorded to the establishments of the diverse categories are justified and in conformity with the provisions of the Resolution, and therefore establishing definitively, *inter alia*, that the Italian Government does not have, with regard to the establishments listed in paragraph 7, any ownership rights whatsoever which should be transferred to Libya.

" The Agent of the Italian Government has alleged that the Libyan Government was bound by the Agreement because the British Government, in concluding it, exercised its powers of Administering Power. The Agent of the Libyan Government, on the contrary, held that only a special agreement between the Italian and Libyan Governments, as provided for by paragraph 3 of Article I of the Resolution, could decide which are the establishments of a public character in whose assets the Italian Government had ownership rights that should be transferred to Libya.

" However, it would be useless to dwell on this controversy in view of the fact that under the terms of the Agreement the Libyan Government has the right to refer to the Tribunal any question whatsoever regarding these establishments, and that the Agent of the Italian Government finally admitted that the Libyan Government can refer to the Tribunal any question regarding these establishments, and request that it declare that the properties or that certain of the properties which, under the terms of the Agreement, were released from custody and restored to their respective owners, should have been transferred to Libya, and that in one or several of the establishments listed in Article 5, paragraph 7, of the Agreement there were interests of the Italian State which should be transferred to Libya.

" On the other hand, it is evident that in the event of disagreement between the Italian and Libyan Governments, as that existing in the present case, the Italian Government was not obliged to await action on the part of the Libyan Government but could take the initiative as it has proceeded to do.

" It is now in order to examine the situation of the different establishments.

" I. Sezione Autonoma per le Case Popolari in Libia; Ente Autonomo Fiera Campionaria di Tripoli; Ente Turistico ed Alberghiero della Libia;

" The Agent of the Italian Government, as hereinabove stated, has recognised that when the Agreement was concluded these three establishments were considered as establishments of a public character in whose assets the Italian State had ownership rights which should be transferred to Libya. The Agent of the Libyan Government contends that all of the assets of the first and third establishments and that possibly all of the assets of the second establishment should be attributed to the Italian State and therefore transferred to the Libyan State.

" In any event the Tribunal is of the opinion that it was rightly decided to release the property of these establishments to duly appointed liquidators in order to determine what should be transferred to Libya.

" It appears that by this decision the rights of Libya were sufficiently safeguarded, the more so because, according to the assertion of the Italian Agent, not contested by the Libyan Agent, the two Governments have reached an agreement on the dismissal of the sole liquidator who had been appointed by the President of the Tribunal of Tripoli on the proposal of the British Administration, and on his replacement by two liquidators for each establishment, one liquidator having been designated by the Libyan Government and one by the Italian Government in each case.

" It should be considered, therefore, that the release to liquidators of the properties of these establishments was in conformity with the provisions of Article I, paragraph 3 (b). As to the conditions which should govern the liquidation, the right of the parties to come before the Tribunal in case of disagreement is reserved.

" II. Istituto Nazionale della Previdenza Sociale (Ramo Assicurazione); Istituto Nazionale per l'Assicurazione contro gli Infortuni sul Lavoro; [and] Istituto per l'Assistenza Sociale nell'Africa Italiana.

" In the first place the Tribunal finds that the evidence which has been produced establishes that the Italian Government has no rights in the capital and property of these establishments.

" Furthermore, the Tribunal is of the opinion that the release of the property of these establishments, without prejudice to the provisions of Article II of the Resolution, can be considered as the most practical measure that could be taken at the time the Agreement was concluded, for, on the one hand, it was then foreseeable that considerable time would elapse before the conclusion of the special agreements provided for in the said Article and in fact the said special agreements are yet to be concluded, and, on the other hand, it does not appear that the rights of Libya were placed in jeopardy by this measure, in view of the fact that the part of the reserves of the said establishments transferable to similar organizations in Libya is to be taken preferably from the real property and fixed assets in Libya of the said organizations. The Tribunal also notes that the Agent of the Libyan Government did not make any serious objections to the said measure, having limited himself to stating that the British Government should have requested instructions from the Tribunal before taking action.

" Given these circumstances, the Tribunal considers that the release of the property of these establishments to their representatives, without prejudice to Article II of the Resolution, was in conformity with the provisions of the said Article and of Article I, paragraph 3 (*b*), of the Resolution. The conformity with the said Article I, paragraph 3 (*b*), implies that the provisions thereof do not apply to these three establishments.

" III. Ala Littoria S.A.; Società Italo-Americana del Petrolio; Nafta Società Italiana pel Petrolio ed Affini; Società Anonima Trasporti Africa; Società Anonima Vacuum Prodotti Petroliferi; [and] Societa Emulsione Bitumi Italiana Colas.

" The Agent of the Libyan Government has declared that it was unnecessary to discuss the case of these establishments in view of the fact that at present they have no property in Libya that could be transferred to Libya.

" On the other hand, it is apparent from the explanations furnished by the Agent of the Italian Government and the documents exhibited by him that the said Government has no rights in the capital and the property of these six establishments.

" It must be considered, therefore, that the provisions of the Agreement relative to these establishments are in conformity with the provisions of Article I, paragraph 3 (*b*), of the Resolution, in that the said provisions do not apply to these six establishments.

" IV. Ente per la Colonizzazione della Libia; [and] Istituto Nazionale della Previdenza Sociale (Ramo Colonizzazione).

" The Agent of the Italian Government has limited himself to stating that it does not seem to be necessary to supply special documentation relating to these establishments, since under the terms of paragraph 9 of Article 5 of the Agreement, final arrangements dealing with the said establishments would be made in due course in accordance with the provisions of Article IX of the Resolution.

" The Agent of the Libyan Government made no mention at all of these establishments.

' The Tribunal, therefore, does not have at its disposal any of the elements which would enable it to examine the request, and it is not even clear if the Agent of the Italian Government persists in the said request.

" Consequently, the parties are invited to supply the necessary explanations in respect of these two establishments.

" V. Società Agricola Coloniale della Stampa Emilio de Bono.

" In his note relative to this establishment, the Agent of the Italian Government has declared:

' that the establishment was constituted in order to execute the work of reforestation of lands, the concession of which had been granted to it by the " general Government in Libya ";

' that having fulfilled all the contractual obligations, the establishment had become the owner of 85% of the said lands, held *pro-indiviso*, whereas the remaining 15% were part of the alienable property (*patrimonio disponibile*) of the State and should be transferred to Libya.'

" Therefore, it cannot be understood why all the lands under consideration have been released to the representatives of the establishment.

" However, the Agent of the Libyan Government has limited himself to stating that he has taken note of the recognition by the Italian Government of Libya's right [to] 15% of the property of the establishment.

" Given these circumstances, the two parties are invited to explain more amply the case of this establishment.

" VI. Banco di Napoli; Banco di Sicilia; Istituto Nazionale per le Case degli Impiegati dello Stato; Istituto Nazionale delle Assicurazioni; Società Anonima Azienda Tabacchi Italiani; Società Anonima Petroli Libia; Reale Automobile Club d'Italia; Ente Italiano Audizioni Radiofoniche; Magazzini Generali di Tripoli; [and] Società Coloniale Italiana.

" Before deciding the case of these establishments, the Tribunal considers it necessary to have the explanations of the Agent of the Italian Government regarding the objections to the request raised by the Agent of the Libyan Government, as well as supplementary evidence in all those instances in which the said Agent complains of the fact that the evidence necessary for him to plead his case has not been presented as, for example, in the cases of the Società Anonima Petroli Libia and the Società Coloniale Italiana.

" The Tribunal also invites the Agent of the Italian Government to exhibit all the documents relative to the negotiations which led to the conclusion of the Agreement under reference, and especially the minutes of the meetings held between March 17 and 30, 1951, which do not form part of Annex 2 to the Rejoinder.

" In view of the foregoing, there are grounds for asking the parties to submit supplementary conclusions containing explanations on the points indicated above, as well as such additional evidence as may be necessary; and because of the divergence of opinion between the two parties as to which are the establishments of public character, the Tribunal invites them to discuss the criteria to be followed in determining which are the said establishments.

" The time-limits for depositing the supplementary conclusions and additional evidence will be fixed by order of the President.

" For these reasons, the Tribunal,

" 1. Rejects the exception to the effect that the request should not be entertained and decides to entertain the request as introducing a dispute, in accordance with Article X, paragraph 1 (b), of the Resolution.

" 2. Declares that the release of the property of:
Sezione Autonoma per le Case Popolari in Libia
Ente Autonomo Fiera Campionaria di Tripoli
Ente Turistico ed Alberghiero della Libia
to their liquidators was in conformity with the provisions of Article I, paragraph 3 (b), of the Resolution, and reserves the right of the parties to come before the Tribunal in case of disagreement with regard to the conditions on which the liquidation is based.

" 3. Declares that the release of the property of:
Istituto Nazionale della Previdenza Sociale (Ramo Assicurazione)
Istituto Nazionale per l'Assicurazione contro gli Infortuni sul Lavoro
Istituto per l'Assistenza Sociale nell'Africa Italiana
to the representatives of these establishments, without prejudice to Article II of the Resolution, was in conformity with the provisions of the said Article and of Article I, paragraph 3 (b), of the Resolution.

" 4. Declares that the provisions of the Agreement relating to:
Ala Littoria S.A. Società Italo-Americana del Petrolio
Nafta Società Italiana pel Petrolio ed Affini
Società Anonima Trasporti Africa
Società Anonima Vacuum Prodotti Petroliferi
Società Emulsione Bitumi Italiana Colas
were in conformity with the provisions of Article I, paragraph 3 (b), of the Resolution.

" 5. Orders the parties to submit supplementary conclusions with regard to the other establishments containing explanations on the points hereinabove indicated as well as additional evidence.

" 6. Declares that the time-limits for depositing the above-mentioned conclusions and evidence will be fixed by order of the President.

" The present sentence has been drawn up in the English and French languages, the French text being authoritative."

[Report: Unpublished.]

NOTE.—After the additional evidence and submissions had been put in, the Tribunal delivered its final judgment in this matter on June 27, 1955. This judgment is reported in *International Law Reports*, 1955, p. 103.

# PART III

# STATE TERRITORY

## A—IN GENERAL

## I.—Nature of Territorial Sovereignty

State Territory—In general—Nature of territorial sovereignty—
Ownership of land by foreign State—Whether limitation of sovereignty.

See p. 2 (*Italy* v. *United Kingdom of Great Britain and Northern Ireland and United Kingdom of Libya. General List No. 1 (Merits)*).

## IV.—Effects of Changes of Sovereignty

[*See also* PART II, STATES AS INTERNATIONAL PERSONS: E, State Succession.]

State territory—Effects of change of sovereignty—Cession—
Property of ceding State—Distinction between public and private
State property—Relevance of " special provisions " regarding
private State property—Treaty of Peace with Italy, 1947, Article
23 and Annex XIV—Scope of renunciation by Italy in Article 23—
United Nations General Assembly Resolution 388 (V) of December
15, 1950.

See p. 2 (*Italy* v. *United Kingdom of Great Britain and Northern Ireland and United Kingdom of Libya. General List No. 1 (Merits)*).

## PART V

# STATE RESPONSIBILITY

## A—NATURE AND KINDS OF STATE RESPONSIBILITY

### II.—For Breaches of Treaty Obligations

State responsibility—For breaches of treaty obligations—European Convention for Protection of Human Rights and Fundamental Freedoms, 1950—Inter-State applications—Exhaustion of local remedies—Actions of State officials—Absence of legal remedies against State—Possibility of civil or criminal proceedings against officials personally—Dependence of criminal proceedings upon leave of State—Prospect of success of civil proceedings—Absence of information regarding identity of officials—Whether local remedies have been exhausted.

*Re* APPLICATION NO. 299/57 (GOVERNMENT OF THE KINGDOM OF GREECE *v.* GOVERNMENT OF THE UNITED KINGDOM OF GREAT BRITAIN AND NORTHERN IRELAND).

*European Commission of Human Rights. October* 12, 1957.

(Berg, Acting President; Waldock, Eustathiades, Faber, Süsterhenn, Petren, Janssen-Pevtschin, Sørensen, Crosbie, Erim.)

### I. *The admissibility of the Application*[1]

THE FACTS (as stated in the decision of the Commission).—The Application lodged by the Greek Government against the United Kingdom Government concerned certain cases of " torture or maltreatment amounting to torture " alleged to have been committed in Cyprus.

By an Order dated July 19, 1957, the President, Mr. Berg, in accordance with Rule 44 of the Rules of Procedure, instructed the Secretary-General of the Council of Europe to give notice of the Application to the United Kingdom Government and invited the said Government to submit to the Commission its observations in writing on admissibility. Written observations of the United Kingdom Government on admissibility were submitted on August 19, 1957.

In its Decision dated August 28, 1957, the Commission, in accordance with Rule 46, paragraph 1, of its Rules of Procedure, invited the Agents and Counsel of the Parties to appear before it on August 30, 1957, and to submit, without entering upon the merits, oral explanations of the admissibility of the Application.

---

[1] See below, p. 168, n. 1, for an explanation of the difference between the treatment by the Commission of questions of admissibility and questions of substance.

Oral explanations were submitted to the Commission during the hearings on August 30 and September 2, 3 and 4, 1957, by MM. Cambalouris, Rolin and Loïzides, Agent and Counsel of the Greek Government respectively, and Mr. F. A. Vallat, Agent of the United Kingdom Government.

In its Decision dated September 4, 1957, the Commission invited the Agent of the Greek Government to furnish details of the forty-nine cases set out in the Appendix to the original Application, and put certain questions to the Agent of the United Kingdom Government. In his Reply of September 16, 1957, the Agent of the Greek Government furnished the Commission with the details requested of him. On September 27, 1957, the Government of the United Kingdom replied to the questions put by the Commission.

Observations were submitted by the Government of the United Kingdom on October 2 and 4, 1957, concerning the aforementioned Reply of the Greek Government dated September 16, 1957.

*Held:* that the application was admissible except in so far as it related to cases in which the perpetrators of the alleged acts were identified.

The Commission said: " The United Kingdom Government holds that the application is inadmissible on the grounds:

" (a) that it does not establish even on a *prima facie* basis any action or omission by the Government of the United Kingdom which amounts to a breach of the Convention for the Protection of Human Rights and Fundamental Freedoms;

" (b) that it does not comply with the Rules of Procedure which govern the proceedings of the Commission;

" (c) that domestic remedies in connection with the matter complained of have not been exhausted as is required by Article 26 of the Convention.

" In considering the admissibility of an application lodged pursuant to Article 24 of the Convention[1] it is not the Commission's task to ascertain whether the applicant Contracting Party establishes ' *prima facie* proof ' of its allegations, since enquiry into such aspects relates to the merits of the case and cannot therefore be undertaken at the present stage of the proceedings. The provisions of Article 27, paragraph 2, of the Convention,[2] as the Commission has already declared when pronouncing on the admissibility of Application 176/56 on June 2, 1956,[3] only refer to applications

[1 Article 24 of the Convention provides as follows: " Any High Contracting Party may refer to the Commission, through the Secretary-General of the Council of Europe, any alleged breach of the provisions of the Convention by another High Contracting Party."]

[2 Article 27, para. 2, provides: " (2) The Commission shall consider inadmissible any petition submitted under Article 25 which it considers incompatible with the provisions of the present Convention, manifestly ill-founded, or an abuse of the right of petition."]

[3 Reported below, p. 168.]

submitted under Article 25[1] and not to applications made by Governments, and are therefore inapplicable to the present case.

" In regard to the complaint that Rule 41 of the Rules of Procedure has not been complied with, it is sufficient to point out that the indications already embodied in the original Application were supplemented by the additional information and proofs furnished by the Greek Government on September 16, 1957, at the Commission's request.

" Under Article 26 of the Convention the Commission may only deal with a matter after all domestic remedies have been exhausted, according to the generally recognised rules of international law. In accordance with the said generally recognised rules of international law it is the duty of the Government claiming that domestic remedies have not been exhausted to demonstrate the existence of such remedies.

" In this connection the United Kingdom Government has shown, firstly, that although no remedies through the courts of law are available against the State itself, either in the form of the British Crown or in the form of the Government of Cyprus, it is possible to address a demand for compensation by petition addressed either to the Governor of Cyprus, or to the Queen. However, such a remedy, being a measure of grace, is not among those which must be exhausted by virtue of Article 26 aforementioned.

" It further emerges from the memorials, documents and pleadings of the United Kingdom Government that civil and criminal actions may be instituted in Cyprus against any official alleged to be responsible for acts of torture or ill-treatment. The main contention of the Greek Government has always been that, since the aim of its application is to establish the responsibility of the United Kingdom as such, the aforesaid actions, directed as they are against the responsibile individuals and not against the State, do not constitute the effective and adequate remedies which are to be exhausted within the meaning of Article 26. The said actions nevertheless make it possible for the courts to find that the alleged facts are of a substantial and illegal character, as well as to fix compensation; and the remedies in question are therefore, in principle, among those which must be tried before the Commission may be seized of the matter.

" In regard to criminal prosecutions, by writ of summons against individuals, under the Emergency Regulations now in force such prosecutions require the leave of the Attorney-General if they are

[1 Article 25 of the Convention provides, in part: " (1) The Commission may receive petitions addressed to the Secretary-General of the Council of Europe from any person, non-governmental organisation or group of individuals claiming to be the victim of a violation by one of the High Contracting Parties of the rights set forth in this Convention, provided that the High Contracting Party against which the complaint has been lodged has declared that it recognises the competence of the Commission to receive such petitions. . . ."]

brought against members of the police or armed forces. The Greek Government regards this demand as an obstacle likely to render such prosecutions particularly ineffectual. It has nevertheless been shown, in the light of the uncontested statements of the United Kingdom Government, that the Attorney-General has so far never refused such leave.

" It is established that any such refusal, or the acquittal of the accused, would not constitute an impediment to the institution of a civil action, except in cases of felony.

" Particularly as regards civil actions, their exhaustion is the more necessary inasmuch as the Greek Government, in its Application, also requests determination of ' the amount of compensation to be paid to the victims of ill-treatment or their next-of-kin ".

" In accordance with the generally recognised principles of international law, the exhaustion of a domestic remedy is nevertheless not required if the applicant party can prove that in the particular circumstances such remedy will probably prove ineffectual or inadequate. It should therefore be ascertained whether the Greek Government has furnished proof of such probability in connection with the facts relating to the cases listed in the Appendix to its Application. The Commission is thus required to examine the facts peculiar to each of the said cases.

" In this regard it appears that in some cases none of the accused was identified, but that the failure to identify is attended by different circumstances: in one group of cases the individuals concerned, or their Counsel, approached the competent authorities in Cyprus for the names of the authors of the alleged acts, but were refused the information requested; in another group of cases the aforesaid authorities were requested to open an investigation or enquiry into the alleged acts, but considered that there was no reason to prosecute; and, lastly, in a third group of cases, no such approach or request was made. The Commission notwithstanding deems it superfluous to distinguish among the three categories of cases in respect of the application of Article 26 of the Convention. The Greek Government has established that the British Authorities displayed no readiness to indicate the names of the perpetrators of the alleged tortures or ill-treatment, even though an express request for such information was addressed to them and although in all probability such a request would consequently not have produced any more positive result in the cases belonging to the second and third categories mentioned above.

" The absence of any information as to the identity of the accused makes it impossible in practice to exercise the aforementioned remedies in the cases appearing in the Appendix to the Greek Application under numbers . . .

" In the remaining cases, on the other hand, those who claim to be victims, or their next-of-kin, can identify the perpetrators of the alleged torture or ill-treatment, or at least some of them, and would therefore have been able to institute civil or criminal proceedings against them, but did not in fact do so.

" The Greek Government has nevertheless emphasised that in most of the cases concerned those claiming to be victims are at present in custody and therefore ' have not the necessary freedom to institute legal proceedings against the officials of the Authorities '. The said Government, however, has not satisfactorily shown that the fact of detention has in itself prevented the individuals concerned from asserting their rights before the Courts, nor has it shown that the bringing of an action by a person in custody against an official would be fraught with special risks to the person in custody.

" In all those cases, therefore, where the perpetrators of the alleged torture or ill-treatment, or some of them, have already been identified, the Commission considers that, in conformity with Article 26 of the Convention, the aforementioned domestic remedies ought first to have been exhausted. In all these cases, which appear in the Appendix to the Greek Application under numbers 1, 4, 9, 15, 17, 18, 19, 23, 24, 25, 30, 31, 33, 38, 41, 42, 43, 45, 46 and 49, the plea of inadmissibility entered in accordance with Article 27, paragraph 3, should consequently be accepted."

[Report: *Yearbook of the European Convention on Human Rights*, 1958–1959, p. 187.]

## II. *The merits*

On January 7, 1958, a Sub-Commission of seven members was constituted.[1] This Sub-Commission met several times during 1958; in particular, it held meetings in the presence of the Parties on June 30 and July 1, and from November 12 to 19, 1958.

While the Sub-Commission was engaged in establishing the facts, the situation in the island of Cyprus was radically changed by the conclusion of the Zurich and London Agreements, which brought about a political settlement of the Cyprus question.

In view of this new situation the Greek and United Kingdom Governments together requested the Commission to close the case without entering upon the substance of the Application.

In considering this request the Commission pointed out that under Article 19 of the Convention it had been set up " to ensure the observance of the engagements undertaken by the High Contracting Parties in the (present) Convention ". It added that " when an Application alleging a breach of the Convention had been referred to the Commission, the withdrawal of the Application was a matter which concerned the Commission as well as the Parties and the

---

[1] Footnote omitted.

Commission must satisfy itself that the termination of the proceedings was calculated to serve, and not to defeat, the purposes of the Convention".

In view of the significance of the Zurich and London Agreements as a means of restoring to the population of Cyprus the full enjoyment of their rights and freedoms, and since, according to the information received, the terms of the Convention were again being fully observed in Cyprus, the Commission *decided* at its eighteenth session to terminate proceedings in regard to Application No. 299/57 without judging its merits. This decision was recorded in a report transmitted to the Committee of Ministers on July 16, 1959.

On December 14, 1959, at its twenty-fifth session, the Committee of Ministers, having received the report in question, *decided* [Resolution (59) 32] that "no further action was called for".

[Report: *Ibid.*, pp. 178–180.]

**State responsibility—For breaches of treaty obligations—European Convention for Protection of Human Rights and Fundamental Freedoms, 1950—Individual applications—Exhaustion of local remedies—Appeal open—Relevance of absence of prospect of success—Relevance of existence of alternative remedy—Duty to lodge claims within reasonable time.**

See p. 172 (*Re Application No.* 214/56 (*De Becker* v. *Belgium*)).

**State responsibility—For breaches of treaty obligations—By subsequent inconsistent treaty—Obligation to exercise due diligence to avoid conflict.**

See p. 190 (*Re Application No.* 235/56 (*Mr. X. and Mrs. X.* v. *German Federal Republic*)).

**State responsibility—For breaches of treaty obligations—European Convention for Protection of Human Rights and Fundamental Freedoms, 1950—Individual applications—Exhaustion of local remedies—Remedies in the ordinary courts and whole system of legal remedies available in State—Whether both must be exhausted.**

See p. 216 (*Re Application No.* 332/57 (*Lawless* v. *Republic of Ireland*)).

**State responsibility—For breaches of treaty obligations—European Convention for Protection of Human Rights and Fundamental Freedoms, 1950—Individual applications—Exhaustion of local remedies—Relevance of time-limits in municipal courts.**

See p. 230 (*Re Application No.* 352/58 (*X.* v. *Federal Republic of Germany*).

# VI.—For Wrongs Unconnected with Contractual Obligations

## i.—Acts and Omissions of State Organs and Officials

(a) DENIAL OF JUSTICE. EXHAUSTION OF LEGAL REMEDIES

State responsibility—For wrongs unconnected with contractual obligations—

—Acts and omissions of State organs—Exhaustion of local remedies—Rule of—Applicability in arbitration proceedings—Absence of special provision for application—Case not involving claim on behalf of individual—Request for interpretation of Agreement as between States—Effect of—Exhaustion of local remedies under Agreement on German External Debts, 1953.

—Acts of judicial organs of State—Denial of justice—Error of law—Error in application of Treaty—Whether State responsible.

SWISS CONFEDERATION v. GERMAN FEDERAL REPUBLIC (No. 1).

*Arbitral Tribunal for the Agreement on German External Debts.*

(Daehli, President; Michelson, Barandon, Wolff, Richard, Phenix, von Caemmerer, Members ; Makarov and Hinderling, Additional Members.[1])

*July* 3, 1958.

THE FACTS (as stated by the Tribunal).—" The Aargauische Hypothekenbank, a company limited by shares (*Aktiengesellschaft*), whose head office is at Brugg in Switzerland, had acquired a plot of land situated in Stuttgart at a forced auction sale in order to safeguard a mortgage on this land registered in its name. It then sold the land by a contract dated July 31, 1931 to the merchants Max and Moriz Lindauer in Stuttgart. A postponement of the payment of the balance of the purchase price amounting to Goldmarks 300,000 was granted to the purchasers; in order to secure this claim a mortgage on the purchased land was registered in favour of the ' Aargauische Hypothekenbank, Aktiengesellschaft, at Brugg, Switzerland '. The provisions of the contract of sale which are relevant for the present dispute read as follows:

" § 1. The Aargauische Hypothekenbank, with its head office at Brugg, remained the highest bidder at the forced auction sale of the land located within the boundaries of Stuttgart and entered in the Land Register,

---

[1] Appointed respectively by the Government of the German Federal Republic and the Swiss Federal Council.

Stuttgart, Volume No. 1996, Part I, No. 1, in the name of the firm J. Mack, Stuttgart,

Boundaries of Stuttgart,

| Building No. 65 Königstrasse | | |
|---|---|---|
| Dwellinghouse | —: | 2 a 17 qm |
| Yard | —: | 14 qm |
| Corner shared with Building No. 2 Poststrasse | —: | 07 qm |

—: 2 a 38 qm

and the said land was allotted to it by a decision announced on July 14, 1931, by Bezirksnotar Küstner, Stuttgart.

" § 2. The Aargauische Hypothekenbank with its head office at Brugg hereby sells the land described in § 1 of this minute to Messrs. Max Lindauer, merchant of Stuttgart, and Moriz Lindauer, merchant of Stuttgart, who acquire the land to hold jointly in undivided moieties.

" § 5. Interest is payable on the total purchase price from October 1, 1931, at 6½ per cent. annually. The interest is to be paid at the end of each calendar quarter and for the first time on December 31, 1931, free of charge to the vendor or to a pay office (or ' payee ', in German ' Zahlstelle ') to be specified by it; the same applies to the payment of the purchase price and the several instalments.)

The creditor has not specified a pay office.

" The merchants Lindauer sold the land by contracts of sale and transfer of November 16, 1937, to the Kommanditgesellschaft Conrad Tack & Cie, shoe factory, with its seat then at Berlin-Tempelhof, now at Weinheim a. d. Bergstrasse. The Tack firm took over as debtor the mortgage claim entered on behalf of the Aargauische Hypothekenbank as a set-off against the purchase price. Conrad Tack & Cie, GmbH. at Weinheim a. d. Bergstrasse, is also liable for the mortgage claim; it has been entered in the Land Register as owner since May 9, 1956. After repayment of an instalment on November 26, 1940, the mortgage debt has amounted to Goldmarks 220,000.

" After the Agreement on German External Debts of February 27, 1953 (hereinafter referred to as 'the Debt Agreement '),[1] came into force, the creditor requested the firm of Tack & Cie to settle the mortgage debt as a debt with a specific foreign character on the basis of a conversion rate of 1 : 1. The firm of Tack & Cie thereupon addressed themselves, in a correspondence extending over years in which the creditor also intervened, to the authorities competent to pass upon such an agreement for settlement (Bank deutscher Länder, now Deutsche Bundesbank, Oberfinanzdirektion Karlsruhe, Ministry of Finance of Baden-Württemberg) in order to secure the indemnity envisaged in §§ 52 et seqq. of the Federal Law of August 24, 1953, for the Implementation of the Agreement of February 27, 1953, on

[1 *U.N.T.S.*, vol. 333, p. 4.]

German External Debts (*Bundesgesetzblatt*, I, p. 1003) in case of an admission of the conversion rate of 1 : 1. The Deutsche Bundesbank refused to take position on the question of the conversion rate so long as an agreement for settlement had not been reached between the creditor and the debtors. The Finance Authority did not maintain its original objection that the amount owed, being a debt for a balance of purchase money, did not have a specific foreign character, but it expressed the opinion that the contract of July 31, 1931, did not contain an express agreement on a place of payment abroad and that the Goldmark claim secured by mortgage did not have a specific foreign character.

" On February 27, 1957, the Swiss Legation at Cologne addressed the following *Note Verbale* to the Foreign Office at Bonn:

" ' Differences have arisen between Swiss creditors and German Finance Authorities with regard to the fundamental question whether the so-called unpaid balance of a purchase price arising out of the purchase of German land, when postponed over many years and secured by mortgage, can be considered a debt resulting from a financial transaction of the nature of a loan. Thus the Aargauische Hypothekenbank, of Brugg/Switzerland, is of the opinion that its claim against the firm of Tack, of Weinheim a.d. Bergstrasse, for the balance of purchase money is of a specific foreign character within the meaning of Annex II in conjunction with Annex VII to the London Debt Agreement. The enclosed Opinion of *Rechtsanwalt* Miller [of] Düsseldorf, contains exhaustive information regarding the facts of the case and the legal position.

' The negotiations undertaken up to now by the creditor with the debtors, the Bank deutscher Länder, as well as with the Finance Authorities of the *Land* of Baden-Württemberg, have been without result. Pursuant to the letter of December 13, 1956, a photostat copy of which is enclosed, the Ministry of Finance at Stuttgart have finally adopted the view " that the claim of the Aargauische Hypothekenbank of Brugg/ Switzerland against the firm of Tack is not of a specific foreign character within the meaning of the London Debt Agreement and that, therefore, the firm of Tack is not entitled to claim compensation from the *Land*, in pursuance of the Law implementing the London Debt Agreement ".

' As, on the one hand, the Aargauische Hypothekenbank is not prepared to accept the negative decision quoted and, on the other hand, the Swiss Federal Council are prepared to accept the creditor's legal interpretation as their own, the Legation request the Foreign Office to obtain, as soon as possible, the comments of the Government of the Federal Republic of Germany on the point in dispute.'

" On July 22, 1957, the Foreign Office, in a *Note Verbale*, informed the Swiss Embassy of the following:

" ' The Foreign Office have the honour to refer to their *Note Verbale* No. 72/57 of 30. 4. 1957 regarding the liability of the firm of Tack & Cie GmbH. towards the Aargauische Hypothekenbank at Brugg, and to confirm to the Swiss Embassy that the Federal Minister of Justice supports the view expressed in the letter from the Oberfinanzdirektion, Karlsruhe, dated 12. 4. 1957, with regard to the opinion on the specific foreign character of the disputed Goldmark claim. The Federal Minister of Justice bases his view—agreeing, in essence, with the other Authorities concerned—on the wording of § 5 of the contract of sale, which reads as follows:

' " The interest is to be paid at the end of each calendar quarter and for the first time on December 31, 1931, free of charge to the vendor or to a pay office (or payee) to be specified by it; the same applies to the payment of the purchase price and the several instalments."

" ' As this clause determines merely to whom but not where the payments are to be made, it cannot be regarded as an agreement on the place of payment. In a case like this, the question of the place of payment (place of performance—Leistungsort) can be determined only in accordance with legal provisions. Even if this should mean a place of payment abroad—which would not be the case if German law were applied—it would not suffice, in view of Annex VII, Section I, para. 2 (a), to affirm the specific foreign character. Even if interpretation were to show that the clause of agreement mentioned contains a stipulation of the place of payment, this could, in any case, not be regarded as an " express " agreement within the meaning of Annex VII to the Debt Agreement. This being the position in law, the Federal Minister of Justice has not examined further the question whether, in the case presented, the claim for an unpaid balance of purchase price is of a specific foreign character within the meaning of Annex VII to the Debt Agreement.'

" In August 1957, the Tack firm brought an action against the Land Baden-Württemberg before the Landgericht, Karlsruhe, by submitting the application:

" ' that the Plaintiff, in the settlement of its debt owed to the Aargauische Hypothekenbank, Brugg/Switzerland, amounting to GM 220,000, which is entered in the Land Register of Stuttgart, Volume No. 1996, Part III, No. 19, as a mortgage charge in favour of the Aargauische Hypothekenbank, is entitled to an indemnity under §§ 63 and 66 of the Law implementing the London Debt Agreement.'

" This proceeding was suspended sine die upon the request of both parties at the hearing of November 12, 1957 ' because of the proceeding pending before the Arbitral Tribunal at Koblenz '.

" The Swiss Confederation, whose Government is a Party to the Debt Agreement, has now resorted to the Arbitral Tribunal requesting that

' the Arbitral Tribunal render the following decision:

" ' that, within the meaning of Annex VII, Section I, para. 2 (a), to the Agreement on German External Debts of February 27, 1953, it has expressly been agreed by the contract of July 31, 1931, between the Aargauische Hypothekenbank Aktiengesellschaft and Messrs. Max and Moriz Lindauer that the place of payment of the Goldmark claim created by the contract was situated abroad.'

" The Federal Republic of Germany, whose Government is also a Party to the Debt Agreement, requested as Respondent

" that the Application of the Swiss Confederation be dismissed as inadmissible.

In case this request should not be complied with, the Respondent has requested

" that the Application of the Swiss Confederation be rejected as unfounded.

" The contract of July 31, 1931, concerns, as is undisputed, a debt relationship which is subject to settlement pursuant to Annex II to the Debt Agreement. According to Article V, para. 3, of said Annex, ' such financial debts and mortgages, expressed in Goldmarks or in Reichsmarks with a gold clause, as had a specific foreign character shall be converted into Deutsche Mark at the rate of 1 Goldmark, or 1 Reichsmark with a gold clause, = 1 Deutsche Mark.'

" The criteria constituting a specific foreign character in the case of such pecuniary debts are determined pursuant to Annex VII to the Debt Agreement. The provision of Annex VII which is relevant in this connection is the provision contained in Section I, para. 2 (a), which, in so far as it has bearing on the present dispute, reads as follows:

" ' In respect of the claims and rights specified below it is recognized that they have a specific foreign character within the meaning of the above-mentioned provisions:

1. . . . . .

2. Claims expressed in Goldmarks, or in Reichsmarks with a gold clause or a gold option, arising from other loans or advances resulting from financial transactions and raised abroad by German debtors, including claims of this kind secured by mortgage charges; if

(a) it was expressly agreed under the original written debt arrangements that the place of payment or the ·competent court is situated abroad or foreign law is applicable.'

The introductory sentence of this quotation refers to the provisions now contained in Sub-Annex D to Annex I, No. 2, in Article V, para. 3, of Annex II and in Article 6, para. (2), of Annex IV.

" In order to substantiate their submissions, the parties used the following arguments.

" The Applicant expressed the opinion that §§ 1, 2 and 5 of the contract of July 31, 1931, contained an express agreement, within the meaning of Annex VII, Section 1, para. 2 (a), to the Debt Agreement, that the place of payment was to be situated abroad, *viz.* in Brugg/ Switzerland, the head office of the creditor. It was the general legal opinion that the conception of an express agreement of a place of payment abroad within the meaning of Annex VII, as well as the remaining provisions of that Annex, must be given a wide interpretation according to the sense emerging from the text and from their origin. With regard to the conception of an express agreement of a place of payment abroad within the meaning of Annex VII to the Debt Agreement, the Applicant invoked Section 244, para. 1, of the German Civil Code as well as a number of legal opinions and court decisions, including the decision of the Mixed Commission of November 27, 1956, in the case of *Bodenkreditbank in Basel* v. *Gebrüder*

*Rohrer GmbH*.[1] The Applicant furthermore pointed out that the 'head office at Brugg' was mentioned twice in the contract; it maintained that it emerged from this fact as well as from the provision of the contract that the purchase price, the instalments thereof and interest were to be paid free of charge to the vendor or to a pay office (*or* payee) to be specified by it, that Brugg had been expressly agreed upon as the place of payment.

" In the opinion of the Applicant, the Arbitral Tribunal has jurisdiction under Article 28, para. (2), of the Debt Agreement because the dispute which had arisen between the Applicant and the Respondent concerning questions of interpretation of Annex VII could not be settled by negotiation. Nor, in the opinion of the Applicant, was the jurisdiction of the Arbitral Tribunal excluded in the present case by Article 28, para. (5), of the Debt Agreement since the Arbitration and Mediation Committee envisaged under Article IX of Annex II to the Debt Agreement had not yet been established.

" The Respondent in the first place contested the competence of the Arbitral Tribunal and argued as follows:

" The prerequisites for a resort to the Arbitral Tribunal did not exist in the present case if only because, according to a generally accepted rule of international law, the private parties whose interests are involved in the case must themselves first have exhausted unsuccessfully the remedies open to them before the courts competent under national law for the prosecution and enforcement of their interests, before resort can be had to an international arbitral tribunal competent to decide disputes between States. The Respondent pointed out in this connection that the private party in question in the present case, *viz.*, a Swiss bank as creditor, had not only not exhausted the remedies before the courts at its disposal but had not even begun to do so. It relied in this connection on a number of decisions of international courts and on the views of certain authors.

" The Respondent furthermore expressed the opinion that the competence of the Arbitral Tribunal could not be deduced from Article 28 of the Debt Agreement in cases like the present. The nature of the Applicant's request alone excluded the jurisdiction of the Arbitral Tribunal under Article 28 of the Debt Agreement, since it could not be the task of the Arbitral Tribunal to decide a dispute which, by its nature, was a dispute between two private parties, merely because it had been clothed with the appearance of an international dispute between States by the Application of the Applicant. The Respondent argued that the jurisdiction of the Arbitral Tribunal, as set out in Article 28, para. (2), of the Debt Agreement and in so far as it concerned the application of the Agreement, covered only claims against a Party to the Agreement, as, *e.g.*, claims resulting from the obligations which the Federal Republic of Germany had assumed in Articles 7, 8 and 10 of the Debt Agreement. Furthermore, the

[1 Reported below, p. 326.]

jurisdiction of the Arbitral Tribunal which might exist was excluded by Article 28, para. (2), if the dispute concerned a question of interpretation or application of an Annex to the Debt Agreement, and an arbitral body established pursuant to such Annex was competent to decide a dispute concerning the interpretation or application of that Annex. In the present case the dispute concerned the interpretation or application of Annex VII to the Debt Agreement which, in so far as it was applicable to the present case, was relevant only in conjunction with Annex II to the Debt Agreement and constituted only a Sub-Annex to that Annex. The arbitral body competent to decide disputes concerning the interpretation or application pursuant to Annex II to the Debt Agreement, *viz.*, the Arbitration and Mediation Committee envisaged in Article IX of Annex II to the Debt Agreement, had in the meantime been established and was able to take up its functions at any time.

" In order to substantiate its alternative request that the Application of the Swiss Confederation be rejected as unfounded, the Respondent maintained that with regard to the debt in question there was no agreement at all on the place of payment. It contradicted the opinion of the Applicant according to which such an agreement could be deduced from the mention of the ' head office at Brugg ' or from the provision of § 5 of the contract of July 31, 1931. It went into lengthy explanations regarding the conception of the place of payment in general and, in particular, within the meaning of Annex VII to the Debt Agreement. Setting out from the principle that the place of payment is the place where the debtor has to take the action necessary for the satisfaction of the pecuniary debt, the Respondent explained Sections 269 and 270 of the German Civil Code to mean that, according to German law, pecuniary debts are either callable debts (place of payment is the residence of the debtor) or deliverable debts (place of payment is the residence of the creditor) or transmissible debts (place of payment is the residence of the debtor who is, however, obliged to transmit the money owed at his cost and risk to the creditor). A number of foreign legal opinions were also cited in this connection which, the Respondent maintained, showed that this legal situation had also been recognized abroad. The Respondent argued that in the present case the debt was transmissible (place of payment is the residence of the debtor) and that § 5 of the contract of sale of July 31, 1931, did not contain a place-of-payment clause but a typical transmission clause. The place of payment therefore was, in any case, Stuttgart. The fact that the place of payment must be determined according to German law resulted also from the rule of German private international law, which was generally accepted in legal science and jurisprudence, and according to which the applicable law was determined by the centre of gravity of the debt relationship. This centre of gravity was situated in Germany, for the case concerned the sale of land situated in Germany to a German. The sale was authenticated by a German notary public, the purchase price was specified in German currency and secured by a mortgage on a German plot of land.

" The applicant made detailed observations in reply to the objections of the respondent to the admissibility of the proceeding and to the competence of the Arbitral Tribunal. It argued, in particular, that in the present case the dispute concerned the interpretation of not only one, but several, Annexes to the London Debt Agreement and that, therefore, the Arbitral Tribunal was competent under Article 28, para. (2), of the Agreement, irrespective of the establishment of the Arbitration and Mediation Committee under Annex II. Nor was it a private dispute disguised as a dispute between States, because the individual foreign creditor was confronted not by the individual German debtor but by the latter's State and its authorities as his true opponents whenever these authorities denied the specific foreign character of the debt, so that every such case became a ' State affair '. The Applicant countered the objection of the non-exhaustion of local remedies by arguing that the Debt Agreement, as a self-contained *lex specialis*, did not permit the application of the rule of the exhaustion of local remedies. Furthermore, pursuant to Article 17, para. 1 (a), of the Debt Agreement in conjunction with § 2, para. 1, of the German Law implementing the Debt Agreement, the foreign creditor had the right, but not the duty, to resort to German courts and to submit himself definitively to this jurisdiction.

" In the substantive dispute concerning the question of the place of payment abroad the applicant argued in detailed observations that the conception of the place of payment within the meaning of the Debt Agreement could only be taken from the Agreement itself, and in accordance therewith the place of payment was the place where, pursuant to the written arrangements, the creditor was actually to receive payment of his pecuniary claim, *i.e.*, in the present case Brugg (Switzerland). Moreover, the express agreement on the place of payment abroad resulted both from the document of July 31, 1931, and from the attendant circumstances.

" The parties set out their contradictory legal opinions, the principal points of which have been reproduced above, in exhaustive pleadings, basing themselves on numerous decisions, legal opinions and statements of public authorities.

" The question asked by some members of the Arbitral Tribunal as to how the respective debtors had effected the interest payment due on December 31, 1931, and all subsequent interest payments was answered by the parties as follows:

" The Applicant submitted: The debtors Lindauer had transferred interest for the total debt of Goldmarks 300,000 in quarterly instalments to the head office of the creditor at Brugg (Switzerland) in the period from December 31, 1931, to September 30, 1933. After

September 30, 1933, only the interest on the free capital part of Goldmarks 220,000 had been transferred by the debtors Lindauer in quarterly instalments directly to the head office of the creditor, while the interest on the capital part of Goldmarks 80,000 had been transferred to the creditor through the German-Swiss clearing system *viâ* the Conversion Office for German External Debts. The Tack firm had continued this mode of payment. They had also transferred the interest on the free capital part of Goldmarks 220,000 through their bank connection, the Deutsche Bank at Berlin, freely and directly, and the interest on the remaining part through the Conversion Office for German External Debts to the head office of the creditor. After repayment of a capital part of further Goldmarks 79,089.84 to a blocked account of the creditor with the Deutsche Bank at Berlin, interest payment on the remaining capital part of Goldmarks 220,000 had continued to be effected in quarterly instalments to the head office of the creditor. The last interest payment before the end of the war had been made on June 30, 1944. Additional interest payments which had been made had not been received by the creditor.

" The Respondent submitted: No statements could be made regarding the manner of interest payment for the time prior to November 16, 1937, the day of the purchase of the land by the Kommanditgesellscahft Conrad Tack & Cie. So far as the time after November 16, 1937, was concerned, interest had been transferred either through the bank connection of the debtor or, in so far as the amounts due were not freely convertible, through the Conversion Office. The transfers had been effected in such a manner that the Deutsche Bank had received orders to transfer the transferable interest to a Swiss bank at Basle or Zurich for the account of the creditor or to pay the amounts in question to the Conversion Office."

*Held*—*On the question of competence* (unanimously): that the Arbitral Tribunal was competent to adjudicate upon the present dispute.

*On the merits* (by five votes to four—Barandon, Wolff and von Caemmerer, Members, and Makarov, Additional Member, dissenting): that the request of the applicant must succeed. The term " place of payment " as used in Annex VII to the Agreement on German External Debts " should be interpreted as denoting the place where the creditor was entitled actually to receive his money, whether directly from the debtor or by transmission through the post or by any other agency ". In the present case the creditor was entitled to receive payment in Switzerland. Thus it must be concluded that " within the meaning of Annex VII, I, 2 (*a*), to the Agreement on German External Debts of February 27, 1953, it was expressly agreed in the contract of July 31, 1931, between the Aargauische Hypothekenbank AG. and Herren Max and Moriz Lindauer that the place of payment of the Goldmark claim created by the said contract was situated abroad."

The Tribunal said:

1. " *On the question of Competence*
" I.

" Pursuant to Article 6 of the Charter of the Arbitral Tribunal (Annex IX to the Debt Agreement), the Arbitral Tribunal must, in the interpretation of the Agreement and the Annexes thereto, apply the generally accepted rules of international law. There can be no doubt that the rule of the exhaustion of local remedies (*Grundsatz der Erschöpfung der landesrechtlichen Instanzen; règle de l'épuisement des instances internes*) is also a generally accepted rule of international law and must, therefore, be applied by the Arbitral Tribunal in its decisions concerning the interpretation of the Debt Agreement and the Annexes thereto. The rule of the exhaustion of local remedies, as a generally accepted rule of international law, is applicable to the interpretation of an international treaty also in cases in which that treaty does not expressly stipulate the observation of this rule (see the criticism voiced in Guggenheim, *Lehrbuch des Völkerrechts*, Basle 1951, Vol. II, in Note 2 on p. 531, of the opinion expressed by Judge van Eysinga in his Dissenting Opinion to the decision of the Permanent Court of International Justice in the case of the *Panevezys-Saldutiskis Railway*[11]). It is true, however, that the application of the rule of the exhaustion of local remedies may also be expressly excluded in a bilateral or multilateral agreement, which is not the case here.

" The question is, however, whether in view of the internationally generally accepted content of the rule of the exhaustion of local remedies the Respondent can in the present case invoke this rule in order to prove its contention that the Arbitral Tribunal is not competent to deal with and to decide this case.

" In legal text-books and decisions by the Permanent Court of International Justice and the International Court of Justice, as well as in treaty practice, the application of the rule of the exhaustion of local remedies has always been taken into consideration only in connection with a discussion of the question of the international responsibility of a State for an unlawful act (*Unrecht; l'acte contraire au droit*) committed on its territory against a national of another State and for a refusal to grant reparation of this unlawful act, *viz.*, a denial of justice (*Rechtsverweigerung; déni de justice*). The invocation of the rule of the exhaustion of local remedies as a generally accepted rule of international law is justified only if a claim is made against a State, in particular a claim for reparation or damages, and such claim is based on the fact that a national of the State which makes the claim has been impaired in his rights in

[1 *P.C.I.J.*, Series A/B, No. 76; *Annual Digest*, 1938–1940, Case No. 103, at p. 314.]

violation of international law, if the State against which the claim is made can be held responsible therefor under international law and the person whose rights have been infringed has not exhausted the remedies legally available to him in the State against which the claim is made, in order to assert the infringement of his rights.

" As far as legal text-books are concerned, special reference may be made in this connection to

" Dionisio Anzilotti, *Corso di Diritto Internazionale* (Volume I of the complete edition of the works), Padua 1955, pp. 384 *et seqq.*, 423; Bin Cheng, *General Principles of Law as Applied by International Courts and Tribunals*, London 1953, pp. 163 *et seqq.*, 170 *et seqq.*, 177 *et seqq.*; Frede Castberg, *Folkerett*, Oslo 1948, pp. 150 *et seqq.*; Louis Cavaré, *Le droit international public positif*, Paris 1951, Volume II, pp. 270 *et seqq.*, 292 *et seqq.*; J. E. S. Fawcett in *The British Year Book of International Law*, 1954, pp. 452 *et seqq.*, Note: ' The Exhaustion of Local Remedies: Substance or Procedure? '; Paul Guggenheim, *Traité de Droit international public*, Genève 1954, Volume II, pp. 1 *et seqq.*, 12 *et seq.*, 21 *et seqq.*; Charles Cheney Hyde, *International Law*, Boston 1951, Volume II, pp. 909 *et seqq.*; Franz von Liszt, *Das Völkerrecht*, 12th edition, edited by Max Fleischmann, Berlin 1925, pp. 279 *et seqq.*, 283; Lord McNair, *International Law Opinions*, Cambridge 1956, pp. 293 *et seqq.*, 311 *et seqq.*; L. Oppenheim, *International Law*, 8th edition, edited by Sir H. Lauterpacht, London, New York, Toronto 1955, Volume II, p. 361; Alf Ross, *Lehrbuch des Völkerrechts*, German translation of the Danish original, Stuttgart and Cologne 1951, pp. 231 *et seq.*, 240 *et seqq.*, 250 *et seqq.*; Georg Schwarzenberger, *International Law*, 2nd edition, London 1949, Volume I, pp. 233 *et seq.*, 235 *et seq.*; Paul Schoen, ' Haftung, völkerrechtliche der Staaten ', in Strupp's *Wörterbuch des Völkerrechts und der Diplomatie*, Volume I, Berlin and Leipzig 1924; Halvar G. F. Sundberg, *Folkrätt*, Stockholm 1950, pp. 211 *et seqq.*; Alfred Verdross, *Völkerrecht*, 3rd edition, Vienna 1955, p. 308, p. 329.

" Nor does a different interpretation of the rule of the exhaustion of local remedies emerge from the Judgments of the Permanent Court of International Justice cited by the Respondent in the proceeding instituted by Estonia against Lithuania concerning the *Panevezys-Saldutiskis Railway*,[1] of the International Court of Justice in the proceeding instituted by France against Norway conerning *Certain Norwegian Loans*,[2] or from the decision of the Arbitrator, Algot Bagge, in the dispute between Finland and Great Britain concerning the use of various *Finnish ships*[3] during the First World War.

" So far as the Lithuanian-Estonian dispute is concerned, the issue was that the Lithuanian Government was charged with having refused to recognize rights of the owners and concessionaries of the railway line Panevezys-Saldutiskis and to grant compensation for the illegal seizure and use of this railway line. Consequently, a

[1 *P.C.I.J.*, Series A/B, No. 76; *Annual Digest*, 1938–1940, Case No. 103.]
[2 *I.C.J. Reports*, 1957, p. 9; *International Law Reports*, 1957, p. 782.]
[3 *Annual Digest*, 1933–1934, Case No. 91.]

claim for damages was made against the Lithuanian Government. The Permanent Court of International Justice decided in its Judgment of February 28, 1939, that the application submitted by the Estonian Government was inadmissible and that the objection of the non-exhaustion of local remedies raised by the Lithuanian Government was well founded. See . . . ' Publications de la Cour Permanente de Justice Internationale ', Série A/B No. 76, in particular p. 5 and p. 22.

" In the dispute between France and Norway the question was whether the gold clause contained in certain loans which had been issued by the Norwegian State and by two Norwegian banks, for which the Norwegian State had assumed a full guarantee, should continue to be observed. The French Government supported this view by reasoning that the loans in question were international loans and that it followed from the nature of such loans that payments to the foreign owners of bonds of such loans had to be effected without any discrimination. The Norwegian Government, on the other hand, relied primarily on the declarations made by the litigating parties of November 16, 1946, and of March 1, 1949, which contained a restriction of the obligatory jurisdiction of the International Court of Justice. It, furthermore, invoked a Norwegian Law of December 15, 1923, by virtue of which the servicing of loans expressed in gold had been modified in a certain manner—further details are not interesting in this connection. Lastly, it also argued that the bondholders, on whose behalf the French Government thought it was justified in resorting to an international court, had not exhausted local remedies in Norway. The decision of the International Court of Justice is dated July 6, 1957. The Court considered itself not competent, in view of the declaration of the French Government of March 1, 1949, which, in the opinion of the Court, contained a reservation with regard to the obligatory jurisdiction of the Court and upon which the Norwegian Government could rely from the point of view of reciprocity. The Court, therefore, did not deem it necessary to deal with the further objections raised by the Norwegian Government. For details, see ' Report of Judgments, Advisory Opinions and Orders ', Judgment of July 6th, 1957; ' Recueil des Arrêts, Avis Consultatifs et Ordonnances ', Arrêt du 6 Juillet 1957, in particular pp. 13, 16, 17, 19 and 27.[1]

" Consequently, there is in this case no decision of the International Court of Justice concerning the applicability of the rule of the exhaustion of local remedies. It is true, however, that the Judge Sir Hersch Lauterpacht dealt with the question of the applicability of this rule in his very exhaustive Separate Opinion, which differs from the decision of the Court. With reference to the rule in question, he said: ' It is a rule which international tribunals have applied with a considerable degree of elasticity '. (Page 39 of the

[1 *International Law Reports*, 1957, p. 782.]

publication of the decisions of the International Court of Justice in the above-mentioned official Reports.) But whether this opinion is correct or not, the fact remains that the observations of Sir Hersch Lauterpacht refer only to the dispute submitted to the International Court of Justice in which the French Government charged the Norwegian Government with an infringement of rights and made a claim based on this alleged infringement because Norway had not treated the owners of an international loan impartially. Moreover, Sir Hersch Lauterpacht's observations on the ' elasticity ' in the application of the rule of the exhaustion of local remedies do not concern the question whether and when this rule is applicable, but the question of the method of its application, *i.e.*, the question how the rule is to be applied in each case.

" The dispute between Finland and the United Kingdom of Great Britain and Northern Ireland, which was decided by the Arbitrator, Algot Bagge, in 1931, concerned a claim for damages made by Finland against the United Kingdom. This claim was based on the fact that during the First World War Finnish ships had first been requisitioned by Russia and had then been taken to British ports where they were taken over by British authorities. The Finnish shipowners had requested compensation for this (see Schwarzenberger, *op. cit.* p. 235, as well as Bin Cheng, *op. cit.* p. 911, Note 9, and p. 917). In this case, too, the claim for damages was based on the contention that there had been an infringement of rights for which the State against which the action was brought was legally responsible.

" It is in accord with the opinion of the various international arbitral bodies, as reflected in the above-mentioned decisions, that in the *Ambatielos* case (Greece versus the United Kingdom of Great Britain and Northern Ireland), the Commission of Arbitration which had been established pursuant to an agreement between the litigants, in its decision of March 6, 1956 (Her Majesty's Stationery Office, London, 1956,[1] see in particular p. 27[2]), formulated the rule of the exhaustion of local remedies as follows:

" ' It means that the State against which an international action is brought for injuries suffered by private individuals has the right to resist such an action if the persons alleged to have been injured have not first exhausted all the remedies available to them under the municipal law of that State.'

" In international treaty practice, too, the rule of the exhaustion of local remedies has always been applied only in the same sense in which legal text-books and international decisions termed it a generally accepted rule of international law. The more recent treaties cited by the Respondent do not speak against the assumption, as remains to be shown in a different context.

[1 *International Law Reports*, 1956, p. 306.]
[2 *Ibid.*, p. 334.]

" But the opinions quoted by the Respondent, as they have of late been expressed in international bodies on the rule of the exhaustion of local remedies, also merely confirm that the rule can only be valid as a generally accepted rule of international law as formulated above and in connection with the responsibility of States for infringements of rights. The Respondent itself mentions that the Rapporteur of the International Law Commission of the United Nations, Garcia Amador, made his observations on the problem of the Exhaustion Rule in connection with the question of ' International Responsibility '. The resolution adopted at the meeting of the Institut de Droit International at Granada (April 1956) also proceeds from the assumption that a State contends ' *que la lésion subie par un de ses ressortissants dans sa personne ou dans ses biens a été commise en violation du droit international* ' and that in that case any diplomatic or judicial intervention is inadmissible if the national legislation of the State which is alleged to have committed the injury provides remedies which had been available to the injured person and which would probably also have been effective and sufficient, and if and so long as the use of these remedies has not been exhausted. In connection with this resolution, reference may also be made to the *travaux préparatoires* of the Granada meeting and to the particularly illuminating remarks on the questionnaire of the Rapporteur, J. H. W. Verzijl, by the Rapporteur himself as well as by Alf Ross, Roberto Ago, Paul Guggenheim and Alfred Verdross (*Annuaire de l'Institut de Droit International*, Session de Granade 1956, pp. 14 *et seqq.*, 21 *et seqq.*, 24 *et seqq.*, 31 *et seqq.*, 47 *et seq.*).

" This is not a case in which the rule of the exhaustion of local remedies, in so far as it is to be considered a generally accepted rule of international law in accordance with the above observations, could be applied.

" In certain circumstances, however, the rule of the exhaustion of local remedies could also be effectively invoked in a proceeding concerning the interpretation or application of the Debt Agreement or the Annexes thereto before the Arbitral Tribunal. This would be the case if a creditor country alleged that one of its nationals had been refused the enforcement of his rights pursuant to Article 17 of the Debt Agreement before the German courts by not having his complaint entertained at all; this could then constitute a dispute which would be subject to the jurisdiction of the Arbitral Tribunal. In that, presumably purely theoretical, case the Arbitral Tribunal could only be resorted to once the creditor country had proved that its national had tried in vain, by exhausting all the remedies at his disposal, to bring an action against the debtor which was admissible under Article 17 of the Debt Agreement. If, however, the German courts have dealt with the action in due form and if only the creditor's contention that the debt due to him had a specific foreign character within the meaning of Annex VII to the Agreement has remained unsuccessful after he has exhausted all remedies at his disposal under German law, the State of which the creditor is a national could nevertheless not resort to the Arbitral Tribunal and possibly bring an action for damages against the Federal Republic. For the declaration of the German courts that a claim does not have a specific foreign character would, at the most, represent a legal error for which the Federal Republic would not be responsible under international law, and it would never be a violation of international law or a denial of justice for which the Federal Republic would have to bear the international responsibility. The present case, however, as has been said before, is not such as to make possible the application of the rule of the exhaustion of local remedies, at any rate not in so far as it has been generally accepted as a binding rule of international law in what may be termed its classical form, as described above. The Applicant has not made a claim for damages against the Federal Republic. The Applicant makes no claim whatsoever, but merely requests a decision of the Arbitral Tribunal on the interpretation and application of Annex VII in conjunction with Annex II to the Debt Agreement in a particular dispute.

" In the present case, therefore, the lack of jurisdiction of the Arbitral Tribunal cannot be alleged by invoking the rule of the exhaustion of local remedies in the form more precisely defined above—and only in that form, as has been explained previously has it been recognized as a generally binding rule of international law.

" The Respondent, however, as can be deduced in particular from its arguments in the oral proceedings, also tried to show that there are obvious tendencies in the more recent development of international law which amount to an extension of the applicability of the rule of the exhaustion of local remedies. In this connection, the Respondent refers in particular to the observations made by the Judge Sir Hersch Lauterpacht in his Separate Opinion to the decision of the International Court of Justice in the dispute between France and Norway concerning *Certain Norwegian Loans* of July 6, 1957, as well as to some recent treaties in which, in the opinion of the Respondent, the rule has been applied in a wider sense than hitherto. It mentions, in this connection, the Pact of Bogotá of April 30, 1948 —American Treaty on Pacific Settlement—(printed in *United Nations Textbook*, Leiden 1954, p. 385[1]), the Agreement between the Federal Republic of Germany and the Austrian Republic concerning the Facilitation of Frontier Clearance for Transport by Rail, Road and Waterways of September 14, 1955 (*Bundesgesetzblatt*, 1957, II, Vol, I, p. 582), the Agreement between the Federal Republic of Germany and the Austrian Republic concerning the Regulation of the Frontier Crossing of Railways of October 28, 1955 (*Bundesgesetzblatt*, 1957, II,

[1 Also in 30 *U.N.T.S.* 55.]

Vol. I, p. 599), and the Agreement between the Federal Republic of Germany and the Kingdom of Sweden concerning German Property in Sweden of March 22, 1956 (*Bundesgesetzblatt*, II, Vol. I, p. 811).

" The observations by Lauterpacht to which the Respondent refers have already been dealt with above. They are also based on the opinion that the invocation of the rule of the exhaustion of local remedies is, at any rate, subject to a claim having been made by one State against another which is based on an infringement of rights. This follows also from the formulation which Sir Hersch Lauterpacht himself has given of the rule in the newly edited text-book on International Law by Oppenheim (Oppenheim-Lauterpacht, *International Law*, 8th edition, 1955, London, New York, Toronto). It is said therein on p. 361 in § 162 a:

" ' It is a recognised rule that an international tribunal will not enter-tain a claim put forward on behalf of an alien on account of alleged denial of justice unless the person in question has exhausted the legal remedies available to him in the State concerned.'

" In the Pact of Bogotá which, as is made clear by its official title, ' American Treaty on Pacific Settlement ', was a political treaty, the rule of the exhaustion of local remedies is to be found in Article 7. According to the formulation of this provision, the impression might be created that a somewhat more extensive applicability of the rule of the necessity to exhaust local remedies before taking diplomatic steps or resorting to international jurisdiction was to be admitted in inter-American relations, as compared with the former practice of international law. In the opinion of the Arbitral Tribunal, however, this is not the case either. On the contrary, the words used in Article 7 of the Pact of Bogotá ' in order to protect their nationals ' make it clear that the American States, too, which concluded the Pact, proceeded from the assumption that it is possible to invoke the rule of the exhaustion of local remedies only if the State which wishes to invoke this rule is held responsible for an unlawful act committed on its territory and if claims resulting therefrom are being made against it. Nor is it to be assumed that precisely when con-cluding a purely political treaty concerning the general relationship of the American States to one another, such as the Pact of Bogotá, the contracting Parties had the intention of creating an extension, binding on the Contracting States, to the field of applicability of the rule in question.

" Nor can it be deduced from the Agreements which the Federal Republic recently concluded with Austria and Sweden that inter-national law is about to admit the possibility of applying the rule of the exhaustion of local remedies also in cases in which no claim based on an infringement of rights is made against the State which wishes to invoke this rule. The Treaties cited merely contain the provision customary in recent treaties that in the case of differences of opinion between the Contracting Parties resort shall be had to an arbitral tribunal, and they lay down details as to the composition of this arbitral tribunal. The Treaties do not say anything about the question under what further conditions the arbitral tribunal can be resorted to in the case of disputes concerning their interpretation and application.

" Nor is it evident from international decisions that there might be tendencies in international law from which an application of the rule of the exhaustion of local remedies more extended than hitherto practised could be concluded. It is certainly true that the International Court of Justice has, with regard to the establishment of its jurisdiction, always adopted a very cautious attitude towards the objection that local remedies had not been exhausted. This attitude, however, does not concern the substantive prerequisites for the application of the rule of the exhaustion of local remedies in accordance with the general principle of international law, but merely the question whether, assuming the applicability of this rule, the local courts had, in fact, rendered a final decision or not (see Sir Hersch Lauterpacht, *The Development of International Law by the International Court*, London 1958, pp. 100 to 102). Consequently, the International Court of Justice also remains of the opinion that the above-mentioned rule can be applied only ' in the field of State responsibility ' for an international unlawful act (see Sir Hersch Lauterpacht, *op. cit.*, p. 350).

" But even if the recent development of international law showed the tendencies alleged by the Respondent with regard to the application of the rule of the exhaustion of local remedies, this would nevertheless not mean that a generally accepted rule of international law has already evolved which the Arbitral Tribunal, too, would have to take into account when rendering its decisions. Under Article 6 of its Charter (Annex IX to the Debt Agreement), it is bound only by the generally accepted rules of international law. The rule of the necessity to exhaust local remedies before the opening of diplomatic negotiations or the resort to international jurisdiction is valid as a generally accepted rule of international law only in the formulation contained in the resolution of the Institut de Droit International as adopted at the Granada meeting in April 1956, which was also quoted by the Respondent. (See *Annuaire de l'Institut de Droit International*, 1956, p. 358.)

" If, therefore, the resort to the Arbitral Tribunal in disputes like the present is not subject to a prior exhaustion of the remedies which were available for the settlement of the civil suit forming the basis of the dispute, it is not necessary to examine what possibilities the creditor would have had of enforcing its claims against the debtor; whether, *e.g.*, the special requirements for a resort to the German courts by a foreign creditor laid down in Articles 15 and 17 of the Debt Agreement existed in the present case. Nor is it relevant, therefore, whether, as the Applicant contends, the debtor made an offer of settlement pursuant to Article 15 of the Debt Agreement and was willing to recognize the specific foreign character of the debt in question provided the indemnity to which it is entitled under §§ 63 *et seqq.* of the German Law implementing the Debt Agreement and which is to be paid by the *Land* [of] Baden-Württemberg was secured, or whether, as the Respondent contends, an agreement between creditor and debtor regarding the terms of settlement had not, in fact, been reached.

" II

" If, therefore, the objection of the Respondent which is based on the rule of the exhaustion of local remedies fails, the question must now be examined whether any other circumstances following from the Debt Agreement itself might exclude the jurisdiction of the Arbitral Tribunal in the dispute pending before it.

" The decisive point, consequently, is what, according to the wording, sense and context, Article 28, para. (2), in conjunction with Article 28, para. (5), of the Debt Agreement provides with regard to the jurisdiction of the Arbitral Tribunal. The jurisdiction of the Arbitral Tribunal pursuant to Article 28, para. (3) (jurisdiction of the Arbitral Tribunal to decide questions regarding Annex IV which are of fundamental importance for the interpretation of that Annex and which are submitted to it by any Party to the Agreement), and pursuant to Article 28, para. (4) (jurisdiction of the Arbitral Tribunal in appeals from decisions of the Mixed Commission), may be disregarded in this connection.

" According to Article 28, para. (2), in conjunction with Article 28, para. (5), of the Debt Agreement, the Arbitral Tribunal has exclusive jurisdiction in all disputes between two or more of the Parties to the Agreement regarding the interpretation or application of the Agreement, or the Annexes thereto, which the Parties are not able to settle by negotiation, unless a dispute concerns solely the interpretation or application of an Annex to the Agreement if an arbitral body established pursuant to such Annex is competent to decide the question of interpretation or application concerned.

" The jurisdiction of the Arbitral Tribunal under these provisions is exclusive. This means that, for a decision in disputes between two or more of the Parties to the Debt Agreement regarding the interpretation or application of the Agreement or the Annexes thereto, no resort can be had to other international arbitral bodies, such as the International Court of Justice at The Hague or the Arbitration Tribunal established under Article 9 of the Convention on Relations between the Three Powers and the Federal Republic of Germany of May 26, 1952 (in the version of the Protocol of October 23, 1954). The term ' exclusive ' in Article 28, para. (2), of the Agreement has obviously no other meaning.

" According to Article 28, para. (2), of the Debt Agreement, the dispute must be one which the Parties concerned have not been able to settle by negotiation. By means of the above-mentioned exchange of Notes, an attempt has been made to settle by negotiation a dispute which had arisen between the Swiss Confederation and the Federal Republic of Germany out of an individual case regarding the interpretation of Annex VII to the Debt Agreement. Originally, the dispute concerned only the question whether claims for a balance of purchase money must also be considered ' loans or advances resulting from financial transactions ' within the meaning of the provision contained in Section I, para. 2, of Annex VII to the Debt Agreement or whether they must at least be placed on the same footing as such loans or advances. In the *Note Verbale* of the Foreign Office of July 22, 1957, however, it was then said that the Federal Minister of Justice had not further examined this point at issue; for he was of the opinion that the specific foreign character of the claim of the Swiss creditor had to be negatived if only for the reason that no place of payment abroad had been expressly agreed in the relevant contract of sale of July 31, 1931. The Swiss Embassy did not reply to this *Note Verbale* but instead submitted to the Arbitral Tribunal the Application of October 19, 1957, concerning which a decision must now be reached. The Respondent thinks that the diplomatic exchange of views as to the question what the requirement of an express agreement on a place of payment abroad must be taken to mean, according to the sense and purpose of Annex VII to the Debt Agreement, might possibly have led to agreement if it had been continued. The Arbitral Tribunal, however, is not of the opinion that, in order to establish its competence to decide a dispute between two or more of the Parties to the Agreement, diplomatic negotiations must always have reached a point where the litigating Parties have stated expressly that they have not succeeded in settling the dispute by negotiation. It suffices, on the contrary, that it can be assumed from the circumstances that a continuation of the diplomatic exchange of letters will not make possible the settlement of the dispute. This is the case here. As follows from the subsequent attitude of the litigants, the legal opinion held by the Federal Minister of Justice with regard to the meaning of the clause contained in Annex VII to the Debt Agreement concerning the necessity of an express agreement on a place of payment abroad, which was communicated to the Swiss Embassy in the *Note Verbale* of the Foreign Office of July 22, 1957, was of such fundamental importance precisely for the Swiss creditors that it was not to be expected that the Swiss side would eventually adopt this legal opinion. It is thereby established, within the meaning of Article 28, para. (2), or the Debt Agreement, that the dispute which has arisen between the Parties out of the present case between individuals concerning the interpretation of Annex VII to the Debt Agreement could not be settled by negotiation.

" If the Arbitral Tribunal is to be competent to decide a dispute between two or more of the Parties to the Debt Agreement, the subject of the dispute, according to Article 28, para. (2), of the Debt Agreement, must be the interpretation or application of the Debt Agreement or the Annexes thereto. This could also apply if a claim is made against the Federal Republic of Germany on the basis of the Debt Agreement, *e.g.*, on the basis of Article 2 or Article 10. This would, in fact be a case in which there is a dispute concerning the application of the Debt Agreement.

" However, as follows also from Article 28, para. (2), of the Debt Agreement, the jurisdiction of the Arbitral Tribunal is not limited to disputes in which a claim of some kind is made against the Federal Republic of Germany. But, irrespective of the cause of the dispute and irrespective of whether a claim is made against the Federal Republic of Germany or not, the Arbitral Tribunal is, in any event, competent only if the interpretation or application of the Agreement or the Annexes thereto is in question.

" The dispute to be decided in this case concerns primarily a question of the interpretation of the Debt Agreement and the Annexes thereto within the meaning of Article 28, para. (2), of the Agreement, *viz.*, a question of the interpretation of Annex VII in conjunction with Annex II. The question for decision is what this Annex means when it provides that, for the recognition of the specific foreign character of a claim in cases like the present, a place of payment abroad must have been expressly agreed in the original written debt arrangements. It is only in the second place, *i.e.*, after the question of interpretation as formulated above has been decided, that the question arises whether an express agreement on a place of payment abroad has been made within the meaning of this decision in the relevant contract of sale of July 31, 1931. It is, therefore, not correct that the real subject of the dispute is merely the interpretation of a contract under private law and that, as the Respondent contends, the Arbitral Tribunal is thus not competent because it could not be its task to decide a dispute which, by its nature, is a dispute between two private parties, *viz.*, between a Swiss bank as creditor and a German firm as debtor, but which the Applicant had clothed in the appearance of an international dispute between States by the Application it submitted to the Arbitral Tribunal. On the contrary, in the circumstances of the case this is a dispute between States which can be decided only by the Arbitral Tribunal pursuant to Article 28, para. (2), of the Debt Agreement.

" Nor can it be deduced from Article 28, para. (5), of the Debt Agreement that the Arbitral Tribunal is not competent to decide the present dispute. The said provision excludes the jurisdiction of the Arbitral Tribunal only if a dispute concerns exclusively the interpretation of an Annex to the Debt Agreement and if an arbitral body established pursuant to such Annex is competent to decide the question of interpretation concerned. It is true that the dispute has arisen out of a private dispute which was concerned with the claim of a Swiss creditor falling under the settlement provided in Annex II to the Debt Agreement. However, the dispute does not concern a question of the interpretation of provisions of Annex II itself, but a question of the interpretation of Annex VII which (the Respondent is quite right on that point) also constitutes a Sub-Annex supplementing Annex II. At the same time, however, it is a Sub-Annex which supplements Annexes I and IV, as is shown by the editorial remark on the letter addressed by the head of the German Delegation for German External Debts, Hermann J. Abbs, and the chairman of Negotiating Committee B at the Conference on German External Debts, N. Leggett, to the chairman of the Tripartite Commission on German External Debts of November 21, 1952. The provisions of Annex VII are, therefore, relevant for the settlement of Goldmark loans of German municipalities under Annex I to the Debt Agreement (see Sub-Annex D to Annex I) as well as for the settlement of debts expressed in Goldmarks or in Reichsmarks with a gold clause or a gold option, which fall under Annex II and Annex IV. Moreover, as results from their wording and context, the Annexes to the Debt Agreement cannot be interpreted separately but must be interpreted in the light of their interrelation and in conjunction with the Debt Agreement itself so that this will, in many cases, restrict the jurisdiction of the arbitral bodies provided [for] in the various Annexes. Annex VII, in particular, concerns several Annexes, *viz.*, as has already been mentioned, Annexes I, II and IV, and it is, consequently, also of importance for the whole Debt Agreement. Therefore, this is not a case envisaged in Article 28, para. (5). On the contrary, the Arbitral Tribunal is competent without restriction under Article 28, para. (2).

" For this reason, too, it is therefore irrelevant whether the attitude of the debtor towards the creditor after the coming into force of the Debt Agreement must be considered to reflect a readiness in principle to settle the claim on the basis of Annex II to the Debt Agreement.

" It also follows therefrom that the Arbitral Tribunal is competent to decide the present dispute irrespective of whether the Arbitration and Mediation Committee under Annex II has been established or not.

" If it were otherwise, there would be no judicial body the resort to which could eliminate the possibility of conflicting decisions on the interpretation of Annex VII by the arbitral bodies established pursuant to Annexes II and IV. Nor would there be anything to prevent the Arbitration and Mediation Committee competent under Annex II from answering the question of the specific foreign character of a claim owned by a foreign creditor in the negative, while the Mixed Commission competent under Annex IV affirms the question of the specific foreign character of another claim, owned by the same creditor, although this claim had been created in the same manner and in the same conditions as the claim the character of which had to be decided by the Arbitration and Mediation Committee. Such differences in the appreciation of identical legal situations would result, in particular, from the fact that the line of demarcation between claims which must be settled under Annex II and those which are subject to settlement under Annex IV has been drawn more or less arbitrarily in Article III of Annex II and in Article 2 of Annex IV, and in many cases depends on purely external circumstances (amount of the original debt, period of the loan). However, once conflicting decisions have been rendered by the two arbitral bodies competent under Annexes II and IV, respectively, it would no longer be possible to restore uniformity. It is true that a Party to the Debt Agreement could appeal to the Arbitral Tribunal from a decision pursuant to Article 31, para. (7), of the Debt Agreement if it were of the opinion that the Mixed Commission was wrong in assuming the specific foreign character of the claim, by basing this appeal on the ground that the decision concerned a question of general or fundamental importance. If the Arbitral Tribunal then confirmed the decision of the Mixed Commission, the decision of the Arbitral Tribunal would, pursuant to Article 28, para. (10), of the Debt Agreement, thenceforth be binding also on the Arbitration and Mediation Committee competent under Annex II to the Debt Agreement. However, the decision of the latter, which is final and binding on the private litigants according to Article IX, Section 1, para. (2), first sentence, of Annex II to the Debt Agreement, would not have been annulled.

" The conflict between the two decisions of the Mixed Commission and the Arbitration and Mediation Committee would, therefore, continue to exist. It must therefore be possible, by means of a resort to the Arbitral Tribunal, to prevent conflicting decisions by the arbitral bodies in question concerning the interpretation of an Annex to the Debt Agreement even before such decisions have been pronounced, thus guaranteeing a uniform and identical treatment of a disputed question of interpretation. This was obviously also the tendency in the discussions which the Tripartite Commission for German Debts had with the German Delegation for External Debts in London in the period from September 16, 1952, to February 26, 1953, regarding the formulation of the various provisions of the Debt Agreement (see the minutes of the meetings of December 12, 1952, No. 1 et seqq., p. 112, and of February 11, 1953, No. 9 et seqq., p. 171, as well as No. 32 et seqq., p. 173).

" However, even if it were assumed that in the present case only the interpretation of one Annex to the Debt Agreement, viz., the interpretation of Annex VII in conjunction solely with Annex II, was at issue, the Arbitral Tribunal would be competent to pronounce a decision on the Application submitted by the Swiss Confederation. At the institution of the proceeding, the Arbitration and Mediation Committee under Annex II was undoubtedly not yet established. The Respondent submitted only shortly before the beginning of the oral proceedings that it had now been established. According to the principle of *perpetuatio fori*, the jurisdiction of the Arbitral Tribunal in the present case remains unaffected by the establishment, after the institution of the proceeding, of the Arbitration and Mediation Committee under Annex II to the Debt Agreement to which the creditor might have resorted. In the *Nottebohm* case (dispute between Liechtenstein and Guatemala) the International Court of Justice made the following observations on the validity of the principle of *perpetuatio fori* in its decision of November 18, 1953 (*Reports of Judgments, Advisory Opinions and Orders* [1953, p. 111]—see in particular pp. 122 and 123) :[1]

" ' . . . the filing of the Application is merely the condition required to enable the clause of compulsory jurisdiction to produce its effects in respect of the claim advanced in the Application. Once this condition has been satisfied, the Court must deal with the claim; it has jurisdiction to deal with all its aspects, whether they relate to jurisdiction, to admissibility or to the merits. An extrinsic fact such as the subsequent lapse of the Declaration, by reason of the expiry of the period or by denunciation, cannot deprive the Court of the jurisdiction already established.'

" This refers to the principle, which is generally valid, at any rate in proceedings before international arbitral bodies, that, once the competence of the arbitral body has been established by the submission of the application for a decision, extrinsic facts and circumstances no longer affect this competence. This principle must also be valid for the competence of the Arbitral Tribunal in the present case, which has already been established by the submission of the Application of the Swiss Confederation. Therefore, the invocation by the Respondent of Article 28, para. (5), of the Debt Agreement is unfounded also in this respect.

" Nor is it correct that, as the Respondent maintains, a jurisdictional rule, as deduced from Article 28 of the Debt Agreement according to the above observations, would establish the competence of the Arbitral Tribunal also for the decision of disputes between individuals, for which the Debt Agreement precisely envisages special arbitral bodies, *viz.*, those of Anexes II and IV. Nor can it be said that the Debt Agreement does not, under any circumstances, offer a choice between a creditor bringing an action against his debtor before the competent ordinary German court or the arbitral bodies provided in the Debt Agreement for disputes between creditors and debtors and the creditor country as such, *i.e.*, as a Party to

[1 *International Law Reports*, 1953, p. 567, especially at pp. 575–576.]

the Debt Agreement, making the case the subject of a dispute between States before the Arbitral Tribunal. It is true that in general there will be no such alternative. According to the text and meaning of Article 28 of the Debt Agreement, the Arbitral Tribunal is, of course, not qualified to decide disputes between creditors and debtors. However, in certain circumstances a dispute may exist which either the private parties concerned would have to resolve by resorting to one of the arbitral bodies provided in Annexes II and IV to the Debt Agreement (in the case of a resort to the Mixed Commission pursuant to Article 16 of Annex IV in conjunction with Article 31 of the Debt Agreement, possibly with the participation of the Government of the creditor country or of the debtor country or both) or which would have to be taken to the Arbitral Tribunal as a dispute between Parties to the Debt Agreement. This would be the case in particular if, as in the present dispute, the question at issue is not how a contract is to be interpreted in the light of an Annex to the Debt Agreement, but two Parties to the Debt Agreement have entered into a dispute regarding the interpretation of a provision which is contained in several Annexes; that is, in particular if, again as in the present case, the point at issue is the interpretation of Annex VII which contains several provisions supplementing other Annexes. In such cases it is possible, pursuant to Article 28, para. (2), of the Debt Agreement, for a Party to the Agreement to resort to the Arbitral Tribunal, primarily in order to secure uniform decisions by the arbitral bodies which are competent for the interpretation or application of the Annexes in question. In those cases, the dispute need not first be submitted by the private party to one of the arbitral bodies provided for in the relevant Annex. On the contrary, such a case will then call for a decision in a dispute between two Parties to the Debt Agreement as defined in Article 28, para. (2), of that Agreement, although it will have arisen out of a dispute between individuals, which will be the rule, at least when the decision of the Arbitral Tribunal is requested concerning the interpretation of Annexes to the Debt Agreement. But even if a Party to the Debt Agreement formulated its Application for a decision by the Arbitral Tribunal in a theoretical form, *i.e.*, without naming the private parties concerned, the dispute would have arisen out of an individual case or a group of individual cases and the Arbitral Tribunal would have to examine the disputed question of the interpretation of the Annexes in the light of this individual case or group of individual cases, according to the jurisdiction conferred upon it by the Debt Agreement.

" Lastly, it is also not correct that, as the Respondent contends, the provision of Article 28, para. (11), of the Debt Agreement, according to which the Arbitral Tribunal can be requested to render advisory opinions regarding the interpretation or application of the Debt Agreement (except with respect to the interpretation or application of Article 34 of the Agreement), also reflects the obviously highly restrictive view of the Debt Agreement in the question of the jurisdiction of the Arbitral Tribunal. This contention fails to recognize the relation existing between the provisions of paras. (2) and (11) of Article 28 of the Debt Agreement. The fact that the Arbitral Tribunal is competent to decide disputes between two or more of the Parties to the Debt Agreement not only in the case of international disputes in the traditional sense, follows already from the above observations. Disputes between Governments which have arisen out of private disputes can also be the subject of the jurisdiction of the Arbitral Tribunal and, as has already been remarked, will normally be its subject if the dispute, as defined in Article 28, para. (2), of the Debt Agreement, concerns the interpretation or application of the Debt Agreement or the Annexes thereto, and if Article 28, para. (5), of the Debt Agreement does not exclude the jurisdiction of the Arbitral Tribunal. The request that the Arbitral Tribunal render a non-binding advisory opinion pursuant to Article 28, para. (11), will be made only as long as there is, as yet, no dispute between two or more of the Parties to the Debt Agreement, in particular, *e.g.*, if a Party to the Debt Agreement makes this request in order to come to a conclusion on the question whether it wishes to raise an issue of interpretation or application which it will then submit to the Arbitral Tribunal for its decision.

" For these reasons the Arbitral Tribunal unanimously declares: The Arbitral Tribunal is competent to adjudicate upon the present dispute. "

2. *"On the Merits*

" The question which has been submitted by the Swiss Federal Council for decision by the Tribunal is whether, within the meaning of Section I, 2 (*a*) of Annex VII to the Debt Agreement, it was expressly agreed under the original written debt arrangements (*i.e.*, the contract of sale of July 31, 1931) that the place of payment is situated abroad.

" This question is twofold:
" (*a*) What meaning is to be assigned to the words in Annex VII ' it was expressly agreed under the original written debt arrangements that the place of payment . . . is situated abroad ?'
" (*b*) Is this requirement fulfilled in the contract of sale between the Aargauische Hypothekenbank and Max and Moriz Lindauer?

" In order to answer question (*a*) it is necessary first to ascertain what method of interpretation should be employed. The problem is of especial relevance in connection with the meaning to be assigned to the term in Annex VII, I, 2 (*a*) ' place of payment ' (in the German text ' *Zahlungsort* ', in the French text ' *que le paiement serait fait à l'étranger* ') which has a significance varying according to the rule of interpretation which is applied.

" It has been contended by the Respondent that the correct method is to find the proper law applicable to each contract and then to interpret the above-cited provision of Annex VII in accordance with this law.

" It is the opinion of the Tribunal that the use of this method presents certain grave inconveniences. In the first place, contracts of precisely the same wording would be interpreted differently according to the law which is applicable to them. In the second place—and this is a more serious objection—there would in every case be a preliminary problem requiring solution before the criteria contained in Section I, 2 (a) of Annex VII could be applied, namely, the ascertainment of the proper law of the contract. This is often a matter of great complexity giving rise to protracted legal proceedings. Indeed, the very method to be employed for its ascertainment has been the subject of conflicting legal theories and judicial decisions. On the one hand it has been laid down that the law which the parties intended to apply must be sought for; on the other hand it has been decided that the proper criterion is what law the parties, as reasonable men, should have intended to apply, had they addressed their minds to the question. That law has been held to be the law of the country with which the contract has the more substantial links. See ' The Significance of *The Assunzione* ' by G. C. Cheshire, (*British Year Book of International Law*, 1955/56, page 123). The solution of this problem might require a resort to one of the arbitral bodies set up under the Agreement or to a German court or other tribunal, and might give rise to a subsidiary dispute as to what tribunal is competent to decide the question of the proper law of the contract.

" The possibility of such controversies arising would frustrate the object which the parties to the agreement contained in Annex VII had in mind, which was to provide a guide to the easy recognition of a claim with a specific foreign character as referred to in Annexes I, II and IV of the Debt Agreement. For these reasons, preference should be given to a method of interpretation which can be simply and uniformly applied.

" The rule commonly applied to the interpretation of Treaties should be applied to the interpretation of Annex VII. According to the practice of the International Court of Justice, words and phrases are to be given their normal, natural, and unstrained meaning in the context in which they occur.

" The practice of the International Court of Justice coincides with the resolution of the Institut de Droit International passed at Granada at the Session of April 1956 (*Annuaire*, p. 349):

" 'Article premier

' 1) L'accord des parties s'étant réalisé sur le texte du traité, il y a lieu de prendre le sens naturel et ordinaire des termes de ce texte comme base d'interprétation. Les termes des dispositions du traité doivent être interprétés dans le contexte entier, selon la bonne foi et à la lumière des principes du droit international.

' 2) Toutefois, s'il est établi que les termes employés doivent se comprendre dans un autre sens, le sens natural et ordinaire de ces termes est écarté.'

" The word ' *Zahlungsort* ' in the German text of Annex VII is not to be found in sections 269 and 270 of the German Civil Code (*Bürgerliches Gesetzbuch*, BGB). According to the dictionary ' *Der Grosse Brockhaus* ', the word ' *Zahlungsort* ' signifies ' *Erfüllungsort für eine Geldschuld* ' (the place of liquidation of a money debt).— Section 270, first paragraph, of the German Civil Code provides: ' *Geld hat der Schuldner im Zweifel auf seine Gefahr und seine Kosten dem Gläubiger an dessen Wohnsitz zu übermitteln.*' The English translation is: ' In case of doubt the debtor has to send the money at his own risk and expense to the creditor at the latter's residence.' —However, the fourth paragraph of Section 270 provides: ' *Die Vorschriften über den Leistungsort bleiben unberhürt.*' In English: ' The provisions relating to the place of performance remain unaffected.'

" The fourth paragraph of Section 270 signifies that the provisions of Section 269 of the German Civil Code concerning the place of performance of obligations in general, ' *Leistungsort* ', are to be applied when nothing to the contrary has been agreed. It is not necessary to examine the wording of Section 269 as according to German jurisprudence and nearly unanimous German theory the word ' *Leistungsort* ' means the place of performance also for money debts, where nothing else has been agreed, and is the place of the residence of the debtor, also when the residence of the creditor is at another place. According to German law, however, this does not signify that the creditor has got what is due to him and that the money debt has been extinguished if the creditor has not actually received the money. If through no fault of the creditor he does not actually receive the money, the debtor has to pay again. However, the debtor is not liable in damages for delay or failure on the part of his bank or the postal service in transferring the money for him to the creditor, since, strange as it may look, the bank and the post are not, according to German conception, considered as the debtor's representatives (agents) in the above-mentioned cases.

" What is of importance for the Tribunal is that, in spite of the particular technical meaning of the word ' *Leistungsort* ', even under German law the creditor is not considered as having actually received what is due to him and the debt is therefore not extinguished until the creditor has actually received the money or, in case of postal or bank transfers, until his account has been finally credited with the remittance. (Palandt: *Bürgerliches Gesetzbuch*, 17th edition, p. 221, Erman: *Handkommentar zum Bürgerlichen Gesetzbuch*, 2nd edition, 1958, p. 333).

" The word ' *Zahlungsort* ' in the German text of Annex VII is not necessarily synonymous with the word ' *Leistungsort* ' used in Sections 269 and 270 of the BGB. The word ' *Leistungsort* ' is a more general term than the word ' *Zahlungsort* '—the latter concerning only money debts—and has in German law a particular and absolutely technical meaning.—Some German jurists are even of the opinion that according to Section 270 of the German Civil Code the place of performance (' *Leistungsort* ') of money debts may be at the residence of the debtor; but that this does not affect the ' place of payment ' or ' place of fulfilment ' (' *Zahlungsort* ' or ' *Erfüllungsort* '), which is determined by the residence of the creditor, because no payment has been finally executed and the debt extinguished before the creditor has actually received the money due to him (either in cash or by final statement of credit from the creditor's bank or his post office). (Franz Leonhard: *Schuldort und Erfüllungsort* (1907), and *Allgemeines Schuldrecht des BGB* (1929), p. 232; Arwed Koch: *Die Allgemeinen Geschäftsbedingungen der Banken* (Jena, 1932), p. 241.)

" On the other hand, in English and American law the term ' place of payment ' is not a term of art; it is interpreted in its natural meaning, namely, the place where the creditor is entitled actually to receive payment.

" The difference between the German and the English and American conceptions is well illustrated by the following passages from pp. 174 and 175 of the second edition of *The Legal Aspect of Money, with Special Reference to Comparative, Private and Public International Law* ', by F. A. Mann:

" ' 2. It is not unlikely that the meaning to be attached to the term " place of payment " may not be the same in all countries. Although there is no direct English authority on the point, it is suggested that in English law the place of payment is the place where, according to the express or implied terms of the contract, payment ought to be made, not the place where payment is actually made. Moreover, in English law the conception " place of payment " connotes the place at which the creditor is entitled actually to receive the money due to him, not the place from which the money is to be dispatched to him or at which any other step preparatory to payment must be taken.

' It it is desired to ascertain the equivalent, in a foreign legal system, of the place of payment in the English sense, it is, accordingly, necessary to ask where, in the eyes of the foreign law, the creditor is entitled to the money contractually due to him. It would be dangerous to stop short at what the foreign law calls the place of payment.

' It is the function, not the terminology, that matters. Thus, German law provides that the place of the debtor's residence at the time of the contract usually is the place of performance, but the debtor must transmit the money at his risk and expense to the place where the creditor resides. This, therefore, is the place where, under German law, the creditor is entitled to be paid, and is the equivalent of the English conception of the place of payment. It is irrelevant that German law calls it the place of destination or delivery and describes the place of the debtor's residence at the time of the contract as the place of performance.'

"The following passage from Nussbaum, ' *Money in the Law, National and International* ', at pages 147 *et seqq.* is also relevant:

"'The Central European Codes therefore distinguish between the place of performance ("*Erfüllungsort*") or more specifically place of payment ("*Zahlungsort*"), which in case of doubt is the place of the debtor's domicile, and the "place of destination" ("*Bestimmungsort*") which ordinarily is the place of the creditor's domicile. Normally the debtor has to "pay" at his own domicile with the concomitant obligation of sending the money at his cost and risk to the creditor's domicile. By this artificial device the law favours the debtor with regard to jurisdictional and Conflict-of-Laws requirements, but favours the creditor with regard to the risks of payment. The price paid for this solution, which to a certain extent may be explained historically, is a complete distortion of the place-of-payment conception, nothing being actually "paid" at the place since the real payment is made at the place of "destination". This has led to considerable confusion.

'While the Latin legal systems, by contrast with the Central European, have refrained from overemphasizing the place-of-payment concept, they still cling to the traditional rule that the debtor's domicile is in doubtful cases the proper place of payment. This adherence to tradition, however, has not prevented the French *Cour de Cassation* from imposing upon the debtor the risk involved in sending money to a creditor abroad.'

'In more recent times both common law and civil law courts have resorted, in Conflict-of-Laws situations, to the criterion of the place of payment. The results reached are frequently, if not in the majority of cases, unsound. As long as money was actually transported for outside payments, the place of payment carried a certain weight. But under modern banking conditions this is no longer true. Suppose a London debtor has to pay a New Yorker in dollars. If for one reason or another (probably jurisdictional) London was stipulated as the place of payment the debtor will send the creditor a check on London or make a remittance on a London bank unless he simply pays by check on New York.

'All [things] considered, the place of payment is in our day no more than a matter of postal or banking facilities. While in some situations it furnishes a helpful criterion, its value has been greatly exaggerated in the practice and doctrine of private international law.'

"The French text of Annex VII, I, 2 (*a*), reads ' *qu'il ait été expressément convenu dans les accords initiaux écrits relatifs à la dette que le paiement serait fait à l'étranger . . .*'.

"Since Article 1247 of the French Civil Code lays down that, in the absence of a contrary agreement, a debt is payable at the residence of the debtor, although the *Cour de Cassation* has imposed upon the debtor the risk of sending the money to a creditor abroad (Cass., March 30, 1925, DP 1927 I 168), it might be argued that the term employed in the French text has a technical meaning. Nevertheless, the words of the French text of Annex VII, ' *le paiement serait fait à l'étranger* ', are equally susceptible of the natural interpretation that the payment should actually be made and received abroad.

" The parties have discussed the rules of law in various other countries also concerning the place at which the debtor is obliged to pay his money debt in the absence of any agreement. Since, however, the application of the Swiss Government is necessarily based upon an allegation of the existence of an agreement on this point, these rules are irrelevant except in so far as they may be thought to throw light upon the meaning of the word ' payment '. It is therefore sufficient to mention that, whereas in Germany, France and Belgium, in the absence of agreement the so-called place of performance of a money debt is fixed as the debtor's residence, in England, Switzerland, the United States of America, the Netherlands, Italy, Greece, Hungary and the Scandinavian countries the place of payment is the place where the creditor resides.

" It is noteworthy that the International Law Association at its 47th Conference held at Dubrovnik in 1956 considered a Revised Draft Convention concerning the payment of foreign money liabilities in which the term ' place of payment ' is used in several Articles. In order to eliminate the ambiguity attaching to this term the draftsmen inserted Article 10, which reads as follows: ' The place of payment referred to in the preceding Articles shall be the place where payment is due.'—The French text of this Article reads: ' *Le lieu de paiement au sens des articles qui précèdent est le lieu où le paiement est dû.*'—This definition does not, however, cure the ambiguity since there is no definition of ' the place where payment is due '. This was recognized by the Committee on Monetary Law, since in paragraph 18 of their Report they write:

" ' The words " place of payment " are ambiguous in that they may contemplate the place where payment ought to be made or the place where payment is in fact made. Art. 10 suggests that the expression should be given the former meaning.'
(*Report of the Forty-Seventh Conference of the International Law Association*, Annexes I and II, pp. 287 to 289.)

" The Tribunal is of the opinion that the natural meaning of ' place of payment ', ' *Zahlungsort* ', ' *que le paiement serait fait à l'étranger* ', contained in Annex VII is to be preferred to the technical and artificial meaning advanced by the Respondent. This is even more evident when it is borne in mind that Annex VII does not use the technical term ' *Leistungsort* ' found in Sections 269 and 270 of the German Civil Code.

" The Tribunal is confirmed in this opinion when it examines both the origin of Annex VII to the Debt Agreement as it emerges from the preparatory documents to the Debt Agreement and its Annexes which were published in connection with the Agreement, and the legal position of the creditors as it was at the time of the

London Conference. But although the parties to this case have referred to what they claim occurred during the negotiations between representatives of debtors and creditors at the London Conference and during the subsequent special negotiations resulting in Annex VII, the Tribunal does not feel that in interpreting Annex VII it can give any evidential value to such assertions, based as they are on no published record, even should the parties agree as to their accuracy. —At any event, in so far as the so-called material referred to bears on the substance of such negotiations it permits of no compelling conclusion to the effect that the terms ' Zahlungsort ', ' place of payment ', ' que le paiement serait fait à l'étranger ' were to have the narrow and technical meaning asserted by the Respondent and were thus to lead to an extraordinary and inequitable denial of ' specific foreign character ' to claims [such] as the one discussed. The whole history of the origin of the London Debt Agreement also contradicts any such narrow interpretation.

" By Article XVI (16) of Military Government Law No. 63 (Conversion Law) of June 27, 1948, it was provided that, in principle, Reichsmark claims (which for the purpose of that Law were defined to include claims expressed in Goldmarks) were to be so converted into Deutsche Mark claims that the debtor should be obliged to pay to the creditor one Deutsche Mark for every ten Reichsmarks due. But by Article XV (15) of that Law, as amended by Articles 1 and 2 of Law No. 46 of the Allied High Commission (*Bundesanzeiger* No. 31 of February 14, 1951), it was provided, in effect, that the provision for conversion should not apply to debts owing to United Nations nationals whenever a creditor refused to agree to payment in accordance with Article XVI (16). Accordingly, at the date of the Conference on German External Debts held in London from February to August 1952, the United Nations creditors arrived at the conference table with their claims to be paid in accordance with the gold clause unimpaired by the provisions of the Conversion Law. The fact that the present case concerns a Swiss claim and not one of a United Nations national is irrelevant since the plan of the London Conference for the settlement of external debts comprised the totality of these debts (except those owed to Eastern Europe), and the principle underlying this plan was that of non-discrimination (see Article 8 of the Debt Agreement).

" The Conference set up among other committees four negotiating Committees to deal with the following categories of debts (see paragraph 8 of the Report of the Conference which is reproduced as Appendix B to the Debt Agreement):

Committee A.—*Reich* debts and other debts of public authorities;

Committee B.—Other medium and long-term debts;

Committee C.—Standstill debts;

Committee D.—Commercial and miscellaneous debts.

" The recommendations of these Committees, which were appended to the Report of the Conference adopted on August 8, 1952, appear as Annexes I to IV to the Debt Agreement. That part of the Report of the Conference which deals with the gold clause appears in paragraph 30 and reads as follows:

" ' 30. On the question of the gold clause in general the Tripartite Commission informed the Conference that, as part of the arrangements agreed on in order to make a comprehensive settlement of the German debt problem possible, the Governments of France, the United Kingdom and the Unites States of America had decided that, in so far as the German debt settlement was concerned, gold clauses should not be maintained but might be replaced by some form of exchange guarantee.

' With respect to the Young Loan, they of course regarded it as essential that the equality of treatment for the different issues of that Loan provided for under the loan contract should be maintained. The representatives of the European bondholders have expressed their regret at the decision to depart from the contractual right of the bondholders of this international Loan to payment in their own currencies on a gold basis. They have inserted in the "Agreed Recommendations for the Settlement of *Reich* debts and debts of other public authorities' (Appendix 3) the provision there included solely in view of this Governmental decision.

' Corresponding provisions had been included in other reports where appropriate.'

" These ' corresponding provisions ' are those contained in paragraphs (1), (2) and (3) of Sub-Annex D to Annex I (dated November 19, 1952), paragraphs 2 and 3 of Article V of Annex II and Articles 6 to 8 of Annex IV, which cover both Foreign Currency Debts with gold clauses and German Currency Debts with gold clauses. With regard to the latter, the principle was accepted that such debts (claims) and mortgages, expressed in Goldmarks or in Reichsmarks with a gold clause, as had a specific foreign character should be converted into Deutsche Mark at the rate of 1 Goldmark, or 1 Reichsmark with a gold clause, = 1 Deutsche Mark. The Annexes continue:

" ' The definition of the criteria constituting the specific foreign character of the above indebtedness shall be the subject of further negotiation. Both sides reserve their position as to the question in which cases and in which way the above principle can be implemented . . .'

" The present dispute involves a loan which falls within the provisions of Annex II. Article V of that Annex prescribes the terms of settlement, and paragraph 1 thereof states: ' There shall be no reduction in the outstanding principal amount.' This statement would have been more accurate if it referred to the outstanding ' nominal ' amount, since by agreeing to the non-application of provisions in original contracts calling for repayment in terms of gold or currency of equivalent gold value the London Debt Conference in effect resulted in a substantial loss to some foreign creditors.

" Article V of Annex II deals with two principal categories of debts. In respect of ' *Foreign* Currency Debts with Gold Clauses ' it provides that

" ' . . . debts expressed in gold dollars or gold Swiss francs . . . shall be computed on the basis of 1 currency dollar equalling 1 gold dollar and 1 currency Swiss franc equalling 1 gold Swiss franc . . .'

and that in the case of other non-German currencies with gold clauses

" ' the amounts due shall be payable only in the currency of the country in which the loan was raised . . . the amount due being computed as the equivalent at the rate of exchange when the amount is due for payment of a sum in U.S. dollars " reached " by converting the amount of the obligation expressed in the currency of issue into U.S. dollars at the rate of exchange ruling when the loan was raised . . .'

provided, however, that the amount of currency issue so reduced shall not be less than

' if it were computed at the rate of exchange current on 1st August 1952.'

" In all non-German currency debts with gold clauses, therefore, the principle of repayment in depreciated foreign currencies (including U.S. dollars and Swiss francs) is established regardless of the original gold clauses, and equality of treatment is maintained.

" The other category of debts covered by Article V is ' *German* Currency Debts with Gold Clauses '. Here a similar principle is followed, namely, that such of these debts as have ' specific foreign character ' shall be settled on the basis of 1 Deutsche Mark (which is the same as 1 currency Deutsche Mark) for each Goldmark or Reichsmark with a gold clause, just as one depreciated currency dollar and one depreciated currency Swiss franc were made the equivalent, for settlement purposes, of one gold dollar and one gold Swiss franc respectively. But since debts expressed in Goldmarks or Reichsmarks with a gold clause do not *prima facie* possess foreign character, special safeguards had to be introduced to ensure that such German currency debts be genuine external debts. These safeguards were established in paragraph 3 of Article V of Annex II, which provides that German currency debts with gold clauses must have a ' specific foreign character ' to entitle the creditor to repayment at the rate of 1 Deutsche Mark for each Goldmark or Reichsmark with a gold clause. (The Deutsche Mark, though, is of lesser value than were the Goldmark or Reichsmark.)

" The criteria for determining the ' specific foreign character ' of debts covered by Annexes I, II and IV are set forth in Annex VII, which incorporates the agreement reached on November 21, 1952, after a month of negotiations between the German Delegation for External Debts and a delegation of British, American, Swiss and Netherlands creditor representatives.

" The task of the negotiators was not an easy one; its purpose was, as far as possible, not to place foreign creditors of foreign loans expressed in German currency with a gold clause in a more unfavourable position than creditors of foreign loans expressed in non-German currencies with a gold clause, provided, of course, that there was no *mala fide* acquisition of rights. It cannot be assumed that the Signatories of the London Debt Agreement could have intended to single out for discriminatory further loss foreign creditors having claims expressed in German currencies with a gold clause.

" In this respect the Tribunal believes the Respondent has been led astray by a wrong interpretation of the German word ' *Zahlungsort* ' in the German text of Annex VII. Considering only German law, the word ' *Zahlungsort* ' in the German text may well conjure up in the mind of a German jurist the special technical significance with which German law and custom have endowed the word ' *Leistungsort* '. As shown above, however, the Tribunal regards that interpretation as too limited and not consistent with the clear purpose of the relevant Annexes to the London Debt Agreement.

" In this connection it should also be mentioned that the Governments Signatory to the Debt Agreement made amongst others the following declarations in its Preamble:

" ' . . .

' Considering that, for about twenty years, payments on German external debts have not, in general, conformed to the contractual terms . . . and that the Federal Republic of Germany desires to put an end to this situation;

' Considering that . . . the Governments of the French Republic, the United Kingdom of Great Britain and Northern Ireland and the United States of America were prepared to make important concessions with respect to . . . their claims for post-war economic assistance . . . on condition that a satsifactory and equitable settlement of Germany's pre-war external debts was achieved;

' Considering that such a settlement of German external debts could be achieved only by a single overall plan which would take into account the relative positions of the various creditor interests, the nature of various categories of claims and the general situation of the Federal Republic of Germany;

' . . .'

" The application of the principle of interpreting treaties according to the natural sense of the words is therefore particularly appropriate to this case, where the natural meaning seems to coincide with the intention of the parties as deduced from the circumstances of the case. For all these reasons the Tribunal is of the opinion that the terms 'place of payment', '*Zahlungsort*', '*que le paiement serait fait à l'étranger*', should be interpreted as denoting the place where the creditor was entitled actually to receive his money, whether directly from the debtor or by transmission through the post or by any other agency.

" There remains to be decided the question whether, in the contract of sale of July 31, 1931, it was ' expressly agreed ' that the place of payment, as defined above, was situated abroad.

" Much has been said on behalf of both Parties as to the effect to be given to the terms ' expressly agreed ', ' *ausdrücklich festgelegt* ', ' *expressément convenu* ', as used in Annex VII. On the one hand it is contended that these words are equivalent to ' *expressis verbis* ' and that the agreement must therefore state in express words that the place of payment is abroad. On the other hand it is contended that it is sufficient that there should be a written agreement which clearly and unambiguously establishes that the place of payment is situated abroad.

" To apply the term ' *expressis verbis* ' to the English text would do violence to the meaning. The English words are ' expressly agreed ', not ' agreed in express terms ' (the equivalent of ' *expressis verbis* ').

" Moreover, there are decisions of the highest German Courts to the effect that the term ' *ausdrücklich* ' as used in Section 244 of the German Civil Code requires only unambiguous evidence of the intention of both parties.

" Thus in the case of *D. Bank & Disk. Ges., Filiale D. v. S. Rh. Giro-Zentrale und Prov.-Bank* reported at p. [384] of volume 153 (1937) of the ' *Reichsgerichtsentscheidungen in Zivilsachen* ', the German Supreme Court held, following earlier decisions of the same Court, that where the plaintiff had opened a credit in foreign currency in favour of the defendant ' by way of loan ' (' *leihweise* '), that expression implied ' effective ' repayment in foreign currency. Consequently, the effective repayment in foreign currency had in the opinion of the Court been ' expressly stipulated for ' (' *ausdrücklich bedungen* ') within the meaning of Section 244, para. 1, of the German Civil Code, and it was not necessary for the word ' effective ' to be used.

" In a case decided by the Federal Supreme Court (*Bundesgerichtshof*) on January 25, 1954 (Lindenmaier-Möhring No. 5 to Section 275 of the German Civil Code), the plaintiff bank had obtained from its client, the defendant, a promissory note (*eigener Wechsel*) for the like principal amount in the same effective currency as the amount of the credit granted to the plaintiff bank by a London bank. This procedure was laid down in paragraph 7 (1) (*a*) (i) of the German Credit Agreement of 1939 made between a committee representative of banking, commercial and industrial concerns in Germany, and the Reichsbank and the Deutsche Golddiskontbank on the one hand, and several committees representative of banking institutions in the United States of America, Belgium, England,

France, Holland and Switzerland on the other hand. The Court of Appeal had held that, although the German Credit Agreement only affected the relations of banks to each other, yet it should be applied *mutatis mutandis* to the obligation of the defendant towards the plaintiff as there was a specific reference to the Credit Agreement. This reference was a sufficient contractual stipulation that the loan was to be repaid in foreign currency. This being so, the payment in foreign currency had been expressly made a part of the contract.

" In its judgment the Federal Supreme Court said:

" ' According to the jurisprudence of the *Reichsgericht*, which is adopted, repayment of a credit in foreign currency will only be " expressly stipulated for " if the intention of both parties as to an effective payment in foreign currency is unambiguously evident to a special degree. In this connection the word " effective " need not be used (RGZ 158, 383 (385) and note). The Court of Appeal regards the reference to the Credit Agreement in particular as constituting such evidence. That can legally not be contested. The Court of Appeal has stated that the arrangement which is contained in the Credit Agreement, and was binding only on the banks which were parties to it, was also applicable *mutatis mutandis* to the obligation of the defendant, whose attention has specifically been called to the Credit Agreement. Thus, it bases itself decisively upon the fact that the credit was granted, according to the written confirmation, " within the scope of the Credit Agreement " and therefore considers that the payment in £–currency was expressly stipulated for. This conclusion is logically possible.'

" The English case of *Charlton* v. *Lings* (1868) L.R.C.P. 374 deals with the word ' expressly ', the Court stating:

" ' The difficulty, if any, is created by the use of the word "*expressly* ". But that word does not necessarily mean " expressly excluded by words " ... The word " expressly " often means no more than plainly, clearly, or the like, as will appear on reference to any English dictionary.'

" The words ' expressly agreed ', ' *ausdrücklich festgelegt* ', and ' *expressément convenu* ' are words found in an international multilateral agreement. As pointed out earlier, the usual practice in interpreting words and phrases in a treaty is to give them a reasonable, as distinguished from a restricted or technical, meaning.

" In this connection, one may refer to Hackworth's *Digest of International Law* (Washington 1927) on page 223 of Volume V, where it is said:

" ' ... courts have usually held that where treaties are open to two constructions, one restricting the rights which may be claimed under it and the other enlarging those rights, the more liberal interpretation is to be preferred, bearing in mind the purpose of the treaty and the fact that diplomatic relations between nations require the utmost good faith.'

" ' Reasonable ' as distinguished from ' restricted or technical ' meanings of the English words ' expressly agreed ' and their French equivalent can be found in dictionary definitions. Among other

definitions, the *Oxford English Dictionary* (Oxford 1933) defines
'express' as 'definite, unmistakable in import' and the word
'expressly' as 'in direct or plain terms; clearly, explicitly, definitely,
distinctly, positively'. Bouvier's *Law Dictionary* (West Publishing
Co., 1914) defines 'express' as 'stated or declared, as opposed to
implied. That which is made known and not left to implication'.
*Larousse Universel* (Paris, 1948) defines '*expressément*' both as
'*en termes exprès*' and '*d'une façon nette, précise, claire*'.

" The Tribunal is of the opinion that the language of Annex VII
becomes unclear or obscure only when there is imported into the
meaning of the word '*Zahlungsort*' in the German text the unique
and restricted definition given under German law to the word
'*Leistungsort*'. There was no 'express' or even implied agreement
in the contract of July 31, 1931, as to '*Zahlungsort*' in the strictly
German sense of the word '*Leistungsort*', but there was 'express'
agreement defined as 'clear', 'definite', 'unmistakable in import'
as to the place where the creditor was entitled actually to receive
the money due to him.

" The Tribunal finds that the terms 'expressly agreed', '*ausdrücklich festgelegt*' and '*expressément convenu*' as used in Annex
VII mean agreed 'clearly' or 'definitely' or 'distinctly' or 'unmistakable in import', and that to fulfil the requirement of Annex
VII in this respect it was not necessary for a place of payment
to have been in specific terms geographically located in the contract of July 31, 1931. It is sufficient that the place where the
creditor was entitled to receive the money due to him was clearly
and unmistakably set forth in the text of the contract as being
situated abroad.

" The Aargauische Hypothekenbank is incorporated under Swiss
law, having its head office in Brugg, Switzerland, and with branch
offices elsewhere in Switzerland. Neither at the date of the contract
nor thereafter has the bank had a branch office in Germany. Whenever the Aargauische Hypothekenbank is mentioned in the contract
by name (twice), the name is coupled with the phrase 'with its head
office at Brugg' ('*mit Hauptsitz in Brugg*'); elsewhere the bank
is called the vendor. Article 5 oι the contract provides for payment
of principal and interest to be made to the vendor (*an die Verkäuferin*)
The Respondent has asserted that this calls for payment *to* a person
but not *at* an agreed place, and that the words ' with its head office
at Brugg' ('*mit Hauptsitz in Brugg*') are significant only in so
far as they state ' the address to which the debtor had to transmit
the amounts due " free of charge " ', that is, that Article 5 establishes
' to whom, but not where the debtor has to discharge his obligation
" free of charge " '.

" In the light of its interpretation of Annex VII the Tribunal does
not accept this contention. If the debtors are obliged to make payments *to* the ' *Aargauische Hypothekenbank mit Hauptsitz in Brugg*'

they are no less obliged to make those payments *in* Switzerland, since that is the only country where the Aargauische Hypothekenbank is located. In this case the ' to whom ' and ' where ' are clearly connected. If it was ' expressly agreed ' under the 1931 contract ' to whom ' the payments due were to be made—and that cannot be disputed—it was no less ' expressly agreed ' that the ' place of payment', namely, the place at which the creditor was entitled actually to receive payment, was in Switzerland. Moreover, the German debtor could not, without the consent of the Swiss creditor, have discharged his liability by making a payment into an account of the creditor in a German bank even assuming the creditor had such an account, since this would leave the creditor with nothing but a foreign claim (Enneccerus, *Recht der Schuldverhältnisse* 1954, § 61, II; v. Tuhr-Siegwart, *Allgemeiner Teil des Schweizerischen OR*, Vol. II, p. 439).

" Finally, it should be noted that according to a formal statement by the creditor the Reichsmark interest payments made by the debtors from 1931 to 1944 were transferred with the authorization of the German foreign exchange authorities and paid to the creditor in Brugg in Swiss francs.

" For these reasons the Arbitral Tribunal, by five votes to four, declares: that, within the meaning of Annex VII, I, 2 (*a*), to the Agreement on German External Debts of February 27, 1953, it was expressly agreed in the contract of July 31, 1931, between the Aargauische Hypothekenbank AG. and Herren Max and Moriz Lindauer that the place of payment of the Goldmark claim created by the said contract was situated abroad."

President Daehli delivered the following Individual Opinion on the question of competence:

" I agree with the other Members of the Arbitral Tribunal that the objection to the jurisdiction of the Arbitral Tribunal raised by the German Federal Government fails. However, I prefer to base my opinion upon the following reasons which I consider sufficient:

" Article 28 (2) of the Debt Agreement provides that ' the Tribunal shall have exclusive jurisdiction in all disputes between two or more of the Parties to the present Agreement regarding the interpretation or application of the Agreement, or the Annexes thereto, which the Parties are not able to settle by negotiation, except that any dispute respecting the interpretation or application of Article 34 of the present Agreement shall not be within the jurisdiction of the Tribunal or of any other court or tribunal . . .' There is one exception to this clear provision of paragraph (2), namely, that contained in Article 28 (5). According to that provision, the Arbitral Tribunal ' shall not have jurisdiction in any dispute which is concerned solely with the interpretation or application of an Annex to the present Agreement, if an arbitral body established pursuant to such Annex is competent to decide the question of interpretation or application concerned.'

" According to the exposition given by the majority of the Members of the course of the proceeding, the submissions and the facts, the present case concerns the interpretation or application of Annex VII to the Debt Agreement, which affects Annexes I, II and IV. Annex VII is a supplement to each of those three Annexes. No special arbitral body is provided for the interpretation or application of Annex VII and in reality the interpretation or application of Annex VII involves the simultaneous interpretation or application of the three Annexes I, II and IV.

" It follows therefrom that it is irrelevant for the treatment of the present Application whether an arbitral body had been established for the interpretation or application of Annex II, for the above-mentioned provision of Article 28 (5), which contains a restriction on the jurisdiction of the Arbitral Tribunal, cannot be applied to disputes concerning the application or interpretation of Annex VII.

" It follows both from the system of the Agreement and the Annexes thereto and from the preparatory negotiations which can be taken from the published Minutes of the Agreement, that the negotiating Parties intended the Arbitral Tribunal to have such an absolutely unrestricted jurisdiction, which is clearly expressed in Article 28. Therefore, there is nothing to prevent a State which is a Party to the Debt Agreement from submitting to the Arbitral Tribunal pursuant to Article 28 (2) an application originating from a dispute between individuals in which the private parties are directly concerned, such as is the case in the present dispute.

" Article 28 (2) does not contain the restriction which is expressed in the subsequent paragraph (3), *viz.*, that the questions submitted to the Arbitral Tribunal have ' fundamental importance '. However, it is not to be assumed that the Governments will make insignificant questions the subject of applications under Article 28 (2).

" I do not deem it necessary to deal with the international rule of the ' exhaustion of local remedies ' (' *Prinzip der Erschöpfung der landesrechtlichen Instanzen* ', ' *règle de l'épuisement des instances internes* ') in detail since, in my opinion, there can be no doubt but that this rule cannot be applied to the present case for the following reasons:

" First I should like to state that in agreement with the other Members I am of the opinion that according to international jurisprudence and theory the application of the rule is limited to claims for violation of public international law. According to international decisions and theory, a State is free to exclude the application of the rule of the exhaustion of local remedies either by an international treaty or in an individual case. However, in some international agreements of recent origin concerning obligatory rules of arbitration, the parties deemed it necessary expressly to reserve the application of the rule of the exhaustion of local remedies because they desired to prevent the possibility of this rule not being applied (Louis Cavaré, *Le Droit International Public Positif*, Paris 1951, Tome II, p. 295).

" The Agreement on German External Debts is an international instrument designed to establish a plan for an orderly and complete settlement of German pre-war external debts in a manner as quick, satisfactory and just as possible. The Agreement and all the Annexes thereto are of a particularly technical and complicated nature. The provisions of Article 28 of the Agreement concerning the jurisdiction of the Arbitral Tribunal have, therefore, a very limited and specific application. The Parties to the Agreement have no possibility of having their disputes regarding the interpretation or application of the Agreement or the Annexes thereto decided by national courts or other arbitral bodies. Nor could they have desired this. In fact, the only practical arrangement whereby an authoritative solution to questions of principle could be found as quickly as possible, while at the same time achieving a maximum degree of legal uniformity in decisions of the innumerable administrative and judicial bodies, was just the possibility given to the Governments through the jurisdiction of the permanent Arbitral Tribunal under the Debt Agreement to obtain a decision on disputes concerning the interpretation or application of the Agreement or the Annexes thereto by means of international judicial proceedings.

" Although the jurisdiction of the Arbitral Tribunal is somewhat restricted by the provision of Article 28 (5), this has no bearing on the right of the Parties envisaged in the Agreement to submit disputes concerning the interpretation or application of the Agreement or the Annexes thereto directly to the Arbitral Tribunal since private parties, creditors or debtors, cannot submit their disputes to the Arbitral Tribunal for its decision but have to obtain a decision from other judicial bodies. The Parties to the Debt Agreement, *viz.*, the Governments, do not depend on the creditor or debtor having accepted a settlement of the debt pursuant to the provisions of the Agreement and the Annexes thereto, nor do they depend on the wishes of the creditor or debtor in an individual case, if the question concerns the institution of judicial proceedings. If a Party to the Agreement is interested in obtaining a judicial decision on a question of interpretation or application of the Agreement or the Annexes thereto disputed with another Government, the former Party is completely free to submit an application to the Arbitral Tribunal without regard to the wishes of the creditors or debtors.

" The Parties to the Debt Agreement created an obligatory international arbitral jurisdiction within the framework of that Agreement since there was no possibility for national courts to decide disputes between Governments on the interpretation or application of the international instrument. Such a possibility would have been irrational and, in my opinion, even illogical. According to the national codes of legal procedure—and this was confirmed for the Federal Republic by its Agent—it is not open to the Governments to address themselves to the national courts in order to obtain judicial decisions on their disputes concerning the interpretation or application of the Agreement or the Annexes thereto."

Mr. Michelson, Member of the Tribunal, delivered the following Individual Opinion on the merits:

" While I concur in the judgment of President Daehli, Monsieur Richard, Mr. Phenix and Professor Hinderling, I wish, in exercise of the right conferred by rule 44 (*c*) of the Rules of Procedure of the Tribunal, to add the following remarks of my own:

" Any loan raised abroad would ordinarily be considered to be an ' external ' or ' foreign ' loan, and one would expect a loan of ' a specific foreign character ' to be also repayable abroad. Now, Article III of Annex II, which is headed ' Debts Covered ', provides that ' the present Agreement ', that is, Annex II, should apply to every bonded loan and to every non-bonded loan issued or raised outside Germany, subject to certain specified conditions of which repayment abroad is not one. The distinction between an external loan or debt and debts having ' a specific foreign character ' is first made in Article V, para. 3, of Annex II.

" Article V of Annex II deals in paragraph 2 with ' Foreign Currency Debts with Gold Clauses ' and provides that:

' . . . debts expressed in gold dollars or gold Swiss francs . . . shall be computed on the basis of 1 currency dollar equalling 1 gold dollar and 1 currency Swiss franc equalling 1 gold Swiss franc . . .'

and, in the case of other non-German currencies with gold clauses, that

' the amounts due shall be payable only in the currency of the country in which the loan was raised . . . the amount due being computed as the equivalent at the rate of exchange when the amount is due for payment of a sum in U.S. dollars " reached " by converting the amount of the obligation expressed in the currency of issue into U.S. dollars at the rate of exchange ruling when the loan was raised."

" Paragraph 3 of Article V deals with German Currency Debts with Gold Clauses. It seems to me that the object and effect of Annex II read in conjunction with Annex VII is to assimilate German currency debts with gold clauses, so far as possible, to foreign currency debts with gold clauses in cases, but only in cases, where, under the terms of the original contracts, they were repayable abroad, as would normally be the case with foreign currency debts. The alternative conditions of the competent court being situated abroad or foreign law being applicable do not seem to have great importance, since one would rarely expect to find either of these conditions in a contract for a foreign loan unless payment abroad had also been stipulated for.

" The attention of the Tribunal was drawn to various documents published after the date of the signature of the Debt Agreement, in particular to the Message of the Swiss Federal Council to the Federal Assembly dated May 15, 1953, in which it is said (at page 8) that the creditors, especially the Swiss representatives, had argued on the basis that there were debts which were subject to foreign law, for which reason they should not be treated according to German law, including the conversion at the rate of 10 : 1, which view was ultimately accepted on the German side. These documents, including the Message of the Swiss Federal Council, were not mentioned in the pleadings, either written or oral, nor were they put to the Agents or Counsel of the parties at the oral hearing. For this reason, I think that the Tribunal should not take them into consideration. In any case their value would be very doubtful as they represent unilateral statements for internal use, made after the signature of the Debt Agreement.

" It would require plain and unambiguous words to justify the conclusion that creditors who had been deprived against their will of the benefit of the gold clause and had consented to a substantial reduction of their interest, intended to forgo nine-tenths of the remainder of their claim in cases in which the debtor had contracted to transmit his debt to the creditor abroad, *e.g.*, through a bank or by post, instead of, notionally, bringing the debt personally to the creditor at his residence, which, under modern banking conditions, would occur only exceptionally. For this would be the result of the adoption of the artificial meaning of ' *Zahlungsort* ' contended for by the Respondent. In order to express that meaning plainly and unambiguously it would be necessary to use words like the following: ' It was expressly agreed under the original written debt arrangements that the place at which, according to the law applicable to such arrangements, the debt is deemed to be payable, is situated abroad.'

" The term ' expressly agreed ' in the English text, in my opinion, requires that there should be an express agreement from which it clearly and unambiguously emerges that the ' place of payment ' is situated abroad. This means that the intention of the parties must be expressed and not left to inference, as is the case in an implied contract, such as, for instance, a warranty implied by law in a contract for the sale of goods.

" There can be no doubt that the parties to the contract of July 31, 1931, have in § 5 entered into an express agreement as to payment. The dispute between the litigants concerns not the existence but the effect of this express agreement. The paragraph in question is worded (in translation) as follows:

" ' Interest is payable on the total purchase price from October 1, 1931, at 6½ per cent. annually. The interest is to be paid at the end of each calendar quarter and for the first time on December 31, 1931, free of charge to the vendor or to a pay office (*or* " payee " *or* " address ") (in German " *Zahlstelle* ") to be specified by it; the same applies to the payment of the purchase price and the several instalments.'

" Now the vendor, the Aargauische Hypothekenbank, is a corporation incorporated under Swiss law, having its fixed seat at Brugg in Switzerland and having no branch office outside Switzerland. In §§ 1 and 2 of the contract the vendor is described as ' with its head office at Brugg '. Such a corporation cannot, like a private individual, easily change its seat without observing strict formalities; and it seems to me that the undertaking to pay money to the vendor can be fulfilled only at the head office at Brugg or, possibly, at one of the branch offices of the bank. A debtor who contracted to pay to the Bank for International Settlements would, in the absence of a special agreement, expressly agree to pay at Basle, although no place was specifically mentioned.

" If the effect of § 5 were merely to designate the person to whom payment was to be made, the reference to the vendor would be unnecessary, since, as was indeed admitted by the Agent of the Respondent in the course of the oral proceedings, it goes without saying that payment should be made to the vendor. The meaning of § 5, properly interpreted, seems to me to be that the interest is to be paid ' either to the vendor itself or to a person to be designated by it '.

" If that be so, the case seems to me analogous to those cited by the Applicant, in which the German Federal Financial Authorities decided that a clause which provided for payment to be made ' to the vendor himself ' was a sufficient compliance with the provision of clause I, 2 (a), of Annex VII. I agree with the principle underlying these decisions in so far as it implies that an agreement to pay to the creditor himself constitutes, in the case of a corporation, and in the absence of other indications, an agreement to pay at the seat of the creditor. I would not, however, wish to be understood as saying that this principle should necessarily be made applicable to debts owed to natural persons.

" I agree that the Application of the Swiss Federal Council should be granted."

Messrs. Barandon, Wolff and von Caemmerer, Members of the Tribunal, and Mr. Makarov, Additional Member, delivered the following joint Dissenting Opinion on the merits:

" While agreeing with those parts of the judgment which deal with the question of the competence of the Arbitral Tribunal, we very much regret being unable to share the position taken up in the judgment on the merits for the following reasons:

" I.

" In order to arrive at the correct interpretation of Annex VII to the Debt Agreement one must bear in mind the true purpose of the settlement contained in Sub-Annex D to Annex I, in Article V, para. 3, of Annex II and in Article 6, para. (2), of Annex IV, which has subsequently only been laid down in greater detail in Annex VII. The meaning and purpose of this settlement was to provide for certain loans and pecuniary claims expressed in Goldmarks or in Reichsmarks with a gold clause or a gold option an exception from the principle that claims of this kind due to foreign creditors should be converted into Deutsche Mark at a rate of 10 : 1, in the same manner as corresponding claims of inland creditors. A conversion at the rate of 1 : 1 of such claims due to foreign creditors was to be effected only under certain conditions, viz., only in exceptional cases and not under all circumstances. The criterion adopted for the distinction between preferred and non-preferred claims is the determination whether the claim has a specific foreign character or not, whether, in other words, the debt relationship ' is subject to foreign law ' or not (see the Message of the Swiss Federal Council to the Swiss Federal Assembly concerning the London Debt Agreement of May 5, 1953, p. 8), whether, consequently, the centre of gravity of the debt relationship is situated abroad or not. Therefore, it in no way suffices, as is also made clear by the wording of the above-mentioned relevant provisions, that the pecuniary claim has a foreign character which might—at least possibly—be admitted if only the creditor is a foreigner or has his seat or residence abroad. A *specific* foreign character is required if the conversion is to be effected at the rate of

1 : 1. Only this special prerequisite justifies a conversion at the rate of 1 : 1, differing from the treatment of other foreign Goldmark claims or Reichsmark claims with a gold clause or a gold option. Thus, even the wording of the provisions quoted makes it unmistakably clear that the Contracting Parties desired to restrict such a conversion to special, *i.e.*, specific, cases and that, guided by this intention, they established the criteria according to which it was to be ascertained whether and when a pecuniary claim expressed in Goldmarks or in Reichsmarks with a gold clause has a specific foreign character. Precisely this concept of the specific foreign character, however, which had already been used in the above-mentioned provisions of Annexes I, II and IV, required further clarification, which was then given in the provisions of Annex VII. But there can no longer be any question of such a clarification if the terms used to achieve it are interpreted and used in a manner which will eventually convert something intended to be specific into an unintended general rule. In the case of a special settlement, such as Annex VII to the Debt Agreement represents in accordance with the above observations, ' an extensive application of the provisions is not permitted ' (see Gurski, *Das Abkommen über deutsche Auslandsschulden*, 1955, p. 649).

" The fact that this is so is confirmed by the origin of the provisions of the Debt Agreement which are in question.

" At the London Debt Conference the creditors had at first requested that an exception be made for all Goldmark liabilities and Reichsmark liabilities with a gold clause due to a foreign creditor from the conversion into Deutsche Mark at the rate of 10 : 1 which was generally applicable under German currency legislation after the elimination of the gold clause for inland creditors. Subsequently, however, they soon renounced the claim, as in the case of foreign currency debts, for full maintenance of the gold clause and thus performance on the basis of the original gold clause. Moreover, this was only a necessary consequence in view of the development which the question of the adherence to gold as a standard of value for currencies had in the meantime taken. Even on the occasion of the devaluation of the U.S. dollar, the Joint Resolution of June 5, 1933, had practically declared the gold clause null and void. In the course of subsequent currency devaluations the gold clause was, accordingly, to a very large extent abolished, the only exceptions being cases in which, as in England, it had not played a practical rôle (see Nussbaum, *Money in the Law*, 1950, pp. 280 *et seqq.*). Accordingly, the Occupation Powers, by means of the Mark=Mark Law of 1947, had abolished all value clauses, including the gold clause, in the discharge of Reichsmark liabilities in the territory of the three Western occupation zones and in Greater Berlin. The Tripartite Commission for German Debts took this development into account when deciding that, in the settlement of German external debts, gold clauses should no longer be maintained (see Paragraph 30 of the Report of the Conference on German External Debts—Appendix B to the Debt Agreement). The creditors, therefore, were finally prepared to content themselves with the claim that the relevant German liabilities should be discharged in Deutsche Mark at the rate of 1 : 1. The German delegation at the London Debt Conference resisted this claim for a long time. They were guided not so much by a consideration of the transfer problem for, in principle, this problem existed equally for all German external debts, but by the consideration of the principle of equality in [the] treatment of nationals and foreigners which, in general, governs the settlement of German external debts (see the express emphasis on the principle of national treatment in Article 14, para. (2), of the Agreement).

" However, the foreign creditors had sound reasons for arguing that certain Goldmark liabilities and Reichsmark liabilities with a gold clause or a gold option owned by German debtors had a *specific* foreign character and therefore deserved a preferential treatment. The Swiss creditors, in particular, insisted that a special arrangement had to be made for private liabilities of that kind. The result was a compromise and, in the above-described circumstances, the German delegation found itself induced to give up its original legal position and to accept, in the interest of the re-establishment of German credit abroad, a conversion at the rate of 1 : 1 for Goldmark liabilities and Reichsmark liabilities with a gold clause or a gold option which have a specific foreign character. Negotiations on the reservation contained in the above-mentioned provisions of Annexes I, II and IV, that the definition of the criteria constituting the specific foreign character of a claim should be the subject of further negotiations, were held only after the close of the London Debt Conference. Their result is contained in the Goldmark Agreement of November 21, 1952, and in the relevant provisions which were agreed upon subsequently. It now constitutes the contents of Annex VII to the Debt Agreement and the Sub-Annex thereto. See, in this connection, the Memorandum on the Agreement for German External Debts which the Government of the Federal Republic of Germany submitted to the *Bundestag* simultaneously with the draft Law concerning the London Debt Agreement—Paper No. 4260 of the 1st election period 1949, the Message of the President of the United States concerning the Agreements with the Federal Republic of Germany of April 10, 1953, with the report of the Secretary of State to the President of April 4, 1953, p. 223, as well as the Message of the Swiss Federal Council to the Swiss Federal Assembly concerning the London Debt Agreement of May 5, 1953, p. 8. There is no doubt that the Tribunal can consider these official publications as well as all other literature concerning the Debt Agreement. They carry particular weight if it is shown that the interpretation arrived at from the wording, sense and purpose of the provisions of the Agreement concurs with the opinion of the Governments concerned with regard to the contents of the Agreements concluded.

" As emerges also from the essentially concurring arguments of the litigating parties in this case, the provisions contained in Section I, para. 2 (*a*), of Annex VII, which alone are of interest here, originated as follows:

" According to the draft for these provisions submitted by the creditor side, the establishment of the specific foreign character of a claim should depend only on whether the debtor had known at the time he contracted the debt that the creditor was a foreigner, either directly or through the intervention of a trustee, or had his residence or seat abroad, or whether the creditor belonged to those persons who were exempt from German interest or payment restrictions. The German delegation countered this proposal by arguing that such a sweeping formulation did not take into account the instruction which consisted of precisely defining the criteria for the *specific* foreign character of a claim. If the proposal of the creditors had been adopted, the number of foreign claims to be taken into consideration for a conversion at the rate of 1 : 1 would, as the German delegation realized immediately, have increased to such an extent that only few claims would have been left for the normal conversion of 10 : 1 which was to be the rule.

" Thus, the German proposal which was then made represented an attempt to define the criteria for the specific foreign character of a claim more precisely. It made, in so far as it is relevant in this connection, the establishment of the specific foreign character dependent upon the condition that under the debt arrangements, and in the case of claims secured by mortgage charges under the debt document which formed the basis of the entry in the Land Register, the place of payment had to be a place abroad. The Swiss creditors opposed this proposal, but without success. They, on their part, then suggested that a pecuniary claim should be considered specifically foreign if a German place of payment had not been expressly agreed. The German proposal then became the basis of the present version of the provisions contained in Section I, para. 2 (*a*), of Annex VII to the Debt Agreement, after agreement had also been reached on the criteria of an agreement on a foreign forum or on the applicability of foreign law, which might take the place of the criterion of a place of payment abroad.

" It is generally recognized that an international tribunal must take into account the purpose of the agreed provisions when interpreting a treaty and may, to this effect, also consider the origin of that treaty. Thus, Art. 2 (2) (a) and (c) of the resolution adopted by the Institut de Droit International at its meeting in Granada (1956) mentions precisely also ' le recours aux travaux préparatoires ' and ' la prise en considération des buts du traité ' as legitimate means of interpretation (Annuaire de l'Institut, pp. 358 and 359).

" However, the origin of Annex VII also makes it clear, as has been explained above, that the parties who had to negotiate the definition of the criteria of the specific foreign character of a claim considered it essential to find a formulation which was to prevent all claims of creditors who had their residence or seat abroad at the time of the creation of the debt relationship having, with only a few exceptions, to be recognized as being specifically foreign. The result of the negotiations concerning the formulation of Annex VII shows rather that the debts with a specific foreign character were to be the exception and that it was to depend upon special, that is, specific, criteria, whether a claim should, by reason of its centre of gravity being unequivocally abroad, enjoy the advantages of a conversion at the rate of 1 : 1. However, in the cases in question, the centre of gravity of a debt will only be situated abroad pursuant to Section I, para. 2 (a), of Annex VII to the Debt Agreement, if in the case of such claims the loan or advance was raised abroad and if it was expressly agreed under the original written debt arrangements that either the place of payment or the competent court is situated abroad or foreign law is applicable.

" The present case concerns exclusively the question whether a place of payment abroad has been expressly agreed in the contract of July 31, 1931, or not. The remaining criteria of the specific foreign character are not of interest here: an express agreement of a foreign court or the applicability of foreign law is undoubtedly not contained in the contract of July 31, 1931. And the question whether the brothers Max and Moriz Lindauer raised a credit abroad when purchasing the land situated in Stuttgart from the Aargauische Hypothekenbank, the latter granting them a postponement for the balance of the purchase money, is not submitted to the Arbitral Tribunal for a decision. On the contrary, the Respondent declared that it did not intend to call in question that the specific foreign character of the claim for the balance of purchase money concerned would have to be recognized if a place of payment abroad had been expressly agreed in the original written debt arrangements. Accordingly, the Applicant submitted only the question of the express agreement of a place of payment abroad to the Arbitral Tribunal for a decision.

" The provision in Section I, para. 2 (a), of Annex VII to the Debt Agreement does not specify what ' place of payment ' must be taken to mean. The concept of the place of payment is not defined in the Annex, but taken for granted. The Applicant is of the opinion that the concept of the place of payment must, for the purposes of the Debt Agreement, be defined irrespectively of its meaning under the various national laws. However, no such indication whatsoever is to be found in the Agreement. The attempt to find a natural, non-technical meaning of the term ' place of payment ' which might be applied to Annex VII does not, as will be shown in greater detail in Section III, make possible a decision precisely in those cases in which there may be doubts as to where the place of payment is situated. Nor does the idea of establishing the meaning which the term ' place of payment ' might have in Annex VII by means of comparative law lead to a positive result, in view of the great differences in the concepts of the legal systems concerned. In certain cases it permits the negative ascertainment that a certain place does not meet the requirements generally made of a place of payment. However, a positive concept which could be used in all cases for the application of Annex VII cannot be obtained in this manner. This will also be explained at greater length in Section III.

" It would, therefore, seem correct to take the concept of the place of payment, which has not been defined in Annex VII but which has obviously been taken for granted, from that law which generally governs the debt to be settled. This is the most natural solution in the case of an Agreement which settles existing liabilities subject to specific laws. It will, in any case, lead to a clear answer to the question what ' place of payment ' must be taken to mean, while avoiding a violation of the sense of the Agreements between the parties.

" It is true that doubts have been expressed as to whether it is admissible to take the concept of the place of payment from the law which is applicable to the contractual relations of the parties. Reference is made in this connection to the apparently similar problems of private international law. This calls for the following observations:

" As far as private international law is concerned, it must indeed be admitted that in cases in which the determination of the applicable law depends on the place of performance, there are objections to taking the concept of the place of performance from this law itself. In those cases, prevailing practice and theory base themselves on the concept of the place of performance resulting from the rule of conflict (see, *e.g.*, Lewald, ' Règles générales des conflits de lois ', *Rec. des Cours*, 1939, III (69), pp. 85 *et seqq.*). However, the situation is different when determining the place of performance under Annex VII, so that the above-mentioned objections cannot be extended to it. In the first place and in contrast to the above-mentioned rules of conflict, the Debt Agreement does not contain any concept of the place of payment or performance which could be resorted to. Furthermore, the question is different in so far as it is not the determination of the applicable law but the establishment of the specific foreign character of the liability which depends on the place of payment. In contrast, the law applicable to the contract is certain irrespective of the question of the place of payment and is, therefore, best suited to supply information as to which is the place of payment of the liability.

" One further point of view speaks in favour of this solution. The criterion of the express agreement of a place of payment abroad is laid down as an alternative to the express agreement of a foreign court or the applicability of foreign law. If there are any doubts as to whether the last mentioned agreements have been effectually concluded, they can be resolved solely according to the law which is applicable to the contract. It is, therefore, fair to proceed in the same manner with respect to the place of payment and to let the proper law of the contract decide about it.

" This treatment of the question is, at the same time, that which can best do justice to the interest of the parties. If, *e.g.*, a German enterprise were to raise a loan in the U.S.A. the applicability of American law, without being expressly agreed, could nevertheless result from the fact that the loan contract was concluded in New York in the English language, on the basis of New York forms of contract, with the legal terms and clauses customary there. In such a case the law of New York must be decisive also for the determination of the place of payment. The American creditor can expect that the concept of the place of payment under New York law, which is decisive for the contract, will also be the criterion for the question whether there exists an express agreement on a place of payment abroad. On the other hand, no injustice is thereby done to the German debtor, for he must realize that his liability under the loan contract is subject to the law of New York in every respect.

" In the case to be decided there is no doubt that the contract of July 31, 1931, for the sale of the land which created the debt for the balance of the purchase money, the specific foreign character of which is now at issue, is subject to German law.

" The contract between the Aargauische Hypothekenbank, as vendor, and the brothers Max and Moriz Lindauer of Stuttgart, as purchasers, was concluded before a notary public at Stuttgart and concerned the sale of land situated in Stuttgart. The purchase price is expressed in German currency and secured by a mortgage on the land situated in Germany. According to Swiss private international law, German law is applicable to such a contract as *lex rei sitae*, since the transfer of the ownership of the land is the performance characteristic for the contract, so that this is the closest point of contact (BGE, 82, II, 550, see also 79, II, 295 (297); Schnitzer, *Handbuch des internationalen Privatrechts*, II, 4th edition, 1958, p. 590, Note 73, pp. 633 *et seqq.*, p. 690). German private international law holds the same view. The present contract of sale of the land has its centre of gravity in Germany. German law is to be applied as that law with which the debt relationship has the most important points of contact and the application of which also corresponds, at the same time, to the presumed intention of the parties. (See BGHZ 7, 231 *et seqq.* (235); 9, 221 *et seqq.*; 17, 89 *et seqq.* (92) and 19, 110 *et seqq.*; Palandt-Lauterbach, preliminary remark 2 *a* before EGBGB, Art. 12; Erman-Arndt, preliminary remark I C before Art. 12, EGBGB; Soergel-Kegel, preliminary remark III 1 (p. 46) before Art. 7, EGBGB).

" If the rules of conflict of the legal systems concerned with the facts concur, these rules must also be used as a basis by an international tribunal (Rebel, *Z. f. ausländ. u. internat. Privatrecht*, 1, 1927, pp. 33 to 47; Martin Wolff, *Das internationale Privatrechts Deutschlands*, 3rd edition, 1954, p. 33). Moreover, and going beyond this, it can be said in the present case that a quite predominant opinion has developed in the whole world with regard to the treatment under private international law of contracts for the sale of land. According to this opinion, such contracts must be judged under the *lex rei sitae* unless another point of contact suggests itself conclusively for particular reasons. This is the point of view of English, French, Italian and many other laws of conflict and, at the same time, the opinion of numerous international bodies (as, *e.g.*, the proposals of the Institut de Droit International made at its meeting in Florence as early as 1908; see Rabel, *Conflict of Laws*, III, 1950, pp. 104 *et seq.* with detailed references). Therefore, the Arbitral Tribunal can follow this opinion without hesitation in its decision. The liability at issue is thus to be judged according to German law.

" This leads to the following conclusions in the case to be decided:

" The place of payment is the place where the debtor has to fulfil his obligation to pay. According to Sections 269, para. 1, and 270, para. 4, of the German Civil Code, the place of performance of the obligation to pay the purchase price resulting from the contract of July 31, 1931, is Stuttgart, since Messrs. Max and Moriz Lindauer had their residence there at the time the contract was concluded. This is where they had to fulfil their obligation by sending the money to the creditor. The fact that they had, in accordance with the provision ' in case of doubt ' of Section 270, para. 1, of the German Civil Code, assumed the cost of transmission to the creditor in § 5 of the contract does not change the fact that Stuttgart remained the place of payment for the purchasers; this follows from the provisions, which are unequivocal in this respect, of Section 269, para. 3, and Section 270, para. 4, of the German Civil Code, which stem from the General German Commercial Code (ADHGB, Art. 325; also Austria, ABGB § 905); (see in this connection Larenz, *Schuldrecht*, I, 1957, § 17, IV c, pp. 162 *et seq.*; Palandt-Danckelmann BGB, § 270, Note 1 *a*, § 269, Notes 1 and 3; Erman-Goerke, BGB, § 270, Note 1, § 269, Notes 1 and 5). If, as is almost a matter of course in a notarial deed, the seat of the creditor is mentioned in the text of the deed, this merely indicates to the debtors where they have to address the money. . This does not, however, constitute a statement concerning the place of payment.   On the contrary, according to Sections 270, para. 4, and 269, para. 1, of the German Civil Code, the place of payment remains the residence of the debtors at Stuttgart.

" If, consequently, the place of payment of the obligation for the purchase price created in the agreement of July 31, 1931, is situated in Germany, the Application of the Swiss Confereration for the declaration that this place was to be situated abroad according to this agreement should be rejected as unfounded.

" III.

" While the determination of the place of payment according to the proper law of their contract, with which the parties are familiar, will always lead to clear and practicable solutions, one enters into very complicated lines of reasoning when attempting to determine the concept of the place of payment for Annex VII to the Agreement in an autonomous manner.  This method may be supposed not to be the right one if only for the reason that it can hardly be assumed that the authors of the Debt Agreement wanted to make the criteria of the specific foreign character dependent upon such complicated reasoning as becomes necessary here.  In the present case, moreover, this road would not lead to any other decision and result.

" 1.  As has already been indicated, it might first occur to one to try to find a ' natural ', not ' technical ', meaning of the term ' place of payment ' and to use it in the interpretation of Annex VII to the Debt Agreement. However, if one attempts to do so one overlooks the fact that the terms ' payment ' and ' place of payment ', as well as the two remaining criteria used in Section I, para. 2 (a), for the specific foreign character, are legal terms. They must be interpreted by taking into account the purpose which the enumeration of these criteria is to serve.  By means of these criteria, liabilities of which the centre of gravity is situated abroad are to be distinguished from those which do not possess such a centre of gravity.   The attempt to find a natural, non-technical, meaning of the term ' place of payment ' does not do justice to this consideration.  Moreover, one will not succeed in elaborating such a natural, non-technical, meaning which could also be used in deciding cases of doubt.

" It is true, however, that in certain cases the determination of the place of payment does not present any difficulties, so that a natural concept thereof seems to offer itself without hesitation.  This is the case when debtor and creditor reside at the same place so that payment and receipt of the money happen at the same place.  There can be no doubt about the place of payment then.  The same applies when the debtor has his residence or seat elsewhere but he has undertaken to transport the money to the place of the creditor, to make it available there and to pay it there so that the banks or post-office which he uses in order to make the money available to the creditor are his agents (*Erfüllungsgehilfen*), for whose possible failure he is responsible.  This is the case, for instance, under [Annex VII], Section I, para. 1 (*b*), when bonds are payable in foreign countries only.  It is then incumbent upon the debtor to have the redemption monies available there so that the bond can be honoured upon presentation by the creditor.  There is no doubt in this case that payment and receipt of the money are to take place at this place of redemption.

" Difficulties in the determination of the concept of the place of payment will occur only if the obligation of the debtor, as is the case in the contract of July 31, 1931, is limited to posting the money to the address of the creditor. It must be decided in this case whether the place of payment is to be in the place where the debtor pays, *i.e.*, peforms the action of payment incumbent upon him, which consists of the posting of the money, or whether the place of payment is to be the place where the creditor receives the money.

" The fact that not only the place where the creditor receives his money can be considered a ' natural ' conception of the place of payment, is shown by the parallel problem of the determination of the place of delivery. The question whether the place of dispatch or the place of destination is to be considered the place of performance in this connection is wide open in the language of commercial intercourse. In the case of a c.i.f. transaction, *e.g.*, it is customary to designate that place as place of delivery where the goods are shipped and dispatched by the vendor, and not the place of destination where the buyer receives the goods (see Almén-Neubecker, *Das skandinavische Kaufrecht*, I, pp. 118 *et seqq.*, II 310; Rabel, *Recht des Warenkaufs*, pp. 317 *et seqq.*).

" Consequently, he who attempts to decide the question whether the place of dispatch or the place of destination is to be considered the place of payment according to a ' natural ', ' non-technical ', meaning of the term ' place of payment ' runs the risk, although unconsciously, of taking the concept of the place of payment with which he is familiar and which corresponds to the provisions of his own law, which are applicable in the absence of agreement, to be the natural concept.

" 2. Therefore, if one is of the opinion that the concept of the place of payment under Annex VII must be determined independently and irrespectively of the proper law of the contract of the parties, the only way left is that of a clarification, by means of comparative law, of what may be meant by place of payment. In the case of such a comparative formation [formulation] of the concept, one must, at the same time, consider and ponder most carefully the purposes which Annex VII pursued in establishing the requirement of an express agreement on a place of payment abroad.

" In this connection, it must be stated at the outset that there is no difference in the meaning of the German, English and French texts of the Agreement, which are all three equally authentic. While the German and English texts speak of ' *Zahlungsort* ' and ' place of payment ', respectively, which must be situated abroad, the French text requires the agreement ' *que le paiement serait fait à l'étranger* '. This is the same formula as is used in Art. 1247, para. 2, of the French Civil Code in order to express that in case of doubt the place of payment is the residence of the debtor. The French formulation is thus synonymous with the German and English formulation and cannot be taken to be an indication that not the place of the action of payment is meant, but the place of the receipt of the money. Therefore, it is not the texts of the Agreement which are different, but merely the provisions, applicable in the absence of agreement, of the law involved.

" These provisions differ greatly from one another. According to the law of the French Civil Code (Art. 1247, para. 2) and numerous laws following it, the residence of the debtor is the place of payment, According to German and Austrian law (German Civil Code §§ 269, 270, para. 4; Austrian ABGB § 905) which go back to the General German Commercial Code, Art. 325, the place of payment is also the residence or seat of the debtor, but in case of doubt the debtor is obliged to dispatch the money to the address of the creditor. Anglo-American law, on the other hand—although with an important restriction which will be discussed below—applies the rule: ' The debtor must seek the creditor ', according to which the pecuniary debt must be discharged at the residence or seat of the creditor. Among the Continental European laws, too, more recent codes have adopted the establishment of the place of payment at the residence of the creditor in the absence of agreement (Switzerland, OR, Art. 74, para. 2, No. 1; Italy, Codice Civile, Art. 1182, para. 3; 1498, para. 3; Greece, Civil Code, Art. 321).

" There can thus be no question of a uniform legal opinion which could be used as a basis for the interpretation of the Debt Agreement. The question is whether, for any reason, the concept of those laws which make the residence of the creditor decisive, as being the predominant rule in the Anglo-American legal area and of late being frequently followed outside this area, could have priority in the interpretation of the Agreement. This question must be answered in the negative.

" When appreciating the existing profound differences it must be remembered that the emphasis on the residence of the debtor in the legal area of the French Civil Code and of German and Austrian law has its root in the fact that the place of payment was considered to be the centre of gravity of the debt relationship. Therefore, the forum and the applicable law depended upon it, and it did not seem tolerable to submit the debtor without ado to the court or law of the creditor merely because he had to dispatch the money to the creditor. Wherever in modern laws the residence of the creditor is declared the place of payment, this is connected with the progressive separation of the question of the place of payment from the question of the forum and the applicable law (see Nussbaum, *Money in the Law*, 1950, pp. 146 to 149). Therefore, the concepts developed in those laws which consider the place of payment irrelevant for the localisation of the legal relationship have no bearing on Annex VII to the Agreement, in which the criterion of the place of payment is used precisely in order to establish the foreign centre of gravity of a liability.

" Moreover, it must be taken into account when appreciating the rule of Common Law, ' the debtor must seek the creditor ', that the place of payment determined in accordance therewith never had any significance for the ' proper law of the contract '. Above all, however, it must not be overlooked that the rule, at least in American Common Law, applies only if creditor and debtor live in the same state. Otherwise, the place where the contract was concluded is decisive (see 40 *American Jurisprudence*, Payment §§ 16 to 19, where the same is assumed also in respect of English law; furthermore, Williston, *On Contracts*, IV, § 1812, in particular Note 6; *Weyand* v. *Park Terrace* Co., 1911, 202 N.Y. 231, 95 N.E. 723). In English law the legal situation is not quite so clear. It is certain, however, that the rule according to which the debtor must seek the creditor and make payment at this place applies only if the creditor has his residence or seat of business in England (Chitty's *Treatise on the Law of Contracts*, 20th edition, 1947, with Suppl. 1952, p. 271). Consequently, the rule that the residence of the creditor is the place of performance is completely irrelevant for external liabilities (Rabel, *Conflict of Laws*, III, 1950, p. 8). It would, therefore, be wrong to use a concept of the place of payment which takes up the rule ' the debtor must seek the creditor ' for the establishment of the specific foreign character of a debt under the London Debt Agreement.

" The Applicant placed emphasis on the formulation by F. A. Mann, *The Legal Aspect of Money*, 1953, p. 175, that the concept of the place of payment in English law means the place ' at which the creditor is entitled actually to receive the money due to him, not the place from which the money is to be dispatched to him . . .' If this were the concept of English law, it would not have any decisive bearing on the interpretation of the Debt Agreement, for the reasons discussed above. This is true all the more since the starting-point of French and German law, the concepts of which must be given at least the same significance for the Agreement, is an opposite one. But F. A. Mann is also very careful in his contention and stresses that this is his personal opinion (' it is suggested '), since there is no ' authority ' in this field. This is due to the fact that English law does not attribute to the centre of gravity of the debt relationship, to the forum or to the applicable law any legal consequences in connection with the concept of the place of payment comparable to the treatment under continental laws. The courts have therefore no reason to clarify the concept of the place of payment, which thus carries so much less weight under English law than it does under continental laws.

" For the rest, however, it may be assumed that even under English law the place where, according to the saying ' the debtor must seek the creditor ', the creditor is to receive the money is, at the same time, the place at which the debtor has to perform his contract. If the debtor does not perform his contract in person but makes use of the services of the post-office or of a bank, these latter are his agents (*Erfüllungsgehilfen*), for whose possible mistakes he is responsible. Therefore, the debtor is responsible for payment at the seat of the creditor. If the bank makes a mistake he is liable and in default, and bound to repair the damage caused by his default.

" In the present case the debtors are only bound to dispatch the money, according to German law, which in this respect is undoubtedly decisive. They have thus done all that is required of them once they have sent off the money. The bank and post-office are not their agents. Therefore, by designating the place where the creditor receives the money as the place of payment, even in such a case one uses a concept of the place of payment which is foreign also to the practice of English law and which, as far as is evident, does not appear in any law of the world.

" The place where the creditor receives the money can thus be considered the place of payment within the meaning of Section I, para. 2 (*a*), of Annex VII to the Agreement only if the debtor is responsible for performance being made there. This is also the only concept of the place of payment which corresponds to the reasoning behind the provisions of Annex VII to the Agreement. The object is, as has been explained under I, to establish a differentiating criterion within the meaning of Annex I, Sub-Annex D, para. 2, Annex II, Art. V, para. 3 (*b*), and Annex IV, Art. 6, para. (2), whereby external debts of *specific* foreign character are to be taken out of the mass of all other external debts. If the mere mention of the foreign address of the creditor sufficed to achieve this, practically all external debts would have a ' specific ' foreign character. This would, consequently, not be a differentiating criterion. The only exception would be those debts for which, which will hardly happen in practice, a place of payment in Germany was expressly agreed. An application of the Swiss delegation to establish the criteria of the specific foreign character in this manner was, as has already been emphasized, expressly rejected in the negotiations. Nor did the request originally put forward by the creditor side, that it should suffice for the specific foreign character of a liability if the creditor had his seat or residence at the time of the creation of the debt abroad and the debtor was aware of this, meet with acceptance. It is not possible subsequently, by way of interpretation, to introduce into the Agreement a settlement which was not desired by the Parties to the Agreement, and thus to turn the settlement which was adopted into its opposite.

" Even the placing side by side of the alternative criteria of the agreement on a foreign court, the applicability of foreign law or a place of payment abroad makes it clear that they must be criteria according to which the centre of gravity of the legal relationship is situated abroad and the debt relationship ' is subject to the foreign law ', as it has been appropriately expressed in the above-mentioned Message of the Swiss Federal Council (p. 8). However, this would not be the case if one wishes to take the place of payment abroad to mean the mere foreign address of the creditor. Precisely in view of the modern technique of transactions without actual currency, it is practically irrelevant for the determination of the centre of gravity of a debt relationship to what address the money is to be sent. The only important point is how far the responsibility of the debtor goes.

" If, in the present case, the brothers Max and Moriz Lindauer were responsible for the money being available on maturity in Brugg in Switzerland for the Aargauische Hypothekenbank, then, according to international legal opinion, which is unanimous in this respect, the place of payment was at Brugg. But this is not the case here. The debtors were obliged only to dispatch the money from Stuttgart and had done all that was incumbent upon them when having effected the dispatch. It is true that, according to the rule of Section 270, para. 1, of the German Civil Code, in case of doubt the debtors bore the cost and risk of the dispatch, *i.e.*, they had, if necessary, to pay once again if the money was lost. But they were not responsible for the payment at Brugg; the German and Swiss banks which transmitted the money were not their agents. If the money did not arrive or arrived late at the creditor's, due to a mistake on the part of these banks, the debtors could not be held liable for damages, since their liability and responsibility ended with the dispatch of the money in Stuttgart. In such a case it cannot be assumed that the place of payment within the meaning of Annex VII, Section I, para 2 (*a*), is situated abroad. If this were assumed, *i.e.*, if the concept of the place of payment were based merely on the consideration that the creditor must eventually receive the amount of his claim, this would mean that all claims have a specific foreign character if only the creditor is a foreigner, which, as has been mentioned previously, cannot be intended according to the sense and purpose of the settlement concluded in favour of claims of a specific foreign character.

"Therefore, the Application of the Swiss Confederation should be rejected as unfounded also from this point of view.

" IV.

" However, it is not to be assumed that the Parties to the London Debt Agreement and the Annexes thereto wished to make the establishment of the specific foreign character of a debt dependent upon the result of such rather complicated considerations. Nor have they done so, for they required that the place of payment must be agreed ' expressly ' (' *ausdrücklich* ', ' *expressé-ment* ') in the original written arrangements. This refutes the criticism which was occasionally voiced in the course of the proceedings that the determination of the place of payment under German law (and under other laws based upon the residence of the debtor, see Nussbaum, *Money in the Law*, 1950, pp. 146 *et seq.*) was too complicated and difficult for outsiders to understand. If, as is indicated, the requirement of expressness is taken seriously, cases of doubt will hardly occur. If the contracting parties agreed in a clause such as is customary, particularly with banks—the external debts of specific foreign character are to a large extent claims of banks and insurance companies—that the business premises of the bank which grants the loan are to be the place of payment, such an express agreement practically excludes doubts as to the interpretation which might result from the different concept of the place of payment under the various laws. The same is true for all other place-of-payment clauses customary in business transactions, such as ' payable in X ', ' place of payment in X ', ' place of payment at the residence of the creditor in X ', ' place of fulfilment for both parties in X ', and the like.

" What must the ' express ' written agreement that the place of payment is to be situated abroad be taken to mean?

" Normally, in modern law the effect of express and implicit or tacit declarations of intention is exactly the same, as it has, *e.g.*, been laid down in general and in principle in Art. 1, para. 2 (see also Art. 74, para. 1, and Art. 176, para. 3), of the Swiss Law of Obligations and, similarly, in Section 164, para. 1, second sentence, of the German Civil Code. ' *En principe, la volonté tacite a autant de force que la volonté expresse du moment où elle est établie* ', says Esmein (Planiol-Ripert-Esmein, *Traité pratique de droit civil français*, VI, 1952, No. 105). The same is stated in Anglo-American literature, where it is said at times that there is no difference between express contracts and implied contracts, apart from the question of proof (see Williston, *On Contracts*, II, 1936, § 3, pp. 6 *et seqq.*; Corbin, *On Contracts*, 1952, §§ 18 *et seqq.*, p. 26; 12 *American Jurisprudence*, Contracts, §§ 4 *et seqq.* and § 239).

" However, there are cases even in modern law in which the legislator demands an express agreement for good reasons. This means—at least if, as in Annex VII, Section I, para. 2 (*a*), an express *written* agreement is required—an agreement ' *expressis verbis* '. In such a case a declaration is express if its meaning results unequivocally from the words used without regard to the circumstances (see von Tuhr, *Allgemeiner Teil des Deutschen Bürgerlichen Rechts*, II, p. 416; Heinrich Lehmann, *Allgemeiner Teil*, 1957, § 30, II, 2). The content of the declaration must have found full and unequivocal expression in the written declaration itself (RGZ 65, 177 *et seqq.* [180]). The contrast thereto is a determination of the meaning of the declaration by way of deduction or through an interpretation of the circumstances. When the legislator demands expressness in this sense, the purpose is to make sure that both the party making the declaration and the party receiving it are aware of the significance of the declaration (RGZ 65, 177 *et seqq.* [181]). The requirement of expressness has been used in this sense, *e.g.*, in Section 700, para. 2, of the German Civil Code and in modern legislation, in particular in the Law of Deposits (*Depotgesetz*), Section 5, para. 1, second sentence; Section 10, para. 1; Section 12, para. 1 (see Heinrich Lehmann, *op. cit.*, § 30, II, 2; Baumbach-Duden HGB, 1955, Appendix I to § 406, p. 848).

" Similarly, Swiss law also knows cases in which the declaration must be express (OR, Art. 459, para. 2; 462, para. 2; 481, para. 3; ZGB, Art. 294). In such cases, the Swiss Federal Court requires that the intention must be declared *expressis verbis*, *i.e.*, in words from which this intention emerges directly and as their essential sense and content according to current usage of the language. The Court maintains that expressness does not coincide with clarity and unequivocality; an intention can emerge very clearly from the conduct of the parties but it is not thereby expressly declared (BGE 63, II, pp. 8 *et seqq.*; in the same sense v. Tuhr-Seigwart, *Allgemeiner Teil des schweizerischen Obligationenrechts*, 1942, p. 153; Oser-Schönenberger, *Obligationenrecht*, V, 3, 1945, Art. 481, Note 6).

" As far as French legal language is concerned, the observations by Esmein may be considered representative. He points out that the Civil Code requires a '*stipulation expresse*' or ' *des termes exprès* ' in certain cases in order to draw the attention of the parties to the importance of a given agreement. In such cases, a tacit or implicit declaration of intention does not suffice (Planiol-Ripert-Esmein, VI, 1952, No. 105; also Aubry et Rau, IV, § 343, No. 3).

" In Anglo-American law, too, the express agreement is in contrast to what can be deduced by interpretation from the circumstances. ' Express contracts are those in which the terms of the agreement are fully and openly incorporated.' Express is ' declared in terms; set forth in words ', ' made known distinctly and explicitly, and not left to inference ', ' manifest by direct and appropriate language ', in contrast to ' implied ' (see 12 *American Jurisprudence*, Contracts, § 4, and Black's *Law Dictionary*, 1951, under ' express ' with reference to judicial decisions; 15 A *Words and Phrases* (permanent edition) under ' express ', ' express contract ', p. 520, p. 528; Williston, *On Contracts*, § 3, p. 6). The same usage of language exists in English law: ' Contracts which are completely set forth in words either by mouth or writing are called express; those which are either wholly or partly not so set forth are called implied contracts ' (Chitty's *Treatise on the Law of Contracts*, 1947, with Suppl. 1952, p. 3; Wharton's *Law Lexicon*, 1938, under ' express ').

" Observations which seem to obliterate this contrast are . . . to be found in another connection which is not of interest here. These observations confront genuine contracts which are not only ' express contracts ' but also ' contracts implied in fact ' with fictitious contracts, ' contracts implied in law ', ' quasi contracts ', or ' constructive contracts ' (which concern cases of *negotiorum gestio* or of undue enrichment) (Williston, *On Contracts*, II, § 3, pp. 6 *et seqq.*; 12 *American Jurisprudence*, Contracts, §§ 4 *et seqq.*). Such observations must, therefore, not be misunderstood in the sense that even in cases where the law requires an express agreement, an agreement ' by implication ' would suffice.

" In an individual case, of course, the requirements to be made depend always on the reason for which a given provision laid down the requirement of expressness (RGZ 65, 177 et seqq. (179); RGR Kommentar BGB, 1953, preliminary remark 2 before § 116). In the case of the provision in question of Annex VII, the point is that an agreement on the place of payment can be considered to have a particularly close link [with] a foreign country only if this agreement has been express. This regulation of Annex VII is in accord with the point of view held for the treatment under private international law of credit contracts. In these cases one is convinced that an express agreement on the place of payment is important for the applicable law, . . . otherwise no importance can be atached to the place of payment (Rabel, *Conflict of Laws*, III, 1950, p. 7).

" Above all, however, the requirement of an express agreement was obviously meant to create a clear situation and to exclude issues like the present. This is the reason why the agreement on the applicability of foreign law is also required to be in an express form. From a substantive point of view, the case would be the same if, *e.g.*, the application of English law followed unequivocally from the use of English contract forms and legal concepts. Art. 2 of the Hague Convention on International Purchase Law[1] would consider this sufficient. With regard to the determination of the applicable law by the parties, it provides: ' *Cette désignation doit faire l'object d'une clause expresse, ou résulter indubitablement des dispositions du contrat.*' The provision of Annex VII, Section 1, para. 2 (*a*), however, is narrower and does not consider this latter definition sufficient. In accordance therewith, only the express agreement on a place of payment which excludes all doubts carries enough weight to establish the specific foreign character.

" In the cases up to now decided by the Mixed Commission and by the German courts in which the specific foreign character of a debt was affirmed there has, accordingly, always existed an express place-of-payment clause meeting the requirements. In the case of the *Bodenkreditbank Basel* v. *Rohrer* (judgment of the Mixed Commission of November 7, 1956)[2] it was agreed that the seat of the creditor should be the place of payment. In the judgment of the *Bundesgerichtshof* of July 4, 1957—VII ZR 257—BGHZ 25, 111 et seqq., the clause reads: ' All payments are to be made at the residence of the creditor.' In the case decided by the *Bundesgerichtshof* in its judgment of November 11, 1957—VII ZR 201/56—, the business premises for the time being of the creditor at Basle were envisaged as the place of performance for all contractual obligations. If, in conclusion, the judgment of the *Bundesgerichtshof* contains the words ' in so far the designation of the place of payment abroad was not even required; it sufficed, on the contrary, that the Swiss place of performance and payment followed unequivocally from the circumstances ', this refers to the fact that (as in the *Rohrer* case) the case concerned a loan granted by a German trustee of the Swiss creditor. In this case, which is regulated by the last paragraph of Section I of Annex VII, an express agreement of a Swiss

---

[1 Draft Hague Convention on Conflicts of Law in the Matter of Sales of International Character of Corporeal Movable Property, 1955. For text, see Conférence de la Haye de Droit International Privé, *Actes de la Septième Session* (1951), pp. 382–384 (in French).
  An (unofficial) translation into English appears in *American Journal of Comparative Law*, 1 (1952), p. 275. Article 2 there reads:
    "A sale is governed by the internal law of the country designated by the contracting parties.
    " Such designation must be contained in an express clause, or unambiguously result from the provisions of the contract.
    "Conditions affecting the consent of the parties respecting the law declared applicable are determined by such law."]
[2 Reported below, p. 326.]

place of payment in the contract concluded between the German trustee as the formal lender and the German debtor is practically not even conceivable. In this case it must, therefore, suffice that the circumstances and, in particular, the preliminary agreements indicated unequivocally a Swiss place of payment. But apart from this trusteeship case, it cannot suffice for the requirement of an express agreement that the place of payment results merely from the circumstances.

" In the case of the notarial contract of July 31, 1931, there can be no question of an express agreement on the place of payment abroad which would meet the necessary requirements as described above. It does not contain anything about the place of payment. § 5 of the contract merely makes it clear that the debtors have to bear the cost of transmission to the creditor. It hereby eliminates the doubts which might still be possible under Section 270, para. 1, of the German Civil Code. Apart from that, it is agreed in addition that the debtors have to bear the cost of transmission even if the creditor instructs them to make payment to a pay office to be specified by it, *i.e.*, to another payee. This is an agreement on the cost of payment and not on the place of payment. None of the provisions of the notarial contract of July 31, 1931, fulfils the sense of making the debtor aware of the fact that by the agreement concluded he had submitted himself to a foreign legal system and had assumed a debt with a clearly foreign centre of gravity, exactly as he would have done in the case of an express argeement on a foreign forum or the applicability of foreign law.

" Therefore, the Application of the Swiss Confederation ought to be rejected as unfounded also because the agreement on a place of payment abroad was not express.

" V.

" The requirement of expressness is, indeed, sometimes also understood in a somewhat wider sense. It is true that such an interpretation cannot be applied as a matter of principle if, as in the present case, an express ' written ' agreement is required (RGZ 65, 177 *et seqq.* [181]). But in cases where a written agreement is not prescribed and the requirement of expressness is made for declarations which may also be expressed orally, there may sometimes be a departure from the usual meaning of the requirement of an express agreement. In those cases, one is satisfied with declarations which represent ' a particularly unequivocal expression of the intention to that effect, be it by words or facts of inescapable conclusiveness ' (RGZ 107, 111).

" German judicial decisions proceed in this manner in the case of Section 244, para. 1, of the German Civil Code (see the above mentioned decision RGZ 107, 110 [111] as well as RGZ 111, 316 [317]; 153, 384 *et seqq.*; BGH of January 25, 1954—IV ZR 94/53—Lindenmaier Möhring No. 5 to Section 275 of the German Civil Code). The basic decision RGZ 107, 111, which the other judgments mentioned follow, emphasizes very clearly that this interpretation of the requirement of expressness is limited to the case of Section 244, para. 1, of the German Civil Code and is based on the sense of the purpose of precisely this provision. It must, indeed, suffice in the case of Section 244, para. 1, of the German Civil Code that the purpose of actually receiving foreign currency in order to use it, *e.g.*, for travel abroad, emerges unequivocally from the circumstances (Martin Wolff, *Ehrenbergs Handbuch des Handelsrechts*, IV, 1, p. 640). The requirement of expressness came to be incorporated in the provision only because it had been taken over into general civil law by way of Art. 336, para. 2, ADHGB from the law of bills of exchange (ADWO Art. 37). In the law of bills of exchange, however, the requirement of expressness had its sound reason for the insertion of the ' effective clause '. This explains why jurisprudence is somewhat liberal here in the interpretation of the requirement, which does not quite fit into Section 244, para. 1, of the German Civil Code.

" This is not decisive for other cases (Heinrich Lehmann, *Allgemeiner Teil*, 1957, § 30, II, 2; see also Palandt-Danckelmann, § 244, Note 4 c: ' however, express here means only . . .' (' *doch bedeutet ausdrücklich hier nur . . .*'), and RGR Kommentar BGB, preliminary remark 2 before § 116). Moreover, in contrast to Section 244, para. 1, of the German Civil Code, Annex VII requires an express written agreement. Therefore, the Applicant is wrong in basing itself on these decisions.

" Moreover, the agreement of July 31, 1931, does not even meet the reduced requirement of a particularly unequivocal agreement on a place of payment abroad. To do so it would be necessary to eliminate in an unequivocal manner doubts which exist or are possible with regard to the place of payment. This, however, is not the case.

" In the first place, every contract and every declaration of the parties must be interpreted on the basis of the law governing them. The contract, therefore, would have to be such as to eliminate the doubt existing under Sections 269, para. I, and 270, para. 4, of the German Civil Code whether the basic rule is to remain in force that the residence of the debtor is the place of performance. As has been explained above under II, the contract does not only not do so in a clear and unequivocal manner, but it does not do so at all.

" But even when disregarding the existence of the rules under Sections 269 and 270 of the German Civil Code, and considering the contract as having been concluded so to speak *in vacuo*, nothing unequivocal can be deduced from it with respect to the place of payment.

" It is said in §§ 1 and 2 of the contract that the Aargauische Hypotheken-bank, with its head office at Brugg, had acquired the land at a forced auction sale and was thereby disposing of it to other purchasers. The provisions laying down the duties of the purchasers thus indicate, apart from the name of the vendor, also the head office of the latter, without this having any bearing—at least not at first—on the obligations of the purchasers.

" The main content of § 5 of the contract, on which the Applicant relies, is primarily the stipulation of the interest rate for the purchase price and the interest dates. It is added that payment thereof is to be made free of charge and that the same terms, *viz.*, maturity at the end of each calendar quarter and the bearing of the cost, apply also to the payment of the purchase price and the several instalments. This provision does not mention the place of payment.

" The Applicant, however, considers the fact that § 5 lays down the additional obligation of the debtors to pay the purchase price, if so instructed, not to the vendor but to a pay office to be specified by it, to constitute an element of locality. It argues that, if the provision for payment to such a pay office is to be understood in the sense of indicating a place, then the payment to the vendor mentioned in § 5 also receives this sense of locality, which furnishes the justification for attaching to the mention of the head office of the vendor at Brugg the importance of an agreement on the place of payment. If this argument were correct, the conclusion reached thereby would, at any rate, be very complicated and indirect. It could not be said of it that it contained ' a particularly unequivocal expression ' of the intention to agree on a place of payment. Therefore, there would be no express agreement even if that line of reasoning were correct.

" The above-mentioned argument does not stand the test even from the point of view of its content. By means of § 5 of the contract, the creditor is merely given the right to name in its stead another payee, in particular a trustee, as is often done by Swiss banks in the case of such credits. Therefore, the clause says something about the person to whom payment is to be made and nothing about the place of payment. The case is different from those cases in which the debtor undertook to make payment ' at the residence of the creditor at Basle ' or in which the seat of the creditor at Zurich is agreed as the place of payment or place of performance. In such cases, the Swiss localisation of his debt has been clearly impressed upon the debtor. In the contract of July 31, 1931, on the contrary, this has not happened. Under this contract, the question is open whether the place of payment is Stuttgart, Brugg or a third place.

" If the creditor had had branch offices in Germany (which is not the case) or if it had had current accounts with banks in Berlin, Frankfurt or Stuttgart, the debtor would have been entitled without any doubt, when disregarding the relevant provision of Section 270, para. 1, of the German Civil Code, to pay to such an account of the creditor, *e.g.*, in Stuttgart, according to the text of the contract. Such a transfer is admissible whenever the creditor has bank accounts which were made known in the usual manner and nothing to the contrary results from the individual contract (see Schoele, *Das Recht der Überweisung*, 1937, pp. 236 *et seqq.*; von Caemmerer, ' Girozahlung ', *Juristenzeitung*, 1953, pp. 446 *et seqq.*; Erman-Westermanm BGB, 1958, § 362, Note 2). As a remittance to an account to the Aargauische Hypothekenbank, this would have been payment ' to the creditor ' and not payment ' to a pay office ' within the meaning of § 5 of the contract. This observations also shows that the contract leaves the question of the place of payment wide open.

" The question whether the debtors had to pay in Stuttgart or in Brugg or elsewhere can thus not be answered from the contract alone without investigating the existence of foreign branch offices, bank accounts and other circumstances, and without consulting the relevant rules of the law decisive for the contract. This being necessary, however, one cannot, even when taking this requirement in its widest sense, speak of an express contractual designation.

" The clause contained in § 5 does not say anything which would not be a matter of course, *viz.*, that payment is to be made to the creditor and that the debtors have to bear the cost of payment. This is mentioned only because it is to apply also in case the creditor designates another payee. If, by way of interpretation, this is at the same time considered to constitute the assumption of the obligation to let the creditor have the money, the question remains open how this duty is to be understood. It can only be answered through supplementary law. If German or Austrian law is to be used to supplement the agreement the debtors have only to dispatch the money, thereby having done all that is incumbent upon them. If the contract is interpreted according to Swiss or English law the debtors would be obliged to pay at the seat of the creditor. But something which can only be deduced on the basis of the relevant provisions of the law applicable to the contract is not expressly agreed in any sense which can be given to this requirement.

" If the mention of the foreign address of the creditor in the debt contract (a natural stipulation that the debtor is obliged to pay his debt to the creditor) were to justify the conclusion that the place of payment at the residence of the creditor has thereby been agreed, the meaning of Annex VII would be converted into its opposite and the criterion of the agreement on a place of payment abroad would be deprived of every mark distinguishing the group of external liabilities with specific foreign character."

[Report: *Reports of Decisions and Advisory Opinions*, 1958, p. 3.]

NOTE.—The above decision is discussed by Johnson, " Case No. 1, between the Swiss Confederation and the Federal Republic of Germany, under the Arbitration Tribunal for the Agreement on German External Debts", in *British Year Book of International Law*, XXXIV (1958), p. 363.

State responsibility—For wrongs unconnected with contractual obligations—Exhaustion of local remedies—Convention on the Settlement of Matters Arising out of the War and Occupation, 1952–1954—Right to submit a case pending in municipal court to Arbitral Commission.

See p. 524 (*Levis and Levis* v. *German Federal Republic* (*Jurisdiction*)).

State responsibility—For wrongs unconnected with contractual obligations—Exhaustion of local remedies—Understanding between parties on suspension of further proceedings before municipal court—Whether bar to jurisdiction of Arbitral Commission.

See p. 527 (*Scheidt* v. *German Federal Republic* (*Jurisdiction*)).

State responsibility—Nature and kinds of—Responsibility for wrongs unconnected with contractual obligations—Acts of judicial organs—Whether Supreme Restitution Court in Germany a judicial organ for which Germany responsible—International character of Tribunal—Position of Court of Restitution Appeals—Relevance of fact that it functions in Germany—Effect on responsibility of Germany for decisions of inferior courts—" Absorption " of responsibility.

See p. 190 (*Re Application No. 235/56* (*Mr. X. and Mrs. X.* v. *German Federal Republic*)).

## B—CLAIMS

## II.—Nationality of Claims

State Responsibility—Claims—Nationality of claims—Examination by Conciliation Commission of certificate of nationality—Probative value of certificate in international law—Question of legal system applicable—Provisions of Peace Treaty as *lex fori*—Ouster of national law—Need for caution in absence of serious doubts as to nationality invoked—Review of validity of naturalization of ancestor on which claim to nationality *jus sanguinis* based—Refusal to examine circumstances of naturalization and subsequent conduct of ancestor—Relevance of fact that ancestor not a party to proceedings—Examination of relevant laws of naturalizing State—Review of statements made by claimant to passport authorities, etc.—Expatriation—Effect of ancestor's expatriation on nationality of claimant—Relevance of *animus redeundi*—The law of the United States of America—Bancroft Treaties between United States and German States, 1868—Irrelevance of cancellation of treaties on outbreak of war between Parties to Treaty—Irrelevance of fact that party to dispute not Party to Treaty—Question of supremacy of municipal law subsequent to treaty—Duty of Commission to give priority to international law—Interpretation of Treaty concerning nationality—Relevance of decisions of municipal court in similar cases—Theory of effective nationality—Allegation of " apparent nationality "—Invocation of nationality for sake of temporary material advantage—Principle of " estoppel " or " *non concedit venire contra factum proprium* "—Rejection of doctrine—Question whether claimant " a United Nations National " or whether " treated as enemy " within Treaty of Peace with Italy, 1947, Article 78, paragraph 9—Examination of texts of treaties—Reconciliation of conflicting meaning in various languages—Relevance of " purpose aimed at by the Parties "—Sale of claimant's shares in Italy at undervalue—Allegation of obstruction of sale by Italian authorities—Rejection of argument that delay constitutes hostile treatment—Critical dates for applicability of restitution provisions of Treaty of Peace of 1947—Necessity for claimant to be national of claiming State on date when damage sustained.

FLEGENHEIMER CLAIM.

*Italian-United States Conciliation Commission. September 20, 1958.*

(Sauser-Hall, Matturri, Sorrentino.)

THE FACTS.—This was a claim under Article 78 of the Treaty of Peace with Italy of 1947 for cancellation of the forced sale in 1941, at an undervalue, of certain property of the claimant in Italy. The Italian Government opposed the claim on the ground that the claimant was not a United Nations national within the meaning of Article 78, paragraph 9, sub-paragraph (a), of the Treaty.[1]

The decision involved a consideration of the life history of the claimant and that of his father, Samuel Flegenheimer, who was born in 1848 in the Grand Duchy of Baden. In 1864 (or 1866) Samuel Flegenheimer emigrated to the United States, and in 1873, after attaining his majority and having fulfilled the requisite condition of five years' residence, he became a United States citizen by naturalization. In 1874, however, he returned to Germany and settled in Wurttemberg. He married there, was naturalized in 1894, and died there in 1929. He thus resided no more than eight or ten years in the United States and spent the rest of his life—fifty-five years—in Wurttemberg.

Three of Samuel Flegenheimer's children, including Albert, the present claimant, were included in his naturalization in 1894. Albert was born in 1890 and lived in Germany continuously until 1937, when, in view of the political situation then existing, " he began to feel the threat of persecution ". At that time, he discovered that his father had been naturalized in the United States and he endeavoured to ascertain whether he himself had retained that nationality or whether he could eventually recover it. He made, however, no formal claim for recognition of his American nationality. In November 1937, he was compelled to sell all his property at a nominal price, and later he was ordered to leave Germany. He went to Italy, where he owned certain assets, but in 1938 the Italian Government enacted certain anti-Jewish laws and Flegenheimer left Italy for Switzerland. In February 1939, he went to Canada where he had his German passport renewed. In November of that year he submitted to the United States Consulate at Winnipeg his first formal claim to be recognized as a United States national on the ground that he had not lost his United States nationality under American law. The Board of Special Inquiry of the Immigration and Naturalization Service of the United States decided that Flegenheimer was not a United States national, but admitted him to the country for a limited period while the examination of the question of his nationality was pending. In December 1939, the Department of State informed him that he could not be registered as a United States national because he was not one and because for many years he had " manifested an adherence to German nationality ".

---

[1] Article 78, para. 9 (a), of the Peace Treaty with Italy of 1947 provides as follows:
" 9. As used in this Article:
" (a) ' United Nations nationals ' means individuals who are nationals of any of the United Nations, or corporations or associations organized under the laws of any of the United Nations, at the coming into force of the present Treaty, provided that the said individuals, corporations or associations also had this status on September 3, 1943, the date of the Armistice with Italy.
" The term ' United Nations nationals ' also includes all individuals, corporations or associations which, under the laws in force in Italy during the war, have been treated as enemy;".

In the meantime, while in America, Flegenheimer had, without his knowledge, been divested of his German nationality under the German Law of July 14, 1933, concerning the withdrawal of naturalizations and the forfeiture of German nationality; the decree of April 29, 1940, confirming the forfeiture was published in the *Reichsanzeiger* of May 4, 1940. Flegenheimer was informed of this forfeiture of his German nationality shortly afterwards.

In 1941, the claimant sold for 277,860.60 U.S. dollars his holding in Italy of 27,907 shares of the Società Finanziaria Industriale Veneta, which formed the subject of the present dispute. In connection with this sale, the claimant alleged that the actual value of the shares was between four and five million dollars and also that he had been " treated as enemy " by the Italian authorities who, in particular, held up the transactions and raised difficulties in connection with the transfer of the proceeds to the claimant, qualifying him as a " Jew, formerly a German national ". Canada having, since 1940, been at war with Italy, the money was on his instructions sent to him in New York on June 6, 1941. On June 10, 1941, the claimant, who had left America and had been travelling about, was permitted to re-enter the United States for a temporary sojourn. At that time he was in possession of large sums in dollars and it was his intention to do all in his power to remain in the country until the end of the war.

On December 8, 1941, the United States entered the war, and the claimant's position became difficult because he had entered the country on a German passport. A few days later he applied for an extension of his sojourn permit and was submitted to examination in January 1942. He testified on oath that he had lost his German nationality in May 1940, by the forfeiture decree. After a " supplementary inquiry " in February 1942, the Immigration and Naturalization Service of the Department of Justice ordered that the claimant be " given the status of American national "; and, after some delays, the State Department issued a passport to him in October 1946 (and subsequently renewed it).

On May 8, 1952, the claimant applied for a certificate of United States nationality. On receipt of the application, the Immigration and Naturalization Service asked the State Department for information concerning the enquiries which the claimant stated that he had made between 1933 and 1939 at certain European Consulates and at an Embassy of the United States for the purpose of obtaining recognition of his American nationality. The State Department answered that prior to Albert Flegenheimer's application made at Winnipeg in 1939, there existed no document in its files establishing that steps in that direction had been taken by the claimant. The State Department added that even if Albert Flegenheimer had had an occasional conversation with one of the consular or diplomatic agents of the United States, this would have been the subject of a report which would have been sent to it [the State Department], because " it was well known to citizenship officers in Europe that a person who came in to discuss his status but who declined to execute a formal application when invited to do so, would be likely to apply at some other office and attempt to conceal information which he learned would be damaging to his case."

On May 8, 1952, the claimant was again examined and the report of the examining officer contained the following paragraph:

" It appears highly improbable that the three foreign service officials to whom he says he spoke in three different cities and in different years all neglected to follow the established procedures and customs of the Department of State. This factor plus the subject's own evidence containing correspondence giving the reason why he made no claim to citizenship during this period, leads to the conclusion that he did not, between 1933 and 1939, assert any claim of United States citizenship but on the contrary continued by his actions to show an election of the German nationality which had been conferred upon him by naturalization of his father in 1894 when he was a minor and included in his father's naturalization. . . . It is therefore recommended that the application of Albert Flegenheimer for a certificate of citizenship be denied."

Nevertheless, on July 10, 1952 (more than a year after the institution of the present proceedings), the American authorities ordered that a certificate of citizenship be issued to Albert Flegenheimer. The conclusions reached by the officer of the Department of Justice dealing with the application, and which led to the issue of the certificate of citizenship, included the following:—

" The subject's case has twice been decided on the question of election. In 1939 the State Department stated he had elected German nationality, and in 1942 the Service stated there was no evidence to show he had elected German nationality and, therefore, he should be considered a United States citizen. While much of the new evidence that has been added to the case is conflicting . . . there is much to support his allegation that he did attempt to claim United States citizenship many times between 1933 and 1939. It is true his story is in conflict with the known practice of the Department of State in connection with such matters, but it is difficult to believe one could fabricate a story specifically naming so many people and then have many of those people prepare affidavits corroborating him. . . . Accordingly, while no formal application for a United States passport or of registration as a United States citizen was made, the subject did what he thought was appropriate to claim United States citizenship. . . . It must also be borne in mind that during all the crucial period between 1933 and 1939 Nazism had risen to great power in Germany and, being Jewish, many of the subject's activities were influenced by a fear of the concentration camp. . . . It is a matter of placing credences in the subject's explanations. If he had to be believed only as to certain items, which are they? Only those supported by affidavits of others? It appears there is no choice but to believe all his statements or none.

" In the foregoing it is conceded for the moment that the subject was unaware until 1933 that he had a claim to United States citizenship. Evidence has now been introduced establishing that when the subject was married in Stuttgart in 1920 he had to furnish evidence of his German nationality. To accomplish this a copy of the German naturalization certificate relating to his father's naturalization was furnished. He disclaimed any knowledge of such a certificate. The registrar at Stuttgart has stated such documents were requested when one's citizenship status was in doubt. . . . From all this it appears that in 1920 the subject could have become aware of his father's former United States citizenship if he had read the German naturalization certificate he allegedly submitted. He swears he never saw that certificate or any other German certificate of citizenship. Since . . . he denies knowledge of such certificate, it is not possible to establish that he did have such knowledge.

" The allegation that the father, Samuel Flegenheimer, had never mentioned during his entire lifetime to his sons the fact of his former American citizenship would appear to be plausible in the light of a general attitude prevailing in Germany . . . displaying it to be a lack of patriotism. . . . Again it is a matter of credence. . . . Accepting that, there is no alternative to accepting all of the subject's statements. . . .

" Inasmuch as there is no evidence of any voluntary acts of the subject which may have expatriated him, it is further concluded the subject is a citizen of the United States."

The question of Albert Flegenheimer's American nationality was thus settled by an administrative authority; it was never made the subject of a decision of a judicial tribunal.

The point at issue between the parties was this. Paragraph 9 of Article 78 of the Treaty of Peace provided, in effect, that in order to benefit by the compensation and restitution provisions of the Article a claimant had to be a national of one of the United Nations at both September 3, 1943 (the date of the Armistice with Italy), and September 15, 1947 (the date of the coming into force of the Treaty). The Italian Government maintained that that condition had not been fulfilled by Flegenheimer and that it could not recognize the latter's American nationality on the basis of the documents which he had submitted to the Commission; it was contended that " in order to be in a position to be permitted to exact from Italy the heavy obligations imposed on her by the Treaty of Peace in favour of certain given United Nations nationals, it is necessary that the bond of nationality with one of the United Nations be positive and not subject to denial or criticism." In particular, in connection with the payment of the proceeds of sale of the Italian shares, the Italian Government alleged that the claimant had availed himself of his German nationality in order to obtain authorization for such payment by Italy, a State allied to Germany, in the United States, which were still neutral; and contrasted that attitude with the position adopted by the claimant in the present proceedings, namely, that he had been a United States national since birth.

The Government of the United States contended that it had in the certificate of citizenship of July 10, 1952, submitted full and sufficient proof of the claimant's United States nationality and that he therefore fulfilled the conditions required by the Law of Nations to entitle him to the diplomatic protection of the United States.

*Held:* that the claim must fail. Flegenheimer could not be regarded as a United Nations national within the meaning of Article 78, paragraph 9, of the Treaty of Peace. Although at birth he had United States nationality, he lost that nationality as a result of his father's acquisition of German and Wurttemberg nationality in 1894, combined with five years' residence in Germany. He therefore held German and Wurttemburg nationality until it was forfeited by the decree of May 4, 1940, when he became stateless. He had not proved that he had been treated as enemy by the Italian authorities during his stay in Canada and the United States. He was never naturalized in the United States and the certificate of citizenship issued on July 10, 1952, " is not of a nature to prove, to the full satisfaction of law, that Albert Flegenheimer fulfills the conditions required by Article 78, para. 9 (*a*), sub-para. 1, of the Treaty of Peace with Italy, for the purpose of being considered as a United Nations national".

With regard to the contentions respecting the payment in the United States of the proceeds of sale of the Italian shares, the Commission said: " The Commission . . . can give no consideration to this criticism, because at that time Albert Flegenheimer was unaware of the forfeiture of German nationality decreed against him and he could justifiably claim no other citizenship than that which appeared on his identity papers. The Italian Ministry of Foreign Exchange was in any event aware of Albert Flegenheimer's legal position, and proof of this is the letter which has been introduced in the record, written on March 11, 1941, to the ' Società Finanziaria Industriale Veneta ', authorizing the transfer of dollars to the United States, and qualifying *expressis verbis* the Flegenheimer brothers as ' ex German Jews '. The German nationality of the individual concerned therefore was not a determinant factor in the conclusion of this financial operation."

With regard to the other matters raised, the Commission said:

" A. *Power of the Conciliation Commission, established pursuant to the Treaty of Peace with Italy of February 10, 1947, of examining the probative value of certificates of nationality submitted by the parties to a dispute.*—As the signatory States of the Treaty of Peace have entrusted the Commission with the task of settling, under the terms of Article 83 of the aforesaid Treaty, all disputes giving rise to the application of Articles 75 and 78, as well as Annexes XIV, XV, XVI and XVII, part B, the Commission has no other powers than those resulting from said Treaty; and the Treaty is its Charter.

" In the exercise of its powers, it has the right to examine all questions concerning its jurisdiction, and amongst these questions, one should make a distinction between those which concern its competence and those which concern the admissibility of the Petition.

" The competence of the Commission in the instant case is not in doubt. It is based on Article 78, paragraph 3, of the Treaty of Peace which reads as follows:

" ' The Italian Government shall invalidate transfers involving property, rights and interests of any description belonging to United Nations nationals, where such transfers resulted from force or duress exerted by Axis Governments or their agencies during the war.'

" It is not disputed between the Parties that the Petition of the United States Government is based on this provision: the merits of the case are based on the legal justification of the claim involved.

" On the other hand, the admissibility of the Petition of the Government of the United States is uncertain, because there exists a dispute between the High Parties on an element of fact required by Article 78, paragraph 9, letter (a), of the Treaty of Peace with Italy which provides:

" ' (a) " United Nations nationals " means individuals who are nationals of any of the United Nations, or corporations or associations organised under the laws of any of the United Nations, at the coming into force of the present Treaty, provided that the said individuals, corporations or associations also had this status on September 3, 1943, the date of the Armistice with Italy.

' The term " United Nations nationals " also includes all individuals, corporations or associations which, under the laws in force in Italy during the war, have been treated as enemy.'

" The Italian Government denies that Albert Flegenheimer was a United Nations national on the relevant dates in accordance with the foregoing provision, namely, September 3, 1943, and September 15, 1947, and it is necessary that the Commission settle this issue in order to determine whether the Petition submitted by the Government of the United States is admissible or inadmissible.

" It is clear that the afore-mentioned provision of the Treaty of Peace, in explaining the meaning of ' United Nations nationals ' refers to an unquestionable principle of international law according to which every State is sovereign in establishing the legal conditions which must be fulfilled by an individual in order that he may be considered to be vested with its nationality.

" The lengthy arguments developed both in the written proceedings and in the oral hearings by the Agents, and Counsel, for both Parties on the title to nationality of the United States, suffice to establish that they (the Parties) consider this right to be determinant in deciding Albert Flegenheimer's nationality and that the Commission will have to submit to the jurisprudential or conventional legal content thereof when it has extablished the rules that must be applied; in other words, the Commission will have to admit or reject, at the international level, a nationality, the existence or inexistence of which shall be established, in its opinion in full compliance with the law, at the national level.

" Nevertheless, the Commission recalls that, according to a well established international jurisprudence, where international law and the international law bodies who must apply that law are concerned ' national laws are simple facts, an indication of the will and the activity of States, just like judicial decisions or administrative measures '. (P.C.I.J., Decision of May 25, 1926, *Case relating to Certain German Interests in Upper Silesia*, Series A, No. 7, p. 19.[1])

" The result is that, in an international dispute, official declarations, testimonials or certificates do not have the same effect as in municipal law. They are statements made by one of the Parties to the dispute which, when denied, must be proved like every other allegation. It is the duty of this Commission to establish Albert Flegenheimer's true nationality at the relevant dates specified in Article 78, paragraph 9, of the Treaty of Peace, and it has a right to go into all the elements of fact or of law which would establish whether the claimant actually was, on the aforementioned dates, vested with the nationality of the United States; these investigations are necessary in order to decide whether the international action instituted in his behalf, fulfills the conditions required by the Treaty of Peace from which the Commission cannot deviate. It must therefore freely examine whether an administrative decision such as that taken in favour of Albert Flegenheimer in the United States, was of such a nature as to be convincing.

" The profound reason for these broad powers of appreciation which are guaranteed to an international court for resolving questions of nationality, even though coming within the reserved domain of States, is based on the principle, undenied in matters of arbitration, that complete equality must be enjoyed by both parties to an international dispute. If it were to be ignored, one of the parties would be placed in a state of inferiority *vis-à-vis* the other, because it would then suffice for the Plaintiff State to affirm that any given person is vested with its nationality for the Defendant State to be powerless to prevent an abusive practice of diplomatic protection by its Opponent.

" The right of challenge of the international court authorizing it to determine whether, behind the nationality certificate or the acts of naturalization produced, the right to citizenship was regularly acquired, is in conformity with the very broad rule of effectivity which dominates the Law of Nations entirely and allows the court

[1 See *Annual Digest*, 1925–1926, Case No. 4.]

to fulfill its legal function and remove the inconveniences specified.

" During these proceedings, the agent of the United States and his Counsel have nevertheless persistently contended that the certificate of nationality issued to Albert Flegenheimer on July 10, 1952, under American law, constitutes legally valid proof of his nationality, and that the nature of this proof is such as to be binding on this Commission, unless it were proved that the aforesaid certificate was obtained by fraud or favoritism such as to allow the claimant to avail himself of the diplomatic protection of the United States and, as a consequence, benefit by the reparation provisions of the Treaty of Peace with Italy, and of the Commission's jurisdiction. In the latter part of their allegations, they contended that it would be sufficient for Albert Flegenheimer's American nationality to be plausibly established in order to avoid any challenge and investigation by the Commission.

" They invoke several precedents, principally the *Rau*[1], *Meyer Wildermann*[2] and *Pablo Najero*[3] cases.

" The *Rau Case* was brought before the German-Mexican Claims Commission and decided by that Commission on January 14, 1930; the allegations of the Agent of the Mexican Government were based on the unconstitutionality of a Mexican Law concerning nationality; these allegations were rejected because the Commission held it had ' no power to pass on the constitutionality of Mexican laws '. This precedent is not pertinent with regard to the situation which this Commission is called upon to examine, because in Albert Flegenheimer's case there is no question of constitutionality of the law that is to be applied; the Commission must only investigate whether,[1] in actual fact, the nationality invoked is that resulting from the law applicable to this case in the United States.

' The *Pablo Najero* case, decided on October 19, 1928, by the Franco-American Claims Commission, gave rise to the following statement by the Commissioners:

" ' A legal presumption militates in favor of the regularity of all official acts of public officers. An international Tribunal in face of declarations of option accepted by the Government concerned is fully justified in considering these declarations as regular options, and in refraining from entering into an independent examination of the conditions on which their validity depends.' (*Annual Digest*, 1927–1928, [at] p. 302.)

" In support of its theory denying the international court the right of interpretation in matters of nationality when this fact is plausibly established, the Plaintiff Party also lays stress on the *Meyer Wildermann* v. *Héritiers Stinnes et Consorts* decision, rendered by the German-Roumanian Mixed Arbitral Tribunal on June 8,

[1 See *Annual Digest*, 1931–1932, Case No. 124.]
[2 *Ibid.*, 1933–1934, p. 112.]
[3 *Ibid.*, 1927–1928, Case No. 196.]

1926, wherein, in connection with the verification of a certificate of nationality, it is stated:

" ' It is hence the duty of the Tribunal to verify whether the Rumanian Minister of the Interior has performed an act of favor or of justice . . . The Arbitral Tribunal cannot impose in interpretation of municipal law. It must be acknowledged that the Rumanian authorities, when applying their own law and investigating the circumstances of the instant case, have the same latitude enjoyed by tribunals and, above all, administrative courts everywhere. The hypothesis of an act of favor shall be discarded if the challenged decision is reconcilable with a *plausible* interpretation of Rumanian law and of the circumstances of fact.' (*T.A.M.* [*Recueil des Décisions des Tribunaux Arbitraux Mixtes*], vol. VI, p. 493.[1])

" The Agent of the Government of the United States and his Counsel also attach great importance to the Instructions given on November 30, 1881, by Secretary of State Blaine to the United States Commissioner on the Spanish-American Reparations Commission, established under the Treaty of February 11/12, 1871, in connection with a decision rendered in the *Buzzi Case* on April 18, 1881; Secretary of State Blaine said:

" ' . . . I refuse to recognize the power of the Commission to denationalize an American citizen. When a court of competent jurisdiction, administering the law of the land, issued its regular certificate of naturalization to Pedro Buzzi, he was made a citizen of the United States, and no power resides in the Executive Department of this government to reverse or review that judgment. And what the power of the Executive can not do in itself it cannot delegate to a commission which is the mere creation of an executive agreement.' (Moore, [*International Arbitrations* (1898)], vol. III, pp. 2592 to 2642, particularly pp. 2618–2619.)

" In sharp contrast with this point of view, the Agent and Counsel of the Italian Government before this Commission deny the correctness, as regards the merits, of Secretary of State Blaine's Instruction of 1881 to the United States Commissioner on the Spanish-American Commission. They refer to other instructions given by other American Secretaries of State, on the basis of that same 1871 Treaty, and concerning the same Commission, some of which are prior to while others are subsequent to Secretary of State Blaine's Instruction, so that the latter appears as isolated in American practice and in conflict with the opinions of his predecessors and successors.

" In his Instruction of November 18, 1870, prior to the operation of the Spanish-American Commission, Secretary of State Fish expressed himself regarding the manner in which the said Commission was to exercise its powers, as follows:

' Naturalized citizens of the United States will, if insisted by Spain, be required to show when and where they were naturalized, and it will be open to Spain to traverse this fact, or to show that from any of the causes named in my circular of October 14, 1869, the applicant has forfeited his acquired rights; and it will be for the commission to decide whether each applicant has established his claim.' (Moore, *Arb.*, vol. III, p. 2563.)

" Blaine's immediate predecessor, Secretary of State Evarts, developed this point of view in his letter to the Spanish Minister in Washington, dated March 4, 1880:

' The Government of the United States from the first considered, as it still maintained, that the Commission established under the Convention of 1871 was an independent judicial tribunal, possessed of all the powers and endowed with all the properties which should distinguish a court of high international jurisidiction, alike competent in the jurisdiction conferred upon it to bring under judgment the decisions of the local courts of both nations, and beyond the competence of either Government to interfere with, direct or obstruct its deliberations.' (Moore, *Arb.*, vol. III, p. 2599.)

" Secretary of State Evarts then pointed out that certificates of American nationality of claimants could always be impeached by Spain when it was established that the proofs submitted were inadmissible in form, or that they were the result of fraud or that, taken together, such proofs were insufficient to establish the demand of American citizenship.

" Secretary of State Frelinghuysen who succeeded Blaine made an attempt at clarifying what he defined as the ' true rule ' in a letter written by him on September 25, 1882, to the United States counsel before said Commission, wherein he stated:

' The true rule to govern this Commission is, that when an allegation of naturalization is traversed, and the allegation is established prima facie by the production of a certificate of naturalization, or by other and sufficient proof, it can only be impeached by showing that the court which granted it, was without jurisdiction or by showing, in conformity with the adjudications of the courts of the United States on that topic, that fraud, consisting of intentional and dishonest misrepresentation or suppression of material facts by the party obtaining the judgment, was practised upon it, or that the naturalization was granted in violation of a treaty stipulation or a rule of international law.' (Moore, *Arb.*, vol. III, p. 2620.)

" The American and Spanish Commissioners accepted this Instruction of Secretary of State Frelinghuysen for themselves on December 14, 1882, and transmitted it to the Umpire as a matter of policy.

" Therefore, Blaine's Instruction only played an incidental role in the jurisprudence of international commissions when they are called upon to deal with matters of nationality: it was promptly disavowed and abandoned, to the point where all cases giving rise to this question and brought before the Spanish-American Commission, either before or after Blaine's statement, have resulted in decisions refusing to recognize foreign judgments on this subject.

(Van Dyne, *Treatise on the Law of Naturalization of the United States* (1907), p. 172-173, 177.)

" The Agent of and Counsel for the Italian Government before this Commission were not satisfied with this refutation and contended that every international jurisdiction is fully at liberty to investigate the existence or inexistence of a nationality invoked before it.

" They affirm that the principles invoked by the Government of the United States in these proceedings do not correspond to positive law and that, in particular, when a certain given nationality is the very condition for the existence of an obligation sanctioned by an international treaty, the international body who must interpret and apply said treaty, is entitled and has the duty to examine, in the utmost freedom, whether such a condition exists in accordance with the Treaty, in order that it may not impose charges on the debtor State, and that it may not confer to the creditor State rights which do not come under the intentions of the High Contracting Parties.

" They stress that the Law of Nations itself does not contain any rule by which the acquisition and loss of nationality is established, and on this point reference is made by them to the municipal law of the various States; but this reference is not absolute: it is limited by the powers vested in a body, whose duty it is to give judgment between the Parties, to investigate, by verification and appraisal of the facts, whether nationality was actually acquired or lost, to exclude fraud, favoritism, error and inconsistencies with treaties and general principles of law, even if the rules of municipal law, which may not contain a strict system of regulating the manner of disputing the acquisition or the loss of nationality, or which may be organized in a special manner, would result in recognition in a given person of the quality of a national of a given State. In other words, the international court, even though having the power of applying rules of municipal law in order to establish the nationality of an individual has, in addition, the power to dismiss these rules and to reach, for instance on the basis of a conception of fraud directly inspired by the Law of Nations and which might differ from the notion which it would have in municipal law, the conclusion that the quality of national of a given State should be denied a given individual. The result is that nationality could exist with regard to municipal law, although inoperative in international proceedings, without requiring that the international body express an opinion on this nationality under municipal law, or annul it.

" They draw the conclusion from the foregoing allegations that this Commission has the power to examine, within the framework of international law and particularly of Article 78, paragraph 9, of the Treaty of Peace with Italy, the correctness of the administrative document of the United States dated July 10, 1952, which recognizes in Albert Flegenheimer the quality of United States

national; if in its appraisal it reaches a conclusion that differs from
that of the competent administrative bodies of the United States,
the interested person would still remain an American national for
the authorities of the United States, but this quality would not be
recognized in him by this Commission on the basis of the documents
introduced in the record and by the arguments developed during the
proceedings.

" In fulfilling its duties, the Commission can draw its authority
from a long series of arbitral precedents, as well as from important
qualified legal writings distinctly affirming the power of investigation by the international court in matters of nationality.

" The first case in which the question was dealt with is the
*Medina* case, decided by the United States–Costa Rican Claims
Commission on December 31, 1862.   This case has a certain analogy
with the instant case, in that the Government of Costa Rica contended that Medina's naturalization was not valid because it was
not in conformity with United States law; the American Commissioner answered that the Commission must respect a decision which,
rendered by an American judge, had the authority of a *res judicata*
and, as such, is not contestable in any other jurisdiction, even an
international jurisdiction, at least until it was annulled by the
judge that had rendered it; it was a judicial and not a merely
administrative act, entailing an interpretation of United States laws
and had to be recognized in Costa Rica.   But Umpire Bertinatti
rejected this argument and stated:

' An act of naturalization, be it made by a judge *ex parte* in the exercise
of his *voluntaria jurisdictio*, or be it the result of a decree of a king bearing
an administrative character; in either case its value, on the point of
evidence, before an international commission, can only be that of an
element of proof, *locus regit actum*, both intrinsically and extrinsically,
in order to be admitted or rejected according to the general principles in
such matter.' (Moore, *Arb.*, vol. III, p. 2587.)

" In the *Salem Case*[1] between the United States and Egypt,
which gave rise to an arbitral decision on June 8, 1932, in connection
with the nationality of the interested party, the majority of the
Commission affirmed:

' The Arbitral Tribunal is therefore entitled to examine whether the
American citizenship of Salem really exists.   Such examination is not
impeded by the principle of international law that every foreign State
is, generally speaking, sovereign in deciding the question as to which
persons he will regard as his subjects, because the bestowal of citizenship
is a manifestation of his international independence.   In fact, as soon as
the question of nationality is in dispute between two sovereign powers,
it cannot be exclusively decided in accordance with the national law of
one of these powers.   In the present case it should be ascertained whether
one of the powers, by bestowing the citizenship against general principles

[1 See *Annual Digest*, 1931–1932, Case No. 98.]

of international law, has interfered with the rights of the other power, or if the bestowal of the citizenship is vitiated because it has been obtained by fraud.' ([United Nations, *Reports of International Arbitral Awards*], vol. II, p. 1184.)

" In the *Hatton Case*[1], decided on September 26, 1928, by the United Mexican States–United States of America General Claims Commission, United States Commissioner Nielsen, who had rendered a dissenting opinion in the *Salem case*, affirmed that:

' However, it is proper to observe with reference to this point that, as has already been pointed out, convincing proof of nationality is requisite not only from the standpoint of international law, but as a jurisdictional requirement.' ([*U.N.R.I.A.A.*], vol. IV, p. 331.)

" In the *Russel Case*, which was brought before this same Commission, United States Commissioner Nielsen expressed the opinion that nationality, in international law, is justification for the intervention of Government in the protection of persons or property in another country; that the jurisdictional articles of the Convention of September 8, 1923, between Mexico and the United States of America for the settlement of claims, were established within the framework of this principle, and added:

" ' . . . The Commission, created by that Convention has the power to deal with the merits of claims only in cases where the claimants possess American nationality. It must of course dispose of the preliminary jurisdictional question of nationality before deciding a case on the merits.' (Nielsen, *International Law Applied to Reclamations* (1933), p. 596–597.)

" In the *Flutie Case*, decided in 1903 by the American–Venezuelan Commission, the following opinion was rendered:

' The American citizenship of a claimant must be satisfactorily established as a primary requisite to the examination and decision of his claim. Hence the Commission, as the sole judge of its jurisdiction, must in each case determine for itself the question of such citizenship upon the evidence submitted in that behalf. . . . And the fact of such citizenship, like any other fact, must be proved to the satisfaction of the Commission or jurisdiction must be held wanting.' (Ralston and Doyle, *Venezuelan Arbitrations of* 1903.)

" A similar point of view is to be found in the decision of June 8, 1926, rendered by the Rumanian-German Mixed Arbitral Tribunal in the *Meyer Wildermann* v. *Heirs Stinnes et Consorts Case* (*T.A.M.*, vol. IV, p. 848[2]); in the *Case of Religious Property* between France, the United Kingdom and Spain on the one hand, and Portugal on the other, brought before the Permanent Court of Arbitration and decided on September 4, 1920 (*U.N.R.I.A.A.*, vol. I, p. 27[3]); in

[1 See *Annual Digest*, 1927–1928, Case No. 335.]
[2 *Ibid.*, 1923–1924, Case No. 120.]
[3 *Ibid.*, 1919–1922, Case No. 165.]

the *Carlos Klemp Case*, decided in 1925 by the German–Mexican Mixed Claims Commission (*Am. J. Int.* 24 (1930) p. 622[1]); in the *Lynch Case*, decided on November 8, 1929, by the Mexican–British Claims Commission (*U.N.R.I.A.A.*, vol. V, p. 227[2]); in the *Durcatte Case*, decided by the Franco–Mexican Commission, wherein, against the opinion of the French Commissioner, it was admitted that claimant did not possess French nationality inasmuch as he had lost it by virtue of the provisions of the French Civil Code (Ralston, *The Law and Procedure of International Tribunals* (1926)).

" The majority of international tribunals has thus accepted this concept. It would be purposeful to mention, further, from a series of precedents which could still be lengthened, the following excerpt appearing in the decision rendered by the Franco–Mexican Reparations Commission, Prof. Verzijl acting as Umpire, on April 6, 1928, in the *Georges Pinson Case*:

" ' . . . It is the duty of an international tribunal to determine tne nationality of claimants in such a manner that, insofar as the tribunal is concerned, this nationality is positive, irrespective, in principle, of the requirements of the national laws of each claimant individually. The national provisions are not devoid of value in this respect, but it is not bound by them.' (*U.N.R.I.A.A.*, vol. V, p. 371.[3])

" The foregoing point of view is, in any event, that which has been upheld on many occasions by the Agents of the Government of the United States during international proceedings.

" Hence, in his Answer concerning the *Castaneda and de Leon Case*, which was pending before the American and Panamanian General Claims Commission in 1926, the Agent of the Government of the United States said:

' It is admitted by the Government of the United States that proof of the nationality of claimants is of fundamental importance, since the jurisdiction of the Commission depends upon the proof thereof, and the facts regarding citizenship must be established in the record before the Commission, to bring the claim within the jurisdiction of the Commission under Article 1 of the Convention.' (*Hunt's Report*, State Department Publication No. 593 (1934), p. 663 [and noted at *A.J.*, 28 (1934), p. 71].)

" The same point of view was further expressed in the *Yanquez Case* which was pending before the same Commission in 1926; the Government of the United States then contended that:

' Numerous claims have been dismissed by Claims Commissions, not only for the lack of evidence regarding the citizenship of the claimant, but also because of the inadequacy of such evidence.' (*Ibid.*, p. 723.)

" Lastly, it is purposeful to quote, in part, the answer given by United States Secretary of State Evarts on February 9, 1880, to a protest of the Minister of Spain who expressed dissatisfaction with a

[1 See *Annual Digest*, 1931–1932, Case No. 121.]
[2 *Ibid.*, 1929–1930, Case No. 134.]
[3 *Ibid.*, 1927–1928, Case No. 194.]

decision of the United States–Spanish Claims Commission, concerning American nationality:

' I sincerely hope that the views I have had the honour to submit to you may satisfy you that the contention on the citizenship of the claimants, dependent upon naturalization, is as fully a question of judicial determination for the tribunal in respect to the admissibility of evidence, its relevancy and its weight, and in respect to the rules of jurisprudence by which it is to be determined, as any other question in controversy in the case.' (Moore, *Arb.* (1898), vol. III, p. 2600.)

" Abundant doctrine in international law confirms the power of an international court to investigate the existence of the nationality of the claimant, even when this is established ' prima facie ' by the documents issued by the State to which he owes allegiance and in conformity with the legislation of said State. This opinion is supported, in particular, by distinguished American authors of international law, such as the late Professors Borchard and Hyde. The former expresses himself as follows in his report to the Institute of International Law on the diplomatic protection of citizens abroad:

" ' . . . It is the duty of the defendant State to look into the question as to whether the individual, in whose behalf the Petition is submitted, actually is a national of the plaintiff State. . . . Therefore, a mere statement by the claimant State concerning the fact that claimant is its national should not be sufficient.' ([*Annuaire de l'Institut de Droit international*], 1931, vol. I, p. 277–278.)

" The latter author makes a more specific reference to the practice followed by the United States and sums it up as follows:

' If the validity of the naturalization of an individual claimant (or of one through whom a claim is derived) is challenged in a case before an international tribunal, the Department of State appears to recognize the reasonableness both of the right of contest and of the decision of the question by the arbitral court. The consent to its jurisdiction is believed to be implied from the agreement for the submission of claims. Such tribunals have not hesitated to impeach certificates of naturalization when the evidence warranted such action.' (Hyde, *International Law, Chiefly as Interpreted and Applied by the United States* (2nd revised Edition, 1945), vol. 2, p. 1130–1131.)

" See also Makarov, *Allgemeine Lehren des Staatsangehörigkeitsrechts* (1947), p. 329, who wrote that international jurisdictions were not satisfied, in many cases, with the submission of an act of naturalization and proceeded themselves with an investigation of its legal validity, by looking into whether the conditions of naturalization had been fulfilled; he notes that qualified legal writings were able to draw from these precedents the conclusion that the possibility of subjecting to a new investigation the validity of naturalization acts was ' well established ' by international tribunals. The same opinion is voiced by Sandifer, *Evidence Before International Tribunals* (1939), p. 149.

" This Commission does not intend to espouse an argument which would lead to extremes the logical consequences of the freedom of international jurisdictions when examining questions of nationality.

" It could not disregard the scope of the presumption of truth *omnia rite acta praesumuntur* of the decisions rendered by the official authorities of a State acting in the sphere of their duties and in matters over which they have internal jurisdictional power. But there is here involved only a *juris tantum* presumption which could be reversed by contrary evidence.

" The Commission is thus faced with the question of the law that is applicable to the evidence of disputed nationality. In the jurisprudence of the various States, this law is either the *lex fori* or the *lex causae*, namely, the law of the State with which, it is contended, the individual has a bond of citizenship.

" Now the Commission has no other *lex fori* than the provisions of the Treaty of Peace which it must apply and the general rules of the Law of Nations; and neither the former nor the latter contain any requirements as regards evidence of a disputed nationality. It must further notice that the application of the *lex causae* could constitute an obstacle to the jurisdictional mission entrusted to it by the signatory States of the Treaty of Peace, because this law could, by the operation of formal evidence, force it to recognize a nationality the actual existence of which it has the right and the duty to investigate.

" Umpire Bertinatti affirmed the foregoing in his decision rendered on December 31, 1862, by the Commission for Claims against the United States and Costa Rica, in the *Medina Case*, the most important excerpt thereof being the following:

" ' The certificates exhibited by them being made in due form, have for themselves the presumption of truth; but when it becomes evident that the statements therein contained are incorrect, the presumption of truth must yield to the truth itself.

" ' It has been alleged in behalf of the claimants that even admitting that their acts of naturalization are intrinsically void, it is not in the power of the Commission to reject them as proof, if they are not first set aside as fraudulent by the same tribunal from which they were obtained.

" ' To admit this would give those certificates in a foreign land or before an international tribunal an absolute value which they have not in the United States, where they may eventually be set aside, while Costa Rica, not recognizing the jurisdiction of any tribunal in the United States, would be left with no remedy. Moreover, this Commission would be placed in an inferior position, and denied a faculty which is said to belong to a tribunal in the United States.

" ' . . . Consequently this Commission judges according to truth and justice, and cannot be prevented from examining the intrinsic value of an act exhibited as evidence by any limitation or extrinsic objection arising from a matter of form established by the municipal law of the United States. The claimants having chosen to place themselves under the jurisdiction of this Commission, must bring before it proofs which are really true and not merely considered so by a fiction introduced by the municipal law of the United States.' (Moore, *Arb.* (1898), vol. III, p. 2587-2588.)

"This Commission cannot neglect remarking that this decision by Umpire Bertinatti, the first which has affirmed the powers of investigation of the international court in matters of nationality, was the subject of severe criticism on the part of two distinguished French jurists, the late Professors de la Pradelle and Politis who do not accept that the international court may, when an act of naturalization is valid in form, ' investigate whether the authority that issued such certificate did or did not do so in conformity with the laws '; it can only require that the act be in conformity with international law and issued without ' fraud ' ([de la Pradelle et Politis, *Recueil des Arbitrages Internationaux*] (1923), vol. II, p. 176). But this restrictive interpretation of the powers of the international court is not predominant in international jurisprudence. If it is correct that a body established by States cannot freely interpret municipal law, this Commission intends to follow the jurisprudence of the International Court of Justice which permits it to ' verify, by its own knowledge, the application of municipal law in connection with the facts alleged or denied by the parties in order to determine whether these are correct or incorrect '. Decision of April 6, 1955, *Nottebohm Case* (2nd Phase): *I.C.J. Reports* 1955, p. 52,[1] *Liechtenstein* v. *Guatemala*.

"A similar viewpoint has already been adopted by the Permanent Court of International Justice (Decision of March 26, 1925, *Case of the Mavrommatis Concessions in Jerusalem, Greece* v. *Great Britain*: P.C.I.J., Series A, No. 5, p. 30[2]).

"It has been further alleged by one of the jurists for the Plaintiff that, in order to successfully deny a nationality, proof of which consists in an official statement of the national State, the other Party must establish the existence of so serious a cause as to affect the validity of the acquisition of nationality within said national State; if the irregularity alleged is not liable to entail cancellation under the municipal law of that State, this irregularity cannot be brought up before an international court.

"But this restriction, in its absolute form, does not appear to find support in international jurisprudence; in the *Salem Case*, the Arbitral Tribunal certainly held that the international court must examine municipal law of the State which contends that a person is its national, but the opinion has not been expressed that the nullity in municipal law must be presupposed so that the other

[1 See *International Law Reports*, 1955, p. 349, at p. 379 (Dissenting Opinion of Guggenheim, Judge *ad hoc*).]
[2 See *Annual Digest*, 1925-1926, Case No. 148.]

State may contest the nationality. It is the opposite idea that emerges from the following excerpt of that decision:

" ' In order to decide the question of fraud it will be necessary to examine if the false representations with which the nationality of a certain Power has been acquired refer to those points on which, according to the law of that Power, the acquisition of nationality is essentially dependent. So far the notion of fraud cannot be construed without taking into consideration the national law of the Power which bestowed the citizenship, . . . The objection of the American Government that such proof can only be furnished to the American courts who, under the Law of June 29, 1906, section 23, are competent to deprive any naturalized person of citizenship, if fraud is proved, is not admissible before an international arbitral tribunal. The judgment of a national court may be indispensable to engender the legal effects of such a fraud under national law, but nevertheless in a litigation between States regarding the nationality of a person the right of one State to contest, as acquired by fraud, the nationality claimed by the other State cannot depend on the decision of the national courts of this State.' (*U.N.R.I.A.A.* (1949), vol. II, p. 1185.[1])

" One could also add that from the standpoint of practice it may frequently be impossible for the international court to have knowledge of the grounds of nullity, under municipal law, in matters of nationality, as the laws are often silent in this respect and jurisprudence does not cover all the eventualities that might occur, and this is exactly so in the *Flegenheimer* case, *i.e.*, a case of ' first impression ' submitted to the court for the first time.

" The Commission, in conformity with the case law of international tribunals, holds that it is not bound by the provisions of the national law in question, either as regards the manner or as regards the form in which proof of nationality must be submitted. And this is in harmony with the opinion expressed by the Franco–Mexican Reparations Commission in the *Georges Pinson* Case:

' An international tribunal . . . may lay down stricter requirements than those contemplated under national legislation, for instance for the purpose of unmasking naturalizations obtained *in fraudem legis* but it may also be satisfied with less strict requirements in cases where it does not appear to it to be reasonably necessary to set in motion the entire apparatus of formal proofs . . . it is much more logical not to bind the tribunal to any national system of proof, but to give it complete freedom of investigation of the evidence submitted, as the case may warrant.' (*U.N.R.I.A.A.*, vol. V, p. 371.[2])

" The Commission, on the basis of the research made in jurisprudence and authoritative doctrine, holds that its powers of investigation as to whether Albert Flegenheimer validly acquired United States nationality is all the less disputable in that no American judgment of naturalization has been introduced during these

[1 *Annual Digest*, 1931–1932, Case No. 98, at p. 191.]
[2 *Ibid.*, 1927–1928, Case No. 194.]

proceedings but a mere administrative statement which, according to the international practice commonly followed, is subjected to the valuation of every court, whether national or international, to which the question of the validity of a nationality is submitted.

" The Commission nevertheless considers that the observations made by the commentators of the *Medina Case* cannot be ignored, and that international jurisdictions must act with the greatest caution and exercise their powers of investigation only if the criticism directed by one Party against the allegations of the other, not only are not manifestly groundless, but are of such gravity as to cause serious doubts in the minds of their Members with regard to the reality and truth of the nationality invoked.

" In the instant case, the grounds for doubt in connection with Albert Flegenheimer's nationality are so numerous and so patent, that the Commission could allow him to benefit by Article 78 of the Treaty of Peace with Italy only if all the doubts, raised in its mind over the facts on the basis of which the certificate of United States nationality was issued, were dispelled.

" These facts are first of all connected with the validity of Samuel Flegenheimer's naturalization in the United States from which flows the acquisition *jure sanguinis* of his son Albert's American nationality; subsequently with the loss by the latter of his American nationality as a result of his naturalization together with his father in Wurttemberg in 1894, when he was still a minor; with the long sojourn of the interested party, as a German national, in Germany from 1904 to 1937, with his entry into Canada on February 10, 1939, before the outbreak of World War II, on a German passport which was renewed to him a few days later by the German Consulate at Winnipeg, and then in 1941 by the Swiss Consul in that city, who had taken over the protection of German interests.

" The Commission's grounds for doubt are further increased when acquiring knowledge, from the documents in the record, of the fact that all inquiries for information made by Albert Flegenheimer at consular offices and even at an Embassy of the United States in Europe in connection with his American nationality only resulted in negative or dubious answers; that, if he succeeded in obtaining an authorization of making, at the outset, only temporary sojourns in the United States, his case gave rise to conflicting decisions by the State Department and by the Immigration Service of the Department of Justice of the United States; that at the time of the inquests to which he was subjected by American officials, he made statements which are not entirely consistent; that the authorization which was accorded to him to enter the United States as a German national was only modified by a decision of the Immigration and Naturalization Service of February 24, 1942, in the sense that he was thereafter qualified as a citizen of the United States, but that the subsequent inquests which resulted in this amendment of the record of his entry, are defined as irregular by the American counsel for the Italian Government in these proceedings.

" This Commission cannot fail to take notice of the fact that the State Department on May 14, 1946, refused at first to issue an American passport to Albert Flegenheimer, and that if later, on October 24, 1946, it did decide to issue a passport, it specified that this document would not be renewed; that even after the institution of legal action before this Commission on behalf of Albert Flegenheimer on June 26, 1951, the application for a certificate of citizenship made by him gave rise to a dispute between the State Department and the Department of Justice of the United States; that on May 8, 1952, Albert Flegenheimer then swore to an *ex parte* affidavit in which he explained his case; that the ' Examining Officer ' nevertheless concluded that his application should be refused, but the ' Acting Assistant Commissioner ' held that the petitioner was to be considered as a United States citizen on the basis of his own statements, on the scarcely convincing grounds that there could be no other alternative than that of considering them as completely incorrect or entirely correct; that he concluded by following this latter course which resulted in the issuance of the certificate of nationality of July 10, 1952, more than one year after the Petition was submitted to this Commission. Lastly, this Commission cannot but be impressed by the fact that the precedent of the Supreme Court of the United States in the *Perkins* v. *Elg* Case (1939),[1] which instigated the decision of the American administrative authorities in Albert Flegenheimer's favor, was already known at the time the preceding negative decisions were rendered, and that the effects which the Bancroft Treaties might have had on the nationality of Albert Flegenheimer were not examined by the American authorities. Hence, Albert Flegenheimer's nationality is far from presenting such a character of certitude and of clarity as to entail conviction.

" This Commission owes it to itself, as it owes it to the two States who have placed their confidence in it so as to assure a correct application of Article 78 of the Treaty of Peace with Italy, to make an objective search for the truth and to clarify the legal position which, as far as the Commission, in its capacity as an international organ, is concerned is Albert Flegenheimer's factual position.

" In the fulfilment of this duty, the Commission feels it is not bound by the unilateral statments of either of the two States. It cannot directly consider, without a thorough investigation, an assertion of faith made by an official of the United States in connection with the statements of the interested person to the point of giving rise to certain international obligations to be borne by the Italian Republic but it cannot lightly reject a nationality which is recognized by the Plaintiff State, because its powers of investigation

[1 See *Annual Digest*, 1938–1940, Case No. 116.]

are not so extensive as the Agent of and Counsel for the Italian Government would have it believe.

" It is therefore important to establish in as precise a manner as possible the limits within which an international jurisdiction is entitled to investigate the acquisition or the loss of nationality by a person whose nationality is established ' prima facie '. These limits may concern the form in which a certificate of citizenship is issued; they may also concern the merits when an official certificate, regular as to form, is inconsistent with the conditions of merit required by law, by the case law of the State whose nationality is claimed or by the international treaties to which said State is a party.

" From the standpoint of form, international jurisprudence has admitted, without any divergence of views, that consular certificates as well as certificates issued by administrative bodies which, according to the national legislation of the subject State do not have absolute probative value, are not sufficient to establish nationality before international bodies, but that the latter are nevertheless entitled to take them into consideration if they have no special reasons for denying their correctness.

" From the standpoint of merit, even certificates of nationality the content of which is proof under the municipal law of the issuing State, can be examined and, if the case warrants, rejected by international bodies rendering judgment under the Law of Nations, when these certificates are the result of fraud, or have been issued by favor in order to assure a person a diplomatic protection to which he would not be otherwise entitled, or when they are impaired by serious errors, or when they are inconsistent with the provisions of international treaties governing questions of nationality in matters of relationship with the alleged national State, or, finally, when they are contrary to the general principles of the Law of Nations on nationality which forbid, for instance, the compulsory naturalization of aliens. It is thus not sufficient that a certificate of nationality be plausible for it to be recognized by international jurisdictions; the latter have the power of investigating the probative value thereof even if its ' prima facie ' content does not appear to be incorrect. This is particularly true before international arbitral or conciliation commissions who are called upon to adjudicate numerous disputes following troubled international situations, that are the outcome of war, internal strife or revolutions.

" B. *On Albert Flegenheimer's jure sanguinis acquisition of United States nationality.*—The Government of the United States contends that Albert Flegenheimer acquired United States nationality through filiation, *jure sanguinis*, at birth, on July 4, 1890, in German territory, because he was born of a father who at that date was vested with United States nationality and had not yet been naturalized in Wurttemberg.

" The Italian Government denies this and claims that Samuel Flegenheimer secured his naturalization in the United States in 1873 in a fraudulent manner, and that, consequently, it was null and devoid of effects; furthermore, even supposing, by way of hypothesis, that he had validly secured the said naturalization, he could have lost his American nationality because of the lack of *animus revertendi* to the United States and as a result of his having taken up permanent residence in Germany since 1874, so that, on the date of the birth of his son Albert, in 1890, he could not have transmitted to him *jure sanguinis*, a nationality which he had never acquired or which he has previously lost.

" This Commission is hence called upon to pass on the validity and the actual existence of the American nationality of an individual who, in any event, had possession thereof from 1873 through 1894, the year in which he was naturalized in Wurttemberg, without it ever being contested, and to decide whether the nullity of the citizenship of an individual who died in 1929 can still be raised before it (the Commission).

" Although, at first sight, the opening of an inquiry regarding a person now many years deceased would appear to be somewhat unusual, the Commission does not intend to shun the issue, because the very nature of acquisition of nationality by filiation entails a probatory examination which necessarily extends to the citizenship of the claimant's ascendants; it can hence embrace many generations if the law which is recognized as applicable by the Commission does not exclude proof *ad infinitum* by laying down certain presumptions like that, for instance, of the French nationality Code (Article 143).

" In order to evaluate Samuel Flegenheimer's naturalization in the United States in 1873—likewise in order to decide whether it must admit or deny the effects of the American nationality of his son Albert—the Commission must naturally make an analysis of United States law such as it existed at the time when the facts entailing the acquisition or the loss of American nationality of these persons occurred, exclusive of all developments, amendments or restrictions this law may have been subjected to subsequently, either by the enactments of laws, by international treaties or by jurisprudence.

" The XIVth Amendment of the United States Constitution provides:

" ' All persons born or naturalized in the United States and subject to the jurisdiction thereof, are citizens of the United States and of the State wherein they reside.'

In the instant case, the regularity of Samuel Flegenheimer's naturalization, as to form, is not questioned; likewise, the fact that he complied with the five-year residence condition in the United States before naturalization, in conformity with the Act of February 10

1855, chapter 71, section I (10 Stat. 604/1855) is not denied by the High Parties. The criticism raised by the Italian Agent and his Counsel is directed at the following points:

" (a) Samuel Flegenheimer, it is objected, at the time of his naturalization, had no intention of residing permanently in the United States.

" Even though this condition was required by a United States statute only in the Law of June 29, 1906 (34 Stat. 596/1906), the Supreme Court expressed the opinion that this condition was implicitly contained in previous laws; in fact, in 1913, it rules that:

" ' . . . by necessary implication the prior laws conferred the right to naturalization upon such aliens only as contemplated the continuance of a residence already established in the United States. . . . By the clearest implication those laws show that it was not intended that naturalization could be secured thereunder by an alien whose purpose was to escape the duties of his native allegiance without taking upon himself those of citizenship here, or by one whose purpose was to reside permanently in a foreign country and to use his naturalization as a shield against the imposition of duties there, while by his absence he was avoiding his duties here. Naturalization secured with such a purpose was wanting in one of its most essential elements—good faith on the part of the applicant . . . True, it was not expressly forbidden neither was it authorized. But, being contrary to the plain implication of the statute, it was unlawful, for what is clearly implied is as much a part of a law as what is expressed.' (*Luria* v. *United States*, 231 U.S. 9 (1913).)

" In its decision the Supreme Court ordered that the certificate of nationality issued to Luria be cancelled, on the grounds ' that the taking up of a permanent residence in a foreign country shortly following naturalization has a bearing upon the purposes with which the latter was sought and affords some reason for presuming that there was an absence of intention at that time to reside permanently in the United States is not debatable '.

" In the case *United States* v. *Ellis*, 185 Fed. 546 (Circuit Court, Eastern District of Louisiana, 1911) a similar judgment was rendered.

" (b) Samuel Flegenheimer, it is also objected, acted in bad faith when he submitted his application for naturalization because he had no intention to reside permanently in the United States; and the Supreme Court, in the case cited above, admitted that this intention was an element of good faith required of candidates to naturalization.

" (c) Samuel Flegenheimer, it is further objected, went to the United States at the age of sixteen (or eighteen), in 1864 (or in 1866), just prior to being called up for military service in his country or origin, the Grandduchy of Baden, at a time when Germany was living through a troubled period known as the Bismarck era, and to have abandoned his new home country less than one year after securing naturalization, not for the Grandduchy of Baden, where he was liable to indictment for violation of his military duties, but for Wurttemberg, of which country he was not a citizen prior to his emigration to America, and where he secured naturalization as soon as he reached an age to be dispensed with every obligation of serving in the American armies; he lived there uninterruptedly until he was eighty-one. This conduct was considered as a fraudulent naturalization by the Supreme Court of the United States in the *Knauer* case, concerning an individual who was naturalized in 1937 and who, after having taken an oath of allegiance to the United States, swore loyalty to Hitler. The Court said:

" ' Moreover, when an alien takes the oath with reservations or does not in good faith forswear loyalty and allegiance to the old country, the decree of naturalization is obtained by deceit. The proceeding itself is then founded on fraud. A fraud is perpetrated on the naturalization court.' (*Knauer* v. *United States*, 328 U.S. 654 (1945).[1])

" In order to establish that this conception was that expressed by American statesmen at the time when Samuel Flegenheimer secured naturalization, the Italian Government invokes a communication written by Secretary of State of the United States Fish to Bancroft, then Minister to Berlin, in which he indicates the reasons justifying a revision of the nationality treaties between the United States and several specific States of the German Empire:

" ' A German can now come to America, obtain his naturalization papers through the operation of our laws, return to Germany and reside there indefinitely as an American citizen, provided he does not reside the requisite time for renunciation in the territories under the jurisdiction of the particular power of whom he was formerly a subject. It is true that such a course would be a fraud upon the United States and a fraud upon the German Empire.... It is for the interest of neither to perpetuate this.' (Letter, June 4, 1873; *vide* Wharton, *International Law Digest*, pp. 377–378.)

" (d) Lastly, the Respondent Party finds support in the fact that as Samuel Flegenheimer left the United States a few months after acquiring naturalization without *animus revertendi*, he must be deemed to have had the intention of expatriating himself and to have lost, on these grounds, his American nationality, even if it were to be assumed that he had acquired it in good faith and without fraud.

" In this connection the Respondent Party refers to the Act of March 2, 1907 (Ch. 2534), section 2, para. 2, which established a presumption of expatriation against all aliens who leave the United States after securing naturalization and who reside at least two years in their country of origin or five years in another State. The Respondent Party can, however, cite only one judicial decision in support of its theory, a decision which is prior to the enactment of the aforesaid law; it was rendered by the Court of Appeals of Kentucky, in connection with Mr. and Mrs. Alsberry, United States nationals who extablished their residence in Texas in 1824, at a

[1 See *Annual Digest*, 1946, Case No. 51.]

time when this State was not yet a part of the United States. The Court said:

" ' . . . As Thomas Alsberry and his wife settled themselves in Texas, in 1824, with the ostensible purpose of making it their permanent home, and especially as she remained there, with the same apparent intention, for years after his death, and even until after revolutions had been effected in the political relations of that country, its independence had been declared, and a new consitution, to which she should be presumed to have been a party, had been adopted, we are of the opinion that she as well as he, should be deemed to have ceased—so far as by her own act she could cease—to be a citizen of the United States . . .' (*Alsberry* v. *Hawkins*, 39 Ky. (9 Dana) 177 to 180 (1839).)

" The Respondent Party contends that, although prior to the Law of 1907, statutes did not contain an accurate description of the acts which could entail the loss of United States nationality, it was nevertheless clearly admitted that departure of a naturalized national from the United States without *animus revertendi* automatically entailed the loss of American nationality; the Respondent Party cites, in this connection, numerous assertions made by statesmen, including many Secretaries of State of the United States, and of American jurists. The Respondent Party also refers to the decision rendered in 1952 by the Supreme Court in the *Mandoli* v. *Acheson* case (344 U.S. 133, 136–137[1]).

" In examining these various arguments, this Commission must note that they are not of such a nature as to give it certainty that, during the period under consideration, and under the laws then in force in the United States, Samuel Flegenheimer did not regularly acquire the nationality of that Power by naturalization or that he had lost the benefits thereof.

" It is admitted by the American authors themselves that nationality laws, especially during the period of time that must be taken into consideration, namely, from 1873 through 1890, did not have the same technical accuracy which they acquired after the beginning of the twentieth century, especially the Laws of June 29, 1906, and March 2, 1907, the provisions of which were used and developed by more recent Laws, the Nationality Act of October 14, 1940, and the Immigration and Nationality Act of 1952 as well as the copious jurisprudence which ensued therefrom.

" In the Commission's opinion, neither these legislative texts, nor the principles of jurisprudence set forth by the United States' courts following the beginning of the twentieth century, can be retroactively applied, unless an exception is expressly provided by positive law, in order to deny the American nationality of an individual who was vested in it for decades, without his status, as an American citizen, having ever given rise to a dispute while he was living, so that it represented a veritable possession of a status; this

[1 *International Law Reports*, 1951, Case No. 64.]

could only be contested on the basis of formal texts or a judicial decision concerning the interested person directly, subsequent to an analysis of his particular condition. If the Commission were to follow a different path, it would be led, by an abstract reasoning, to conclusions which would conflict with the content of the records introduced in the case, and thus with reality; it would be faced with the impossibility of establishing the exact date on which Samuel Flegenheimer ceased to be an American national, and consequently of determining whether he transmitted *jure sanguinis* some kind of nationality to his son Albert, or whether the latter should be considered as stateless since birth.

" The Commission is strengthened in its conviction that its manner of envisaging the situation, in holding that criticism which is directed against the validity of Samuel Flegenheimer's naturalization, leads to subjective provisions of a psychological nature which escape a definite judicial appraisal in the absence of the party concerned.

" Although the whole of Samuel Flegenheimer's conduct raises serious suspicions, they only concern the motives underlying the various changes of nationality which he underwent at a time when those motives were not contemplated by the positive laws of the United States.

" As Samuel Flegenheimer had already lost his American nationality following his naturalization in Wurttemberg in 1894, more than ten years before the enactment of the Law of June 29, 1906, the Commission entertains serious doubts as to whether the absence of the intention to permanently reside in the United States could, under the circumstances, entail the invalidity of his naturalization in that State. The American judicial decisions ruling on the nullity of American nationality on these grounds, which have been cited during these proceedings, concern cases which were decided after the enactment of the Law of June 29, 1906. Unlike what is provided in this latter Law, former legislation did not require from a candidate to naturalization any statement under oath regarding his intention to permanently reside in the United States, whereas he did have to take such an oath under the 1906 Act.

" Nevertheless, in the *Luria* case [*supra*], which raised the question of the validity of a naturalization secured as early as 1894, the naturalization was cancelled by the Supreme Court on October 20, 1913, because the interested party had left the United States only a few months after being naturalized, to take up residence in South Africa. The Supreme Court rendered its decision on the basis of the Law of June 29, 1906, by admitting a presumption of revocation of a naturalization, extended by the last paragraph of section 15 of this Law, to naturalizations accorded under the authority of former Laws, because this presumption was. implicitly included in the latter. It should be pointed out, however, that proceedings could be instituted in an American court after 1894 because Samuel Flegenheimer had already lost his American nationality at that time, as the result of his naturalization in Germany. On these first grounds the Commissin holds it cannot take into consideration, without reservations, the *Luria* case precedent in order to declare that Samuel Flegenheimer's naturalization in the United States was null and void because of lack of *animus manendi*.

" It must furthermore take note of the fact that no judicial action for nullity was instituted against the interested party by the American authorities, as was the case in the *Luria* proceedings. In fact, it appears from the text of the Law of June 29, 1906, that cancellation of a naturalization, because of the lack of *animus manendi*, is not incurred under the Law; this only creates a presumption of fraud which the person concerned can rebut by countervailing evidence; the Law expressly provides for this in section 15 which reads as follows:

" ' That it shall be the duty of the United States district attorneys for the respective districts, upon affidavit showing good cause therefor, to institute proceedings in any court having jurisdiction to naturalize aliens in the judicial districts in which the naturalized citizen may reside at the time of bringing of the suit, for the purpose of setting aside and cancelling the certificate of citizenship on the ground of fraud or on the ground that such certificate of citizenship was illegally procured. In any such proceedings the party holding the certificate of citizenship alleged to have been fraudulently or illegally procured shall have sixty days personal notice in which to make answer to the petition of the United States; and if the holder of such certificate be absent from the United States or from the district in which he last had had residence, such notice shall be given by publication in the manner provided for the service of summons by publication or upon absentees by the laws of the State, or the place where such suit is brought. If an alien who shall have secured a certificate of citizenship under the provisions of this Act shall, within five years after the issuance of such certificate, return to the country of his nativity, or go to any other foreign country, and take permanent residence therein, it shall be considered prima facie evidence of lack of intention on the part of such alien to become a permanent citizen of the United States at the time of filing his application for citizenship, and, in the absence of countervailing evidence, it shall be sufficient in the proper proceeding to authorize the cancellation of his certificate or citizenship as fraudulent . . .'

" It is not denied by the High Parties to this dispute that a suit for cancellation of Samuel Flegenheimer's naturalization could not be instituted at this time because the law requires that he be notified of the petition and that it be followed by a hearing of the individual concerned and by the submission of defenses and procedural acts which can no longer be accomplished by reason of his demise.

" Therefore, the first argument raised by the Italian Government against the validity of Samuel Flegenheimer's naturalization cannot be accepted.

" The same thing can be said, and for the same reasons, of the second argument of the Italian Government which consists in denying that Samuel Flegenheimer acted in good faith. It is true that there has been introduced in the record of the case an excerpt of the application, submitted under oath, by Samuel Flegenheimer on November 7, 1873, to the Court of Pittsburgh (Pennsylvania, U.S.); he swore that the facts set out in his application were true and that for the past three years he had had the *bona fide* intention of becoming a United States national. But, evidently, this statement can only be referred to the naturalization conditions, such as they existed, at that time, required of and known by the candidates. In the *Luria* case, the Supreme Court did not exclude *a priori*, a change in the candidate's intention which would not exclude good faith; it affirmed that, if, in actual fact, the candidate, at the time he submitted his application, intended to reside permanently in the United States, and that if his subsequent residence abroad was established on grounds which were reconcilable with that intention, he was completely at liberty to prove it, because there were involved elements of a decision on which he alone was in a position to supply the necessary information. Now, at this time, no useful inquiry could be carried out to that effect by this Commission.

" The whole of the Italian Government's allegations concerning the interested nature of the motives underlying Samuel Flegenheimer's naturalization, who is said to have obeyed, above all, the urge of evading military service in Germany, is plausible, even though it is not proved by the documents of these proceedings that he was compelled to do active service in the army of his country of origin, when it was proven his son Albert was exempted. It is nevertheless not decisive because, at the time he secured naturalization, the United States was not concerned with the motives which induced a candidate to apply for naturalization. This was noted by American Secretary of State Frelinghuysen, in his Instruction of September 25, 1882:

" ' The only question in each case, is whether the person claiming to be naturalized citizen has been naturalized. There is no law of the United States requiring the applicant to disclose the motive which induces him to change his nationality.' (Moore, *Arb.* (1898), p. 2620.)

" If, at that time, naturalization secured by candidates for the only purpose of evading their military duties in their respective countries grew to such an extent as to constitute a genuine evil custom against which the American authorities have vigorously reacted as a consequence, it is no less certain that on the date of Samuel Flegenheimer's naturalization in the United States, these practices were not forbidden by positive law and did not constitute a violation of the naturalization laws. The citations of declarations and opinions of American statesmen and learned jurists who condemned them and which are abundantly reproduced in the written defenses and supporting opinions submitted by the Italian Government, were directed at obtaining an amendment of the laws or of the international treaties then in force; manifestly, they concerned the *lex ferenda* and not the *lex lata*. The Commission thus holds that it cannot consider them for the purpose of evaluating Samuel Flegenheimer's naturalization.

" Lastly, the final argument of the Italian Government does not seem to be better founded, namely, that even if Samuel Flegenheimer's naturalization could not be considered as null and devoid of effects by the Commission on the grounds of fraud against the American law, he lost the benefits of said nationality by his expatriation resulting from his return to Germany, because the term expatriation does not have the mere material meaning of abandonment of residence in the United States, but the legal meaning of the loss of American nationality.

" In this connection the Commission is again led to conclude that the Act of March 2, 1907, entitled ' an Act in reference to the expatriation of citizens and their protection abroad ', does not appear to be applicable in order to decide whether, in 1890, Samuel Flegenheimer was still a national of the United States. Likewise, the decision of the Supreme Court in the *Mandoli* v. *Acheson* case, referred to by the Italian Government[1], because it was rendered in 1952, that is, many decades after the enactment of the Act of 1907, is not of such a nature as to clarify Samuel Flegenheimer's legal position, as it existed in 1874, the year of his return to Germany, and in 1890, the year in which his son Albert was born. It should in fact be noted that, in the aforesaid decision, the Supreme Court made an analysis of the origins of said Act of 1907 and came to the conclusion that the Congress of the United States did not accept the proposal of sanctioning an extensive doctrine on expatriation by emigration, but confined itself to introducing in the new Law a mere presumption of loss of American nationality limited to naturalized persons, ' native born ' citizens being excluded. This restriction refutes all arguments tending to describe the Act of 1907 as a synthesis of the principles indisputably recognized and previously followed by unwritten law. The situation is similar to that which existed prior to the Act of 1907 with regard to the effects of a naturalization obtained without a sincere desire to permanently reside in the United States. At that time, American law on expatriation was not very clear and gave rise to uncertain interpretations, wherefore it was impossible to establish whether the departure of a naturalized citizen without *animus revertendi* entailed, as a consequence, the loss of American

[1 See above, p. 116.]

nationality, or merely an interruption thereof which involved a refusal by the Administration to extend diplomatic protection. It was only under the ' Nationality Act ' of 1940 that expatriation, that is, the complete loss of American nationality, was automatically connected with the materialization of cetain objective conditions, laid down by law, without any consideration of the intention of the individual concerned.

" The Act of March 2, 1907, Section 2, on the contrary, provided that:

" ' When any naturalized citizen shall have resided for two years in the foreign State from which he came, or five years in any other foreign State, it shall be presumed that he has ceased to be an American.'

Also, according to this provision, it is a question of a *juris tantum* presumption which can be reversed by countervailing evidence during the course of judicial proceedings, which were never instituted against Samuel Flegenheimer; the requirement of a special action for cancellation in order that the nullity of a naturalization may be decided, has been admitted in a recent case, the *Laranjo* v. *Brownell* suit, adjudicated in 1954 by the United States District Court of California.[1]

" But as regards the period prior to 1907, and expecially that between 1874 and 1890, United States law did not provide for such presumption of loss of citizenship by expatriation, and, unlike section 5 of the Act of June 29, 1906, no retroactivity was assigned by the legislator to section 2 of Act of March 2, 1907 (Hackworth, *Digest of International Law*, vol. III (1942), p. 300). Borchard comments on the Act of 1907, which appears to admit only a loss of diplomatic protection, as follows:

" ' By paragraph 2 of the Act of 1907, two years' residence of the naturalized citizen in the country of origin or five years' residence in any other country create a presumption that he has ceased to be an American citizen, and unless that presumption is rebutted by showing some special and temporary reason for the change of residence, the obligation of protection by the United States is deemed to be ended.' ( *Diplomatic Protection of Citizens Abroad* (1915), p. 531.)

" Even though preserving its freedom in evaluating the facts which, as far as the Commission is concerned, are the laws, administrative practice and the jurisprudence of States, the Commission cannot adopt results which would be inconsistent with such positive rules of international law like those linking nationality with diplomatic protection. If these two institutions appear to be separate in the law of the United States, prior to 1907, this is only a consequence of the discretionary power recognized to all States in the field of diplomatic protection because these do not give rise to a subjective right to the benefit of the individual but are dominated by reasons

[1 See *International Law Reports*, 1954, Note on p. 191.]

of expediency which the State freely evaluates.  But the Court cannot draw therefrom any conclusion with regard to the legal nationality of persons who have been refused diplomatic protection. It is hence clear that the Commission cannot insert in American positive law, preceding the Act of 1907, a cause for the loss of nationality by emigration without *animus revertendi* which is not provided for therein, and which, even under the authority of the Law which subsequently sanctioned it, gave rise in the United States to disputes with regard to its scope and veritable meaning.

" Furthermore, as the Commission does not have jurisdictional powers to decide on the nationality of persons who are not directly connected with the dispute between the High Parties, which it has been called upon to adjudicate, it is of the opinion that, in order to determine Samuel Flegenheimer's nationality, it should abide by the formal evidence submitted to it; it must therefore eliminate from the investigations all questions implying an evaluation of the subjective intentions of a person whose interests are not at stake and who cannot be heard. The Commission can thus only notice that no positive proof of the loss of American nationality, undeniably acquired by naturalization by Samuel Flegenheimer in 1873, has been introduced.   The *Alsberry* v. *Hawkins* precedent invoked,[1] apart from the fact that it is old, does not appear to be determinant by reason of the fact that if the emigration of Mr. and Mrs. Alsberry to Texas goes back to a date that is prior to the incorporation of that State into the American Union, the decision of expatriation of the Federal Court of Kentucky was rendered subsequent to the declaration of independence of Texas, during a time of political transition, whose influence on the decision is difficult to specify; the interested persons lived in Texas and had acquired citizenship by virtue of the Common Law, at a time when rules on nationality had not yet been made uniform in the United States by Federal Law.

" The result of the foregoing considerations is that the Commission must take notice of the fact that on the date of Albert Flegenheimer's birth, July 4, 1890, Albert's father, Samuel Flegenheimer, was still vested with the nationality of the United States and that he therefore transmitted to his son, *jure sanguinis*, the quality of a national of the United States, under the Act of February 10, 1855, Revised Statutes 604, Section 1993 of which reads as follows:

" ' All children heretofore born or hereafter born out of the limits and jurisdiction of the United States, whose fathers were or may be at the time of their births citizens thereof, are declared to be citizens of the United States; but the rights of citizenship shall not descend to children whose fathers never resided in the United States.'

" The conditions of this legal provision are fulfilled, because even though Albert Flegenheimer was born in Germany, it is not

[1 See above, pp. 115–116.]

denied and it is moreover proved that his father, an American national, had previously resided in the United States. They can thus benefit by the XIVth Amendment to the Constitution of the United States.

"C. *On the loss, following naturalization in Wurttemberg, of the United States nationality of Albert Flegenheimer.*—It is henceforth expedient to investigate whether, as a result of his naturalization in the United States in 1873, Samuel Flegenheimer lost his nationality of origin, namely, that of the Grand Duchy of Baden, and whether later, following his naturalization in the Kingdom of Wurttemberg in 1894, he lost his title to United States nationality and if, possibly, this latter expatriation was extended to his son Albert who was a minor at the time it occurred.

" The two High Parties to this dispute concur in admitting that United States law considers the voluntary naturalization of an American national abroad as cause of loss thereof, under reservation of special clauses introduced in international treaties, because naturalization abroad was considered, subsequent to the nineteenth Century, as the most manifest and effective proof of expatriation, although this is not the only manner in which expatriation can occur.

" The Act of March 2, 1907, sanctioned this principle in Section 2, which reads as follows:

" ' That any American citizen shall be deemed to have expatriated himself, when he has been naturalized in any foreign State, in conformity with its laws, or when he has taken an oath of allegiance to a foreign State.'

" The Parties disagree, however, on the question as to whether or not Albert Flegenheimer's position is governed by the Bancroft Treaties stipulated by the United States with the Grand Duchy of Baden on July 19, 1868, and with Wurttemberg on July 27, 1868. This is affirmed by the Agent of the Italian Government and is categorically denied by the Agent of the Government of the United States. The Parties also disagree on the effects of the father's expatriation on the nationality of his son, then a minor: Italy affirms, while the United States denies, that Albert Flegenheimer lost his American nationality as the result of his naturalization in Wurttemberg, at a time when he was still a minor.

" The so-called Bancroft Treaties constitute a pattern of agreements concluded by the United States with a large number of European and American States with a view to settling certain nationality conflicts, and, in fact, to put a stop to the malpractices committed by European emigrants who acquired American nationality for the sole purpose of avoiding their military duties in their respective countries, and later returned thereto when in possession of United States citizenship papers, without any intention of returning to this latter country.

" The first of these Treaties was negotiated by George Bancroft, United States Minister in Berlin, with the Northern German Confederation, on February 22, 1868, and it was followed, in that same year, 1868, by four treaties with the Grand Duchy of Baden, with Bavaria, with the Grand Duchy of Hesse and with Wurttemberg. The United States concluded similar treaties with Austria–Hungary, Belgium, Denmark, Great Britain, and Sweden and Norway, between 1868 and 1872. Later, between 1902 and 1928, the United States concluded further treaties of this kind with the States of Central and South America and other European States. All these treaties go under the general name of Bancroft Treaties, even though they were not all negotiated by this diplomat, because they have certain common features. But they do not contain provisions that are wholly alike; there are two types of Bancroft Treaties and even those concluded with the five afore-mentioned German States do not all belong to the same category. They can therefore be interpreted one for the other only with caution because many of them have certain peculiarities which are not to be found in the treaties concluded with other States. The Agent of the Government of the United States and his counsel have nevertheless contended that it was necessary to interpret the Treaty with the Confederation of North Germany in order to establish the meaning of the Treaties with the Grand Duchy of Baden and with Wurttemberg but did not notice that their provisions do not fully agree. They are not, therefore, mutually complementary.

" It is also expedient to point out that the five treaties concluded with specific German States are not interchangeable, even if the provisions of some of them are alike. It should not be denied that, in confederations of States and in federated States, the member States of which have maintained a limited international sovereignty permitting them to conclude agreements with foreign States in certain spheres, the treaties binding on a particular State cannot be extended to another member of the Union, even if this latter member were linked with that same foreign State by a Treaty containing similar provisions.

" The legal position was not modified by the establishment of the German Empire, on January 18, 1871, because the United States did not conclude similar treaties with all the members of the new federative State, but only with the States of the old Confederation of North Germany and the other four which have been mentioned; it is therefore not possible to admit that the conditions established by one of these treaties, conditions which in any event are not entirely alike, can be applied to all Americans of German origin, whatever the particular State in which they have gone to reside. The question is an important one in the case submitted to this Commission, because if Samuel Flegenheimer applied for naturalization in the United States when he was a citizen of Baden, he did not return to the Grand Duchy of Baden after securing his

American naturalization, but to Wurttemberg, so that the provisions of both treaties should apply to him, one for his connection with the Grand Duchy of Baden and the other for his connections with Wurttemberg. This solution must be unquestionably resorted to, because the American authorities themselves have admitted that each one of the Bancroft Treaties referred to above, concluded with the various German States, had its own territorial sphere of application; this is the reason why, as early as 1873, they proposed to the Government of the Reich in Berlin to extend to the whole of the German Empire the provisions of the Treaty concluded in 1868 with the Confederation of North Germany, but the German Government did not act on this proposition (Sieber, *Das Staatsbürgerrecht im internationalen Verkehr* (1907), vol. I, p. 520; Hackworth, *Digest of International Law*, vol. III, p. 384; Moore, *Digest of International Law*, vol. III, pp. 364 *et seq.*).

" The right of the Italian Government to find support in the Bancroft Treaties was denied by the Government of the United States for two reasons: in the first place because the Treaties are no longer in force; and in the second place because as far as Italy is concerned they are a *res inter alios acta* in view of the fact that she was not a party thereto.

" Neither of these two objections is [well] founded.

" It cannot be denied that the Bancroft Treaties between the United States and the German States expired on April 6, 1917, as the result of the fact that the United States entered World War I, by virtue of the rules of the Law of Nations which provide that treaties between States are cancelled by the outbreak of war between the signatory States, with the exception of treaties concluded in contemplation of war and of collective treaties which are merely interrupted between the belligerent States, but continue to deploy their effects between neutral and belligerent States. They (the Bancroft Treaties) were not subsequently resumed.

" The Bancroft Treaties nevertheless fully deployed their effects until April 6, 1917 (Hackworth, [*op cit.*] vol. III, p. 334, and vol. V, p. 386), that is, during the whole of the critical period during which Samuel Flegenheimer changed nationality for the first time in the United States, and a second time in Wurttemberg, hence from 1874 to 1894. Their provisions may have exercised influence, first on the loss of Samuel Flengenheimer's Baden nationality as the result of his naturalization in Pittsburgh, the validity of which is admitted by the Commission, and, subsequently, on his own American nationality and on the American nationality of his son Albert Flegenheimer, whose *jure sanguinis* acquisition of United States nationality is likewise admitted by this Commission. The result is that, in order to examine the political status of these two individuals *vis-à-vis* Germany, it is indispensable to take into consideration the law that was applicable at the time at which these changes in nationality occurred, that is, in the first place, the Bancroft Treaties in the German–American relationships and, in the second place, in a supplementary and subsidiary manner, if it was established that these treaties had no influence on the nationality of the individuals concerned, the provisions of German municipal law on the loss of nationality, namely, the provisions of the German Imperial Law of June 1, 1870, concerning the acquisition and loss of the nationality of the Empire and of the States. The facts which must be legally examined, in fact, occurred under the authority of these conventional and legal provisions.

" The objection raised that Italy has no title to invoke the Bancroft Treaties because she was not a party thereto, is also unfounded. It is a foregone conclusion that Italy is obligated to bear the heavy burdens of reparation and restitution which she accepted under the Treaty of Peace of 1947, only if the persons involved are nationals of one of the ' United Nations '. She has no obligation of this kind, under a reservation which will be examined in letter F of this Decision [*infra*, p. 153], towards nationals of other States, especially not towards persons of German nationality. She has a right to require that the ' United Nations ' nationality be established in each case, and to oppose all rebuttal evidence against the allegations of the opponent Parties.... if this rebuttal evidence flows from conventional provisions concluded with a third State, there is no reason why Italy should not invoke them, preliminarily, in so far as they create objective conditions which can be forced not only upon her but on every other State as well. In other words, the treaty is a legitimate source of nationality *vis-à-vis* third States as the provision of municipal law of a State which is not a party to an international dispute and which is invoked by one of the States engaged in this controversy. No distinction should be made according to whether a rule establishing the nationality of a person is contained in the municipal law of a State or in a treaty concluded by the State with another State. It is the duty of this Commission to clarify, by resorting to these Treaties, Samuel and Albert Flegenheimer's nationality; and their effects on the legal position of these persons have operated long before this dispute between the United States and Italy arose.

" The Commission further adds to the foregoing considerations that the question of priority of a subsequent law on the rights acquired by an international treaty does not arise for the United States, because the ' Nationality Act ' of 1940 provides in Section 504:

" ' The repeal herein provided shall not terminate nationality heretofore lawfully acquired nor restitute nationality heretofore lost under any law of the United States or any treaty to which the United States may have been a party.'

" By this express provision the United States legislature intended to preserve the prior status of nationality of a person, whether he or she acquired or lost, by virtue of a treaty concluded with the United States, his or her nationality, thus deviating, in an obligatory manner, from the jurisprudence generally adopted by the American courts, according to which municipal law and an international treaty have equal value, so that a legal provision can modify or abrogate a treaty in force prior to its enactment, in the same way as it can be modified or abrogated by a treaty concluded subsequently. This Commission is all the more justified in abiding by Section 504 of the Nationality Act of 1940, regarding the consideration of a status established by an international treaty, in that this provision is in conformity with the principle of priority of international law which it must follow in that it is an international body and has the duty of observing international law, in conformity with the jurisprudence of the Permanent Court of International Justice which has affirmed:

" ' It is a generally accepted principle of international law that in the relations between Powers who are contracting Parties to a treaty, the provisions of municipal law cannot prevail over those of the treaty.' *P.C.I.J.*, Series B, No. 17, p. 32;[1] in the same sense, Series A, No. 24, p. 12;[2] Series B, No. 5, p. 26;[3] Series A/B, No. 46, p. 167[4].)

" The Parties to this dispute are in complete disagreement on the meaning of the Bancroft Treaties. The Agent of the United States and his Counsel consider them as agreements whose essential purpose is to eliminate disputes between States in connection with the diplomatic protection of persons naturalized in a State and returning subsequently to their country of origin, while the Agent of the Italian Republic and his Counsel consider them mainly as conventions governing the nationality of the subjects of one of the contracting States residing in the other, and containing therefore provisions on the acquisition and the loss of title to citizenship of persons whose legal position the signatory State have agreed to settle.

" In order to determine their exact scope, it is indispensable to go back to the origin of these Treaties; their conclusion was due to the initiative of the Government of the United States.

" As the United States owed its prosperity to a constant flow of European immigrants, beginning with the nineteenth century, it was concerned with attaching legally and in a final manner all this new population to the territory wherein it resided. It forcefully affirmed the right of every individual to change his nationality and to expatriate. In this policy of assimilation of aliens the United

[1 Advisory Opinion in the *Greco-Bulgarian "Communities" Case*: *Annual Digest*, 1929–1930, Case No. 2, at p. 5.]
[2 Order in the *Case concerning the Free Zones of Upper Savoy and the District of Gex*: *Annual Digest*, 1929–1930, Case No. 6, at p. 16.]
[3 Advisory Opinion on the *Status of Eastern Carelia*: *Annual Digest*, 1923–1924, Case No. 219.]
[4 Judgment in the *Case concerning the Free Zones of Upper Savoy and the District of Gex*: *Annual Digest*, 1931–1932 Case No. 362.

States clashed with the law of numerous European States which were desirous of preserving, often for military reasons, their emigrated nationals, either because these States constantly followed the principle of perpetual allegiance, or because they subjected the loss of the nationality of origin to governmental authorization (acts of manumission) which was frequently refused to individuals who were still liable to military service in their home country, or, further, because they did not admit that naturalization abroad entailed, by operation of law, the loss of the nationality of origin of their nationals and required the fulfilment of formalities (application for expatriation, specific renunciation) in order to liberate the naturalized individuals from all ties and bonds with the State of origin.

" The United States set out with the idea that the naturalization of all aliens established in its territory was to entail immediately the loss of their previous nationality; it inversely admitted that naturalization of its nationals abroad directly caused the loss of American nationality. Following a long and concordant practice which goes back to 1793, when American Secretary of State Jefferson affirmed the rights of every American national to divest himself of his nationality, it (the United States) enacted the Law of June 27, 1868, which admitted the right of expatriation to be one of the fundamental principles of the Republic (Revised Statutes, tit. XXV, section 1999). Later this Law was drawn up in statute form by the Act of March 2, 1907, which provides:

" ' Sec. 2. That any American citizen shall be deemed to have expatriated himself when he has been naturalized in any foreign State in conformity with its law, or when he has taken an oath of allegiance to any foreign State.'

" It defended this principle in its international intercourse with regard to both American nationals naturalized abroad and aliens naturalized in America, without however succeeding in having it prevail completely with respect to the latter. Numerous disputes arose, above all, in connection with immigrants who applied for naturalization for the sole purpose of avoiding their civic and military duties in their country of origin and who returned to that country after having obtained title to American nationality, and requested the diplomatic protection of the United States against their former country, when the latter still intended to consider them as its own nationals and required them to accomplish their military service. These cases cropped up by the thousand beginning from the middle of the nineteenth Century.

" The conflict between American law on naturalization and the law of numerous foreign States, who thwarted the freedom of expatriation of their nationals, caused a very considerable increase of persons in possession of dual nationality and gave rise to disputes over diplomatic protection. The Bancroft Treaties are, above all, treaties establishing the nationality of persons, and in a manner which is not alike in all of these treaties, as the United States has not always succeeded in obtaining recognition of the principle of the loss, by operation of law, of the nationality of origin as the result of the naturalization of nationals of one of the contracting Parties in the territory of the other. Diplomatic protection was considered only incidentally.

" The genesis of the Bancroft Treaties, historically, is to be found in the tendency of the United States to abolish, to the greatest extent possible, the dual nationality resulting from the conflicts of laws between conditions governing naturalization and conditions governing expatriation. When analyzing their provisions this purpose should be borne in mind.

" All the Bancroft Treaties concluded with the German States reveal one peculiarity in common: they sanction the following principle, the pertinence of which is manifest in the instant case:

> The nationals of one of the contracting Powers who have been naturalized in the territory of the other Party and have resided therein uninterruptedly for a period of five years shall be held to be nationals of the naturalizing State by their country of origin and shall be treated as such.

On the other hand, the content of all the Bancroft Treaties is not alike in connection with the legal position of naturalized persons who return to reside in their country of origin. In this respect one is confronted with two diversities in these Treaties:

" (a) In some of these Treaties these naturalized persons are considered to have renounced their nationality of adoption when they do not intend to return to the country of their naturalization, as *animus revertendi* was presumed to be lacking after two years' residence in their country of origin (Confederation of Northern Germany, Bavaria, Hesse and Wurttemberg).

" (b) In the Treaty with Baden, these naturalized persons cannot be compelled to re-acquire their nationality of origin, but they can renounce their naturalization and be voluntarily redintegrated in their nationality of origin, without the necessity of observing any time limit with regard to residence before obtaining recognition of the nationality of their country of origin.

" It is evident that these two types of Bancroft Treaties can have different effects on the nationality of persons falling under their provisions.

" Under reservation of particular agreements between the contracting States, such as concordant statements or annexed protocols, it has been contended that in the treaties of the former type, like the one concluded with the Confederation of Northern Germany, the question of dual nationality was not settled and the point as to

whether or not, subsequent to naturalization in one of the contracting States, the question of nationality of the immigrant still existed
*vis-à-vis* his State of origin, was not resolved by the Treaty and was
left to the municipal legislation of the other Party. The naturalized
immigrant was to be treated solely as an alien in his country of origin
until it was presumed that he had *animus manendi*. The treaty merely
interrupted his citizenship of origin and did not annul it; it did
therefore settle only the question of diplomatic protection between
the United States and the aforesaid Confederation, and it was for
the municipal legislation of the latter to decide whether the nationality of origin of a person naturalized in the United States still
existed or had come to an end. This is the viewpoint of the Agent
of the United States and his Counsel in the instant case; it is based
on the *Bericht der Vereinigten Ausschüsse des Bunderats für das
Landheer und Festungen und Justizwesen* (Dzialoszynski, *Die Bancroft
Verträge* (1913), p. 45.)

" This Commission cannot render an opinion on the foregoing
interpretation because the Bancroft Treaty between the United
States and the Confederation of Northern Germany is not applicable
in the instant case. It will confine itself to point out that this interpretation cannot be extended, by way of analogy, to the provisions
of the other Bancroft Treaties concluded with German States, where
the question was clearly settled by special protocols; these provide
that the naturalized immigrant who returns to reside in his country
of origin without the intention of going back to the country of his
naturalization, does not recover his nationality of origin by the mere
fact of taking up residence therein but can be redintegrated in the
nationality of this latter country only by a new naturalization, just
like any other alien. This is the solution which is sanctioned in the
relationships between the United States and Bavaria, Hesse and
Wurttemberg. The result is that these treaties have a direct bearing
on nationality, that they do away with dual nationality, as the
citizenship of origin is undeniably lost by a naturalization abroad
accompanied by a five-year residence, because in case of return to
the former country, the person concerned must become naturalized
in order to re-acquire it.

" In the latter type of Bancroft Treaties, that concluded with the
Grand Duchy of Baden, it is undeniable that the contracting States
intended to settle directly the question of the nationality of naturalized persons, because it is stated therein, *expressis verbis*, that the
nationality of origin can be recovered, in cases where the person
concerned returns to reside in his former home-country, only if the
latter files an application, in other words, it is lost as the result of
naturalization in the other contracting State. The accumulation of
nationalities was hence done away with by the Treaty itself. This
stipulation is also to be found in the Bancroft Treaties with Austria,
Belgium, Denmark and Sweden and Norway.

" After a careful analysis of these conventional texts, the Commission is convinced that the Bancroft Treaties with the Grand Duchy of Baden and Wurttemberg, in the relationship with the United States, not only had the purpose of regulating the diplomatic protection of naturalized persons but of determining their nationality as well. There now remains to be examined what bearing these Treaties had on the status of Samuel and Albert Flegenheimer.

" By his naturalization in the United States in 1873, Samuel Flegenheimer lost his nationality of origin, that of Baden, in application of the Naturalization Convention of July 19, 1868, concluded by this State with the Grand Duchy of Baden, Article I of which stipulates:

" ' Citizens of the Grand Duchy of Baden who have resided uninterruptedly within the United States of America five years, and before, during or after that time have become or shall become naturalized citizens of the United States, shall be held by Baden to be American citizens and shall be treated as such.'

" The expressions ' shall be held ' and ' shall be treated ' do not only refer to the obligation of the Grand Duchy of Baden to consider its nationals who have been naturalized and who have resided for five years in the United States as American nationals and to treat them as such, that is to say, not to impose upon them the execution of civic duties nor of interposing in their behalf through diplomatic channels, but imply a loss of the Baden nationality, by virtue of the Treaty of July 19, 1868. This can in no way be doubted because of the existence of Article IV of the aforesaid Treaty which provides:

" ' The emigrant from the one State, who, according to the first article, is to be held as a citizen of the other State, shall not on his return to his original country be constrained to resume his former citizenship; yet if he shall of his own accord reacquire it and renounce the citizenship obtained by naturalization, such a renunciation is allowed, and no fixed period of residence shall be required for the recognition of his recovery of citizenship in his original country.'

" It clearly appears from the foregoing text that naturalization in the United States entailed the loss of Samuel Flegenheimer's Baden nationality, because, if he had returned to his former home-country, he could have recovered this nationality only by making an application therefor and renouncing his American nationality. A case of dual nationality never arose in the person of Samuel Flegenheimer, because, at the very time when he acquired American nationality, all the conditions causing the loss of his Baden nationality were fulfilled, namely, his naturalization in the United States and his five-year residence in that country.

" After being naturalized in the United States, Samuel Flegenheimer returned to Germany, but did not take up residence in his former country of origin, namely, the Grand Duchy of Baden, so that the Bancroft Treaty of July 19, 1868, concluded with that State was not applicable, as regards the consequences of this return, to his nationality. He did not lose his United States nationality under this Treaty, because, on the one hand, he did not fulfil the conditions of Article IV which contemplated a return of the naturalized person to the Grand Duchy of Baden itself, and, on the other hand, even supposing that it was applicable to him, the aforesaid Article IV does not, unlike the provisions made in many other Bancroft Treaties, provide for the automatic loss of the nationality acquired in the United States in cases where the naturalized person returns to reside in his country of origin, without *animus redeundi* to America.

" He thus took up permanent residence in Wurttemberg as an American national, and it is likewise in this quality, and not as a former Baden national, that he applied for and obtained Wurttemberg naturalization in 1894, following an uninterrupted residence of twenty years. As the result of this naturalization he directly and finally lost his United States nationality by virtue of Article 1, para. 2, of the Bancroft Treaty of July 27, 1868, concluded between the United States and Wurttemberg, wherein it is provided that:

" ' Reciprocally: citizens of the United States of America who have become or shall become naturalized citizens of Wurttemberg and shall have resided uninterruptedly five years within Wurttemberg shall be held by the United States to be citizens of Wurttemberg and shall be treated as such.'

" In the foregoing text, like in the corresponding text of the Treaty with the Grand Duchy of Baden of July 19, 1868, the expression ' shall be held ' and ' shall be treated ' do not have the meaning of a mere interruption of the American nationality and of the loss of title to the diplomatic protection of the United States, but of a complete annulment of the title to the nationality of that State, by virtue of the Treaty itself. The Commission must reach this conclusion when faced with the Protocol signed at Stuttgart, on the same date as the Treaty, July 27, 1868, which, although making specific reference to Article 4 of the Treaty, explains very clearly that naturalized persons, in application of Article 1, lose, as a result of their naturalization, their preceding naturalization; Part III of this Protocol reads as follows:

" ' It is agreed that the fourth article shall not receive the interpretation, that the naturalized citizen of the one State, who returns to the other State, his original country, and there takes up his residence, does by that act alone recover his former citizenship; nor can it be assumed, that the State, to which the emigrant originally belonged, is bound to restore him at once to his original relation. On the contrary it is only intended, to be declared, that the emigrant so returning, is authorized to acquire the citizenship of his former country, *in the same manner as other aliens* in conformity to the laws and regulations which are there established. Yet it is left to his own choice, whether he will adopt that course, or will preserve the citizenship of the country of his adoption. With regard to this choice, after a two years' residence in his original country, he is bound, if so requested by the proper authorities, to make a distinct declaration, upon which these authorities can come to a decision as the case may be, with regard to his being received again into citizenship or his further residence, in the manner prescribed by law.'

" The Commission could interpret this document established by common agreement of the High Contracting Parties, in no other way than as a recognition of the principle constantly defended by the American authorities in their relationship with foreign States, namely, that the nationality of origin is lost *ipso jure*, by virtue of the Bancroft Treaty concluded with Wurttemberg; it draws the conclusion therefore that even a Wurttemberg national, if naturalized in the United States, when returning to reside in his country of origin can re-acquire the nationality of this latter country only like any other alien, this means without the slightest doubt that he had lost that nationality as a result of his naturalization in the United States, by virtue of Article 1 of the aforesaid Treaty, and that, in application of the principle of reciprocity which is at the basis of the Bancroft Treaties, this is all the more so in the case of an American who secures naturalization in Wurttemberg.

" The Commission is of the opinion that Article 4 of the Bancroft Treaty with Wurttemberg of July 27, 1868, is not applicable to the instant case; it reads as follows:

" ' If a Wurttemberger naturalized in America renews his residence in Wurttemberg without the intention to return to America he shall be held to have renounced his naturalization in the United States. . . . The intent not to return may be held to exist when the person naturalized in the one country resides more than two years in the other.'

" Samuel Flegenheimer never fell under the provisions of this Article, because he was not a Wurttemberg national naturalized in the United States, but an individual of Baden origin. On the other hand, the Bancroft Treaty of July 10, 1868, with the Grand Duchy of Baden (Article 4) fails to recognize this loss of American naturalization as the result of the return to reside in the country of origin without *animus revertendi* to the United States; it only provides for a new naturalization in the country of origin accompanied by a voluntary renunciation of the naturalization secured in the United States; but this provision also was inapplicable to Samuel Flegenheimer who could not be qualified as a Baden national returning to his country of origin. The two Treaties are not complementary and the provisions of one cannot be invoked in order to make good the inapplicability of the provisions of the other. It is therefore by virtue of Article 1, para. 2, of the Treaty between Wurttemberg and the United States that Samuel Flegenheimer and the members of his family, under his control and guardianship as a husband and as a father, lost their American nationality.

" Samuel Flegenheimer's naturalization in Wurttemberg was formally extended, by the very act under which he secured said naturalization, to his wife and to his minor children, namely, Joseph who was then 18 years old, Eugen who was 6 and Albert who was 4. The three of them, through their father, lost under the Bancroft Treaty concluded between the United States and Wurttemberg, the American nationality they had acquired *jure sanguinis*. The collective effects of Samuel Flegenheimer's naturalization on the members of his family, under his control and guardianship as a husband and as a father, are explicitly confirmed by the excerpt from the Register of families of the Schwäbisch-Hall district, as well as by a statement, introduced in the record, of the Government of the district of his domicile in Wurttemberg *Königliche Kreisregierung*) of August 23, 1894. They fulfilled the conditions of domicile required by the Treaty of July 27, 1868; although Albert was only four years old on the date of the naturalization of his father, he too falls under the provisions of this Treaty. The Protocol annexed thereto explicitly provides in Part I (1):

" ' It is of course understood, that not the naturalization alone, but a five years uninterrupted residence is also required, before a person can be regarded as coming within the treaty, but it is by no means requisite that the five years residence should take place after the naturalization.'

" It is therefore immaterial whether the five-year uninterrupted residence is placed before or after the grant of naturalization; it is in any event established that Albert Flegenheimer resided uninterruptedly for more than five years in Wurttemberg, since birth and immediately after his naturalization. One could admit that he lost title to United States nationality only in 1895, a chronological verification that is devoid of all pertinence for the purpose of settling this dispute.

" Moreover, the Bancroft Treaty of July 27, 1868, like the others, does not specifically decide the question of the extension, to the minor children of an American national, of the loss of United States nationality by the head of the family who secured naturalization in Wurttemberg. As the collective effects assigned to a naturalization under the laws of a State do not have as a necessary corollary an expatriation with collective effects in the State of origin, the laws of which may have adopted, by way of hypothesis, the principle of individual expatriation, the question must be settled by an interpretation of the Treaty that is binding on the two Parties.

" A literal interpretation of Article 1, para. 2, of the Treaty between Wurttemberg and the United States of July 27, 1868, leads to the recognition that all of Samuel Flegenheimer's minor children, who were naturalized with him, lost by this fact, like him, their American nationality.

" The starting point of the *processus* of all interpretation of an international treaty is the text on which the two Parties have agreed; it is evident that the main point of an international agreement lies in the concordant intent of such parties and that, without this concordance, there are no rights or obligations which arise therefrom. The written word, Max Huber of the Institute of International Law affirmed, in the art of interpreting texts, has just as important a place as mathematics have in the art of engineering; it aims at precision and this can be obtained only by a choice, after extremely careful thought, of the expressions employed. As Vattel, the Swiss jurist, pointed out already in the eighteenth century,

'. . . when an act is worded in clear and precise terms, when the meaning is manifest and does not lead to anything that is absurd, there is no reason for refusing this act the meaning that it naturally displays. To search elsewhere for probable inferences so as to restrict or extend it, means an intent to evade it.' (*Le Droit des Gens*, vol. II, chap. XVII, para. 263.)

" International jurisprudence has made an extensive application of this rule of interpretation. The Permanent Court of International Justice in fact affirmed:

' The Court's task is clearly defined. Having before it a clause which leaves little to be desired in the nature of clearness, it is bound to apply this clause as it stands, without considering whether other provisions might with advantage have been added to or substituted for it.' (Advisory Opinion of September 15, 1923, *Acquisition of Polish Nationality*: *P.C.I.J.*, Series B, No. 7, p. 20.[1])[2]

" The Treaty of July 27, 1868, does not afford any exception to the rule of the loss of American nationality following the naturalization in Wurttemberg of minor children included in their father's change of nationality. There is therefore no ground for inserting it in the text of the Treaty and taking it for granted: ' *ubi lex non distinguit, nec nos distinguere debemus* '. Such is the wisdom of centuries.

" A teleological interpretation of the aforesaid Treaty does not lead to a different result. As the genesis of the Bancroft Treaties discloses, the main concern of the United States in concluding these treaties was to put a stop to the evil usage and inconveniences of dual nationality, by adopting the rule that every naturalization in the United States accompanied by a permanent residence, entailed as a consequence, automatically, the loss of the former allegiance; and the United States succeeded in obtaining this result only by

[1 See also *Annual Digest*, 1923–1924, Case No. 168.]
[2] See also Series B, No. 2, p. 22 [*Competence of the International Labour Organization (Regulation of Conditions of Work of Persons Employed in Agriculture*)]; and Decision of the Mixed Claims German-American Commission of November 1, 1923, concerning the interpretation of the Treaty of August 25, 1921, between the United States and Germany (*The Lusitania Case*) in Witenberg, *Decisions of the Commission* (1926), vol. I, p. 37 [*Annual Digest*, 1923–1924, Case No. 196].

admitting, in their turn, by way of reciprocity, that American nationality would not continue to exist following naturalization, accompanied by permanent residence, of an American national abroad. Therefore, the principal purpose of these treaties is to link every naturalization in a State, the seriousness and sincere character of which is proved by a durable residence, with expatriation in the other State.

" A search for the agreed intent of the contracting Parties, at the time the Bancroft Treaties were concluded, does not lead to another result.

" In German law, in the interest of the unity and nationality of the family, the naturalization of the father as well as his expatriation was extended to his wife under his marital control and authority, and to his children under his fatherly control and authority (para. 11, 14a, 19, 21, sub-para. 2, of the German Nationality Law of June 1, 1870, that was applicable at the time of Samuel Flegenheimer's naturalization in the United States in 1873 and in Wurttemberg in 1894).

" The same conditions applied in the United States where, beginning with the first Naturalization Act of March 26, 1790, it was admitted that the naturalization of the parents was extended to their minor children who resided with them in the United States.

" The same collective effects on the nationality of minor children were attributed to the expatriation of Americans, heads of families, following naturalization abroad. In the case of Baldura Schmidt, who was included in the naturalization of his father in Germany, in 1923, Secretary of State Stimson affirmed:

" ' The Department knows of no sufficient ground for contending that the nationality of a minor child cannot be changed, without the child's consent, by the act of a parent in obtaining naturalization in a foreign State; especially in view of the fact that the law of this country provides for the naturalization of a parent in the United States, without requiring the consent of the child . . . Such being the case, it would be inconsistent for this Government to hold that Americans who have been naturalized in foreign countries during minority through naturalization of their parents have retained their American nationality.' (Hackworth's Digest, vol. III, p. 238.)

" It was nevertheless admitted in Steinhauler's case in 1875, that the native-born child of a naturalized parent, subsequently included in the restoration of the latter into his country of origin, has the right to elect American nationality upon reaching majority, provided he returns to the United States. Several Instructions of Secretaries of State in this direction were given to American diplomatic representatives abroad. (Moore, [International Arbitrations (1898)], vol. III, pp. 542-544, 548.)

" Although this right of election was not included in any positive law, at that time, it was considered as a legal rule constantly admitted and sanctioned by the Supreme Court in the *Perkins* v. *Elg* case in 1939, subject to the provisions contained in international treaties.

" This right of option was never analyzed very thoroughly by American jurists, so that it was not possible to establish whether for the minor children involved, it is a question of loss of American nationality under a resolving condition of option and of return to the United States, or of redintegration in their American nationality suspensively conditioned upon option and return to the United States. In the first case, these minors would lose their American nationality as a result of the naturalization of their father abroad, and would only be vested with the nationality of their father during the whole of their minority, but could re-acquire their American nationality by an option entailing the cancellation of the loss which had previously occurred; in the second case these minor children would maintain their nationality during their minority, they would thus have simultaneously the quality of American nationals and of nationals of the country of naturalization of their father, but would still be required to elect in favor of American nationality and to return to the country of their birth; failing the option, they would lose this latter citizenship and would remain vested only with the nationality acquired by their naturalized father.

" The Commission must note that the Treaty of 1868 with Wurttemberg contains no reservation in favor of this right of option. If it had been the intent of the contracting parties to admit it, they would have introduced certain provisions in their agreement which the Commission cannot presume. It is in fact the custom of introducing in international conventions, directed at combating or preventing dual nationality, special rules if the right of option is reserved to minor children naturalized with their parents in one of the contracting countries, as is particularly the case in the Franco-Swiss Convention of July 23, 1879, and of establishing, very accurately, this right of option which must be made use of within certain time limits and before certain designated authorities.

" The gap of the Treaty in this connection leads the Commission to note that Wurttemberg has always applied, in its municipal law, the principle of naturalization and expatriation with collective effects, and that the same principle was generally followed by the United States until 1939, and this fact appears, *inter alia*, from the *Tobiassen Case* which, although criticised by the Supreme Court in the *Perkins* v. *Elg* case, establishes the status of American law prior to 1939. The *Tobiassen Case* involved a minor child (a girl), an American national who, when eight years old, was included in her father's re-acquisition of Norwegian nationality; this case was

M

brought before the United States courts in 1932, where Attorney General Mitchell affirmed:

> " ' The law of Norway . . . is analogous to our statutes . . . by virtue of which foreign-born children of persons naturalized in the United States are declared to be citizens of this country . . . Inasmuch as under our laws a foreign-born child obtains a citizenship status through the naturalization of the father, it seems to me inconsistent . . . to deny a like effect to similar laws of Norway.' (36 Op. Attys. Gen. 535 (1932).)

The Commission concludes therefrom that the contracting Parties did not so much intend to deviate from this principle in a treaty, like the Bancroft Treaty concluded on July 27, 1868, as they intended to do away with cases of dual nationality and the abuse which had arisen therefrom.

" It is impossible for the Commission to admit that Albert Flegenheimer retained the nationality of the United States and that he was consequently vested with German-American dual nationality from 1894 until the German Decree of April 29, 1940, under which he forfeited his German nationality, when the clear text of an international treaty classifies him in the category of Americans expatriated by naturalization and when proven facts establish that he considered himself as vested with German nationality alone.

" In any event, the principle of collective expatriation was only recently clearly specified in paragraph 401 (a) of the 1940 Nationality Act in the following terms and established that Albert Flegenheimer forfeited his right of option since 1913, should this Law be applicable to him, which is not the case, however:

> " ' A person who is a national of the United States, whether by birth or through naturalization shall lose his nationality by : (a) Obtaining naturalization in a foreign State, either upon his own application or through the naturalization of a parent having legal custody of such person: *Provided, however,* that the nationality shall not be lost as the result of the naturalization of a parent unless and until the child shall have attained the age of twenty-three years without acquiring permanent residence in the United States.'

" Even under this principle, the legal position of Albert Flegenheimer would not be modified.

" Hence, on this point the Commission reaches the conclusion that Albert Flegenheimer, following his naturalization in Germany in 1894, lost his American nationality and that he was never simultaneously vested with both German and United States nationality.

" D. *On the question as to whether Albert Flegenheimer recovered, subsequent to his naturalization in Germany, his title to United States nationality.*—The Agent of the Government of the United States and his Counsel, after having denied that the Bancroft Treaties could have caused the loss of American nationality of minor children included in their father's naturalization in Germany, lay heavy stress on the right of election recognized to these minors, after reaching majority, in favor of United States nationality provided they establish their permanent residence in that country.

" In this connection they invoke numerous American judicial precedents, and among these the *Perkins* v. *Elg* case,[1] adjudicated in 1939, and the *Mandoli* v. *Acheson* case,[2] adjudicated in 1952, both of them by the United States Supreme Court.

" The Claiming Party attaches a decisive importance to the *Perkins* v. *Elg* precedent, because it was decided in favor of a minor person, falling under the provisions of the Bancroft Treaty of May 26, 1869, concluded between the United States on the one hand and Sweden and Norway on the other, and because the Supreme Court specifically recognized, in the person concerned, a right of election, after reaching majority, in favor of American nationality.

" Miss Elg's position in fact and in law is not the same as that of Albert Flegenheimer.

" Miss Elg was born in New York in 1907 of Swedish parents who had acquired United States nationality by naturalization in 1906. In 1911, at the age of four, her mother took her to Sweden where she resided until 1929. In 1922 her father went to Sweden in his turn and never returned to the United States; in 1934 he made a statement before an American Consul in Sweden, under the terms of which he expatriated himself voluntarily, because he did not wish to preserve his American nationality and intended to remain a Swedish national.

" In 1928, shortly before reaching majority, Miss Elg inquired at an American Consulate in Sweden what the possibilities were to receive an American passport in order to return to the United States; in 1929, eight months after her twenty-first birthday, she obtained this passport and returned to the United States as a national of that country, where she permanently resided. In 1935-1936 her title to American nationality was challenged by the American authorities and the legal proceedings which followed terminated in a decision of the Supreme Court wherein Miss Elg was recognized to be an American national.

" The Court based its opinion on the administrative precedents wherein an American minor, born in the United States, who had acquired a foreign nationality through his father, had been recognized the right to elect between this and the American nationality, at the age of twenty-one, by his return to the United States, in view of the fact that expatriation, except for treaties, can only be the consequence of voluntary naturalization abroad and is not extended to minor children who are passively included in that of their parents. The Supreme Court admitted that this administrative practice was a consequence of the constitutional provision conferring title to

[1 307 U.S. 325; *Annual Digest*, 1938–1940, Case No. 116.]
[2 344 U.S. 133; 73 Sup. Ct. 135; *International Law Reports*, 1951, Case No. 64.]

nationality to all persons born in the United States and submitted to its jurisdiction.

" The Court, after formally reserving contrary conventional rules, examined the Bancroft Treaty of 1869 between the United States and Sweden and Norway, and in view of the fact that the case involved the return of a naturalized person to the United States, his country of origin, took as a basis Article III of that Treaty and the Protocol annexed thereto; the aforesaid Article III reads as follows:

" ' If a citizen of the one party, who has become a recognized citizen of the other party, takes up his abode once more in his original country and applies to be restored in his former citizenship, the government of the last named country is authorized to receive him again as a citizen *on such conditions as the said government* may think proper.'

" In connection with this Article the Protocol provides:

" ' It is further agreed that if a Swede or Norwegian, who has become a naturalized citizen of the United States, renews his residence in Sweden or Norway without the intent to return to America, he shall be held by the Government of the United States to have renounced his American citizenship.'

" In interpreting these texts, the Supreme Court admitted that they specifically authorized the United States to receive ' as a citizen on such conditions as the said Government may think proper ' a child born in America and who, taken to Sweden when he was still a minor, chose to return to the United States upon reaching majority. The Court further affirmed:

" ' And if the Government considers that a native citizen taken from the United States by his parents during minority is entitled to retain his American citizenship by electing at majority to return and reside here, there would appear to be nothing in the treaty which would gainsay the authority of the United States to recognize that privilege of election and to receive the returning native upon that basis. Thus, on the facts of the present case, the treaty does not purport to deny to the United States the right to treat respondent as a citizen of the United States, and it necessarily follows that, in the absence of such a denial, the treaty cannot be set up as a ground for refusing to accord to respondent the rights of citizenship in accordance with our Constitution and laws *by virtue of her birth in* the United States.' (307 *U.S.* (1939), p. 338.)

" This Commission believes that this precedent, the importance of which it does not deny, is applicable, in the interpretation of an international treaty to the specific case of election of American nationality by a minor child born in the United States territory, of parents who were naturalized in the United States, and later taken by them to their country of origin where the latter re-acquired, by virtue of a special applicable authorization of the Bancroft Treaty, their nationality of origin, under conditions established at the discretion of the Government of that country, hence without a naturalization procedure; election of nationality must be accompanied by a return to the United States shortly after the minor child reaches majority.

" None of these particular circumstances have occurred in the instant case. Albert Flegenheimer's position in fact differs from that which appeared in the *Perkins* v. *Elg* case, on essential and numerous points.

" (a) In the first place, Miss Elg was born in the United States of parents who resided in that country. She thus had the status of a *jure soli* native born American national, by virtue of the Constitution of the United States, whereas Albert Flegenheimer was born in Germany of a father who had been a resident of that country for many years and who had been formerly naturalized in the United States; he thus acquired American nationality *jure sanguinis*, by virtue of Section 1993 of the Revised Statutes.

" (b) In the second place, Miss Elg was taken to Sweden by her mother when she was four years old, while her father remained in the United States until she was fifteen years old; it has not been established that she was included in the Swedish decree of naturalization granted to her father, because the latter confined himself to declare he no longer wished to retain his American nationality; whereas Albert Flegenheimer who was specifically included in his father's act of naturalization in Wurttemberg, resided uninterruptedly with his parents in Germany during the whole of his youth and, after attaining majority, until 1937, that is, a total of 47 years; he left Germany because of the political events which disturbed Germany after the coming into power of the National-Socialist régime; the reasons of his emigration are comprehensible, but do not prevent the Commission from noting that all his family and business interests were in Germany where he created a family, where his children were born, that he received a German education, that he never lived in America until he was almost fifty and that his assimilation into the American people and life had not even begun in 1939, when he filed his first application for recognition of his American nationality.

" (c) In the third place, even before reaching majority, Miss Elg secured information on her American nationality and went to the United States shortly after her twenty-first birthday. She proceeded without delay in her election of nationality, thus giving proof of a real attachment to the country of her birth; she resided permanently in that country, and her nationality was challenged only six years later; whereas Albert Flegenheimer did not make an election in favor of American nationality until he was 49 years old, under the pressure of political events and in the furtherance of his business.

" In the *Perkins* v. *Elg* decision the Supreme Court many times stressed the fact that the right of election in favor of American nationality must be exercised ' on attaining majority ' (pp. 329, 334, 338, 339, 340 and 346[11]), and although no peremptory time limit is provided by positive law, the decision affirms that Miss Elg ' promptly made her election and took up her residence in this country accordingly '. Albert Flegenheimer tries to explain away the delay in his election of American nationality and comes to the conclusion that he is not barred from this privilege. He explains it on the following grounds :

" In the first place, he contends that he was unaware of his father's naturalization in 1873 and of his own *jure sanguinis* title to American nationality until 1933, after the death of his father, when he learned of the latter's American passport; he claims he can furnish proof of this by the numerous affidavits and statements introduced in the records of the case. The Commission, by virtue of its freedom of evaluation of evidence, is all the less inclined to recognize the probative force of *ex parte* affidavits and statements established by third parties, inasmuch as it is difficult to reconcile them with the birth certificate of the individual concerned wherein it is stated that his father, Samuel Flegenheimer, was naturalized in Wurttemberg in 1894 together with his family; although this document does not show the American nationality of his father, it seems hardly likely that Albert Flegenheimer did not have the slightest curiosity in this respect and did not try to discover what the former nationality of his father was, a fact which he could have very easily discovered by consulting the register of marriages, which is public in Germany, and in which Samuel Flegenheimer's American nationality is mentioned; it also seems strange that he never had knowledge of Wurttemberg's *Kreisregierung*'s attestation establishing his own naturalization in that State.

" Subsequently, Albert Flegenheimer refers to the requests for information made by him at various United States Consulates and an Embassy in Europe, between 1933 and 1939, which, in his opinion, establishes his election of American nationality. But these were intermittent steps, devoid of all legal meaning, because no trace of them was ever discovered in the files of the State Department, prior to his formal application submitted to the United States Consulate in Winnipeg on November 3, 1939. Even if one were to accept Albert Flegenheimer's version with regard to his late discovery of Samuel Flegenheimer's naturalization in the United States, his election of American nationality, which occurred 49 years after his birth, 28 years after reaching majority, and 6 years after the date on which he claims he discovered he had a right of election, would

[1 Reference is to 307 U.S. 325. See also *Annual Digest*, 1938–1940, at pp. 354, 355, 356.]

appear to the Commission to be too dilatory to justify the application to his case of the jurisprudence of the Supreme Court in the *Perkins* v. *Elg* case, and, consequently, of Article 78 of the Treaty of Peace with Italy.

" (d) In the fourth place, the Bancroft Treaty concluded with Sweden and Norway confers a discretionary power on the contracting State, which applied to Miss Elg's case, for establishing the conditions of redintegration of a naturalized person in her nationality of origin, whereas the Bancroft Treaty with Wurttemberg contains very clear and precise provisions to the contrary, namely, the naturalized person who returns to his country of origin can recover the nationality thereof only ' in the same manner *as other aliens* in conformity to the laws and regulations which are there established' (Protocol and Art. IV of the Treaty).

" This Commission holds that, unlike what was admitted by the Supreme Court in the *Elg* case, Albert Flegenheimer was never vested with dual nationality and that, therefore, the *Perkins* v. *Elg* case is not applicable to his case by reasons of fact and of law.

" Albert Flegenheimer's nationality was established by the special provisions of the Bancroft Treaty with Wurttemberg which do not harmonize with those of the Treaty concluded by the United States with Norway and Sweden on the point analysed herein; they lead to a conclusion other than the one admitted in the *Perkins* v. *Elg* case.

" One could object that since April 6, 1917, this Treaty is no longer in force and that it could therefore no longer prevent the dilatory exercise of the right of election by Albert Flegenheimer on November 3, 1939. But the Commission has already pointed out that, in order to determine the conditions and the effects of a naturalization, the legal and conventional provisions at the time the act was accomplished apply, an issue which is in any event admitted by the Agent of the United States and his Counsel. Now, from 1894, the date of Albert Flegenheimer's naturalization, until he attained majority in 1911, and even later during a period of five years, until April 1917, the Bancroft Treaty with Wurttemberg was actually in force and definitively established the nationality of the individual concerned. The Commission is of the opinion that, even if only by way of hypothesis the jurisprudence developed by the Supreme Court in the *Perkins* v. *Elg* case were to apply, he lost his American nationality before the repeal of the aforesaid Treaty.

" In analysing the practice followed by the Department of State subsequent to the principles affirmed by the Supreme Court in the *Perkins* v. *Elg* case, it was not contended that no retroactive application thereof was made by the Administration to cases which had been dealt with many decades before. The practice of the Department of State was modified soon after the subject decision was rendered by the Supreme Court, and it is summed up in the following manner in a judgment of the District Court of New Jersey of November 17, 1953, concerning the *Rueff* v. *Brownell* case (116 F. Supp. 298, 302–303, 1953):

" ' . . . a minor, being a citizen of the United States who acquired derivatively the nationality of a foreign state through the foreign naturalization of a parent will not, in the absence of specifically applicable treaty stipulations, be considered by the Department as having lost his or her citizenship of the United States *provided shortly before or shortly after attaining majority the person concerned manifests his or her election to retain American citizenship and to return to the United States to reside.*' (Emphasis by the Court.)

" The Commission recalls that Section 504 of the Nationality Act of 1940, to which it already had had occasion to refer, specifically preserves that nationality status previously established by a person, whether this person has acquired or lost American nationality, and does not confer any retroactive effects on the provisions of the new law. Finally, the Commission notes that Albert Flegenheimer's older brothers, who were in the identical legal position in which he stood, very logically came to the conclusion that they could not acquire American nationality by election and applied for and secured their naturalization in the United States, in 1944 and 1947 respectively. This was the only method to be followed in order to regularly obtain the status of American nationals.

" The second precedent of the Supreme Court, invoked by the Plaintiff Party, is of no interest in the solution of the dispute submitted to the Commission.

" The *Mandoli* v. *Acheson* case, adjudicated in 1952,[1] involved a conflict between a *jure soli* and a *jure sanguinis* nationality. Mandoli was born in the United States of parents who had not been naturalized in that country; he thus had the status of a native born citizen by virtue of American law, and that of an Italian national, in application of Italian law. His parents returned to reside in Italy when he was still a minor; when he was 15 years old he made unsuccessful attempts to return to the United States; he renewed these attempts when he was 29 or 30 years old and, later, twice during the following eleven years. He finally obtained permission to enter the United States in order to obtain judicial recognition of his title to American nationality. On the basis of these facts, the Court decided that Mandoli had not expatriated himself, a solution which was unavoidable because the individual concerned had been vested with two nationalities since birth and the *Perkins* v. *Elg* doctrine on the expatriation of minors included in the naturalization of their parents abroad was not involved; it was not a question of election in favor of American nationality, but the recognition of title to nationality acquired *jure soli* in the United States and which had given rise to a dispute. The Commission does not consider this

[1 See *International Law Reports*, 1951, Case No. 64.]

precedent to be pertinent for the purpose of resolving the question of Albert Flegenheimer's nationality.

" The judicial decisions rendered by the lower courts of the United States, cited by the Plaintiff Party in support of its conclusions, are not pertinent; they were, in any event, all rendered subsequent to the Nationality Act of 1940.

" The case which has the greatest similarity with the Albert Flegenheimer case, is the *Rueff* v. *Brownell* judgment, which was decided by the District Court of New Jersey on November 17, 1953. The Petitioner was born in Germany in 1910 of United States native born nationals, and she herself was a *jure sanguinis* United States national; she was naturalized in Germany during minority, in 1918, together with her mother who had emigrated to that country. Following several steps taken at American Consulates, beginning in 1934, she applied, in 1939, shortly after the *Perkins* v. *Elg* decision, for an American passport which was refused; she went to the United States in 1945 and renewed her request to be issued a certificate of nationality in 1949. Following another refusal by the Administrative authorities, she submitted her request to the American courts. The District Court held she was an American national by virtue of Section 1993 of the Revised Statutes.

" The *Rueff* v. *Brownell* case is similar to the Albert Flegenheimer case because of certain peculiarities in common; birth of the person involved outside of the United States, collective effects of naturalization abroad, delay in election of American nationality. But they differ, on the other hand, on some very important points: American origin of Rueff's parents, whereas Samuel Flegenheimer was a naturalized American of Baden origin who promptly abandoned the United States; tardiness in the exercise of the right of election overstepping all tolerable measures in the Albert Flegenheimer case; and, above all, absence of a nationality treaty stipulation in the *Rueff* Case, since all Bancroft Treaties concluded with the various German States were repealed on April 6, 1917, prior to her mother's naturalization. This precedent is therefore not pertinent to the case submitted to this Commission.

" The other decisions invoked by the Plaintiff Party were rendered by United States Courts of Appeals, and they too do not appear to have sufficient analogy with the instant case for them to be considered by the Commission.

" The *Perri* v. *Dulles* case, decided by the Court of Appeals on July 24, 1953,[1] involved an Italian, born in Italy in 1913 of a father of Italian origin, naturalized as an American national, later redintegrated in his Italian nationality in 1926 together with his son, then a minor. The nationality of the latter was not established by treaty stipulation because Italy concluded no Bancroft Treaty with the

[1 3 Cir., 206 F. 2d 586; *International Law Reports*, 1953, at pp. 256 and 258.]

United States. The Court considered him to be exactly like a dual national, namely, an American national *jure sanguinis* and an Italian national by the collective effects that Italian law attributes to the redintegration of the father in Italian nationality; the Court applied the Nationality Act of 1940 and sent the case back to the District Court for examination as to whether or not the individual concerned could benefit by the supplementary delay in election provided for in Section 401 (a) of said Act.

" The *Lehmann* v. *Acheson* case was decided by the Court of Appeals on July 29, 1953;[1] here too a dual nationality was involved. Lehmann, a Swiss who was born in the United States in 1921, was brought to Switzerland in 1924; his father remained in America and was naturalized as an American national without thereby losing his Swiss nationality. The son, who also had title to Swiss citizenship, performed his militiary service in Switzerland and the Court decided that this compulsory service did not have the effect of depriving him of his American nationality with which he was vested *jure soli*. There are no treaty stipulations on nationality between the United States and Switzerland, but merely a convention of November 11, 1937, relating to the military obligations of certain dual nationals.

" The *Podea* v. *Acheson* case, decided on January 10, 1950,[2] and the *Richter* v. *Dulles* case, decided on May 17, 1957, only concern questions of expatriation as a result of oaths taken to foreign States by native born Americans and do not raise any naturalization problem.

" E. *On the inadmissibility of the Petition on grounds other than the absence of United States nationality.*—The Commission, taking as a basis the Bancroft Treaty concluded on July 27th, 1868, between the United States and Wurttemberg, is of the opinion that Albert Flegenheimer lost his American nationality through the naturalization of his father in Wurttemberg, in 1894, and that he never subsequently recovered it, either because he did not have a legal possibility to do so by virtue of laws which were applicable at the time of his naturalization in Germany, or, in the hypothesis most favorable to him, because it must be admitted that the right of election he claims he had in favor of American nationality was exercised too late by him.

" The Commission can therefore dispense with entering upon the remedy of law based on expatriation, resulting from an absence of *animus redeundi*, of persons naturalized in the United States, as the result of prolonged residence in their country of origin or in another foreign State. In the interest of an exhaustive analysis of Albert Flegenheimer's position *vis-à-vis* the United States, the Commission nevertheless considers it its duty to investigate whether the other remedies of law invoked are well founded or groundless.

[1 206 F. 2d 592; *International Law Reports*, 1953, p. 255.]
[2 179 F. 2d 306; *Annual Digest*, 1949, p. 197.]

" The Commission is of the opinion that it can reject outright the argument of the Respondent Party affirming that, by virtue of Section 2 of the Act of March 2, 1907, Albert Flegenheimer lost his title to American nationality, to all intents and purposes of law, for having taken an oath of allegiance to the Kingdom of Wurttemberg, because a clear, categorical and convincing evidence of this oath has not been submitted. The Italian Government assumes this oath was taken because the Constitution of the Kingdom of Wurttemberg of September 25, 1819, which remained in force until May 20, 1919, required that the oath of allegiance was to be taken by all native born Wurttemberg citizens, upon attaining the age of 16, or by all naturalized citizens on the date of their naturalization (Constitution of the Kingdom of Wurttemberg, Chapter III, Article 20).

" The Commission is of the opinion that Albert Flegenheimer, who was born in Wurttemberg as a United States national, does not fall under the category of persons who were to take the oath of allegiance when 16 years old; on the other hand, as he was four years old on the date of his naturalization, he could not have taken the oath at that time; it is possible that the subject oath was required of his father, Samuel Flegenheimer, but no document has been introduced in the record proving that this oath was actually taken by him. The Commission could not be satisfied with evidence based on inference in order to determine the nationality of the individual concerned.

" The Respondent Party attaches much importance to the theory of effective nationality, according to which, even supposing that Albert Flegenheimer was solely an American national, this nationality could not be productive of effects in the intercourse with Italy in order to obtain the application of Article 78 of the Treaty of Peace, in view of the fact that, during half a century, the individual concerned was considered as and considered himself to be a German national by his conduct, his sentiments, his interests. The Respondent Party contends that a nationality is not effective when it confines itself to establishing a nominal link between a State and an individual and is not supported by a social solidity resulting from a veritable solidarity of rights and duties between the State and its national. As was decided by the International Court of Justice in the *Nottebohm Case*, between Liechtenstein and Guatemala, in its decision of April 6, 1955,[1] and from which Italy intends to gain advantage:

' Conferred by a State, it only entitles that State to exercise protection *vis-à-vis* another State, if it constitutes a translation into juridical terms of the individual's connection with the State which has made him its national.' (*I.C.J. Reports*, 1955, p. 23.[2])

" Italy therefore considers that no effective bond of nationality exists between the United States and Albert Flegenheimer, even if

[1] *I.C.J. Reports.* 1955, pp. 12–26; *International Law Reports*, 1955, p. 349.]
[2] *Ibid.*, at p. 360.]

it were to be admitted that he was an American national on purely legal and nominal grounds. Italy concludes by saying that, on the international level, and whatever Albert Flegenheimer's position may be in connection with American municipal law, the United States is not entitled to exercise, in his behalf, the right of diplomatic protection, nor can they resort to the Commission to plead his case.

" The Agent of the Government of the United States and his Counsel rebut this argument in pointing out that their Opponents cannot, inasmuch as they are in a position of a third State, raise the question of effective nationality, because Italian nationality is not at stake, and, furthermore, if it were intended to apply this doctrine, it would be necessary to admit, at least beginning from the forfeiture of German nationality decreed in 1940 by the German authorities against the individual concerned, that American nationality was the only effective nationality, because Albert Flegenheimer left Germany definitively in 1937 to take up residence in the United States in 1941, the seat of his domicile, of his family and business interests.

" The Commission is of the opinion that it is doubtful that the International Court of Justice intended to establish a rule of general international law in requiring, in the *Nottebohm Case*, that there must exist an effective link between the person and the State in order that the latter may exercise its right of diplomatic protection in behalf of the former. The Court itself restricted the scope of its Decision by affirming that the acquisition of nationality in a State must be recognized by all other States,

' subject to the twofold reservation that, in the first place, what is involved is not recognition for all purposes but merely for the purposes of the admissibility of the Application, and, secondly, that what is involved is not recognition by all States but only by Guatemala.'

The Court further clarified its thought by affirming:

" ' The Court does not propose to go beyond the limited scope of the question which it has to decide, namely, whether the nationality conferred on Nottebohm can be relied upon as against Guatemala in justification of the proceedings instituted before the Court.' (*I.C.J. Reports*, 1955, p. 17.[1])

" The Court has thus distinctly affirmed the relative nature of its decision, and this Commission is of the opinion that the doctrine in support thereof cannot be opposed to the Government of the United States in this dispute.

" The theory of effective or active nationality was established, in the Law of Nations, and above all in international private law, for the purpose of settling conflicts between two national States, or two national laws, regarding persons simultaneously vested with both nationalities, in order to decide which of them is to be dominant,

[1 *International Law Reports*, 1955, at pp. 353–354.]

whether that described as nominal, based on legal provisions of a given legal system, or that described as effective or active, equally based on legal provisions of another legal system, but confirmed by elements of fact (domicile, participation in the political life, the center of family and business interests, etc.). It must allow one to make a distinction between two bonds of nationality equally founded in law, which is the stronger and hence the effective one.

" Application thereof was made in cases of dual nationality, like the *Carnevaro Case*, decided on May 3, 1912, by the Court of Permanent Arbitration [*sic*.], between Italy and Peru, as well as in many decisions rendered by Mixed Arbitral Tribunals established under the Treaties of Peace from 1919 to 1923, especially the Franco–German Tribunal in its decision of July 10, 1926, in the *Barthez de Montfort* v. *Treuhänder* case,[1] and the Hungary–Jugoslav Tribunal in its decision of July 12, 1926, in the *Baron de Born* case (*Revue générale de droit international public*, 1913, p. 329; *T.A.M.*, vol. VI, pp. 806, 809 and pp. 499, 503[2]).

"The 1930 Hague Convention concerning certain questions relating to the conflicts of nationality laws has, likewise, placed this theory at the basis of its Article 5, which is strictly limited to cases of multiple nationality and which reads as follows:

" ' In a third State, the individual possessing more than one nationality shall be treated as if he were vested with one nationality only. Without prejudice to the rules of law applied in the third State in matters of personal status and subject to the conventions in force, this State may, in its territory, recognize exclusively amongst the nationalities possessed by such individual, either the nationality of the country in which he mainly and principally resides, or the nationality of the State to which, according to the circumstances, he appears to be more attached in fact.'

" The theory of effective or active nationality was nevertheless limited in its application by the principle of the unopposability of the nationality of a third State, which, in an international dispute caused by a person with multiple nationalities, permits the dismissal of the nationality of the third State, even when it should be considered as predominant in the light of the circumstances; this was the decision rendered on June 8, 1932, by the Arbitral Tribunal in the *Salem Case*, disputed between the United States and Egypt, when this latter country invoked the Persian nationality which the claimant possessed, besides Egyptian nationality, to obtain a rejection of the claim of the United States (*U.N.R.I.A.A.*, vol. II, p. 1188[3]).

" Reference should also be made, in the same sense, to the decision rendered on June 10, 1955, by the Italian–United States

[1 *Annual Digest*, 1925–1926, Case No. 206.]
[2 *Ibid.*, Case No. 204.]
[3 *Ibid.*, 1931–1932, Case No. 98.]

Conciliation Commission, completed by a Third Member, de Yanguas Messia, in the *Strunsky Mergé Case*[1] involving a native born American national who had married an Italian subject whose nationality she had acquired, without, however, losing her American nationality, and was hence in the legal position of a person vested with dual nationality; the Commission took into consideration the Italian nationality which it held to be predominant, but pointed out that effective nationality does not allow a Respondent State to invoke, against the Plaintiff State that accords protection to one of its nationals, the fact that the latter is also in possession of the nationality of a third State; the result is that American subjects who are not in possession of Italian nationality, but of the nationality of a third State, can be considered as United Nations nationals under Article 78 of the Treaty of Peace, even when the predominant nationality is that of the said third State (*Archives of the Commission*, No. 55).

" But when a person is vested with only one nationality, which is attributed to him or her either *jure sanguinis* or *jure soli*, or by a valid naturalization entailing the positive loss of the former nationality, the theory of effective nationality cannot be applied without the risk of causing confusion. It lacks a sufficiently positive basis to be applied to a nationality which finds support in a state law. There does not in fact exist any criterion of proven effectiveness for disclosing the effectiveness of a bond with a political collectivity, and the persons by the thousands who, because of the facility of travel in the modern world, possess the positive legal nationality of a State, but live in foreign States where they are domiciled and where their family and business center is located, would be exposed to nonrecognition, at the international level, of the nationality with which they are undeniably vested by virtue of the laws of their national State, if this doctrine were to be generalized.

" The Commission wishes to specify that it is by virtue of the rules of State positive law, and not on the grounds of social, family, sentimental or business effectiveness, that it is led to determine objectively that Albert Flegenheimer, who was never vested with dual nationality, lost title to his American nationality, in application of the international treaties concluded by the United States. Likewise, it is also on the basis of an American State law that he acquired American nationality at birth through a German father who became a naturalized American.

" The Agent of the Italian Government and his Counsel, in connection with the foregoing, have further contended that, always working on the assumption that Albert Flegenheimer had preserved his American nationality, the United States Petition should be rejected by virtue of what they describe as apparent nationality.

[1 *International Law Reports*, 1955, p. 443 (*sub nom. Mergé Claim*).]

The explanation of this theory lies in the fact that the allegedly injured individual, at the time of the March 18, 1941, transaction, availed himself of his German nationality in order to obtain, in matters of transfer of currency, certain advantages which were reserved by Italy to countries that were her allies; they contend that because Albert Flegenheimer always used a German passport, even after his *ex autoritata* denationalization in Germany, in 1940, he could not now avail himself of his American nationality in order to benefit by the advantages which the Treaty of Peace guarantees to United Nations nationals. Italy envisages therein additional grounds for affirming that the proceedings instituted in behalf of the protection of Albert Flegenheimer's interests are inadmissible even if the latter's nationality was effective and at the same time the only legal one.

" The Agent of the Government of the United States and his Counsel deny the existence of a rule of public international law permitting the granting of predominance to a nationality invoked by an allegedly injured party when he does not possess that nationality.

" The Commission cannot follow, on this point, the Italian Government's arguments; they appear to be unfounded in fact and in law.

" In fact, the Commission has noted that Albert Flegenheimer's German nationality was not a decisive factor when the Italian Ministry of Exchange and Foreign Currency, on June 6, 1941, authorized the payment of 277,860.60 dollars in New York, because the said Ministry described the Flegenheimer brothers in its authorization as ' Ebrei ex-germanici ' (former German Jews) and had knowledge at that time of the fact that Albert Flegenheimer had lost his German nationality (see . . . the considerations of fact No. 15 [above, p. 96]).

" From the legal viewpoint, the Commission notes that the doctrine of apparent nationality cannot be considered as accepted by the Law of Nations. In international jurisprudence one finds decisions based on the ' *non concedit venire contra factum proprium* ' principle which corresponds to the Anglo-Saxon institution of estoppel; it allows a Respondent State to object to the admissibility of a legal action directed against it by the national State of the allegedly injured party, when the latter has neglected to indicate his true nationality, or has concealed it, or has invoked another nationality at the time the fact giving rise to the dispute occurred, or when the national State has made erroneous communications to another State thus fixing the conduct to be followed by the latter.

" *Wilson Case*, Moore [*International Arbitrations* (1898)], vol. III, No. 2, p. 555;

" Decision of July 26, 1927, of C.P.J.I., *Chorzów Industrial Plant [Factory] Case* (Jurisdiction), P.C.I.J., Series A, No. 8, p. 31.[1]

" See also Borchard [in *Annuaire de l'Institut de Droit International*], 1931, I, p. 368 and 399 *et seq.*

" The *Rothmann*[2] precedent invoked by the Respondent Party seems to be of little pertinence. That case, which was adjudicated by the tripartite Commission between the United States, Austria and Hungary in 1928, concerned a former Austrian national who had been naturalized in the United States, had returned to Austria where he had resided for a number of years posing as an Austrian and had been drafted into military service in Austria during World War I, after the American diplomatic mission in that State had affirmed, upon being questioned by the Austrian authorities, that Rothmann had lost his American nationality by virtue of the Act of 1907. When the war was over, Rothmann was redintegrated in his American nationality, by virtue of Section 2, para. 2, of the Act of 1907, by rebutting the presumption of voluntary expatriation following a prolonged sojourn in his country of origin. The United States accorded him its protection for obtaining from Austria compensation for the damage he had suffered as the result of having been drafted in the Austrian Army. Judge Parker rejected the Petition filed by the United States, without referring to any so-called doctrine of apparent nationality, but merely taking as a basis the fact that on the date on which the damage occurred, the American authorities did not consider Rothmann as a United States national. Judge Parker affirmed:

" ' The Commissioner rejects the contention that the subsequent overcoming of the presumptions (of expatriation) can affect the nationality of this claim which has arisen during the time when the claimant was not entitled to recognition and protection as an American citizen; especially as the very existence of the claim turns on the state of claimant's citizenship at the time it arose.' (*Am. J. Int. [Law]*, vol. XXIII, p. 182 *et seq.* (186).)

" If the predominance of an apparent nationality over every other nationality were a rule of general international law, Judge Parker could have all the more easily adopted it in that the legal appearance of the loss of American nationality had been created by an official statement of the American authorities later claiming compensation for their national who was injured by that very statement. In this case there is no apparent nationality artificially created either by a third State, Germany, or by the individual concerned, Albert Flegenheimer; the latter was in good faith when he used his German passport, subsequent to the issuance of a decree of

[1 *Annual Digest*, 1927–1928, Case No. 342.]
[2 *Ibid.*, Case No. 168 (*sub nom. Rothmann v. Austria and Hungary*).]

which he was unaware and under which he forfeited his German citizenship, because he was vested with German nationality and German nationality alone from 1894 to 1940.

" The predominance of apparent nationality over legal nationality, on the other hand, was dismissed in the *Wildermann* v. *Stinnes* case, by the decision of the Mixed German–Rumanian Tribunal of June 8, 1926,[1] which refused to give any importance to the non fraudulent use of a foreign passport; in this decision it is affirmed that:

' It is an established fact that the petitioner was requested to lecture at Oxford University, that until 1922 he passed himself off as a Russian and that in 1922 he had his Russian passport renewed in England. The Minister of Home Affairs did not envisage thereby a tacit renunciation of Rumanian nationality. . . . On the other hand, so long as the petitioner did not succeed in having his Rumanian nationality recognized, he was forced to use the only passport which he could obtain, that is to say, a Russian passport. The compulsory renewal of this Russian passport could have no meaning and the petitioner's whole attitude, beginning from the time when he gained knowledge of his rights in Rumania, manifestly rules out his alleged tacit renunciation of his Rumanian nationality.' *T.A.M.*, vol. VI, 485 *et seq.* (495).)

" Barring cases of fraud, negligence or serious errors which are not proved in the instant case, the Commission holds that there is no rule of the Law of Nations, universally recognized in the practice of States, permitting it to recognize a nationality in a person against the provisions of law or treaty stipulations, because nationality is a legal notion which must be based on a State law in order to exist and be productive of effects in international law; a mere appearance cannot replace provisions of positive law governing the conditions under which a nationality is granted or lost, because international law admits that every State has a right, subject to treaty stipulations concluded with other States, to sovereignly decide who are its nationals.

" F. *On the question of the applicability to Albert Flegenheimer of Article 78, para. 9 (a), sub-para. 2, of the Treaty of Peace with Italy.*— Article 78, para. 9 (a), sub-para. 2, of the Treaty of Peace with Italy of February 10, 1947, places persons who were treated as enemies in Italy during World War II on the same level as United Nations nationals; it reads as follows:

" ' The term " United Nations nationals " also includes all individuals, corporations or associations which, under the laws in force in Italy, during the war, have been treated as enemy '.

" In its Order of February 18, 1956, the Commission decided to examine the question of Albert Flegenheimer's nationality firstly. In the Brief submitted by the Agent of the United States on this question on May 30, 1956, resuming the arguments already developed

[1 *Annual Digest*, 1923–1924, Case No. 120.]

in its Reply of November 17, 1952, the question of the applicability of this provision was raised; the Agent of the Italian Government dealt with this question in his Reply Brief, filed on October 15, 1956, and the two Agents conclusively explained their respective positions on this point in their final Rebuttal Observations, by the Agent of the Government of the United States on October 28, 1957, and in the final Counter Reply, by the Agent of the Italian Government on November 9, 1957. The Commission intends all the more to affirm that this question cannot be eliminated from the discussions in that it is closely linked with the question of Albert Flegenheimer's nationality, by virtue of the Treaty of Peace itself.

" The Agent of the Government of the United States contends that the aforesaid Article 78, para. 9 (a), sub-para. 2, of the Treaty of Peace has the effect of including in the expression ' United Nations nationals ' all individuals, who were not necessarily ' treated ' as enemies, but considered as such under the legislation in force in Italy during the war.

" He bases this interpretation on the Russian text of the aforementioned article, where the word ' rassmatrivat ' which is used therein has only one meaning, that of ' considering ' because the expression ' treated ' can be obtained in Russian by the words ' obchoditsia ' or ' podvergnut dejstwiyu ', which terms are not employed in the Russian text of the Treaty. As Article 90 of the Treaty considers the English, French and Russian texts as authenticated originals, the United States Agent contends that the Russian text also should be taken into consideration in order to obtain the exact meaning of Article 78, para. 9 (a), sub-para. 2, and in this connection he refers to Decision No. 2 of the French-Italian Conciliation Commission of August 29, 1949, which affirmed:

' whatever the genesis of the two texts may be, it is not lawful to give exclusive consideration to one of these texts (French and English); the interpreter should rather try to clarify one by making use of the other.' (Recueil des Décisions, 1er fasc., p. 100.[1])

" He justifies the preference to be given to the Russian text by the Italian translation of the Treaty, where the term ' traités ', or ' treated ', is translated by the expression ' considerate ', which corresponds exactly with the Russian text. Although the Italian translation does not have the value of an authenticated origin, the United States Agent contends that it can be opposed to the Italian Government in the instant case, in that it expresses in a clear and unequivocal manner the meaning attached by it to that Article of the Treaty. He reaches the conclusion that the word ' traités ' or ' treated ', was intended by the contracting Parties to mean ' considered ' and that the Italian Government is not allowed, by virtue

[1 *International Law Reports*, 1951, Case No. 128 (*sub nom. Re Italian Special Capital Levy Duties*), at p. 409.]

of the doctrine of estoppel, to give that provision another meaning in order to modify the extent of its obligations.

" On the basis of this argument, the Agent of the United States invokes Article 3 of the Italian War Law (Law Decree 1415) of July 8, 1938, establishing the two following conditions under which a person, who is not a national of an enemy State, can nevertheless be considered as an enemy subject: (1) if said person is stateless; (2) if said person resides in an enemy country. He draws the conclusion therefrom that on the date of the conclusion of the allegedly vitiated contract as the result of duress, that is, March 18, 1941, Albert Flegenheimer fulfilled these two conditions because he had forfeited his German nationality and resided in Canada, a country then at war with Italy; in his opinion, Albert Flegenheimer is thus entitled to the benefits of Article 78 of the Treaty of Peace.

" The Italian Government denies the correctness of this argument and contends that the mere possibility of being considered as enemy is not sufficient to entitle one to the restitution and restoration imposed by this Treaty on Italy, but that it is necessary that these actually have been treated as enemy, and invokes the jurisprudence established by the Conciliation Commission in similar cases.

" This Commission holds that the arguments of the Plaintiff Party are not well founded because:

" (a) The Commission does not deny that the texts of the Treaty, prepared in three languages, all have the same value of authenticated originals, and that the interpreter must reconcile them one with the other.

" In French, the *Littré* dictionary gives no less than twenty-three meanings to the word ' *traiter*,' none of which has the purport of ' *considérer* '; that which comes closest is that of ' giving such and such qualification '; but it is not the usual meaning. It is universally admitted in international law that the natural meaning of the terms used must be taken as the starting point of the *processus* in interpreting treaties. In its natural sense, the word ' *traiter* ' in French means: ' to act towards a person in such and such a manner '. The usual meaning of the English word ' treat ' is no different, according to the Harrap's *Standard French and English Dictionary*. The expression ' *considéré* ', in French, may have five meanings, according to the *Littré* dictionary, and the following are those that could be taken: ' have regard to, take into account, believe, esteem '; the same applies in English.

" Therefore, the expression used in the Russian text cannot be reconciled exactly with the French and English texts of the Treaty; it would mean that the said Treaty would have to be applied to persons who, under the provisions of the laws in force in Italy, were believed, or seemed to have been enemies. Article 78, para. 9 (a), sub-para. 2, would not be thereby devoid of meaning, but it must be admitted that it would lead to a solution which would conflict with the other provisions of the Treaty. The preference accorded to the Russian text by the Plaintiff Party is the result of a true and proper vicious circle, because it offers as proof of the correctness of its solution the very supposition from which it started.

" On the other hand, it is not admissible to take the Italian translation of the Treaty to corroborate one of the three authenticated originals, nor to contend that the Italian Government is bound by the Italian text, on the grounds that this translation should be an indication of the manner in which Italy has understood her obligations arising out of the Treaty. The Commission holds that the principle of ' estoppel ' or ' *non concedit venire contra factum proprium*', could be opposed to the Respondent Party only if, by declarations to the contracting States, or by conclusive acts, or even by an attitude regularly taken towards them, it had given Article 78, para. 9 (*a*), sub-para. 2, of the Treaty of Peace an interpretation corresponding to the Russian text, but not by a translation devoid of official value, and which, according to the allegations of the Agent of the Italian Government, is, in actual fact, the collective work of all the contracting States, who purposely refused to give it any character of authenticity. It is therefore devoid of all international legal significance and Italy has never accepted the meaning resulting out of the Russian text.

" It cannot be denied that the interpretation of the text of a treaty can be made only by using the versions that have been declared to be authenticated originals by the Treaty itself.

" (*b*) When the texts of an international treaty prepared in different languages cannot be exactly reconciled with one another, the Commission, according to the teachings of international law, believes that adjustment should be made on the basis of a common denominator which answers the meaning of all the texts stated to be authenticated originals by the Parties. It is universally admitted that treaties can confer rights and impose obligations on the contracting States only within the limits within which the intent of these States became manifest in a concordant manner. It is clear that the expression ' *considérés* ' of the Russian Treaty [text], includes ' *traités* ' or ' treated ', because a person who was not a United Nations national, but who was treated as enemy by the Italian Government, must have forcibly been first considered as enemy by the aforesaid Italian Government, whereas the reverse proposition is not correct.

" (*c*) The true and proper meaning of all international treaties should always be found in the purpose aimed at by the Parties.

" The Russian text of Article 78, para. 9 (*a*), sub-para. 2, of the Treaty of Peace, does not seem to answer the intent of the contracting Parties, at the time they drew up the Part VII concerning property, rights and interests, particularly Nos. 1 to 4 of Article 78, for the purpose of assuring restoration to persons injured by exceptional war measures introduced in Italian legislation. A restoration of property, rights and interests is not conceivable unless these were previously injured in such a manner as to engage the responsibility of the Italian State, subject only to material and direct war damage caused by military operations.

" This is especially evident in Article 78, No. 3, of the Treaty of Peace which provides:

" ' The Italian Government shall invalidate transfers involving property, rights and interests of any description belonging to United Nations nationals, where such transfers resulted from force or duress exerted by Axis Governments or their agencies during the war.'

" A person can be ' believed to be, or esteemed to be ' an enemy without any injury resulting thereby either to himself or to his property, rights or interests; for such injury to materialize, it is necessary that there be a concrete course of action by the state authorities, having prejudicial consequences for the person against whom such course of action is taken. The negotiators did not aim at creating an ' enemy status ' whereby it would be sufficient for the subject conditions to materialize under Italian law to make the provisions of the Treaty of Peace applicable. The meaning to be given to the Article in question is hence one of concrete, effective treatment, meted out to a person by reason of his enemy status, and not by abstract considerations envisaging the mere possibility of subjecting him to a course of action by the State of such a nature as to cause injury on the grounds that such a person would fulfil the conditions for being considered, under the terms of a legal provision of municipal law, as an enemy person.

" (d) It should be furthermore considered that the provision contained in Article 78, para. 9 (a), sub-para. 2, of the Treaty of Peace, is a rule of an exceptional character, in that it extends the diplomatic protection of the United Nations to persons who are not their nationals; like every exception, it must be interpreted in a restrictive sense, because it deviates from the general rules of the Law of Nations on this point. Likewise for this reason the English and French texts of the Treaty answer the intentions of the co-contracting Parties better than the Russian text.

" (e) The interpretation of the Article in question of the Treaty of Peace through Article 3 of the Italian War Law of July 8, 1938, does not lead to the conclusion proclaimed by the Plaintiff Party. If it is correct that the Treaty refers to this Law for determining who are non-enemy persons and can nevertheless be held to be an enemy ' under the terms of the legislation in force in Italy during the war ', it adds, in the French and English texts, which the Commission considers to be the correct expression of the intent of the Parties, that they must have been treated as enemies. Two conditions must hence be simultaneously fulfilled for entailing the application of Article 78, para. 9 (*a*), sub-para. 2, of the Treaty of Peace:

" (1) A regulation of principle, contained in Italian legislation in force during the war, of considering certain persons as enemies, even though they did not possess the nationality of a State at war with Italy; this is the case of stateless persons residing in enemy countries;

" (2) Implementation of this provision by actual treatment meted out to a person because he is enemy.

" The interpretation set forth herein confirms in full the interpretation which had already been given this Article in several previous decisions of the Italian–United States and the French–Italian Conciliation Commissions.

" In the *Bacharach Case* (No. 22), decided on February 19, 1954,[1] by agreement of the Representatives of the United States and Italy, without resort to a Third Member, this viewpoint was adopted in the following terms:

" ' The Agent of the Government of the United States of America refers also to the provisions of Article 3 of the Italian War Law which declares that stateless persons residing in enemy countries are considered enemy nationals; but this provision contains an abstract statement which is not sufficient in itself alone to constitute treatment as enemy; this provision could become important only in the event that it were the basis for any restrictive measure that may have been taken against the claimant or her property, which does not seem to be the case. . . . To be treated as enemy necessarily implies on the one hand that there be an actual course of action on the part of the Italian authority (and not an abstract possibility of adopting one), and on the other hand that said course of action be aimed at obtaining that the individual who is subjected to it be placed on the same level as that of enemy nationals.' (Archives of the Commission.[2])

" The Agent of the Government of the United States points out that this decision refers to a position of fact which differs from that of Albert Flegenheimer, because Mrs. Bacharach was a Jewish person who left Italy before war broke out, on September 7, 1938, for fear of the racial persecutions, and left her furniture in a storage room in Milan where it was destroyed as a result of an air raid on August 12–13, 1943; in the Albert Flegenheimer case, the cancellation of a derogatory contract is involved. The Commission believes that if the facts are different, the applicable principles are the same, because the property of the person concerned was not subjected to sequestration or other measures of control on the part of the Italian Government or its agents.

" The argument contained in the *Bacharach* decision with respect to the meaning of Article 78, para. 9 (*a*), sub-paragraph 2, of the Treaty of Peace, was confirmed by three decisions rendered by the

[1 *International Law Reports*, 1955, p. 646.]
[2 *Ibid.*, at p. 648.]

Italian–United States Conciliation Commission, completed by a Third Member, on September 26, 1956; these decisions involved the *Treves*, *Levi* and *Wollemborg* cases,[1] in which the Commission distinctly established that the applicability of this Article presupposes a concrete course of action by the Italian authorities on the basis of the legislation in force in Italy during the war, actually subjecting the person concerned to measures intended for enemy nationals (Archives of the Commission). The French-Italian Conciliation Commission, completed by a Third Member, adopted the same interpretation in the case of " *Società Generale dei Metalli Preziosi* ", in its Decision No. 167 of March 9, 1954; this case involved a company established under Italian law but attached by the Italian authorities by reason of the importance of a French company's participation in its capital stock. The Commission affirmed:

' Because the measures, described above, were taken against her in Italy the Società Generale dei Metalli Preziosi, under Article 78, para. 9 (*a*), sub-para. 2, must be considered as having been treated as enemy by the Italian Government.' (*Recueil des Décisions*, 5e fasc., p. 12.)

" The Agent of the United States has nevertheless tried to establish that Albert Flegenheimer was actually treated as enemy during the war, under the Italian laws. He points out, a fact which cannot be denied, that beginning on April 29, 1940, Albert Flegenheimer became a stateless person because his German nationality was forfeited, and that furthermore, as he had resided in Canada in 1940 and in 1941, he was domiciled at that time in a State that was at war with Italy, thus fulfilling the conditions required by the Italian War Law of 1938 for the purpose of treatment as enemy. As proof of actual treatment as enemy by the Italian authorities, the Agent of the United States cites the three documents, described below, connected with the sale of Albert Flegenheimer's 47,907 shares of the Società Finanziaria Industriale Veneta:

" (*a*) A letter dated June 15, 1940, written by his general attorney, Mr. Valenti, in Milan, to Mr. Montesi, reading as follows:

" ' I have been informed that ISTCAMBI, because of the measures taken against subjects of enemy States, has *deferred* the transfer of the Finanziaria shares.

" ' I have, in turn, hastened to explain to the informer that no restrictive measures can be applied against Mr. Flegenheimer, a German national, because the circumstance that he resides in Canada is irrelevant.'

" (*b*) A certificate of the Italian Consul General in New York dated September 18, 1940, affirming that Albert Flegenheimer submitted a German passport from which it appeared that he was a German national and resided at 1795 Riverside Drive, New York.

[1 *International Law Reports*, 1957, pp. 313, 303 and 654, respectively.]

" (c) A letter dated March 11, 1941, written by the ' Ministero Scambi e Valute ' to the ' Società Finanziaria Industriale Veneta ', the most important excerpts of which are the following:

" ' We refer to your letters of February 26th ult., with which you have forwarded a list of the foreign Corporations which will purchase, cash payment, your shares owned by the Flegenheimer brothers, Albert and Joseph, jewish persons formerly German nationals, and at present deposited in Italy in the " Foreign Jews " dossier.

" ' . . . In connection with the foregoing, we confirm our agreement to the operation indicated above, while, in order that appropriate instructions may be issued to the competent bodies, we request you to specify the amounts for which the subject shares are to be transferred to the " Distilleria di Cavarzere ".'

" The Plaintiff Party believes that Albert Flegenheimer, on the basis of these documents, inasmuch as he was a stateless person residing in an enemy country during World War II, fulfilled the conditions of Article 3 of the Italian War Law of 1938, and that it was for this reason that the Italian authorities, prior to the derogatory contract of March 18, 1941, raised difficulties in connection with the transfer of the price of the sold shares, because the authorization to pay the $277,860.60 in New York was given only three months after the conclusion of the contract, namely, on June 11, 1941; he was thence actually treated as enemy at a time when the Italian authorities could no longer consider him as a German national because they themselves qualified him as a Jew, formerly a German national.

" The Agent of the Government of the United States contends that the Italian Government, after alleging in the course of these proceedings that the remittance in dollars to New York had been possible only because Flegenheimer had deceived the Italian Government by invoking his German nationality in order to benefit by a treatment reserved to the nationals of an allied State, can now no longer justify a measure it had taken in favor of the person by stating that it was once more misguided by the fact that Albert Flegenheimer had told the Italian Consul General in New York that he was domiciled in that city, at a date (June 1941) when the United States was not yet at war; the principle of estoppel would oppose this.

" He concludes therefrom that the Italian authorities treated Albert Flegenheimer as enemy twice, first in 1940 and then in 1941; insofar as necessary, he formulated his conclusions in this connection under No. V.

" This Commission fails to discover, either in these documents or in these allegations, proof of a treatment as enemy meted out to the individual concerned by the Italian authorities.

" Lawyer Valenti's letter of June 15, 1940, refers to a former deed of sale of May 1, 1940, with the ' Société Générale de Sucreries et

Raffineries Roumaine ', in Brussels (a company of the Montesi Group); this sale related to the same 47,907 shares of the ' Società Finanziaria Industriale Veneta ' which were the property of Albert Flegenheimer; the price of $239,535 was to be paid to the ' Société Générale de Belgique ' in Brussels as soon as possible, in favor of the Bank of Manhattan Company at New York. The shares were to remain on deposit with the ' Banca Popolare Cooperativa Anonima di Novara ' until confirmation was received by this Italian bank from the aforesaid ' Société Générale de Belgique ' that the amount in dollars had been received. A stake of 1,400,000 lire was the object of a supplementary contract of May 16, 1940. It had been agreed that if within the time limit of ten days after the Italian bank had received the sold shares, the amount due in dollars was not paid, the contract would be cancelled and considered null and void. In the supplementary contract, it was furthermore provided that the amount in lire was to be paid ' as soon as " Istituto Nazionale per i Cambi con l'Estero " has confirmed . . . the authorization to effect the operation already given by the " Ministero Scambi e Valute " in its communication of April 1, 1940, . . . and April 30, 1940 . . . against the withdrawal of the sold shares.' It was further stipulated that the sale of the shares would be revoked and cancelled if the remittance of the sold shares was not made within the time limit of one month beginning from May 16, 1940, and that the contract would likewise be invalidated and cancelled if the purchasing company did not effect payment of the $239,535 due to the ' Société Générale de Belgique ', or failed to obtain from this latter company a statement establishing that it had effected remittance of this sum to the Bank of Manhattan Company at New York.

" As Italy entered the war on June 10, 1940, these contracts do not fall under the provisions of Article 78, paragraph 3, of the Treaty of Peace which contemplates only contracts conluded during the war, under force or duress exerted by the Italian Government or its agents. Lawyer Valenti's letter of June 15, 1940, does not furnish proof that the Italian authorities ordered the withholding of the transfer of Albert Flegenheimer's shares; the difficulties which were pointed out were in any event promptly removed as the result of the German nationality which was at that time attributed to the individual concerned. There is no indication permitting one to admit that he was treated as enemy by reason of his statelessness, because the Italian authorities were unaware at that time, as Flegenheimer himself was unaware of the fact that he had lost his German nationality a few days before the conclusion of the contract, namely, on April 29, 1940, because the forfeiture decreed against him by the authorities of his country of origin was published in the ' Deutscher Reichsanzeiger und Preussischer Staatsanzeiger ', No. 103, only on May 4, 1940, thus subsequent to the conclusion of the principal contract of May 1, 1940. This lack of knowledge as to the true status of the individual concerned appears also from the statement of the Italian Consulate General in New York of September 18, 1940, affirming Albert Flegenheimer's German nationality on the basis of the German passport submitted by the latter and affirming, further, that he was domiciled in New York. It appears that the Agent of the United States wishes to take advantage of this incorrect information in order to rebut the theory of apparent nationality propounded by Italy; but this criticism is badly directed, because it is not a question of ascertaining whether the individual concerned made improper use of his German nationality, but whether or not the Italian authorities treated him as enemy, notwithstanding his apparent nationality, because he was a stateless person and was residing in an enemy country at the same time. This question must be settled negatively.

" In actual fact, the execution of the former contract was impeded by the German invasion of Belgium, which began on May 10, 1940, as the purchasing Company's head office was in Brussels. Neither Albert Flegenheimer's statelessness, nor his domicile in Canada were the cause of the impediment. Proof of the foregoing is found in lawyer Valenti's letter of July 16, 1940, wherein it is noted that the ' Istituto Nazionale per i Cambi con l'Estero ' had authorized the transfer of Albert Flegenheimer's 47,907 Finanziaria shares. The impossibility to pay the price of the sale at Brussels in favor of a New York bank is due to the measures taken by the occupying Power in Belgium during World War II, and it is as the result of the application of the stipulations concurred [in] by the parties that the contracts of May 1 and May 16, 1940, became null and void and could not be carried out.

" They were replaced by the contract of June 6, 1941, which was concluded with an Italian company of the Montesi group, before the United States entered the war on December 8, 1941, at a time when Albert Flegenheimer resided there. His status of statelessness was known on that date, but he was not domiciled in a country that was Italy's enemy. He thence did not fulfil the necessary conditions for being considered as an enemy person under the terms of Article 3 of the Italian War Law of 1938, and, in fact, he was not treated as such. The letter dated March 11, 1941, of the ' Ministero per gli Scambi e per le Valute ', invoked by the Agent of the Government of the United States, establishes that the operation of the sale had not been hindered by the Italian Government or its agents; on the contrary, the latter authorized the payment to the Bank of Manhattan Company at New York of the price established in the new contract of sale, namely, $277, 860.60, which sum, however, was immediately blocked upon arrival because the American nationality of the individual concerned had not been recognized by the United States, which country he had entered on a German passport.

" Treatment as enemy, according to the final written observations (Rebuttal) of the Plaintiff Party would flow from a delay of less than three months in the transfer of dollars to the New York bank, effected on June 6, 1941, while the second contract was dated March 18, 1941, delay which the Plaintiff attributes to the knowledge of Albert Flegenheimer's statelessness by the Italian authorities and to his residence in Canada, an enemy country, so that, in their opinion, he automatically fell, under the terms of the Italian legislation, within the category of persons considered as enemy. This argument does not appear to be sufficient to establish that the individual concerned was treated as enemy by Italy, as the 1938 War Law provided that enemy nationals, or individuals considered as such, were under prohibition to perform any operation in connection with their securities or property (Article 312), under penalty of having their securities or property sequestered (Article 295) or, possibly, of submitting these securites or property to forced sale and sequestration of the proceeds. It is not alleged that any such measure was taken against the individual concerned by the Italian authorities, who, on the contrary, authorized a bank transfer of the price in dollars, in free currency and without any reduction, and liberated the securities owned by Albert Flegenheimer from the blocking applied to all foreigners, under the Italian laws on currencies, without consideration of their nationality or religion. The Commission fails to see in this three months' delay, which appears to be normal in time of war, a hostile treatment, as this must have the characteristics of a discriminatory and prejudicial treatment which was not applicable to all non-Italian property, rights or interests.

" This Commission is of the opinion that the English and French texts of Article 78, para. 9 (a), sub-para. 2, of the Treaty of Peace with Italy correspond better than the Russian text to the intention of the negotiators and the conditions which they intended to settle and, therefore, these must prevail over a less adequate text drawn up in another language.

" Furthermore, as the Plaintiff has not established that Albert Flegenheimer was even plausibly treated as enemy by the Italian authorities, under the terms of Italian legislation, the Commission holds as non-pertinent the conclusion directed at obtaining from the Italian Government the production of all the acts and documents in the possession of the Italian authorities, for the years 1940 and 1941, concerning foreign exchange operations of the ' Società Finanziaria Industriale Veneta ', of the corporations controlled by the said Company, as well as those concerning Mr. Montesi personally, particularly those relating to the purchase of Albert Flegenheimer's ownership interest in Finanziaria.

" In the Lovett-Lombardo Agreement, concluded on August 14, 1947, and described as ' Memorandum of Understanding between the Government of the United States of America and the Italian Government concerning the settlement of certain wartime claims and related matters', invoked by the Plaintiff Party, the Italian Government, as a result of the waiver by the Government of the United States of certain claims based on the Treaty of Peace and the concession by the latter of certain advantages to Italy, in particular that of allowing her to rebuild the tonnage of her commercial fleet, consented to a broad extension of the protection accorded by Article 78 of the aforesaid Treaty to American nationals who claimed the restitution of their property and interests which had been transferred as the result of measures of seizure or control on June 10, 1940, or thereafter.

" The Commission is of the opinion that in the instant case this Agreement cannot obtain the effect of giving Article 78, of which it is only a broad interpretation, the authority of according American nationals, on certain claims, an extension of protection; this protection, in fact, rests completely on the fundamental condition established by this Article, that is, title to United States nationality with which the individual concerned must be vested in order that he may avail himself of the subject Agreement. It therefore presupposes that the injured party must be in a position to submit evidence, to the full satisfaction of law, of his status of United Nations national, a condition which the Commission cannot hold as having been fulfilled in Albert Flegenheimer's case.

" G. *On the relevant dates for the applicability of Article 78 of the Treaty of Peace with Italy.*—Articles 78, para. 9 (*a*), sub-paragraph 1, of the Treaty of Peace with Italy provides:

" ' " United Nations nationals " means individuals who are nationals of any of the United Nations, or corporations or associations organized under the laws of any of the United Nations, at the coming into force of the present Treaty, provided that the said individuals, corporations or associations also had this status on September 3, 1943, the date of the Armistice with Italy.'

" Therefore, the dates which serve as criteria are September 3, 1943, and September 15, 1947 (coming into force of the Treaty).
" The Lovett-Lombardo Agreement contains another solution in its Article V:

" ' For the purpose of this *Memorandum* of Understanding, the term " nationals " means individuals who are nationals of the United States of America, or of Italy, or corporations or associations organized under the laws of the United States of America and Italy, at the coming into force of this *Memorandum* of Understanding, provided that under Article 3 above, nationals of the United States of America shall, for the purpose of receiving compensation, also have held this status either at the time at which their property was damaged or on September 3, 1943, the date of the Armistice with Italy.'

" A lengthy dispute arose between the High Parties to these proceedings on the question as to whether the admissibility of a Petition for restoration or restitution is subject to proof of United Nations nationality:

(a) on the date on which the damage was suffered by one of their nationals as well as on the other two dates established by the Treaty of Peace; or

(b) on the dates of September 3, 1943, and September 15, 1947, if this nationality was acquired subsequent to the date of the damage; or

(c) alternatively, either on the date of the damage, or on that of the Armistice (Lovett-Lombardo Agreement); or even

(d) only on the date of the coming into force of the Treaty of Peace (September 15, 1947), when the damage occurred after the Armistice, because the military operations continued until the surrender of the German troops in Italy.

" The Government of the United States contends that no consideration should be given to the date of the damage and that it is sufficient that the claimant was in possession of the nationality of the United Nations on the dates specified by the Treaty of Peace in order that he be admitted to the benefits of Article 78 of this Treaty, whereas the Italian Government contends, on the contrary, that the date on which the damage occurred must always be given consideration and that the claim of the United States in behalf of Albert Flegenheimer, who alleges to have suffered injury by a contract concluded under duress on March 11, 1941, cannot be accepted by the Commission because of the absence of a fundamental condition of the general Law of Nations requiring that the injured party be a national of the claiming State on the date on which he sustained damage.

" The Commission holds that this question can be left open in the instant case because it would be important only if Albert Flegenheimer's title to American nationality were proved to the satisfaction of law, which in the Commission's opinion it is not, in which case consideration would have to be given to the German nationality of the individual concerned, by virtue of either the effective nationality theory or the apparent nationality theory, which the Commission also rejects. It is sufficient for the Commission to note that Albert Flegenheimer has failed to prove that he was a United Nations national on either of the dates specified in Article 78, para. 9 (a), sub-para. 1, of the Treaty of Peace, namely, on September 3, 1943, and September 15, 1947. It would be the same if, in application of the Lovett-Lombardo Agreement, consideration were to be given to the date of the damage, June 11, 1941, or to the date of the Armistice with Italy, September 3, 1943.

## " Conclusions

" On the basis of the foregoing considerations of fact and of law, this Commission concludes:

" 1. that Albert Flegenheimer acquired by filiation the nationality of the United States, at birth, in Wurttemberg on July 4, 1890;

" 2. that he acquired German and Wurttemberg nationality as the result of his naturalization in Wurttemberg on August 23, 1894, and thereby lost, after five years' residence in his new home country, his American nationality, under the Bancroft Treaty concluded on July 2, 1868, between the United States of America and Wurttemberg;

" 3. that he never re-acquired his American nationality after reaching majority;

" 4. that he was therefore vested solely with German and Wurttemberg nationality, after five years' residence in Germany, that is, beginning from 1895 until the German Decree of April 29, 1940, published on May 4, 1940, declaring he had forfeited that nationality;

" 5. that he became stateless beginning from this latter date, but that he did not prove that he was treated as enemy by the Italian authorities during his stay in the countries at war with Italy, Canada first and later the United States;

" 6. that he was never naturalized in the United States since he took up residence in that country in 1941/1942;

" 7. that the certificate issued to him by the United States authorities on July 10, 1952, subsequent to the filing of the Petition in the case with this Commission, on June 25, 1951, and after the new administrative investigations by the American authorities in 1952, which were also held subsequent to the date of the pending legal action, is not of a nature to prove, to the full satisfaction of law, that Albert Flegenheimer fulfills the conditions required by Article 78, para. 9 (*a*), sub-para. 1, of the Treaty of Peace with Italy, for the purpose of being considered as a United Nations national; nor does he fulfil the conditions required by Article V of the Lovett-Lombardo Agreement;

" 8. that it is not established that he fulfils the conditions of Article 78, para. 9 (*a*), sub-para. 2, of the aforesaid Treaty of Peace.

" For the foregoing reasons, and dismissing all contrary conclusions of the High Parties to this dispute,

## " Decides

" I.—That Albert Flegenheimer cannot be considered a United Nations national for the purposes of Article 78, para. 9 (*a*), sub-para. 1, of the Treaty of Peace with Italy;

" II.—That Albert Flegenheimer cannot be considered a United Nations national within the meaning of Article 78, para. 9 (*a*), sub-para. 2, of the Treaty of Peace with Italy;

" III.—As a consequence, the Petition filed in his behalf on June 25, 1951, by the Government of the United States is rejected on grounds of inadmissibility;

" IV.—That this decision is final and obligatory.

" The dispositions of this decision are adopted by unanimous vote, although on some points of law the Representative of the United States of America is not in agreement."

[Report: Unpublished (Decision No. 182).]

NOTE.—The question of the nationality of Albert Flegenheimer was the subject of an Opinion of the Attorney General of the United States, of January 19, 1960, addressed to the Legal Adviser of the Department of State.

The decision of the Conciliation Commission is the subject of extensive comment by Goldschmitt, " Recent Applications of Domestic Nationality Laws by International Tribunals ", in *Fordham Law Review*, 28 (1959–60), p. 689. See also 53 *A.J.I.L.* (1959), p. 944, for a digest of the decision by W. W. Bishop, Jr.

PART VI

# THE INDIVIDUAL IN INTERNATIONAL LAW

## A—IN GENERAL

### I.—Position of Individuals in International Law. Human Rights and Freedoms

[See also PART I, INTERNATIONAL LAW IN GENERAL: IV, Relation to Municipal Law; and PART VIII, TREATIES: VII, B, Operation and Enforcement of Treaties.]

**The individual in international law—Human rights and freedoms —European Convention for Protection of—European Human Rights Commission—Inter-State applications—Admissibility of—Relevance of requirement of exhaustion of local remedies—Whether affected by scope of application—Application alleging incompatibility of legislation with provisions of the Convention—Derogations made under Article 15—Whether relevant to question of admissibility—" A public emergency threatening the life of the nation "—Whether Commission competent to investigate existence thereof—Limits of discretion of Government.**

*Re* APPLICATION NO. 176/56 (GOVERNMENT OF THE KINGDOM OF GREECE *v.* GOVERNMENT OF THE UNITED KINGDOM OF GREAT BRITAIN AND NORTHERN IRELAND).

*European Commission of Human Rights.*[1] *June 2, 1956.*

(Berg, Acting President; Waldock, Eustathiades, Faber, Beaufort, Dominedo, Fuest, Süsterhenn, Petren, Akbay, Janssen-Pevtschin, Sørensen, Crosbie.)

THE FACTS.—By an Application introduced on May 7, 1956, the Greek Government submitted that the derogation from the provisions of the Convention notified by the British Government and applied to Cyprus by virtue of Article 15 of the Convention[2] was irregular in form and, furthermore, that the conditions required by the Article were not present in this case. It also maintained that a

---

[1] Where its decisions concern the admissibility of Applications, the Commission has considered that it is fulfilling a judicial function and that decisions not bearing on the substance of the Application can be published. Accordingly, in the present case, the statement of facts on the substance of the Application and the manner in which the Commission dealt with it is to be found in a note appearing in *Yearbook of the European Convention on Human Rights*, 1958–1959, p. 175, while the report can be found *ibid.*, p. 182. The present report is derived from both those sources.

[2] *Cf. Notes Verbales* of October 7, 1955, and April 13, 1956 (*ibid.*, vol. I (1955–56–57), pp. 49–50).

Article 15 provides, in part: " (1) In time of war or other public emergency threatening the life of the nation any High Contracting Party may take measures derogating from its obligations under this Convention to the extent strictly required by the exigencies of the situation, provided that such measures are not inconsistent with its other obligations under international law."

series of emergency laws and regulations in force in Cyprus were incompatible with the provisions of the Convention. It alleged, in particular, that the legislation providing for the imposition of whipping and various forms of collective punishment was an infringment of Article 3 of the Convention[1] which, under Article 15, the Contracting Parties may not depart from even in time of war or other public emergency. For its part the British Government denied that it violated the Convention, relying partly on the definition of the rights and freedoms recognised by the Convention and partly on the existence in Cyprus of a "public emergency threatening the life of the nation" within the meaning of the aforesaid Article 15.

The British Government also contested the admissibility of the Application.

1. *The admissibility of the Application.*—The detailed facts relating to the admissibility of the Application were (as stated in the decision of the Commission) as follows:

An Application dated May 7, 1956, was presented by the Greek Government against the Government of the United Kingdom alleging violation of human rights and fundamental freedoms in Cyprus. The Agent of the Government of the United Kingdom in a communication dated May 25, 1956, indicated that the Government of the United Kingdom considered that a period of three months would be required for the submission of their written comments on the admissibility of the Application of the Greek Government.

The Greek Government in a communication dated May 28, 1956, requested the Commission to decide in the course of its present session as to the admissibility of the Application.

The Commission decided on May 28, 1956, to give precedence to the matter.

The Commission further decided, on the same date, to invite the Agent of the British Government to appear before it on Friday, June 1, 1956, at 10 a.m., to clarify to the exclusion of any grounds of objection on the merits, the grounds of objection to admissibility which the British Government might have in mind possibly to raise and to invite the Agent of the Greek Government to be present at the above-mentioned sitting in order to submit its comments.

The Commission heard, at its meeting on June 1, 1956, Mr. Vallat, Agent of the United Kingdom Government, and Mr. Cambalouris, Agent of the Greek Government, as well as Mr. Rolin and Mr. Christides, counsel for the Greek Government.

The Agent of the Greek Government in the course of the hearing on Friday, June 1, limited the object of the application to certain legislative measures and administrative practices of the British authorities in Cyprus and consequently withdrew section B I (*a*)

---

[1] Article 3 of the Convention provides: "No one shall be subjected to torture or to inhuman or degrading treatment or punishment." ·

of the Application, reserving all the rights of his Government to reintroduce it by a new Application.

*Held:* that the application was admissible.

The Commission said: " The provisions of Article 27, paragraphs 1 and 2, of the Convention only refer to petitions submitted under Article 25 and not to applications made by Governments, and are therefore inapplicable to the present cases. The provisions of Article 26 concerning the exhaustion of domestic remedies according to the generally recognised rules of international law does not apply to the present Application, the scope of which is to determine the compatibility with the Convention of legislative measures and administrative practices in Cyprus. The effects of derogations made by the Government of the United Kingdom under Article 15 of the Convention relate to the merits of the case and not to the admissibility of the Application. The conditions laid down in Article 41, paragraph 1, of the Rules of Procedure of the Commission have been satisfied in this case. No other grounds for considering the Application inadmissible have been found."

II. *The merits.*—After being declared admissible, the Application was referred to a Sub-Commission of seven members[1] charged with establishing the facts and seeking a " friendly settlement of the matter " (Articles 28 and 29 of the Convention). As no settlement was reached, the plenary Commission, basing itself on the conclusions of the Sub-Commission (several of whose members visited Cyprus from January 13–28, 1958, in order to enquire into the position on the spot[2]), drew up a report containing the views of both the majority and the minority as to whether the facts found disclosed a violation of the Convention (Article 31).[3]

The question arose as to what were the powers of the Commission when a State, invoking Article 15, departed from the obligations laid down in the Convention. The Commission considered that it was " competent to pronounce on the existence of a public danger which, under Article 15, would grant to the Contracting Party concerned the right to derogate from the obligations laid down in the Convention ". The Commission also considered that it was " competent to decide whether measures taken by a Party under Article 15 of the Convention had been taken to the extent strictly required by the exigencies of the situation ". It added that " the Government should be able to exercise a certain measure of discretion in assessing the extent strictly required by the exigencies of the situation."

---

[1] *Cf.* Composition of Sub-Commission, *ibid.*, p. 102.

[2] *Cf.* Law No. 1 of 1958 of the Government of Cyprus granting diplomatic privileges and immunities to members of the European Commission of Human Rights (see *ibid.*, p. 198).

[3] It should be noted that during the proceedings the Government of Cyprus revoked or relaxed many of the regulations complained of in the Application.

The report of the Commission was transmitted to the Committee of Ministers of the Council of Europe on October 2, 1958.

Neither Greece nor the United Kingdom had accepted as compulsory the jurisdiction of the European Court of Human Rights (Article 46 of the Convention). Greece made a declaration giving its consent *ad hoc* to the reference of this particular case to the Court. In the absence, however, of a similar declaration by the British Government, the Committee of Ministers was called upon to examine the question, in accordance with Article 32 of the Convention,[1] whether there had been a violation of the Convention.

In the meantime, the States most directly concerned with the Cyprus problem succeeded in reaching agreement on the status of the island.

Having noted with satisfaction this political settlement of the Cyprus problem, the Committee of Ministers decided, on April 20, at their twenty-fourth session, on the joint proposal of Greece and the United Kingdom, that " in accordance with Article 32 of the European Convention for the Protection of Human Rights and Fundamental Freedoms, no further action was called for ".

[Report: *Yearbook of the European Convention on Human Rights* 1958–1959, p. 182.]

[1] Article 32 of the Convention provides as follows:

" (1) If the question is not referred to the Court in accordance with Article 48 of this Convention within a period of three months from the date of the transmission of the Report to the Committee of Ministers, the Committee of Ministers shall decide by a majority of two-thirds of the members entitled to sit on the Committee whether there has been a violation of the Convention.

" (2) In the affirmative case the Committee of Ministers shall prescribe a period during which the High Contracting Party concerned must take the measures required by the decision of the Committee of Ministers.

" (3) If the High Contracting Party concerned has not taken satisfactory measures within the prescribed period, the Committee of Ministers shall decide by the majority provided for in paragraph (1) above what effect shall be given to its original decision and shall publish the Report.

" (4) The High Contracting Parties undertake to regard as binding on them any decision which the Committee of Ministers may take in application of the preceding paragraphs."

**The individual in international law—Human rights and freedoms —European Convention for Protection of—European Human Rights Commission—Individual applications—Right of individual to reside in his own country—Freedom of expression—Retroactivity of penal legislation—Competence *ratione temporis*— Continuing violations—Compatibility of existing legislation with provisions of Convention—Exhaustion of local remedies—Concept of ordinary remedy—Insufficient remedy—Six months' period for application to Commission—Retroactive interpretation—Meaning of term " manifestly ill-founded "—Concept of *prima facie* violation—Limited power of Commission to examine substance in deciding admissibility.**

*Re* APPLICATION NO. 214/56 (DE BECKER *v.* BELGIUM).

*European Commission of Human Rights. June* 9, 1958.

(Waldock, President; Eustathiades, Berg, Faber, Beaufort, Dominedo, Süsterhenn, Petren, Janssen-Pevtschin, Sørensen, Crosbie, Skarphedinsson, Erim.)

THE FACTS (as stated in the decision of the Commission).— " The Applicant, a journalist and writer of Belgian nationality, was resident in Paris. On July 24, 1946, he was condemned to death by the Brussels *Conseil de Guerre* for having, between June 13, 1940, and October 5, 1943, collaborated with the German authorities in Belgium in divers ways and capacities, principally in the exercise of his functions as general editor of the Belgian daily newspaper " Le Soir ". De Becker was found guilty, in particular of having collaborated with the enemy's transformation of legal institutions or organisations, of having undermined the loyalty of Belgian citizens to the King and the State in time of war, and of having knowingly furthered the enemy's policy and design; of having deliberately directed, practised, promoted and encouraged propaganda against resistance to the enemy and the enemy's allies; of having by his writings, directly and with the effect intended, incited Belgian nationals to commit the crime of taking up arms against their country and its allies by knowingly performing for the enemy tasks including fighting, transport, mounting guard and others normally carried out by the enemy forces and their auxiliary services; and of having directly, as well as through intermediaries or acting himself in the capacity of an intermediary, supplied the enemies of the State with troops and manpower.

" The judgment of the *Conseil de Guerre* carried with it forfeiture by the Applicant of the rights set out in Article 123 sexies [§ 6] of the Belgian Penal Code.

" The Brussels Military Court, to which the Applicant appealed on July 20, 1946, while confirming the facts and the Applicant's criminal intent, allowed the existence of extenuating circumstances, namely, the Applicant's opposition to the 'annexionist and separatist' intentions of the German authorities, which opposition had led to his arrest by the said authorities in October 1943, and deportation to Germany for two years. In its judgment of June 14, 1947, the Court therefore commuted the death penalty pronounced by the lower Court to one of life imprisonment. It confirmed the judgment in all other respects, including therefore the forfeiture of the rights enumerated in Article 123 sexies of the Penal Code.

" This Article, incorporated in the Code by the decree (*arrête-loi*) of May 6, 1944, and first amended by the Decree (*arrête-loi*) of September 19, 1945, stated at the time that:

' Any person convicted of an offence or attempted offence under Section I, Vol. 2, Chapter II of the Penal Code, or Articles 17 and 18 of the Military Penal Code, committed in time of war, shall, *ipso facto*, be deprived for life of the following rights:

' (*a*) the rights set out in Article 31 of the Penal Code, including the right to vote and the right to be elected;

' (*b*) the right to appear on any roll of barristers, honorary counsel or probationary barristers;

' (*c*) the right to take part in any capacity whatsoever in instruction provided by a public or private establishment;

' (*d*) the right to receive remuneration from the State as a minister of religion;

' (*e*) the right to have a proprietary interest in or to take part in any capacity whatsoever in the administration, editing, printing or distribution of a newspaper or any other publication;

' (*f*) the right to take part in organising or managing any cultural, philanthropic or sporting activity or any public entertainment;

' (*g*) the right to have a proprietary interest in or to be associated with the administration or any other aspect of the activity of any undertaking concerned with theatrical production, films, or broadcasting;

' (*h*) the right to exercise the functions of director, and/or manager or authorized representative of a private company, limited shareholding partnership, co-operative society or credit union; the functions of manager of a Belgian establishment, under Article 198 (2) of the consolidated Commercial Companies Acts; to follow the profession of stockbroker, broker's agent or bank auditor, the profession of banker, or exercise the functions of director, governor, manager or authorised representative of a bank as defined in Royal Decree No. 185 of July 9, 1935, or those of manager of the Belgian branches of foreign Banks specified in Article VI of Royal Decree No. 185 of July 9, 1935;

' (*i*) the right to be associated in any way with the administration, management or direction of a professional association or a non-profit-making association;

' (*j*) the right to be a leader of a political association.'

" Article 123 sexies of the Belgian Penal Code was subsequently modified by the Laws of June 14, 1948, and February 29, 1952, but only in respect of the nature of the conviction to which it applied. In its present form it applies only to a criminal offence entailing a sentence of more than five years' imprisonment. Hence, the terms of this Article remain valid in the case of the Applicant.

" In 1950, the sentence of life imprisonment was reduced by the executive authorities to 17 years.

"On February 22, 1951, the Minister of Justice granted the Applicant's release, on condition, firstly, that he would not engage in politics, and secondly, that he would give a voluntary undertaking to take up residence in France within one month of his release. After some time in Switzerland, the Applicant took up residence in Paris.

" On December 10, 1952, De Becker asked the Belgian Minister of Justice to lift the ban on his residing in Belgium and practising his profession, and undertook to abstain from all political activity. He renewed this appeal on June 1, 1953, suggesting this time that he be authorised initially, if not to take up residence in Belgium, at least to establish legal domicile there. On October 12, 1953, the Director of the Belgian Department responsible for the provisional and conditional release of prisoners informed him, on the Minister's behalf, that there could be no question of his residing in Belgium and that he must continue to reside abroad, but that if he succeeded in establishing legal domicile in Belgium, that department could not prevent him from doing so. As a result, the Applicant did in fact establish legal domicile in Brussels. In letters dated April 26, 1954, and July 1, 1955, he again submitted his case to the Minister of Justice but received no reply."

The applicant's complaints related to the two following points:

(1) De Becker did not contest the validity of the above-mentioned judgment of June 14, 1947, but only that of his forfeiture of rights under Article 123 sexies of the Belgian Penal Code. In his view, this forfeiture of rights contravened two Articles of the European Convention of Human Rights. In the first place, it violated Article 7, which laid down the principle of legality of offences and penalties, since Article 123 sexies was incorporated in the Code by a Decree taking effect retrospectively. Furthermore, they disregarded Article 10, guaranteeing to everyone the right to freedom of expression, since they prevented De Becker from exercising his profession as a journalist and writer. In general, they were contrary to human dignity, since their effect was to leave the Applicant with four equally unacceptable courses: to refrain from any expression at all, to express himself under a pseudonym, to write abroad and renounce any circulation in Belgium which would hardly have been aceptable to his publishers, or, lastly, to disregard the injunction and expose himself to a further term of imprisonment under Article 123 nonies [§ 9] of the Penal Code.

(2) De Becker's second complaint concerned what he called his *de facto* exile. This exile, for which no provision was made under Belgian Law or in the Constitution, was simply the result of the terms of the Applicants' conditional release on February 22, 1951. The

Applicant regarded this exile as incompatible with Article 5 of the Convention whereby " everyone has the right to liberty and security ", and with Article 9 of the Universal Declaration of Human Rights [1948] which states that " no one shall be subjected to arbitary arrest, detention or exile ". De Becker added that he gave this undertaking to reside abroad and respected it only under moral pressure, that is to say, under the threat of a refusal to release him and, at the present time, under the threat of re-imprisonment, as well as because he had been led to expect that the measure would be lifted rapidly. However, his *de facto* exile had lasted for several years, and the Belgian authorities, apparently unwilling to put an end to it, were legally in a position to prolong it until July 14, 1973, the date of his final release.

The Applicant, for family reasons as well as for reasons of principle, claimed the recognition of his right to reside in Belgium, and the right to express himself by all legal means in accordance with the spirit of the Convention, and particularly with Article 17; he asked the Commission to invite the Belgian Government, preferably under the terms of a friendly settlement (Article 28 (*b*) of the Convention), to lift the measures of which he complained, and, in so far as this might necessitate certain legislative steps, to suspend the said measures in the meantime.

The first stage of the procedure under the Convention was an examination by the Commission of the admissibility of the Application, without regard to the substance of the case; accordingly the following steps were taken:

On March 8, 1957, the Commission decided, in accordance with Rule 45, para. 3 (*b*), of its Rules of Procedure, to give notice of the Application to the Belgian Government and invite it to submit to the Commission its observations in writing on the admissibility of the Application.

The written comments of the Belgian Government reached the Secretariat on May 10, 1957, and the Applicant's reply on June 24, 1957.

On July 19, 1957, the Commission gave the following partial decision:

" . . . . *Whereas* the Applicant was convicted and condemned to death on July 24, 1946, for collaboration during the war with the German authorities occupying Belgium and this sentence was afterwards changed to one of perpetual imprisonment;

" *Whereas* in 1950 the sentence was commuted as an act of grace to one of seventeen years, and whereas on February 22, 1951, the Minister of Justice granted the Applicant his liberty on two conditions, one of which was that he should undertake voluntarily to remove himself out of the country within one month, and the Applicant was set free and fulfilled the said condition;

" *Whereas* it therefore appears that the Applicant is residing out-side Belgium under the terms of an arrangement for his release from prison as an act of mercy and whereas the right of an individual to reside within the territory of his own State is not specifically as such guaranteed under any of the provisions of the Convention;

" *Whereas* it follows that the Application, in so far as it complains of the condition of residence abroad imposed by the Minister of Justice on February 22, 1951, is incompatible with the provisions of the Convention and hence inadmissible under Article 27 (2) thereof;

"*Whereas* Article 7 of the Convention provides that :

' No one shall be held guilty of any criminal offence on account of any act or omission which did not constitute a criminal offence under national or international law at the time when it was committed. Nor shall a heavier penalty be imposed than the one that was applicable at the time the criminal offence was committed ';

" *Whereas* the Applicant contends that Article 123 sexies of the Belgian Penal Code, in virtue of which he is deprived of his right to exercise his profession, is a provision of criminal law and that its application to his case was a violation of Article 7 of the Convention;

" *Whereas* Article 7 (2) of the Convention expressly states that this Article shall not prejudice the trial and punishment of a person guilty of any act or omission which, at the time when it was com-mitted, was criminal according to the general principles of law recognised by civilised nations;

" *Whereas* the offence committed by the Applicant falls within the terms of this exception, as the preliminary work of Article 7 of the Convention clearly confirms;

" *Whereas* it follows that the Applicant's complaint concerning the deprivation of his right to exercise the profession of a journalist, in so far as it is based on an alleged breach of Article 7 of the Con-vention, is incompatible with the terms of the said Article and, consequently, inadmissible under Article 27 (2) of the Convention;

" *Whereas* the Applicant further contends that Article 123 sexies of the Belgian Penal Code is in conflict with Article 10 of the Con-vention, under which everyone has the right to freedom of ex-pression, including the freedom to hold opinions and to receive and impart information and ideas without interference by public authority and regardless of frontiers;

" *Whereas* the Government of Belgium maintains that Article 123 sexies is a civil security measure falling under paragraph 2 of Article 10 of the Convention, in virtue of which the exercise of the freedoms provided for in the said Article, since it carries with it duties and responsibilities, may be subject to such formalities, conditions, restrictions or penalties as are prescribed by law and are necessary in a democratic society, in the interests of national security, territorial integrity or public safety, for the prevention of disorder and crime, for the protection of health or morals, for the protection of the reputation or rights of others, etc. . . . ;

" *Whereas* Article 26 of the Convention provides that the Commission may only deal with the matter after all domestic remedies have been exhausted, according to the generally recognised rules of international law, and within a period of six months from the date on which the final decision was taken;

" *Whereas* the Government of Belgium in any case alleges as a preliminary objection to the admissibility of the Application that it does not fulfil the above-mentioned condition under which the Commission may only deal with the matter within a period of six months from the date on which the final decision was taken;

" *Decides*, before taking its decision on the admissibility of this part of the Application,

" (1) To communicate to the Belgian Government the Applicant's reply of June 21, 1957;

" (2) To ask the Belgian Government to inform the Commission what, if any, legal procedures are now available to the Applicant in Belgium for the purpose of seeking a modification of the restrictions imposed on him by Article 123 sexies of the Belgian Penal Code;

" (3) To inform the Belgian Government that it may at the same time, if it so desires, submit its observations on the Applicant's reply dated June 21, 1957;

" (4) To ask the Belgian Government to supply the information and observations referred to in paras. 2 and 3 above within six weeks of the date of notification of the present decision."

The Belgian Government supplied the information and observations asked for in the form of a further memorial, which reached the Secretariat of the Commission on September 20, 1957, and to which the Applicant replied in a letter of December 9, 1957.

By a decision taken on December 18, 1957, the Commission, by virtue of Rule 46, para. 1 *in fine*, invited the parties to appear at the twelfth plenary session to supply oral explanations on the three following points, without going into the merits of the case:

" (a) Having regard to the date on which the Convention came into force in respect of Belgium (June 14, 1955), is the claim that Article 123 sexies of the Belgian Penal Code violates Article 10 of the Convention admissible or not, *ratione temporis*, according to the generally recognised principles of international law?

" (b) Does the six months' period specified in Article 26 of the Convention apply in this case and, if so, has the Applicant complied with this condition?

" (c) Is the claim referred to in paragraph (a) above manifestly ill-founded within the meaning of Article 27 (2) of the Convention? In other words, since the problem is not to determine whether the claim is justified, but simply whether it is admissible, does or does not the examination of the file disclose a *prima facie* violation of Article 10 of the Convention by Article 123 sexies of the Belgian Penal Code? "

The hearing in the presence of the parties took place on March 18, 1958. In accordance with Rules 36 and 37 of the Rules of Procedure, the Applicant, Mr. Raymond De Becker, and for the respondent, Me Gomrée and Me Van Ryn, Agent and Counsel for the Belgian Government respectively, appeared and their explanations were heard by the Commission.

On March 19, 1958, the Commission postponed its decision on the admissibility of the Applicant's claim mentioned above until its thirteenth plenary session.

*Held:* that the application was admissible.

The Commission said: " The Commission is called upon, at this stage in the proceedings, to pronounce on the various problems involved in considering the admissibility of the Application, in so far as this concerns the Applicant's claim that Article 123 sexies of the Belgian Penal Code violates Article 10 of the Convention; [1]

" I. *As regards admissibility ' ratione temporis '.*—

" The judgment of the Brussels *Conseil de Guerre* and that of the Military Court, as a result of which the provisions of Article 123 sexies became applicable to the Applicant, date back respectively to July 24, 1946, and June 14, 1947, that is, to a period before June 14, 1955, on which date the European Convention for the Protection of Human Rights and Fundamental Freedoms came into force in respect of Belgium. The question then arises whether the above-mentioned claim is inadmissible *ratione temporis.* It is true that this is not one of the grounds for inadmissibility enumerated in Articles 26 and 27 of the Convention, for Article 66 of the Convention merely determines when the Convention shall come into force, without specifying the date from which its entry into force shall have effect. However, inadmissibility on *ratione temporis* grounds derives from the generally recognised principle of international law that treaties and conventions are not retrospective in effect. In a number of decisions, the Commission has already acknowledged that by virtue of this principle the Convention applies, as regards each Contracting Party, only to facts subsequent to the date of its entry into force in respect of that Party.

" The Applicant maintains that the above-mentioned judgment of the Brussels Military Court merely marked the beginning of a state of affairs whereby, in his view, his right to freedom of expression is being repeatedly and perpetually violated. He points out, furthermore, that such a state of affairs might lead to his being convicted again were he at any time to exercise his right to freedom of expression. He deduces therefrom that the essential feature of Article

[1 For text of Article 10 see below, p. 186.]

123 sexies of the Belgian Penal Code is not the judgment as a result of which it becomes applicable, but the perpetual character of the forfeiture of rights it entails, which, in his view, gives rise to repeated violations of Article 10 of the Convention. He further states that, consequently, the purpose of his Application to the Commission is not to appeal against an isolated decision which, at a given moment, might have been considered contrary to the Convention, but against legislation which is permanently in conflict with it.

" The Belgian Government claim that the Applicant cannot dissociate the Belgian Law of which he complains, and which still forms part of Belgian legislation, from its application to his case by the Brussels Military Court. They invoke Article 25 of the Convention, according to which only an individual or corporate body claiming to be the victim of a violation, by one of the High Contracting Parties, of the rights set forth in the Convention, can validly make an application to the Commission. They deduce from this Article that an Applicant is not entitled to dispute the compatibility of any law with the Convention unless he can complain of its application to himself, and that therefore the decision which resulted in the application of Article 123 sexies to the Applicant must be primarily taken into account.

" The Application would be inadmissible *ratione temporis* if and so far as it concerned the validity or justification of the judgment of June 14, 1947, an isolated act which occurred prior to the entry into force of the Convention in respect of Belgium. An examination of the file shows, however, that the Applicant does not protest against the decision of the Brussels Military Court as such, but solely against the forfeiture of his rights which was imposed upon him by Article 123 sexies and which was the automatic and perpetual result of the above decision.

" The Commission is therefore called upon to examine whether the above-mentioned claim on the part of the Applicant concerns facts which, although prior in origin to the date on which the Convention came into force in respect of the respondent Government, might constitute a continuing violation of the Convention extending after that date. This is a specific question on which the Commission must reach a decision in the light of the special circumstances of the case.

" It should be pointed out in the first place that the judgment of the Brussels Military Court which resulted in De Becker losing the rights set out in Article 123 sexies of the Belgian Penal Code, was delivered prior to June 14, 1955, on which date the Convention came into force in respect of Belgium. Moreover, the subsequent entry into force of the Convention cannot have invalidated retrospectively the forfeiture of rights complained of for all the preceding period, since the Convention, according to the generally recognised rules of international law, did not take effect retrospectively. It follows that the Applicant cannot legally claim, for the period in question, to have been the victim of a violation of rights guaranteed by the Convention, even if the state of affairs complained of is of a permanent nature.

" It should nevertheless be noted, in respect of the period subsequent to June 14, 1945, that any person to whom the provisions of Article 123 sexies of the Belgian Penal Code are applied, is, in accordance with the very terms of that Article, deprived *ipso facto* and for life of the rights in question. De Becker thus finds himself permanently deprived of the rights enumerated in Article 123 sexies and, in the event of an infringement of the provisions of the said Article, he may at any time be convicted under Article 123 nonies.

" It appears, in these circumstances, that the decision of the *Conseil de Guerre* and the Brussels Military Court merely initiated the automatic application of a legal provision giving rise to a permanent situation and that, therefore, the Commission is being asked to examine not the compatibility of the above decisions with the Convention, but that of the said legal provision.

" It should be recalled, in this connection, that, in accordance with the general principles of international law, borne out by the spirit of the Convention as well as by the preliminary work, the Contracting Parties have undertaken, without prejudice to the provisions of Article 64 of the Convention, to ensure that their domestic legislation is compatible with the Convention and, if need be, to make any necessary adjustments to this end, since the Convention is binding on all the authorities of the Contracting Parties, including the legislative authority. It follows that the Commission is competent to consider whether the domestic legislation of the Contracting Parties is compatible with the Convention, and that this competence exists likewise in respect of Laws promulgated before the date on which the Convention came into force, if, like Article 123 sexies of the Belgian Penal Code, they remain in force after that date.

" It therefore appears that the Applicant finds himself in a continuing situation in respect of which he claims to be the victim of a violation of the right to freedom of expression guaranteed by Article 10 of the Convention and that the Application, in so far as it concerns this continuing situation extending after June 14, 1955, is consequently not inadmissible *ratione temporis*.

" II. *On the fulfilment of the conditions of Article 26 of the Convention.*—

" According to Article 26 of the Convention, the Commission may only deal with the matter after all domestic remedies have been exhausted, according to the generally recognised rules of international law, and within a period of six months from the date on which the final decision was taken. Under Article 27 (3) of the Convention, the Commission shall reject any petition which it considers inadmissible under Article 26.

" Article 26 lays down two different rules: in the first place, that of the exhaustion of domestic remedies; in the second place, that of the period of six months from the date of the final decision after which no application may be lodged.

" The Commission has to consider whether the Applicant has complied with these two rules in respect of the claim according to which Article 123 sexies of the Belgian Penal Code constitutes a violation of Article 10 of the Convention.

" (a) *On the exhaustion of domestic remedies.*—The Commission is called upon to confirm, first, whether in the present case all domestic remedies have in fact been exhausted, according to the generally recognised rules of international law.

" The Applicant was entitled to appeal against the judgment of the Brussels Military Tribunal before the Belgian *Cour de Cassation*, but did not avail himself of that right. It seems clear, however, from the memorials and pleadings of the parties that the latter agree that, in view of the nature of his claim, De Becker was under no obligation to lodge such an appeal. Article 17 of the Belgian Law of August 14, 1832, defining the competence of the *Cour de Cassation* shows indeed that the Applicant could not dispute, before this Court, the validity of the forfeiture of rights imposed by Article 123 sexies of the Belgian Penal Code, since the Brussels Military Court had applied this Article correctly and, moreover, the *Cour de Cassation* was not empowered to release the Applicant from the application of this Article, which is a legal provision binding the *Cour de Cassation* to the same extent as the lower Courts.

" Furthermore, the Belgian Government have admitted that there is no further legal remedy available to the Applicant in Belgium to waive or mitigate the forfeiture of rights incurred by virtue of Article 123 sexies of the Belgian Code.

" The Belgian Government have nonetheless drawn the Commission's attention to the fact that the Law of April 25, 1896, as amended by that of February 8, 1954, makes it possible to sue for re-instatement. However, in the Commission's view, such an action under the two above-mentioned Laws, does not seem to constitute an ordinary remedy to be exhausted according to the generally recognised rules of international law, since its purpose is to obtain a favour and not to vindicate a right. Moreover, as admitted by the Belgian Government, it follows from Article 1 (3) of the Law of April 25, 1896, that the Claimant shall not be entitled to take such action until five years after his final release, *i.e.*, as from July 14, 1978, so that in any event such a course proves inadequate in the present case.

" It is clear from the foregoing that all domestic remedies have been exhausted according to the generally recognised rules of international law.

" (b) *On the six months' period.*—The Belgian Government claims that the Applicant has not fulfilled the second condition of Article 26 of the Convention, for he did not apply to the Commission until more than six months after the date of the final decision. In the view of the said Government, the Application must consequently be declared inadmissible, by virtue of Article 27 (3) of the Convention, on the grounds that it was lodged too late.

" It should be recalled that the judgments entailing for De Becker the loss of the rights set out in the said Article 123 sexies date back to July 24, 1946, and June 14, 1947, that the Convention came into force in respect of Belgium on June 14, 1955, that the competence of the Commission in respect of individual applications was accepted by Belgium on July 5, 1955, and that De Becker lodged his Application with the Commission on September 1, 1956.

" The Applicant points out, in the first place, that neither at the time of the judgment of the Brussels Military Court, nor in the six months following, was he able to apply to the Commission and deduces therefrom that, even from the point of view of the Belgian Government, the question of the six months' period can only be considered after the incorporation of the Convention into Belgian legislation, and this with all due regard for his own special circumstances.

" With regard to these circumstances, De Becker points out that no domestic remedy exists for him, nor, consequently, has there been any final decision in his own country within the meaning of Article 26 of the Convention. He claims, however, that the loss of the right to freedom of expression constitutes a permanent state of affairs unable to give rise to any domestic decision from which a given period could be said to run. Lastly, he makes the [alternative] plea of excusable ignorance of the Convention, by reason of his absence from Belgium, at the time of the acceptance by the Belgium Government of the individual right of application. He submits that this acceptance was not made known to him until March 3, 1956, by a person whom the Commission could call as a witness if they so desired, and he lodged his Application less than six months after that date.

" The Belgian Government objects, primarily, that the Contracting Parties were concerned to impose on all applicants, in a general way, the obligation to lodge their applications within six months of the final decision on their appeal to domestic authorities, *i.e.*, in this case, within six months of the date of the judgment of the Brussels Military Court on June 14, 1947. In this Government's view, the intention of the Contracting Parties was to prevent final decisions on appeals by individuals against measures taken under national legislation from being constantly called into question. According to the respondent's submissions, Article 26 means that the Convention is concerned with the future, and, as regards the past, only with decisions taken less than six months before its entry into force, and the intention was to obviate or at least reduce the risk of the Commission being overwhelmed by individual applications.

" The Belgian Government maintains in particular that Article 26 makes no distinction between a final decision entailing immediate forfeiture of rights on the part of an applicant and one entailing a lasting loss of rights. In the event of the Commission concurring on this point with the Applicant's view, the said Government contends, as a secondary consideration, that the sole result would be to place the beginning of the six months' period at the date of the entry into force of the Convention in respect of the State of which the Applicant is a national, in this case June 14, 1955. Lastly, with regard to the Applicant's plea of excusable ignorance of the Convention, the Belgian Government claims, again as a secondary consideration, that De Becker had ample time to learn of the existence of a document as widely publicised as the Convention, particularly as he was certainly paying close attention to events in Belgium at the time, especially to the ratification of a Convention such as this. The Belgian Government points out, furthermore, that the Applicant had not even invoked circumstances allegedly making it materially impossible for him to have lodged his Application at the right time, and that the assertion that he was not informed of the fact that the Convention had come into force does not constitute a valid excuse in the eyes of the law.

" It should be noted that before June 14, 1955, the Convention, which did not then have any binding effect with regard to Belgium, could not impose on De Becker the six months' rule laid down in Article 26. It follows that the decision of the Brussels Military Court prior to that date, cannot mark the beginning of the six months' period. It should be stressed, moreover, that until July 5, 1955, on which date Belgium accepted the right of individual application to the Commission, the Applicant was unable to lodge with the Commission an application against that State and that there could not be any question of invoking against him the six months' rule for the period between June 14 and July 5, 1955. It follows that the six months' rule can apply in the Applicant's case only to the period after July 5, 1955.

" Further, as regards the six months' rule, the main problem facing the Commission in this case is that of deciding to which final decision Article 26 of the Convention can be said to relate.

" The Commission notes, in this connection, that the two rules contained in Article 26, concerning the exhaustion of domestic remedies and concerning the six months' period, are closely inter-related, since not only are they combined in the same Article but they are also expressed in a single sentence whose grammatical construction implies such correlation; the term ' final decision ', therefore, in Article 26 refers exclusively to the final decision concerned in the exhaustion of all domestic remedies according to the generally recognised rules of international law, so that the six months' period is operative only in this context.    Furthermore, the preparatory work of the Convention, in particular the report prepared in June 1950 by the Conference of Senior Officials, confirms this interpretation.

" The Commission has already noted that Belgian legislation does not at present offer De Becker, for the purpose of challenging the validity of his loss of rights under Article 123 sexies of the Penal Code, any domestic remedy which he would be obliged to exhaust.    Moreover, in view of the nature of his claim, which is concerned with the compatibility of a legal provision with the Convention, the Applicant has never had an opportunity to make such an appeal.    In particular, the judgment of the Brussels Military Court on June 14, 1947, does not therefore constitute, for the above-mentioned claim, a final decision for the purposes of Article 26 of the Convention.

" Moreover, the Applicant does not complain of an act occurring at a given point in time nor even of the enduring effects of such an act, but, as the Commission has already noted when ruling on the admissibility of the Application *ratione temporis*, of a legal provision giving rise to a constant and even perpetual state of affairs, against which no domestic remedy is available to him. The existence of the six months' period specified in Article 26 of the Convention is justified by the wish of the High Contracting Parties to prevent the past judgments being constantly called into question.    This legitimate concern for order, stability and peace cannot be allowed to stand in the way of the consideration by the Commission of the permanent state of affairs of which De Becker complains, in so far as this state of affairs is not a thing of the past but still continues and, in the present state of the Belgian legislation, will continue in principle for the rest of the Applicant's life, without any domestic remedy being available to him.    Since there is no justification for the application of the rule in the present case, there can be no question of the Applicant being debarred by lapse of time. When the Commission receives an application concerning a legal provision which gives rise to a permanent state of affairs for which there is no domestic remedy, the problem of the six months' period specified in Article 26 can arise only after this state of affairs has ceased to exist.    In the circumstances, it is exactly as though the alleged violation was being repeated daily, thus preventing the running of the six months' period.

" It might be claimed, indeed, in support of the applicability of the six months' period in the present case, that by insisting, in Article 26 of the Convention, on the need to observe this rule, the intention of the Contracting Parties was to exclude discussion of the past and that, in the event of doubt as to the exact scope of this rule, the *ratio legis* should prevail. It would follow that when there is no final domestic decision within the meaning of Article 26, the six months' period shall run from the date on which the state of affairs complained of came into existence.

" However, in the Commission's view, this argument would in any case be pertinent only if the said state of affairs had already ceased to exist at the time of the lodging of the Application. There is no justification for invoking *ratio legis* if, as in the present case, the state of affairs complained of is still in existence at the time when the Commission is asked to consider it, since it cannot reasonably be assumed that the Contracting Parties, by including the six months' rule in Article 26, intended to exclude the present or, *a fortiori*, the future.

" Furthermore, it should be noted that the provisions of Article 26 relating to the six months' period, read with those of Article 27 (3) of the Convention, have the effect that in certain circumstances the right of application will lapse or be forfeited, and, therefore they normally call for a restrictive interpretation according to the general principles of law. It should be recalled, in the same connection, that, by specifying that application must be made to the Commission within a certain period, Article 26 introduces an exception to the two preceding Articles, namely, 24 and 25, which confer competence. Restrictive provisions of this kind do not lend themselves to a broad interpretation, as was stated by the Permanent Court of International Justice in its [Advisory] Opinion of February 7, 1923, on the *Nationality Decrees in Tunis and Morocco* (Series B, No. 4, p. 25)[1] and in its Judgment of May 25, 1926, on *Certain German Interests in Polish Upper Silesia* (Series A, No. 7, p. 76).[2] These technical points have special force in the field covered by the Convention, which is that of the protection of human rights and fundamental freedoms.

" It follows from the foregoing that the six months' period referred to in Article 26 of the Convention is inapplicable to the present case. It is superfluous, in these circumstances, to examine whether De Becker's plea of excusable ignorance of the Convention is well-founded and pertinent or otherwise.

" Nonetheless, it might be asked whether, in such special circumstances in which the ' *lex specialis* ' of Article 26 is no longer applicable, the ' *lex generalis* ', according to which all international appeals must be lodged within a reasonable time, does not again obtain. However, there is no need to consider this question in the present case, as it is sufficient to observe that the Claimant has

[1 *Annual Digest*, 1923–1924, Case No. 203.]
[2 *Ibid.*, 1925–1926, Case No. 60.]

lodged his application within a reasonable time, according to the generally recognised rules of international law.

" It appears, consequently, that the Application, in so far as it questions the compatibility of Article 123 sexies of the Belgian Penal Code with Article 10 of the Convention, cannot be declared inadmissible as being out of time.

" III. *On the argument that the Application is manifestly ill-founded.*—

" According to Article 27 (2) of the Convention, the Commission shall consider inadmissible any application submitted under Article 25 which it considers manifestly ill-founded.

" The Belgian Government, invoking this provision, asks the Commission to reject the Application as being manifestly ill-founded.

" In order to settle this point, the Commission should set out the respective arguments of the parties on the compatibility of Article 123 sexies of the Belgian Penal Code with Article 10 of the Convention, whereby:

' (1) Everyone has the right to freedom of expression. This right shall include freedom to hold opinions and to receive and impart information and ideas without interference by public authority and regardless of frontiers. This Article shall not prevent States from requiring the licensing of broadcasting, television or cinema enterprises.

' (2) The exercise of these freedoms, since it carries with it duties and responsibilities, may be subject to such formalities, conditions, restrictions or penalties as are prescribed by law and are necessary in a democratic society, in the interests of national security, territorial integrity or public safety, for the prevention of disorder or crime, for the protection of health or morals, for the protection of the reputation or rights of others, for preventing the disclosure of information received in confidence, or for maintaining the authority and impartiality of the judiciary.'

" The Applicant claims that the fact of conviction and conditional release do not in themselves constitute an obstacle to the admissibility of an application relating to the exercise of the right to freedom of expression. In support of this, he points out that Article 10 accords this right to ' everyone ' and, unlike Article 4 relating to forced or compulsory labour, does not restrict this right specifically in the case of prisoners on conditional release. He also invokes, to prove the same point, the terms of Article 14 (' Without discrimination on any ground ' and ' or other status '). He argues from this that any person convicted or released conditionally has the same right to freedom of expression as any other citizen, subject to the general conditions, restrictions or penalties prescribed by law set out in paragraph 2 of Article 10.

" With regard to the formalities, conditions, restrictions or penalties mentioned in Article 10 (2), the Applicant points out, firstly, that under Western systems of law the right to freedom of expression has never been among those forfeited in the event of conviction, and that in Belgium such a measure has never existed in ordinary law. He concludes that Article 123 sexies of the Penal Code was an exceptional measure understandable in 1944 and 1945, but that nothing can justify its retention in time of peace.

" De Becker also recalls that this Article places disabilities on him for life and stresses the absolute character of the forfeiture of rights of which he complains. He claims that this is shown first by the modes of expression prohibited. He asserts, in this connection, that he has freedom of expression only in private conversation and correspondence, as was the case even under the dictatorship whose recurrence the Convention seeks to prevent. He claims that he is subject not to restrictions within the meaning of Article 10 (2), but to a total abolition of the right to freedom of expression. De Becker maintains that this absolute character is further demonstrated by the fact that Article 123 sexies deprives those to whom it is applicable of the right to publish anything whatever, irrespective of its content, and certain Belgian citizens having, like De Becker, suffered a loss of rights under this Article, have been convicted recently of publishing non-political works abroad. In these circumstances, according to the Applicant, the Article resulting in the loss of these rights is directed not only against certain actions but against individuals. Moreover, he submits that the measures in question cannot be classified as general measures known to all in advance but as individual measures taken *ratione personae* and *ex post facto*. He maintains that this is the fundamental difference between Article 123 sexies of the Penal Code and Article 10 (2) of the Convention, the primary aim of which is to link the notion of freedom to that of responsibility, the notion of rights to that of obligations and the concept of the individual to that of the community. The Applicant maintains that the formalities, conditions, restrictions or penalties mentioned in Article 10 (2), being of an anonymous and general nature, are intended merely to govern the exercise of the right to freedom of expression and penalise any abuse of it and could never be invoked to abolish freedom of expression in the future even for a delinquent. De Becker states that he could understand that, in respect of persons who, rightly or wrongly, are regarded as having participated in activities leading to the abolition or restriction of democratic freedom, the right to freedom of expression should be subject to the giving of certain undertakings, such as an undertaking to respect thereafter the principles of democracy and the spirit of the Convention on Human Rights. In his view, however, there is no comparison between conditions or restrictions of this kind, which leave the right itself intact, and the provisions of Article 123 sexies which abolish it completely.

" The Belgian Government claims that Article 123 sexies, as part of Belgian legislation under the democratic Belgian Constitution, is in no way an exceptional measure, and that although Article 10 of the Convention forbids restrictions dictated by motives alien to the common interest and welfare, such as revenge, imposed by a majority on their former political opponents, nothing of this sort has ever occurred in Belgium.

" The said Government also point out that Article 10 (2) of the Convention expressly states that the exercise of freedom of expression carries with it duties and responsibilities which are, as it were, its counterpart, and that the paragraph in question implies that any person wishing to enjoy this freedom must be conscious of his duties and responsibilities, this being the reason why the said paragraph allows the Contracting Parties to lay down in their laws formalities, conditions, restrictions or penalties leading inevitably to the restriction of freedom of expression. In the view of the Belgian Government the loss of rights imposed by Article 123 sexies of the Penal Code are a good example of the application of this clause of the Convention, since they are only conditions, restrictions or penalties justified by the need to ensure national security, territorial integrity, public safety, and the prevention of disorder or crime. In support of this assertion, the Belgian Government quote several passages from the report of the Council of Ministers stating the reasons for the incorporation of Article 123 sexies. They also stress the fact that the persons convicted by the Brussels Military Court on June 14, 1947, in particular De Becker, were leaders of the movement in favour of intellectual collaboration with the invader and that the purpose of their activities, or at any rate their undoubted result, was to expose Belgium to those very dangers which Article 10 (2) of the Convention itself regards as sufficiently serious to justify restrictions on the right to freedom of expression.

" Lastly, the Belgian Government maintains that the measures set out in Article 123 sexies do not abolish the right to freedom of expression as laid down in Article 10 of the Convention, since they do not affect freedom to hold opinions or the freedom to receive information or ideas, and since even the freedom to communicate information or ideas is restricted only in so far as this has been deemed necessary for national reasons in the Belgian democratic society. They submit that these restrictions are, in fact, only concerned with any weapon of propaganda and the Applicant remains free to impart information and ideas by word of mouth, even in public, by letter or by any other means not included in those limited restrictions listed in Article 123 sexies.

" At this stage of the proceedings, the Commission is called upon only to decide whether the Application is admissible, in so far as it contests the compatibility of Article 123 sexies of the Belgian

Penal Code with Article 10 of the Convention. It is true that Article 27 (2) of the Convention obliges the Commission to declare inadmissible any individual application which it considers ' manifestly ill-founded '. The preparatory work for the Convention shows that this special terminology and unusual extension of the notion of admissibility is explained by the concern of the Contracting Parties to prevent applications unworthy of the Commission's attention. However, the Commission is not thereby entitled to reject, at the stage of its decision as to admissibility, an application which is not obviously ill-founded. It follows that in the present decision the Commission is not called upon to pronounce upon the existence of a violation, to the detriment of the Applicant, of the rights and freedoms guaranteed by the Convention. Moreover, it affirms from the well-established jurisprudence of the Commission that the latter declares an application inadmissible as being manifestly ill-founded only when an examination of the file does not disclose a *prima facie* violation [of any of the rights and freedoms set forth in the Convention].

" It is evident from the file that there are complex problems involved in assessing the compatibility of the disabilities complained of with the provisions of Article 10 of the Convention. These problems, which turn essentially on whether the disabilities are necessary within the meaning of Article 10 (2), require for their solution an examination of the substance of the case.

" It appears, therefore, that, inasmuch as it disputes the validity of the forfeiture of rights provided for in Article 123 sexies of the Belgian Penal code, the Application cannot be considered inadmissible as manifestly ill-founded within the meaning of Article 27 (2) of the Convention.

" The Commission finds no other ground for inadmissibility."

[Report: *Yearbook of the European Convention on Human Rights*, 1958-1959, p. 216.]

The individual in international law—Human rights and freedoms —European Convention for Protection of—European Human Rights Commission—Individual applications—Supreme Restitution Court of German Federal Republic—As international tribunal—Whether within jurisdiction of Federal Republic—Court of Restitution Appeals—Whether within jurisdiction of Federal Republic— Alleged miscarriage of justice by Tribunal within jurisdiction of Contracting Party—Absorption by decision of international tribunal—Such decision not subject to review by Commission.

Re APPLICATION NO. 235/56 (MR. X. AND MRS. X. *v.* GERMAN FEDERAL REPUBLIC).

*European Commission of Human Rights. June* 10, 1958.

(Waldock, President; Eustathiades, Berg, Faber, Beaufort, Dominedo, Süsterhenn, Petren, Janssen-Pevtschin, Sørensen, Crosbie, Skarphedinsson, Erim.)

THE FACTS (as stated in the decision of the Commission).— " The Applicants were resident in ——, Germany, and German subjects. In November 1932 the first Applicant left and went to Israel, where he eventually settled and at some date acquired Palestinian, later Israeli, nationality.

" The second Applicant, Mrs. X., was the first Applicant's wife. She and the children of the marriage remained in ——, where she divorced the first Applicant on March 14, 1935. She and her children left Germany at about the end of the year 1936 and went to live in England, where Mrs. X. was naturalised a British subject on August 30, 1948.

" By agreement between the Applicants, the benefit of the property in Germany and of the claim pursued in the German courts was vested in the second Applicant in about 1934 and the proceedings in Germany which are the subject matter of this Application were carried on at her expense and in accordance with her instructions, the first Applicant, Mr. X., being merely her agent. The benefit of the claim is therefore vested in Mrs. X. and for that reason her name was added to the Application.

" The first Applicant was the owner of business premises at —— which on or about June 24, 1936, acting through an agent he sold for RM 100,000 to Mr. and Mrs. Otto ——. RM 58,345.66 was paid by them direct to the German Revenue Authorities on account of so-called Flight Tax. It was at all times the first Applicant's contention that the fair market value of the property was RM 180,000 to 200,000.

" On or about November 10, 1947, there was introduced in what was then known as the United States Zone of Germany a law called the Restitution Law, the material provisions of which are as follows:

'*Article 1: Basic Principles*

' 1. It shall be the purpose of this Law to effect to the largest extent possible the speedy restitution of identifiable property (tangible and intangible property and aggregates of tangible and intangible property) to persons who were wrongfully deprived of such property within the period from January 30, 1933, to May 8, 1945, for reasons of race, religion, nationality, ideology or political opposition to National Socialism. For the purpose of this Law deprivation of property for reasons of nationality shall not include measures which under recognised rules of international law are usually permissible against property of nationals of enemy countries.

' 2. Property shall be restored to its former owner or to his successor in interest in accordance with the provisions of this Law even though the interests of other persons who had no knowledge of the wrongful taking must be subordinated. Provisions of law for the protection of purchasers in good faith, which would defeat restitution, shall be disregarded except where this Law provides otherwise.

'*Article 2: Acts of Confiscation*

' 1. Property shall be considered confiscated within the provisions of this Law if the person entitled thereto has been deprived of it, or has failed to obtain it despite a well-founded legal expectancy of acquisition, as the result of:

' (a) A transaction *contra bonos mores*, threats or duress, or an unlawful taking or any other tort;

' (b) Seizure due to a governmental act or by abuse of such act;

' (c) Seizure as the result of measures taken by the N.S.D.A.P., its formations or affiliated organisations,

provided the acts described in (a) to (c) were caused by or constituted measures of persecution for any of the reasons set forth in Article 1.

' 2. It shall not be permissible to plead that an act was not wrongful or *contra bonos mores* because it conformed with a prevailing ideology concerning discrimination against individuals on account of their race, religion, nationality, ideology or their political opposition to National Socialism.

' 3. Confiscation by a governmental act within the meaning of paragraph 1 (b) shall be deemed to include, among other acts, sequestration, confiscation, forfeiture by order or operation of law, and transfer by order of the State or by a trustee appointed by the State. The forfeiture by virtue of a judgment of a criminal court shall also be considered a confiscation by a governmental act, if such judgment has been vacated by order of an appropriate court or by operation of law.

' 4. A judgment or order of a court, or of an administrative agency, which, although based on general provisions of law, was handed down solely or primarily with the purpose of injuring the party affected by it for any of the reasons set forth in Article 1 shall be deemed a specific instance of the abuse of a governmental act. The abuse of a governmental act shall also include the procurement of a judgment or of measures of execution by exploiting the circumstances that the opponent was, actually or by law, prevented from protecting his interests by virtue of his race, religion, nationality, ideology, or his political opposition to National Socialism. The Restitution Authorities (Restitution Agency, Restitution Chamber and Oberlandesgericht) shall disregard any such judgment or order of a court or administrative agency whether or not it may otherwise be appealed or reopened under existing law.

'  *Article 3: Presumption of Confiscation*

' 1. It shall be presumed in favour of any claimant that the following transactions entered into between January 30, 1933, and May 8, 1945, constitute acts of confiscation within the meaning of Article 2:

' (*a*) Any transfer or relinquishment of property made during a period of persecution by any person who was directly exposed to persecutory measures on any of the grounds set forth in Article 1;

' (*b*) Any transfer or relinquishment of property made by a person who belonged to a class of persons which on any of the grounds set forth in Article 1 was to be eliminated in its entirety from the cultural and economic life of Germany by measures taken by the State or the N.S.D.A.P.

' 2. In the absence of other factors proving an act of confiscation within the meaning of Article 2, the presumptions set forth in paragraph 1 may be rebutted by showing that the transferor was paid a fair purchase price. Such evidence by itself shall not, however, rebut the presumptions if the transferor was denied the free right of disposal of the purchase price on any of the grounds set forth in Article 1.

' 3. A fair purchase price within the meaning of this Article shall mean the amount of money which a willing buyer would pay and a willing seller would take, taking into consideration, in the case of a commercial enterprise, the normal goodwill which such enterprise would have in the hands of a person not subject to persecutory measures referred to in Article 1.

'  *Article 4: Power of Avoidance*

' 1. Any transaction entered into by a person belonging to a class referred to in paragraph 1 (*b*) of Article 3 within the period from September 15, 1935 (the date of the first Nuremberg Laws) to May 8, 1945, may, because of the duress imposed on such class, be avoided by a claimant where such transaction involved the transfer or relinquishment of any property unless:

' (*a*) The transaction as such and with its essential terms would have taken place even in the absence of National Socialism or

' (*b*) The Transferee protected the property interests of the claimant (Article 7) or his predecessor in interest in an unusual manner and with substantial success, for example, by helping him in transferring his assets abroad or through similar assistance.

' 2. In determining under paragraph 1 (*a*) whether the transaction would have taken place even in the absence of National Socialism, the fact that

the transferor himself offered to sell the property to the transferee or

the transferor received a fair purchase price (see Article 3, paragraph 3) the free right of disposal of which was not denied him on any of the grounds set forth in Article 1, shall be considered by the Restitution Authority together with all other facts, but neither fact, either singly or in conjunction with the other, shall be sufficient to show that the transaction would have taken place even in the absence of National Socialism.

' 3. Similarly neither of these facts, either singly or in conjunction with the other, shall be sufficient to show that the claimant is estopped from exercising the power of avoidance by reason of his own previous conduct or that of his predecessor in interest.

' 4. The term " claim for restitution " as used in this Law shall be deemed to include all claims based on the right to exercise the power of avoidance. The exercise of the power of avoidance shall have the effect that the property transferred or relinquished pursuant to the voided transaction shall for the purposes of this Law be deemed to be confiscated property.

' 5. The filing of a claim for restitution shall, whether or not it is specifically stated, be deemed to be an exercise of the right of avoidance on behalf of the person entitled to exercise such right.'

" In due course the first Applicant applied for restitution under the said Law.

" By a decision of December 2, 1952, the Court of First Instance, the District Court (*Landgericht*) at ——, dismissed the claim. The Applicants state that the reason given by the Court was that the first Applicant was not a member of the group of persons protected by Article 1 of the Restitution Law, because he had sold the property at a time when he was living outside Germany.

" The Applicants further state that the Court made no findings of fact on any of the matters referred to in Articles 3 and 4 of the said Law, except that the first Applicant left Germany for reasons not connected with National Socialism. In particular, the Court did not find that the price of RM 100,000 was fair nor that the assessment of Flight Tax was free from discrimination.

" The first Applicant, in accordance with the provisions of the Restitution Law, appealed to the Court of Appeal (*Oberlandesgericht*) at ——, which Court, so the Applicants state, did not have the power to find facts.

" On June 2, 1953, the first Applicant applied to the Court of Appeal for an oral hearing. This was not granted.

" On October, 6 1953, the first Applicant's appeal was dismissed with costs by a decision which was not pronounced publicly.

" The Applicants state that the Court held that:

" (a) the District Court was not in error in holding that the first Applicant was not persecuted within the meaning of Article 1 of the said Law, and

" (b) the assessment of Flight Tax was the dominant motive of the sale and that, since this assessment was not conditioned by persecution, the first Applicant would have sold the property even in the absence of National Socialism, there being no evidence that the amount of the price resulted from persecution.

" The Applicants allege that the second of these grounds was plainly untenable.

" On December 16, 1953, the first Applicant submitted a Petition for Review to the Court of Restitution Appeals, which had been set up under Law No. 21 of the United States High Commissioner for Germany as a tribunal to review restitution cases decided in the United States Zone of Germany.

" In accordance with an Order previously made by the said Court, oral argument took place at Nuremberg on May 5, 1954. The first Applicant was represented by Dr. —— who, according to the Applicants, argued at length on the fundamental question of law involved in the appeal, *viz*: whether the first Applicant was or was not a member of the protected class contemplated by Article 1 of the said Law, or more particularly, whether Jews living outside Germany at the time of a sale could invoke the Restitution Law.

" Having concluded his submissions on this point, the first Applicant's Counsel intended to proceed with his argument on the requirements of Articles 3 and 4 of the said Law, *i.e.*, on the question of the fairness of the price, its payment at free disposal, the conclusion of the transaction as such and with its essential terms even in the absence of National Socialism and the absence of ' other facts '.   He was, however, stopped by the President in circumstances which are set forth in paragraph 5 of the first Applicant's petition for a re-hearing and in paragraph 3 of Dr. ——'s Statutory Declaration submitted therewith.

" The Applicants allege that the Court of Restitution Appeals failed to render a decision within a reasonable time or at all.

" The Applicants state that, at some time unknown to them, but between June 2 and October 12, 1955, the case was referred to the Third Division of the Supreme Restitution Court which replaced the Court of Restitution Appeals under the terms of Article 6 of Chapter 3 of the Convention on the Settlement of Matters arising out of the War and the Occupation (hereinafter referred to as " the Settlement Convention ").

" The Applicants allege that the first Applicant was invited to move for new oral arguments before this Court, that he did so move on October 17, 1955, and sent reminders on January 3, 1956, February 3, 1956, and April 24, 1956. The Applicants further allege that on May 24, 1956, the Clerk of the Court informed the first Applicant that ' it will not be necessary for further oral arguments to be heard inasmuch as two of the Justices who heard the original arguments are members of the present Court '.

" On June 29, 1956, the Supreme Restitution Court filed a decision with the Clerk of the Court, without pronouncing it publicly.

" The Applicants declare that:

" (a) on the fundamental question of law involved in the appeal, the Court held that the ruling of the Court of Appeal was in error in ruling that a foreign Jew was not entitled to the presumption of confiscation under Article 3 of the Law No. 59;

" (b) that the Court of Appeal was not in error in drawing the conclusion from the facts found by the District Court, that the transaction with its essential terms would have taken place even in the absence of National Socialism.

" The Applicants state that a copy of the said decision was received by the first Applicant's Counsel on August 7, 1956; that on August 8, 1956, the first Applicant made a motion for re-argument which was supported by a Statutory Declaration; that on October 2, 1956, the Clerk informed the first Applicant 'that no further proceedings may be initiated respecting the case'; that under German law there does not lie any further appeal against the decision of the Supreme Restitution Court; finally, that in the course of further correspondence the first Applicant failed to obtain an answer to his question whether a record of the oral argument had been made and transcribed and also failed to obtain a copy of the record, if any.

" The Applicants allege a violation of Article 6 of the Convention for the Protection of Human Rights and Fundamental Freedoms, whereby 'in the determination of his civil rights and obligations ... everyone is entitled to a fair and public hearing within a reasonable time' and where 'judgment shall be pronounced publicly'.

" In particular they allege:

" (1) that Article 6 was violated by the Court of Appeal in that:

" (a) it did not grant the first Applicant a public hearing;

" (b) it did not pronounce judgment publicly;

" (2) that Article 6 was violated by the Court of Restitution Appeals in that it failed to decide the appeal within a reasonable time so as to render the hearing of May 5, 1954, unfair.

" (3) that Article 6 was violated by the Supreme Restitution Court in that:

" (a) it refused a public hearing;

" (b) it failed to pronounce its judgment publicly;

" (c) it rendered a decision more than 25 months after the hearing before the Court of Restitution Appeals on May 5, 1954;

" (d) it failed to give the first Applicant a fair hearing because:

" (i) its decision was rendered by five judges, only one of whom was present at the hearing on May 5, 1954, although the first Applicant was informed that two judges who were present at that hearing were members of the Court;

" (ii) it refused to hear oral arguments;

" (iii) it dismissed the first Applicant's appeal on a ground which:

" (aa) at the express suggestion of the Court and as a result of the arrangement made on May 5, 1954, was excluded from the oral argument;

" *(bb)* had not been investigated by the only fact-finding tribunal, the District Court;

" *(cc)* if investigated or argued would have proved to be untenable.

" The Applicants claim from the Federal Government damages estimated at DM 325,000 arising from the above judgments of the Court of Appeal and Supreme Restitution Court.

" *Matters on which the views of the parties were specially invited by the Commission*

" In relation to the above-mentioned facts the Applicants and the Federal Government were particularly invited, in accordance with the Commission's decisions of March 8 and July 18, 1957, respectively, to state their opinions as to whether, having regard to Article 1 of the Convention of Human Rights,[1] the Federal Government was responsible under the Convention for the acts of the United States Court of Restitution Appeals and the Supreme Restitution Court.

" On February 26, 1958, the parties were informed that the President had decided to invite them, in accordance with Rule 46, paragraph 1, of the Rules of Procedure, to make oral explanations before the Commission concerning the admissibility of the Application and again in particular concerning the responsibility of the Federal Government under the Convention in respect of the alleged proceedings before the Court of Appeal, the Court of Restitution Appeals and the Supreme Restitution Court, and it was also indicated to the parties that they should take into account Article 26 of the Convention, which relates to the exhaustion of the local remedies.

" In a further letter of March 13, 1958, the attention of the parties was drawn to the decision of the Arbitral Tribunal in the *Salem* case (*Reports of International Arbitral Awards*, Vol. II, pp. 1163 *et seq.*[2]).

" At the conclusion of the oral hearing on March 21, 1958, the parties were invited:

" *First*, to present, in writing, if they thought fit, a final statement of their views concerning the relevance and inter-relation of the provisions of the Paris Agreements[3] and of German municipal law on the question of the Federal Republic of Germany's power to control the procedure of the Supreme Restitution Court:

" *Secondly*, to present any additional observations which they might think useful on the question how far the Federal Republic, when concluding subsequent treaties, was bound to take account of its obligations under the European Convention of Human Rights

[1 Article 1 of the Convention provides:
" The High Contracting Parties shall secure to everyone within their jurisdiction the rights and freedoms defined in Section I [Articles 2–18] of this Convention."]
[2 *Annual Digest*, 1931–1932, Case No. 98.]
[3 Bonn/Paris Conventions, 1952–1954, terminating the occupation régime in Western Germany (*U.N.T.S.*, vol. 331, pp. 253, 327; vol. 332, pp. 3, 157, 219, 387).]

and, in particular, how far it was under an obligation to insure, when concluding the Paris Agreements, that the Supreme Restitution Court would be bound to respect the provisions of the European Convention of Human Rights.

"*Thirdly*, to present any additional observations which they might think useful on the application of Article 26 of the Convention[1] to the present case, in the event that the Supreme Restitution Court should be held to be an international tribunal for whose acts or omissions the Federal Republic is not responsible under the Convention.

" And in responding on the third point, concerning the application of Article 26, the parties were invited in particular:

" (*a*) to take into consideration the fact that appeals from the decision of the Court of Appeal of ——— to the Court of Restitution Appeals and to the Supreme Restitution Court were open to, and in fact had been brought by, the first Applicant under, respectively, the relevant provisions of the Occupation Laws and the Paris Agreements;

" (*b*) to consider whether any proceedings were open to the Applicants under German law for the purpose of instituting a claim against the Federal Republic in respect of breaches of the European Convention of Human Rights alleged to result from the acts or omissions of the Court of Appeal of ——— and from the subsequent failure of the Court of Restitution Appeals and Supreme Restitution Court to remedy those alleged breaches.

" The replies of the Applicants and the Federal Government to the above-mentioned points were submitted in letters of April 30 and May 7, 1958, respectively, and are taken into account in the summary of their arguments which is given below:

" *The Arguments of the Parties*

" The arguments of the parties may be summarised as follows:

" I. *Responsibility of the German Government*

" The Applicants contended:

" In accordance with Article 1 of the Convention, the Federal Government was bound to secure to everyone within its jurisdiction the rights and freedoms defined in Section 1 of the Convention; that the Federal Government was, therefore, responsible internationally for alleged breaches of the Convention by [the] Courts sitting at ——— and ———, respectively, and therefore within its territorial jurisdiction.

" The Court of Appeal at ——— formed part of the German judicial system and the Federal Government's responsibility for the acts of that Court was therefore evident.

[1 Article 26 of the Convention provides: " The Commission may only deal with the matter after all domestic remedies have been exhausted, according to the generally recognised rules of international law, and within a period of six months from the date on which the final decision was taken."]

" For purposes of international law the Court of Restitution Appeals was a Court within the Federal Republic's jurisdiction for which the Federal Government was internationally responsible, even although until the coming into force of the Settlement Convention, on May 5, 1955, this Court was admitted by the Applicants to be an American Court and that the Federal Government had no control over it.

" The Supreme Restitution Court was a Court within the Federal Republic's jurisdiction; . . . it resulted from the constitution of the Court, as established in the Charter contained in the Annex to Chapter 3 of the Settlement Convention, that the Federal Government was at least jointly responsible for its acts; . . . the Federal Republic had international responsibility for the acts of the Supreme Restitution Court both originally by reason of its own defaults and indirectly by reason of its vicarious responsibility for the defaults of the Court itself.

" The Applicants developed their argument in regard to the original responsibility of the Federal Republic for the alleged violation of the Convention by the Supreme Restitution Court as follows:

" The Federal Government, being a High Contracting Party to the Human Rights Convention, failed to secure a procedure of the Court compatible with the Convention on Human Rights and, in particular, with Article 6 of the said Convention.

" The Federal Government, in accordance with Chapter 3, Article 2, of the Settlement Convention, undertook ' to implement ' the legislation referred to in Article 1 thereof and ' to entrust a Federal Agency with ensuring the fulfilment ' of this obligation. By Article 3 (2) thereof, the Federal Republic was given the right to ' exercise all legislative powers exercisable by the Three Powers or any of them pursuant to such legislation in a manner not inconsistent therewith, by means of Federal legislation or of ordinances of the Federal Government '. The Federal Republic, therefore, had the power and the right to exercise the sovereign right of legislation and thus to exercise ' jurisdiction '; it had a corresponding duty, the fulfilment of which was partly entrusted to a Special Federal Agency and otherwise vested in the Federal Parliament.

" By virtue of Chapter 3, Article 6 (2), of the Settlement Convention, the Court of Restitution Appeals ' shall within three months decide those cases in process of final disposition '; the fulfilment of this obligation was undertaken by the Federal Republic when it signed the said Convention; the Federal Republic failed to exercise its jurisdiction under the said Articles 2 and 3 (2) by appointing a Federal Agency or otherwise in order to ensure the performance of the obligation arising under the said Article 6 (2).

" By virtue of Article 1, paragraph 2, and Article 3 of the Convention on Relations between the Three Powers and the Federal Republic (hereafter referred to as ' the Relations Convention '), of the above Articles of the Settlement Convention and of the provisions of Article 69 of Law No. 59, the Federal Republic had the overriding sovereign power of making rules of practice and procedure, while the making of such rules was also, by delegation, in the competence of the Supreme Restitution Court pursuant to Article 9 (1) (c) of its Charter as contained in the Annex to Chapter 3 of the Settlement Convention. The Federal Republic failed to exercise such power so as to make rules of procedure adequate to ensure the observance of the Human Rights Convention.

" Alternatively, if the Settlement Convention should have to be so construed as to require or permit a breach of the Human Rights Convention, the conclusion of the Settlement Convention by the Federal Republic was of itself a breach of the Human Rights Convention.

" The Applicants further developed their arguments in regard to the vicarious responsibility of the Federal Republic for the alleged violation of the Convention by the Supreme Restitution Court as follows:

" The Supreme Restitution Court, being within the territory of the Federal Republic, was within the Federal Republic's jurisdiction.

" Alternatively, the Federal Government had, at least, a joint responsibility, for the acts of the Supreme Restitution Court.

" Alternatively, under the Settlement Convention the Federal Republic had such measure of control over the Supreme Restitution Court as brought it within its jurisdiction in the sense of Article 1 of the Human Rights Convention.

" Alternatively, the Supreme Restitution Court, deriving its powers from the Settlement Convention which became part of German law pursuant to a Law of March 24, 1955 (BGBl 1955 II 213), had its legislative origin in a sovereign act of the Federal Republic and was therefore within the Federal Republic's jurisdiction.

" In reply, the Federal Government contended that the obligation of the High Contracting Parties, as stated in Article 1 of the Convention on Human Rights, is to ' secure to everyone within their jurisdiction the rights and freedoms defined in Section 1 of this Convention '; . . . in consequence an application against a High Contracting Party which is founded on an alleged breach of the rights defined in Section 1 through the decision of a Court must have as its basis a decision found to be the decision of a Court of the State against which the application is lodged.

" With regard to the alleged breach of Article 6 of the Convention by the Court of Appeal at ——, the decision of this Court must be disregarded since the first Applicant was entitled to have, and did in fact have, recourse by way of appeal to a further tribunal in accordance with the provisions of the prescribed legal procedure.

" With regard to the alleged breach of the Convention by the Court of Restitution Appeals, the Federal Government contended that, as was admitted by the Applicants, that Court did not form part of the German judicial system and did not exercise jurisdiction under the Federal Republic of Germany; the Federal Government had accordingly no control over that Court.

" In regard to its supposed original responsibility for the alleged violation of the Convention by the Supreme Restitution Court, the Federal Government replied:

" The relevant part of Chapter 1, Article 1, of the Relations Convention stated as follows:

" 'The Federal and *Land* Authorities shall have the power, in accordance with their respective competences under the Basic Law of the Federal Republic, to repeal or amend legislation enacted by the Occupation Authorities, *except as otherwise provided in the Convention on Relations between the Three Powers and the Federal Republic of Germany or any of the related Conventions listed in Article 8 thereof.*'

" One of the ' related Conventions ' was the Settlement Convention; . . . the provisions, in particular Articles 1, 2 and 3, of the latter Convention and the fact that Article 69 of Military Government Law No. 59, on which the Applicants relied, had already been abolished by Article 8 of the Allied High Commission Law No. 21, had the effect that the exclusive power to make regulations had been transferred directly from the American High Commission to the Court of Restitution Appeals and thereafter to the Supreme Restitution Court. This was further shown in the Preamble to the Rules of Procedure which were issued by the Supreme Restitution Court and which came into force on March 7, 1957. The power to make regulations was accordingly never acquired by the Federal Republic, which, furthermore, by the provisions of the Settlement Convention, was bound under international law to respect such exclusive competence of the Supreme Restitution Court.

" Although the Human Rights Convention came into force before the Settlement Convention, the Federal Republic only acquired sovereignty under the latter Convention, and that sovereignty was limited in various ways, in particular by exclusion of control over the Supreme Restitution Court.

" The exclusive power of the Supreme Restitution Court to draft its rules of procedure was provided for in the Settlement Convention signed on May 26, 1952, and this provision could not be amended by the Federal Republic at the time of the conclusion of the Protocol thereto on October 23, 1954.

" In regard to the supposed vicarious responsibility of the Federal Republic for the alleged violation of the Convention by the Supreme Restitution Court, the Federal Government contended in reply:

" The Charter of the Supreme Restitution Court, annexed to Chapter 3 of the Settlement Convention, and, in particular, Articles

2, 3, 5, 6 (1), 7 (3) and 9 of the said Charter, made it clear that the Supreme Restitution Court was an international court over which the Federal Republic had no control; and . . . the Applicants did not in any event come under the sovereignty of the Federal Republic either before or after the Supreme Restitution Court was set up.

" Alternatively, the Supreme Restitution Court was not a Civil Court or Criminal Court for the purposes of Article 6 of the Human Rights Convention but had the character of an administrative court.

" In regard to the Applicants' claim that the Federal Republic is responsible for the acts of the Supreme Restitution Court as being a Court based on a German Law of March 24, 1955, the Federal Government conceded that this Law was the essential German legal instrument; whereas, however, it disputed that the said law had the effect of making the Supreme Restitution Court a court based on German law for the purposes of the Human Rights Convention, arguing as follows:

" Article 1 of the said Law merely provided:

' Consent is hereby given to the Protocol signed in Paris on October 23, 1954, concerning the termination of the occupation régime in the Federal Republic of Germany together with Lists I to V annexed thereto, to the exchange of Letters of October 23, 1954, which referred to Letters exchanged in 1952, and to the exchange of Letters of October 23, 1954, concerning facilities for Embassies and Consulates '.

" The effect of this Article was to put the President of the Federal Republic in a position to deposit the instrument of ratification with respect to the Protocol in the Article; and that the exchange of instruments of ratification effected by the President with the other Contracting Parties is an executive act in German law and not an act of substantive legislation.

" While a further effect of the said Law was to transform the Protocol and the various international agreements annexed thereto into internal German law, the passing of the law by the Federal Parliament did not make these Agreements immediately binding within the German law; . . . , on the contrary, the international agreements in question did not become binding as internal German law until the subsequent exchange of ratifications which created their binding force internationally; and . . . , if those agreements for any reason ceased to be binding internationally, they would automatically cease to be binding internally in German law.

" In consequence, the Supreme Restitution Court is to be regarded as based on the international agreements in question, not on German law.

" II. *Exhaustion of domestic remedies*

" The Applicants contended that an appeal against the decision of the Court of Appeal at —— had been made to the competent tribunal, namely, the Court of Restitution. Appeals, and thereafter to the Supreme Restitution Court.

" No appeal lay from the Supreme Restitution Court to the Federal Constitutional Court or any other tribunal in the Federal Republic.

" It was clear from the provision of Section 90 (2) of the Law of the Federal Constitutional Court that it was unlikely that the Federal Constitutional Court would have admitted a remedy from the Court of Appeal and . . . , therefore, there was no reasonable expectation that such appeal to the Federal Constitutional Court would succeed.

" It had not been open to the first Applicant to pursue simultaneous lines of appeal to the Federal Constitutional Court and the Court of Restitution Appeals, respectively, and . . . he had, therefore, chosen the normal remedy expressly provided for under Law No. 21, namely, recourse to the Court of Restitution Appeals.

" The Federal Government admitted that the first Applicant had exhausted those domestic remedies which led to the Supreme Restitution Court, from which, it also admitted, there was no further appeal.

" The Government contended, however, that the first Applicant could have pursued, previously or at least simultaneously, a line of appeal from the Court of Appeal to the Federal Constitutional Court, and that Section 90 (2) of the Law on the Federal Constitutional Court, together with Article 103 of the Basic Law (*Grundgesetz*), provided for substantial recourse on the particular grounds alleged.

" The second Applicant was not a party to the proceedings before the District Court and the Court of Appeal and had not, therefore, exhausted those domestic remedies.

" The parties were agreed that no proceedings were open to the Applicants under German law for the purposes of instituting a claim against the Federal Republic in respect of breaches of the Human Rights Convention alleged to result from the acts or omissions of the Court of Appeal at —— or from the subsequent failure of the Court of Restitution Appeals and the Supreme Restitution Court to remedy those alleged breaches."

*Held:* that the application must be dismissed.

The Commission said: " The Applicants allege that, in dealing with the first Applicant's claim to restitution under the relevant Laws and Agreements in force, three courts successively committed violations of Article 6 of the Convention, and that the Federal Republic is responsible for the alleged defaults of each of these courts.

" In chronological order, the first of these courts was the *Oberlandesgericht* at ——, an appellate court forming part of the hierarchy of courts within the Federal Republic. The first Applicant's claim was dealt with by this Court under Military Government Law No. 59

in the United States Zone of Occupation, which conferred upon the Court an appellate jurisdiction in matters of restitution covered by the provisions of the said Law.

" In chronological order, the second of these Courts was the Court of Restitution Appeals at ――――. The first Applicant's claim was partially considered by this Court under Law No. 21 of the United States High Commissioner for Germany, which conferred upon the Court jurisdiction to review the decisions of German courts in matters of restitution within the United States Zone of Occupation. The claim had not been decided by this Court before the entry into force of the Paris Agreements for the termination of the occupation régime in the Federal Republic.

' " In chronological order, the third of these Courts was the Supreme Court of Restitution Appeals at Nuremberg. The first Applicant's claim was dealt with by this Court under the provisions of Chapter 3 of the Settlement Convention, Article 6 of which transferred to the Third Division of the said Court jurisdiction to hear and determine cases left undecided by the above-mentioned Court of Restitution Appeals.

" The alleged injustice of which the Applicants complain culminated in the final rejection of the first Applicant's claim by the last mentioned Supreme Court of Restitution. The Commission's decision as to the responsibility or otherwise of the Federal Republic for the acts or omissions of the Supreme Restitution Court may have consequences for its decision as to the responsibility of the Federal Republic for the acts or omissions of the *Oberlandesgericht* of ――――. Accordingly, the Commission will first examine the Federal Republic's responsibility in regard to the Supreme Restitution Court.

" *The responsibility of the Federal Republic in regard to the Supreme Restitution Court.*—The Commission considers that the Supreme Restitution Court without doubt possesses the character of an international tribunal, *inter alia*, for the following reasons:

" (1) The Court was established by Article 6, Chapter III, of the Settlement Convention, an international Convention concluded between the three Occupying Powers and the Federal Republic, and the said Article 6 expressly provided that the composition, jurisdiction, powers and duties of the Court should be as prescribed in a Charter drawn up by the Four Powers and annexed to the Convention;

" (2) Article 1, paragraphs 1 and 2, together with Article 9 of the Charter of the Court provided that the Court should consist of three Divisions, one for each former Zone of Occupation, and that each Division should be composed of at least *five* justices; and Article 2 of the said Charter further provided that of these five justices two were to be appointed by the former Occupying Power, two by the Federal Republic and one was to be the national of an outside State and appointed by agreement between the Federal Republic and the former Occupying Power or, failing such agreement, by the President of the International Court of Justice. In short, the provisions of Article 2 are similar to those found in numerous international treaties for the establishment of international mixed arbitral tribunals;

" (3) Article 3, paragraph 5, of the said Charter provided that all justices of the Court, other than German nationals, should enjoy during their term of office not merely immunity from guilt in respect of acts performed in the exercise of their official duties but also ' the same privileges and immunities as are accorded members of diplomatic missions '.

" (4) Article 1 of the said Charter mentions a number of matters the determination of which needs the approval of the three former Occupying Powers and the Federal Government, while paragraph 7 of the same Article obliges the Presidential Council to render annual reports to the Governments of the three Powers and the Federal Government setting forth its requirements for personnel in the ensuing twelve months.

" The Applicants, nevertheless, maintain that, regardless of the international character of the Supreme Restitution Court, the Federal Republic has responsibility under the Convention for the defects of its proceedings because they contend that the entry into force of the Paris Agreements on May 5, 1955, put the Federal Government into a position to control and amend the procedure of the Court.

" However, the arguments advanced by the Applicants in support of their last-mentioned contention do not appear to the Commission to be well-founded for the following reasons:

" (1) It is true that Article 1, paragraph 2, of the Relations Convention laid down that the Federal Republic should thenceforth have ' the full authority of a Sovereign State over its internal and external affairs '. It is also true that Article 1 of Chapter 1 of the Settlement Convention expressly provided that the Federal *Land* Authorities should ' have the power, in accordance with their respective competences under the Basic Law of the Federal Republic, to repeal or amend legislation enacted by the Occupation Authorities '. The latter provision, however, was made subject to the very important qualification that the Federal and *Land* authorities should not have this power where any of the various Conventions in question otherwise provided.

" (2) In the opinion of the Commission the procedure of the Supreme Restitution Court was a matter where other provision was made in the Settlement Convention with the result that the Federal and *Land* authorities were not empowered by the Paris Agreements to legislate in regard to the procedure of that Court.

Articles 1 and 5 of the Charter of the Court, annexed to the said Convention, provided that the constitution of the Supreme Restitution Court should include a Presidential Council, which was invested with power to determine the arrangements and regulate the proceedings of the Court. This Presidential Council was to consist of nine justices, three being drawn from each Division as follows: the justice appointed from outside the nationals of the High Contracting Parties, one of the justices appointed by the Occupying Power concerned and one of the justices appointed by the Federal Republic. The said Convention and the said Charter contained no provisions which might be construed as giving the Federal Republic control of, or reponsibility for, the Presidential Council.

" On the contrary, Article 1, paragraphs 6 and 7, of the said Charter contained clear indications that any control of, or responsibility for, the Presidential Council was to be vested in the three Occupying Powers and the Federal Republic acting together.

" (3) As to the power to control the justices in the performance of their judicial duties, Article 2, paragraph 4, of the said Charter made it plain that this power was not given to any of the High Contracting Parties but was to be vested in the Presidential Council. Paragraph 4 provided that it was for the Presidential Council to declare a vacancy in the event of a justice failing to perform his duties diligently.

" (4) As to the power to draw up or amend the rules of procedure of the Supreme Restitution Court, it is clear that the effect of Article 5, paragraph 5, of the Charter was to vest this power in the Presidential Council and not in the Federal Republic. In the first place, it is a general rule of international law that, in the absence of any express provision to the contrary, international tribunals have power to determine their own rules of procedure and the Presidential Council was the organ designated by the said Charter to consider questions of common interest to the three Divisions and to be generally responsible for the administration of the Court as a whole. In the second place, Article 5, paragraph 5 (c), expressly vested in the Presidential Council the powers formerly exercised by the United Kingdom High Commissioner, under British Military Government Law No. 59, to approve rules of procedure in restitution appeals in the British Zone. In other words, the power to approve rules of procedure for the Second Division of the Supreme Restitution Court was by this provision expressly placed in the hands of the Presidential Council and not in those of the Federal Republic. Although the said Charter contains no similar provision for the French and United States Zones, it appears to the Commission to be completely inconceivable that the High Contracting Parties intended to differentiate between the three Divisions of the Court in regard to the Presidential Council's power to approve rules of procedure.

"No possible reason can be imagined which might lead the High Contracting Parties to intend to place the power of approving rules of procedure for the Second Division in the hands of the Presidential Council but that for the other two Divisions in the hands of the Federal Republic. On the other hand, the reason why it was thought necessary to make express mention of the transfer of the powers of the former United Kingdom High Commissioner to the Presidential Council, while saying nothing about a similar transfer in regard to the French and United States High Commissioners, is not far to seek. In the former United Kingdom Zone of Occupation the High Commissioner, while permitting the Restitution Court of Appeal (called the Board of Review) to draw up its own rules of procedure, had made these rules expressly subject to subsequent approval by himself. In the other two Occupation Zones, however, there was no such express reservation of power to the High Commissioner and it was not therefore thought necessary to say anything in the Charter of the Supreme Restitution Court concerning a transfer of the power to approve rules of procedure from the High Commission to the Presidential Council. As the Commission has already stated, it appears inconceivable that the High Contracting Parties intended to create a difference between the three Divisions of the Council on this point. Accordingly, the very fact that Article 5, paragraph 5 (c), of the said Charter expressly transferred the power of approving rules of procedure in regard to the Second Division to the Presidential Council appears to the Commission to be fatal to the Applicants' contention that in regard to the Third Division the same power was transferred to the Federal Republic under the provisions of the Paris Agreements.

"It follows that, for the purposes of determining the responsibility of the Federal Republic in the present case, the Supreme Restitution Court must be regarded as an international tribunal with respect to whose procedure the Federal Republic had no powers of legislation or control. Also it is clear that, in general, a State does not have responsibility for the acts or omissions of an international tribunal merely by reason that [the tribunal] has its seat and exercises its functions on the territory of that State; otherwise it could be said that, for example, the Netherlands Government had responsibility for the acts or omissions of the International Court of Justice itself, which sits at The Hague. In the present case, however, there has to be taken into account the special fact that the Supreme Restitution Court was established as an international tribunal to review in matters of restitution the decisions of courts which were undoubtedly courts of the Federal Republic.

"On this aspect of the Federal Republic's alleged responsibility for the proceedings of the Supreme Restitution Court, the nearest parallel to the present case appears to be the *Salem Case* decided by a United States-Egyptian Mixed Arbitral Tribunal in 1932.

In that case the Tribunal had under consideration Egypt's responsibility for an alleged denial of justice by one of the so-called Mixed Courts established by Agreements between Egypt and Foreign Powers to hear cases involving the interests of foreigners. The Tribunal, as a secondary ground for its refusal to hold Egypt responsible for the acts or omissions of the Mixed Courts, expressly held that the Egyptian Government could not be made responsible at all for the errors of the Mixed Courts, and set out its reasons for so holding as follows:

'*The Arbitral Court has already pointed out that this jurisdiction was instituted and is continued not only through the will of the Sovereign Egyptian State, but by conventions concluded with the capitulatory powers.* Both Parties, by executing these Conventions in form of corresponding national legislations, made a sacrifice of their sovereignty; the capitulatory powers resigned a part of their jurisdictional prerogatives on Egyptian territory by waiving for a time the civil jurisdiction of their consuls; the Egyptian Government resigned likewise a part of their jurisdictional sovereignty by undertaking to let themselves be judged in civil cases, especially in cases for alleged violation of foreigners' rights on the part of Egyptian authorities, by a court composed of a majority of foreigners. *If the Mixed Courts are at fault, the Egyptian Government is unable to prevent the repetition of such faults; they can neither remove the judges nor punish them by disciplinary action—this action is reserved to the Mixed Court of Appeal—nor can they modify the laws in accordance with which the court is composed and has to decide its cases.* None of these measures could have been taken during the period provided by the international conventions for the functioning of the mixed jurisdiction without the consent of the capitulatory powers.

'The responsibility of a State can only go as far as its sovereignty; in the same measure as the latter is restricted, that is to say, as the State cannot act in a free and independent manner, the liability of the State must also be restricted.'[1]

" Although there are certain differences between the legal circumstances of the *Salem Case* and those of the present case, the reasons which led the Tribunal in the *Salem Case* to refuse to hold the territorial State responsible apply with equal and even greater force in the present case; they apply with even greater force because, in the present case, the Supreme Court is an independent international tribunal which pronounces its judgments in its own name, whereas the Mixed Courts in Egypt formed part of the Egyptian judicial system and pronounced their judgments in the name of the King of Egypt.

" In sum, the Commission is clearly of the opinion that the Supreme Restitution Court is an international court, [and] is not a court within the jurisdiction of the Federal Republic nor subject to its sovereign power or control. Accordingly, the Commission rejects the submissions of the Applicant in so far as they seek to

[1 *Annual Digest*, 1931–1932, Case No. 98, at pp. 197–198.]

attribute responsibility to the Federal Republic on the basis that the Supreme Restriction Court was a court within its jurisdiction or a court subject to its power of legislation and control.

" The Applicants further contend that the Supreme Restitution Court had as its basis a German Law of March 25, 1955, and that the Federal Republic has responsibility under the Convention for that Court, as being a court based on German law.  However, a clear distinction must be drawn between the legal instrument on which the Supreme Restitution Court was based and the legal instrument by which the establishment of that Court was recognised by the Federal Republic for the purposes of its internal law.  In the opinion of the Commission, there can be no doubt that the legal instrument on which the Supreme Restitution Court was based was the Settlement Convention and the Charter annexed thereto, and that this instrument was an international agreement deriving its essential force from international, not German, law.  Although the passing of the above-mentioned German Law of March 24, 1955, may, as a matter of internal German law, have been essential for authorising the President of the Federal Republic to deposit on its behalf the instrument ratifying the Settlement Convention, that fact does not warrant the conclusion that the Supreme Restitution Court was based on the said Law of March 24, 1955.  Accordingly, the Commission considers that, for the purposes of the application of the European Convention of Human Rights, the Supreme Restitution Court has to be regarded as a court based on an international agreement and not one based on a German law.  It follows that the submissions of the Applicant founded upon a contrary view of the legal basis of the Supreme Restitution Court must be rejected.

" The Applicants, in seeking to establish an alternative ground for the responsibility of the Federal Republic, have contended that, by reason of its prior ratification of the Human Rights Convention, the Republic was under an obligation, when it signed the Paris Agreements, expressly to insure that the procedure of the Supreme Restitution Court should be in conformity with the provisions of the Human Rights Convention.  In consequence, if the Federal Republic failed to reserve for itself in the Paris Agreements sufficient powers to enable it to control the procedure of the said Court, that failure amounted to a lack of due diligence in the performance of its obligations under the Human Rights Convention which entailed the responsibility of the Federal Republic.

" It is clear that, if a State contracts treaty obligations and subsequently concludes another international agreement which disables it from performing its obligations under the first treaty, it will be answerable for any resulting breach of its obligations under the earlier treaty.  However, this is very far from being the position of the Federal Republic in the present case by reason of the following considerations:

" Before the entry into force of the Paris Agreements the Federal Republic did not possess the authority of a sovereign State in matters of restitution, which were then subject to the legislation and control of the Occupying Powers. It was only as a result of the Paris Agreements that the Federal Republic secured the termination of the Occupation Régime and obtained the authority of a sovereign State in matters of restitution. It follows that, when negotiating the terms of the Settlement Convention and of the Charter of the Supreme Restitution Court annexed thereto, the Federal Republic was not negotiating concerning the restriction of a sovereignty in matters of restitution which it already possessed but was, on the contrary, negotiating for the transfer to itself of the authority in matters of restitution which then belonged to the Occupying Powers.

" It may be a question whether in these circumstances there is any basis for applying the principle invoked by the Applicants that the Federal Republic, in concluding the Paris Agreements, was under an international obligation to insure that the Charter of the Supreme Restitution Court was in conformity with the Federal Republic's obligations under the Human Rights Convention. However, it is unnecessary for the Commission to decide the point since neither the Settlement Convention nor the Charter annexed thereto contained any provision which was either expressly or implicitly inconsistent with the provisions of the Human Rights Convention.

" In the opinion of the Commission, a Party to a Convention which establishes an independent international tribunal is entitled to presume that the tribunal will adopt such rules of procedures and will so order its proceedings as to conform to the recognised standards of the administration of international justice. Therefore, the mere fact that the Federal Republic did not take steps to secure the insertion in the Settlement Convention or in the Charter annexed thereto of an express provision requiring the Supreme Restitution Court to observe the prescriptions of the Human Rights Convention, cannot be considered to constitute a lack of due diligence on the part of the Federal Republic with respect to its obligations under the Human Rights Convention.

" If the complaint of a lack of due diligence on the part of the Federal Republic is put upon the ground that it failed to make representations or to take other steps to secure the insertion in the Supreme Restitution Court's Rules of Procedure of provisions which might have prevented the alleged breaches of the Human Rights Convention, it suffices to observe that these Rules of Procedure were not officially published until after the alleged breaches had occurred.

" If the complaint of lack of due diligence is put upon the ground of the failure of the Federal Republic to establish a federal agency entrusted with the task of insuring the fulfilment of its obligations in matters of restitution, as provided by Article 2 of Chapter 3 of the Settlement Convention, it suffices to observe that under the express terms of this Article the federal agency was only to be concerned with the fulfilment of the obligations of the Federal Republic in matters of restitution, and was given no mandate with respect to the proceedings of the Supreme Restitution Court. The Supreme Restitution Court, although a tribunal established to hear appeals in matters of restitution, has been held by the Commission to be an independent international tribunal for whose alleged acts or omissions the Federal Republic was not responsible. It follows that the failure of the Federal Republic to establish a federal agency, as contemplated in the said Article of the Settlement Convention, cannot be considered to be a failure of due diligence on the part of the Federal Republic with respect to its obligations under the Human Rights Convention.

" The Commission accordingly decides that the Federal Republic is not responsible in law for the alleged acts or omissions of the Supreme Restitution Court.

" *The Court of Restitution Appeals.*—It is common ground between the parties that the Court of Restitution Appeals was a United States Court in the United States Zone of Occupation and that the Federal Republic at no time had any power of legislation or control over the said Court. It follows that the said Court was not a Court within the jurisdiction of the Federal Republic for the purposes of Article 1 of the Human Rights Convention.

" The Commission accordingly decides that the Federal Republic is not responsible in law for the alleged acts or omissions of the Conrt of Restitution Appeals.

" *The Oberlandesgericht at*——.—It is not disputed that at all material dates the *Oberlandesgericht* at——was a German court subject to the legislation and control of the Federal Republic. It follows that the *Oberlandesgericht* at——is a court for which the Federal Republic in principle has responsibility.

" However, the responsibility of a State under the Human Rights Convention does not exist until, in conformity with Article 26, all domestic remedies have been exhausted according to the generally recognised rules of international law. The system of remedies in matters of restitution, provided by the Occupation Laws and afterwards by the Paris Agreements, was a very special one, the lower courts being German courts and the final court being in the earlier period a court of the Occupying Power and afterwards the Supreme Restitution Court. In the present case the first Applicant appealed from the allegedly defective decision of the *Oberlandesgericht* to the Court of Restitution Appeals. After the entry into force of the Paris Agreements the appeal, being then still undecided, was transferred to the Supreme Restitution Court whose decision rejecting the appeal finally exhausted the remedies provided under the Occupation Laws and the Paris Agreements. It follows that, if regard is had exclusively to the system of remedies prescribed under the Occupation Laws and the Paris Agreements, the first Applicant had exhausted all the remedies available to him.

" In principle, if all remedies have been exhausted without an alleged maladministration of justice by a lower court having been redressed, and an application has been made within six months of the final decision, the Commission may take up the matter and examine into the alleged maladministration of justice. However, the position is different when the final decision was rendered by an independent international tribunal which rejected the Applicant's claim, because, by taking up the matter, the Commission would in effect be setting aside the decision of another international tribunal duly invested with competence to determine the case. Moreover, the Commission has held that the Supreme Restitution Court is an international tribunal for whose decision the Federal Republic does not have responsibility under the Convention. The Commission considers that any alleged maladministration of justice on the part of the *Oberlandesgericht* at ——, so far as concerns the responsibility of the Federal Republic, must be regarded as absorbed by the higher decision of the Supreme Restitution Court whose decisions are not subject to examination by the Commission under the Convention.

" The Commission, accordingly, decides that the Federal Republic is not responsible in law for the alleged maladministration of justice by the *Oberlandesgericht* at ——.

" Finally, the grounds alleged by the Applicants as establishing violations of the Convention by the *Oberlandesgericht* at —— were that it refused them an oral hearing and dismissed their appeal by a judgment which was not pronounced publicly. The Federal Republic having been held on other grounds not to be responsible in law for the alleged maladministration of justice by the said Court, the Commission finds it unnecessary to enter into the question whether in the circumstances of the present case the Application might also be inadmissible as manifestly ill-founded with reference to the decision of the *Oberlandesgericht* at ——.

" The Commission, for all the reasons which are set out above, decides that the Federal Republic does not have any responsibility under the Convention for the alleged acts or omissions of the *Oberlandesgericht* at —— or of the Court of Restitution Appeals or of the Supreme Restitution Court, and rejects the Application as manifestly ill-founded."

[Report: *Yearbook of the European Convention on Human Rights*, 1958–1959, p. 256.]

The individual in international law—Human rights and freedoms
—European Convention for Protection of—European Human
Rights Commission—Individual applications—Right to liberty and
security of person—Arrest and preventive detention—No *prima
facie* violation—Suspending effect of application to Commission
—Exhaustion of local remedies.

*Re* APPLICATION NO. 297/57 (X. *v.* GERMAN FEDERAL REPUBLIC).

*European Commission of Human Rights. March* 22, 1958.

(Waldock, President; Eustathiades, Berg, Faber, Beaufort, Dominedo,
Süsterhenn, Petren, Janssen-Pevtschin, Sørensen, Crosbie, Skarphedinsson, Erim.)

THE FACTS (as stated in the decision of the Commission).—
" The Applicant, a commerical representative, was a German
national.  He was arrested and placed in preventive detention on
May 22, 1957, on a warrant for his arrest issued on that date by the
District Court (*Amtsgericht*) of —— (Federal Republic of Germany).
He was accused of having knowingly contravened the decision of
August 17, 1956, of the Federal Constitutional Court (*Bundesverfassungsgericht*), which ordered the dissolution of the German
Communist Party (K.P.D.) as unconstitutional.  According to the
indictment, the Applicant had held a leading position in ' a clandestine association ' (Article 128 of the German Penal Code), furthered
clandestinely in the capacity of ' *Rädelsführer* ' and ' *Hintermann* '
an ' association whose aims or activities involve the commission
of offences ' (Article 129 of the German Penal Code) and violated the
provisions of Article 90 of the German Penal Code and Articles 42
and 47 of the Law on the Federal Constitutional Court (*Gesetz über
das Bundesverfassungsgericht*).    The Applicant was accused, in
particular, of having made use of his occupation, which enabled him
to travel frequently, for the purpose of maintaining contact of all
kinds with the clandestine organisations of the German Communist
Party.

" The warrant gave as the grounds for X.'s preventive detention
the seriousness of the suspicions against him, the danger that he
might abscond and the danger that he might destroy the evidence
against him.

" On the day of his arrest, the Applicant lodged an appeal (*Beschwerde*) for his provisional release.  The appeal was disallowed on
May 25, 1957, by the —— Court of First Instance (*Landgericht*)
on the same grounds as those given in the warrant.  On June 11, 1957,
the Applicant lodged a ' second appeal ' (*weitere Beschwerde*) against
the decision (*Beschluss*) of the *Landgericht*, in which he denied the
accusations made against him and, in particular, the existence of a
danger that he might abscond or destroy the evidence.  He requested
the Court to inform him of the grounds for the accusations made
against him and the names of the witnesses for the prosecution.

Lastly, he requested his provisional release at least on account of his poor state of health. The —— Court of Appeal (*Oberlandesgericht*) disallowed X.'s ' second appeal ' by an interlocutory judgment (*Beschluss*) of June 20, 1957. On July 19, 1957, the —— District Court, having reviewed his detention, ordered it to be continued. The Applicant lodged an appeal against this order with the —— Court (*Landgericht*). The appeal was disallowed on July 30, 1957. A ' second appeal ' was disallowed by the —— Court of Appeal (*Oberlandesgericht*) on August 21, 1957. The Applicant was released from preventive detention on October 15, 1957, and the warrant for his arrest was withdrawn on October 17, 1957, at the request of the Public Prosecutor, who considered, as a result of further investigation, that circumstances no longer justified prolonging the detention.

" The Applicant's lawyer, in his letters of July 1 and October 7, 1957, formally denied the accusations against his client and declared that the latter's numerous journeys were a normal feature of his activities as a commercial representative. He alleged violation of Articles 5, 6, 7, 8, 9, 10, 11, 13 and 14 of the European Convention on Human Rights. He contended further that, even if the accusations mentioned above were founded, X.'s preventive detention violated the provisions of Article 5 (3) of the Convention,[1] since he had not yet appeared before the Court competent to try him and had thus been denied his right to ' trial within a reasonable time ', as set forth in the aforesaid article.

" The Applicant asked the Commission to declare his application admissible and to intervene with the authorities of the Federal Republic of Germany on his behalf in order to secure his immediate release. He requested the Commission, in the event of its proving impossible to secure his release through a friendly settlement, to declare that the Federal Republic of Germany had violated the Convention and to submit the case to the Committee of Ministers of the Council of Europe.

" The Government of the Federal Republic of Germany, in their written comments of February 10, 1958, stated that the length of X.'s preventive detention was due to the fact that examination of his statements, particularly those on the purpose of his journeys, demanded exhaustive and complicated enquiries. The grounds for ordering and prolonging X.'s preventive detention had been twice examined by various courts, all of which had found the detention to be justified by circumstances. When the Public Prosecutor had decided, as a result of further investigation, that those circumstances no longer existed, he had himself requested withdrawal of the warrant

[1 Article 5, para. 3, of the Convention provides: " (3) Everyone arrested or detained in accordance with the provisions of paragraph 1 (*c*) of this Article shall be brought promptly before a judge or other officer authorized by law to exercise judicial power and shall be entitled to trial within a reasonable time or to release pending trial. Release may be conditioned by guarantees to appear for trial."]

for arrest. It was then clear that preventive detention had not been prolonged beyond a ' reasonable time ' within the meaning of Article 5 (3) of the Convention. The Government of the Federal Republic also stated that no charge could yet be brought against X. before the competent court, as the investigation was still incomplete on account of the difficulties mentioned above. Finally, the Federal Government contended that, if X. did not consider his application to be settled, it should be rejected under Article 27 (2) of the Convention as manifestly ill-founded.

" The Applicant's lawyer, in his reply of March 12, 1958, to the aforesaid written comments of the Federal Government, maintained that X. had been unlawfully detained from May 22 to October 15, 1957. He submitted that the Federal Government themselves had apparently acknowledged the illegality of the measure by cancelling the detention order on October 17, 1957. In his view, the comments of the Federal Government could not justify the Applicant's continued detention.

" The Applicant's lawyer also stated that the Federal Government had violated Article 6 of the Convention, alleging that the Public Prosecutor had submitted to the Judges dealing with the case documents containing unfavourable secret information respecting X. although neither he nor his representative had been allowed access to the file and no copy of the said documents had subsequently been transmitted to them, and this constituted a flagrant violation of the rights of the defence.

" The Applicant claimed compensation for the damage suffered through his detention. He furthermore contended that, apart from any other consideration, the mere fact that the Application of the German Communist Party was pending before the Commission in May 1957 should have required the German Government to await the finding of the Commission before prosecuting him under the decision of the Federal Constitutional Court against the Communist Party.

" Lastly, the Applicant complained that a letter which he had written to his wife on September 22, 1957, was confiscated as abusive under a decision (*Beschluss*) of September 26, 1957, of the —— District Court (*Amtsgericht*). He claimed that his right to freedom of expression had thereby been infringed."

*Held:* that the application must be dismissed.

The Commission said: " *With regard to the Applicant's complaint as to his alleged wrongful arrest and preventive detention.*—An examination of the file, including an examination made *ex officio*, does not disclose a *prima facie* violation of the rights and freedoms set out in the Convention, in particular under Articles 5 and 6. The conditions required by Article 5, paragraph 1 (c), of the Convention were in fact satisfied. It therefore appears that the Application is in this respect manifestly ill-founded. The Application should, in pursuance of Article 27, paragraph 2, of the Convention, accordingly be rejected.

" *With regard to the Applicant's complaint in respect of the duration of his preventive detention.*—An examination of the file, including an examination made *ex officio*, does not disclose a *prima facie* violation of the rights and freedoms set out in the Convention, in particular under Article 5, paragraph 3. It appears in fact that the said detention cannot be regarded as having been unduly prolonged, in view of the complex nature of the Applicant's case and in view of the fact that the grounds of his detention were under continual consideration by the German courts as a result of the many applications submitted by X., and speedier proceedings as to his activities and doings were thereby prevented. It therefore appears that the Application is in this respect manifestly ill-founded and should, in pursuance of Article 27, paragraph 2, of the Convention, accordingly be rejected.

" *With regard to the Applicant's contention that the Government of the Federal Republic of Germany should have refrained from prosecuting him until the Commission had given a ruling on Application No. 250/57, being an Application submitted by the German Communist Party against the Federal Republic of Germany which was declared inadmissible on July 20, 1957.*[1]—The Convention does not contain any such obligations binding upon the High Contracting Parties as invoked by the Applicant. Moreover, the Convention does not contain any provision giving the Commission competence to order provisional measures. It therefore appears that the Application is in this respect incompatible with the provisions of the Convention and should, in pursuance of Article 27, paragraph 2, of the Convention, accordingly be rejected.

" *With regard to the alleged infringement of the Applicant's freedom of expression.*—According to Article 26 of the Convention, the Commission may only deal with a matter after all domestic remedies have been exhausted, according to the generally recognised rules of international law, and within a period of six months from the date on which the final decision was taken. The Applicant failed to have recourse to such remedies as were available to him in this matter. Moreover, an examination of the file, including an examination made *ex officio*, does not disclose the existence of any special circumstances which would have released the applicant, according to the generally recognised rules of international law, from the obligation to exhaust the domestic remedies at his disposal. It therefore appears that the Applicant has not satisfied the conditions laid down in Article 26 of the Convention as regards the exhaustion of local remedies. The application should in this respect, in pursuance

[1 *International Law Reports*, 1957, p. 349.]

of Article 27, paragraph 3, of the Convention, accordingly be rejected.

" *With regard to all other allegations contained in the letter dated March* 12, 1958, *by the Applicant's lawyer.*—According to Article 26 of the Convention, the Commission may only deal with a matter after all domestic remedies have been exhausted . . . . The Applicant failed to have recourse to such remedies as were available to him in this matter and did not, in particular, lodge a disciplinary action (*Dienstaufsichtsbeschwerde*) with regard to the submission by the Public Prosecutor of unfavourable secret information respecting the Applicant which the latter had no opportunity to see or contest. Moreover, the Applicant still has the right to make a submission in this respect when a charge is brought against him before the competent court. Moreover, an examination of the file, including an examination made *ex officio*, does not disclose the existence of any special circumstances which would have released the Applicant, according to the generally recognised rules of international law, from the obligation to exhaust the domestic remedies at his disposal. It therefore appears that the Applicant has not satisfied the conditions laid down in Article 26 of the Convention in regard to the exhaustion of local remedies and the Application should, also in this respect, in pursuance of Article 27, paragraph 3, of the Convention, accordingly be rejected.

[Report: *Yearbook of the European Convention on Human Rights*, 1958–1959, p. 204.]

**The individual in international law—Human rights and freedoms —European Convention for Protection of—European Human Rights Commission—Individual applications—Exhaustion of local remedies—Ineffective remedy—Article 17 of Convention—Acts and activities aimed at destruction of rights and freedoms set forth in Convention—Article 15—Derogations—Article 27 (2)—Whether application " manifestly ill-founded "—Whether application an " abuse of the right of petition "—Limit of power of Commission to consider admissibility of application.**

*Re* APPLICATION NO. 332/57 (LAWLESS *v.* REPUBLIC OF IRELAND).

*European Commission of Human Rights. August* 30, 1958.

(Waldock, President; Eustathiades, Berg, Faber, Beaufort, Dominedo, Süsterhenn, Petren, Janssen-Pevtschin, Sørensen, Crosbie, Skarphed-insson, Erim.)

THE FACTS (as stated in the decision of the Commission).—The Applicant stated that he was a builder's labourer, an Irish national, and domiciled in Ireland.

" On May 14, 1957, the Applicant was arrested and on May 16, 1957, he was charged in the Dublin District Court under Sections 12 and 24 of the Offences Against the State Act, 1939 (hereinafter referred to as 'the Act of 1939') with, respectively, 'possession of incriminating documents' and 'membership of an unlawful organisation by possession of such documents'. He was sentenced to one month's imprisonment on the first, but acquitted on the second, charge.

"On July 11, 1957, the Applicant was again arrested, and detained in the Bridewell Police Prison in Dublin under Section 30 of the Act of 1939, as being a suspected member of an illegal organisation.

"On July 12, 1957, the Chief Superintendent of Police, acting under Section 30 of the Act of 1939, made an Order that the Applicant be detained for a further period of 24 hours expiring at 7.45 p.m. on July 13, 1957.

"In the morning of July 13, 1957, the Applicant was transferred to the Curragh Military [Internment] Camp, County of Kildare, and was first detained in a Military Detention Prison and later, on July 17, 1957, in an Internment Camp. On July 13, 1957, while in the Internment Camp, he was handed a copy of an Order made on July 12, 1957, by the Minister of Justice pursuant to Section 4 of the Offences Against the State (Amendment) Act, 1940 (hereinafter referred to as 'the Act of 1940') and ordering his arrest and detention.

"On July 11, 1957, the Applicant [had been] informed in writing that he would be released forthwith on giving a written undertaking that he would respect the Constitution and Laws of Ireland and would not be a member of, or assist, any organisation declared unlawful under the Act of 1939. The Applicant [had] declined for alleged political and religious reasons to give such an undertaking.

"On September 8, 1957, the Applicant applied to the Government to have the continuation of his detention considered by a Commission set up under Section 8 of the Act of 1940 (hereinafter referred to as 'the Internment Commission').

"The Internment Commission held sittings on September 17 and September 20, 1957, in the presence of the Applicant and his Counsel. At the session of September 20 the hearing was adjourned *sine die*, pending the outcome of proceedings regarding a Conditional Order of *Habeas Corpus ad subjiciendum*, which the Applicant had applied for on September 18, 1957, and subsequently obtained from the High Court. The said Order was directed to the Commandant in charge of the Curragh Internment Camp.

"The Motion of the Applicant, dated September 30, 1957, for an Order to have the Conditional Order made absolute notwithstanding cause shown, was heard on October 8, 1957, by the High Court which, after further hearings on October 9, 10, 11 and 16, 1957, allowed the cause shown and discharged the Order.

"On October 14, 1957, the Applicant appealed from the Order of the High Court to the Supreme Court asking that that Order be reversed, the appeal be allowed and the Conditional Order of

*Habeas Corpus* be made absolute. The hearing of this Appeal began on October 21 and was concluded on October 31, 1957. On November 6, 1957, the Supreme Court announced its decision refusing the appeal and affirming the Order of the High Court allowing the cause shown and on December 31, 1957, delivered its judgment.

" On December 6 and 10, 1957, the Internment Commission continued its hearings, during the course of which the Applicant filed an affidavit denying various allegations which had been submitted in the Police Report as being parts of the grounds for the Applicant's detention.    Following the reading of this affidavit, the Attorney-General stated that he would be prepared to recommend the Applicant's release if the latter would give assurance that he would not in the future engage in any illegal activities. The Applicant agreed provided that the Attorney-General would undertake to re-investigate the charges made against the Applicant before the Internment Commission. The Attorney-General indicated that he would take this course. On December 11, 1957, the Applicant was released from detention.

" It is now alleged by the Applicant that his arrest and imprisonment under the Act of 1940 without charge or trial constituted a breach of the [European Convention for the Protection of Human Rights and Fundamental Freedoms, 1950] and, in particular, of the provisions of Articles 5 and 6 thereof.

" In his Statement of Complaint and Claim of November 8, 1957, the Applicant requested the Commission to take all steps within its competence to secure:

" (a) ' the immediate release from imprisonment;

" (b) ' The payment of compensation and damages by the Irish Government for his imprisonment from July 12, 1957, to the date of his release;

" (c) ' the payment by the Irish Government of all the costs and expenses of and incidental to the proceedings instituted by the Applicant to secure his release in the Irish Courts and before the Commission of Human Rights.'

" The Applicant stated in a letter of December 16, 1957, to the Secretary-General of the Council of Europe that, notwithstanding his release from internment, he wished to maintain his application before the Commission and that his claim was solely for damages.

" The Applicant declared in his Statement of Claim, filed on June 20, 1958, that he claimed payment of compensation and damages for his imprisonment by the Respondent Government:

" (a) ' From July 12, 1957 (the date upon which the Warrant for the imprisonment of the Complainant pursuant to the provisions of the Offences Against the State (Amendment) Act, 1940, was signed by a Minister of the Respondent Government), to December 11, 1957;

" (b) ' In the alternative, as and from 6 a.m. on July 13, 1957 (the hour at which the Complainant was removed from the Bridewell Police Prison) to December 11, 1957.

" (c) ' In the further alternative, as and from 8 a.m. on the said July 13, 1957 (the hour at which the Complainant became a prisoner at the Military Internment Camp) to December 11, 1957.'

" The Applicant further claimed payment by the Respondent Government of all the costs and expenses of, and incidental to, the proceedings instituted by him in the Irish Courts and before the Commission.

" The Respondent Government has requested the Commission to reject the Application and declare it inadmissible, on grounds which may be summarised as follows:

" (i) the Applicant did not comply with Article 26 of the Convention in that he failed to exhaust the domestic remedies which were open to him;

" (ii) the Application is an abuse of the right of recourse;

" (iii) the Application is inadmissible under the provisions of Article 17 of the Convention;[1]

" (iv) the Application does not disclose any violation of the rights set forth in the Convention;

" (v) Article 15 of the Convention permits derogation and the Irish Government addressed in this respect a letter to the Secretary-General of the Council of Europe, dated July 20, 1957.

*Held:* that the application was admissible.

The Commission said:

" 1. *As regards the exhaustion of domestic remedies.*—Article 26 of the Convention provides that ' the Commission may only deal with the matter after all domestic remedies have been exhausted, according to the generally recognised rules of international law, and within a period of six months from the date on which the final decision was taken '.

" It is not disputed that under the laws in force in the Republic of Ireland a person claiming to be illegally detained has available to him certain remedies before the ordinary courts, and in particular proceedings for *habeas corpus* and an action for false imprisonment.

" The Applicant sought to obtain his release by proceedings for *habeas corpus* in the High Court. The responsible officers of the Republic made answer that the Applicant was detained under powers conferred on them by Section 4 of the Act of 1940. The High Court held,

[1 Article 17 of the Convention provides: " Nothing in this Convention may be interpreted as implying for any State, group or person any right to engage in any activity or perform any act aimed at the destruction of any of the rights and freedoms set forth herein or at their limitation to a greater extent than is provided for in the Convention."]

" (1) that the Act of 1940 is not open to challenge on constitutional grounds since the Supreme Court has already ruled that its provisions are not in conflict with the Constitution (*In re Article 26 of the Constitution and the Offences against the State, Amendment, Bill*, 1940: 1940 Irish Reports, p. 470);

" (2) that the European Convention for the Protection of Human Rights and Fundamental Freedoms does not have the force of law within the Republic of Ireland, so that, even if it were to be assumed that a conflict exists between the provisions of the Act of 1940 authorising detention without trial and the provisions of the Convention concerning liberty and security of the person, that would not affect the right of the Government to invoke and rely upon the provisions of the Act of 1940 in the Courts of the Republic; and

" (3) that, in consequence, it was a sufficient answer to the Applicant's proceedings for *habeas corpus* to show that he was detained by the responsible officers of the Government under powers conferred on them by the Act of 1940.

" The decision of the High Court was upheld by the Supreme Court on substantially the same grounds, and no further appeal was open to the Applicant.

" It appears evident that the grounds which led the High Court and the Supreme Court to dismiss the Applicant's claim in the proceedings for *habeas corpus* would have equal force in proceedings by the Applicant for false imprisonment or in any other proceedings in the ordinary Courts of the Republic brought by the Applicant with respect to his detention under the Act of 1940. Therefore, any such further proceedings open to the Applicant in the ordinary Courts of the Republic with respect to his detention under the Act of 1940 did not offer him a reasonable prospect of success and must be regarded as ineffective remedies. It follows that under the generally recognised rules of international law it was not necessary for the Applicant to have recourse to such further domestic remedies before submitting his case to the Commission.

" However, the Respondent Government points out that the Applicant's claim is for compensation with respect to his detention from July 12, 1957, to the date of his release, that from July 12 until early on July 13 he was held in the Bridewell Police Prison under powers contained in the Act of 1939 and that on July 13 he was removed by police officers from that prison to the Curragh Internment Camp, where he was detained under an order made by the Ministry of Justice pursuant to the Act of 1940. It also points out that in the *habeas corpus* proceedings before the High Court and Supreme Court the Applicant complained that, when he was removed from the prison to the camp, he was not informed of the place where he was being brought nor the grounds on which he was being taken there into custody. It further states that the Supreme Court itself intimated in the *habeas corpus* proceedings that, if these allegations were well-founded, that part of the Applicant's arrest was illegal. The Respondent Government contends that, at any rate in respect of the brief period covering the transfer of the Applicant from the Bridewell Police Prison to the Curragh Internment Camp, the Applicant had available to him an action for false imprisonment which he made no attempt to use. It further contends that, even if this ground of objection should appear to be somewhat technical, it ought to be given full weight since, in the Government's view, the Applicant's claim is politically inspired and unmeritorious.

" At the oral hearing Counsel for the Applicant conceded that an action for false imprisonment could technically have been maintained with respect to a period of approximately two hours covering the period of his transfer from the Bridewell Police Prison to the Curragh Internment Camp. However, he also stated that the Applicant did not consider it to be worth while to pursue that action.

" In paragraph 24 of the Application the Applicant's claim was formulated in general terms as a claim to compensation and damages ' for his imprisonment in violation of the Convention from the 12th July, 1957, to the date of his release '. The Order made by the Minister for Justice ordering the Applicant's detention under the Act of 1940 was in fact made on July 12, 1957, although it was not actually executed until early the following morning. The detention of the Applicant from ' July 12, 1957, to the date of his release ' extended in all over a period of 153 days. Therefore, whatever action for false imprisonment may have been open to the Applicant with respect to the brief period of two hours covering his transfer from the Bridewell Police Prison to the Curragh Internment Camp, or with respect to any other period between July 12, 1957, and his detention under the Act of 1940 at the Camp at 8 a.m. the following day, relates to an infinitesimal part of the period of detention which is the subject of his claim. A judgment in the Applicant's favour in any such action for false imprisonment could not in any way have altered his position with respect to the subsequent period of his detention under the Act of 1940. It follows that the Commission must hold any such action for false imprisonment to have been an ineffective remedy with respect to the claim which is the subject of the Application.

" It remains a question whether the Applicant's failure to institute an action for false imprisonment with respect to some brief period before his detention in the Curragh Internment Camp has the consequence that his claim to compensation with respect to that period must be excluded from consideration. However, the facts relating to this question form an integral link in the facts on which the Applicant's whole claim is based. For this reason the Commission considers it desirable to defer its decision on this question until after the investigation of the facts of the case. Accordingly, the Commission reserves its decision on this question until a later stage in the proceedings.

" In general, with respect to the subject of this Application, the Applicant must be held to have exhausted the domestic remedies available in the ordinary Courts of the Republic according to the generally recognised rules of international law.

" However, the generally recognised rules of international law required the Applicant to exhaust not merely the remedies in the ordinary Courts but the whole system of legal remedies available in the Republic.

" The Act of 1940 provided in Section 8 for the establishment of a special Commission, namely, the Internment Commission, to which persons detained under the Act might apply to have their cases examined. Section 8 provided that the Commission should consist of three persons, of whom one should be a commissioned officer of the Defence Forces with not less than seven years' service, and the other two should be barristers or solicitors of not less than seven years' standing or should be or have been a judge of the Supreme Court, High Court, Circuit or District Court. Section 8 further provided that on an application being made to the Government by a detained person to have his case examined:

" (a) ' the Government shall, with all convenient speed, refer the matter of the continuation of such person's detention to the Commission;

" (b) ' the Commission shall inquire into the grounds of such person's detention and shall, with all convenient speed, report thereon to the Government;

" (c) ' the Minister for Justice shall furnish to the Commission such information and documents (relevant to the subject-matter of such inquiry) in the possession or procurement of the Government or of any Minister of State as shall be called for by the Commission;

" (d) ' if the Commission reports that no reasonable grounds exist for the continued detention of such person, such person shall, with all convenient speed, be released.'

" It clearly appears from paragraph (d) that a report of the Commission recommending the release of a detained person is binding upon the Government and effective to secure his release. Moreover, it is common ground between the Parties that, if the Internment Commission were to decline to examine a case or to render a report, it would be open to the detained person to apply for a mandatory order from the High Court to compel the Internment Commission to examine the case and to render a report.

" Therefore, the question is raised by Section 8 of the Act of 1940 whether the right which it gives to persons detained under the Act to have recourse to the Internment Commission is to be considered a domestic remedy the exhaustion of which is required by Article 26 of the Convention. However, it is unnecessary for the present Commission to pronounce upon this question because:

" (a) the Applicant is no longer in detention and the Application, although originally framed so as to include a demand for the Applicant's release, is now confined to a demand for compensation and damages;

" (b) it clearly appears from Section 8—and this is not disputed by the Respondent Government—that the power of the Internment Commission is confined to a power to recommend the release of the detained person and does not extend to recommending an award of damages or compensation;

" (c) the right of recourse to the Internment Commission under Section 8 is not therefore an effective remedy for the purpose of securing the redress which now forms the object of the Application.

" It is true that the Application was filed on November 8, 1957, at which date the Applicant was still in detention and his case was still under consideration by the Internment Commission. It is also true that at that date the Application, as previously stated, included a demand for the Applicant's release; and on the hypothesis that the right of recourse to the Internment Commission is a domestic remedy within the meaning of Article 26 of the Convention, the respondent Government contends that the Commission ought not to entertain the Application because the conditions laid down in that Article had not been fulfilled when it was filed.

" Even if it be accepted that the Application was out of order when it was filed on November 8, 1957, by reason of the Applicant's failure to exhaust the domestic remedies available for obtaining his release, account has to be taken of the facts that subsequently the Applicant obtained his release from detention and wrote to the Commission amending his claim so as to limit it to compensation and damages. The present Commission, as an international tribunal, is not bound to treat questions of form with the same degree of strictness as might be the case in municipal law (*Mavrommatis Palestine Concessions Case*, Permanent Court of International Justice, 1924, Series A, No. 2, page 34).[1] The Applicant's letter of December 16, 1957, stating that, notwithstanding his release, he wished to maintain his Application with respect to the claim for compensation and damages, should properly be regarded as in substance a re-submission of his Application amended so as to exclude the demand for his release and to confine it to a demand for compensation and damages. The Commission has already held that the right of recourse to the Internment Commission is not an effective domestic remedy with respect to the Applicant's demand for compensation and damages. It follows that, even if the original Application is regarded as having been defective in that it was filed without first exhausting the remedy before the Internment Commission, 'the Application was

[1 *Annual Digest*, 1923-1924, Case No. 181.]

not subject to that defect in the form in which it was presented to the Commission in the letter of December 16, 1957.

" It has also been contended by the respondent Government that the Applicant could have secured his release from detention at any time by giving an undertaking to respect the Constitution and the laws and by agreeing not to be a member of any unlawful organisation. On July 11, 1957, while under detention in the Bridewell Police Prison, the Applicant was informed that he could secure his release by this means; and by not availing himself of this means of obtaining his release, the Applicant failed to exhaust a domestic remedy open to him.

" It suffices to observe that the signing of such an undertaking by a detained person and the release of a detained person upon signing such an undertaking was not a procedure for which provision was made by law. In consequence, that procedure cannot be considered to be a domestic remedy within the meaning of the generally recognised rules of international law concerning the exhaustion of domestic remedies, and is not a remedy the exhaustion of which is called for under Article 26 of the Convention.

" Finally both the original Application and the letter of December 16, 1957, amending it, were filed within six months of the date on which the Supreme Court gave its final decision on the Applicant's proceedings for *habeas corpus*.

" *The Commission decides* that, for the several reasons above stated, the contention that the Application is inadmissible on the ground of an alleged failure to comply with the provisions of Article 26 of the Convention must be rejected.

" 2. *As regards Article 17 of the Convention.*—Article 17 of the Convention provides:

' Nothing in this Convention may be interpreted as implying for any State, group or person any right to engage in any activity or perform any act aimed at the destruction of any of the rights and freedoms set forth herein or at their limitation to a greater extent than is provided for in the Convention.'

" The respondent Government contends that prior to June 1956, the Applicant was known to be a member of an unlawful organisation, the so-called Irish Republican Army (hereinafter referred to as the I.R.A.). After a split in that organisation the Applicant was a member of a minority group, which committed a number of armed outrages. On September 21, 1956, the Applicant was one of four men discovered by the *Garda Siochana* in a disused shed at Keshcarrigan, County of Leitrim. These men were in possession of arms and admitted that they were members of the I.R.A. and one of them was identified as the Applicant. On October 18, 1956, the four men were charged in the Dublin District Court under the Fire Arms Act of 1925 and the Criminal Justice Act of 1951. On October 25, 1956, at a hearing in the said Court the

Applicant admitted that he was a member of the I.R.A. The acquittal of the Applicant by the Dublin Circuit Criminal Court on November 23, 1956, did not involve a declaration of innocence, but was decided on the ground that the technical requirements of proving that the accused did not hold firearms certificates had not been fully complied with. On May 14, 1957, the Applicant was arrested on suspicion of engaging in unlawful activities and, when searched, a sketch map was found of the border village of Pettigo with markings to indicate a British Customs and Police Barracks and with the words 'Infiltrate, Annihilate, Destroy' written on the map. The Applicant admitted ownership of that map. On May 18, 1957, the Applicant was sentenced in the Dublin District Court to one month's imprisonment for possession of incriminating documents. His acquittal on the same occasion on a charge of membership of an unlawful organisation was no proof of his innocence since, having convicted him on the first count of possessing incriminating documents, the Court simply dismissed the remaining charges without investigating them. While in prison [the Applicant] consorted with members of the above-mentioned minority group and after his release from prison he resumed his association with the same group.

"The Government submits that these several circumstances show that the Applicant was a member of a subversive organisation engaged in activities aimed at undermining the institutions of the Republic established to protect the rights and freedoms guaranteed in the Convention. The Applicant was himself a person engaged in activity aimed at the destruction of such rights and freedoms. including notably the most fundamental right of all, the right to life. In consequence, he is debarred by Article 17 from himself invoking the protection of the Convention in the present case.

"The Applicant, in his affidavit of February 21, 1958, stated that he had ceased to be a member of any unlawful organisation at the time of his arrest on July 11, 1957. He had in fact withdrawn his support from, and severed all connections with, the I.R.A. and the above-mentioned minority group. The Applicant relied, *inter alia*, upon his acquittal by the Dublin District Court on May 18, 1957, of a charge of being a member of an unlawful organisation. He submitted that in general the allegations of the Respondent Government in regard to him were untrue or exaggerated.

"In Application No. 250/57, *German Communist Party Case*,[1] the Commission held that members of an organisation which was found to be engaged in activities aimed at the destruction of the rights and freedoms set forth in the Convention, were debarred by Article 17 from invoking in their own favour the provision of the Convention concerning freedom of association. The possibility that the principle applied in the *German Communist Party Case* may be applicable in

[1 *International Law Reports*, 1957, p. 349.]

the present case is not excluded by a *prima facie* consideration of the statements of the Parties and the evidence so far submitted to the Commission. However, in the present case there is a direct conflict of view between the Parties on a crucial point of fact, namely, whether the Applicant had or had not ceased to be a member of an illegal organisation or group engaged in activities of the kind covered by the provisions of Article 17, when he was arrested on July 11, 1957, and subsequently detained under the Act of 1940. The Commission is not in possession of sufficient evidence to enable it to pronounce now upon that point of fact. Also, that point of fact is closely connected with matters arising upon the merits of the Applicant's claim.

" *The Commission decides* to join to the merits the respondent Government's preliminary objection founded upon Article 17 of the Convention.

" 3. *As regards Article 15 of the Convention.*—Article 15 of the Convention provides:

' (1) In time of war or other public emergency threatening the life of the nation any High Contracting Party may take measures derogating from its obligations under this Convention to the extent strictly required by the exigencies of the situation, provided that such measures are not inconsistent with its other obligations under international law.

' (2) No derogation from Article 2, except in respect of deaths resulting from lawful acts of war, or from Articles 3, 4 (paragraph 1) and 7 shall be made under this provision.

' (3) Any High Contracting Party availing itself of this right of derogation shall keep the Secretary-General of the Council of Europe fully informed of the measures which it has taken and the reasons therefor. It shall also inform the Secretary-General of the Council of Europe when such measures have ceased to operate and the provisions of the Covention are again being fully executed.'

" The Department of External Affairs of the Respondent Government addressed a letter to the Secretary-General of 'the Council of Europe, dated July 20, 1957, which read as follows:

' I have the honour to inform you that Part II of the Offences against the State (Amendment) Act, 1940, was brought into force on the 8th July, 1957, when a Proclamation made by the Government of Ireland on the 5th July, 1957, under section 3 of the Act was published in the Irish *Oifigiuil*, the official gazette. A copy of the Proclamation, together with a copy of the Act, is attached to this letter.

' 2. In so far as the bringing into operation of Part II of the Act, which confers special powers of arrest and detention, may involve any derogation from the obligations imposed by the Convention for the Protection of Human Rights and Fundamental Freedoms, I have the honour to request you to be good enough to regard this letter as informing you accordingly, in compliance with Article 15 (3) of the Convention.

'3. The detention of persons under the Act is considered necessary to prevent the commission of offences against public peace and order and to prevent the maintaining of military or armed forces other than those authorised by the Constitution.

'4. I have the honour also to invite your attention to section 8 of the Act, which provides for the establishment by the Government of Ireland of a Commission to inquire into the grounds of detention of any person who applies to have his detention investigated. The Commission envisaged by the section was established on the 16th July, 1957.'

" If the arrest and detention of the Applicant under the Act of 1940 should be considered by the Commission to have been inconsistent with the provisions of Articles 5 and 6 of the Convention, the Respondent Government relies on its powers under Article 15, paragraph 1, to take measures derogating from its obligations under the Convention; and it refers to its letter of July 20, 1947, as a sufficient notification of such measures to the Secretary-General and of the reasons for them.

" The Applicant contests the view of the Government that in July 1957 there was in the Republic of Ireland ' a public emergency threatening the life of the nation ' within the meaning of Article 15, paragraph 1, and the view that, if there was such a public emergency, the special powers of arrest and detention exercisable under the Act of 1940 were measures ' strictly required by the exigencies of the situation '. The Applicant further appears to challenge the right of the Government to rely upon its letter of July 20, 1957, as a notification to the Secretary-General under paragraph 3 of Article 15.

" Both the question whether, in July 1957, there was in existence a ' public emergency, threatening the life of the nation ', and the question whether the special powers of arrest and detention exercisable under the Act of 1940 were measures strictly required by the exigencies of the situation depend on matters of fact which are in dispute between the parties. The Commission is not in possession of sufficient evidence to enable it to form an opinion now upon these matters of fact. These matters of fact are closely connected with matters arising upon the merits of the Applicant's claim.

" *The Commission decides* to join to the merits the Respondent Government's preliminary objection founded upon Article 15 of the Convention.

" 4. *As regards the question whether the Application is inadmissible under Article 27, paragraph 2, of the Convention as being manifestly ill-founded.*—Article 27, paragraph 2, of the Convention provides that the Commission shall declare inadmissible any Application filed under Article 25 which it considers to be manifestly ill-founded.

" The Respondent Government represents that the Applicant was arrested and detained in July 1957 in order to restrain him from persisting in a course of conduct violating the obligations of loyalty to the Republic imposed on all citizens by the Constitution and endangering the lives and limbs of others. It contends that such arrest and detention was justifiable because Article 5, paragraph 1 (b), of the Convention expressly envisages that in accordance with a procedure prescribed by law a person may be made the subject of a lawful arrest or detention ' in order to secure the fulfilment of any obligation prescribed by law ' and because paragraph 3 of that Article, which requires an arrested or detained person to be brought before a judge or other judicial authority within a reasonable time, does not apply to cases under paragraph 1 (b). Alternatively, it contends that the arrest and detention of the Applicant was justifiable because paragraph 1 (c) of Article 5 expressly envisages that, in accordance with a procedure prescribed by law, a person may be made the subject of a lawful arrest or detention ' for the purpose of bringing him before the competent legal authority on reasonable suspicion of having committed an offence or when it is reasonably considered necessary to prevent his committing an offence ' and because, in its view, paragraph 3 is not applicable to the case of a person arrested when it was reasonably necessary to prevent him from committing an offence, in view of the impossibility under Irish law of putting a person on trial merely for intending to commit a crime.

" However, the Applicant contends that either the obligation imposed upon him by Article 9, Section 2, of the Constitution constitutes a civil obligation within the meaning of Article 6, paragraph 1, of the Convention, or alternatively the breach thereof must be a criminal offence. In either case [he contends] he was entitled under Article 6 of the Convention to a fair and public hearing within a reasonable time by an independent and impartial judicial tribunal, established by law. If the breach of the said constitutional obligation constituted an ' offence ' within the terms of Article 5 (1) (c), the Applicant was likewise entitled to a trial within a reasonable time or to release pending trial by virtue of Article 5 (3) of the Convention. The interpretation which the Respondent Government seeks to place on Article 5, paragraph 1 (b), would negative the provisions of Article 5, paragraph 3, and Article 6, paragraph 1, of the Convention and deprive them of all force and effect, and cannot therefore be correct. [He further contends] that if the breach of the constitutional obligation constitutes an ' offence ', the lawful arrest or detention of a person on reasonable suspicion of having committed such an offence or where it was reasonably considered necessary to prevent his committing such offence, which is authorised by Article 5, paragraph 1 (c), can only be an arrest or detention for the purpose of subsequently bringing him before the competent legal authority for trial and not for the purpose of indefinite detention without trial.

" At this stage of the proceedings the Commission's task, in deciding whether the Application is inadmissible under Article 27, paragraph 2, as manifestly ill-founded, is limited to determining whether a *prima facie* examination of the facts of the case and the statements of the Parties does or does not disclose any possible ground on which a breach of the Convention could ultimately be found to be established. It cannot be concluded from a *prima facie* examination of the facts and the statements of the Parties in the present case that there is no possible ground on which a breach of the Convention could ultimately be found to be established.

" *The Commission accordingly rejects* the Respondent Government's contention that the Application is inadmissible under Article 27, paragraph 2, of the Convention, as being manifestly ill-founded.

" 5. *As regards the question whether the Application is inadmissible under Article 27, paragraph 2, of the Convention as being an abuse of the right of petition.*—The Respondent Government contends that it was open to the Applicant at any time to secure his own immediate release by signing the above-mentioned undertaking to respect the Constitution and the laws and by agreeing not to be a member of any unlawful organisation. It also contends that, by refusing to do so, the Applicant failed to make use of a means which he had in his own hands to put an end to his detention, and by thus failing to mitigate the damage disentitled himself from claiming compensation. It further contends that the Application was inspired by motives of publicity and political propaganda. It submits that for these various reasons the Application should be held to be vexatious and an abuse of the right of petition within the meaning of Article 27, paragraph 2, of the Convention.

" The Applicant takes the position that the Government by the act of detaining him committed a violation of the Convention; that the signing of an undertaking to obtain release was not a procedure which had any legal basis; and that he himself had certain scruples in regard to the signing of the undertaking.

" The question as to what extent the Applicant could and should have mitigated the damage is a question which relates to the merits and cannot be determined at this stage of the proceedings, and the fact that the Application was inspired by motives of publicity and political propaganda, even if established, would not by itself necessarily have the consequence that the Application was an abuse of the right of petition. In any event, that fact is not one which can be determined until after a full examination of the merits of the case. In general, the question whether the present Application constitutes an abuse of the right of petition depends upon the outcome of the issue whether or not the Applicant has been the victim of a fundamental breach of the Convention, which issue essentially belongs to the merits and cannot be decided at this stage of the proceedings.

"*The Commission accordingly rejects* the Respondent Government's contention that the Application is inadmissible under Article 27, paragraph 2, of the Convention, as being an abuse of the right of petition.

" To sum up:

" 1. *As regards the exhaustion of domestic remedies under Article 26 of the Convention.*—The Commission rejects the contention of the Respondent Government that the Application is inadmissible on the ground of an alleged failure to comply with the provisions of Article 26 of the Convention with regard to the exhaustion of domestic remedies.

" 2. *As regards Article 17 of the Convention.*—The Commission decides to join to the merits the Respondent Government's preliminary objection founded upon Article 17 of the Convention.

" 3. *As regards Article 15 of the Convention.*—The Commission decides to join to the merits the Respondent Government's preliminary objection founded upon Article 15 of the Convention.

" 4. *As regards the question whether the Application is inadmissible under Article 27, paragraph 2, of the Convention as being manifestly ill-founded.*—The Commission rejects the Respondent Government's contention that the Application is manifestly ill-founded.

" 5. *As regards the question whether the Application is inadmissible under Article 27, paragraph 2, of the Convention, as being an abuse of the right of petition.*—The Commission rejects the Respondent Government's contention that the Application is an abuse of the right of petition."

[Report: *Yearbook of the European Convention on Human Rights*, 1958–1959, p. 308.]

**The individual in international law—Human rights and freedoms —European Convention for Protection of—European Commission of Human Rights—Individual applications—Failure to exhaust local remedies—No *prima facie* violation of Convention.**

*Re* APPLICATION NO. 352/58 (X. *v.* FEDERAL REPUBLIC OF GERMANY).

*European Commission of Human Rights. September 4, 1958.*

(Waldock, President; Eustathiades, Berg, Faber, Beaufort, Dominedo, Süsterhenn, Petren, Janssen-Pevtschin, Sørensen, Crosbie, Skarphedinsson, Erim.)

THE FACTS (as stated in the decision of the Commission).—" The applicant, a Swiss national, born and resident in Germany, stated that he had appeared before the District Court (*Amtsgericht*) of ——in 1953, charged with unlawful wounding. On April 28, 1953,

the said Court nevertheless acquitted him on the grounds that
' at the moment of the act ' concerned X. ' was not capable of understanding the unlawful character of his act, nor of acting in the light
of his own reason, as a result of a pathological disturbance of his
mind' (Article 51 (1) of the German Penal Code). In its judgment
the Court also found that the act in respect of which the applicant
was prosecuted would, in the circumstances of the case, only be
regarded as criminal ' if the relevant depositions made by the victim
were true.'

" Accordingly, this judgment was recorded in the applicant's
police record, in accordance with Article 9 of the Ordinance of
February 17, 1934, concerning police records. Under this Article,

' there shall be recorded in the police record . . . judgments given by
German courts acquitting . . . a person in accordance with the provisions of paragraph 1 of Article 51 of the Penal Code without ordering
his transfer to a mental institution.'

" The applicant claimed that this provision could not apply to
his case, since, in his opinion, the Court of——had expressly made
the validity of its judgment subject to the condition that the depositions of the victim of the act in respect of which the prosecution
was brought, were true. Accordingly, he asked the Ministry of Justice
of Baden-Württemberg to remove from his police record all mention
of the judgment in question, but on September 30, 1954, the Ministry
refused this request.

" The applicant apparently challenged this decision before the
Administrative Court (*Verwaltungsgericht*) of——, which dismissed his
application on January 4, 1956. He appealed to the Administrative
Court of——, which affirmed the decision of first instance on November 29, 1956. At the same time, the Court refused, in accordance with
Article 53 of the Law concerning the Federal Administrative Court,
to allow the applicant to appeal from its decision.

" The applicant lodged an application (*Beschwerde*) against this
refusal, but this was rejected by the Federal Administrative Court
(*Bundesverwaltungsgericht*) of Berlin on October 30, 1957.

" On November 12, 25 and 29, 1957, the applicant addressed
to the Federal Court requests for a further examination of his case.
On December 11, 1957, the Court declared these requests to be
inadmissible. It held, in particular, that the last judicial decisions
given in the applicant's case were final and enforceable.

" On January 14, 1958, the applicant lodged with the Federal
Constitutional Court (*Bundesverfassungsgericht*) an appeal (*Verfas-
sungsbeschwerde*) which was rejected on February 7, 1958, by virtue
of Article 91 (*a*), sub-paragraph 2, of the Law concerning the Federal
Constitutional Court. Under that Article, such an appeal can be
rejected when ' a decision on the merits could not help to resolve a
question of constitutional law ' and when ' the fact of the Court's
not pronouncing on the merits would not cause serious and inevitable

injury to the applicant.' Before this order was made, and in accordance with the procedure provided for by Articles 24 and 91 (a), the President of the First Chamber of the Court had, in a letter dated January 23, 1958, drawn the applicant's attention to the fact that his appeal was faced with the following obstacles:

" (a) In so far as the applicant was challenging the decision of the Federal Administrative Court of December 11, 1957, his application was inadmissible because it was directed against a judicial decision concerning the exercise of an extraordinary form of appeal not provided by law;

" (b) In so far as the applicant apparently challenged the last final judicial decision, namely, the Order of October 30, 1957, of the Federal Administrative Court, his appeal was also inadmissible on the ground of non-observance of the time-limit of one month provided by the existing law in the matter of constitutional appeals.

" The applicant maintains that the authorities of the Federal Republic of Germany have violated Articles 5, 8 and 13 of the European Convention for the Protection of Human Rights and Fundamental Freedoms. He asks the Commission to require the Ministry of Justice of Baden-Württemberg to correct the entries contained in his police records; and he claims in addition DM 10,000 damages."

*Held:* that the application must be rejected.

The Commission said: " As regards the constitutional appeal instituted by the applicant, and in so far as that appeal challenged the above-mentioned decision of October 30, 1957, in accordance with the provisions of Article 26 of the European Convention for the Protection of Human Rights and Fundamental Freedoms the Commission may only deal with a matter after all domestic remedies have been exhausted, according to the generally recognized rules of international law, and within a period of six months from the date of the final domestic decision. In order to satisfy the provisions of that Article, applicants must not only submit their cases to the competent internal courts, but they must also act within the time-limits provided by the law. The applicant did not lodge his constitutional appeal against the decision of October 30, 1957, within the period of one month available to him under Article 93 of the Law concerning the Federal Constitutional Court.

" In addition, an examination of the file, even *ex officio*, does not disclose the existence of special circumstances which would relieve the applicant, according to the generally recognised principles of international law, from the duty to lodge the appeal in question within the time-limit provided by the applicable national law. It follows that the applicant has not satisfied the provisions of Article 26 of the Convention with regard to the exhaustion of domestic remedies and the application should accordingly be rejected on this ground in accordance with Article 27 (2) of the Convention.

" In addition and in any event, an examination, even *ex officio*, of his file, as it stands, does not disclose any *prima facie* violation of one of the rights and freedoms recognized in the Convention, in particular in Articles 5, 8 and 13. It appears, therefore, that the application is manifestly ill-founded and it must accordingly be rejected on this ground by virtue of Article 27 (2) of the Convention."

[Report: *Yearbook of the European Convention on Human Rights*, 1958–59, p. 342 (in French).]

**The individual in international law—Human rights and freedoms —European Convention for Protection of—European Human Rights Commission—Inter-State applications—Allegations of torture or maltreatment amounting to torture—*Prima facie* case not relevant in considering admissibility of inter-State application —Exhaustion of local remedies.**

See p. 27 (*Re Application No.* 299/57 (*Government of the Kingdom of Greece* v. *Government of the United Kingdom of Great Britain and Northern Ireland*)).

## II.—Before International Tribunals

**The individual in international law—In general—Before international tribunals—Admitted as party before Arbitral Commission—Right to invoke provisions of Treaty creating such Commission.**

See p. 522 (*Veerman* v. *German Federal Republic* (*Interim Protection*)).

## B—NATIONALITY

## I.—In General. Proof of Nationality

**Nationality—Proof of—Examination by Conciliation Commission of certificate of nationality—Probative value of certificate in international law—Review of validity of naturalization of ancestor on which claim of nationality *jus sanguinis* based—Refusal to examine circumstances of naturalization and subsequent conduct of ancestor—Examination of relevant Laws of naturalizing State— Review of statement made to passport or other authorities— Theory of effective nationality—Allegation of " apparent nationality "—Invocation of nationality for sake of temporary material advantage—Principle of " estoppel " or " *non concedit venire contra factum proprium* "—Rejection of doctrine.**

See p. 91 (*Flegenheimer Claim*), at pp. 98–100, 112 *et seq.*

**Nationality—Proof of.**

See p. 349 (*Zgainski* v. *German Federal Republic*), at p. 353.

## II.—Acquisition of Nationality.  Nationality as Affected by Changes of Sovereignty

Nationality—Acquisition of—United States of America—Nationality Act, 1940—Naturalization—" First papers "—Whether conferring United States nationality.

PERSITZ-KELLER *v.* GERMAN FEDERAL REPUBLIC.

*Arbitral Commission on Property, Rights and Interests in Germany, Third Chamber.*

(Lagergren, Vice-President; Arndt, Phenix.)

*February* 1, 1958.

THE FACTS.—This was an appeal to the Commission under Article 12, Section 1 (*a*), of Chapter Ten of the Bonn Settlement Convention, 1952–1954, from a decision of the Federal Restitution Office (*Bundesamt für die Prüfung ausländischer Rückgabe– und Wiederherstellungsansprüche*) dated November 30, 1956, rejecting for want of jurisdiction the complainant's claim for restitution of property allegedly owned by her and the restoration of her alleged rights and interests therein.  The claim was for the restoration of a one-half interest in certain real estate located in Weil am Rhein, Germany.  The property in question had been acquired by the city in 1942 at a forced sale of which complainant stated she had no notice and which, she asserted, constituted discriminatory treatment.  It was sold by the city in 1954.  The complainant asked that the sale be held null and void, submitting her claim under Chapter Ten of the Bonn Settlement Convention, 1952–1954.

The Federal Restitution Office held that the complainant was entitled to claim and that the claim had been filed within the prescribed time-limits, but that there was no basis for the claim under Article 1, Chapter Ten, of the Convention, since she had not been deprived of property nor had any rights or interests of hers been impaired by discriminatory treatment.  As to deprivation, the Restitution Office denied that the complainant held title to any part of the property in dispute and asserted that the official land records of the city of Weil am Rhein, covering the disputed property, contained neither her name nor the names of those from whom she alleged she had inherited a one-half interest.  As to discriminatory treatment, it denied any discrimination, asserting that the representatives of the owners of record had agreed to the forced sale for unpaid taxes and because German legislation regarding forced sales was applicable to all property owners regardless of nationality.  Since the claim could not, therefore, fall within the provisions of the said Article 1, the Restitution Office held that the complainant had no cause of action and rejected the application.

The complainant then appealed to the Arbitral Commission, and, in response to the Commission's request for further information, she stated that she was a Swiss national from 1919 to 1947 and had been a citizen of the United States since 1947.

The defendant's reply of June 13, 1957, argued that if the complainant were in fact a Swiss national from 1919 to 1947, she was not a national of one of the United Nations when the alleged deprivation and discrimination occurred and was therefore not qualified to claim under Article 1, Chapter Ten, of the Bonn Settlement Convention. The defendant argued further that even if the complainant were qualified, the claim must fail, because neither she nor her alleged predecessor in interest held title to any part of the disputed land under German law and because, the forced sale proceedings being applicable to all property owners, whether German or foreign, they did not constitute discriminatory treatment.

The Commission ordered that the preliminary objection raised by the defendant should be made the subject of a separate decision.

*Held:* that the preliminary objection of the defendant must be sustained and the appeal of the complainant must be dismissed. The complainant, in view of her nationality in 1942, was not entitled to put her claim before the Commission.

The Commission said: " The record before the Commission contains the complainant's uncontested statement that she was a Swiss national from 1919 to 1947, when she became an American citizen (letter from complainant to the Commission dated April 20, 1957). However, under date of October 24, 1957, complainant states that she received ' U.S. First Papers ' in December 1940, apparently on the theory that possession of ' first papers ' established some claim to United States citizenship.

" The significance she attaches to the so-called ' first papers ' does not legally exist. Such ' first papers ' were merely the ' Declaration of Intention ' to became a United States citizen as required under the Nationality Act of 1940 (U.S. Code annotated Title 8, page 78, commentary on the Immigration and Nationality Act by Walter M. Besterman). Under the 1940 statute a person desiring to be naturalized as a United States citizen was required to execute a ' Declaration of Intention ' not less than two, nor more than seven, years prior to his petition for naturalization, such declaration containing the statement ' It is my intention in good faith to become a citizen of the United States and to reside permanently therein ' (Nationality Act of 1940, Section 331). Not less than two nor more than ten years thereafter, an applicant had to file with the clerk of a naturalization court a ' Petition for Naturalization ' praying that he ' be admitted a citizen of the United States ' (Section 332). Every final hearing on such petitions had to be held in open court (Section 334) and the petitioner was required to take oath also in open court, *inter alia*, that he would support the Constitution of the United States and that he renounced all other allegiances (Section 335). Upon admission to citizenship by the naturalization court after final hearing the new citizen was entitled to receive a ' Certificate of Naturalization ' showing, among other things, the date of his naturalization (Section 336). In the instant case this certificate would appear from the complainant's own statement, no copy thereof having been furnished to the Commission, to have shown a naturalization date in 1947, and the Commission assumes that to be the fact. It is thus clear that the complainant had not in 1942 acquired the nationality of one of the United Nations, namely, of the United States of America, nor is there any evidence that complainant was a direct successor by inheritance or testamentary disposition of a national of one of the United Nations. She is, therefore, not entitled to claim under Article 1, Chapter Ten, of the Bonn Settlement Convention, . . .

" For These Reasons the Arbitral Commission orders that: (1) the preliminary objection of the defendant is sustained; (2) the appeal from the decision of the *Bundesamt für die Prüfung ausländischer Rückgabe- und Wiederherstellungsansprüche* is dismissed; (3) each party to the proceedings shall pay it own costs."

[Report: *Decisions of the Arbitral Commission*, I (1958), Case No. 10, p. 139.]

**Nationality—Acquisition of—*Jure sanguinis*—Examination of circumstances of acquisition of nationality of ancestor—Relevance of *animus redeundi*.**

See p. 91 (*Flegenheimer Claim*), at pp. 112–123.

**Nationality—Acquisition of—As result of change of sovereignty— Cession of North Schleswig by Germany to Denmark in 1920— Danish subjects—Service in German Waffen-SS during Second World War—Whether conferring German nationality.**

See p. 513 (*Jürgensen* v. *German Federal Republic*).

**Nationality—Acquisition of—United States of America—Naturalization—" First papers "—Whether conferring United States nationality.**

See p. 357 (*Fürth-Perl and Fürth-Strasser* v. *German Federal Republic*).

# V.—Naturalization

Naturalization—

—Consequent loss of nationality of origin.

—Recovery of nationality of origin—Consequent loss of nationality of naturalization.

—Effect on wife and minor children of person naturalized.

—Option by children of person naturalized upon attaining majority.

—Child of naturalized person who acquired further nationality by naturalization—Recovery of parent's former nationality of naturalization.

—For avoidance of military service—Prevention of—Bancroft Treaties between United States of America and German States.

See p. 91 (*Flegenheimer Claim*), at pp. 123 *et seq.*, 134, 136–146.

# VI.—Expatriation. Loss of Nationality

Nationality—Expatriation—Effect of expatriation of ancestor—Relevance of *animus redeundi*—The law of the United States of America.

See p. 91 (*Flegenheimer Claim*), at pp. 123 *et seq.*

Nationality—Loss of—Loss of nationality of origin on naturalization abroad—Loss of nationality on re-naturalization—Effect on minor children.

See p. 91 (*Flegenheimer Claim*), at pp. 123 *et seq.*, 134, 136–146.

Nationality—Expatriation—Loss of nationality—Polish law.

See p. 349 (*Zgainski* v. *Federal Republic of Germany*), at p. 353.

# VII.—Denationalization

Nationality—Denationalization—Nazi legislation—Non-recognition of validity of—Convention with Germany on the Settlement of Matters Arising out of the War and Occupation, 1952–1954—Application by Arbitral Commission.

See p. 357 (*Fürth-Perl and Fürth-Strasser* v. *German Federal Republic*).

# VIII.—Double Nationality

Double nationality—

—Theory of effective nationality.

—Doctrine of apparent nationality—Rejection of.

See p. 91 (*Flegenheimer Claim*), at pp. 147–153.

# PART VIII

# TREATIES

## A—IN GENERAL

### I.—Conception and Function of Treaties

Treaties—Conception and function of treaties—*Pactum de contra-hendo*—Treaty containing requirement of further " special agreement "—Effect of action taken in absence of special agreement—Whether valid—General Assembly Resolution 388 (V).

See p. 2 (*Italy* v. *United Kingdom of Great Britain and Northern Ireland and United Kingdom of Libya. General List No.* 1 (*Merits*)).

## B—CONCLUSION AND OPERATION OF TREATIES

### I.—Signature. Accession and Adhesion. Tacit Renewal

Treaties—Conclusion and operation of—Accession—Accession in advance—Whether possible.

See p. 540 (*Leupold-Praesent* v. *German Federal Republic*).

### III.—Parties to Treaties. Right to Conclude Treaties. Composite and Dependent States and Territories

Treaties—Parties to—Composite States—Effect of unification—Treaties with German States—Effect of establishment of German Empire.

See p. 91 (*Flegenheimer Claim*), at pp. 124-125.

### V.—Reservations

Treaties—Operation of—Reservations and exceptions—Implied terms—Reservation of public policy—Relevance to conventions on private international law—Whether international tribunal entitled to review application of municipal public policy—Relevance of reasonableness and good faith—Obligations of parties in relation to burden of proof—Hague Convention of 1902 on Guardianship of Infants.

See p. 242 (*Case concerning the Application of the Convention of 1902 Governing the Guardianship of Infants*), at pp. 246, 253, 256 *et seq.*, 265, 267 *et seq.*, 276–280, 284, 287 *et seq.*, 301, 312.

Treaties—Operation of—Exception clauses—European Convention for Protection of Human Rights and Fundamental Freedoms, 1950 —Article 15 (right of derogation)—Existence of "public emergency threatening the life of the nation "—Whether subject to review by Commission.

See p. 216 (*Re Application No.* 332/57 (*Lawless* v. *Republic of Ireland*).

## VI.—Ratification of Treaties. Entry into Force

Treaties—Conclusion of—Entry into force—Applicability to events occurring before entry into force—Principle that treaties have no retrospective effect—Continuing nature of unlawful act—European Convention for Protection of Human Rights and Fundamental Freedoms, 1950.

See p. 172 (*Re Application No.* 214/56 (*De Becker* v. *Belgium*)).

## VIII.—Effect of Treaties on Third Parties

Treaties—Conclusion and operation of—Effect on third parties— Invocation by third State of treaty affecting nationality.

See p. 91 (*Flegenheimer Claim*), at p. 126.

## IX.—Effect of Municipal Legislation

Treaties—Conclusion and operation of—Relation to municipal law —Effect of inconsistent municipal legislation—Whether treaty violated—Relevance of alleged difference of subject matter— Whether guardianship distinguishable from protective upbringing —Hague Convention of 1902 on Guardianship of Infants.

See p. 242 (*Case concerning the Application of the Convention of 1902 Governing the Guardianship of Infants*), at pp. 250–255, 263, 285–287, 297, 310.

Treaties—Conclusion and operation of—Effect of subsequent legislation.

See p. 91 (*Flegenheimer Claim*), at pp. 126, 127.

## X.—Miscellaneous

Treaties—Conclusion and operation of—Inconsistent treaties— Effect of—Responsibility for breach of earlier treaty—Requirement of exercise of due diligence to avoid conflict.

See p. 190 (*Re Application No.* 235/56 (*Mr. X. and Mrs. X.* v. *German Federal Republic*)).

## C—TERMINATION OF TREATIES

### I.—By Operation of Law

#### iii.—Outbreak of War

[*See also* Part XI, War and Neutrality]

Treaties—Termination of—Outbreak of war.

See p. 91 (*Flegenheimer Claim*), at p. 125.


## D—INTERPRETATION OF TREATIES

### I.—Agencies of Interpretation

Treaties—Interpretation of—Agencies of interpretation—Arbitral Tribunal—Interpretation by.

See p. 33 (*Swiss Confederation* v. *German Federal Republic (No. 1)*), at pp. 50–57.


### II.—Principles and Rules of Interpretation

Treaties—Interpretation of—Principles and rules of—Intention—Purpose of Convention—Whether construction permissible which leads to impossibility—Relevance of social purpose of Convention—Relevance of practice of Parties—Hague Convention of 1902 on Guardianship of Infants.

See p. 242 (*Case concerning the Application of the Convention of 1902 Governing the Guardianship of Infants*), at pp. 265, 303, 311.


Treaties—Interpretation of—Principles of Interpretation—

—Effectiveness—Interpretation of arbitral undertakings—Possibility of conflicts between international tribunals—Whether to be avoided.

—Reference to purposes—Intention of Parties—Liberal interpretation—Reasonableness—Use of preamble—Methods which can be simply and fruitfully applied—Reference to—Natural meaning—Surrounding circumstances.

—Interpretation by Parties subsequent to conclusion—Weight to be attached—Permissibility of reference to evidence of interpretation if not referred to in argument.

—Use of treaties of municipal law terms—Reference to municipal law for purposes of interpretation—Permissibility of—Multilingual treaties.

—Preparatory work—Consideration of—Confirmatory character of—Absence of published record—Assertions of Parties as to content of—Whether of evidential value—History of origin of Agreement.

See p. 33 (*Swiss Confederation* v. *German Federal Republic* (No. 1)), at pp. 53–54, 58–62, 66, 71, 73, 77–86.

Treaties—Interpretation of—Principles of—Grammatical interpretation—Restrictive interpretation of exceptions—Consideration of preparatory work—European Convention on Human Rights, 1950.

See p. 172 (*Re Application No.* 214/56 (*De Becker* v. *Belgium*)).

Treaties—Interpretation of—Whether right of an international organization to delegate its powers can be implied—*Inclusio unius est exclusio alterius*—European Coal and Steel Community Treaty, 1951.

See p. 369 (*Meronie et Cie, Industrie Metallurgiche, S.P.A.* v. *The High Authority*).

Treaties—Interpretation of—Rules of—Function of articles setting out fundamental aims of treaty—Elaboration of fundamental aims to be read as one with them—General principles of law of member States—European Coal and Steel Community Treaty, 1951.

See p. 379 (*Groupement des Hauts Fourneaux et Acieries Belges* v. *The High Authority*).

Treaties—Interpretation of—Principles and rules of interpretation—Treaty to be read as a whole—Treaty of Peace with Italy, 1947, Article 78, paragraph 6.

See p. 313 (*Re Application to Swiss Nationals of the Italian Special Capital Levy Duty*).

Treaties—Interpretation of—Principles of interpretation—

—Interpretation by analogy with other treaties.

—Clear meaning of text.

—Intention of the Parties.

—*Lacuna* in treaty—Filled by reference to municipal law of one Party.

—Interpretation by reference to dictionary.

—Interpretation by reference to purpose aimed at by the Parties.

—Restrictive interpretation of treaty provision deviating from international law.

—Interpretation by reference to relevant legislation of one Party.

—Effect of subsequent " Memorandum of Understanding " between the Parties.

—Interpretation by Reference to decision of municipal court on similar treaty.

—Texts of multilingual treaties—Authenticated originals—Reconciliation of texts—Comparison of texts in different languages.

See p. 91 (*Flegenheimer Claim*), at pp. 129–132, 135–137, 154–157, 163–164.

Treaties—Interpretation of—Principles of—Literal construction—Agreement on German External Debts, 1953.

See p. 326 (*Bodenkreditbank in Basel and the Swiss Confederation* v. *Gebrüder Rohrer Gmbh. and the German Federal Republic*).

## V.—Miscellaneous

Treaties—Interpretation of—Miscellaneous—Protocol signed by Parties—Not published or ratified—Whether Protocol can be used in relation to interpretation of another Agreement concluded by same Parties.

See p. 540 (*Leupold-Praesent* v. *German Federal Republic*).

## E—SPECIAL KINDS OF TREATIES

Treaties—Special kinds of—Private international law—Hague Convention of 1902 on Guardianship of Infants—Interpretation of—Whether Convention subject to an implied exception of *ordre public*—Relationship between Convention and municipal law of the parties—Law of guardianship—Nature of Swedish law on protective upbringing.

CASE CONCERNING THE APPLICATION OF THE CONVENTION OF 1902 GOVERNING THE GUARDIANSHIP OF INFANTS.

(NETHERLANDS *v.* SWEDEN.)

*International Court of Justice. Judgment of November* 28, 1958.

(Klaestad, President; Zafrulla Khan, Vice-President; Basdevant, Hackworth, Winiarski, Badawi, Armand-Ugon, Kojevnikov, Sir Hersch Lauterpacht, Moreno Quintana, Córdova, Wellington Koo, Spiropoulos, Sir Percy Spender, Judges; Sterzel and Offerhaus, Judges *ad hoc.*)

THE FACTS.—By an application filed on July 10, 1957, the Government of the Netherlands asked the Court to declare that certain measures taken by the Swedish authorities in Sweden in respect of Marie Elisabeth Boll during the period 1954–1956 were not in conformity with the obligations of Sweden towards the Netherlands under the 1902 Convention on the Guardianship of Infants.

The facts, as stated by the Court, were as follows: [62] " The essential and undisputed facts underlying the present case are as follows: Gerd Elisabeth Lindwall, the wife of Johannes Boll and mother of Marie Elisabeth Boll, having died on December 5th, 1953, Johannes Boll, the latter's father, thereupon became her guardian by the operation of Article 378 of the Civil Code of the Netherlands. On March 18th, 1954, on the application of the father and without any reference then being made to the Dutch nationality of the infant, the Second Chamber of the Court of First Instance at [63] Norrköping in Sweden registered the guardianship of the father and appointed Emil Lindwall as *god man* of Marie Elisabeth, pursuant to Swedish law of guardianship.

" On May 5th, 1954, the Child Welfare Board at Norrköping, confirming the decision made on April 26th, 1954, by the President of the Board, decided to place the infant under the régime of protective upbringing under Article 22 (*a*) of the Swedish Law of June 6th, 1924.

" The Amsterdam Cantonal Court, on June 2nd, 1954, appointed Jan Albertus Idema, of Dutch nationality, residing at Dordrecht, deputy-guardian of the infant, Marie Elisabeth Boll, her father being her guardian by operation of law.

" The latter, jointly with the deputy-guardian, appealed against the institution of protective upbringing to the Provincial Government of Östergötland, which, by decision of June 22nd, 1954, confirmed the decision of the Child Welfare Board.

" On August 5th, 1954, the Court of First Instance of Dordrecht, upon the application of the Guardianship Council of that town and with the consent of Johannes Boll, discharged the latter from his functions as guardian of Marie Elisabeth Boll and appointed Catharina Postema as guardian. The same judgment ordered that the child should be handed over to the guardian.

" The Second Chamber of the Norrköping Court of First Instance, on September 16th, 1954, cancelled the previous registration of the guardianship of Johannes Boll and ordered that guardianship should no longer be administered according to Swedish law. In the same decision the Court dismissed an application for the removal of Emil Lindwall as *god man* of the infant Marie Elisabeth. The Court of Appeal of Göta, by decision of January 21st, 1955, maintained the *god man*, but a judgment of the Supreme Court of July 2nd, 1955, quashed this decision and discharged the *god man* of his functions.

" An appeal having been lodged by Johannes Boll, Jan Albertus Idema and Catharina Postema, against the decision of the Provincial Government of Östergötland of June 22nd, 1954, the Supreme Administrative Court of Sweden, by a judgment of October 5th, 1954, maintained the measure of protective upbringing.

" The Child Welfare Board of Norrköping, having before them a letter from the father of the infant Marie Elisabeth Boll, and an application by Jan Albertus Idema, decided on June 3rd, 1955, to obtain a further medical report before reviewing the measure of protective upbringing. On October 28th, 1955, the Provincial Government of Östergötland, on appeal by Catharina Postema and Jan Albertus Idema against this decision, ordered the measure of protective upbringing to be terminated. On appeal by the Child Welfare Board against that decision, the Supreme Administrative Court, by a judgment of February 21st, 1956, maintained the measure adopted by that Board on June 3rd, 1955.

[In an earlier part of the Judgment the Court had referred to the institution of proceedings.]

[56] " In a letter of July 9th, 1957, received in the Registry on July 10th, 1957, the Minister for Foreign Affairs of the Netherlands transmitted an Application dated July 9th, 1957, instituting proceedings in a dispute with the Government of the Kingdom of Sweden concerning the application of the Convention of 1902 governing the guardianship of infants. At the same time, the Minister for Foreign Affairs of the Netherlands notified the Registry of the appointment of M. W. Riphagen as Agent for the Netherlands Government in the case.

[57] " The Application thus filed in the Registry on July 10th, 1957, expressly refers to Article 36, paragraph 2, of the Statute of the Court and to the acceptance of the compulsory jurisdiction of the International Court of Justice by the Kingdom of Sweden on April 6th, 1957, and by the Kingdom of the Netherlands on August 1st, 1956. It refers to a measure taken and maintained by the Swedish authorities in respect of the infant Marie Elisabeth Boll, a Dutch national, born at Norrköping on May 7th, 1945, of the marriage of Johannes Boll, of Dutch nationality, and Gerd Elisabeth Lindwall, who died on December 5th, 1953, and who was of Swedish nationality before her marriage. The Application alleges that the Swedish authorities acted contrary to the provisions of the Convention of 1902 governing the guardianship of infants, which provisions are based on the principle that the national law of the infant is applicable and the national authorities are competent.

" Pursuant to Article 40, paragraph 2, of the Statute, the Application was communicated to the Government of the Kingdom of Sweden and, pursuant to paragraph 3 of the same Article, other Members of the United Nations as well as non-member States entitled to appear before the Court were notified of it.

" Since the Application referred to the provisions of the Convention governing the guardianship of infants, signed at The Hague on

June 12th, 1902, the States other than those concerned in the case which are Parties to the Convention were notified in accordance with Article 63, paragraph 1, of the Statute."

After referring to the time-limits for the filing of the pleadings, to the holding of oral hearings and the development of the submissions of the parties, the Court stated the final submissions of the parties:

On behalf of the Government of Sweden, as presented at the hearing of October 1, 1958:

[**60**] " May it please the Court
" *As to admissibility :* to hold

" (1) that the rights pertaining to custody and control, to upbringing and all other rights exercised by Johannes Boll over the person of his daughter until August 5th, 1954, derived from his *puissance paternelle* and not from guardianship within the meaning of the 1902 Convention; that this was more particularly so in the present case inasmuch as on his application his guardianship was originally instituted in accordance with Swedish law, which does not regard as falling within this institution rights relating to the person of the child; that the decision of May 5th, 1954, could accordingly not infringe any rights protected by the Convention;

" (2) that when the Dutch authorities had subsequently instituted the guardianship of Johannes Boll in accordance with the law of the Netherlands and later released Johannes Boll from his functions, replacing him by Catherine Postema, the Swedish Courts terminated the guardianship instituted by them;

" (3) that notwithstanding, Sweden not being bound by the 1902 Convention to recognize the validity of the Dutch decision putting an end to the *puissance paternelle* of Johannes Boll, nor consequently of the transfer of these rights to Catherine Postema, any breach of those rights would not constitute a violation of the Convention.

" *As to the merits*: to hold

" that the rules pertaining to conflict of laws which form the subject-matter of the 1902 Convention on the guardianship of infant children do not affect the right of the High Contracting Parties to impose upon the powers of foreign guardians, as indeed of foreign parents, the restrictions called for by their *ordre public*;

" that these rules leave unaffected in particular the competence of the administrative authorities responsible for the public service of the protection of children;

" that the measure of protective upbringing taken in respect of Elisabeth Boll cannot accordingly in any way have contravened the 1902 Convention relied upon by the Netherlands;

" that it is furthermore not for the Court, in the absence of any allegation of denial of justice, to judge the grounds on which the competent Swedish authorities decided to decree or to maintain the said measure;

[**61**] " In the premises,

" May it please the Court to declare that the claim is neither admissible nor well-founded; in the alternative, before adjudication, to invite the Respondent to produce the file of the administrative enquiries which led to the disputed decisions."

On behalf of the Government of the Netherlands, as presented at the hearing of October 3rd, 1958:

" May it please the Court to declare:

" I. that the ' *skyddsuppfostran* ' (protective education) curtails Netherlands guardianship as protected by the 1902 Convention governing the guardianship of infants;

" II. that *ordre public* cannot prevail against the Convention, because *ordre public* generally cannot be invoked against conventions;

" III. that, even if *ordre public* could be invoked against the Convention:

" A. the Court, in virtue of its powers under the Statute, is fully competent to appreciate, in the light of all the relevant facts and circumstances and the nature of the municipal legal provisions applied thereto, whether or not the conditions for *ordre public* have been complied with;

" B. in the present issue *ordre public* is not warranted,

(i) either by the character of the case,

(ii) or by the character of the provision of Swedish law as applied to the case.

" Therefore

" May it please the Court to adjudge and declare:

that the measure taken and maintained by the Swedish authorities in respect of Marie Elisabeth Boll, namely the ' *skyddsuppfostran* ' instituted and maintained by the decrees of May 5th, 1954, June 22nd, 1954, October 5th, 1954, June 3rd, 1955, and February 21st, 1956, is not in conformity with the obligations binding upon Sweden *vis-à-vis* the Netherlands by virtue of the 1902 Convention governing the guardianship of infants;

" That Sweden is under an obligation to end this measure."

*Held* (by twelve votes to four): that the claim of the Government of the Netherlands must be rejected.

The Court said: [**62**]  " The dispute upon which the Court is called on to adjudicate has been clearly defined by the Parties in their Pleadings and oral arguments. The Court has before it a concrete case: did the Swedish authorities, by applying the measure of protective upbringing (*skyddsuppfostran*) to the Dutch infant, Marie Elisabeth Boll, fail to respect obligations resulting from the 1902 Convention on the guardianship of infants? The task of the

Court is thus limited. It is not concerned with the correctness of the application of the Swedish Law of June 6th, 1924, on the protection of children and young persons, nor has it to pass upon the proper appreciation of the grounds on which the challenged decisions are based, or on the circumstances to which those grounds are related. These questions are not within the terms of the present dispute and would raise points which are outside the proceedings.

" The final Submissions of the Government of the Netherlands, before asking the Court to adjudge and declare that Sweden, in taking and maintaining the measure complained of, is in breach of its obligations under the 1902 Convention, ask it to ' declare ' certain propositions relating to the effect of protective upbringing and to *ordre public*. These propositions are, in reality, the essential considerations which, in the view of the Government of the Netherlands, must lead the Court to adjudge and declare that Sweden is in breach of its obligations. In a less categorical form, the Submissions of the Government of Sweden are set out in a similar way. The Court has to adjudicate upon the subject of the dispute; it is not called upon, as it pointed out in the *Fisheries* case, to pronounce upon a statement of this kind (*I.C.J. Reports* 1951, p. 126).[1] It retains its freedom to select the ground upon which it will base its judgment, and is under no obligation to examine all the considerations advanced by the Parties if other considerations appear to it to be sufficient for its purpose."

The Court then stated the facts, as printed above (pp. 242 *et seq.*) and continued:

[64] " These decisions given in Sweden and in the Netherlands relate to the organization of guardianship and to the application of the Swedish Law on the protection of children. The Court is not concerned with the decisions relating to the organization of guardianship. The dispute relates to the Swedish decisions which instituted and maintained protective upbringing. It is of these decisions that the Government of the Netherlands complains, and it is only upon them that the Court is called upon to adjudicate.

" The Government of the Netherlands submits that these decisions are not in conformity with the provisions of the 1902 Convention. The institution of protective upbringing in the case of Marie Elisabeth Boll prevents the infant from being handed over to the guardian for the exercise of her functions. The 1902 Convention provides that the guardianship of an infant shall be governed by his national law, and the Government of the Netherlands draws the conclusion that the Swedish authorities could take no measure once the national authorities had taken decisions organizing guardianship of the infant. The limitation on the principle of the national law contained in Article 7 of the Convention, according to the Government of the Netherlands, is not applicable to the present case because Swedish protective upbringing is not a measure permitted by that Article and because the condition of urgency required by that provision has not been satisfied.

" The Government of Sweden does not dispute the fact that protective upbringing temporarily impedes the exercise of custody to which the guardian is entitled by virtue of guardianship under Dutch law; this fact, however, does not constitute a breach of the 1902 Convention or a failure by Sweden to fulfil her obligations thereunder. In support of its contentions the Government of Sweden relies upon the following grounds:

" (1) The right to custody, at the time when the infant was placed under the régime of protective upbringing, belonged to her father, and it was in his case an attribute of the *puissance paternelle*, which is not governed by the 1902 Convention on guardianship. In the circumstances in which guardianship and the right to custody were conferred on Mme Postema, the 1902 Convention is equally inapplicable to that right, which was merely the continuation of the father's right to custody.

" (2) The Swedish Law for the protection of children of June 6th, 1924, applies to every infant residing in Sweden, and the jurisdiction which that Law confers upon the Swedish authorities remains outside the Convention, which governs only conflicts of law and of jurisdiction in respect of the guardianship of infants and which does not extend to the settlement of other conflicts of law. The Law for the protection of children being a law within the category of *ordre public*, the protective upbringing decreed by the Swedish authorities does not constitute a breach of the 1902 Convention, the Conven-[65]tion being incapable of affecting the right of the contracting States to make the powers of a foreign guardian, as indeed foreign parents, subject to the restrictions required by *ordre public*.

" With reference to the first ground relied upon by the Swedish Government, the Court observes that in the written and oral proceedings a distinction appears to have been made between the period during which Johannes Boll was invested with the guardianship of his daughter under Dutch law, the law applicable in accordance with Article 1 of the 1902 Convention, and the period after he had been released from guardianship when the latter was entrusted to Mme Postema. That may lead to a distinction being drawn between the original institution of the régime of protective upbringing in respect of the infant and her maintenance under this régime in face of the guardianship conferred upon Mme Postema. The Court does not consider that it need be concerned with this distinction. The grounds for its decision are applicable to the whole of the dispute.

" The Court has before it a measure taken in pursuance of the Swedish Law of June 6th, 1924, on the protection of children and young persons. It has to consider this measure in the light of what it was the intention of the Swedish Law to establish, to compare it with the guardianship governed by the 1902 Convention and to determine whether the application and the maintenance of the measure in respect of an infant whose guardianship falls within that Convention involve a breach of the Convention.

" It has been contended that the measure is one ' virtually amounting to guardianship ', that it constitutes a ' rival guardianship ' in competition with the Dutch guardianship so that the latter, as a result of the measure, ' is completely absorbed, whittled away, overruled and frustrated '.

" To judge of the correctness of this argument it is necessary to consider the attitude adopted with regard to the Dutch guardianship by the judgments given in Sweden.

" So far as the administration of property is concerned, the judgment of the Norrköping Court of September 16th, 1954, and the judgment of the Supreme Court of July 2nd, 1955, both proceeded on the basis of recognition of the Dutch guardianship. With regard to the capacity of the guardian to concern herself with the person of the infant, that capacity was recognized in the decision of the Supreme Administrative Court of October 5th, 1954, given on an appeal lodged by the guardian; reference was there made to the fact that the decision of the Dordrecht Court, appointing Mme Postema as guardian, extended to the custody of the child and to the claim of the guardian that the régime of protective upbringing should be terminated; this claim was dismissed, not on the ground that it was inadmissible, but after it had been considered on the merits and because it appeared to the Court that to uphold it would, [66] at that time, have constituted a serious danger to the mental health of the ward.

" The judgment of the Supreme Administrative Court of February 21st, 1956, merits particular attention. This judgment was given on an appeal against a decision of the Provincial Government of Östergötland which had held that the measure of protective upbringing should be terminated: if matters had ended there, there would have been no subject for dispute. There is a subject for dispute only as a result of the judgment of February 21st, 1956, which decided that the measure should be maintained. The judgment was given, as the decision appealed against had been, in the light of and taking into account the desire expressed by the guardian, Mme Postema, to entrust the infant to M. and Mme Törnquist, at Norrköping. The Supreme Administrative Court did not question Mme Postema's capacity to take proceedings before it, and it thereby recognized her capacity as guardian and her right to concern herself with the person of the infant; it did not raise protective upbringing to the status of an institution, the effect of which would be completely to absorb the Dutch guardianship; it confined itself, for reasons outside the scope of the Court's examination, to finding that the desire of the guardian and the satisfactory information which she gave with regard to the household which enjoyed her confidence did not constitute sufficient grounds for terminating the régime of protective upbringing applied to the infant. Finally, under the régime thus maintained, the person to whom the Child Welfare Board has entrusted the infant has not the capacity and rights of a guardian. He receives her, watches over her, provides for the care of her health: the infant is entrusted to his care as she would have been entrusted to the care of the Törnquist family if the guardian's wish had been carried out.

" The protective upbringing applied to the infant, as it appears in these decisions, *i.e.*, according to the facts in the present case, cannot be regarded as a rival guardianship to the guardianship established in the Netherlands in accordance with the 1902 Convention.

" The Swedish measure of protective upbringing, as instituted and maintained in respect of Marie Elisabeth Boll, placed obstacles in the way of the full exercise by the guardian of her right to custody. Before the Supreme Administrative Court she relied, as has been recalled, upon her intention to entrust the infant to a home of her choice: that intention clearly corresponded to an exercise by the guardian of her right to custody. The guardian was not, however, asking that her intention should simply be acted upon; she relied upon it as a reason for terminating the régime of protective upbringing. The Supreme Administrative Court, by its judgment of February 21st, 1956, dismissed her claim. In dismissing it, the Court limited itself no doubt to adjudicating upon the maintenance of protective upbringing, but, at the same time, it placed an [**67**] obstacle in the way of the full exercise of the right to custody belonging to the guardian. Does this constitute a failure to observe the 1902 Convention, Article 6 of which provides that ' the administration of a guardianship extends to the person . . . of the infant '?

" In order to answer this question, it is not necessary, as has already been said, for the Court to ascertain the real or alleged reasons which determined or influenced the decisions complained of. It is called upon to pronounce only on the compatibility of the measure with the obligations binding upon Sweden under the 1902 Convention. It has before it a measure instituted pursuant to a Swedish Law which impedes the exercise by the guardian of the right to custody conferred upon her by Dutch law in accordance with the 1902 Convention. Are the imposition and maintenance of such a measure incompatible with the 1902 Convention?

" The Court is not confronted by a situation in which it would suffice for it to say that a national Law cannot override the obligations assumed by treaty. It is asked to say whether the measure taken and impugned is or is not compatible with the obligations binding upon Sweden by virtue of the 1902 Convention. To do that, it must determine what are the obligations imposed by that Convention, how far they extend and, especially, it must determine whether, by stipulating that the guardianship of an infant is governed by the national law of the infant, the 1902 Convention intended to prohibit the application to a foreign infant of a law such as the Swedish Law on the protection of children.

" The 1902 Convention, as indicated by its preamble, was designed to ' lay down common provisions to govern the guardianship of infants '. It provides for the application of the national law of the infant for the institution and operation of guardianship by expressly extending in Article 6 the administration of a guardianship to the person and to all the property of the infant. It goes no farther than that, and indeed it has been pointed out that it does not make complete provision for guardianship, which should serve as a warning against any construction which would extend it beyond its true scope. In providing that guardianship and, in particular, that the guardian's right to custody should be governed by the national law of the infant, the Convention was intended to determine what law should be applied to settle these points. It was intended, in accordance with the general purpose of the Conferences on Private International Law, that it should put an end to the divergences of view as to whether preference ought to be given in this connection to the national law of the infant, to that of his place of residence, etc., but it was not intended to lay down, in the domain of guardianship, and particularly of the right to custody, any immunity of an infant or of a guardian with respect to the whole body of the local law. The local law with regard to guardianship is in principle excluded, but not all the other provisions of the local law.

[68] " There may be some points of contact between matters governed by the national law of the infant which is applicable to guardianship and matters falling within the ambit of the local law. It does not follow that in such cases the national law of the infant must always prevail over the application of the local law and that, accordingly, the exercise of the powers of a guardian is always beyond the reach of local laws dealing with subjects other than the assignment of guardianship and the determination of the powers and duties of a guardian. If, for instance, for the purposes of the administration of guardianship in respect of the person or the property of an infant, a guardian finds it necessary to travel to some foreign country, he will, so far as his journey is concerned, be subject to the laws relating to the entry and residence of foreigners. This is something outside the scope of guardianship as regulated by the 1902 Convention.

" If, in a country in which a foreign infant, to whom the 1902 Convention applies, is living, laws relating to compulsory education and the sanitary supervision of children, professional training or the participation of young people in certain work, are applicable to foreigners, in circumstances assumed to be in conformity with the requirements of international law and of treaties governing these matters, a guardian's right to custody under the national law of the infant cannot override the application of such laws to a foreign infant. In adopting the national law of the infant as the proper law to govern guardianship, including the guardian's right to custody, the 1902 Convention was not intended to decide upon anything other than guardianship, the true purpose of which is to make provision for the protection of the infant; it was not intended to regulate or to restrict the scope of laws designed to meet pre-occupations of a general character.

" The same must be true of the Swedish Law on the protection of children and young persons. Considered in its application to children of Swedish nationality, the Law is not a law on guardianship, it does not relate to the legal institution of guardianship. It is applicable whether the infant be within the *puissance paternelle* of the parents or under guardianship. Protective upbringing, which constitutes an application of the Law, is superimposed, when that is necessary, on either, without bringing either to an end but paralyzing their effects to the extent that they are in conflict with the requirements of protective upbringing.

" Is the 1902 Convention to be construed as meaning—tacitly, for the reason that it provides that the guardianship of an infant shall be governed by his national law—that it was intended to prohibit the application of any legislative enactment on a different subject-matter the indirect effect of which would be to restrict, though not to abolish, the guardian's right to custody? So to interpret the Convention would be to go beyond its purpose. That purpose was to put an end, in questions of guardianship, to diffi-[69] culties arising from the conflict of laws. That was its only purpose. It was sought to achieve it by laying down to this end common rules which the contracting States must respect. To understand the Convention as limiting the right of contracting States to apply laws on a different topic would be to go beyond that purpose.

" The 1902 Convention determines the domain of application of the laws of each contracting State in the matter of guardianship. It does this by requiring each contracting State to apply the national law of the infant. If the 1902 Convention had intended to regulate the domain of application of laws such as the Swedish Law on the protection of children and young persons, it would follow that that Law should be applied to Swedish infants in a foreign country. But no one has sought to attribute such an extraterritorial effect to that Law. The 1902 Convention is therefore not concerned with the determination of the domain of application of such a law.

" A comparison between the purpose of the 1902 Convention and that of the Swedish Law on the protection of children shows that the purpose of the latter places it outside the field of application of the Convention.

" The 1902 Convention did not seek to define what it meant by guardianship, but there is no doubt that the legal systems, as between which it sought to establish some harmony by prescribing what was the proper law to govern that situation, understood and understand by guardianship an institution the object of which is the protection of the infant: the protection and guidance of his person, the safeguarding of his pecuniary interests and the fulfilling of the functions rendered necessary by his legal incapacity. Guardianship and protective upbringing have certain common purposes. The special feature of the régime of protective upbringing is that it is put into operation only in respect of children who, for reasons inherent in them or for causes external to them, are in an abnormal situation—a situation which, if allowed to continue, might give rise to danger going beyond the person of the child. Protective upbringing contributes to the protection of the child, but at the same time, and above all, it is designed to protect society against dangers resulting from improper upbringing, inadequate hygiene, or moral corruption of young people. The 1902 Convention recognizes the fact that guardianship, in order to achieve its aim of individual protection, needs to be governed by the national law of the infant; to achieve the aim of the social guarantee which it is the purpose of the Swedish Law on the protection of children and young persons to provide, it is necessary that it should apply to all young people living in Sweden.

" Protective upbringing is not, as is guardianship, applied for a pre-ordained period during which it is maintained. The public service of the protection of children is much more flexible, just because the measures taken depend upon the circumstances, and [70] can be modified in accordance with alterations in those circumstances. Its functions correspond to preoccupations of a moral and social order. The Swedish Law being designed to provide a social guarantee, it was presented, on behalf of the Government of Sweden, as a law of *ordre public* which, as such, is binding upon all those upon Swedish territory. The consequences to be drawn from such a characterization were argued at length before the Court. It was contended that a proper interpretation of the 1902 Convention must lead to recognition that this Convention, bringing about the unification as between the contracting States of certain rules for the settlement of conflicts of law, must be understood as containing an implied reservation authorizing, on the ground of *ordre public*, the overruling of the application of the foreign law recognized as normally the proper law to govern the legal relationship in question. It has been argued that such an exception is recognised in the systems of private international law of those countries which joined in the partial codification of this branch of the law. The Court does not consider it necessary to pronounce upon this contention. It seeks to ascertain in a more direct manner whether, having regard to its purpose, the 1902 Convention lays down any rules which the Swedish authorities have disregarded.

" The 1902 Convention had to meet a problem of the conflict of private law rules. It presupposes the hesitation which was felt in the choice of the law applicable to a given legal relationship: the national law of an individual, the law of his place of residence, the *lex fori*, etc. It gave the preference to the national law of the infant and thereby prescribed to the courts of each contracting State that they should apply a foreign law when the infant involved was a foreigner. It is perfectly conceivable that the courts of a State should in certain cases apply a foreign law.

" Very different is the sense of the question if it be asked what is the domain of the applicability of the Swedish Law or of the Dutch law on the protection of children. The measures provided for or prescribed by Swedish law are applied, at least in the first stage as was done in the present case, by an administrative organ. Such an organ can act only in accordance with its own law: it is inconceivable that the Swedish Child Welfare Board should apply Dutch law to a Dutch infant living in Sweden and equally inconceivable that the competent Dutch organ should apply Dutch law to such an infant living abroad. What a Swedish or Dutch Court can do in matters of guardianship, pursuant to the 1902 Convention, namely, apply a foreign law—Dutch law or Swedish law as the case may be—the authorities of those countries cannot do in the matter of protective upbringing. To extend the 1902 Convention to such a situation would lead to an impossibility. It is not permissible so to construe the Convention as to bring about such a result.

[71] " The 1902 Convention was designed to put an end to the competing claims of several laws to govern a single legal relationship. There are no such competing claims in the case of laws for the protection of children and young persons. The claim of each of these laws is that it should be applied in the country in which it was enacted: such a law has not and, as has been seen, cannot have any extraterritorial aspiration, for that would exceed its social purpose as well as the means of which it disposes. The problem which was at the basis of the 1902 Convention does not exist in respect of these laws, and the only danger which could threaten them would lie in the negative solution which would be reached if, as a result of an extensive construction which has not heretofore been considered justified, the application of Swedish law was refused to Dutch children living in Sweden; since Dutch law on the same subject could not be applied to them, the protection of children and young persons, desired both by Swedish law and by Dutch law, would be frustrated. The 1902 Convention never intended that a negative solution should

be reached in the domain with which it is concerned: this confirms that what is understood by the protection of children and young persons does not fall within the domain of the Convention.

" It is scarcely necessary to add that to arrive at a solution which would put an obstacle in the way of the application of the Swedish Law on the protection of children and young persons to a foreign infant living in Sweden would be to misconceive the social purpose of that Law, a purpose of which the importance was felt in many countries particularly after the signature of the 1902 Convention. The social problem of delinquent or even of merely misdirected young people, and of children whose health, mental state or moral development is threatened, in short, of those ill-adapted to social life, has often arisen; laws such as the Swedish Law now in question were enacted in several countries to meet the problem. The Court could not readily subscribe to any construction which would make the 1902 Convention an obstacle on this point to social progress.

" It thus seems to the Court that, in spite of their points of contact and in spite, indeed, of the encroachments revealed in practice, the 1902 Convention on the guardianship of infants does not include within its scope the matter of the protection of children and of young persons as understood by the Swedish Law of June 6th, 1924. The 1902 Convention cannot therefore have given rise to obligations binding upon the signatory States in a field outside the matter with which it was concerned, and accordingly the Court does not in the present case find any failure to observe that Convention on the part of Sweden.

" This finding makes it unnecessary to examine a further submission put forward by the Government of the Netherlands after the main submission which is not upheld by the Court. Furthermore, in view of the reply given to the main submission put forward by [72] the Government of Sweden, it is unnecessary to examine its alternative submission."

[Report: *I.C.J. Reports*, 1958, p. 55.]

Judge Kojevnikov made the following statement (at p. 72):

" that he is unable to concur either in the reasoning or in the operative clause of the Judgment because, in his opinion, on the basis of the principle *pacta sunt servanda*, having regard to the fact that the rights and obligations of the Parties under the 1902 Convention governing the guardianship of infants are abundantly clear, having regard to the character of the case and the available facts, as well as the legitimate interests of the infant concerned —who is of Dutch nationality—the Court ought to have held that the measures taken by the Swedish administrative authorities in respect of the said infant, which impede the exercise of the right of guardianship based on the Treaty, are not in conformity with the obligations binding upon Sweden *vis-à-vis* the Netherlands by virtue of the aforementioned 1902 Convention, in particular Articles 1 and 6 of the Convention."

Judge Spiropoulos made the following statement (at p. 72):

" that, although he shares the opinion of the Court that Sweden cannot be held to have failed to respect her obligations under the 1902 Convention in this case, he considers that the rejection of the claim of the Government of the Netherlands ought rather to be based upon the character of *ordre public* [73] of the Swedish Law on the protection of children and young persons. In his opinion, this character enables the Law to override the 1902 Convention, since the 1902 Convention must be understood as containing an implied reservation authorizing, on the ground of *ordre public*, the overruling of the application of the foreign law recognized as the proper law, in accordance with the Convention, to govern the legal relationship in question."

Judges Badawi, Sir Hersch Lauterpacht, Moreno Quintana, Wellington Koo and Sir Percy Spender appended statements of their Separate Opinions (see below).

Vice-President Zafrullah Khan stated (at p. 73) that he agreed generally with Judge Wellington Koo.

Judges Winiarski and Córdova, and M. Offerhaus, Judge *ad hoc*, appended statements of their Dissenting Opinions (see below).

### Judge Badawi

[74] "I am in agreement both with the operative clause of and the grounds for the Court's Judgment. As reasons for its decision, however, the Court did not think it necessary to pronounce upon the interpretation of the Law on protective upbringing as a law of *ordre public* aiming to provide a social guarantee, nor of the Convention of 1902 as containing an implied reservation authorizing, on the ground of *ordre public*, the overruling of the application of the foreign Law recognized as the proper law to govern the legal relationship in question. The Court confined itself to giving a careful and closely reasoned analysis of the differences between the purpose of the Convention and the purpose of the Law. In view of these differences, the Court considered that the Convention could not overrule the Law, quite apart from the fact that unless the Law prevailed, a negative solution would be arrived at, according to which the infant would lose in Sweden, where she lives, both the benefit of the Law on protective upbringing and of the corresponding Dutch system of placing under supervision, this system only being applicable in the Netherlands by the Dutch national organs.

" For my part, I take the view that this justification alone is not decisive, since, apart from the differences between the Convention and the Law, there is the fact that the application of the latter affects the effects of the former. There is thus opposition between the two, and it is necessary to make one prevail over the other.

"Now, the Law is a national instrument, while the Convention is an international instrument. In favour of the latter there is a presumption of primacy, and it has been established by many judicial decisions that a State cannot evade the obligations imposed by an international convention by invoking its own law, or indeed even its own constitution.

"It is not enough, therefore, that the subject-matter of the Law should be different from the subject-matter of the Convention. One must further take the view, either that this particular Law is superior to the Convention, or that the Convention should be interpreted as embodying a tacit reservation which authorizes in certain cases the preference being given to the *lex fori*— in other words, that the Law constituting the *lex fori* is a law of *ordre public*.

" The first alternative is clearly to be excluded. The second one remains. Now, despite its apparent incongruity in the case of international conventions, the concept of laws of *ordre public* is a common one in private international law.

"It is universally recognized in national systems of conflicts of laws as inseparable from these systems, notwithstanding that this [75] general formula of *ordre public* is considered a vague, indefinite and relative concept and one that varies according to place and time.

" Is the situation the same in international conventions relating to the system of the conflict of laws? International conventions on this subject are, in fact, simply designed to achieve the unification of the system, without creating specific obligations. They merely constitute an alignment of States upon a uniform solution, without changing the nature of this solution as it is generally adopted in national legal systems.

" Some doubt however appears to have been cast upon the invariability of this conclusion in the case of international conventions. Some take the view that, in the Convention of 1904 on succession, signed by the representatives of a large number of States, Article 6 regarding *ordre public*, which was redrafted so many times, made the Convention abortive, for it was never ratified, and that in 1913 France denounced the three Conventions of 1902, also for a reason of *ordre public*.

" However that may be, it is somewhat significant to note that recent conventions of private international law expressly provided for the exception of *ordre public*.

" During the drawing up of the Convention of 1902 on guardianship, there were, indeed, lengthy discussions on the adoption of a general formula of *ordre public*. The trend of opinion opposed to its inclusion in the Convention prevailed by invoking its vagueness and generality, as well as the fear that national tribunals might reduce the Convention to nothing in giving the formula a broad interpretation. According to this view, the Convention adopted a system of special treatment by providing for the only cases which deserved to be regarded as exceptions to the general rule laid down by the first article of the Convention.

" Articles 3, 6 and 7 of the Convention have been cited as cases in which, on the grounds of *ordre public*, the national law is excluded. According to this interpretation, a similar exception would not be justified in any other case.

" But, leaving aside paragraph 2 of Article 6, the provisions of Article 3 and 7 are, in fact, concerned with details of application or with hypotheses in which the application of the national law cannot be contemplated, not on grounds of *ordre public*, but on account of factors inherent in those very hypotheses. Under Article 3, it is as a result of the failure of the national law that the local law will be applied, while Article 7 is concerned only with provisional measures taken pending the institution of guardianship under the national law or measures taken in cases of urgency.

" Apart from this argument drawn from the Convention and on the basis of the discussions at the Hague Conferences, must one conclude that in the absence of an exception of *ordre public* expressly provided for in the Convention, no such exception should be [76] admitted? But no special provisions for individual cases could be sufficient or adequate to meet the needs of every legal situation, since the cases of *ordre public* cannot be fixed and listed in advance. The human contingencies which may give rise to a divergence between a rule determined by the system adopted for conflict of laws and another rule of the *lex fori* are numerous and often unforeseeable, quite apart from the fact that new laws may give rise to cases in which similar divergencies may be revealed.

" The absence of a general formula of *ordre public* cannot, therefore, be interpreted as a negation of this reservation. In fact, this tacit reservation forms part of the technical structure of private international law which, by settling a conflict between two systems of law by means of the all-inclusive acceptance of one of them, cannot obviate another conflict between a particular rule of the system chosen and a rule of the *lex fori*. And it is precisely the exception of *ordre public*, implied in any system of conflict of laws, that constitutes the criterion for the settlement of conflict, which can be foreseen but not determined in advance.

" But, if the omission to provide for the exception of *ordre public* in a convention does not mean that the convention denies its existence, such an omission could, in the mind of its supporters, have served as a means of minimizing the violations of the convention which would result from an abusive use of the exception. Perhaps it was thought that, without an arbitration voluntarily agreed to by the contracting Parties to the Hague Conventions, in case of the abusive use of the exception—a cumbersome, costly, and not very appropriate method—the parties would have been unable to obtain justice.

" Notwithstanding this probable mental reservation, the fact that the Convention is silent with regard to the exception cannot properly be construed as a denial of its existence. The view that it would, in one form or another, be admissible has always been held, because the exception is inseparable from the system of conflict of laws.

" In fact, the exclusion of the exception of *ordre public* in the application of an international convention on the conflict of laws is only conceivable on the assumption that the contracting States impliedly intended to accept the obligation not to reserve for their own sovereign action any right to apply the rules of their own legislation which might directly or indirectly run counter to the effects of the application of the convention.

" Such an interpretation is, however, neither admissible nor in conformity with the facts. It is not admissible because it would reject the implication of the exception of *ordre public* to substitute for it a more serious implication.

[77] " It is not in conformity with the facts because even the extremist opponents of the exception cannot deny that certain limitations to the application of the Convention do in fact exist, in particular in penal matters, notwithstanding that these limitations have not been expressly provided for and that they can only be the result of an interpretation by implication. Without attempting a definition of *ordre public*, which the Conferences were not able to establish, it is not difficult to admit that the limitations which may be justified on grounds similar to or as valid as the limitation mentioned above should benefit by the same treatment. They would involve a comparison between the obligation resulting from the Convention and the local law. If the courts of a contracting State, under the possible ultimate supervision of an international jurisdiction, hold that the law, in view of its importance and its serious nature, should not be applied only to nationals of the country, either as a right or a privilege, or as an obligation or duty, but to all the inhabitants of the country as being a law of *ordre public*, they cannot be held to be contravening the intentions of the contracting States in making the law prevail over the Convention. It is, in fact, a question to be decided in each case, having regard to the convention and the law involved.

" With regard to the present case, it is sufficient to recall that the Netherlands, notwithstanding the omission of any allusion in the Convention to the exception, recognize that the Convention cannot be invoked with regard to the custody of a child under guardianship against the carrying out of a penalty or of a measure of reformation pronounced against the child for an offence which it has committed, in the same way as they would recognize that the protective upbringing exercised in cases (*b*), (*c*) and (*d*) referred to in Article 22 of the Swedish Law of June 6th, 1924, would override the application of the Convention, but not case (*a*)—which is that of Elisabeth Boll—because that case only relates to the private interests of the child and thus constitutes a case of guardianship and hence a rival guardianship to that provided for in the first article of the Convention.

" But it is arbitrary, where the law has put the different grounds on a footing of equality, to consider that one of them is connected with the private interests of the child, while the others have in view the interests of society—especially bearing in mind the evolution that has taken place in ideas concerning children and young people.

" How, moreover, [and] on what basis, is the respective seriousness of the grounds laid down in Article 22 to be determined, when the Law establishes and puts at the disposal of the Board measures which are not determined by the differences in those grounds—a certain measure being applied for a certain ground—but only by the appropriateness of the measure in regard to the specific case? [78] A case (a) may be more serious than a case (b), and may call for a graver measure; and the contrary can also be true.

" In order to contest the exception of *ordre public*, the vagueness and generality of the concept have often been invoked, as also the fear that it may be abusively or arbitrarily applied; but, apart from the fact that that is a hypothetical and exaggerated danger, the objection is not valid to exclude a rule of law of which it postulates the truth in principle. At the most, the only value of the objection would be to call for greater circumspection in its application.

" In the present case, the issue does not in reality bear on the principle of the exception of *ordre public*, nor on the fact that it constitutes an implied reservation to the first Article of the Convention of 1902, nor on the general scope of the Law on protective upbringing, but on the application of one of its provisions to the case submitted to the Court, by detaching the first paragraph of Article 22 of the Law of June 6, 1924, from the sytem as a whole and by contesting its character of *ordre public*.

" The presence of the element of a substantive link considered as a condition of the exception of *ordre public* has also been disputed, but the uninterrupted residence of the infant in Sweden leaves no doubt, in the present case, of the existence of such an element.

" From the foregoing considerations it may be concluded that the Law on protective upbringing is a law of *ordre public* and that, as such, it overrides the application of the Convention of 1902.

" This reason should therefore be added to the reasons adopted by the Court, of which it is a necessary complement.

" The rejection of the Submissions of the Netherlands arrived at on the basis of the arguments of the Parties themselves would then be even more convincing."

Judge Sir Hersch Lauterpacht delivered the following Separate Opinion:

[79] " While, for reasons which I deem it incumbent upon me to state, I am unable to accept some of the contentions advanced by the defendant Government and upheld by the Court, I arrive on other grounds at the same results as does the Judgment. I do so by reference to considerations of public policy, of *ordre public*—a question which occupied the main part of the written and oral pleadings, which figures exclusively in the formulation of the legal issue in the final Conclusions of both Parties, and which I feel therefore bound to examine in the present Opinion.

" The facts underlying the controversy between the Parties are stated in detail in the Judgment of the Court. For the purpose of this Opinion it is sufficient to recapitulate briefly the crucial aspect of the dispute: The Hague Convention of 12th June, 1902, on Guardianship of Infants, to which both Sweden and the Netherlands are Parties, provides in Article 1 that the guardianship of an infant shall be governed by the national law of the infant. It is clear from the various articles of the Convention, and it is not disputed by the Parties, that such guardianship extends normally to the custody of the person of the minor. In accordance with the provisions of the Convention, a

Dutch guardian was appointed in 1954 by a Dutch Court over Elisabeth Boll who, although born in Sweden and permanently resident there since her birth, is of Dutch nationality. In the same year, various Swedish authorities, in a series of decisions and in circumstances which appear from the Judgment, applied to Elisabeth Boll the Swedish Law of 1924 concerning the Protection of Children and Young Persons (Child Welfare Act)—which will be referred to in this Opinion as the Law on Protective Upbringing. By one of these decisions the custody of the person of Elisabeth Boll was taken over in 1954 by the Child Welfare Board at Norrköping, the place of residence of Elisabeth Boll. The Board, in turn, entrusted the custody of Elisabeth to her maternal grandfather—such custody to be exercised on behalf of the Board. That measure was finally confirmed by the Supreme Administrative Court of Sweden. It must be noted that in a series of decisions the Swedish courts and authorities otherwise recognized the guardianship appointed by the Dutch court.

" The principal justification which the Swedish Government adduced for the action taken by the Swedish authorities was that [80] the Law on Protective Upbringing is a measure of *ordre public* and that the reliance on it, far from being in violation of the Convention, is implied in it. In the course of the written and oral pleadings subsidiary arguments were relied upon by the Swedish Government. One of them was the contention that the Convention of 1902, being a Convention on Guardianship, does not cover the Swedish Law on Protective Upbringing said to pursue a different object and to lie in a different field. It is that line of argument which has acquired prominence in the present case and which must be examined in the first instance.

" That manner of approach, as expressed in or as underlying the Swedish argument, may be summarized as follows: There is no incompatibility between the Guardianship Convention and the Law on Protective Upbringing. The Convention, which is concerned with guardianship, does not cover protective upbringing. The latter is outside the Convention. This is so although the effect of the Law on Protective Upbringing is such as to render impossible, for the time being, the exercise by the Dutch guardian of the right of custody of the person of Elisabeth Boll. The object and purpose of the Law on Protective Upbringing is wholly different from that of the Guardianship Convention. The Court is not concerned with the incidental effects of the Law on Protective Upbringing, but with its nature and purpose. Guardianship and protective upbringing are wholly different institutions. The former is concerned with the interests of the minor, the latter with the interests of society. Guardianship is in the sphere of private law. Protective upbringing is in the sphere of public law. The Convention, which is one on *private* international law, can be violated only by legislation in the sphere of private international law. From the point of view of their nature and purposes, the Convention and the Law on Protective Upbringing operate on wholly different planes and there is, therefore, no question of the Law and the measures taken thereunder being incompatible with the Convention.

" The reasoning underlying these contentions raises important questions, transcending the issue immediately before the Court, of interpretation and observance of treaties. If a State enacts and applies legislation which, in effect, renders a treaty wholly or partly inoperative, can such legislation be deemed not to constitute a violation of the treaty for the reason that the legislation in question covers a subject-matter different from that covered by the treaty, that it is concerned with a different institution, and that it pursues a different purpose? I have considerable difficulty in answering that question in the affirmative. The difficulty is increased by the fact that the conflict between the treaty and the legislation in question may be concealed, or made to be concealed, by what is no more than a doctrinal or legislative difference of classification. An identical provision which in the law of one country forms part of a law for the protection of children may, in [81] another State, be included within the provisions relating to guardianship. That, as will be shown, is no mere theoretical possibility. It is in fact a conspicuous feature of the present case.

"What is the meaning of the expression: The Convention of 1902 does not cover a system such as that set up in the Swedish Law on Protective Upbringing? It is admitted that guardianship under the Convention covers the right to decide on the residence and education of the minor—a right claimed and exercised by a Swedish authority and, on its behalf, by the Swedish maternal grandfather acting in pursuance of the Law on Protective Upbringing. If that is so, then the Convention does cover, in one of its essential aspects, the same powers and functions which are now exercised by Swedish authorities in pursuance of the Law on Protective Upbringing. The substance is the same although the purpose of the Convention and of the Law may be different. It may be said that what matters is not the substance of these functions but their object. It is not easy to follow that distinction. When a State concludes a treaty it is entitled to expect that that treaty will not be mutilated or destroyed by legislative or other measures which pursue a different object but which, in effect, render impossible the operation of the treaty or of part thereof.

"The treaty covers every law and every provision of a law which impairs, which interferes with, the operation of the treaty. It has been said that the Law in question may have an adverse effect upon the subject-matter of the treaty without being covered by the treaty. However, what the Court must be concerned with is exactly the effect of the Law inasmuch as it impairs the operation of the treaty, and not the notional identity or otherwise of the objects pursued by the Law and the treaty. The treaty prohibits interference with its operation unless there is a justification for it, express or implied, in the treaty; that justification cannot be found in the mere fact that the Law pursues an object different from the object pursued by the treaty. It can be found only in the fact that that particular object is expressly permitted by the treaty or implicitly authorized by it by virtue of some principle of public or private international law—a principle such as stems from public policy or from a cognate, although more limited, principle, which is often no more than another formulation of public policy, namely, that certain categories of laws, such as criminal laws, police laws, fiscal laws, administrative laws, and so on, are binding upon all the inhabitants of the territory notwithstanding any general applicability of foreign law.

"The following example will illustrate the problem and the consequences involved: States often conclude treaties of commerce and establishment providing for a measure of protection from restrictions with regard to importation or export of goods, admission and residence of aliens, their right to inherit property, functions of consuls, and the like. What is the position of a State which has concluded a treaty of that type and then finds out that the other Party [82] whittles down, or renders inoperative, one after another, the provisions of that treaty by enacting laws ' having a different subject-matter ', such as reducing unemployment, social welfare, promotion of native craft and industry, protection of public morals in relation to admission of aliens, racial segregation, reform of civil procedure involving the abolition of customary rights of consular representation, reform of the civil code involving a change of inheritance laws in a way affecting the right of inheritance by aliens, a general law codifying the law relating to the jurisdiction of courts and involving the abolition of immunities, granted by the treaty, of public vessels engaged in commerce, or any other laws ' pursuing different objects '? It makes little or no difference to the other Party that the treaty has become a dead letter as the result of laws which have so obviously affected its substance, but which pursue a different object. As stated, some of these laws may be justified as being within the domain of public policy or for some cognate reason. However, the argument here summarized does not proceed on these lines. It is based on the allegation of a difference between the Treaty and the Law which impedes its operation.

" Another example, directly relating to the Convention of 1902, will illustrate the problem from a different point of view. Article 2 of the Convention lays down that in some cases the diplomatic or consular agents authorized by the law of the State of which the infant is a national may make provision for guardianship in accordance with the law of that State. What is the position if a Contracting Party enacts a general law—a law of public character on a quite different plane—relating to the immunities and functions of foreign diplomatic and consular representatives providing that in the future foreign diplomatic and consular representatives shall not perform any act affecting private rights in the territory of that State? Can that State plead that, as the Convention and the Law pursue a quite different purpose, it does not matter that the effect of the Law is to frustrate one of the provisions of the Convention?

" The conspicuous fact in the present case is that the Dutch guardian acceptable to the father of the infant and appointed under Dutch law in accordance with the Convention was replaced, in respect of the exercise of the right of custody, by the Swedish maternal grandfather of Elisabeth Boll acting on behalf of the Children's Bureau. The Dutch authorities and the Dutch guardian may not unnaturally hold the view that the custody exercised by the Swedish grandfather is, in fact and in the circumstances of the case which reveal some dissension between the Dutch and the Swedish branches of the family, to a large extent a rival guardianship. They may find it difficult to appreciate the suggestion that there is no conflict between the Convention and the measures taken [83] seeing that they lie on a different plane and pursue different objects. The situation is not affected by the continuing right of the Dutch guardian to administer the property of the child or to institute proceedings for the restoration of her functions of custody. So long as the exercise of the right of custody is vested in the hands of the Swedish authority and the Swedish maternal grandfather of Elisabeth Boll acting on its behalf, there is a nullification of the essential attributes of the guardianship as instituted by the Convention. There may be—and as will be suggested later on, there is—a full justification for that measure in considerations of a different character. That justification cannot be found in the allegation, which is controversial, that the Dutch guardianship and the Swedish protective upbringing are wholly different institutions.

" A State is not entitled to cut down its treaty obligations in relation to one institution by enacting in the sphere of another institution provisions whose effect is such as to frustrate the operation of a crucial aspect of the treaty. There is a disadvantage in accepting a principle of interpretation, coined for the purpose of a particular case, which, if acted upon generally, is bound to have serious repercussions on the authority of treaties. As stated, the Convention and the particular provision of the Law on Protective Upbringing cover, in relation to the present dispute, the same ground and the same subject-matter. It has been said that there is a technical difference, inasmuch as they lie on different planes, between the Convention and the Law on Protective Upbringing. Assuming that there is a technical difference, it may still be considered undesirable that a dispute between two Governments shall be decided by reference to a controversial technicality in a case relating to significant issues of substance—a technicality which, if acted upon generally, would introduce confusion or, worse, in the law of the operation of treaties. Once we begin to base the interpretation of treaties on conceptual distinctions between actually conflicting legal rules lying on different planes and for that reason not being, somehow, inconsistent, it may be difficult to set a limit to the effects of these operations in the sphere of logic and classification.

" The view has been put forward that there can be no conflict between a Convention on Guardianship and the Law on Protective Upbringing for the reason that the Convention of 1902 is a convention of private international law and that guardianship with which it is exclusively concerned is an institution of private law, in particular of family law, while the Law of Protective Upbringing and the various measures authorized therein are in the sphere of public law seeing that they are concerned with safeguarding the interests of society. Even if these reasons were otherwise acceptable, an essentially doctrinal classification and distinction provides a doubtful basis for judging the question of the proper observance of [84] treaties. However, there is in the present case a particular difficulty in acknowledging the force of that distinction.

" An examination of the main systems of municipal law in the matter of guardianship does not corroborate the view that it is a mere family institution of a purely private law nature. The principal justification for that view is that, by way of traditional classification, guardianship finds a place in codes of private law and that it creates numerous rights and duties in the sphere of private law. However, at the same time guardianship can rightly be described as an institution in which the guardian acts as an organ of the State, as it were, and therefore partakes of the nature of an institution of public law. He acts under the active supervision of the State which may step in at any time—in the interest of both the child and society—and supplant the guardian, wholly or in part. There are very few countries the law of which is based exclusively upon a private law and family conception of guardianship. The law of the majority of States, including Holland and Sweden, on this matter is characterized by an active intervention of the State as an organ of control and supervision at every stage. In some countries, such as Germany, the protection of minors is entrusted mainly to the State, which acts through a special tribunal—the Guardianship Court—and it is only by way of exception that these functions are delegated to the family council. It is of interest to note that prior to the Hague Conferences which examined the various drafts of the Convention on Guardianship, the difference between the two systems— ' tutelle de famille ' (family guardianship) and ' tutelle d'autorité ' (authority guardianship)—was clearly recognized. That distinction was, for instance, elaborated in 1902 by M. Lehr, Secretary of the Institute of International Law, which had a substantial share in the preparation of the first drafts of the Convention (Lehr, ' De la tutelle des mineurs d'après les principales législations de l'Europe ', Revue de droit international et de législation comparée, 2nd series, Vol. 4 (1902), pp. 315 et seq.). He classified both the Dutch and Swedish systems of guardianship as belonging to the group of ' tutelle d'autorité ' (pp. 320, 326, 329).

" In view of this, it does not seem to me possible to accept the argument based on the notion of a purely private law and family character of guardianship. How artificial are the distinctions between the supposed private law character of guardianship and the assumed public law character of systems of protective supervision or upbringing of children, apart from the normal operation of guardianship, may be gauged from the fact that the matter is entirely a question of legislative technique and drafting. That may be seen, for instance, from the provisions of the Dutch Civil Code relating to guardianship and contained in Part XV of Book I of the Code. Section A 1 of Part XV covers Paternal Power; Section B 2 covers Paternal Guardianship; while Section B 3, which according to Section B 9 is applicable to guardianship, embodies largely the same [85] provisions as are embodied in that part of the Swedish Law on Protective Upbringing which was applied in the case of Elisabeth Boll. That Section, in language almost identical with that of the above-mentioned Swedish Law, provides, in paragraph 365, for the taking of certain steps ' if a child grows up in such a way as to be threatened with moral or physical harm '. These steps may be taken at the instance of Guardianship Councils, for which provision is made in the same part of the Law and which, under the authority of courts of law, fulfil functions similar to those of the Children's Bureau under the Swedish Law of 1924 (Sections 461 *et seq.*). The same Section A 3 makes provision for children in that situation being placed by the Judge of the Children's Court in an observation centre for mental or physical examination, or, if the child needs special observation, in an institution selected for that purpose (paragraph 372 *a* and *b*). The German Civil Code, in the Section on Guardianship, provides in a single Article—Article 1838—that the Guardianship Court can order the placing of the minor with an appropriate family or in an educational or reformatory institution—a kind of provision which is found in the Swedish Law of 1924. It is a matter of legislative technique and drafting whether the provisions for the protection of children in relation to whom normal guardianship has proved insufficient are, as in Holland, made part of the legislation relating to guardianship or whether, as in the case of Sweden, they are embodied in a separate enactment. In both instances they are intended to protect both the child and the society.

" For it is clear that the distinction between the protection of the child and the protection of society is artificial. Both the laws relating to guardianship and those relating to protective upbringing are laws intended primarily for the protection of children and their interests. At the same time, the protection of children—through guardianship or protective upbringing—is pre-eminently in the interests of society. They are part of it—the most vulnerable and most in need of protection. All social laws are, in the last resort, laws for the protection of individuals; all laws for the protection of individuals are, in a true sense, social laws. There is an element of unreality in making these two aspects of the purpose of the State the starting-point for drawing legal consequences of practical import. It is wholly unreal to insist that the measures taken under the Law on Protective Upbringing for the safety, health and happiness of Elisabeth Boll were measures taken not primarily in the interest of that child—and therefore not measures of guardianship of her person—but primarily in the interest of society at large and therefore falling within a quite different category. It is in the light of these considerations that it is necessary to judge the view that as the Guardianship Convention of 1902 is concerned only with a private law institution of family relationship devoid of any public element, there can be no conflict between it and an enactment [**86**] of an exclusively public law character such as the Swedish Law on Protective Upbringing. Even if every link of that proposition could be substantiated by reference to national law as operating in most countries—and that does not appear to be the case—there would still remain the difficulty of assessing the content of the statement that there can be no conflict between a treaty regulating a sphere of private law and a national enactment in the realm of public law.

" Undoubtedly, the Convention of 1902 was intended to regulate conflicts of law in the sphere of guardianship. But there is no persuasive reason for accepting the suggestion that the relevant provisions of the Swedish Law on Protective Upbringing, under which the custody of Elisabeth Boll was entrusted to the care of her maternal grandfather in his home under the authority of the Children's Board, has nothing to do with guardianship, seeing that they are of a public law nature. Similarly, it is difficult to accept the suggestion that guardianship, instituted in the private interest of the child, is devoid of a substantial public element of social purpose. The rights of the parties, especially in an international dispute, ought not to be determined by reference to the controversial mysteries of the distinction between private and public law. The fact that the purpose of the Convention of 1902 is to establish rules for avoiding conflicts of laws in the sphere of guardianship does not mean that that sphere is confined to laws *described* as guardianship; it covers all laws, however described or classified, which fulfil an essential function of guardianship. It is part of the firmly established jurisprudence of this Court that with regard to national laws bearing upon treaty obligations what matters is not the letter of the law but its actual effect.

" However, it is not necessary to labour this point. The preceding considerations are, in my view, sufficient to show the decisive difficulties inherent in the proposition that a State can properly claim to depart from the obligations of a treaty by enacting laws which, although they impair the operation of the treaty, are said not to conflict with it on the ground that they lie on different planes or are concerned with a different subject-matter.

" Clearly, the guardian does not enjoy immunity from the operation of local law, such as criminal law, which may deprive him of the custody of the minor placed in a penal or reformatory institution. The guardian is subject to laws relating to education, health, revenue and so on. However, although, in the absence of a more substantial justification than differences of classification, the guardian enjoys no immunity from local law, he is entitled, in principle, to immunity from being deprived permanently or semi-permanently of [87] some of the main attributes of guardianship, such as custody of the child—especially if such custody is made the subject of what, in the circumstances of the case, is apt to give the impression of a rival guardianship. There may be a justification for such deprivation, but that justification cannot properly be based upon factors which are essentially of a technical character. In my view, the more accurate approach to the question is not that the system of protective upbringing is outside the Convention or that it pursues a different object but, rather, that it is not inconsistent with the Convention. In other words, that it is both covered and permitted by the Convention by virtue of public policy—*ordre public*—or some similar reason based on the right, conceded by international law, of a State to apply a particular law impairing or preventing the operation of the Convention.

" In fact, it is in that sense that I understand—and concur in—that part of the Court's Judgment which stresses the beneficent social objects, of an urgent character, of the Swedish Law in question. That is a consideration closely related to those underlying the notion of *ordre public*. It is this aspect of the question which I deem it incumbent upon me to examine in some detail in the present Opinion.

" Prior to that, reference must be made to an ancillary submission of Swedish Counsel bearing upon the possible effects of a ruling that the Swedish Law on Protective Upbringing does not apply to children of Dutch nationality. It was pointed out on behalf of the Swedish Government that any such interpretation of the Convention would result in a dangerous legal vacuum. It was urged that as Dutch administrative authorities are responsible for giving effect to the provisions of the Dutch Law in the sphere of the protection of children and that as, according to international law, no State can perform administrative acts in the territory of another State, the result would be that Dutch children in Sweden who are in need of care outside guardianship would remain altogether without protection.

" It must be conceded that, if only possible having regard to the intention of the Parties, a treaty ought to be interpreted so as to permit rather than to impede desirable measures of social protection. However, it appears to me that the spectre of a legal vacuum, as pictured on behalf of the Swedish Government in this connection, is illusory. Normally, the Dutch guardian would, in such cases, take the necessary steps to remove the child to Holland. In cases when that is not possible, the Dutch guardian would place the child in an appropriate home (as was, in fact, contemplated for a time by the Dutch guardian of Elisabeth Boll) or take other steps required by the physical or mental condition of the child, [88] such as placing it in an institution for observation or treatment. In exceptional cases in which, for one reason or another, the guardian fails to act or to act satisfactorily, necessary measures would be decreed by the Dutch authorities. However, according to Dutch law these are not administrative authorities. They are judicial authorities applying Dutch law which Sweden, by virtue of the Convention, is bound to recognize and the respect for which she is bound to ensure in good faith without requiring any additional treaty arrangements for that purpose. Thus the above-mentioned Article 365 of the Dutch Civil Code provides that if the child grows up in such a way as to be threatened with moral or physical harm the Judge of the Children's Court may place it under supervision. It is also upon the Judge of the Children's Court that Articles 372 *a* and 372 *b* of the Code confer the power to place the child in an observation centre or, if it needs special discipline, in an appropriate institution. Under Article 461 *c* it is for the Judge, on the initiative of the Guardianship Council, to order the necessary steps when the infant is not under required legal authority or in other cases of urgency. It must be added that such exceptional measures of protection with regard to a child remaining in Sweden would, in practice, be the same as would be taken by Swedish authorities in similar circumstances and that therefore no considerations of Swedish *ordre public* would stand in the way of their execution.

" Undoubtedly, the task of Dutch judicial authorities in taking the measures in question might be rendered somewhat more difficult than would otherwise be the case, seeing that they might have to obtain the necessary information with regard to a situation in a foreign country. But these difficulties—which lie wholly outside any legal problem of the applicability of foreign administrative law—are inherent in a Convention which sanctions and prescribes the operation of the national law of the infant. In days of rapid travel, which makes possible visits by the interested parties or representatives of Guardianship Councils or other institutions, and facilities of postal communication, these difficulties are considerably reduced. In any case, as stated, they refer to a wholly exceptional situation; as such they appear somewhat unreal when adduced as a decisive factor with regard to the interpretation of the Convention. They seem to me an unsubstantial ground for permitting a departure from its language and purpose. For these reasons, I cannot accept that particular argument advanced on behalf of the Government of Sweden.

" As already stated, reliance upon *ordre public*—public policy—constitutes the main feature in the written and oral pleadings of the Parties. This is the only submission, in the nature of legal [89] principle, in the final Conclusions of the Parties. The Court is not rigidly bound to give judgment by exclusive reference to the legal propositions as formulated by the Parties in their Conclusions. However, I consider that I ought not to disregard the Conclusions of the Parties formulating exhaustively the legal issue between them. The position is analogous to that in which the Parties have concluded a special agreement defining the legal issue between them and asking the Court to pronounce upon it as part of its operative decision. It is only when it is abundantly clear that the formulation, adopted by the Parties, of the legal issue cannot provide a basis for the decision and that there is another legal solution at hand of unimpeachable cogency, that I would feel myself free to disregard the Conclusions of the Parties. Neither of these conditions seems to me to obtain in the present case. (It may be pointed out in this connection that the position is here different from that in the *Fisheries* case, in which the Court declined to render judgment by reference to general ' definitions, principles and rules' formulated by *one* Party. *I.C.J. Reports* 1951, p. 126.[1]) Admittedly, the legal issue as thus expressed by the Parties in their pleadings and Conclusions in the present case touches directly upon a difficult and controversial question which has constituted one of the crucial problems in the

[1 *Anglo-Norwegian Fisheries Case*: *International Law Reports*, 1951, p. 86.]

sphere of private international law and which brings into prominence the relation between private and public international law.

" Does the Guardianship Convention of 1902, which contains no express exception of *ordre public*, permit reliance upon it? This seems to be the crucial question. However, before an attempt is made to answer it, there are two preliminary observations which must be made in this connection.

" The first is that caution must be exercised with regard to the manner in which the question is put in the present context. It seems incorrect to put the problem in some such form as: ' Shall the Court apply the Convention or shall it apply *ordre public?* Which comes first? ' For there is no question here of choosing between the Convention and *ordre public*. If that were the alternative, clearly the Court would have no option but to apply the Convention. The question is whether the Convention, viewed in its entirety and in the light of relevant principles of interpretation—and not merely by reference to its bare letter—permits the exception of *ordre public*. For these reasons no assistance can be derived from the various pronouncements of the Permanent Court of International Justice to the effect that national legislation cannot be validly invoked as a reason for non-compliance with an international obligation. The problem now for the Court is, exactly, what is the international obligation at issue.

[90] " The second preliminary question is whether legislation relating to protective upbringing of children is properly comprised within the sphere of *ordre public*, that is to say, whether, notwithstanding any apparent treaty provision to the contrary, *ordre public* covers exceptional measures for the protection of minors in addition to and to the exclusion of guardianship operating in normal circumstances. That question must clearly be answered in the affirmative. Apart from criminal law, it is difficult to conceive of a more appropriate and more natural object of *ordre public*, as generally understood, than the protection by the State of infants, especially when they are helpless, ill, an actual or potential danger to themselves or to society, a legitimate object of its compassion and assistance, and an occasion for public resentment whenever the State fails to measure up to its responsibilities in this respect. There are, in that wide and highly controversial province of *ordre public*, matters which are the object of uncertainty and occasional exaggerations of national prejudice reluctant to apply foreign law. But there is a hard core within that field which is not open to reasonable challenge. The protection of children, in the sense indicated above, is an obvious particle of that hard core. Mention may be made in this connection, as emphasizing this aspect of guardianship (which is exemplified, in its wider sense, in the system of protective upbringing), of the fact that in English law the Crown as the *parens patriae*—the parent of the country as a whole—is the supreme guardian of infants and, through its Courts, exercises its authority in this respect, at every stage, with total disregard of any artificial formalities of the law. The Guardianship Act of 1925 provides in Section 1 that, when in proceedings before any court custody or upbringing of an infant are in question, the Court in dealing with the matter ' shall regard the welfare of the infant as the first and paramount consideration ' and shall not decisively take into account any claim, based on any particular rule of law, of the father or the mother to a superior right of custody and control.

" The notion of *ordre public* is generally used in two meanings: It is either applied as referring to specific spheres of the law, such as territorial laws, criminal laws, police laws, laws relating to national welfare, health and security, and the like; from this point of view, protective upbringing clearly comes within the notion of *ordre public*. Secondly, it is resorted to as embracing, more generally, fundamental national conceptions of law, decency and morality. From this point of view, too, the protection of the interests of the minor through measures such as protective upbringing falls naturally within the notion of *ordre public*. (It may be stated in the present context that although in this Opinion the French term *ordre public* is mainly used, it is not used as implying a substantial difference [91] between it and the notion of public policy in common law countries such as the United Kingdom or the United States of America—although probably the conception of *ordre public* is somewhat wider. It is used here for the reason that it is current in the law of the two States which are parties to the dispute).

" Admittedly, in answering the question as here put we are confronted with the following dilemma: Is it the Swedish *ordre public* by reference to which that question must be answered? If that is so, is the Court competent and in the position to examine a matter of Swedish *ordre public*, of Swedish municipal law? It is clear that that question must be answered in the affirmative. The examination of municipal law, wherever that is necessary, is a proper function of the Court; it has undertaken it on repeated occasions. Neither do the intricacies of *ordre public* set a limit to that legitimate function of the Court. In the *Serbian Loans* case the Court examined the French law and the French judical practice in the sphere of *ordre public* in relation to currency legislation (*P.C.I.J.*, Series A, Nos. 20/21, pp. 46, 47[1]). However, the question that must be answered in this connection is not only whether protective upbringing of children falls, according to Swedish law, within the Swedish *ordre public*, but also whether it can properly be included as falling within that sphere. That question cannot be answered by reference to Swedish law only. It can be answered in reliance on a notion of *ordre public* conceived as a general principle of law—an aspect of the question referred to below.

" If protective education of children falls legitimately within the sphere of public order, then—and only then—there must be considered the main question, namely, whether public order, if not expressly permitted by the Convention, can be invoked at all; whether it has been properly invoked in the present case; and, if so, whether the Law on Protective Upbringing has been applied by the Swedish authorities in a manner which is reasonable and not manifestly contrary to the object and the principles of the Convention.

" Does the conception of *ordre public* operate at all in the present case? This is the central issue before the Court. It can be examined here only in brief outline:

" In the first instance, the Convention now before the Court is a Convention of public international law in the sphere of what is generally described as private international law. This means: (*a*) that it must be interpreted, like any other treaty, in the light of the principles governing the interpretation of treaties in the field of public international law; (*b*) that that interpretation must take [92] into account the special conditions and circumstances of the subject-matter of the treaty, which in the present case is a treaty in the sphere of private international law.

" Secondly, in the sphere of private international law the exception of *ordre public*, of public policy, as a reason for the exclusion of foreign law in a particular case is generally—or, rather, universally—recognized. It is recognized in various forms, with varying degrees of emphasis, and, occasionally, with substantial differences in the manner of its application. Thus, in some matters, such as recognition of title to property acquired abroad, the courts of some countries are more reluctant than others to permit their conception of *ordre public*—their public policy—to interfere with title thus created. However, restraint in some directions is often offset by procedural or substantive rules in other spheres. On the whole, the result is the same in most countries—so much so that the recognition of the part of *ordre public* must be regarded as a general principle of law in the field of private international law. If that is so, then it may not improperly be considered to be a general principle of law in the sense of Article 38 of the Statute of the Court. That circumstance also

[1 *Annual Digest*, 1929-1930, Case No. 278.]

provides an answer to the question as to the nature and the content of the conception of public policy by reference to which there must be judged the propriety of the Swedish legislation in the matter. Clearly, it is not the Swedish notion of *ordre public* which can provide the exclusive standard in this connection. The answer is that, the notion of *ordre public*—of public policy—being a general legal conception, its content must be determined in the same way as that of any other general principle of law in the sense of Article 38 of the Statute, namely, by reference to the practice and experience of the municipal law of civilized nations in that field. It is by reference to some such considerations that I have, in an earlier part of this Opinion, attempted to answer the question whether the Swedish Law on Protective Upbringing can properly be regarded as falling within the domain of *ordre public*.

" For these reasons the correct interpretation of a convention on private international law must take that general recognition of public order fully into account. The same result is reached by way of another, no less cogent, principle of interpretation: In a case concerned with the interpretation of a treaty relating to a particular matter with regard to which the law and practice of both parties recognize the applicability of certain principles, due weight must be given to those principles. To give an example: If the law and practice of Sweden and Holland were to recognize that the distance of twenty miles is the proper limit of territorial waters, and if these two States were to conclude a treaty laying down that their vessels shall be bound to submit to certain restrictions within their [93] respective territorial waters, then the expression ' territorial waters ' would have to be interpreted in the sense attached to it by the law and practice of those two States, namely, as extending to twenty miles. By the same token, if the law of Sweden or Holland recognizes the exception of public order in the sphere of private international law, then that factor must be considered as relevant to the interpretation, as between them, of the treaty in question. It is well known, and it is admitted by both Parties, that both in Sweden and Holland *ordre public* constitutes a valid reason for the exclusion of foreign law. Accordingly, the fact that a particular subject of private international law is covered by a convention does not, in the absence of an express prohibition to the contrary, in itself exclude the operation of *ordre public*, even if the convention is otherwise silent in the matter—provided always that the State invoking *ordre public* is, if its decision to invoke it is challenged, willing to submit to an impartial judicial or arbitral determination of the issue. The latter condition follows inevitably from the principle that a State which invokes an exception not expressly recognized by the treaty cannot claim the right to determine unilaterally whether that exception applies.

" At the same time, and this is the third main consideration in the present context, the circumstance that the Parties are bound by treaty in relation to a particular subject of private international law sets a limit to the application of *ordre public*. It does so in three respects:

" In the first instance, the existence of the treaty imposes upon municipal courts an obligation of restraint in invoking *ordre public*—a restraint additional to that which they impose upon themselves in matters of private international law generally. This is admitted by both Parties. In fact, it is one of the objects of a treaty bearing upon private international law to set some further limit to reliance upon *ordre public*.

" Secondly, the existence of a treaty limits the discretion of national courts in determining whether a particular subject is within the domain of *ordre public*; it limits it in the sense that in case of a dispute, and provided that an international tribunal is endowed with the requisite jurisdiction, it is for that tribunal to determine the matter. This, too, is in substance admitted by both Parties.

" Thirdly—a view contended for by Holland but denied by Sweden—in the case of a dispute as to the manner in which the national authority has applied the exception of *ordre public*, that question is subject to review and determination by an international tribunal, if otherwise competent in the matter. That aspect of the question is examined later in this Opinion.

" Applied to the present case, these principles mean, in general, that the exception of public order is admissible within proper limits [94] and that, there being a dispute as to whether these limits have been observed, it is for the Court to decide whether the notion of public order has been properly invoked and applied. As stated, I have come to the conclusion that reliance on *order public* in relation to a Law on Protective Upbringing is fully justified and that, therefore, *ordre public* has been properly invoked. I will revert presently to the question whether the proper *application* of *ordre public* has been satisfactorily proved in this case.

" Reference must be made in this connection to certain views expressed during the written and oral proceedings with regard to *ordre public*, in particular the opinion that reliance upon it is inconsistent with the purpose of treaties on private international law and that *ordre public* ought to be interpreted restrictively in that sphere or refused recognition altogether. In particular, it was argued that because of its comprehensiveness and elasticity it has been the cause of uncertainty and confusion, that it has been a disturbing element in that field, and, more emphatically, that it has been destructive of private international law. There is some substance in these considerations. However, they cannot in any way be decisive.

" Admittedly, the notion of *ordre public*—like that of public policy—is variable, indefinite and occasionally productive of arbitrariness and abuse. It has been compared in this respect, not without some justification, with the vagueness of the law of nature. Admittedly also, it has often been the instrument or the expression of national exclusiveness and prejudice impatient of the application of foreign law. Yet these objections, justified as they are, do not alter the fact that the principle permitting reliance on *ordre public* in the sphere of private international law has become—and that it is—a general principle of law of most, if not all, civilized States. More than that: It is, on its own merits, part and parcel of the entire doctrine and practice of private international law almost from its very inception; the two are inseparable, not only as a matter of history but also of necessity; they have grown together in a mutual interaction and compromise. The purpose of private international law is to make possible the application, within the territory of the State, of the law of foreign States. This is an object dictated by considerations of justice, convenience, the necessities of international intercourse between individuals and indeed, as has occasionally been said, by an enlightened conception of public policy itself. But there is an obvious element of simplification in the view that the law of a State should be deemed to have consented or that it should reasonably be expected to consent in advance to the application of foreign law without any limitations, in any circumstances whatsoever, without [95] a safety valve, without a residuum of contingencies in which, because of the very nature of its structure and the fundamental legal, moral and political conceptions which underlie it, it should be able to decline to apply foreign law.

" Within the State, the judicial use of public policy—of *ordre public*—has often been exposed to criticism. But it is seldom, if ever, suggested that it is not an indispensable instrument of the interpretation, application and development of the law. If that is so in relation to the national law of the State which may be changed by ordinary legislative processes, it is particularly so in relation to foreign law over which the State has no control and which, in certain circumstances, its courts may find it inconceivable to apply. History

—modern history—has occasionally produced examples of legislation manifesting eruptions of malevolent injustice, or worse, to which courts of foreign countries may find it utterly impossible to give effect and with regard to which the right to denounce the treaty may not provide a timely or practicable remedy.

" It is that residuum of discretion, it is that safety valve, which has made private international law possible at all, and which, if kept within proper limits, is one of the principal guarantees of its continued existence and development. It is significant that an important part of the contribution of the most illustrious exponents of private international law—such as Story, Savigny and Pillet—lay in their effort to formulate the notion of *ordre public* and the limits, often wide and general, of its application. *Ordre public* is, and ought increasingly to be, subject to reasonable limitations in accordance with the main purpose of private international law. But the problem cannot be solved by the device of shelving it. It can be alleviated by the existence of international remedies of judicial control and review whenever there exists the requisite jurisdiction of an international tribunal. The present case afforded an opportunity for acting in that way.

" The preceding considerations may also offer assistance in answering the question whether the existence of a treaty sets a limit to reliance on public policy in the sense that the latter cannot be properly invoked unless the treaty contains an express exception to that effect. That question must be answered in the negative. Obviously, the treaty may expressly, or by implication, prohibit recourse to *ordre public*. Thus it is occasionally maintained that the Hague Convention of 1902 on the Conclusion of Marriage contained such prohibitive implication by enumerating exhaustively the [96] reasons for which the *lex fori* could disregard the impediments to marriage established by foreign law. (Yet it is significant that, in spite of the Convention, practically all the parties to it refused to recognize, prior to the Second World War, the impediments established by the German Nuremberg Laws. Although Dutch Courts applied the Convention in this respect, they often found circuitous means of defeating the Nuremberg Laws in question.)

" However, apart from an express or clearly implied prohibition, the correct principle seems to be that a convention in the sphere of private international law does not exclude reliance on *ordre public*. Nothing short of an express prohibition can rule out reliance on a firmly established principle of private international law. This seems to me to be the fairly unanimous view of writers. They include authorities of the calibre of Professors Batiffol and Niboyet. This is also the emphatic view of an author who has devoted special attention to questions of private international law in relation to treaties (Plaisant, *Les règles de conflit de lois dans les traités*, 1946, pp. 91–94). Professor Lewald, a balanced and authoritative writer to whose views I attach importance, provides no clear exception to that virtual unanimity. In 1928, writing in the *Revue de droit international privé* (pp. 164 *et seq.*), he stated, though with very considerable hesitation, that, *a priori*, if the treaty is silent on the question of *ordre public*, the latter cannot be invoked. In 1930, when writing in the *Répertoire de droit international* (Vol. 7, p. 308), he expressed a different view, namely, that in such cases the answer to the question depends on the interpretation of the particular treaty and that it is impossible to give an answer *a priori*. There is little judicial practice directly applicable to this matter.

" In this connection reference may also be made to the preparatory work of the Convention of 1902. The study of that preparatory work shows that there was opposition—effective opposition—to incorporating in the Hague Conventions any general clause permitting reliance on *ordre public* (though no discussion on the subject took place with regard to the Convention on Guardianship). Does that mean that there was an intention to exclude altogether recourse to *ordre public* [except] in cases expressly authorized? It may be doubted whether that was so. The authors of the Conventions wished to avoid the complications of a general and express authorization, of a general blank cheque, with regard to a notion so elastic and so comprehensive as *ordre public*. It is natural that they did not wish to inject into the Conventions, in express terms, a potential source of controversy or abuse. But does that mean that, by mere silence, the authors of the Conventions excluded indirectly from the operation of the Convention a firmly-established principle of private [97] international law? That is not probable. It is doubtful whether Governments would have signed and ratified these Conventions if they had expressly denied the right to invoke, in any circumstances, their *ordre public* as a reason for excluding foreign law.

" There is one factor of importance which is directly relevant to the question whether *ordre public* can be invoked by the Parties in the present case in relation to the Convention of 1902. That factor is that in this respect the Court is confronted with a substantial measure of agreement between the Parties. The Dutch Government has repeatedly, although in a highly qualified manner, given an affirmative answer to that question—subject to the obligation of the parties to the Convention to proceed with particular caution, with special restraint and with exacting meticulousness in limiting the operation of the treaty by reference to *ordre public*. That attitude was maintained in Conclusion II of the Netherlands, in which the denial of the right to invoke *ordre public* is qualified by the word ' generally ' and, even more so, in Conclusion III, A and B, which asserts the power of the Court to determine whether the conditions of *ordre public* have been complied with, having regard to the character of the case and the provisions of the Swedish Law on Protective Upbringing—a conclusion which can be understood only on the assumption that there was no intention to deny, in principle, the right to invoke *ordre public*. This—the agreement of the parties on a matter of basic principle —is a significant legal aspect of the situation; it makes it difficult to maintain that public order cannot be invoked unless specifically provided for in the Convention.

" Admittedly, the Dutch Government denies that in the *present case* there is room for resort to *ordre public*. It does so for two reasons: The first is that the obligation of caution and restraint binds the Parties not to invoke it unless there is a requisite element of close territorial connection, and that there is no such connection in the present case. It is difficult to follow that contention. It is not easy to imagine a closer connection between the minor in question and the country which relies on *ordre public*. Elisabeth Boll was born in Sweden; so far as is known, she speaks Swedish only; she has resided permanently in Sweden since her birth. I do not find convincing the argument that, according to Dutch law, Elizabeth Boll shares the legal Dutch domicile of her Dutch guardian or that, if she is not domiciled in Holland, it is only because the Swedish measure of protective upbringing, said to be in violation of the Convention, prevents her from being brought to Holland. The question of domicile, which is a question of fact and intention, is not properly answered by arguments of this nature.

[98] " Neither is it easy to follow the second reason advanced by the Dutch Government in the sense that the necessary territorial connection is lacking, seeing that this is a ' transfer case ', namely, that if only the transfer of the child to Holland were made possible, in accordance with the Convention, then there would be no question of anything happening on Swedish territory which is contrary to Swedish *ordre public*. There is no more force in this argument than in the suggestion that a State has no reason to refuse to hand over a political refugee to prosecution and persecution in a foreign country considering that such prosecution and persecution will take place in foreign territory. Yet it is apparent that in cases such as these the very fact of

intended transfer is decisive for the purpose of relying upon *ordre public*, seeing that the transfer is deemed contrary to the fundamental notions of public law of that State and that it may be productive of a revulsion of public opinion as being flagrantly offensive to national conceptions of decency. Public opinion is not easily reconciled to the view that the moral and social responsibility of the State has been discharged by the simple device of removing to a foreign country the object of possible persecution and suffering. This would be too easy a means of salving the conscience. When, therefore, it is argued that a ' removal case' is not sufficiently connected with the country of the forum to warrant the application of *ordre public*, the correct answer is probably that there are very few occasions in which the connection is more obvious.

" These, then, are the two main grounds—the two only grounds—which the Netherlands have adduced against the application of *ordre public* in this case: the absence of connection and the character of a ' removal case'. Neither of these grounds seems to be acceptable. If they are not acceptable, then there are no grounds which, on the Dutch submission, prevent reliance upon *ordre public*.

" There must now be considered the question of the extent to which the Court is called upon to examine the issue of the propriety of the appeal to and of the manner of application of *ordre public* in the present case. It is upon the answer to a question of this kind that there must, to a substantial degree, depend the position of *ordre public* in the development of this branch of the law.

" Both Parties are in agreement that the Court is competent to decide whether the Swedish Law on Protective Upbringing comes within the sphere of *ordre public* and whether it has been properly invoked for that purpose. In particular, the Government of Sweden does not deny that the Court is competent to determine whether in principle the Swedish Law on Protective Upbringing belongs to the category of *ordre public*. In its Conclusions it asked the Court to [99] hold that the Convention of 1902 does not affect the right of the Parties to impose upon foreign guardians the restrictions called for by their public order. The agreement of the Parties on this question removes, to a large extent, the ground from the criticism directed at reliance on public order by reference to its disintegrating effect as opening wide the floodgates of wholesale nullification of this and similar Conventions by the simple means of asserting unilaterally that a particular law under which the measure was taken is in the domain of *ordre public*. For both Parties agree that it is for the Court, and not for them, to decide that issue.

" At the same time, the Parties are not in agreement on the question whether the Court is entitled to examine the grounds on which, by reference to the Law on Protective Upbringing, the Swedish authorities decided to decree and to maintain the measure which they had taken. Sweden denied such competence in her Conclusions and in the course of the written and oral proceedings. On the other hand, the Government of the Netherlands repeatedly asserted the competence of the Court in that respect. This it did both in the Conclusions and by way of a formal intervention in the course of the oral proceedings. The Agent for the Netherlands insisted that the Court was competent to examine ' every fact, every circumstance, every motive ' pertaining to the application of the Swedish Law and that, this being a case of a treaty obligation, no reliance on a charge of denial of justice was necessary for that purpose.

" I accept the Dutch Conclusion III A, according to which the Court is competent to appreciate, in the light of the relevant facts and circumstances, whether the conditions of *ordre public* have been complied with. The Court is competent to decide not only whether the Law on Protective Upbringing falls within the notion of *ordre public*, but also whether it has been applied reasonably and so as not to defeat the true objects of the Convention. I am unable to accept the Swedish view that the Court, not being a court of appeal, is not entitled to examine that aspect of the question. Suppose the Swedish authorities had decided to apply the Law of Protective Upbringing to a child of Dutch nationality, born in Holland and speaking Dutch only, and who had been resident in Sweden only for one month. Would this Court be precluded from taking these facts into consideration? Recourse to *ordre public*, especially if not expressly authorized by the Convention, is in the nature of an exception. It is a permissible exception. But it is an exception which must be justified with some particularity. If a State takes action which, on the face of it, departs from the language of the Convention, then it cannot confine itself to proving generally that the Law under which it acted falls within the permissible exception; it must show that that exception was applied reasonably and in good faith.

[100] " When there is no treaty binding upon a State, it has very considerable—although not unlimited—discretion in applying its system of private international law in relation to *ordre public*. But when that State is bound by a treaty in relation to a particular subject-matter, it can invoke public order only if, in case its action is challenged, it is prepared to submit the legality of its action to impartial decision. It is that jurisdiction which removes the notion of and recourse to *ordre public* from the orbit of uncertainty, pure discretion and arbitrariness and which endows the treaty with the character of an effective legal obligation. It is that subjection to judicial or arbitral determination, as the very condition of legitimate reliance on *ordre public* in cases not expressly provided by the treaty, which saves *ordre public* in such cases from the reproach of being a cover for a unilateral repudiation of the treaty and which gives it the character of an attempt to secure a just and reasonable interpretation of treaty obligations. The present case provided an opportunity for asserting and giving effect to that principle. The task of such factual examination may be difficult, and, occasionally, invidious. Nevertheless, it constitutes a proper exercise of the judicial function in relation to a dispute which is one both as to law and fact in the meaning of Article 36 of the Statute of the Court.

" In the present case the Parties have not laid before the Court the facts which would enable it to decide with any assurance on this aspect of the question. The Government of Sweden did not act upon the offer, formally made by it in the final Submissions in the Counter-Memorial and repeated during the oral proceedings, to lay before the Court the relevant documents. It is true that it was open to the Court, at any stage of the proceedings, to ask for their production. In particular, Article 49 of the Statute provides that ' the Court may, even before the hearing begins, call upon the agents to produce any document or to supply any explanation '. However, it is not necessary in this connection to consider the problem of the function of the Court, under that and other Articles of the Statute and the Rules, as an agency called upon to clarify and substantiate the basis of its decisions by active initiative in the elucidation of the relevant factors both before and during the oral proceedings. For there was no reason why the Government of Sweden should not have supplied the necessary information of its own accord, in the event that the Court should find that it could properly examine it. A State invoking an exception cannot be too forthcoming in producing evidence in justification of it. It ought not to limit itself to vague—and, from the point of view of ordinary rules of evidence, probably inadmissible—allusions as to the possible contents of the evidence which, by its own decision, it has failed to produce. At the same time, in the exercise of its jurisdiction of review, a legal tribunal must attach importance to the appreciation of the facts by local authorities—the authorities of the State [101] where the child was born and is domiciled. Their decision must not be lightly disturbed. This is so in particular if the applicant Government, while inviting the Court to decide upon the factual aspects of the issue and the motives underlying the decision of the local authorities, has failed to bring to its notice any facts suggesting that the discretion of the Swedish authorities has not been exercised properly and in good faith. In all the circumstances, on such evidence as there is, I am bound to assume that the action of the Swedish authorities was not such as to constitute a misapplication of the Law on Protective Upbringing on which they were clearly entitled to rely as part of their *ordre public*.

" The above considerations explain why, subject to differences of approach and reasoning, I concur in the operative part of the Judgment rejecting the demand of the Government of the Netherlands."

Judge Moreno Quintana delivered the following Separate Opinion:

[102] " To my great regret, although I am fully in agreement with them concerning the judgment at which they arrive in this case, I am unable to share the opinion of the majority of my colleagues who give as the sole determining reason for their decision the fact that the Swedish Law of June 6th, 1924, on the protective upbringing of children is of a different nature from the Convention of 1902 which governs the guardianship of infants as between the Netherlands and Sweden.

" The chief consideration in my mind is that a question of principle has to be settled, namely, the question whether the *ordre public* of one of the Parties in the case can be invoked against an international Convention which is binding on both Parties. The Applicant in this case attaches fundamental importance to this question, as also does the Respondent. Decisive as it is for the settlement of this dispute, the reason first mentioned above does not, in my view, furnish sufficient ground for a decision on a dispute relating to a fundamental question of law. I hold a very definite view on this question, and I must also point out that, far from ruling one another out, the two grounds supplement each other quite logically. For, though the Convention in question is not infringed in this case, because legally it is of a different nature from the Law on protective upbringing, it is the *ordre public* character of that Law which marks the difference. A law of an entirely different nature could never, even in an incidental way, impede the complete accomplishment of an international convention.

" Side by side with its function of deciding ' in accordance with international law such disputes as are submitted to it ', as mentioned in Article 38, paragraph 1, of its Statute, the International Court of Justice has also—notwithstanding the limitation which Article 49 prescribes for its decisions—a doctrinal function of the greatest importance. The Court can and must discharge this function in the present case with a view to the progressive development of international law on the question submitted for its consideration concerning the principle of the relationship between *ordre public* and an international Convention. Paragraph 1 (*d*) of Article 38 of the Statute moreover enjoins the Court to apply ' the teachings of the most highly qualified publicists of the various nations, as subsidiary means for the determination of rules of law'.

" For these reasons, I shall furnish grounds for my separate opinion, which is in favour of the contention advanced by the Respondent, by analyzing the legal scope of the said principle in this case.

[103] " The case before the Court is one which relates to questions within the domain of private international law. Such a situation was dealt with by the Permanent Court in its judgment in the *Serbian Loans Case* in the following terms:

' Any contract which is not a contract between States in their capacity as subjects of international law is based on the municipal law of some country. The question as to which this law is forms the subject of that branch of law which is at the present day usually described as private international law, or the doctrine of the conflict of laws. The rules thereof may be common to several States and may even be established by international conventions or customs, and in the latter case may possess the character of true international law governing the relations between States. But apart from this, it has to be considered that these rules form part of municipal law.' (*Collection of Judgments*, Series A, Nos. 20/21, p. 41.)

" These are notions that are applicable to the present case since treaties which, like that with which it is concerned, are designed to achieve unification of the rules deriving from the application to private persons of particular State laws, undeniably have the character of private international law treaties. The original title: ' Case concerning the guardianship of an infant ' was subsequently, and very wisely, changed to ' Case concerning the application of the Convention of 1902 governing the guardianship of infants ', and this new title is undoubtedly much more in accord with the scope of the judgment to be given by the Court in this case.

" We are confronted with an intervention of what may properly be described as *public* international law in the matter of the interpretation of an international Convention. And it is for the Court, as a judicial organ, to decide the matter. The Court's jurisdiction is clearly established by Article 38, paragraph 1, of the Statute—to which I have already referred—the imperative character of which is beyond doubt. A conversion of private international law into public international law has occurred and this enables the Court to exercise its judicial powers.

" The Court has to adjudicate upon the case of an infant. This infant was the subject of a measure of protective upbringing taken by the competent Swedish authorities which, it is argued, falls outside the legal framework of the Convention and, furthermore, falls within the *ordre public* of Sweden. To this the Applicant has replied that the Respondent is in breach of the Convention which constitutes the legal norm applicable to the guardianship of infants of both countries. It is not precisely a denial of justice that the Applicant alleges against the Respondent, but rather the fact that a measure deriving from the law of Sweden has been applied to a [104] child whose guardianship is governed by the law of the Netherlands. In other words, the Netherlands consider that Sweden has violated her international obligations under the Convention, which provides that the national law of the infant is the norm applicable to its guardianship. Without disputing this view, the Respondent contends that the measure adopted is not covered by the Convention, and that since, in any case, it comes within the domain of *ordre public*, it constitutes a bar to the application of the foreign law.

" A wise rule on the subject which must serve as a point of departure for the decision in the present case is supplied by the great Savigny, in his *Système du droit romain actuel*. The judge, he says, must apply to each legal relationship the norm which is most in conformity with the specific and essential nature of that relationship. This law may be the law of a person's own country or it may be that of a foreign State. But this principle, which establishes a uniformity of law between the different States, is subject to an important restriction—the restriction based upon the existence of several species of laws of a special nature, including laws which are positive and strictly compulsory in character, such as those which are dictated by reason of general interest (*publica autoritas*) (see French translation, Paris, 1860, Vol. 8, para. CCCXLIX).

" In the present proceedings, the crux of the case is constituted by the question whether *ordre public* may validly be invoked against an international convention. That is to say, the question at issue is that of the relationship between the application of the 1902 Convention which governs the guardianship of infants and which is law as between the Netherlands and Sweden, and the measure of protective upbringing taken by Sweden in respect of Marie Elisabeth Boll. Both Parties attribute cardinal importance to this, devoting to it the greater part of their arguments. While the Netherlands claim that the maintenance of the measure is contrary to the Convention on the ground that it impedes the full exercise of guardianship, Sweden contends that she has merely applied her *ordre public* in the present case. However, what are involved are procedures which are of different scope, which are carried out in two different national legal spheres but which affect one and the same situation, the custody of the infant. It is on that point that there is conflict between two Laws, the Dutch Law on guardianship and the Swedish Law on protective upbringing. Sweden has in no wise challenged the legal existence of the guardianship instituted under Netherlands law in accordance with Article 1 of the Convention. In its decision of September 16th, 1954, the Norrköping court rejected the application to this case of the Swedish Law on guardianship. Sweden maintains that her Law on the protective upbringing of infants, of June 6th, 1924, is quite different in object and in scope from the institution of guardianship, a typical institution of family law, to which the 1902 Convention relates. But the difference of the Swedish Law in relation to the 1902 Convention will not [**105**] of itself enable the Law to override the Convention. To do so it must fall within the *ordre public*, a concept which confers upon it the validity which enables it to extend its legal effects on the international plane.

" The concept of *ordre public*, which is so clear and well defined in the legal systems from the so-called *continental* law in the Latin countries, does not seem always to be understood in the same way in other legal systems. As a result, certain of the interpretations given by the Parties in the present case have become somewhat distorted. In order to arrive at a legal solution, there is, I think, no need to construct theories and draw distinctions which merely confuse the issue. I understand *ordre public* to be the whole body of laws and legal instruments whose principles cannot be set at naught either by special conventions or by a conflicting foreign law. Its provisions have retrospective effect and definitively acquired rights cannot be invoked against it. The judges should apply it in spite of any international convention. It finds its basis in the need of each State to provide itself with fundamental institutions in the field of its political and social organization. Those institutions, in particular, which govern the family, child welfare, inheritance and public morals, indubitably have this character.

" The Swedish Government contends in its Rejoinder (pp. 11 *et seq.*) that its Law on protective upbringing falls within the sphere both of public law and of *ordre public*. But although the effect of these two elements may be the same in regard to its invocation as against the application of a foreign law, what are involved are different legal concepts. Indeed, public law has a very specific role: that of providing for the political structure of the State by adjudicating upon interests that are supremely collective. In this connection, the constitution of a country, its economic system or its social organization are manifestations of the activity of its public law. But it is not always easy to draw a hard and fast line between the two branches of law. A single Law, such as that of Sweden on protective upbringing of children, may reveal aspects of public law and aspects of private law. It belongs to public law in so far as it protects children in general; it belongs to private law when it affects the position of individuals. The concept of *ordre public*, being much broader, embraces that of public law. That is why it is unnecessary in the present case to invoke the scope of public law in order to show that the protective upbringing of children is one of the primary institutions of *ordre public*.

[**106**] " In relations which are derived from private international law there is a principle of the limitation of the authority of a foreign law. This principle comes into play whenever the foreign law is in conflict with the *ordre public* of the country where it is to be applied. Each State interprets it by virtue of its national legislation according to the principles which may at a given moment govern its social organization. This concept may vary considerably from State to State, but one common feature is always recognized:

the feature which identifies it with the permanent interests of a nation when that nation provides for its State function of securing respect for individual rights. In those circumstances, the full force of the *lex fori* which has the character of a law of *ordre public* remains unimpaired in the relations flowing from private international law. In its judgment, which I have already cited, in the *Serbian Loans case* the Permanent Court referred to the difficulty of defining *ordre public* ' a conception the definition of which in any particular country is largely dependent on the opinion prevailing at any given time in such country itself . . .' (*Collection of Judgments*, Series A., Nos. 20/21, p. 46). The well-known Cuban international lawyer, Antonio Sanchez de Bustamante, the author of the code of private international law which bears his name, agrees that laws which he calls of domestic *ordre public*, such as those governing the status and capacity of persons, family relationships, inheritance, etc., in a State are peremptory in character; they are binding both on persons having their residence in the State and on the nationals of the State, and prevent the application of a foreign law (Art. 3, para. 1).

" It has also been suggested that there is a difference between national *ordre public* and international *ordre public* on the ground that the latter is of wider scope with regard to its invocation against a foreign law. Many writers recognize that this is so. Others, including myself, consider that only national *ordre public* may constitute a bar to the application of a relationship of private international law. International *ordre public* operates within the limits of the system of public international law when it lays down certain principles such as the general principles of the law of nations and the fundamental rights of States, respect for which is indispensable to the legal co-existence of the political units which make up the international community. The natural society of nations, to which Francisco de Vitoria looked forward, in the 16th century, the society which involved the co-existence of perfect communities within a universal community as propounded by Francisco Suarez in the following century, the *Civitas Maxima* described by Christian Wolff in the 18th century, as constituted by all States on the basis of a tacit covenant, and the legal community of States bound by the performance of certain duties, as defined in the last century by Friedrich Karl von Savigny, are all necessarily based on these principles and these rights. These principles—we are all quite familiar with them because they are very limited—and these rights, [107] too, have a peremptory character and a universal scope. On the one hand, the freedom of the seas, the repression of piracy, the international continuity of the State, the immunity of jurisdiction and the rules governing warfare; and on the other hand the inviolability of treaties, the independence and legal equality of States. But, in any event, what is involved is a conception that is entirely different from the one laid before the Court by the Parties in this case.

" Even in the absence of an express reference, any international agreement laying down rules of private law necessarily runs up against the concept of national *ordre public*. No foreign law is applicable when the principle of the extraterritoriality of laws comes up against a case that is specifically governed by a local law. And, by virtue of their sovereignty, States possess at all times the power to regulate their own *ordre public*. Authors enjoying universal authority assert that this is so beyond any doubt. The decisions of several national courts are also quite decisive on this point. Teachings in this matter are to be drawn from these authors and from these decisions. *Ordre public* is indissolubly bound up with the general principles of law recognized by civilized nations which, under Article 38, paragraph 1 (c), of the Statute, the Court is required to apply as a main source of law in discharging its function of deciding in accordance with international law such disputes as are submitted to it. This means that the application of these principles is the subject of an international undertaking by all Members of the United Nations and by those States which have adhered to the Statute of the Court. *Jus posteriori derogat priori* says the well-known Roman maxim, in accordance with which Article 103 of the Charter of the United Nations prescribes that, in the event of a conflict between the obligations imposed on Member-States by the Charter and obligations arising from any other international agreement, it is the former obligations that shall prevail. The national *ordre public* of Sweden consequently prevails over the provisions of the 1902 Convention which governs the guardianship of infants as between that country and the Netherlands. Moreover, none of the provisions of that Convention, and none of the opinions expressed in the course of the preparatory work for it, justify the view that the application of the principle of *ordre public* was excluded.

" Is the Swedish Law on the protection of infants a law of *ordre public* or is it not? It regulates in great detail the practical methods to be employed in the upbringing of infants who fall within the various categories contemplated in Article 22. In particular, Articles 1, 20 and 21 which relate to the protection of children in each commune, the supervision by the provincial governments [108] with a view to ensuring the welfare of children, and the functions of the Director-General of Social Affairs, are all provisions of *ordre public*. In itself and in so far as the Court is concerned, the Swedish Law in question is no more than a fact. In its Judgment on *German Interests in Upper Silesia*, the Court said: ' From the standpoint of international law and of the Court which is its organ, municipal laws are merely facts which express the will and constitute the activities of States, in the same manner as do legal decisions or administrative measures ' (*Collection of Judgments*, Series A, No. 7, p.19[1]). Consequently the origin of the law, the intention of the draftsman and the possible results to which it may lead are questions which do not fall within the jurisdiction of the Court. It is sufficient for the Court to scrutinize the text of the law in order to ascertain whether or not it is a law of *ordre public*.

" However, before the *ordre public* of a country may be validly invoked against an international convention there must exist a substantive connection between the person concerned and the territory. The Parties to this case agree —and rightly so—that permanent residence by a person in a territory can constitute such a substantive connection. But the Applicant contended that in the case of the infant Boll, her residence in Sweden is a forced residence through the application of the measure of protective upbringing. No proof however has been brought forward by the Applicant to show that the residence of the infant in Sweden is contrary to her personal wish. The Applicant has thought it sufficient to invoke its national law, according to which the domicile of a ward is chosen by its guardian. No reference has been made to any expression of a personal desire. In any case, it is to be presumed—and this is a presumption *juris tantum*—in the absence of any proof to the contrary, that the child's living with her grandparents, her mother's parents, in the place where she was born, where she grew up and where her affections are centred, by no means constitutes a forced residence. *Ubi bene, ibi patria*, says the well-known maxim.

" The facts and the law in this case appear to be as follows. An infant born in Sweden, but of Netherlands nationality because of the nationality of her father and of the nationality acquired by her mother who was originally Swedish, is placed under a measure of protective upbringing in the country which she has not left since her birth. The guardianship of this infant must be governed·by her national law in accordance with a convention between Sweden and the Netherlands. This guardianship has been duly established by decisions of a Swedish court in the first place and subsequently by a decision of a Dutch court, but the right of custody of the infant is impeded by the adoption of this measure of *ordre public*. Is this contrary to international law?

[1 *Annual Digest*, 1925–1926, Case No. 4.]

I do not consider that it is so. The consequences flowing from legal situations produced [**109**] by the application of territorial laws are not in opposition to the obligations flowing from international treaties. This is the special feature of the present case: it is concerned with a territorial Law the application of which does not debar the application of a convention but affects a *de facto* situation constituted by the custody of an infant.

" Any appraisal of *ordre public* in international relations is necessarily a matter for interpretation by a court, provided that such an interpretation does not—to use the words of the Permanent Court in its advisory opinion concerning *Polish Postal Service in Danzig*—' lead to something unreasonable or absurd ' (see *Judgments*, etc., Series B, No. 11, p. 39[1]). And would the Court's decision be unreasonable or absurd if the result of it was to obviate the transplantation and the suffering of a child who would otherwise be torn from the arms of her grandparents, carried away far from the country of her birth and obliged to live in a foreign atmosphere? The law is not a metaphysical creation, a consequence of cold and abstract reasoning of the human mind, which has no regard for social reality. And States like the Netherlands and Sweden, which have incorporated rules of private international law in their international law, surely do not contemplate the application of inhuman solutions. Our own Court stated in the *Anglo-Iranian case* that it could not base itself on a purely grammatical interpretation of the text and that it must seek the interpretation which is in harmony with a natural and reasonable way of reading the text (see *I.C.J. Reports* 1952, p. 104[2]).

" The specific facts of the case, which led the Swedish authorities to take the measures objected to by the Netherlands Government, are not a subject of disagreement between the Parties. That is why the Court decided to adopt no position with regard to them. Knowledge of them might, however, have been extremely useful in determining whether in this particular case Sweden has acted justifiably in putting Marie Elisabeth Boll under protective upbringing. For, if this was not the case, I wonder whether the Respondent would be able, before a judicial organ, to sustain its *ordre public* to impede the effects of a foreign law derived from an international convention. The decision of this Court in the *Nottebohm case*, in which it wisely dissociated the questions of nationality and of diplomatic protection as regard their capacity for functioning independently in different national judicial systems, allows me to think that they would (see *I.C.J. Reports* 1955, p. 26[3]). Not being cognizant of the facts, and no denial of justice having been alleged against the Respondent, I must logically assume that the latter has made a proper use of its *ordre public*."

## Judge Wellington Koo delivered the followed Separate Opinion:

[**110**] " I am in agreement with the operative part of the Judgment of the Court, but I find more direct justification for it in Article 7 of the Convention of 1902 governing the guardianship of infants and I propose to develop the reasons for my opinion.

" I

" The Swedish measure of protective upbringing applied to Marie Elisabeth Boll by the Child Welfare Board of Norrköping is based upon Article 22 (*a*) of the Swedish Law of June 6th, 1924, as amended, for the protection of children and young people. Paragraph (*a*) provides that the Child Welfare Board will take measures concerning

' a child under sixteen who, in the family home, is ill-treated or exposed to serious neglect or any other danger affecting its physical or mental health.'

[1 *Annual Digest*, 1925-1926, Case No. 276.]
[2 *International Law Reports*, 1952, Case No. 114, at p. 510.]
[3 *Ibid.*, 1955, p. 349.]

The application was ordered in respect of Marie Elisabeth Boll for the protection of her mental health as affirmed in the successive decisions of the Child Welfare Board, the Östergötland Provincial Government and the Supreme Administrative Court.

" Article 7 of the Convention of 1902 authorizes the application of such protective measures by the local authorities. It reads:

' Pending the institution of a guardianship, and in all cases of urgency, measures required for the protection of the person and interests of a foreign infant may be taken by the local authorities.'

" Although the laws for the protection of children in several countries, including Sweden, have been enacted after the conclusion of the Convention on Guardianship in 1902, the general subject of child protection had been discussed in the national legislatures, as in the case of Sweden, before the third Hague Conference on private international law in 1900. It appears, therefore, reasonable to presume that the authors of Article 7 of the Convention were not unaware of this legislative interest in the subject of child protection as a function and responsibility of the State.

" II

" The question of the justifiability of the measure of protective upbringing applied to Marie Elisabeth Boll is the crux of the dispute [**111**] in the present case and comprises two aspects: its adoption and its maintenance. Are they both compatible with the obligations binding upon Sweden *vis-à-vis* the Netherlands by virtue of the Convention of 1902 governing the guardianship of infants?

" Marie Elisabeth Boll was placed under protective upbringing on April 26th, 1954, by order of the President of the Norrköping Child Welfare Board, and this order was confirmed by the Board at its meeting on May 5th, 1954. It was stated in the ' Extracts from the Minutes of the Meeting ' placed before the Court that Marie Elisabeth Boll had been placed on April 26th, 1954, in the care of her teacher, Mrs. Birgit Berg, and that she would remain there pending an examination in a psychiatric clinic for children. In confirming the action taken by its President, the Board also resolved to make Marie Elisabeth Boll a ward of the Board pursuant to Article 22 (a) of the Swedish Law of June 6th, 1924, for the protection of children and young people. No reference was made to the Convention of 1902, and understandably so, because it was considered at the time as purely a case of a Swedish ward since the father had been registered as her guardian in accordance with Swedish law on guardianship on March 18th, 1954, by the Norrköping Court on his own application without mentioning his Dutch nationality.

" There can be no doubt that the protective measure was adopted and confirmed as a case of urgency, for the President of the Board took the initial action by virtue of Article 31 of the said Swedish Law, which reads as follows:

' If, in cases covered by Articles 22 or 29, the need for protective upbringing or for transfer to public care is thought to be so urgent that action cannot be postponed until the Infants' Bureau (that is, the Child Welfare Board) has taken a decision, the President will have the right, pending a decision by the Infants' Bureau, to take the person in question in charge.'

" Likewise, the Child Welfare Board, in confirming forthwith the decisions of its President to place the minor under protective upbringing, also acted on the ground of urgency by virtue of Article 25, paragraph 3, of the said Law, as amended by the Law of May 31st, 1934, which provides:

' If the Infants' Bureau considers that the execution of the decision concerning protective upbringing cannot be postponed without risk, it has the right to decree that the decision will be executed without delay.' (Annex E to the Counter-Memorial.)

" Even the plaintiff State in the case, in its Reply to the Counter-Memorial, appears to have acknowledged the element of urgency in regard to the initial adoption of the measure of protective upbringing, for it is therein stated on page 16:

[112] ' Soon after the decease of his wife Mr. Boll was accused, in Sweden, of having committed an infamous crime against his little daughter, then eight years old.

' Now, as long as this accusation was pending, one can well understand and appreciate that the Swedish authorities felt extremely reluctant to abandon the child to a father-guardian whose possible depravity might seriously and permanently endanger its physical and mental health.'

" It is clear that the application of the protective measure to Marie Elisabeth Boll was based upon an urgent need. The fact that no reference was made to Article 7 of the Convention of 1902 is immaterial. The important point is that the measure in question was in fact ordered and applied on the ground of urgency, and as such it clearly falls within the meaning and scope of ' measures required for the protection of the person of a foreign infant ' provided for in the said Article 7. The initial application of the measure of protective upbringing to the infant was therefore clearly compatible with the Convention.

" III

" Is the maintenance of this protective measure justifiable in the face of the Convention of 1902, particularly in view of Articles 1 and 6 thereof?

" It was contended by the plaintiff State that this measure should have been discontinued after the accusation against the father was dropped ' by the end of 1954 or the beginning of 1955 ' and, in any case, after he had been released of his guardianship and replaced by Mrs. Postema, because Sweden is under the obligation to discontinue it in view of the Convention of 1902.

" Now the initial application of the protective measure has been shown to be compatible with the Convention. Whether its maintenance is justifiable in view of the Convention obviously depends upon the question whether the original urgent need which had called for it still continues. If it still exists, clearly the measure cannot be terminated without prejudice to the health of the infant.

" It may be said that Article 7 of the Convention is ancillary to Article 1 and Article 6, which are the predominant provisions of the instrument. But it is also to be noted that the language of Article 7 makes it clear that the effective operation of these two Articles may be retarded for a period of time in an exceptional case when the urgent need for protection of the person or interests of a foreign infant calls for action on the part of the local authorities for the purpose of such protection. The right of the national guardian to custody in the present case is not denied, but its exercise is only incidentally impeded. It is open to the guardian to make a [113] fresh application to the Swedish local authorities to end the protective measure, at which time presumably the need for continuing it will be reconsidered in the light of the prevailing facts and circumstances.

" An examination of the text of Article 7 shows that it authorizes necessary protective measures to be taken by the local authorities for the benefit of the foreign infant in two kinds of circumstances: (a) pending the organization of the guardianship; and (b) ' in all cases of urgency '. Any measure taken under (a) must obviously be ended as soon as the guardianship is organized and known to be organized, thus indicating a time-limit, whereas in the case of a measure taken under (b), there is no indication as to when it should be ended, except the tacit implication that it should be ended when the urgency which has called it into being comes to an end. If this interpretation is sound —and there is no valid reason to doubt this—the continuance of the measure may be justified even after a guardianship based on the national law of the infant has already come into existence. For, unlike the circumstance in (a), the test here is the continuing need of an urgent character.

" In this connection, the plaintiff State contended (Memorial, pp. 4–8) that Article 7 permits only special measures for the protection of the infant and ' does not and cannot permit general measures virtually amounting to guardianship '. As a general proposition this is correct. But it is to be observed that the Swedish measure of protective upbringing does not deal with guardianship, and it does not amount to a virtual guardianship. The Dutch guardianship of Johannes Boll, the father, and his subsequent replacement by Mrs. Postema in accordance with the decision of the Dordrecht Court, was clearly recognized by the judgments of the Court of First Instance of Norrköping, the Court of Appeal of Göta, and finally the Supreme Court of Sweden. To attempt to draw a distinction between special and general measures of protection and to declare that the former is permissible under Article 7 and the latter is not, does not clarify the issue in law. The reason is simple. Although the measure of protective upbringing applied to Marie Elisabeth Boll is part of a general Law for the protection of children and young people, it is, nevertheless, one of several kinds of measures prescribed in the Law and, as such, it can well be considered as a measure of special character chosen to meet the requirements of the particular case.

" Moreover, the Swedish measure in question is aimed at the protection of the person of the infant. For this purpose the nature and degree of the protection must necessarily correspond to the requirements of each case. If it is a matter of protecting the health of the infant, as it is in the present case, appropriate measures must be taken, whether they may be described as general or special in character.

[114] " Finally there remains the argument advanced by the plaintiff State that the concept of urgency must not be confused with the concept of desirability, since a measure is urgent only as far as it is desirable and as far as it cannot suffer any delay. This is undoubtedly correct. The question to consider in the light of this definition, however, is whether the circumstances which called for the application of the measure of protective upbringing continue to exist and whether, in these circumstances, there still persists an element of urgency for the continuance of the measure.

" On the face of things the protective measure applied to Marie Elisabeth Boll appears to have been maintained over an unusually long period. It is four and a half years since it was first ordered by the Child Welfare Board on May 4th, 1954, and more than two and a half years since it was again confirmed by a decree of the Supreme Administrative Court of February 21st, 1956. The important point to determine, however, is whether the need of protection for the infant continues to exist and whether the element of urgency in the need remains. These are questions of fact, and the limited information available to the Court gives no indication as to the present state of the minor's health or as to how or why a change from the existing régime would affect her mental well-being. What is known is the undisputed fact that all of the decisions of the Child Welfare Board, the resolutions of the Provincial Government, and the decrees of the Supreme Administrative Court, acting on application or appeal of the father-guardian, the legal guardian and the deputy-guardian for ending the measure of protective upbringing, alluded to the consideration of the health of the infant and stressed the need of protection from danger to her mental health, with one exception, i.e., the Resolution of the Provincial Government of October 28th, 1955, which was, however, overruled by the Supreme Administrative Court by a decree of February 21st, 1956. Thus the minutes of the Child Welfare Board Meeting of May 5th, 1954, mentioned an examination in a psychiatric clinic for children; the resolution of the Provincial Government of June 22nd, 1952, spoke of an opinion on Marie Elisabeth Boll, rendered by Dr. Eberhard Nyman, M.O. of the Lund

Hospital Psychiatric Clinic, Infants' Division; the decree of the Supreme
Administrative Court of October 5th, 1954, stated that ' the removal of the
child to a wholly strange environment would at present seriously endanger
her mental health '; the minutes of the Child Welfare Board Meeting on
June 3rd, 1955, indicated that the Board ' resolved to obtain further expert
medical advice before deciding whether the girl should be removed from her
present home '; and finally the decree of the Supreme Administrative Court
of February 21st, 1956, after reviewing the evidence produced before the
Provincial Government and the Child Welfare Board, rescinded the resolution
of the former and confirmed the decision of the latter to continue the protective [**115**] measure, because ' according to the evidence in the case, the
child is still in need of wardship '.

" As to the present situation concerning the health of the infant, the
point is left obscure by both Parties. However, it is unnecessary for the Court
to appraise this situation. Since no charge of any abuse of power in applying
and maintaining the measure of protective upbringing has been made against
the Swedish authorities, nor has their good faith in so acting been impugned
in any way, it is reasonable to presume, on the basis of the decisions of the
Swedish authorities referred to above, that the protective measure relating
to Marie Elisabeth Boll has been maintained because of the existence of a
continuing necessity for the protection of her mental health, and that it will,
on review or on application of her guardian, be ended as soon as this necessity
ceases to exist.

" IV

" For the reasons stated, I am of opinion that the application of the
Swedish measure of protective upbringing falls within Article 7 of the Convention of 1902 as a right of permissible exception, even though its exercise
affects for the time being the exercise of the rights of guardianship provided
for by Articles 1 and 6 of the Convention and, that, as of the present moment,
the maintenance of the measure cannot be said to be in contravention of the
Convention."

Judge Sir Percy Spender delivered the following Separate
Opinion:

[**116**] " Whilst concurring in the decision of the Court I deem it appropriate
to deal individually with and to make certain additional observations upon
certain aspects of this case.

" I propose to confine my remarks firstly to the interpretation of the
Convention in relation to the facts of this particular case, and secondly to the
submissions by the Government of the Kingdom of Sweden on *Ordre public*
(Public Policy).

"*Is 'Protective Upbringing' in conformity with the obligations binding upon
Sweden vis-à-vis the Netherlands by virtue of the Convention of 1902?*

" The task with which the Court is confronted may I think be expressed
thus:

(*a*) Is the Swedish Child Welfare Law 1924 as amended or any provision
thereof inconsistent or incompatible with the Convention?

(*b*) Are the measures of protective upbringing taken and maintained in
respect of the child under the provisions of such Law inconsistent or incompatible with the Convention?

" These questions will be determined primarily by the proper construction
to be given to the Convention. It is also necessary to consider the terms of
the Swedish Law under which the measures sought to be impugned by the
Netherlands were taken and to do this in the light of the interpretation to be
accorded the Convention.

" The aim in the interpretation of the Convention must be to determine whether the particular case with which we are called upon to deal, is or is not within its ambit. Our task does not require us to go further.

" The Convention, expressed as it is in general terms, must in my opinion be interpreted and understood according to its subject-matter. The occasion for the Convention, its purpose, the object sought to be obtained are important considerations. Its subject-matter determined in the light of these considerations will mark out its scope and operation.

" What was the situation before the Convention? What were the defects in that situation with which it sought to deal? In what manner was it sought to remedy these defects and for what reasons? These are all pertinent enquiries in the task of interpretation. The answers do not admit of much dispute.

" The Convention was one of a number entered into about the same time dealing with *conflict of laws*. It dealt with problems [**117**] theretofore existing when such conflict occurred in relation to the administration of the guardianship of minors, as between the different States. It sought to formulate rules which would resolve difficulties inherent in this state of affairs and to achieve agreement as between the contracting States as to the proper law which should be applied in order to do this. The task of the drafters was directed to a problem of *conflict of laws* in relation to *guardianship* and its administration. This and this alone was the nature of their task.

" The Convention accordingly sought to lay down rules and to impose obligations upon the contracting States to achieve this end. Its aim was to bring to an end the state of affairs where the law to be applied to the administration of the property and to the custody and control of an infant was the subject of competing and conflicting laws between such States. Its provisions were designed to assimilate within the respective national legal systems of the contracting States certain provisions, in conformity with one another, where a conflict of laws in relation to the administration of guardianship occurred.

" Where previously this conflict of laws was left to operate according to the separate Law of each State, the aim of the Convention was to introduce certain uniform legal rules and provisions and to substitute in cases of conflict of laws thereafter arising these rules and provisions on the administration of guardianship for the national laws of each State thereon.

" In the light of these observations, it is at once obvious that the purpose of the Convention was to resolve a conflict of laws existing at the time of, or which might arise during, its currency between one contracting State and another, in respect of the law to govern guardianship and its administration where a child, the national of one country, was habitually resident in the country of another contracting State, and that in order to accomplish this purpose, it, provided, subject to the provisions elsewhere appearing therein, that the proper law to govern the guardianship should be the national law of the infant.

" It contemplated the contingency of a conflict between the laws of two States—on the subject-matter of guardianship in each State. It was not directed to the laws of States generally. It was confined and limited to a conflict of the laws on guardianship and its administration. It was concerned with that subject-matter and with none other.

" Is *any* limitation or restriction on the guardian's right to custody and control resulting from the operation of a law of a contracting State where the child is habitually resident, which is not a law of or on or dealing with guardianship incompatible or inconsistent with the Convention?

" The answer must turn upon the scope and operation of the Convention and this in turn depends upon its subject-matter.

[**118**] " The characterization or subject-matter of the Convention must be determined by looking at it as a whole. The fundamental questions are: what is its essential character; to what subject-matter in substance does it

relate? The answers are not to be found in any abstract formulation of a general test or criterion but by the considerations to which I have already referred.

" Its essential character is in my opinion clear enough. It is that of guardianship: its administration, and conflict of laws in respect of guardianship and its administration. That is its subject-matter. And that in my view marks out its scope and operation. The Convention must be construed accordingly. So construed it does not confer upon the guardian any such immunity. His exercise of the right to custody and control may be restricted even in a major degree by the effects of other laws dealing with entirely different subject-matters, without any conflict of laws within the contemplation of the Convention arising.

"But are the provisions of the Swedish Child Welfare Law of 1924 as amended, by virtue of which the protective upbringing was brought into being, laws on the subject-matter of guardianship?

" A law may produce an effect in relation to a subject-matter without being a law on that subject-matter. The substance of the relevant law is to be determined by what it does—not by the effects in relation to other matters of what the law does.

" The Swedish Child Welfare Law forms a composite whole. Its provisions are interrelated. Its subject-matter is child welfare and delinquency in the context of the social problem they create, and the protection and welfare of society in relation thereto.

"Child welfare and delinquency recognized increasingly as a vital social problem is of concern to the State not only in the interest of children but primarily in the interest of the community, so that young people may become useful members of society and not a burden upon it. In my opinion, the main purposes of the Swedish law, which gives direction to our enquiry, are:

" (a) the prevention of the creation and the continuance of corrupting homes, and the prevention and reformation of child delinquency, and

" (b) the protection of society against the consequences of the bad upbringing of the young.

" Whatever is the subject-matter of the Swedish Law, it is *not* a law of or in relation to ' guardianship '. I would hardly think any nation that has comparable legislation would itself ever think so.

" It cannot be disputed that the Swedish Law does in certain circumstances produce *effects* which bear on guardianship. In the [119] present case Sweden does not deny that these effects are such as to interfere in a major degree with the guardian's exercise of the right of custody and control. That, however, does not, in my opinion, make it a law on or in relation to or in respect to or of guardianship. Its essential character is *not* determined by the *effects* of the law operating on particular facts and circumstances; or by the acts which may properly be done pursuant to it and their bearing or effect on a guardian's right to custody and control. No conflict of laws with which the Convention is concerned accordingly arises in principle between the Netherlands Law on guardianship and those of the Swedish Law on child welfare. They relate to different subject-matters. Their scope and operation are separate and distinct. The Convention was concerned with and its scope and operation was limited to conflicts of laws arising in relation to the one subject-matter, namely, guardianship. In principle the Swedish Law is outside the domain of the Convention.

" But this does not complete our enquiry. A State, party to the Convention, may not, *whatever* the subject-matter of the Law under which it acts, do anything which contravenes the provisions of the Convention.

" Is then the protective upbringing established in this case a rival guardianship?

" Is its maintenance inconsistent with the Convention or any specific provision thereof?

" As to the first question, the answer must in my view be ' no ' and for the reasons given in the opinion of the Court.

" And if this be so, the answer to the second question must depend upon some specific provision of the Convention, for apart therefrom, for reasons already advanced, no incompatibility between the measure of protective upbringing and the Convention could be said to exist.

" Is there then any specific provision of the Convention with which the protective upbringing may be said to be inconsistent? The only specific provision which I think needs to be adverted to is Article 7.

" Does this Article mean that all other measures which may be said to protect the person of the infant are precluded irrespective of the subject-matter or context of the Law under which or the circumstances in which those measures are taken? In particular does it on its proper construction preclude the measure of protective upbringing?

" I think not. The Article certainly in terms does not so provide. It is in my opinion solely directed to the protection of the person of the child in the contingencies stated therein. It must be read within the scope and operation of the Convention of which it is part. On its proper construction it was never intended to preclude other measures such as protective upbringing which have no relation whatever to guardianship.

[120] " Article 22 (a) of the Swedish Law taken together with the associated articles thereof must be read also within the scope and operation of that Law of which it is an integral part. They cannot be lifted out of their context. These provisions of the Swedish Law and Article 7 of the Convention operate in different fields altogether. Neither the relevant provisions of the Swedish Law nor the protective upbringing established thereunder have anything to do with guardianship as such or with administration; they lie wholly outside the provisions of Article 7 of the Convention. There is no inconsistency or incompatibility.

" One further observation needs to be made.

" If in a particular case it could be shown that a law comparable to the relevant provisions of the Swedish Law had been used by a contracting State not *bona fide* to carry out that Law but for a purpose *aliunde*, for example, to interfere with and restrict a guardian in the exercise of his right of custody and control as such, other and quite different considerations would arise. But that is not the instant case. The Netherlands has very properly conceded that Sweden acted in complete good faith under the provisions of its Law. Nor does any question of denial of justice arise. The challenge of the Netherlands has been exclusively directed to whether the measure of protective custody is itself in conformity with the Convention.

" In my opinion the Netherlands has failed to make out any case that Sweden has not observed the provisions of the Convention.

" *Ordre public* (Public Policy)

" The principal issue to which the Parties to this case directed their attention was whether the Convention should be interpreted as containing an implied reservation authorizing on the ground of *ordre public* or public policy the overruling of the application of the foreign law recognized as normally the proper law to govern the guardian's right to custody and control of the infant. Whilst the opinion of the Court does not pronounce in any way upon this, nor is it necessary to do so, I think it proper, having regard to the manner in which each Party has conducted its case and the importance attached to the issue, that I should express my views on it. For I would not wish any silence on my part to admit of any reason for thinking that the case for Sweden might have successfully rested upon the submissions made by it under this heading.

" The Swedish Government contended that *ordre public* or ' public policy ' is reserved from the Convention, that the Swedish Child Welfare Law, 1924, as amended, is a law of *ordre public*, that accordingly the ' protective upbringing ' established by the Swedish authorities is not a breach of the Convention of 1902.

[121] " Consideration of this branch of the argument raises questions which may be of not inconsiderable importance. Whilst we are concerned with a Convention which relates to a conflict of laws within what may be referrred to as the field of private law, none the less it is in every sense an international convention between sovereign States. Were support given to the Swedish contention that such a reservation should be read into the Convention it could provide a basis for arguments that similar reservations should be read into other and quite dissimilar conventions and treaties.

" The maxim *pacta sunt servanda* is of special significance in considering this contention of the Government of Sweden. One should be constantly alert lest anything that might be said—or, indeed, fail to be said—should give any currency to a view that nations, under ' public policy ', may fashion their own yardstick to determine their obligations under international treaties or conventions (*cf. Greco-Bulgarian Communities, P.C.I.J.*, Series B, No. 17, p. 32[1]).

" Sweden's submissions as formally presented to the Court at the conclusion of argument were as follows:

' That the rules pertaining to conflict of laws which form the subject-matter of the 1902 Convention on the guardianship of infants do not affect the right of the High Contracting Parties to impose upon the powers of foreign guardians, as indeed of foreign parents, the restrictions called for by their *ordre public* (public policy).
' That these rules leave unaffected in particular the competence of the administrative authorities responsible for the public service of the protection of children.
' That the measure of protective upbringing taken in respect of Elisabeth Boll cannot accordingly in any way have contravened the 1902 Convention relied upon by the Netherlands.'

" The argument to substantiate these submissions was developed as follows. Two premises were sought to be established.

" The first was that the application of the personal law of a foreigner must yield before those provisions of the *lex fori* which are within the domain of *ordre public* (public policy), or at least of international *ordre public*.

" The second was that the provisions of Swedish law relating to protective upbringing in fact have that character.

" It is to be noticed that the first premise advanced by Sweden does not state that it is *every* law of the *lex fori* before which the personal law of the foreigner must yield. It is only such laws as are within the domain of *public policy*, or at least within the domain of international public policy.

" Nor is it contended that *every* rule or law of public policy must have priority over the personal law of children nationals of States signatories to the Convention. It is *only* that *part* of *ordre public* (public policy) to which the legislatures clearly attach such [122] importance that, not only do they make it applicable to foreigners upon their territory, but they will not suffer the application of the foreign law. This part of public policy (*ordre public*) is referred to as international *ordre public* or private international *ordre public*.

" I refrain from making any examination of these descriptive words, or any determination whether they do or do not involve any definable concept of law, or are merely indicative in a general sense of certain kinds of laws to which others may attach different descriptive labels. It is important to understand the sense in which these terms are used by Sweden.

" This the Swedish argument proceeded to indicate. A judgment of the Belgian *Cour de Cassation* of 4th May, 1950 (*Pas.* 1950, 1. 624) was quoted as follows:

[1 *Annual Digest*, 1929-1930, Case No. 2.]

' A law of domestic *ordre public* is only of private international *ordre public* in so far as it was the intention of the legislature to lay down by means of its provisions a principle which the legislature regards as essential to moral, political or economic order and which, on that ground, must necessarily, in its eyes, exclude the application, in Belgium, of any rule to the contrary or any different rule in the personal law of the foreigner.'

" So it was argued that public policy (*ordre public*) is applied to cases where:

" (a) the application of foreign law is prevented—the negative effect;

" (b) the application of territorial law is made compulsory—the positive effect.

" Further, it was submitted that territorial measures which are made binding in the public interest, so as to prevail over the foreign law, may in some cases result in complete elimination of the foreign law, and the substitution or enforcement of the *lex fori*; in others the application of the foreign law may be only partially affected.

" It is hardly necessary to refer to the many instances where, in accordance with domestic law of a country, the Courts of that country have, apart from obligations imposed by treaty, refused to recognize foreign laws or judgments or rights arising out of foreign laws, on the grounds of *ordre public* or public policy. Each nation does so to the extent to which it deems its fundamental principles of public policy demand.

" Public policy in every country is in a constant state of flux. It is always evolving. It is impossible to ascertain any absolute criterion. It cannot be determined within a formula. It is a conception. The varying legal approaches made by the different domestic or municipal courts of different countries in the cases on which they have been called to adjudicate, and the wide differences of views on various and important aspects of public policy (*ordre public*) [123] expressed by learned authorities are fairly evident. The truth of the matter is whether *ordre public* (public policy) is based upon considerations analogous to Article VI of the French Civil Code, or on broad principles of moral or political or economic order, or on the imperative nature of domestic laws, or on their territorial application to all people within the State whether foreigners or nationals, or on differences or supposed differences between positive and negative laws, or whether they are public or private laws, administrative or non-administrative laws, or *ordre public* as such or international *ordre public* (or private international *ordre public*), etc.; decisions giving effect to public policy within the municipal domain are based either upon the specific terms of legislative law or upon a more or less elastic conception of what public policy demands or permits in relation to the particular case under consideration.

" It is difficult to ascertain, if indeed that is possible, any common thread or line of reasoning to bind all the different cases together, or to harmonize them one with another, other than the general conception of public policy as developed in each municipal system from law to law, from case to case, and from time to time. Cases, no doubt, may be said to fall within general principles or into wide and somewhat unspecific categories. It is, for example, within one's knowledge that the domestic courts of the same country may vary in their application of principles of public policy to new and evolving sets of circumstances. Some are reluctant to assert any new head of public policy or to extend existing principles to new sets of circumstances. Others are not so reluctant.

" Attempts have been made to discern some definable principle or principles to explain or harmonize the different cases so decided in different countries, and to elevate these principles to the level of rules of international law. For myself, I am bound to say that I do not find them convincing. This is at least understandable. In each country, however, or in reliance upon what domestic laws or general principles it may call in aid, *ordre public* or public policy, is determining for itself, by its legislation, by its administrative agencies, or through its courts, the extent to which, if at all, it will admit or exclude foreign laws, or foreign rights otherwise applicable. It is, in each case, no doubt for good and sufficient reasons in the view of the State concerned, an assertion of national sovereignty.

" It is not, therefore, to be wondered at that, in attempts to enunciate some rules of guidance, laws described as of an absolute and imperative character are divided into two categories (Savigny, English translation by Guthrie, p. 78): those ' enacted merely for the sake of persons who are the possessors of rights ', and those that are [124] not so enacted but rest on moral grounds or on the public interest ' where they relate to politics, police or political economy '.

" We find Brocher describing these two categories as '*Lois d'ordre public interne*' and '*Lois d'ordre public international*', respectively. This distinction is presented for the purpose of indicating that laws within the first category are applicable only where the internal law of the forum applies, whilst the second imperatively demands application even in the sphere of private international law of the country.

" Niboyet has other ideas, and so has Bartin and so has Mancini. The many authorities quoted during the course of the argument on both sides at least should satisfy one, if that were necessary, that *ordre public* (public policy) is but a general description of the operation by which nations reject or refuse to accept foreign laws in the pursuance of, or presumed pursuance of, its fundamental principles of ' public policy ' as understood from time to time (see Dennis Lloyd, *Public Policy: A Comparative Study on English and French Law*, 1953, and *cf. Serbian Loans Case*, P.C.I.J., Series A, Nos. 20/21, p. 46 [1]).

" But whatever may be the position in any municipal system at any given time, once an international agreement or convention or treaty comes before this Court, then the considerations which, in my opinion, are applicable to the problem, are completely different.

" The difficulties in applying public policy (*ordre public*) to treaties and conventions were not underestimated by the Swedish Government. This appears particularly in Sweden's Rejoinder to the Netherlands Reply. The latter had advanced what are, in my opinion, powerful arguments against *ordre public* being invoked against State conventions on conflict of laws. No useful purpose can, I think, be served by referring to the learned authors quoted by each side to support their respective submissions. On the one hand Sweden claims that practically all authors on conflict of laws support their contention that *ordre public* (public policy) can override—or is excepted from —private law conventions, whilst the Netherlands contend the position is the reverse. It seems to me that Sweden felt obliged in its Rejoinder to meet the force of the observations of Wolff (*Das internationale Privatrecht Deutschlands*, p. 70) and Melchior (*Grundlagen*, p. 359), quoted in the Netherlands Reply. These observations are, in my opinion, of such persuasive force that they should be quoted in full:

' Lewald rightly emphasizes the dangers that arise, once *ordre public* is upheld in respect of State conventions. This would enable any State practically to restrict the application of the convention [125] *ad libitum* and, in such manner, to divest the convention of practially its entire value.' (Wolff, *l. c.*)

' In my opinion it should be held, in case of doubt, that within the realm of State conventions on conflict of law, application of *ordre public* cannot be allowed. Normally the States that are parties to the international conventions will intend to create obligations of an equable [*sic.*: equitable] and predictable character. If, however, one admits exceptions by virtue of *ordre public*, one must interfere considerably with the State convention, and this in a manner that can hardly be foreseen on

[1 *Annual Digest*, 1929–1930, Case No. 278.]

contracting, since *ordre public* is less clearly defined than other conflict principles. And if one is to permit the courts to apply *ordre public* within the realm of State conventions, one must necessarily also approve such ulterior laws of a contracting State as undermine the convention in the name of *ordre public*.' (*Melchior, l.c.*)

" Whilst not retreating from the position it had taken up in its Counter-Memorial, Sweden in its Rejoinder presented its argument somewhat differently and within limits which, no doubt, it thought were less susceptible to attack. Having stated the issue as follows:

' The issue is whether the Swedish Government has been guilty of a breach of the 1902 Convention in applying to a Dutch child its law relating to the protection of children, in spite of the Dutch law relating to guardianship which is recognized as being applicable to that child ',
the Swedish case went on to say that the law for the protection of children, being part of the *public* law, is applicable throughout the territory to any foreign child there; that no national or foreign law can stand in the way of its application, and that the 1902 Convention was in no way intended to alter this situation.

" Rules of public (or of administrative) law are, it was submitted by it, absolutely mandatory.

" It seems unnecessary to argue that if a domestic law has been validly passed which, either expressly or by necessary implication, is made clearly to apply, in terms obligatory upon the judicial and adminstrative organs of that country, to all persons or things within the territorial limits of a sovereign and independant State, the mandatory nature of the law upon all persons, foreigners or nationals, within the territorial limits of the State must, within its municipal system, be observed by those judicial and administrative organs. Indeed, assuming the constitutionality and validity of the Act within the domestic legal system of the State concerned, it is competent for a State party to any treaty or convention to pass a law binding on its *own* authorities to the effect that, notwithstanding anything in the treaty or convention, certain provisions thereof [126] binding on that State shall not apply, or to legislate in terms clearly inconsistent with, and intending to override, the terms of an existing treaty (*cf. Sanchez v. United States*, U.S. Supreme Court, Reports, Vol. 216, at p. 167). Whether described as mandatory or otherwise, public or otherwise, that law would have full force and effect within the territorial limits of the State in question. But that in no way would be relevant to the question whether that legislation—or an act done pursuant to it—is or is not in breach of or incompatible with obligations binding upon the State by virtue of a treaty or convention.

" The argument of the Swedish Government on this aspect, as stated in its Rejoinder and as applied to this case, may be stated thus:

" (1) There is a distinction between *public policy* and *public law* as a justification for the application of the *lex fori*.

" (2) This is more than a difference in legal approach.

" (3) *Public policy* may be relied upon as a ground for excluding foreign law otherwise applicable and for applying the territorial law, *by way of exception*.

" (4) On the other hand, the obligatory rules of *public law* are normally and mandatorily applicable to all those resident in the territory, *regardless of any foreign law whatsoever*.

" It is to be observed that Sweden's case is that, whereas ' public policy ' may be invoked by way of exception, the obligatory rules of ' public law ' apply to all resident in the territory regardless of any foreign law whatever, whether arising under convention or treaty or otherwise; ' public law ' does not even admit the *principle* of the applicability of the foreign law. But if either ' public policy ' or ' public law ' may be invoked in respect of the present Convention, it is, I think, clear—however the argument is presented —that this may only be done on the basis of an implied reservation from or exception to the Convention. In my opinion such a reservation should not be implied in the absence of clear necessity that it must be so implied in order to give effect to the intentions of the parties.

" What is the character or definition of a ' public law '? Opinions are varied. There is no agreement.

" In a wide sense, legislative laws are often conveniently categorized as public or private, the former being of general application, directed to the organization of society and applicable to all within the domain of the State concerned, the latter rather directed to special interests of individuals, etc., as distinct from society as a whole.

" But ' public law ', in the context of the present dispute, needs to be more definitively indicated. The Rejoinder of Sweden left me in [**127**] some doubt as to whether the concept of ' public law ' was claimed to be part of, or separate from, that of ' public policy '. In Sweden's final submissions this is still somewhat unclear. But whether it is one or the other, it is reasonably clear that ' public law ', as the term is used in Sweden, is a law which by its terms applies to nationals and foreigners alike within the territorial limits of a State, and which is made obligatory upon all persons and upon all instrumentalities called upon to enforce it. It includes rules of constitutional law, of procedure and of administrative law.

" ' Public law ' is described, if not defined, by others sometimes in similar, sometimes in different, senses. To some it is synonymous with a ' social law '. Others give it the specific role of providing for the political structure of a State and include within it the Constitution of a country, electoral laws, criminal laws, and *certain* administrative and fiscal laws. In this context the field occupied by ' public law ' is different from that occupied by ' public policy '. The two are seen by some as separate concepts whose domains may touch but never overlap.

" Others consider ' public law ' as a special branch of the law whose boundaries are fairly precise and which may be defined ' as the collection of rules—legislative, departmental and Judge-made—which fix, or ought to fix, the relation between the anthorities and the different administrative organizations or public authorities as well with one another as with individuals. It comprises, therefore, constitutional and administrative law.' (' *Droit public* and *ordre public* ', *Transactions of Grotius Society*, 1929, Vol. 15, pp. 83 *et seq.*)

" ' Public law ', so described, seems to me not only to overlap but to occupy a substantial part of the area generally considered as within that of ' public policy '. It presumably would include a public law of the kind indicated by Sweden, but it clearly enough includes very many others. I would think that ' public law ' in the sense used by Sweden is either part of the concept of ' public policy ' or, if a separate concept, occupies with it a substantial area of the same field. It is not, however, for the purpose of this case necessary in my opinion to determine this one way or the other. For, in either case, in whatever words the argument is put, what the Court is being asked to do is read into the Convention a reservation—in other words, to imply a clause or proviso—excepting from the terms and operation of the Convention all laws of ' public policy ' and/or ' public law '. On this basis, the arguments presented by Sweden on each stand or fall together, for that on the one is, in my view, indistinguishable in principle from that on the other.

[**128**] " If, indeed, ' public law ' is to be considered as a concept separate and distinct from ' public policy ' and in no way part of it, the argument for Sweden is, in my judgment, clearly unsound (*cf.* [*Treatment of*] *Polish Nationals in Danzig, P.C.I.J.*, Series A/B, No. 44, p. 24[1]). For, irrespective of *anything* which might appear in this (or any) Convention dealing with conflict of laws, it would be permissible and consistent with the Convention

[1 *Annual Digest*, 1931–1932, Case No. 104.]

for some contracting State to pass a ' public law ' of the character indicated by Sweden which provided, notwithstanding anything to the contrary contained in any such convention, that certain provisions of the ' public law ' should take effect. Even suggested safeguards to keep the invocation of the reservation of ' public policy ' within reasonable or governable limits could hardly find a place where what is done under a reservation, exception or exclusion of ' public law ' *may* be done ' regardless of *any* foreign law whatsoever.'

" I cannot regard a proposition that could lead to such results as sound (*cf.* Advisory Opinion concerning the *Polish Postal Service in Danzig, P.C.I.J.*, Series B, No. 11, pp. 37 and 39[1]).

" Moreover, Sweden appears to have disregarded or paid insufficient attention to the fact that measures which might be made the subject of ' public ' laws in some countries are in others governed by the Civil Code.

" I think the issue in this case would have been clearer had less attention been directed to ' *ordre public* ' (public policy) and ' public law ', and more to consideration of the subject-matter, purpose and scope and operation of the Convention having regard to the terms in which it was drafted and agreed to.

" It is understandable however that the latter received less specific attention than the former since the submissions in favour of a reservation or exclusion of ' public policy ' or ' public law ' depend on considerations which lie largely outside the terms of the Convention. Assuming such a reservation or exclusion exists—which it was the aim of the Swedish case to establish— the terms of the Convention in this particular case were, for the purposes of the argument, of secondary importance. On the submissions of Sweden, all that is necessary to be established is that the law under which the disputed action is taken is one of ' public policy ' or of ' public law ', *that*, in the absence of any allegation of denial of justice, concludes the matter, whatever may be the terms of the Convention.

" Public policy is principally and primarily a concept of municipal law. When, however, an international obligation is involved upon which this Court is called upon to pronounce, as in the present case, we are in a different field altogether. Treaty and convention obligations, whatever they are, must be faithfully observed. The provisions of municipal law cannot prevail over those of a treaty or [129] convention (*Greco-Bulgarian Comunities, P.C.I.J.*, Series B, No. 17, p. 32[2]).

" It should be repeated that what the Court is here being asked to do is to read into, or in legal terms to imply, a reservation—in what precise terms has never been made clear—excepting from the operation of the Convention all laws of contracting States which fall within ' public policy ' or within ' public laws '. The strongest of cases would have to be made out to justify the Court in doing so, for to do so permits States to determine for themselves the extent of their obligations under the Convention. It would permit this to be done even in derogation of what otherwise are obligations the Convention imposes. This could reduce the Convention to a shell. It is difficult to imagine what value the Convention in those circumstances would have, or why, having regard to the problem with which it sought to deal, it was ever entered into.

" Before the Court would be justified in implying a clause or reservation, it would need to be quite satisfied that this was essential to be done in order to preserve the intention of the Parties. For otherwise there would be imposed a new and different agreement upon the contracting States.

" No evidence was forthcoming that this was the intention. Reliance, however, was placed upon a so-called principle that such a reservation or exclusion must be read into conventions dealing with private law. Put in

[1 *Annual Digest*, 1925–1926, Case No. 276.]
[2 *Ibid.*, 1929–1930, Case No. 2.]

another way ' public policy ' operates retroactively, and even definitively acquired rights cannot be invoked against such a Convention.

" It was open to the Parties expressly to stipulate such a reservation. Indeed in Sweden's case it was urged that a reservation of public policy is expressly stipulated in almost all treaties and those that do not do so are the exceptions. The Parties to the present Convention did not so stipulate. It is not I think for the Court to speculate as to why they did not. The minds of the drafters were clearly directed during the preparatory work to the question whether some clause to that effect should or should not be included. They deliberately refrained from including one. It would in my opinion be going against all rules of construction as I understand them to imply such a reservation now.

" It is, I think, proper at this point to offer some general observations on the exercise of having recourse to preparatory work in seeking the proper interpretation to be accorded to treaties and conventions. Recourse to preparatory work of treaties or conventions may, in certain cases, be necessary. But whenever it is permissible it should, I think, be done with caution and restraint. For there is always the danger that, instead of interpreting the relevant treaty or [**130**] convention, one will find oneself tending to interpret the preparatory work and then transferring that interpretation across to the treaty or convention which is the sole subject of interpretation.

" The case before us presents, in my view, an example of this possibility. Some find nothing in the preparatory work of any real value, one way or the other. Others claim that it clearly supports the view that ' public policy ' is excepted from the Convention. Others are equally satisfied that the preparatory work just as clearly supports the opposite view. For my part, I would think this somewhat unsafe ground upon which to base any reasoning.

" Those who contend that such a reservation should be implied are obliged, I think, to concede that—subject to any review by this Court—it is at the discretion of States, applying within their territorial limits their own ideas of public policy, to determine to what extent it will permit the Convention to operate. It is suggested that a State invoking the reservation is under some kind of duty to show that its public policy has been applied reasonably— whatever this in the present context means—and in good faith. The State should be ready to submit its actions to examination. In cases of dispute it is further urged that the acts of the States are subject to review by this Court provided it has jurisdiction. But what if the Court in any given case has not jurisdiction? Moreover, if we are to determine, as we must, the meaning of the Convention at the time it was entered into—1902—any consideration that in event of dispute this Court would be available as a reviewing tribunal, to mitigate the consequences of, or control the unreasonable use by a contracting State of, the reservation, is irrelevant. And what is to be the test or standard of reasonableness that is to be applied? (*Cf. Serbian Loans, P.C.I.J.*, Series A, Nos. 20/21, p. 46[1]).

" Were such a reservation implied it would be a reservation of an indefinable character and there would be little left in any legal sense of any obligations under the Convention. For their content would be variable, quite indefinite, quite unpredictable, depending on the will of different parties. I find it difficult to understand legal obligations so undefined and indefinite.

" In my opinion, the submissions of Sweden on these issues are without substance.

" The views which I have earlier expressed on the proper interpretation of the Convention reject any reservation, exception or exclusion of ' public policy ' or ' public law '.

" In this case—and the decision must, of course, be limited to this case in its surrounding facts and circumstances—the *result* at which [**131**] I arrive

[1 *Annual Digest*, 1929–1930, Case No. 278.]

is the same as that reached by those who support such a reservation, exception or exclusion.

" But the *grounds* on which we reach our conclusion are, in my judgment, not immaterial. They represent not mere methods of approach; they are fundamentally different.

" A reservation or exception of ' public policy ' would, in my judgment, set the Convention at large. What is given by one hand may be taken away by the other. Obligations clearly enough intended thereunder to be imposed upon all contracting States would have no constant—if, indeed, any predictable—meaning. Such obligations could never be defined or ascertainable in terms reciprocally understood and binding on the parties.

" The judgment of the Court, however, in which I have concurred, in my view leaves the Convention unimpaired and intact. It preserves within the domain of the administration of guardianship, to which its scope and operation is limited, the full force and integrity of its provisions and of the obligations thereunder undertaken by the Contracting Parties."

## Judge Winiarski delivered the following Dissenting Opinion:

[132] " To my great regret, I am unable to concur in the Judgment and I believe I must state as briefly as possible the reasons for my dissent.

" The Court is confronted with a specific and particularized case which I have every reason to regard as exceptional. In order to ascertain whether the Submissions of the applicant Party are well-founded in law, the Court must, as it has always done, carefully scrutinize the facts which are at the origin of, and characterize, the disputed situation; it must examine all the facts in the case, including the national laws of the Parties and their application, in order to decide whether these laws, as applied by the national authorities, are or are not inconsistent with the international obligations of the State.

" The decision of the Swedish administrative authorities of April 26th, 1954, is based on Article 22 (a) of the Swedish Law of 1924 on the protection of children and young persons. Paragraphs (b), (c) and (d) contemplate much more serious cases of juvenile delinquency and pre-delinquency. On the other hand, paragraph (a) refers to the case of a ' child under sixteen who, in the family home, is ill-treated or exposed to serious neglect or any other danger affecting its physical or mental health '. Since the documents in the case do not disclose ill-treatment or serious neglect in respect of the infant, it follows that the only reason why the Child Welfare Board took the infant in charge is constituted by ' the danger affecting its physical or mental health '. Indeed, the same reason is to be found in the decision of the Supreme Administrative Court of October 5th, 1954: ' It is obvious that the removal of the infant to a wholly new environment would at present seriously endanger her mental health.'

" 1. The administrative decision of April 26th, 1954, was taken during the brief period of the Swedish guardianship organized on the application of the father of the infant. It is common ground that the Swedish administrative authorities acted correctly in applying the measure of protective upbringing at the time to the infant; the same must be held with regard to the maintenance of the measure during the confused period of transition when, along with the Swedish guardianship, there existed the guardianship of the father-guardian organized in the Netherlands.

" But the situation changed entirely following two judicial decisions: on August 5th, 1954, the Dutch Court of First Instance of Dordrecht released the father from the guardianship, appointed a woman guardian and ' orders the said infant to be handed over to the said guardian'; on September 16th of the same year, the [133] Swedish Court of First Instance of Norrköping, having regard to the Dordrecht judgment, ' orders that the guardianship . . . shall cease to be regulated in conformity with Swedish law'; it thus made way for guardianship within the meaning of the 1902 Convention.

" From that time onwards, the position is clear: by the concurring judicial decision of Dordrecht and Norrköping, the second following the first, the guardianship of the infant is governed by Dutch law in accordance with the Convention.

" 2. Article 1 of the Convention should here be recalled :

' The guardianship of an infant shall be governed by the national law of the infant ',

as well as Article 6, paragraph 1:

' The administration of a guardianship extends to the person and to all the property of the infant, wherever situated.'

" Paragraph 2 provides that this rule may admit of an exception in respect of a certain type of immovable property; no exception, however, is provided with regard to the person. No effort of interpretation could make these clear provisions say what they do not say. The Convention was open only to States represented at the Third Conference of Private International Law and the members of this little family of nations who are bound by this Convention have, with regard to guardianship, a very old common fund of ideas and principles which was formulated in Roman law: *Tutor non rebus dumtaxat, sed et moribus pupilli praeponitur*. And furthermore: *Personae non rei vel causae datur tutor*.

" It should also be noted that Article 6, paragraph 1, does not constitute a rule regarding conflicts of laws. It contains a common substantive rule, in accordance with the intention of the contracting States as expressed in the preamble:

' Desiring to lay down common provisions to govern the guardianship of infants.'

" 3. The legality of the Dutch guardianship is not disputed by Sweden; however, it is respected only as regards the administration of the property and legal representation. On the other hand, the fact is—as has been recognized by the Respondent—that the Dutch guardian is unable to obtain the delivery of the infant to which she is undoubtedly entitled by virtue of Dutch law which is binding on both Parties by virtue of the Convention; her right is confronted by the Swedish administrative measure, taken and maintained by an authority which, as has been said, holds ' a portion of the public power '. The Respondent has recognized in its Counter-Memorial that the measure taken at Norrköping ' constitutes an obstacle ' to the exercise of the right of custody by the regularly instituted guardian. The concurring judicial decisions [134] of the two countries cannot be executed by reason of the Swedish administration with regard to the essential question of rights relating to the person: the right to custody, by virtue of which the guardian may determine where she shall reside with the ward or may send her elsewhere, and necessarily the right of education as well.

" However, although the taking in charge of the infant for protective upbringing was legitimate at the time when it was applied, its legality may be challenged from the moment when: (1) the Swedish Court, informed of the institution of the Dutch guardianship, recognized this guardianship as regularly instituted and cancelled the Swedish guardianship, and (2) the guardian asked for delivery of the infant.

" It might possibly be argued that if the Swedish authorities had wished to find a provision in the Convention to justify the measure taken, it could have sought it in Article 7 which is in the following terms:

' Pending the institution of a guardianship, and in all cases of urgency, measures required for the protection of the person and interests of a foreign infant may be taken by the local authorities.'

" However, the Swedish Government has not relied on Article 7. Indeed, the character of the measure as maintained for four and a half years excludes any idea of urgency, even though protective upbringing could otherwise be regarded as fulfilling the conditions laid down in Article 7.

" 4. Like the Court, I do not regard the Swedish administrative measure as a rival guardianship constituting a direct and deliberate violation of the Convention; I am however unable to regard it as constituting no more than a certain temporary restriction on the exercise by the guardian of her right—and duty—of custody and education.  The measure encroaches deeply upon the attributes of national guardianship which are guaranteed by the Convention and, in the circumstances of the present case, is not compatible with the Convention.

" The infant was nine years old when she was taken in charge by the Swedish administrative authorities.  As the Court is giving its decision in the present case, she is thirteen and a half years old.  The measure has therefore already lasted four and a half years.  There is nothing in the file to indicate that the ending of the measure is in imminent contemplation by the authorities which took it; the last decision in the matter, in which the Supreme Administrative Court briefly found that the infant is still in need of protective upbringing, is dated February 26th, 1956; it was therefore taken two years and eight months ago.  In other words, protective upbringing is being applied to the infant at an age when the measure must necessarily and irrevocably impart to the child a definitive [135] personal, family, professional and national orientation.  That is what constitutes the essence of guardianship, the principal duty and right of the guardian.

" 5. I am unable to content myself with the finding that the Convention was designed to settle conflicts of civil laws, that the case referred to the Court is not a case of a conflict of laws, and that the measure maintained by the Swedish authorities cannot therefore be regarded as incompatible with Sweden's international obligations.

" In the first place, I would recall what I have just said, that Article 6, paragraph 1, does not constitute a rule regarding conflicts of laws but rather a common substantive rule.  Furthermore, I find it difficult to agree that the subject-matter of the Swedish Law is outside the subject of the Convention and that, whatever the Swedish authorities may do in pursuance of that Law, cannot in any way contravene the Convention; for the common factor in the Law and the Convention is, in the final analysis, the infant.  It cannot be asserted at the very outset that since a law has a different aim or purpose, it cannot be inconsistent with the Convention when, in fact, the law paralyzes the effects of the Convention and renders its execution impossible.  I am not referring to cases in which a State, without violating a treaty directly, holds it in check by indirect means of enacting or utilizing laws and regulations which appear to have a different purpose but which in practice make the provisions of a treaty inoperative.  The Swedish Law of 1924 is no doubt not incompatible as such with the 1902 Convention; but our case shows that the manner in which the Law is applied in a specific case may bring it into conflict with the Convention.

" 6. Of course the effect of the Convention cannot be to confer upon the infant or the foreign guardian immunity from the whole of the local legislation.  Without referring to police and security laws, laws relating to the entry and residence of foreigners, foreign exchange regulations, etc., which are not in any way related to guardianship and which extend indiscriminately to all persons who find themselves, even briefly, in the territory of the State, there is no doubt that certain legislative provisions considered to be in the public interest in respect of infants may be applicable to foreign infants residing in the country.  Like the Court, I agree that the Swedish Law of 1924 belongs to this category of laws.  But the conditions in which these laws are applied to foreign infants are not a matter of indifference and it is the application of these laws which makes it possible to decide whether they are in conformity with the international obligations of the State.

" Some of the decisions of the Supreme Court of the Netherlands which have been cited in the proceedings emphasize one of these conditions which is directly relevant to the case before this Court. Those conditions stress the necessity of protecting society ' whenever [136] children living within its territory are endangered by the acts of the parents '; ' the interest which society has that children shall not grow up in Holland in such a way as to be threatened with moral or physical harm '. Völlmar carefully specifies and repeats: children *residing in the country*, a situation which may arise *here*.

" But it is one thing to apply the administrative measure as long as the infant resides in the country for one reason or another, for example, the will of the father or of the guardian; it is a different thing to retain the infant in the country in order to maintain the measure. One example will help to illustrate the problem.

" Let us suppose that the law of the State of residence can overrule the *lex tutelae* by making the infant subject to compulsory primary education until an age that is greater than the one provided in his national law, *i.e.*, sixteen years instead of fourteen. The infant has just reached his fourteenth birthday. If the guardian sought to return with his ward to his national country because primary education there is not compulsory beyond the age of fourteen and the ward could therefore begin to work, the local authorities would certainly not be entitled to prevent the departure of the infant in order to make him enjoy two further years of the compulsory education already initiated; they could not legitimately prevent them from changing their residence.

" It is abundantly clear from the file that the Swedish administrative authorities are not applying the measure of protective upbringing to the infant *because* she has her residence in Sweden but that they are retaining this foreigner in Sweden *in order to* subject her to protective upbringing. This manner of applying the law must be held to be clearly incompatible with the obligations assumed by Sweden under the Convention.

" It appears to be likewise clear from the file that the measure in question is not based upon the supposed insufficiency of the Dutch guardianship (Article 22 *a*) in case the infant were handed over to her guardian, with whom she already has her legal domicile. Indeed, Dutch guardianship, functioning under the effective control of the national authorities, does not provide fewer guarantees with regard to the protection of the interests of the infant than Swedish protective education; the question of the application of Swedish protective education by the Dutch authorities or *vice versa* clearly does not arise. The Netherlands, moreover, possess legislation on the protection of children and young persons that is generally similar to that of Sweden.

" 7. It should be noted that in the Swedish judicial decisions concerning the infant, the question of *ordre public* never arose. The Judgment of the Court of Norrköping which cancelled the registration of the Swedish guardianship and maintained the *god man* referred to the interests of the infant; the Court of Appeal of Göta [137] which confirmed the decision of the Court of First Instance considered the interests of the infant and reached its decision ' having regard, in particular, to the close links between Elisabeth and Sweden '. The Supreme Court, which removed the last traces of the Swedish guardianship by releasing the *god man* from his duties, merely held that the case could not be reduced to one of major necessity as the Court of First Instance had considered.

" The interest of the infant is the *ratio legis*, the purpose and the aim of the legislative or treaty provision. The Swedish courts, which alone were entitled to do so, have not applied the exception of *order public*. This Court cannot substitute itself for a national court in order to decide what is required by the *ordre public* of the country of that court.

" In the Rejoinder, the Respondent partially modified its position and contended that the Applicant wrongly referred to *ordre public* in the specific meaning of the term in private international law.

' Nothing of the sort is involved in the present case ... The Swedish case is that the law for the protection of children, being part of the public law, is applicable throughout the territory and to any foreign child there, that no national or foreign law relating to the status of the child can stand in the way of its application, and that the 1902 Convention was in no way intended to alter this situation. The Government of the Netherlands has clearly lost sight of this absolutely mandatory character of *the rules of public law*, or of administrative law, which perhaps the Swedish Government itself has failed sufficiently to stress.'

" In itself, the distinction is well taken. With regard to the contention, I shall revert to it before I conclude.

" 8. Although the 1902 Convention regulates matters of private law, it is a convention of public international law and, like all international conventions, creates rights and duties in respect of the States which entered into it. The Convention is binding upon the States, of which the courts and administrative authorities are the organs. By signing the Convention, the contracting States could regard it as certain that the decisions of their courts would be in conformity with the rules laid down by the Convention and that execution of these decisions would be effectively secured by the State of the courts concerned.

" It is natural that the Government of the Netherlands should have adopted the cause of its nationals for it thus defends its own right which is guaranteed by the 1902 Convention and which has been disregarded by the Swedish authorities.

" By the Convention, the Netherlands have acquired the right that the guardianship of infants shall be governed by the national law of the infant and in particular that the right relating to the person, right of custody and education should be treated inseparably from guardianship. The Netherlands have acquired this right, [138] not *vis-à-vis* the Swedish Courts but *vis-à-vis* the Swedish State, which must prevent the manner in which its national law is applied by its administrative organs from rendering inoperative the decision which it has taken, in accordance with the Convention, through its Courts. The decisions of the Courts were in conformity with the Convention; in the event of the administrative authorities hesitating between two possible manners of applying the law, the State must prefer the manner which does not bring it into conflict with its international obligations.

" 9. The solution which has my preference does not involve either an interpretation or a criticism of the Swedish Law. In one of its first judgments, the Permanent Court adopted an attitude in this connection from which it never subsequently departed:

' The Court is certainly not called upon to interpret the Polish law as such; but there is nothing to prevent the Court's giving judgment on the question whether or not, in applying that law, Poland is acting in conformity with its obligations towards Germany under the Convention.' (*Case concerning certain German Interests in Polish Upper Silesia*, Series A, No. 7, p. 19.[11])

" With regard to the relationship between an international undertaking and the municipal law, the Permanent Court expressed its view on several occasions:

' It is a generally accepted principle of international law that in the relations between Powers who are contracting parties to a treaty, the provisions of municipal law cannot prevail over those of the treaty.' (*Greco-Bulgarian Communities*, Series B, No. 17, p. 32.[21])

" And again:

[1 *Annual Digest*, 1925–1926, Case No. 4.]
[2 *Ibid.*, 1929–1930, Case No. 2.]

' It is certain that France cannot rely on her own legislation to limit the scope of her international obligations.' (*Free Zones*, A/B, No. 46, p. 167.)

" It has been argued before the Court that the Swedish Law is an enactment of public law. In this conection, the Permanent Court has expressed the following view:

'. . . a State cannot adduce as against another State its own Constitution with a view to evading obligations incumbent upon it under international law or treaties in force.' (*Treatment of Polish Nationals in Danzig*, Series A/B, No. 44, p. 24.[1])

" The Constitution is a classic example of public law.

" I therefore reach the conclusion that the Court ought to have adopted the first Submission of the Government of the Netherlands.

" The second Submission of the Government of the Netherlands merely constitutes a legal consequence of the first Submission. The Government which has created an irregular situation by its administrative measure is under an obligation to end the measure."

## Judge Córdova delivered the following Dissenting Opinion:

[**139**] " Much to my regret, I have to disagree with both the reasoning and the conclusion reached by the Court in this case.

" The judicial authorities of Sweden set up the guardianship of Marie Elisabeth Boll, a minor living in Sweden but of Dutch nationality, on March 18th, 1954. This guardianship, according to Swedish law, only refers to the administration of the interests of the infant, but does not include the custody and control of her person. The same authorities put an end to this guardianship on July 2nd, 1955, when the Supreme Court of Sweden discharged finally the *god man* appointed by the inferior judicial authorities.

" The Swedish administrative authorities, on April 26th, 1954, applying Article 22 (*a*) of the Swedish Law for the Protection of Children and Young Persons (Child Welfare Law) of June 6th, 1924, put Marie Elisabeth Boll under the system called *skyddsuppfostran*, which, according to both Agencies, should be translated into English as ' protective upbringing ', and as ' *éducation protectrice* ' into French.

" This protective measure—which the Swedish authorities still maintain after four and a half years—according to the Swedish Law gives the custody and control of the infant to the Swedish Infants' Bureau.

" On their side, the judicial authorities in Holland, applying the Dutch laws, set up the guardianship of the same infant, and on August 5th, 1954, appointed Mrs. Catharina Postema as her guardian. According to Dutch law, the guardian has the right, as well as the duty, to take custody and control of the infant.

" Neither the judicial authorities of Sweden which first set up and afterwards terminated the guardianship, nor the administrative ones which instituted the protective upbringing, in the whole of their proceedings, made the leightest reference to the Convention governing the Guardianship of Infants, signed by their country and Holland on June 12th, 1902, notwithstanding the fact that this Convention was called to their attention (para 5, Swedish Counter-Memorial).

" In putting an end to their own guardianship, the Swedish authorities applied their own Law of 1904 (Counter-Memorial, Annex D (*a*)). They have, therefore, recognized the Dutch guardian, Mrs. Catherina Postema, with full rights to the administration of the infant's interests, but in fact made it impossible for her to exercise her right of custody and control of the infant's person on account of the infant being subject to the protective upbringing.

" Counsel for Sweden tried to justify this disregard of the Convention —among others of lesser importance with which I do not [**140**] consider it necessary to deal here—on the main contention that the Convention of 1902 should not be considered as applicable, because the Swedish Law of Protective Upbringing of 1924, being a public law and relating to the public order of the State, may be applied to all infants, Swedish and foreign alike, notwithstanding the provisions of the Convention.

" The decision of the Court, although based on different grounds, reaches the same conclusion that the Convention of 1902 is not applicable to the present case.

" Without rejecting expressly the *ordre public* theory relied upon by Sweden, the Decision is predicated upon the theory that the Law for the Protection of Children and Young Persons of 1924—under the authority of which the ' protective upbringing ' was instituted and is still maintained— having a different aim and scope than that of the Convention does not violate the provisions of the latter, even though, in fact, it makes it impossible for the Dutch guardian to fully exercise her rights and fulfil her duties as derived from the Dutch laws and the Convention itself, in so far as it denies her the custody and control of the person of Marie Elisabeth Boll.

" The two theories, that of *ordre public* and public law and that of the different aim and scope, have the same effect with regard to a Convention; they both make it possible for the State, party to the Treaty, to avoid the fulfilment of its obligations as prescribed in the international contract by relying on its own laws. The theory upheld by the Court is nothing less than the same theory of *ordre public* under a different guise; but perhaps still more dangerous in its implications. It is true that the decision does not require of the national law to be a public law or one related to public order, but, as far as giving to a State signatory of a Convention the possibility of infringing its provisions and its natural, logical and expected legal consequences, it opens the door still wider than the theory of *ordre public* to the possibility of raising the national laws as exception against the binding force of treaties.

" In my opinion there is no national law, whatever its classification might be, either common or public or with different aim and scope, which in the face of a treaty dealing with the same subject-matter can juridically claim priority in its application. Laws of procedure, substantive criminal law, political or fiscal legislation, passport regulations, and even laws related to the sovereignty of a State over its own territory, are sometimes put aside and suspended by treaty provisions and, what is more—in some cases—by international law and by international courtesy alone, even in the absence of any treaty stipulation. Such is the case of the régime of capitulations, of diplomatic criminal immunities and fiscal exemptions, and of transfer of territory by treaty provisions. In all these cases the stipulations of a treaty or convention are binding upon the parties, notwithstanding the public character of their affected national legislations. Therefore, in my opinion, there is not much juridical [141] value in the proposition that *ordre public*, or a law with a *scope and aim different* from that of a treaty, can, by themselves alone, be opposed to the application of a convention or treaty, thus making nugatory its intended juridical and practical effects. It seems clear to me that the legislation of a State party to a treaty dealing specifically with a subject-matter otherwise normally regulated by its own laws has to yield before the provisions of such treaty.

" It has been said that treaties and conventions cannot be set up as a barrier to the power to legislate in the future of a State party to such international contract. The argument is not valid, because treaties and conventions usually may be denounced, leaving the parties in complete liberty to change again their legislative principles and laws; and, even when, as in certain cases of transfer of territory, a treaty may not be considered as subject to denunciation, this restriction upon the legislative power which results for a State party to such treaty should be deemed as a consequence agreed upon of its own will by such State. It has also been argued that there is a well-known principle of interpretation of treaties dealing with conflicts of national laws, the so-called Convention of Private International Law, which gives to the parties to such treaties the right to disregard its provisions relying on their own public laws or on their laws relating to public order. I do not believe that there is such principle of Public International Law—the only law between nations; on the contrary, I have always known the time-honoured and basic principle of *pacta sunt servanda*, which makes it impossible for the States to be released by their own unilateral decision from their obligations according to a treaty which they have signed.

" The place to be given to the national laws of *ordre public* and to those with a different scope and aim, whatever their classification might be, depends upon the interpretation of the treaty; but when such interpretation clearly includes within its provisions a subject-matter otherwise normally regulated by those kinds of national laws, the provisions of the treaty should be considered as having priority over them. To decide differently would mean complete anarchy in the relations of States, would leave the binding force of treaties in the unilateral hands of the legislative, judicial and administrative authorities of the States parties to such treaties and, finally, would completely destroy the indispensable hierarchy of the laws of the States and that of the international legislation.

" An international jurisdiction, in the interpretation of a treaty or convention, must determine the extent of the consent of the parties to such instrument. In so doing it must take into consideration the real will of the signatory States as determined by the text of the treaty itself, by the antecedents of the international contract, or by any other means at its disposal.

[142] " I agree with the Court in that the parties to the Convention of 1902 had mainly in mind questions of the conflict of laws with regard to guardianship; and also that they implicitly excluded generally all national laws, either public or common, dealing with subject-matters different from that of guardianship, like criminal laws, those organizing the judiciary and the political structure of the government, passports, and even perhaps the correction of delinquent infants. But I do believe that all matters relating to the guardianship of infants, including all the legal as well as practical effects of guardianship, such as the custody and control of minors, measures relating to the protection and welfare of infants, should be considered as falling within the terms of the Convention, although they might be dealt with by national public laws, laws relating to the public order of the State or by laws with a different aim and scope from that of guardianship. The decision of the Court, although putting aside the theory of *ordre public*, and basing its reasoning on the theory of the aim and scope differing from that of the treaty, nevertheless tries to interpret the Convention of 1902, stating that it was only intended to regulate the conflicts of national legislations regarding guardianship, a subject-matter alien and completely different from the protection of children and young persons, which is the only aim and scope of the Swedish Law of June 6th, 1924. With this basic proposition, I cannot agree.

" In my way of thinking, the 1924 Swedish Law—at least as far as its Article 22 (*a*) is concerned—is far from having an aim and scope different from that of the Convention.

" In substance, guardianship and the laws for the protection of children are remarkably the same, and their means of realizing their purpose is identical: the custody and control of the person of the minor. As far as the intention of both is concerned, the guardianship dealt with in the Convention and the ' protective upbringing ' have one and the same objective: the protection of infants. Guardianship fulfils its purpose by giving the custody and control of the child to the individual parent or guardian, and only when this method of protection fails does this system of State protection intervene by means of the 'protective upbringing' and other similar measures, taking away from the parent or guardian such custody and control.

" In spite of the Netherlands' own admission and Sweden's allegation to the contrary, it is my understanding that Article 7 of the Convention clearly comprehends the protective measures included in Article 22 (a) of the Swedish Law of 1924, when it refers to the possibility of the local authorities to take ' in all cases of urgency ' measures ' required for the protection of the person ' of the infant. In order to prove the contrary, it has been argued that the national laws of all parties to the Convention, dealing with the protection of infants, were enacted a long time [143] after the signing of the Convention, but that is not the case, at least with regard to the two States before the Court, the Netherlands and Sweden. I believe that the reference to protective measures included in Article 7 was not accidental and meaningless. Its inclusion strongly suggests that the necessity to introduce a provision making it possible for the States of residence to apply measures of protection to the foreign infant, according to their present or future legislations, in ' cases of urgency ', was clearly present in the minds of the framers of the Convention. This is the natural and, perhaps, the only reasonable interpretation of Article 7. Moreover, although the Dutch Law introducing the system of protection of infants was enacted after the year 1902, such legislation was already contemplated and prepared since 1901, and Sweden enacted its own Law regarding protective upbringing in the year 1902, which makes it evident that the Netherlands and Sweden had already in mind the application of protective measures. It seems to me that the framers of the 1902 Convention, seeking only the good of the infants, although mainly referring to guardianship, tried to organize the adequate application of the different protective methods of the signatory States, guardianship as well as any other protective measures. They tried to make compatible the institution of national guardianship with the local protective legislations and measures by giving priority to the former (Articles 1 and 6) over the latter (Article 7).

" I hold the above view in spite of the position of both Parties to the litigation before the Court which, as I have pointed out, believe that Article 7 of the Convention is not applicable. If the 1902 Convention had been a bilateral treaty, their common interpretation with regard to one of its Articles—Article 7—would have been enough for me to consider such a construction as final; but the 1902 Convention being a multilateral treaty, it is possible, I believe, to hold a different opinion from that of the two Parties before the Court with reference to the applicability of its Articles.

" Since according to the laws of the Netherlands, this right of custody and control belongs to the guardian, there is sufficient legal reason to decide that Catharina Postema, according to the Convention itself, may rightfully claim the custody and control over Marie Elisabeth Boll, the basic principle of the Convention being that guardianship shall be governed by the national law of the infant (Articles 1, 2, 4 and 8 of the Convention). That is undoubtedly the reason why the Netherlands Court of First Instance of Dordrecht, August 5th, 1954, when appointing Madame Postema as guardian, ordered at the same time that the girl should be handed over to her. But if this were not enough, Article 6 of the Convention will take away the slightest doubt when it says: ' the administration of the guardian extends to the person . . . , of the infant.

[144] " Therefore, I feel safe in concluding that the Convention does regulate both the right to custody and control and the protective measures in general, including, of course, the protective measure called ' protective upbringing ' referred to in Article 22 (a) of the Law for the Protection of Children and Young Persons of June 6th, 1924. As a corollary it necessarily follows that the Convention should have been applied by the Court, and the case of Marie Elisabeth Boll should have been decided exclusively according to its terms. The task of the Court should thus have been very much simplified,

and its decision should have been, in my opinion, the right one.

"Even if the Swedish authorities, on April 26th, 1954, when they instituted the 'protective upbringing', did not know about the Dutch nationality of the infant Boll, and even also if they did not take into account the terms of the 1902 Convention, I believe that the protective measure taken by them to put the Dutch girl under the régime of protective upbringing was a legal act according to the terms of the Convention. Thinking their action urgent, as they must necessarily have judged it, this measure is perfectly justified in the light of Article 7 of the Convention, which makes it possible for the local authorities to take, in ' all *urgent cases*, the measures required for the protection . . . of a foreign infant . . . '. Therefore, the setting up of the protective measure does not constitute in itself a violation of the Convention. I go as far as to believe that the Swedish authorities seem to have been under a moral as well as a legal obligation to take such protective measure judging from the meagre knowledge the Court has of the real situation of the minor Boll.

"It only remains to decide if, according also to the terms of the Convention, the maintenance of such protective measure can be considered compatible with the provisions of the Treaty of 1902. In my opinion this question should have been answered in the negative. An urgency of four and a half years is inconceivable, specially having, as I do, the understanding that the urgency contemplated in Article 7 of the Convention requires two elements, one of fact and the other a legal one. That is to say, a practical need of the infant as well as the lack of an efficient protection, either because the guardian has not yet been appointed or, if already appointed, does not or cannot act efficiently.

"The practical need may extend for an indefinite period of time, but, once the aim of the Convention is fulfilled in the sense that the foreign infant can be considered as sufficiently protected according to the laws of its own nationality, the concept of urgency cannot any more apply; in the present case, as soon as Madame Postema showed herself legally and practically able to take charge of the infant Boll and to exercise her rights and duties as a guardian according to the Dutch laws. I cannot understand the object of Article 6 of the Convention in any other sense than to make obligatory for the local authorities, should they be judicial or [145] administrative, to release the foreign child to the custody and control of the guardian appointed in compliance with the national laws of the infant; therefore, only in the case that the child Boll will remain in Sweden after having been turned over to the Dutch guardian, and the future facts warrant again the State intervention in favour of the child and against the legally appointed guardian, shall the Swedish authorities be entitled—by their own laws and entirely independent of the Convention with which they had already complied—to set up a new ' protective upbringing ', but the provisional one now in existence should be at once discontinued.

"I refuse to accept the idea that the Convention is not applicable in this case, and also the interpretation of the Swedish Law of protective upbringing as giving right to the State of residence to keep a foreign minor—in this case Marie Elisabeth Boll—indefinitely in its territory in order to impose upon her its protection by means of denying the release of the child to the legally appointed guardian—Madame Postema—which is the logical, juridical, intended and expected effect of Article 6 of the Convention.

"The most strange effect of the Law of protective upbringing, to keep a foreign child within the country of residence against the expressed will of the legally appointed foreign guardian, seems to me unwarranted and illegal according to the general principles of international law, even in the absence of a Convention as the one of 1902.

"Such would be the case, for instance, of a so-called public law, or law of *ordre public* which would impose forced labour in the fields upon infants, native and foreign alike, in order to collect the needed crops for the community. This law would certainly have an aim and scope completely different from that of the Convention dealing with guardianship, but could one say that the foreign guardian cannot avoid such forced labour being imposed upon this foreign ward by taking him or her out of the country of residence? Could the local law impede the taking out of the country of the foreign infant because it is a public law or related to the public order, or because it has a different aim and scope than that of the Convention?

" I would reach the same conclusion, I believe, even in the absence of any treaty or convention in the case of any national law different from the penal ones, which would have the effect of denying the right to a foreigner, adult or minor, to leave the country of residence.

" From all that I have said, it is my considered opinion that the Second Final Conclusion of the Dutch Government, which the Agent for the Netherlands included in its Submissions of October 3rd last, that Sweden is under the obligation to end the protective upbringing, should have been granted by the Court."

M. Offerhaus, Judge *Ad Hoc*, delivered the following Dissenting Opinion:

[**146**] " 1. In this case, which concerns the application of the Convention of 1902 on guardianship, the question is one of an infant of Dutch nationality, born on May 7th, 1945, in Sweden, the daughter of a father of Dutch nationality and of a mother Swedish by birth, who had acquired Dutch nationality by her marriage. The mother died on December 5th, 1953, and the father became, by operation of law, guardian of the infant, in virtue of his national law (Art. 378, B[*urgerlijk*] W[*etboek*]. Netherlands).

" The Convention of 1902 governing the guardianship of infants is applicable in this case because according to its Article 9 it applies to the guardianship of infants nationals of one of the contracting States who have their habitual place of residence in the territory of another of those States.

" The organization of the national guardianship in this case passed through various phases before reaching its present state. A deputy-guardian, in the person of M. Idema, was appointed only on June 2nd, 1954. Then, on August 5th, 1954, the Dordrecht Court relieved the father, Johannes Boll, of his functions as guardian, and appointed instead Mme Catharina Trijntje Postema, widow Idema, hereinafter called Mme Postema.

" Meantime, in Sweden, the Swedish authorities had taken measures of ' protective upbringing ' which at once made apparent a conflict with the organization of the national guardianship. On May 5th, 1954, evidently not yet being aware that Dutch nationals were involved, the Child Welfare Board of Norrköping approved the taking in charge of Marie Elisabeth Boll by its President pursuant to Article 22 (*a*) of the Swedish Law of June 6th, 1924, a measure which was confirmed and therefore maintained in the proceedings of June 22nd and October 5th, 1954, and again, on a fresh application, maintained in the first and the last of the three decisions in 1955. After a provisional phase, the child was entrusted to her maternal grandfather, M. Lindwall.

" The decision of June 22nd, 1954, to maintain the measure was taken in full knowledge of the nationality of the parties and of the appointment of M. Idema as deputy-guardian, and that of October 5th, 1954, in full knowledge of the appointment of Mme Postema as guardian in place of the father. Clearly, when the measure of protective upbringing was taken on May 5th, 1954, the Swedish authorities were unaware of the foreign nationality of the infant—which was perhaps also due to the fact that, by mistake, Johannes Boll had, on March 18th, 1954, had himself registered as guardian in Sweden, that is to say as guardian in the limited sense of [**147**] administrator of the child's property, according to Swedish law, in addition to the custody which Sweden allowed him according to Swedish law. This mistake, although regrettable, in my opinion, did not prejudice the father's rights. Moreover, the father's Swedish guardianship was revoked on September 16th, 1954, and the *god man* who had been appointed was discharged on July 2nd, 1955. Only the custody is in issue.

" 2. In the six decisions regarding protective upbringing, no mention was made of an accusation brought against the father, except in the resolution of the Government of the Province of Östergötland of October 28th, 1955, the allusion to a suspicion which existed at the time of the first taking in charge by the Child Welfare Board. In all the decisions, even in the first one, allusion is only made to a danger to the moral or mental health of the child and, after the appointment of the female guardian, to the fear that notwithstanding her powers, the child would remain under her father's influence. Even this fear was based only on negative data, that is on the lack of information regarding the circumstances in which guardianship was being exercised in the Netherlands, and on the presumed ignorance of the Dordrecht Court as to the reasons for the Swedish measures.

" In the Swedish Law of June 6th, 1924, on protective upbringing, Article 22 enumerates the cases in which such measures are permissible. The text of Article 22 runs:

' In conformity with Articles 23–25, the Child Welfare Board will take measures concerning:
(a) a child under sixteen who, in the family home, is ill-treated or exposed to serious neglect or any other danger affecting its physical or mental health;
(b) a child of the same age who, by reason of the immorality or negligence of its parents or of their unsuitability for the duty of educator, is in danger of becoming a delinquent;
(c) a child under eighteen whose delinquency is so serious that special educational measures are required to correct it; and
(d) a person between eighteen and twenty-one who is found to be leading an irregular, idle or immoral life or who exhibits other serious vices, the correction of which calls for special measures on the part of society (Law of April 14th, 1944).'

" Under Article 34, a non-delinquent child will, in the absence of special circumstances, be placed in a suitable family.

" The one case which, in the view of the Swedish authorities, arose in the present instance was that mentioned in paragraph (a). There was no question of the infant's being ill-treated or exposed to serious negligence, the question was of a danger regarding her physical or moral health. Article 22 (a) requires that this danger should be one threatening her in the family home. The Swedish authorities [148] based the measures which they took on the existence of such a danger. This comes under the title of the Law which, according to the French text, concerns ' la protection des enfants et la protection de la jeunesse ' [' the protection of children and young people '].

" It is certainly to be regretted that the Court only knows the decisions and the facts which these bring to light. For whatever reason, neither Government has given the Court more detailed information, and the mystery of incomplete reports and statements has been maintained—marked in the decisions by dots. One does not know whether the child is familiar with her national language nor how she is getting on in the family where she is placed. Following the exhaustion of the local remedies, and pending the Judgment on the Application of the Netherlands Government, the present situation has continued.

" However, the Court had to decide whether at the moment of the institution of the protective upbringing and of its maintenance, these measures were compatible with the Convention, and, if not, whether they should be ended. Therefore, in my view, one must adjudicate on the facts advanced by the Parties which, however incomplete they may be, show that the protective upbringing has only been instituted and maintained for reasons connected with the moral or mental health of the infant. It is the right of the Parties in the case to ask the Court to give its Judgment on these facts alone.

" 3. Although in the Judgment of the Court the measure of protective upbringing is considered as outside the scope of the Convention—an opinion with which I cannot agree—the Court accepts that, in particular in the decision of the Supreme Administrative Court of October 5th, 1954, the capacity of the Dutch female guardian to concern herself with the person of the infant was recognized. This is the starting point for the ensuing considerations in which the Court holds that the protective upbringing cannot be regarded as a rival guardianship to the guardianship instituted in the Netherlands.

" Next, it is said of the protective upbringing that it impedes the exercise by the guardian of the full right to custody which is hers by Dutch law in conformity with the Convention.

" It may indeed be said that the whole dispute concerning the question whether protective upbringing has an object other than the organization of the guardianship presupposes the recognition of the Dutch guardianship.

" None the less, I should have preferred a categorical declaration in which the Court held that the guardianship of the parental guardian and that of Mme Postema, or at least the latter, constituted guardianship within the meaning of the Convention. The Court would thereby have rejected the Swedish Government's contention that Mme Postema's guardianship was based on the *puissance* [149] *paternelle* of Johannes Boll and that it could not, for that reason, be recognized. Furthermore, by such a formal declaration, the Judgment would have interpreted the Convention in a strict and clear fashion. However, in my view, the Judgment will none the less have the same effects.

" For the interpretation of the Convention in this sense, I attach great importance to the indications to be found in the Acts of the Hague Conferences of 1893, 1894 and 1900 which, in this respect, are more important than the representatives of the two Governments have indicated, In particular, it appears that the application of the national law of the infant, as regards the *reasons* for guardianship, mentioned in Article 5, is equally valid for Article 1. For example, if the death of one of the parents deprives the infant of the care of both its parents, there is then a ' guardianship ' in an ' autonomous ' sense acceptable for other countries.

" 4. If it be accepted that the guardianship of the two successive guardians instituted in the Netherlands is wholly governed by the Dutch law of the infant, this means in the first place that the national law is to be applied in the contracting States as regards everything that concerns the exercise of guardianship until that is finally terminated. In the Acts of the Second Hague Conference of 1894 (p. 112, Report of the Fourth Commission), mention is made of the difficulties which the application of a foreign law involves, and the Commission therefore proposed to regulate the matter in such a way that the competence of the courts and of the authorities and the law applicable should coincide. The Commission clarified its point of view by stating that the difficulties were already most embarrassing and that ' those involved in the organization of a complete juridical situation, *in all its phases and with all its complications*, would be even more so '. This same expression ' guardianship in all its phases ' recurs in the commentary on Article 1, also on page 112. Apparently, the aim was to regulate the whole organization of guardianship, in conformity with the Preamble to the Convention, which refers to ' common provisions to govern guardianship '.

" In the second place, for the father-guardian or the mother-guardian, and also as regards the non-parental guardian, guardianship within the meaning of the Convention includes the custody of the person of the infant.

This is also recognized by the Court. If the content of the notion of ' guardian-ship ' is determined by the national law, and if the national law includes custody, the contracting States are bound to recognize this right of custody. Moreover, in the original text of the Swedish Law of July 8th, 1904, which was intended to make possible the accession of Sweden to the Convention (Kosters and Bellemans, p. 723), Article 5 of Chapter 4 regulates the appointment of a delegate to look after the property *and* the person of the infant (*cf.* also the present text in Annex D (*a*) of the Counter-Memorial).

[150] " Guardianship, within the meaning of the Convention, must there-fore include the national guardianship for the whole period of guardianship and for all the care that the person of the infant requires, so to speak, in extrinsic and intrinsic totality. It follows that one may not say that the Convention was only meant to regulate conflicts of laws. Above all, what is important is to determine the scope of the provisions comprised in such a conflict.

" Now, the scope of the Convention is fairly wide. Guardianship formed part of the whole system of international conventions which was in contem-plation at The Hague, including the guardianship of adults, which became the Convention concerning interdiction and similar measures or protection— as, in the 1893 programme, a convention was planned on *puissance paternelle* as well.

" In the Acts of 1894 (pp. 111–112), the Fourth Commission expressed the view that what was involved was protection through guardianship— the word ' protection ' was used three times—and this is asserted in Article 6, which provides that the administration of a guardianship extends to the person and to all the property of the infant, and also in Article 7, which allows measures for the protection of the person and interests of a foreign infant to be taken by the local authorities.

" As regards the extrinsic scope of guardianship, this institution could in no way and nowhere exist or function without intervention and permanent supervision by the courts or the administrative authorities, or bòth. Literally, *tutela* means protection. The institution of guardianship does not fall exclu-sively within the domain of private law. From the outset, the public interest was involved and it is so at present in an even larger measure, in all the con-tracting States.

" The present regulation of Dutch guardianship includes the removal or discharge of a guardian if he neglects his obligations (Art. 419, para. 1, No. 2, *Burgerlijk Wetboek*)—the right of the Department of the Public Pro-secutor to entrust the infant to a Guardianship Council (*Voogdijraad*, since 1955 *Raad voor Kinderbescherming*) in case of the removal of the guardian (Art. 421 *a*)—the discharge of the guardian at the request of the Department of the Public Prosecutor or the Guardianship Council (Art. 423 j° 374 *a*, *B.W.*)—supervision by the deputy-guardian—various rights of the Guardian-ship Council and the Children's Judge—guardianship exercised by bodies, as ordered by the Court (Art. 396). There is always a competent court in the Netherlands, by virtue of the requirement that the deputy-guardian should reside within the territory, as well as a Guardianship Council dealing with infants residing abroad (Art. 461 *a*).

" Further, there are the provisions concerning the placing under super-vision of a child in danger of moral or physical harm which are applicable both in the case of the exercise of parental power and also in that of the exercise of guardianship (Arts. 365 to 373, recently [151] amended by the Law of July 20th, 1955, j° 418 *B.W.*) A family guardian is appointed by the Children's Judge. The latter may place the infant in an establishment or elsewhere. The whole of this institution was described by the Applicant Party as a measure for the assistance of the guardian in the matter of the upbringing of the infant. The guardian may be removed by the Court should he seriously neglect the directions of the family guardian or prevent the application of measures for the placing of the infant (Art. 419, para. 1, No. 7).

" Ever since the entry into force of the codification of 1838, the surviving father or mother has had the guardianship; there has been a deputy-guardian (except in the irrelevant case of Art. 421, *B.W.*); the court has had the right to remove the guardian; the guardian has had the duty of taking care of the person of the infant and, if he had serious misgivings as to the latter's conduct, the guardian could apply to the court for the detention of the infant (Arts. 422, 423, 437, 441, 442, *B.W.*, French translation by G. Tripels, 1886). Thus there was already a system of protective rules which have gradually been increased and improved.

" Sweden, like other contracting States, was in a position to know of this system of protection, as also of the draft law of February 6th, 1901, which came into force on December 1st, 1905, by which the protection of children was modernized.

" In Sweden the first Law on protective upbringing dates from 1901. The consequences of all these laws must have been foreseen before Sweden ratified the Convention in 1904—and afterwards the Convention was not denounced.

" In all the contracting States, legislation on the protection of children, which in the beginning was little developed, has gradually progressed and, as was mentioned in the Swedish arguments, national organizations are, in conferences at Stockholm and elsewhere, still right up to the present concerning themselves with measures to be taken in common agreement.

" The question whether these rules are to be found in the Civil Code or in a special law, is, in this connection, quite formal and secondary. In the Netherlands they are to be found in the Civil Code, both as regards *puissance paternelle* and guardianship. In Sweden, where codification is of another kind and where custody and guardianship are distinguished, they have been dealt with separately, although in the 1949 Law there are various provisions whereby custody is entrusted to the guardian.

" 5. From these considerations I draw the conclusion that the Convention governs the organization of guardianship in its totality, with the aim of protecting children. In principle, it refers to the national law, but this law gives way to the law of the place of residence, as far as may be necessary. As an exception, if guardianship is not or cannot be set up in accordance with Articles 1 and 2, [152] it is instituted and administered in conformity with the law of the place of habitual residence of the infant abroad (Art. 3). As an exception also, Article 7 provides that pending the institution of a guardianship, and in all cases of urgency, measures required for the protection of the person and interests of the infant may be taken by the local authorities.

" As soon as the nationality of the child became known to them, why did the Swedish authorities not study the Convention and, in compliance with Article 8, inform the Dutch authorities of the situation ' as soon as it was known to them '? According to the Swedish Law of July 8th, 1904 (Chapt. 4, Art. 2), a letter to the Swedish Ministry of Foreign Affairs would have sufficed.

" The Swedish authorities might have considered the application of Article 7 as a measure of urgency. But in their decisions there is no allusion to the 1902 Convention.

" I do not share the view that in cases of urgency Article 7 only concerns special or partial measures. Article 7 allows temporary measures of urgency, even if they cover the whole intrinsic sphere of guardianship.

" As to the decisions of the Dutch courts, the applicability of Article 7 has, in my opinion, been affirmed by the Judgment of the Supreme Court (*Hoge Raad*) of May 1st, 1958 (*N.J.* 1958, 432), concerning an infant of German nationality, placed under temporary guardianship in virtue of Article 391

*B.W.* The Supreme Court added—*obiter dictum*, moreover—that, even in the case of a well-founded fear of the interests of the infant being neglected (Art. 391, para. 2), the temporary guardianship should give way to the authority appointed by the national law of the infant, that is to say, that it is for that authority to judge whether, having regard to the child's interests, the measures laid down in the national law of the country to which the child belongs should be *modified*.

" As to the question whether the measure of protective upbringing taken on May 5th, 1954, should, after the event, be described as urgent in the sense of Article 7, I would reply in the affirmative. If there could be any hesitation on this point, it would be for a reason of quite another kind: if one admits that the Child Welfare Board was aware of the foreign nationality of the child, it should have applied Article 8 of the Convention and should then have taken action on the basis of the obligations laid upon it by this Convention.

" Article 7 cannot, after the event, be regarded as applicable to the decision of the Government of the Province of Östergötland of June 22nd, 1954, and to the decisions which followed, because the nationality of the father and the appointment of the deputy-guardian were then known. The Government of the Province should have abstained from taking any such decisions and should have left the child to the care of her guardian and the supervision [153] of the deputy-guardian. After the change of guardian, moreover, it was only the child's health which was regarded as a reason for the decisions. Hence, the situation was thenceforward completely governed by the national law. In the Swedish decisions there is to be found no reproach or fear as regards the guardian Mme Postema, except the fear that the child would remain under the influence of the father. Nothing in these decisions justifies any urgent measure for the moral health of the child.

" 6. The second and the more important conclusion that I draw from a comparison of the two systems, the Dutch and the Swedish, for the protection of infants is the following: the provision of Article 22 (*a*) of the Swedish Law of June 6th, 1924, and the measures taken in execution of this single provision are of the same nature as those laid down in the Dutch Law applicable according to the Convention. Obviously, they are directed towards the interest of the infant. The situation before the Child Welfare Board was one for which the rules regarding Dutch guardianship would have offered a similar solution. The case of the physical and moral health of the child, as also for her intellectual and religious education, the choice of schools, the selection of the place of residence for the child best adapted to her interests, are in the hands of the person who has the child's custody under the supervision of the authorities. Once the Convention is involved, it is not the local law but the national law which prevails. In this case, the application of Article 22 (*a*) has, in fact, in contravention of the Convention, prevented the exercise of the guardian's rights and, consequently, of the rights of the Dutch authorities.

" Thus, it is not permissible to put children who are in a vulnerable condition outside the scope of the Convention. How many children of the present day are so vulnerable! It is a subject of anxiety for all parents. It would be interesting to examine the percentage of such cases among children under guardianship.

" It should not be said that the removal of the infant constitutes a danger in the sense of Article 22 (*a*). It is for the national guardian and for the national authorities to see whether, in the circumstances, a removal is possible or whether, temporarily, the child should stay in Sweden. As we know, the guardian had already made arrangements in this sense.

" For these reasons, I am of opinion that the application of Article 22 (*a*) of the Swedish Law of June 6th, 1924, should in this case, be judged incompatible with the Convention, with the exception of the first taking in charge of the child in so far as that falls under Article 7.

" 7. It follows from the foregoing that no obstacle can be placed in the way of the application of the Convention of 1902, on the ground that the whole subject of the Swedish Law on protective [154] upbringing is outside the scope of the Convention, because of the aim of this Law to provide a social guarantee.

" In considering the object of the whole of this Law, the different cases in which it may be applied are no longer distinguished. The Swedish authorities had in view only the protection of the infant against a danger concerning her physical or moral health, and this in the family home. They applied Article 22 (a) only.

" If one views the four cases enumerated in Article 22 according to the same criterion, there is a whole legislative sphere which is much larger than that involved in the present case. Delictual and quasi-delictual situations are included. There is a risk, therefore, of the social guarantee aspect imposing itself imperatively in cases where the interest of the infant prevails. For the same reason also there is reluctance to admit the apparently unacceptable consequences of a Swedish law which has an extraterritorial effect and which would have to be applied to Swedish infants in a foreign country. But these consequences do not arise because the Swedish law is confined to children ' within a (Swedish) commune ' and because if the Convention was applied to such Swedish infants, this would merely mean that the local authorities tolerate the handing over of such an infant to the person who is in charge of him.

" Without making any imputations as to the aims of the Swedish legislators, I think that it might be an attractive policy to include in local legislation rules governing a whole series of matters which, without such rules, would be covered by the Convention, or to unite in one law provisions of a penal and a civil nature, or to pass legislation covering the whole question of the custody of children from the point of view of a social guarantee—and this in opposition to the legislation of those States which, with a view to the protection of children, have included provisions covering the same matter in their Civil Code. Merely by means of the label affixed to a law, the aim of the Convention could thus be defeated.

" It is not, indeed, a question of another subject, but of another purpose in the legislator's mind. In this connection, the English word ' purpose ' is more indicative than the French word ' objet '. The subject-matter is the legal relationship in question and the rules which are applicable to it. In the present case, the legal relationship is constituted by the personal situation of an infant who is not under the *puissance paternelle* or the parental power of her two parents; the legal rules are the provisions governing the custody of such an infant. This subject-matter is the same in all States.

" What is different is the purpose aimed at by the rules. Here the legislators and the courts are guided by ' pre-occupations of a moral and social order '.

" In fact, what is being done is to make an exception for the application of public law enactments or the principles of [155] international *ordre public*, which thus come in again in disguise by the window after having been chased out of the door.

" The Applicant has rightly made an objection with regard to the category of public law enactments. If indeed such a category exists, it has by its absolute and static character a much wider scope than the exception based on international *ordre public*, which is relativist and dynamic and which, in any case, should be applied with great prudence. This exception does at least allow an examination of the question whether, in a concrete case, the points of attachment to the juridical system of the country of residence are strong enough.

" In the case of the Convention on guardianship, I would reject the general exception based on international *ordre public* because in the Hague Conventions which were drawn up at the Conferences of 1893, 1894 and 1900 the general formula of *ordre public* was deliberately rejected and the system of individual treatment of special cases was adhered to—cases in which, for reasons of public or social interest, a different conflict rule seemed necessary. (*Actes* 1893, I, pp. 37–38, 41, 46–47, 74 *et seq.; Actes* 1894, pp. 15, 48, 118, 125 *et seq.*).

" 8. It cannot be denied that there are other subjects which are not included in the Convention, such as *puissance paternelle* and the interdiction of adults. It is a question of terminology and phrasing for the draftsmen of conventions. The laws on compulsory education, vocational training and health supervision, regulate other matters, but that does not mean that the guardian of an infant of foreign nationality does not retain the right to decide the residence of the infant and that he may not, by such decision, put an end to the application of such laws. And if these laws had to be complied with, the guardian would remain in personal contact with the infant to look after his welfare. Everything here depends on the circumstances of the case, and one must not generalize.

" The distinguishing of the competence of administrative organs, to show the powers of local tribunals, is not decisive. The designation as an administrative or a judicial organ is often accidental or secondary. The Swedish Government has described the decision of its Supreme Administrative Court as a judicial one. In the Netherlands it is the Court which appoints the guardian and directs the supervision of the guardianship.

" Also, the application of the Convention does not lead to negative conflicts of jurisdiction. Clearly, the measures of local supervision are not enforceable in other States, but the institution of guardianship, as a whole, as it is regulated by the national law, meets the needs. With regard to the Dutch institutions, I would refer to the provisions enumerated above, which include the measures to be taken by the courts, as well as the action of the Guardianship [156] Council, the Amsterdam Council being competent as regards every infant of Dutch nationality not residing in the Netherlands (compare Arts. 460 to 461d, *B.W.*). These provisions apply in the case of a Netherlands infant residing in Sweden or elsewhere. The guardian is responsible for the care of the infant's health and well-being and he can be removed or other measures can be applied should he fail to discharge his obligations. The local authorities must respect this application of the national law. Inversely, in the case of a Swedish infant who is in the Netherlands or elsewhere, the local authorities are obliged to respect the measures of guardianship ordered in Sweden. In the ' juridical community ' between the contracting States, which has been invoked as far back as the Acts of 1893, it is the rules of the national law which must be observed, in conformity with that reciprocity which is at the basis of the Convention.

" I conclude that only Article 22 (*a*) of the Swedish Law of June 6th, 1924, is in issue and that the maintenance of the measures of protective upbringing is not in conformity with the obligations binding upon Sweden by virtue of the 1902 Convention."

# I.—Commercial Treaties.   Most-Favoured-Nation Clause

**Treaties—Special kinds of treaties—Establishment conventions—Most-favoured-nation clause—Scope of—Most-favoured-nation treatment with regard to taxation of property of nationals of one party in territory of the other—Whether clause operates to extend benefits of nationals of United Nations under Peace Treaty to nationals of most-favoured-nation—Principle of fiscal equality—Customary international law limitations—Italian-Swiss Establishment and Consular Convention, 1868, Article 5—Treaty of Peace with Italy, 1947, Article 78, paragraph 6.**

*Re* APPLICATION TO SWISS NATIONALS OF THE ITALIAN SPECIAL CAPITAL LEVY DUTY.

*Italian-Swiss Permanent Conciliation Commission. October* 9, 1956.

(Gidel, President; de Yanguas Messia, de Visscher, Members; Ago, Member for Italy; Carry, Member for Switzerland.)

THE FACTS.—The Italian-Swiss Permanent Conciliation Commission, provided for in the Treaty of Conciliation and Judicial Settlement between Italy and Switzerland concluded in 1924,[1] was seised of a dispute between the two parties concerning the application to Swiss nationals of the Italian special capital levy duty.[2] The tax, or levy, was instituted by Legislative Decree No. 143 of March 29, 1947. This Decree was amended several times and the position at the time of the dispute was governed by Decree No. 203 of the President of the Italian Republic dated May 9, 1950, which approved the text of the provisions relating to special levies on capital published in the Ordinary Supplement to the *Gazetta Ufficiale*, No. 107 of May 10, 1950.

The Swiss Government contended that this special levy should not apply to the property of Swiss nationals. Their contention was based on the most-favoured-nation clause in Article 5 of the

---

[1] *L.N.T.S.*, vol. 33, p. 92. Article 3 of the Treaty provides:
" The contracting Parties shall establish a Permanent Conciliation Commission composed of five members.
" Each Party shall nominate one member of its own choosing, the other three being appointed by joint agreement. The latter may not be nationals of the Contracting States, nor be domiciled in their territory nor be employed in their service.
" The President of the Commission shall be appointed by joint agreement from among the jointly selected members.
" So long as the procedure has not begun, each Contracting Party shall have the right to revoke the appointment of its nominee and replace him by another, and also to withdraw its consent to the appointment of any of the three members nominated jointly. In this case the necessary replacement shall be effected without delay.
" Members shall be replaced under the same conditions as were observed in their appointment."
[2] This is a convenient English rendering of the French " *impôt extraordinaire sur le patrimoine* " and of the Italian " *imposta straordinaria sul patrimonio* ".

Italian–Swiss Establishment and Consular Convention of 1868[1]
which, it was argued, operated to oblige Italy to exempt from
the special levy those Swiss nationals who belonged to the same
categories as the nationals of the United Nations who were exempt
from the levy by virtue of Article 78, paragraph 6, of the Treaty
of Peace with Italy, 1947.[2]

The Italian Government maintained that this most-favoured-
nation clause could not be invoked in this way. They based their
argument on the common intention of the Parties at the time of
the conclusion of the Establishment Convention of 1868, alleging
that they contemplated the regulation of normal peaceful relations
and did not intend the most-favoured-nation clause to apply to
circumstances of war and the peace treaties that followed. It was
also submitted that a peace treaty fell into a special category and
resembled an imposed settlement rather than a contractual agreement. The parties having failed to settle the dispute by diplomatic
means, the Permanent Conciliation Commission was called upon to
exercise its functions for the first time.

The Report of the Award[3] contains an account of the procedure
followed by the Commission. During a preparatory period the
parties furnished the Commission with full information as to the
object of their claims and also as to the factual circumstances in
which each found justification for their arguments. The Commission held a preliminary session in Paris on July 4 and 5, 1956,
to establish the procedure to be followed in accordance with the
provisions of the Italian–Swiss Treaty of 1924.[4] It met again from
October 10 to 31, 1956, at Aix-en-Provence for the basic examination
of the dispute.

After having heard the oral arguments of the Agents of the
two parties from October 11 to 16, 1956, the Commission decided
to arrive at a preliminary exchange of views in the absence of the

---

[1] See below, p. 316.

[2] Article 78, para. 6, reads: " United Nations nationals and their property shall
be exempted from any exceptional taxes, levies or imposts imposed on their capital
assets in Italy by the Italian Government or any Italian authority between September 3, 1943, and the coming into force of the present Treaty for the specific purpose
of meeting charges arising out of the war or of meeting the costs of occupying forces
or of reparation payable to any of the United Nations. Any sums which have been
so paid shall be refunded."
The Peace Treaty entered into force on September 16, 1947.

[3] *Atti Relativi Alla Vertenza per l'Applicazione ai Cittadini Svizzeri dell'Imposta
Straordinaria Italiana sul Patrimonio*, (published by the Ministry of Foreign Affairs,
Rome, 1960).

[4] Article 7 of the Treaty provides:
" In proceedings before the Commission both Parties shall be heard.
" The Commission shall draw up its own rules of procedure, regard being had to
the regulations laid down in Title III of the Hague Convention of October 18, 1907,
for the pacific settlement of international disputes, unless the Commission unanimously decides otherwise."
The Hague Convention, 1907, is included in *British and Foreign State Papers*,
vol. 100, 1906–1907, p. 298.

Agents. These provisional conclusions on the legal questions were communicated to the Agents in the course of the plenary session of October 18, 1956, without, however, any mention of the legal argument. The President limited himself to stating that the Commission had pursued its exchange of views far enough, but without taking up a definitive position on the questions comprising the subject-matter of the dispute.

The Commission then wished to hear the economic and financial experts who accompanied the Agents. It was decided to create a sub-commission composed of the two national commissioners assisted by the experts. This sub-commission arrived at a provisional text which was submitted to the Agents by the President. It was this text which, with the approval of the Agents and subject to certain modifications of a purely formal nature, became the regulations which are annexed to the report of the Commission.[1]

A new sub-commission, composed of the President and two commissioners chosen by agreement between the parties, was then set up with the task of formulating the report of the Commission. After amendment on some points by the full Commission, the report was unanimously adopted. Contrary to what had occurred with the proposed regulations, it was not officially submitted to the Agents before being accepted by the Commission.

At the last session, on October 31, 1956, the Commission transmitted its report to the Agents, with the regulations annexed to it. In accordance with Article 13 of the Treaty of Conciliation of September 20, 1924, it allowed the parties a period of six weeks[2] to come to a decision on the proposed regulations. In the interim, the Commission remained seised of the dispute.

*Held:* that the Swiss claim must be rejected. Swiss nationals were not entitled to be exempted from the Italian special capital levy duty by virtue of the operation of the most-favoured-nation clause of Article 5 of the Convention of 1868 with regard to Article 78, paragraph 6, of the Peace Treaty of 1947. However, the Commission found that by virtue of the same Article of the Convention of 1868, Swiss nationals were entitled to equality of treatment with regard to Italian law, and that the Italian legislation imposing the special capital levy duty derogated from this standard of equality. The Commission's proposals for an equitable settlement of the dispute were directed at the attainment of equal treatment for Swiss nationals, particularly corporations, in the operation of the special tax. The proposals were in the form of regulations annexed to the Commission's

[1] See below, p. 322.
[2] Article 13 of the Treaty of 1924 provides:
" The Conciliation Commission shall fix the period within which the Parties will be required to take their decision as regards the Commission's proposals.
" This period shall not, however, exceed three months."

Report and providing for certain modifications of the existing Italian legislation on the capital levy duty in favour of Swiss nationals.

Both Governments accepted the Commission's proposals within the specified time limit,[1] and they became binding on both parties.[2]

The Commission said: " Being required to take account of all the relevant questions of law and of fact, the Commission has drawn up the present Report. It has been unanimously adopted by the five members of the Commission and a copy of it has been sent to each of the High Contracting Parties in the person of their Agents.

" The Commission is of the opinion that it is its duty to consider in the first place the legal aspects of the dispute, enabling itself thereafter to take into account the factual elements to serve as a basis for a proposal for settlement. The legal and factual elements have been distinguished with as much skill as care in the written pleadings, and in the oral arguments of the Agents of the two Governments as well as in the depositions and observations of the experts who accompanied the Agents.

" The legal problem has been posed in its widest form by the introductory request in the case of the Swiss Government, dated January 30, 1956. Relying on the most-favoured-nation clause contained in Article 5 of the Italian–Swiss Establishment and Consular Convention of July 22, 1868, the Government of the Confederation considers that Italy is bound to grant complete exemption from the special capital levy duty, which is stipulated in the Italian Law No. 203, of May 9, 1950, to Swiss nationals who belong to the same categories as the nationals of the United Nations who enjoy the exemption formulated by Article 78, paragraph 6, of the Paris Peace Treaty [with Italy] of February 10, 1947.

" The Italian Government has maintained, on the contrary, that the clause in Article 5 of the Convention of Establishment of July 22, 1868, cannot be invoked with regard to the advantages provided for the nationals of the United Nations and for their property by Article 78, paragraph 6, of the Treaty of Peace of February 10, 1947.

" In view of the formal objection of the Italian Government, the central legal problem is to determine the field of application of Article 5 of the Italian–Swiss Convention of Establishment of July 22, 1868.

" The text of this Article is as follows:

' In time of peace as in time of war, there may not, in any circumstances, be imposed or exacted on the property of a national of one of the two States in the territory of the other, taxes, dues, contributions

---

[1] See above, p. 315.

[2] The agreed settlement was published on January 17, 1957, in the *Recueil officiel des lois et ordonnances de la Confédération suisse* (R. O. 1957, p. 44), and February 27, 1958, in the *Gazzetta Ufficiale* of the Italian Republic (No. 50, p. 816), after having been submitted to the Chamber of Deputies and the Senate of the Republic (Law No. 61).

or charges, other than or heavier than shall be imposed or exacted on the same property if it belonged to a national of the State or to a national of the most-favoured-nation. It is further agreed that there will not be collected or demanded from a national of one of the two States who is in the territory of the other, any tax whatsoever, other than or heavier than those which may be imposed or levied on a national of the State or of the most-favoured-nation.'

" Article 5 of the Italian–Swiss Convention of Establishment of July 22, 1868, thus adopts the principle of fiscal equality: equality for the property which a national of one of the two States possesses in the territory of the other; equality also for the persons of the nationals of one of the two States who are in the territory of the co-contracting State. With regard to the position of the nationals of one or other of the two co-contracting States, it is the municipal legislation which determines the content of the rights of which the nationals of one of the two States may take advantage in the other by virtue of the said equality clause. But the idea of equality may also refer to the position of nationals of a third State, the instrument of this equality being in this case the most-favoured-nation clause. This clause envisages three States, which the usual terminology describes as: the grantor State, the favoured State, and the beneficiary State. In this case, according to the Swiss argument, the grantor State would be Italy; the favoured States would be those whose nationals have been exempted by Italy from the special capital levy duty by the provisions of the Treaty of February 10, 1947, to which Switzerland is not a party, but under which she claims this fiscal advantage in the capacity of beneficiary State in the terms of the most-favoured-nation clause included in Article 5 of the Italian-Swiss Convention of Establishment of July 22, 1868.

" The Italian Government has urged a first consideration against the application of this clause, a consideration in which, despite all the skill with which it has been presented, the Commission is unable to concur. From the fact that the conditions of the Peace Treaty were imposed on Italy, and from the fact that the determination of the conditions was not made the object of free negotiations between the Parties to the Treaty, it has been deduced that the exemption of the nationals of the Allied Powers rests upon mere unilateral decisions of these Powers. Therefore, it has been alleged on the Italian side, the non-contractual advantage which arose for these nationals should be considered as outside the scope of the most-favoured-nation clause. The Commission does not share this opinion. Although it may have been motivated by compulsion, the will of the defeated State nevertheless enters into a Treaty of Peace, into each and every one of the clauses which it contains. If it were not so, then the very character of a treaty would have to be denied to any Treaty of Peace bringing to an end a victorious war.

" The question has already been decided in this way, and precisely in relation to the same Treaty of Peace of February 10, 1947, by the Italian–French Conciliation Commission (*Recueil des décisions de la Commission franco-italienne*, Part 4, No. 136, June 25, 1952[1]) and by the Italian–American Conciliation Commission in the dispute relating to the exercise of diplomatic protection in the case of dual nationality. It was claimed on the American side that, as the Peace Treaty was unilateral, only the will of the American Government was material for the attribution of nationality. The Commission, agreeing unanimously with the opinion of the Third Arbitrator, formally rejected this point of view (Decision of June 10, 1955, in the case of *Strunsky-Mergé* v. *The Republic of Italy*, Case No. 3[2]).

" But, on the other hand, the arguments developed with great skill by the Agent of the Federal Government raise serious doubts. The arguments invoked in support of the Swiss case will be repeated here only in so far as they are indispensable to the statement of the opinion of the Commission.

" In order to extend the operation of the most-favoured-nation clause to the provisions of Article 78, paragraph 6, of the Paris Peace Treaty of February 10, 1947, the absolute form of Article 5 of the Establishment Convention of July 22, 1868, has been relied upon: ' in time of peace as in time of war, there may not, in any circumstances . . . '. It is recognised that the first formula (' in time of peace as in time of war ') has a purely temporal meaning. The second (' in any circumstances ') cannot itself attribute an extravagant function to the clause and one which would be in contradiction to its well known role in international life, which is the role of ensuring equality of treatment to the nationals of different States in normal legal relations. Now, the extension claimed here on the basis of the most-favoured-nation clause would have the effect of extending the exceptional inequality provided for by Article 78 of the Treaty of February 10, 1947. Undoubtedly, the text is clear and, as such, as has been said, it does not need interpretation. But merely to understand a text and to keep it within the limits of its object is not to interpret it.

" The most-favoured-nation clause has limits to its application which are definite and, in the main, hallowed by international practice. Whether or not they are reserved by express provisions, they may be considered as traditional or customary or imposed by the very role of the clause in the relations between States. The Economic Committee of the League of Nations observed (Doc. L. of N., C.20, M 14, 1929, II, p. 11) with regard to restrictions in

[1 *Re Rizzo and Others*: *International Law Reports*, 1952, p. 478.]
[2 *International Law Reports*, 1955, p. 443, sub nom. *Mergé Claim*.]

the matter of the most-favoured-nation clause concerning frontier traffic:

' In any case it must be recognized that the exception concerning frontier traffic is imposed not only by a long tradition, but by the nature of the case and that it is impossible, because of the different factual situations, to establish precisely the extent of the frontier zone destined to benefit from a special régime.'

The same limitations or exclusions are noted particularly in matters of colonial preference, customs or other unions, and double taxation conventions.

" All these limitations have the same basis and the same common feature. All of them, in effect, assume the existence between two or more States of certain relations which are not identical with or have no possible equivalent in the relations between these States and a State which, however, wishes to take advantage of the most-favoured nation clause *vis-à-vis* these States.

" This is exactly the case in the dispute submitted to the Commission. The relations which gave rise to the Treaty of February 10, 1947, between Italy and the Allied Powers were the relations of belligerency and post-belligerency, of conqueror and conquered, and which alone could serve to justify the exemption from the special tax on capital contained in Article 78, paragraph 6, of this Peace Treaty. The absence of similar relations between Italy and Switzerland excludes the operation of the most-favoured-nation clause for the benefit of the latter.

" It is not possible to claim that the exemption clause contained in Article 78, paragraph 6, should be regarded as an autonomous element of the Peace Treaty and without connection with the whole of the Treaty. It is, on the contrary, an inseparable part of the Treaty and one which, detached from its general economic system, would lose all meaning and justification.

" It is equally of little relevance that the clause of Article 5 of the Italian–Swiss Establishment Convention of 1868 is aimed at substantially the same taxes and duties as those from which Article 78, paragraph 6, of the Peace Treaty of February 10, 1947 has provided exemption in favour of nationals of the Allied Nations. Similar identity would indeed allow Switzerland to invoke the benefit of the clause if the exemption from similar fiscal dues granted by Italy for the benefit of nationals of third States tended to favour economic relations of the same kind as those which exist between Switzerland and Italy. This is exactly the case in the two precedents presented in support of the argument of the Swiss Government, but which the Commission does not consider can be relied upon in the sense contended for.

" In 1922, by virtue of Article 6 of the Franco–Swiss Treaty of Establishment of 1882, Switzerland obtained the benefit of the provisions of Article 2, paragraph 2, of the Franco–Spanish Consular Convention of January 7, 1862, and Swiss nationals were thus exempted in France from the special tax on war profits imposed by a French Law of 1916 and which was considered as not applicable to Spanish nationals resident in France. The other case relied upon is that of the forced loans which had been raised in Italy at the time of the wars of liberation, and from which the exemption granted to British nationals by the Treaty of August 6, 1863, was extended to Swiss nationals by the terms of the Declarations of December 10 and 21, 1866. According to the Agent of the Federal Government, these declarations represented an application by anticipation of the most-favoured-nation clause which was to be sanctioned by the Italian–Swiss Convention of July 22, 1868, and therefore furnished an important element for the interpretation of the Convention. It is to be noted, however, that after this last Convention, a Protocol signed on May 1, 1869, provided that the abrogation of these Declarations would take place on October 29, 1873, at the same time as that of the Anglo-Italian Treaty of August 6, 1863. Perhaps the relationship between these various documents remains rather obscure. Moreover, even if it is correct, as the Agent of the Swiss Government maintains, that the Treaty of 1868 did cover the exemption from the Italian forced loans of the wars of liberation, there is still, with regard to the case submitted to the Commission, the fundamental difference that the relations justifying the exemption granted by Italy to British nationals did not differ in any respect from those which existed between Switzerland and Italy. In the present claim of the Swiss Government, on the contrary, it is a question of extending provisions based on a state of belligerency to the relations existing between two States who have only known unchanging friendly relations.

" Such are, in the opinion of the Commission, the indisputably grave objections raised by the argument of the Swiss Government.

" As regards the most-favoured-nation clause, the main basis of the Swiss claim, Article 5 of the Convention of 1868, also contains the provisions, recalled above, which guarantee, whether to the property or to the persons of the nationals of one of the two States in the territory of the other State, a treatment at least equal to that of nationals. It is a question of the clause called the equality clause, mentioned above.

" There is no doubt, in the opinion of the Commission, that by virtue of this clause Switzerland would be fully entitled to demand equality of treatment with regard to Italian law, and in particular with regard to the special capital levy duty. The principle of this equality is mentioned, moreover, in Article 5 of the Legislative Decree No. 1131 of October 11, 1947, (*Testo unico*, No. 203, Article 5). Yet the Italian provisions at present in force have obviously derogated from this equality on an important point. Foreign corporations are subject to the progressive levy on the total amount of capital invested or held in Italy, with a deduction of the registered shares already taxed in the name of physical persons—the levy being established, moreover, on a basis reduced by one-third and limited to a maximum rate of 15 per cent. Italian corporations, on the other hand, bear a proportional tax varying from 2 per cent. to 4 per cent., but with a progressive rate on the shares of the members. The equalization of the treatment of Swiss and Italian corporations in this respect is the object of the present claims on the part of the Federal Government, which, in the opinion of the Commission, seem to be justified.

" The equality of treatment guaranteed to the nationals of the co-contracting States constitutes an impassable limit to fiscal demands. And the desire of the parties engaged in the dispute to develop their relations of commerce and friendship has led them to grant more favourable treatment in many spheres to these nationals than to their own nationals. In the present case, such treatment could be justified in particular by the double taxation which is imposed, in consequence of the different fiscal régimes of the two States, on the movable assets in Italy of Swiss tax-payers resident in Switzerland and by the fact, on the other hand, that Swiss nationals are not entitled to compensation for war damage to their property in Italy.

" Taking into account these different considerations and making use of the factual data which emerged in the course of the negotiations, the Commission has endeavoured to arrive at an equitable settlement of the dispute. It has been greatly assisted in this task by the skill of the Agents of the two Governments and of their experts.

" Therefore, the Commssion has the honour to submit for the approval of the two Governments the annexed Regulations for the settlement of their dispute, adopted unanimously by the members of the Commission. The two texts, French and Italian, should each be considered as expressing precisely the thought of the Commission. The Commission proposes to the two Governments that each of the texts be considered of equal validity.

" It is understood that the opinion of the Commission on points of law may not be invoked by the parties before any tribunal, judicial or arbitral.

" In accordance with Article 13 of the Treaty of Conciliation and Judicial Settlement between Italy and Switzerland of September 20, 1924,[1] the Commission has fixed the period within which the parties are to come to a decision with regard to this settlement and to communicate their decision to the President of the Commission, at six weeks reckoned from November 1, 1956.

[1 See above, p. 315.]

" Until the parties have come to a decision, the Commission remains seised of the dispute."

### Annex to the Report of the Italian–Swiss Permanent Conciliation Commission

The Italian–Swiss Permanent Conciliation Commission proposes to the Italian and Swiss Governments the following settlement of the dispute which has arisen between them as to the application to Swiss nationals of the Italian special capital levy duty:

### Article I

There will be eligible to benefit from the advantages stated in Articles II to V, Swiss taxpayers who, on March 28, 1947, were in the following categories:

(a) physical persons of Swiss nationality who do not at the same time possess Italian nationality, whatever may be their domicile or residence;

(b) partnerships constituted in Switzerland and according to Swiss law;

(c) corporations and other juridical persons constituted according to Swiss law and having their *siège* in Switzerland.

### Article II

1. A special period of 90 days from the entry into force of the present settlement is granted to the Swiss taxpayers designated in Article I for:

presenting a declaration indicating all their taxable property, in accordance with the Italian Law No. 203 of May 9, 1950, or

confirming or completing the declaration which they have already presented.

2. The declaration referred to in the preceding paragraph must be presented to the Italian offices authorized by virtue of Article 45 of the Italian Law No. 203 of May 9, 1950. These will proceed with the assessments in accordance with the Italian Law No. 203 of May 9, 1950, and with the provisions of the present settlement. In the case of disagreement with the Swiss taxpayer, they will transmit the file to the Minister of Finance, ' *Direction générale pour les finances extraordinaires* ', in Rome, who will examine the disputed case and, if appropriate, will hear the Swiss taxpayer.

3. Swiss taxpayers, whose assessment under the head of the Italian special levy duty has already become final before the entry into force of the present settlement will, nevertheless, be able to take advantage of the special period mentioned in the first paragraph of the present Article. In the case where the new assessment based on the present settlement is more favourable than the former assessment, the sums paid in excess will be refunded to them.

4. The Swiss taxpayers mentioned in Article I who have made declarations in accordance with the first paragraph of the present Article will be exempt, as regards their conduct prior to the said declarations, from all sanction or penalty, including interest on overdue payments, provided by the Italian fiscal legislation.

## Article III

1. The physical persons mentioned in Article I (*a*) remain in principle subject to the Italian special progressive capital levy duty. Nevertheless, they enjoy the advantages mentioned in the following paragraphs of the present Article.

2. The Italian administration will proceed with the valuation and assessment of the property of physical persons by accepting the declarations produced by them under the conditions laid down in Article II. This administration will, however, have the power to correct the valuation of the property declared by increasing its value within the following limits:

(*a*) for industrial, commercial and agricultural land, buildings and enterprises of all kinds: up to the value which was inscribed or which ought to have been inscribed in 1947 in the register of the ordinary capital levy duty for the year 1947, it being understood that this value is:

for land and enterprises: the value held for the ordinary capital levy duty for the year 1946, multiplied by the coefficient 10, and

for buildings: the value held for the ordinary capital levy duty for the year 1946, multiplied by the coefficient 5;

(*b*) for ' goodwill' ('*avviamento*') within the meaning of Article 17, paragraph 2, of Italian Law No. 203 of May 9, 1950: up to double the amount of the taxable income established for the enterprise in question in the matter of the '*imposta di ricchezza mobile*' for the year 1947;

(*c*) for shares and other movable securities not quoted on the Stock Exchange: up to an amount not exceeding the lesser of the two following values:

either the value held for the '*tassa di negoziazione*' for the year 1946 (based according to Italian law on the value held for 1945);

or the value which was inscribed or which ought to have been inscribed in 1947 in the register of the ordinary capital levy duty for the year 1947;

(*d*) for shares and other securities quoted on the Stock Exchange: up to the value fixed by Article 18 of Italian Law No. 203 of May 9, 1950, with an overall reduction [*globale et forfaitaire*] of 50 per cent. of that value.

3. It is specified that:

(*a*) intangible property, mentioned in Article 6, No. 9, of Italian Law No. 203 of May 9, 1950, is only taxable as part of the capital of the person who exploits it on Italian territory and not as part of the capital of the person who assigned the property or the right to use it;

(*b*) the assets in Italy of persons resident in Switzerland comprising the proceeds of sale of goods, royalties, interest or dividends, which ought to have been transferred but which were not capable of transfer before March 28, 1947, because of restrictions in the matter of clearing, will not be subject to the Italian tax;

(*c*) no additional duty under the head of "*denaro, depositi e titoli di credito al portatore*" (Article 26 of Italian Law No. 203 of May 9, 1950) will be charged if the taxpayer is not resident in Italy;

(*d*) if a physical person possesses, by right of being a partner with unlimited liability, a share in a partnership constituted in Italy, there will be prepared, for the purpose of the assessment of the partner, an estimate of the different elements of the partnership assets taking into account the valuations provided for in paragraph 2 of the present Article;

(e) if a physical person possesses a share in an ordinary limited partnership constituted in Italy, the valuation of the share will be made according to paragraph 2 (c) of the present Article.

## Article IV

1. The Swiss corporations and juridical persons mentioned in Article I (b) and (c) remain, in principle, subject to the Italian special progressive capital levy duty, reduced by one-third with a maximum rate of 15 per cent. within the meaning of Article 2 and the last paragraph of Article 31 of Italian Law No. 203 of May 9, 1950. However, they enjoy the same facilities for the valuation of their taxable property as those granted to physical persons by Article III, paragraph 2.

2. The Swiss taxpayers mentioned in paragraph 1 of the present Article may ask to be made subject to the proportional capital levy duty provided for in Chapter II of Italian Law No. 203 of May 9, 1950, instead of the progressive capital levy duty calculated according to the rules stated in paragraph 1 above. In this case, the Italian administration will prepare a new assessment of the taxable property and will grant a sufficient period to the Swiss taxpayers concerned for declaring whether they wish to be subject to the progressive levy or to the proportional levy.

3. Whichever levy is applied, progressive or proportional, it is stipulated that:

(a) intangible property, mentioned in Article 6, No. 9, of Italian Law No. 203 of May 9, 1950, is not taxable except as part of the capital of the person who exploits it on Italian territory and not as part of the capital of the Swiss taxpayer who assigned the property or the right to use it;

(b) the assets in Italy of Swiss taxpayers mentioned in the first paragraph of the present Article, comprising the proceeds of sale of goods, royalties, interest or dividends, which ought to have been transferred but which were not capable of transfer before March 28, 1947, because of restrictions in the matter of clearing, will not be subject to the Italian tax;

(c) no additional duty provided for by Article 26 of Italian Law No. 203 of May 9, 1950, will be collected from the Swiss taxpayers mentioned in the first paragraph of the present Article;

(d) the " goodwill " ("avviamento ") within the meaning of Article 17, paragraph 2, of Italian Law No. 203 of May 9, 1950, will only be taken into account, in the event of it being taxable, at the value fixed by Article III, paragraph 2 (b);

(e) the technical reserves of the permanent establishments situated in Italy of Swiss insurance companies are not subject to the special capital levy duty. In consequence, the amount of the said reserves will be deducted from the assets of the permanent establishment, if the tax is imposed on the other elements of those assets;

(f) the provisions of Article III, paragraph 3 (d) and (e), apply equally to Swiss corporations and juridical persons.

## Article V

1. The special capital levy duty due by virtue of Italian Law No. 203 of May 9, 1950, and of Articles III and IV of this settlement, may be paid by the taxpayers referred to in Article I over a period of two years and

in twelve bi-monthly instalments.  This period commences from the date
when, the assessment having become final in whole or in part, the tax
due is inscribed on the register.

2. The suspension of the measures of fiscal execution provided for in
the Italian–Swiss Protocol of Negotiations of December 15, 1951, and confirmed by the circular of the Italian Minister of Finances of February 18,
1952, will remain in force until the present settlement is. put into effect.

### Article VI

1. A joint commission, composed of representatives chosen by the
Italian and Swiss Governments, will be authorized to settle amicably
disputed cases resulting from the application or the interpretation of the
present settlement.

2. This joint commission will meet alternately in Italy and in Switzerland each time that one of the two Governments requests it.  It will be
presided over by one of its members belonging to the State on whose
territory the meeting takes place.

### Article VII

The present settlement will enter into effect on the thirtieth day
from the date on which the Italian–Swiss Permanent Conciliation Commission takes cognizance of the acceptance of the said settlement by the
Italian and Swiss Governments.


[Report: *Atti Relativi alla Vertenza per l'Applicazione ai Cittadini
Svizzeri dell 'Imposta Straordinaria Italiana sul Patrimonio* (published
by the Ministry of Foreign Affairs, Rome, 1960) (in French).]

NOTE.—*Cf.* the award of the Franco-Italian Conciliation Commission
of August 29, 1949, *Recueil des Décisions*, Part 1, p. 95, reported in
*International Law Reports*, 1951, p. 406 (*sub nom. Re Italian Special
Capital Levy Duties*), which deals with a similar Italian capital levy duty
and its application to French nationals.

## II.—Peace Treaties

**Treaties—Special kinds of—Peace treaties—Analogous instruments—Agreement on German External Debts, 1953—Annex IV, Article 6, para. 2, and Annex VII, Section 1 (2)—Interpretation of—Meaning of " specific foreign character " of debts and of " original written debt arrangements "—Principles of interpretation—Literal construction.**

BODENKREDITBANK IN BASEL AND THE SWISS CONFEDERATION *v.* GEBRÜDER ROHRER GMBH. AND THE GERMAN FEDERAL REPUBLIC.

*Mixed Commission for the Agreement on German External Debts.*

(Daehli, President; Michelson, Barandon, Members; Hinderling, Duden, Members *ad hoc.*[1])

*November 7,* 1956

THE FACTS (as stated by the Commission).—" In the years 1927 to 1931 the Applicant, the Bodenkreditbank in Basel, granted loans in Germany, which were secured by mortgages. It procured the money in Swiss francs in Switzerland, partly by the issue of bonds. As security for these bonds the German mortgage deeds were deposited by the Bodenkreditbank with the Schweizerische Treuhandgesellschaft at Basle.

" In the course of this business the Applicant, in the year 1931, granted to the Respondent, Gebrüder Rohrer, a loan to the amount of GM 100,000, of which GM 74,000 have not been repaid. The value of the Goldmark was fixed as ' 1/2790 kilogram of fine gold pursuant to the Ordinance of April 17, 1924 (*RGBl.*, I, p. 415) '.

" ' The seat of the creditors for the time being ' was agreed as the place of payment and of performance.

" No dispute arises as to the amount of the claim.

" The dispute relates to the rate of conversion of the Goldmark claim into Deutschemarks. In the case of an inland claim this rate would be at 10:1, but in the case of a Goldmark claim with a specific foreign character within the meaning of Article 6 (2) of Annex IV and Section I (2) of Annex VII [of the Agreement on German External Debts, 1953[2]], at the rate of 1:1. The Applicant and the Swiss Government, which has become a party to the case, assert that the claim in the present case has such a specific foreign character. The Government of the Federal Republic of Germany, which has also become a party to the case, contests this. The Respondent, Gebrüder Rohrer, would in any case have to bear only the amount which would result from the conversion of an inland claim (rate of 10:1). It would be indemnified in respect of the balance paid

---

[1] Nominated, respectively, by the Swiss Federal Council and the Government of the German Federal Republic.

[2] *U.N.T.S.*, vol. 333, p. 4, Annex VII is entitled: " Agreement on Goldmark Liabilities and Reichsmark Liabilities with a Gold Clause, having a Specific Foreign Character " (*ibid.*, p. 238).]

in application of the conversion rate of 1:1 by the *Land* [of] Baden-Württemberg under §§ 63 *et seqq.* of the German Law of August 24, 1953, for implementing the Debt Agreement. The Respondent is therefore not interested in the result of the dispute and submits to the judgment of the Commission.

" It is the interposition of a German trustee which has given rise to the dispute concerning the nature of the transaction and of the claim; this was effected in the following manner:

" Gerbrüder Rohrer had negotiated with the Bodenkreditbank in Basel concerning the granting of a loan of the amount of GM 100,000, secured by a mortgage. In a letter of February 26, 1931, addressed to Gebrüder Rohrer, the Bodenkreditbank stated:

' We are ready to grant you . . . a loan of GM 100,000 at $7\frac{1}{2}\%$ interest p.a. . . .'

Then come conditions concerning the duration, amortization, security and guarantee and then follows:

' Annexed you will find the offer of the loan in duplicate with the request that you will cause one copy to be returned to us with your signature. We enclose the precedent of our loan deed and would remark that we are transferring our rights under the loan agreement to the Aktiengesellschaft für Kapitalanlagen at Frankfort on Main, in whose favour the mortgage is consequently to be drawn up. As a matter of course we warrant the punctual payment of the amount of the loan and you will incur no expenses by reason of the transfer or payment of interest.'

In the above-mentioned offer of loan, also dated February 26, 1931, the Bodenkreditbank in Basel declares its readiness to grant to Gebrüder Rohrer a loan of GM 100,000 secured by a mortgage on the plot of land situated at Lindenstrasse 14, Stuttgart. After mentioning a number of conditions for the loan it is stated at the end of the loan offer:

' Moreover, in addition to the above-mentioned conditions the general loan conditions of the bank, which are known to the borrowers and which are contained in the general precedent of the debt deed, shall apply.'

" This precedent, which was attached to the offer of loan, is headed ' Debt deed ' (*Schuldurkunde*) and is described as a 'draft'. The names of the officiating notary and of the party who makes the declaration of debt are left blank. After that it reads:

' The persons appearing declared: We acknowledge to have received from the Aktiengesellschaft für Kapitalanlagen at Frankfort a.M. a loan of GM 100,000 in cash, subject to the following agreed conditions: . . .'

It is not, therefore, the Bodenkreditbank which appears here as the lender but the Aktiengesellschaft für Kapitalanlagen. This company was a subsidiary of the Bodenkreditbank. Among the agreed conditions contained in the draft deed, it is stated in paragraph 6:

' The place of payment of the capital and instalments thereof as well as of the interest and all other contractual obligations shall be the seat of the creditors for the time being, where all payments are to be effected at the cost and risk of the borrowers and the landowners. The same applies to the place of performance.'

On March 3, 1931, Gebrüder Rohrer accepted the loan offer of February 26, 1931, to which this precedent of the loan deed was annexed, by means of the following declaration:

' The undersigned borrowers accept in every particular the above offer of the Bodenkreditbank in Basel.'

Following upon this declaration of acceptance a notarial debt deed of Gebrüder Rohrer was executed on March 6, 1931, in the presence of the notary Hermann Heimberger at Stuttgart (appointed by the Bodenkreditbank), in which the Aktiengesellschaft für Kapitalanlagen appears as creditor, and the contents of which correspond to the precedent of the debt deed. To secure the debt the agreed mortgage was on March 10, 1931, entered in the Land Register, again in favour of the Aktiengesellschaft für Kapitalanlagen. The mortgage deed was not transmitted to the creditor mentioned therein, but was sent by the notary to the Bodenkreditbank in Basel. In his accompanying letter of March 14, 1931, addressed to the Bodenkreditbank, the notary describes the loan secured by the mortgage deed as one which was granted by the Bodenkreditbank and describes the mortgage as one to which the Bodenkreditbank is entitled (' your mortgage '). Accordingly, Gebrüder Rohrer in a letter of March 14, 1931, requested the Bodenkreditbank in Basel (not the Aktiengesellschaft für Kapitalanlagen) to pay over the amount of the loan, and again it was the Bodenkreditbank which caused its Swiss banking connexions to pay the amount to the accounts specified by the borrowers.

" Initially, the debtor paid interest into a bank account of the Aktiengesellschaft für Kapitalanlagen at Frankfurt a.M.; for the period beginning October 1, 1931, the instalments of interest and capital which became due from time to time at the end of each period were paid to Basel to the Bodenkreditbank. The mortgage, which was registered in favour of the Aktiengesellschaft für Kapitalanlagen, was assigned by the notarially certified deed of April 9, 1931, to the Bodenkreditbank which, as has been said, was already in possession of the mortgage deed. On December 4, 1931, Gebrüder Rohrer were informed of the assignment to the Bodenkreditbank in Basel.

" By declaration of March 9, 1933, Gebrüder Rohrer ' expressly ' acknowledged the applicability of a decision of the Economic Court of the *Reich* of November 10, 1932, to its mortgage debt. According to this decision a loan secured by a mortgage which the Bodenkreditbank in Basel had granted to the Gemeinnützige Heimstättenbaugesellschaft der B.V.G. Gmbh., Berlin, was to be deemed a financial transaction analogous to a loan effected abroad within the meaning of the Emergency Legislation concerning Reduction of Interest (§ 7, paragraph 2, of the Fourth Emergency Ordinance of December 8, 1931 (*RGBl.*, I, p. 702, first part, Chapter III, Section 1) and Article 17, paragraph 2, of the Executory Ordinance of December 23, 1931 (*RGBl.*, I, p. 793)).

" The loan of the Bodenkreditbank to Gebrüder Rohrer was also continuously treated by the exchange control authorities as a foreign debt within the meaning of the provisions of the above mentioned legislation concerning interest.

" These facts are not disputed. In particular, it is not disputed that the Aktiengesellschaft für Kapitalanlagen was interposed as trustee for the Bodenkreditbank. There remains for decision the question whether, as a result of the above-mentioned facts, the claim of the Bodenkreditbank has a specific foreign character within the meaning of the Debt Agreement and its Annexes.

" The Bodenkreditbank in Basel and the Swiss Federal Council have requested:

' that it be determined that the debt of the debtor, now amounting to GM 74,000, secured by a mortgage on the plot of land situated at Stuttgart, 14 Kienestrasse, entered in the Land Register, Stuttgart, volume No. 7045 (Section III, Serial No. 14), has a specific foreign character within the meaning of Annex IV, Article 6 (2), in conjunction with Annex VII, Section I (2), to the London Agreement on German External Debts of February 27, 1953.'

" The Government of the Federal Republic of Germany has requested :

' that the request of the creditor for the determination of the specific foreign character of its Goldmark claim arising out of a loan of an original amount of GM 100,000 in accordance with the debt deed of March 6, 1931, be rejected, and that it be determined that the said claim does not have a specific foreign character within the meaning of Annex VII to the Agreement on German External Debts of February 27, 1953."

*Held:* that the claim must succeed. The debt had a " specific foreign character ".

The Commission said: " The claim which is the subject of the dispute falls under the provisions of Annex IV to the Debt Agreement, as it is a claim against a ' non-public debtor ' which arose out of a financial transaction and which was originally below the sum of U.S.-$40,000 or its equivalent (at the rate of exchange on July 1, 1952) (Article 2 (2) (*d*) of Annex IV).

" Article 6 of Annex IV reads as follows:

' *Conversion into Deutsche Mark*

' (1) Claims expressed in Reichsmark shall be settled after the foreign creditor has declared his agreement to his claim being converted into Deutsche Mark at the same rate as would apply in the case of a similar claim of a domestic creditor. This applies also to such monetary claims expressed in Goldmark or Reichsmark with a gold clause as have no specific foreign character within the meaning of the following paragraph (2). The German Foreign Exchange Control Authorities shall continue to issue any licence necessary for a conversion pursuant to the Conversion Law or for a modification of the conversion rate pursuant to the legislation on Deutsche Mark balance sheets, to the extent that the creditor is entitled to such conversion or modification.

' (2) The principle is accepted that such monetary claims arising from financial transactions and mortgages, expressed in Goldmark or in Reichsmark with a gold clause, as had a specific foreign character, shall be converted into Deutsche Mark at the rate of 1 Goldmark, or 1 Reichsmark with a gold clause, = 1 Deutsche Mark.

' The definition of the criteria constituting the specific foreign character of such claims shall be the subject of further negotiation. The contracting parties reserve their position as to the question in which cases and in which way the above principle can be implemented. It shall lie with the German Delegation to decide how the solution arrived at can be fitted into the framework of the German laws on currency reform and on the equalization of war and post-war burdens.

' The above-mentioned negotiations between a German Delegation and the creditors' representatives should take place not later than October 31, 1952.'

" This definition of the criteria constituting a specific foreign character was effected by Annex VII to the Debt Agreement: ' Agreement on Goldmark Liabilities and Reichsmark Liabilities with a Gold Clause, having a Specific Foreign Character ', dated November 21, 1952.[1] Section I of this Agreement contains the following provisions:

' I.—In respect of the claims and rights specified below it is recognized that they have a specific foreign character within the meaning of the above-mentioned provisions.

1. Claims expressed in Goldmarks or in Reichsmarks with a gold clause or a gold option arising out of bonds made out by German debtors and issued or placed abroad, if—

(a) they constitute a loan, the conditions of which show that it was intended for investment, sale or negotiation in foreign countries only. Where the interest on any bond has been exempt from taxation of capital yield, the bond shall be considered as forming part of a loan which was intended for investment, sale or negotiation in foreign countries only;

(b) they are payable in foreign countries only under the terms of the bonds.

Any part of a loan which differs from the other parts of the loan in respect of special designation or special treatment in Germany as regards taxation or quotation shall likewise be considered as a loan within the meaning of (a) or (b) above, except where the bonds belonging to such part of a loan were officially quoted on a German Stock Exchange before September 1, 1939.

[1 *U.N.T.S.*, vol. 333, p. 238.]

2. Claims expressed in Goldmarks, or in Reichsmarks with a gold clause or a gold option, arising from other loans or advances resulting from financial transactions and raised abroad by German debtors, including claims of this kind secured by mortgage charges; if

(a) it was expressly agreed under the original written debt arrangements that the place of payment or the competent court is situated abroad or foreign law is applicable; and if

(b) whenever the debt was incurred after July 31, 1931, the equivalent was made available in foreign currency, free Reichsmarks or gold, or originates in a blocked Reichsmark account to which repayments on a Goldmark or foreign currency loan from a foreign country granted before July 31, 1931, had been credited, provided that the foreign creditor has again loaned out the amounts withdrawn from the blocked Reichsmark account, with the consent of the competent German Foreign Exchange Control Authorities, to some other German debtor, stipulating a gold clause or gold option Clause for such renewed loan.

' A loan or advance shall likewise be deemed to have been raised in a foreign country if the debtor was aware, when the indebtedness was incurred, that the German creditor, by virtue of a trusteeship contract, was merely the trustee of a foreign lender. A loan or advance raised from the foreign trustee of a German lender shall not be deemed to have been raised in a foreign country.'

" A Sub-Annex to Annex VII, ' Annex to Agreement of November 21, 1952, on Goldmark Liabilities and Reichsmark Liabilities with a Gold Clause, having a Specific Foreign Character ', reads in part as follows:

' The following provisions shall constitute an Annex to the Agreement dated November 12, 1952:—

1. . . .

2. It is agreed that the existence of a "trusteeship contract", as referred to in the last paragraph of Article I (2) of the Agreement of November 21, 1952, may be proved not only by a document of contract or letters referring to the trusteeship but also by the treatment of the foreign lender as a creditor which was extended to him over the years by the competent German foreign exchange control authorities.'

" The provisions of Annex VII and its Sub-Annexes are also applicable to Goldmark liabilities falling under Annex I and Annex II to the Debt Agreement (see Sub-Annex D (2) and (3) to Annex I and Article V (3) of Annex II).

" The ' specific foreign character' of a pecuniary claim is a term which was created at the London Conference on German External Debts.

" Before the Mixed Commission the question was raised whether the criteria contained in Section I (2) (a) of Annex VII were to be regarded as prerequisites or whether the foreign character of a Goldmark liability can be affirmed on other grounds if these conditions are not fulfilled. The question was raised whether in the present case these criteria are to be found; in particular, which of the documents in the case should be regarded as ' the original written debt arrangements ', and whether one of the conditions contained in Section I (2) (a) is contained in these documents. In connection with this question the further question was raised whether in determining the place of payment regard should be had to the seat of the beneficial owner of the claim or to the seat of the trustee.

"Finally, the last paragraph of Section I (2) of the Agreement contained in Annex VII dealing with trusts was also discussed during the proceedings. According to this provision

> ' A loan or advance shall likewise be deemed to have been raised in a foreign country if the debtor was aware, when the indebtedness was incurred, that the German creditor by virtue of a trusteeship contract was merely the trustee of a foreign lender.'

According to the wording of this last paragraph of Section I (2) of the Agreement, if such a trusteeship contract exists, the loan is to be deemed to have been ' raised in a foreign country ', but in order to constitute a specific foreign character the criteria contained in Section I (2) (a) are also required. On behalf of the Bodenkredit-bank and the Swiss Federal Council it was pointed out that such an interpretation would make the last paragraph meaningless, as it could hardly have been the intention of the parties, when they interposed an inland trustee, to agree expressly on a foreign place of payment in the debt arrangements. In this connection it was mentioned that in Annex VII, Section IV, the word ' prerequisite ' is used in contradistinction to the word ' criteria ' used in the second paragraph of Article 6 (2) of Annex IV.

"The Mixed Commission does not think it necessary either to decide the question whether the foreign character of a Goldmark liability can also be admitted without the presence of the criteria contained in Section I (2) (a) or to clarify the connection between the trusteeship clause in the last paragraph of Section I (2) and the provisions of Section I (2) (a), since it has come to the conclusion that in the present case the requirements of Section I (2) (a) are met.

"This results from the ' original written arrangements ' between the lender and the debtor. The Commission considers that, in a case such as the present, in which the lender was a foreigner, the money was raised abroad, the mortgage security was given for the benefit of the foreign lender, and the trustee relationship was known to the debtor, it should not interpret too narrowly the expression ' original written debt arrangements '. It has not been overlooked that the original legal creditor specified in the mortgage deed was the Aktiengesellschaft für Kapitalanlagen. But the ' original written arrangements ' are not necessarily limited to the written arrangements which are necessary for the creation of the debt. In the present case the assignment of the mortgage by the Aktiengesellschaft für Kapitalanlagen as trustee to the Bodenkreditbank as beneficiary and lender, which was effected immediately following the payment over of the loan and was intended from the outset, must in any event be included amongst the ' original written arrangements '. For the possibility of such an assignment of the mortgage is specifically indicated in the deed of February 26—March 3, 1931, and in the notarial deed of March 6, 1931, in that the seat of the ' creditor for the time being ' was mentioned as the place of payment and of performance; nor could it have escaped the notice of the borrower, which was cognizant of the trustee relationship and knew, moreover, that the Bodenkreditbank had been from the outset in the possession of the mortgage deed, that the lender could require the assignment of the mortgage to itself at any time at its own discretion. The assignment can, therefore, not be detached from the entirety of all the earlier related events and considered in isolation. Since, on the contrary, the assignment was from the beginning recognized contractually as permissible independently of the statutory legal position and, moreover, followed immediately after the payment over of the loan, it seems a natural consequence of the legal position created by the trustee relationship and the arrangements with the debtor, and must be appreciated together with the other ' original ' arrangements as an emanation and a part of them.

" The expression ' original written arrangements ' in Section I (2) (a) of Annex VII to the Debt Agreement, and particularly the English non-technical word ' arrangements ', is a very comprehensive term. It is also more comprehensive than the term used in the other Annexes to the Debt Agreement. In Annex I, Section 7 (1) (e) and (g), and in Annex II, Article II, the expression ' original contract ' is used. The use of the more comprehensive term in Annex VII is a further justification for a more comprehensive consideration of the documents than would be the case in Annex I and Annex II.

" As stated above, one must not overlook the fact that the Aktiengesellschaft für Kapitalanlagen was in point of time the first creditor, but this cannot be decisive of the issue. Moreover, the Bodenkreditbank started with the conception that the rights arising from the granting of the loan would initially enure to its benefit. This is shown by the letter of February 26, 1931, in which the Bodenkreditbank sent the offer of the loan to Gebrüder Rohrer. In that letter the Bodenkreditbank declared:

' that we are assigning our rights arising out of the loan agreement to the Aktiengesellschaft fur Kapitalanlagen at Frankfurt a.M. . . .'

Gebrüder Rohrer did not make any objection. On the basis of this conception, the later assignment of the mortgage by the Aktiengesellschaft für Kapitalanlagen to the Bodenkreditbank did not constitute a modification of the original situation, but merely the restoration of the same by the revocation of the temporary assignment of rights to the Aktiengesellschaft für Kapitalanlagen. This seems to afford an additional reason for including this assignment (or re-assignment) in the ' original written debt arrangements '.

" Since, consequently, in the present case, the assignment (or re-assignment) of April 9, 1931, is to be reckoned among the ' original written debt arrangments ' within the meaning of the provisions of Section I (2) (*a*) of Annex VII, the requirements for the specific foreign character of the loan contained in that Section are fulfilled, for after the assignment of the mortgage by the Aktiengesellschaft für Kapitalanlagen to the Bodenkreditbank in Basel the place of payment was, in accordance with the above-mentioned provisions, contained in the deeds of February 2–March 3, 1931, and March 6, 1931, situated abroad.

" The fact that the assignment' by the Aktiengesellschaft für Kapitalanlagen to the Bodenkreditbank was notified to Gebrüder Rohrer only in December 1931, is not inconsistent with this, since, under § 1154 of the German Civil Code and also under Article 164 of the Swiss Law of Obligations, the assignment became effective before notification to the debtor, and the Bodenkreditbank was already in possession of the mortgage deed.

" The fact that the first payments of interest were made to an account of the Aktiengesellschaft für Kapitalanlagen at Frankfort does not affect the question. It resulted from the assignment of the mortgage to the Bodenkreditbank not yet having been notified to the debtor. The payment of interest to Frankfort during this period without objection from the Bodenkreditbank did not alter the position that as a result of the assignment the agreed place of payment of the debt was Basle; from the time of the assignment the Bodenkreditbank was at all times in the position to notify the assignment to the debtor and to demand payment in Basle instead of in Frankfort.

" It can be left open whether the case would have had to be decided differently if the assignment had been made at a later date.

" As a result of the above-mentioned provisions of the deeds of February 2–March 3, 1931, and March 6, 1931, the foreign place of payment also became ' expressly agreed ' within the meaning of Section I (2) (*a*) of Annex VII after the mortgage had been assigned by the Aktiengesellschaft für Kapitalanlagen to the Bodenkreditbank. It suffices for this purpose that the seat of the creditor for the time being was mentioned as the place of payment in the written arrangements, for in this manner the foreign place of payment clearly emerged from the written arrangements.

" On the question of costs, the Commission assesses the value of the subject matter of the dispute at DM 67,000 and accordingly fixes the fees at DM 3,080 (Article 1, para, 2, of the Annex to the Administrative Agreement concerning the Arbitral Tribunal and the Mixed Commission under the Agreement on German External Debts—*Bundesanzeiger*, Year 7, No. 185, dated September 24, 1955).

" In view of the result of the case the Commission considers it appropriate that the fees be borne by the Government of the Federal Republic of Germany.  Since each of the four Parties has lodged DM 1,000 by way of deposit in respect of costs, the Government of the Federal Republic of Germany has to refund to the Bodenkreditbank in Basel, to Gebrüder Rohrer and to the Swiss Confederation the deposits amounting to DM 1,000 paid by each of them.  The Secretariat of the Commission will refund to the Government of the Federal Republic the sum of DM 920.

" According to Article 7 (7) of the Charter of the Mixed Commission (Annex X to the Debt Agreement), each party tó the proceedings pays its own costs unless the Commission directs otherwise; in the present case the Commission sees no ground for so doing."

[Report: Unpublished.]

**Treaties of Peace—Analogous instruments—Convention on the Settlement of Matters Arising out of the War and Occupation, 1952–1954—Restitution—Conditions of—Restitution under Law No. 8 of Allied High Commission in Germany—Impairment of property rights by war measures—Meaning of—Restitution of rights involving patents.**

SPANIER *v.* GERMAN FEDERAL REPUBLIC.

*Arbitral Commission on Property, Rights and Interests in Germany, Third Chamber.*

(Lagergren, Vice-President; Arndt, Phenix.)

*May 16, 1958.*

THE FACTS (as stated by the Commission).—" This is an appeal under Article 8, paragraph 2 (*a*), of Chapter Ten of the Bonn Settlement Convention against a decision of the *Beschwerdesenat* [Appeal Senate] 1a of the German Patent Office dated June 18, 1953 confirming the decision of the *Patentverwaltungsabteilung* [Patents Administration Division] of the said Office dated March 10, 1952, which denied appellant's request for the restoration and extension of the period of duration of the German patent No. 674724.

" The appellant, who became a citizen of the United States of America on May 16, 1950, initially filed an application in the German Patent Office pursuant to Articles 3 and 5 of Allied High Commission Law No. 8, as amended.

" The grounds for his request were briefly as follows: The appellant was formerly a German national professing the Jewish faith. In 1935, or 1936, the record showing both dates, he left Germany due to the persecution of Jews, which was then developing, and took up his residence in Belgium.  With an effective date of July 8, 1937, he was granted the German patent which is the subject of this appeal. Early in 1940, the appellant's property in Germany was allegedly seized pursuant to the Ordinance of January 15, 1940, on the Treatment of Enemy Property. The appellant himself fled to France when the Germans invaded Belgium and was placed in an internment camp as an enemy alien. This camp, after the fall of France, was transformed into a concentration camp, and the appellant remained imprisoned there until he escaped to Cuba in 1941, allegedly in July. On April 15, 1941, his patent was cancelled for non-payment of the dues for the fourth year. The appellant stated that, since he had been interned in France at the time, it was impossible for him to arrange for the payment of the dues in question and that, in addition, all funds which might have been used for the payment of the dues had been seized as a result of the 1940 Ordinance.

" In denying the appellant's appeal from the decision of the *Patentverwaltungsabteilung*, the Appeal Senate held that the appellant could not be regarded as a ' foreign national ' within the meaning of Law No. 8 at the material time since, although he might have lost his German nationality, he had not yet acquired another nationality. The Appeal Senate also based its decision on the ground that not even under Allied High Commission Law No. 41 could the appellant be regarded as a ' foreign national '. Pursuant to this Law, Law No. 8 also applied to natural persons who, between September 1, 1939, and May 8, 1945, were treated under German war legislation as an enemy and whose industrial property rights in Germany were impaired as a result thereof. The Appeal Senate admitted that the appellant had been subjected to enemy treatment under the 1940 Ordinance, as the appellant had his domicile or permanent residence in Belgium and France, respectively, with which countries Germany was at war at the material time.

" But the Appeal Senate did not find that appellant's rights under patent No. 674724 had been impaired on account of his treatment as an enemy. It held that the appellant's failure to pay the dues for the fourth year had been due to the fact that, according to his own statement, his property had been confiscated under racial legislation enacted before the war.

" The appellant lodged an appeal against the decision of the Appeal Senate with the Patent Appeal Board of the Allied High Commission, alleging that the Appeal Senate should have regarded him as a ' foreign national ' under Article 14 of Law No. 8, as amended, for the purpose of establishing his status as an applicant under Article 3 of the said Law. While he relied principally on his claim under Article 3, the appellant also alleged in the oral proceedings before the Board that his claim to reinstatement would fall under Article 2 of the Law since the impairment of his patent, namely, its revocation for non-payment of dues, resulted from a war measure, namely, the fact that he had been confined in an internment or concentration camp at the time the dues became payable. In this respect, the appellant maintained that he had suffered not only general impairment as envisaged in Article 14 (*b*) (ii) (2) of Law No. 8, as amended, but also impairment in the special sense in which that word is used in Article 2 of that Law.

" The Patent Appeal Board, in its decision of April 29, 1955, was not prepared to examine the merits of the case. However, as it appeared that the appellant had an arguable case to the effect that his appeal might fall within the scope of Article 2 of Law No. 8, as amended, the Board transferred the case to the Arbitral Commission under the provisions of Article 12 of Chapter Ten of the Bonn Settlement Convention.

" Before the Commission, the appellant maintained his earlier submission and arguments and also argued more specifically that his patent rights had been directly impaired as a result of the provisions of Article 6 of the 1940 Ordinance, which prescribed the registration of enemy property in Germany and exposed the appellant to the draconical German treatment of Jewish property, and of Article 9 of the same Ordinance, which prohibited the disposal of enemy property in Germany.

' On August 3, 1957, the Government of the Federal Republic filed an answer, in which it contended that the appeal was inadmissible, expressly presenting this contention as a preliminary objection under Article 58 of the Commission's Rules of Procedure. The defendant pointed out that the facts presented by the appellant came only under Article 3 of Law No. 8, as amended, and that Article 2 of that Law in not applicable since the impairment complained of is not the special impairment defined in Article 2. The defendant argued, therefore, that the challenged decision of the Appeal Senate had already become final by its rendering on June 18, 1953, and was therefore, not subject to appeal to the Patent Appeal Board and, therefore, could not be transferred from the Patent Appeal Board to the Arbitral Commission."

" On December 12, 1957, the Arbitral Commission ordered the preliminary objection to be joined to the merits. A public hearing was thereafter held on March 10, 1958."

*Held:* that the preliminary objection filed by the defendant must be sustained and the appeal dismissed. The appellant was not entitled to obtain restoration and extension of the period of duration of his patent. He was not at the material time a citizen or national of a foreign nation as required by the relevant provision of Law No. 8. Measures taken against him and/or his property by the German authorities did not constitute impairment of his patent in the sense of Article 2 of the said Law.

The Commission said: " The Commission finds that the provisions of Article 12, paragraph 1, of Chapter Ten of the Bonn

Settlement Convention rule out in an unequivocal manner any transfer from the Patent Appeal Board to the Arbitral Commission of appeals from decisions of the Appeal Senate of the German Patent Office other than those which come under Articles 2 and 7 of Law No. 8, as amended, and which were pending before the Board on the entry into force of the Convention, that is, on May 5, 1955. Therefore, in so far as the present appeal falls within the scope of Articles 3 and 5 of Law No. 8, as amended, the Commission has no jurisdiction to entertain the appeal.

" However, the appellant also argues that his claim to reinstatement and extension may be regarded as falling within the scope of Article 2 in connection with Article 5 of Law No. 8, as amended. If that were the case, the Commission would be prepared to admit the appeal although the arguments of the appellant have not throughout the previous litigation been so clearly directed at these Articles as they may now seem to be.

" The Commission then first takes up the question whether the appellant may be regarded as a ' foreign national ' within the meaning of Law No. 8, as amended. In this respect, the Commission concurs with the opinion of the Appeal Senate that the appellant was not at the material time ' a citizen or national of a foreign nation ' as required by Article 14 (b) (i) of Law No. 8, as amended, since he had not at that time acquired a nationality other than his German one. In that connection, the Commission also wishes to make reference to the decision of the *Beschwerdesenat* 1a of June 17, 1953, reported in *Blatt für Patent-, Muster- und Zeichenwesen*, 1953, pp. 377–378.

" With regard to Article 14 (b) (ii), the Appeal Senate held that the appellant undoubtedly had been subjected to enemy treatment during the period in question, referring in that connection to Article 3 of the Ordinance on the Treatment of Enemy Property of January 15, 1940. However, this consideration seems to require some further investigation. First of all, no legislative measures were enacted with respect to Belgian property in Germany until the Ordinance of May 30, 1940, on Treatment of Norwegian, Dutch, Belgian and Luxembourg Property (*RGBl.* I, p. 821), and that Ordinance merely provided for the placing under a custodian of enterprises (*Unternehmen*) [of property] situated in Germany and belonging to nationals from these countries or under the controlling influence of such nationals, and for the application to nationals of such countries not residing in Germany of the provisions of the *Abwesenheitspflegschaft* [Absentee Guardianship] Ordinance of October 11, 1939, but did not involve any obligation of registration of property or prohibition of its disposal. On May 30, 1940, appellant had left Belgium for France, and his status was then changed. Under the Ordinance of January 15, 1940, all property situated in Germany belonging to French nationals or to persons having their domicile or permanent residence in France was, under penalty, subject to registration and prohibition of disposal. (In the appellant's German passport which, according to a prolongation of March 3, 1940, was valid until March 5, 1941, the insertion of the letter ' J ' and a change of the appellant's name to Walter ' Israel ' Spanier had been made in order to identify him as a Jew. He therefore could not benefit from the provisions of the Ordinance of the German Minister of Justice of October 18, 1940, exempting Germans living in occupied France from the terms of the Ordinance of January 15, 1940, but specifically denying such advantage to Jews.) In these circumstances the Commission considers it most probable that during his internment he was legally subject to the provisions of the Ordinance of January 15, 1940, and thus deprived of the right to dispose of his patent, a deprivation which might be claimed to constitute an impairment within the meaning of Article 14 (b) (ii) (2) of Law No. 8, as amended. Since any such impairment would have been a result of the treatment of the appellant as an enemy, he could in such case be considered as a foreign national for the purpose of Article 2 of the Law. The Commission does not express an opinion on these points sin e their determination is not essential for its decision.

" Restoration under Article 2 requires that the foreign national, *inter alia*, be the owner of an industrial property right during the state of war between Germany and the foreign nation concerned, which in the present case can only be considered as France, and that the said property rights be transferred, seized, requisitioned, revoked or otherwise impaired by war measures, whether legislative, judicial or administrative. Admittedly, the appellant owned a patent right during the material time until his right was cancelled for non-payment of dues on April 15, 1941, and undoubtedly the cancellation resulting from appellant's non-payment in the present case, if he qualified as a ' foreign national ' under Article 14 of Law No. 8, as amended, would have entitled him to the relief provided under Article 3 of that Law. But the cancellation of appellant's patent cannot be held to be an impairment of his industrial property right as defined in the frequently mentioned Article 2. There the impairment has to be caused by war measures taken with the specific purpose of impairing industrial, literary or artistic rights or proximately causing the impairment of such rights. Any alleged seizure of appellant's means of payment in Germany as a result of war legislation is therefore without significance so far as Article 2 is concerned, and equally without significance in that connection are the results of the action taken against his person, namely, his internment.

" The Commission then turns to the question whether the prohibition of disposal decreed in the Ordinance of January 15, 1940, which has been deemed applicable to the appellant during the time he was interned in the concentration camp in France, involves an impairment within the meaning of Article 2. In this connection the

Commission quotes with approval the following passage from the decision of the Patent Appeal Board of April 29, 1955, in the case of *Mercedes Büromaschinen Werke A. G.* v. *Federal Republic of Germany*:[1]

' The impairment which is contemplated by Article 2 is of a special nature. It must be by " war measures " and must be the kind of impairment which would be suffered by a person whose patent had been " transferred, seized, requisitioned [or] revoked ". The expression " or otherwise impaired " in Article 2 is of a general nature and follows the specific words mentioned above, and in a case of this sort the Board consider that the *ejusdem generis* doctrine should be applied, to which reference is made in the following terms in Maxwell on *The Interpretation of Statutes*, 10th Edition, p. 337:—

" The general word which follows particular and the specific words of the same nature as itself takes its meaning from them, and is presumed to be restricted to the same genus as those words. In other words, it is to be read as comprehending only things of the same kind as those designated by them, unless, of course, there be something to show that a wider sense was intended, as, for instance a proviso specifically excepting certain classes clearly not within the suggested genus."

" In the present case, the appellant was deprived of the disposal of his patent rights and thus he could not, *inter alia*, sell his patent right or grant any licence on the basis of his invention, but the Ordinance of January 15, 1940, did not by itself have any effect upon the existence of the patent or upon the appellant being recorded as the owner thereof.

" Finally, the Commission cannot find that the appellant's patent was impaired by the mere existence of the obligation of registration under Articles 6 and 7 of the 1940 Ordinance, as the appellant never complied therewith.

" The Ordinance of January 15, 1940, was a ' war measure ' but it did not transfer, seize, requisition, revoke or otherwise impair the patent. Article 2 of Law No. 8, as amended, is therefore inapplicable and the appeal is not admissible.

" For These Reasons the Arbitral Commission orders that: (1) The preliminary objection filed by the Federal Republic of Germany is sustained; (2) the appeal is dismissed; (3) the appellant has to bear his own costs."

[Report: *Decisions of the Arbitral Commission*, I (1958), Case No. 18, p. 165.]

[1 Reported below, p. 548.]

Treaties of peace—Analogous instruments—Convention on the Settlement of Matters Arising out of the War and Occupation, 1952-1954—Restitution provisions—Restoration of rights and interests—Chapter Ten of Convention—Restitution of shares—Conditions of—Discriminatory treatment as prerequisite of return and restoration—Meaning of " discriminatory treatment ".

HEIDSIECK & CIE v. GERMAN FEDERAL REPUBLIC.

*Arbitral Commission on Property, Rights and Interests in Germany, Second Chamber.*

(Sauser-Hall, Vice-President; Schwandt, Marion.)

*June 12, 1958.*

THE FACTS (as stated by the Commission).—" Pursuant to Article 12, Chapter Ten, of the Convention on the Settlement of Matters Arising out of the War and the Occupation of October 23, 1954, an appeal has been lodged with the Arbitral Commission on Property, Rights and Interests in Germany by the firm [of] Heidsieck et Cie. Monopole m.b.H. of Mainz, established under German law, 99 per cent. of whose capital is owned by the Société française Champagne Heidsieck et Cie. Monopole S.A. Reims, against a decision of the Federal Higher Authority of February 8, 1957, rendered pursuant to Article 1 of Chapter Ten of the Settlement Convention and the Annex to this Chapter, by which its application for restoration of rights was rejected. The appeal has been filed in due form within the prescribed time-limit, and the Commission is competent to decide on it pursuant to Article 6, Part II, of its Charter annexed to the Settlement Convention.

" The Commission finds that it is undisputed that the property of the complainant firm had been placed under custodianship by Order of August 9, 1940, issued by the *Oberlandesgericht*, Darmstadt, in implementation of the German Ordinance on the Treatment of Enemy Properties of January 15, 1940, Herr H., manager of the firm [of] Heidsieck and himself to some extent interested in the firm established under German law, thereby being appointed property custodian.

" In its initial application filed with the Federal Higher Authority on May 3, 1956, the firm [of] Heidsieck et Cie. Monopole m.b.H. demanded restoration of its financial situation as on ' January 14, 1940 '. In substantiation of its application, it submitted a list of securities purchased by it during the period from January 15, 1940, to September 9, 1940, to a total value of 234,100 Reichsmark, which partly consisted of shares (nominal value 127,100 Reichsmark) and partly of securities bearing a fixed interest (nominal value 107,000 Reichsmark), such as German Reich Treasury Bonds bought on September 6, 1940 (nominal value 60,000 Reichsmark). The list does not indicate the numbers of the securities. The complainant firm contends that at the time of its being placed under custodianship, its capital consisted only of German shares which, by recommendation or instruction of the *Reichskommissar*, were sold during the period of custodianship, the proceeds having been used to acquire German Reich Treasury Bonds. It asserts that this recommendation or instruction constituted a discriminatory measure as defined by Article 1 of Chapter Ten, as a result of which damage was caused owing to the aforesaid Treasury Bonds completely losing their value.

" The Federal Higher Authority rejected the application for restoration ' for reasons of fact and law '.

" As to the facts, the Federal Higher Authority stated initially that the securities bought and resold between January 15, 1940, and September 9, 1940, on the list submitted by the complainant did not correspond to those which might have been affected by placing the firm under custodianship, since this had not occurred on January 15, 1940, but on August 9, 1940, by which date, instead of securities to the nominal value of 234,100 Reichsmark, as stated on the list, only securities to the nominal value of 59,900 Reichsmark (*recte*: 52,100 Reichsmark) existed, since, by that time, the manager of the firm [of] Heidsieck et Cie. Monopole m.b.H. had already, of his own accord, sold part of the securities at a nominal value of 81,200 Reichsmark (*recte*: 89,000 Reichsmark) shown on the list as having been bought and sold between January 15, 1940, and September 9, 1940, and since he had bought securities at a nominal value of 93,000 Reichsmark only after August 9, 1940, *i.e.*, in September 1940.

" The Federal Higher Authority found that the intervention on the part of the *Reichskommissar*, which the complainant firm considers to have been decisive for the sale of shares and the acquisition of Treasury Bonds, did not aim at a sale of shares but at a possible acquisition of new shares for speculative purposes; that the sales and purchases had been effected in order to ensure the continued running of the champagne firm, and that finally the aforesaid intervention had not consisted of instructions but merely of recommendations.

" As to the law, the decision of the Federal Higher Authority held that the placing of enemy property under custodianship and the control of liquid funds resulting therefrom did not constitute a discriminatory measure within the meaning of Article 1, paragraph 4, of Chapter Ten of the Settlement Convention; that, even if this should be true, the prohibition to buy shares and the order to acquire Treasury Bonds was, in fact, in conformity with the Ordinance on the Treatment of Enemy Properties (paragraph 15) and with Article 19 of the Implementing Regulation of the Reich Minister of Justice of June 20, 1940; that, on the contrary, the acquisition of securities for speculative purposes would have constituted a violation of the legal provisions mentioned above; that, inasmuch as there was no ground for restoration, the application aimed at compensation for loss of value of the Treasury Bonds and could not be based on Article 1 of Chapter Ten, paragraph 6 of which expressly excludes any kind of compensation.

" In its notice of appeal of May 4, 1957, the complainant does not renew its original application for ' restoration of its financial situation as on January 14, 1940 ', filed with the Federal Higher Authority, but applies for: (1) ' Return of a certain number of shares in their present condition ' (without indicating their share numbers), *i.e.*, possibly, in the form of shares of the companies which have succeeded to the firms named; (2) the finding that the forced purchase of Reich Treasury Bonds to the amount of 60,000 Reichsmark was a discriminatory measure.

" In its reply of August 15, 1957, the complainant again modifies its motion under (1) by applying for return of shares as on September 9, 1940, taking into consideration the conditions of conversion resulting from the monetary reform, the subscription rights acquired by shareholders in the course of the past few years and the profit distributed among shareholders. The present total value has been fixed at 233,747.88 Deutsche Mark.

" In its subsequent reply of October 21, 1957, the complainant presented as an alternative motion that, pursuant to Rule 22 (*a*) of the Rules of Procedure, inquiries be ordered concerning the application of the Ordinance of the Reich of December 4, 1941, on share-holdings.

" Finally, the complainant again submitted written motions at the hearing of February 13, 1958, by which it applied for the following modification of its motions of May 4, 1957: (I) ' Restoration by the Federal Republic of its rights and interests as on September 15, 1940, in the collective deposit with the Deutsche Bank, Mainz, according to a list enumerating its securities ' (without indicating their numbers) ' to a total nominal value of 85,000 Reichsmark '; (II) ' the finding that the letters from the *Reichskommissar* of August 30, 1940, and October 17, 1941, constituted discriminatory measures and that the former caused the purchase of Treasury Bonds to the amount of 60,000 Reichsmark.'

" In its various pleadings, the complainant asserts that the Federal Higher Authority has wrongly refused to apply Article 1 of Chapter Ten of the Settlement Convention, thus misjudging the discriminatory treatment to which the complainant was subjected and the damage caused thereby.

" In his answer of August 5, 1957, as in his rejoinders of September 12 and December 12, 1957, the Agent of the Federal Republic, by repeating the reasons of the decision, has moved that this decision be confirmed, but has observed that the complainant could not submit to the Commission an application formulated differently from that which had already been subject to decision and that, inasmuch as it was new, the application was inadmissible.

" Moreover, he moved that the ' application for a declaratory judgment ' under (II) be rejected as inadmissible since it aimed at making apparent a damage which could not be repaired by return or restoration but only by compensation which, according to paragraph 6 [of] Article 1 of Chapter Ten of the Settlement Convention, does not come within the competence of the Arbitral Commission.

" In their replies and rejoinders, respectively, the parties have referred to questions of procedure and competence:

" In its reply of October 21, 1957, the firm [of] Heidsieck et Cie. Monopole m.b.H. stated that by virtue of Rule 58 (a) of the Rules of Procedure, the objection of inadmissibility raised by the defendant was not admissible at this stage of the proceedings since it had not been raised prior to the consideration of the merits of the claim.

" In his aforesaid rejoinders, the Agent of the Federal Republic contended that the question referred to did not constitute an objection but belonged to the sphere of substantive law and that it should, therefore, be considered by the Commission."

*Held:* that the decision of the Federal Higher Authority against Heidsieck & Cie. must be confirmed and all the claims and applications of Heidsieck & Cie. must be denied. The granting of a sum of money as counter-value of shares was not covered by the expression " restoration of rights and interests " as used in Article 1, Chapter Ten, of the Convention on the Settlement of Matters Arising out of the War and Occupation. According to the same Article, the return of shares required identification of the securities; unnumbered shares were not identifiable. There was no discriminatory treatment involving the return and restoration of goods applied for by the complainant. The Commission was not competent to decide on the compensation, nor had it jurisdiction to give a declaratory judgment.

The Commission said:

" *On the procedure.*—It need not to be considered to what extent the successive motions submitted to the Commission, the last of which dates from February 13, 1958, differ in nature and amount claimed from those submitted to the Federal Higher Authority and whether, according to general legal principles, they are thus inadmissible before the Commission inasmuch as they present new submissions, since they are all unfounded. It must be observed, however, that the question of whether a new application is involved or not may be decided only by consideration of the merits, an application of Rule 58 (a) of the Rules of Procedure thus being excluded.

" *On the merits.*—" As to the facts, the parties disagree on the number of shares which may be involved having regard to the date of appointment of the Enemy Property Custodian on August 9, 1940, and that of the inventory on August 17, 1940, as well as on the resulting reinvestment of the proceeds of the shares in Reich Treasury Bonds which are alleged to be valueless. It appears to be unnecessary to clarify these facts since, even if their presentation by the complainant firm were considered to be correct, the application cannot be granted for reasons of law.

" I. The complainant wrongly relies on Article I of Chapter Ten of the Settlement Convention for its claim for restoration of the financial situation as on January 14, 1940, and later on for the return of a certain number of shares, the value of which has been calculated in Reichsmark in some pleadings and in Deutsche Mark in others, the dates of restoration and return varying from January 14, 1940, to September 9, 1940, and September 15, 1940.

" Like the Federal Higher Authority, the Arbitral Commission states that the application for restoration of the financial situation is in itself confused since, regardless of the given date, it covers shares, obligations and liquid funds.

" The firm [of] Heidsieck et Cie. Monopole m.b.H. thus tries to obtain either shares or a counter-value sometimes expressed in Reichsmark and sometimes in Deutsche Mark. The granting of a sum of money as counter-value of shares, however, is not covered by the term 'restoration of rights and interests' as defined by Article I which has been invoked; since, moreover, this would be a case of compensation, it would violate paragraph 6 of the aforesaid Article I, which excludes the question of ' compensation for loss or damage to property, rights or interests.'

" According to Article I, return of property must be effected in ' its present condition ', whereas the application covers securities expressed in Reichsmark as they existed in 1940.

" On the one hand, the return of property—in this case shares of certain companies—requires identification of the securities, while the list of shares submitted does not contain any number which would make identification possible. On the other hand, there are no longer any Reichsmark shares available as a consequence of the monetary reform ordered by Occupation legislation and of German legislation resulting therefrom concerning balance sheets in Deutsche Mark; they have been replaced by shares in Deutsche Mark in accordance with the newly fixed share capital. The complainant does not give any precise definition of the new shares in Deutsche Mark which have replaced the Reichsmark shares, the numbers of which are unknown.

" It is evident that return ' in their present condition ' of the shares existing in 1940 is impossible. Return could, therefore, be effected only indirectly by an acquisition of substitute shares which would amount to compensation violating Article I, paragraph 6, of Chapter Ten of the Settlement Convention. The Federal Higher

Authority justly rejected, therefore, the arguments concerning return and restoration.

" II.  Moreover, the prerequisite for return and restoration provided for in Article 1, that the property must have been subject to discriminatory treatment, has not been met.

" The placing under custodianship of enemy property for its control and safeguarding is generally admissible in modern international law.  This double aim justifies in general the depositing in the State treasury of liquid funds or their conversion into bonds of the State ordering enemy property custodianship.  In the case of industrial or trading companies, the capital required for the running of the firm may be left at the disposal of the property custodian, speculative operations being excluded as contradicting the meaning of the term ' safeguarding '.

" The term ' discriminatory treatment ' has been defined in paragraph 4 (a) and (b) of Article 1, Chapter Ten, of the Settlement Convention specifically with regard to enemy property placed under custodianship.  Anything done or omitted under the German Ordinance on the Treatment of Enemy Properties of January 15, 1940, may be held to amount to discriminatory treatment ' where it appears that: (a) injury to foreign property, rights or interests resulted therefrom; and (b) the injury inflicted could have been avoided without infringing such Ordinance, amendments or regulations.'

" In order to establish discriminatory treatment to its prejudice, the complainant refers to the letters of the *Reichskommissar* of August 30, 1940, and October 17, 1941, addressed to Herr H., alleging that they had caused the latter to sell the shares and to acquire Treasury Bonds.  In the letter of August 30, 1940, it is said:

" ' I inform you that I cannot authorize you to acquire shares for speculative purposes, that is, with the intention to resell them at a profit in the near future.  However, if you wish to acquire securities bearing a fixed interest and shares of stable value quoted on the exchange in order to invest capital and to obtain a higher yield, I shall consent.'

In the letter of October 17, 1941 the *Reichskommissar* states: ' It is considered desirable that mainly securities bearing a fixed interest are acquired . . .'

" Neither of these letters contains an order concerning the sale of shares, return or restoration of which might be applied for; in fact, the first one does not even object to the acquisition of new shares of stable value.  On the contrary, it merely contains recommendations or hints which did not refer to the sale of shares but only contained a prohibition of acquiring in future new shares of a speculative character with the funds available.  The prohibition to buy securities which, in fact, were never owned by the firm under custodianship cannot serve as the basis for a claim for return of property or for restoration of a right.  By interpreting the aforesaid documents in this way, the Federal Higher Authority has rightly assessed the duties incumbent upon an enemy property custodian.

" The complainant's submissions are in fact without foundation: even if they were accepted, they would be without legal effect.

" Even if the recommendations, hints or prohibitions of the *Reichskommissar* are as such in conformity with the provisions of international law they do not, on the other hand, fulfil the two aforesaid conditions of paragraph 4 [of] Article 1 of Chapter Ten of the Settlement Convention.

" As to the first of these conditions, the damage asserted by the complainant was allegedly a result of its having been in possession of valueless Reich Treasury Bonds at the end of the period of custodianship—of uncertain date (no inventory of the property returned after its release having been produced) or in any case at the date of application—whereas the shares the sale of which has been objected to would have retained their value.

" However, neither the sale of shares nor the acquisition of bonds with liquid funds as such constituted a damaging measure. On the contrary, it must be pointed out that the sales proceeds of the shares have served partly for the purchase of goods by the custodian who, being the former manager of the complainant firm in which he had a share, was justified in endeavouring to maintain a certain activity of the firm, which did not call forth any objections on the part of the *Reichskommissar*.

" The alleged damage has not resulted from the sales and acquisitions of securities between 1940 and 1942 but from the subsequent loss of value of the Reich Treasury Bonds caused by the collapse of the Third Reich in 1945. As the damage was not a direct consequence of the measures taken by the custodian and as it is thus not directly connected with the purchase or sale of securities, it was rightly disregarded in the contested decision as not having resulted from these measures.

" As to the second condition, the complainant contends that the provisions concerning enemy property would not have been violated if the property custodian had been authorized to acquire shares of a speculative character and with varying interest, the re-sale of which would have been possible at a profit.

" As is obvious, however, from the Ordinance on the Treatment of Enemy Properties of January 15, 1940 (Articles 9, 10 and 15) and from the Implementing Regulation of the Reich Minister of Justice of June 20, 1940 (Figure 19) it was the main duty of the Enemy Property Custodian ' to preserve and safeguard the property '; in principle, he was prohibited from any act of disposition. Only the Minister of Justice and the Minister of Finance could grant exceptions through their commissioner, the *Reichskommissar*.

" On the one hand, the acquisition of shares for speculative purposes by an enemy property custodian, who prior to his appointment had been manager of a firm dealing in champagne and not in stock exchange operations, would have run counter to the safeguarding of the share capital placed under custodianship.

" If, on the other hand, it is assumed for the sake of argument that the recommendations or instructions of the *Reichskommissar* of August 30, 1940, and October 17, 1941, were of an imperative nature, the enemy property custodian in question obviously would have violated the provisions in force by contravening instructions given to him under legislation.

" The complainant's argumentation concerning the latter condition is no more convincing than that presented in connection with the former.

" III. The new application of the firm [of] Heidsieck et Cie. Monopole m.b.H. presented under II [the second] of the motions of February 13, 1958, that it should be found that the letters of the *Reichskommissar* of August 30, 1940, and October 17, 1941, constitute discriminatory measures and that the first of them had caused the acquisition of Reich Treasury Bonds to the amount of RM 60,000 —assuming its admissibility without it having been submitted to the Federal Higher Authority—does not come within the competence of the Arbitral Commission in so far as this application has no connection whatsoever with proceedings for return or restoration.

" The jurisdiction of the Commission, which is exclusive in certain disputes provided for in the Settlement Convention as an international agreement, cannot be extended for the very reason of its attributive and special character, since no such extension has been provided for in the text; the demand for a declaratory judgment as principal claim is not covered by any of the cases of competence of the Commission provided for in the Settlement Convention.

" IV. The facts as well as the legal arguments presented by thé complainant are without foundation. The recommendations or instructions of the *Reichskommissar*, in so far as they are considered to have caused discriminatory treatment, in no way refer to the sale or acquisition of securities on which the claim for restoration or return has been based, but to a possible investment of liquid funds.

" The application, which has justly been considered as being ambiguous by the decision of the Federal Higher Authority, is based on the loss of value of the Treasury Bonds which have been acquired not in direct replacement of the shares sold but with liquid funds resulting from business transactions; it thus aims at compensation, which is excluded by paragraph 6 of Article 1 of Chapter Ten of the Settlement Convention.

" V. The remaining submissions and motions, which have only been answered implicitly or the answer to which may be inferred, are equally rejected, including the application for investigation and an expert opinion on the application of the Ordinance of December 4, 1941, concerning shareholdings, since it is irrelevant for the decision.

" For These Reasons the Arbitral Commission confirms the decision of February 8, 1957, of the Federal Higher Authority by which the application for restoration of rights filed pursuant to Article 1 of Chapter Ten of the Settlement Convention has been rejected; and denies the firm [of] Heidsieck et Cie. Monopole m.b.H. in Mainz all other claims and applications."

[Report: *Decisions of the Arbitral Commission*, I (1958), Case No. 20, p. 173.]

**Treaties of peace—Analogous instruments—Convention on the Settlement of Matters Arising out of the War and Occupation, 1952–1954—Restitution—restitution of rights and interests— Chapter Ten of Convention—Conditions of restitution—Nationality of claimant—Discriminatory treatment—Meaning of—Measures constituting prejudice, deprivation or impairment of right— Geneva Convention of 1929 on Treatment of Prisoners of War— Article 23.**

ZGAINSKI *v.* GERMAN FEDERAL REPUBLIC.

*Arbitral Commission on Property, Rights and Interests in Germany, First Chamber.*

(Wickström, President; Euler, Bennett.)

*July* 1, 1958.

THE FACTS (as stated by the Commission).—" The complainant, who is at present residing in Federal German territory, submitted a petition to the *Bundesamt für die Prüfung ausländischer Rückgabe- und Wiederherstellungsansprüche* [Federal Restitution Office] in which he stated the following:

" As a Polish lieutenant, he had been a prisoner during the war between the German Reich and Poland. He had been kept in prisoner of war camps and, from September 17, 1939, until May 1, 1945, had received free accommodation and rations as well as a monthly allowance of 81 RM. This payment had merely been an advance, and the greater part of the lieutenant's pay due to him had been withheld. Pursuant to Article 23 of the Geneva Convention on the Treatment of Prisoners of War dated July 27, 1929, officer prisoners of war were entitled to receive the same pay as officers of corresponding rank in the army of the Detaining Power. Such pay was payable to them in full once a month, if possible, and otherwise fell to be credited and handed over upon the termination of captivity, pursuant to Article 24. Germany had not kept to the terms of the Convention as far as Poland was concerned and had paid to Polish officers, as pocket money, only a fraction of the pay to which they were entitled. Owing to the deprivation of the main part of their pay, Polish officers had lost their credit account. Since the failure to credit or pay the amounts so withheld was due to the discriminatory measures adopted by the German Reich, the complainant, pursuant to Article 1, Chapter Ten, of the Settlement Convention, claimed restoration of the rights of which he had been deprived. Until the oubreak of war the pay of a German lieutenant had amounted to 243 RM per month and he [the complainant] had, therefore, been deprived of a monthly amount of 162 RM, a total of 10,854 RM. As a pay claim, this sum should be converted at the rate of 1 RM= 1 DM.

" The complainant petitioned the *Bundesamt* for: (1) restoration of the balance of pay so withheld; (2) conversion of the above at 1 RM = 1 DM; (3) an order for payment of the sum of 10,854 DM.

" The defendant opposed the complainant's application and moved its rejection.

" By decision of October 17, 1947, the *Bundesamt* rejected the application. A brief summary of the reasons given in support of the decision follows:

" On the basis of the complainant's submissions, there was no such deprivation or annihilation of a right as, pursuant to Article 1 of Chapter Ten of the Settlement Convention, would found a claim for restoration if discriminatory treatment were involved. The complainant does not assert deprivation of a right such as, for example, a claim for payment of salary or an account to which the unpaid portions of pay had been credited, but only non-fulfilment of a pay claim due to him. Non-fulfilment of a claim does not constitute deprivation thereof, it does not cancel the claim for fulfilment, and it cannot, therefore, found a claim to restoration. In reality, the complainant does not seek restoration but compensation, as is shown by the phrasing of his application. If he believes that he has been deprived of a Reichsmark claim, it would be logical for him to request restoration of a Reichsmark claim, and he could not move to fix his claim in Deutsch Mark.

" The complainant had not been deprived of any part of the pay to which he had been entitled pursuant to the Geneva Convention. He had received the combat pay (*Wehrsold*) due to a German lieutenant on special assignment in accordance with the German EWGG [*Einsatz-Wehrmachtgebührnisgesetz*—Law governing the Pay of Armed Forces on Special Assignments] of August 28, 1939. Pursuant to that Law and the implementing Ordinance of September 1, 1939, which governs the date of its entry into force, the pay of German officers on special assignment had been altered with effect from September 1, 1939. Since, however, Article 23 of the Geneva Convention did not mention peace-time rates nor refer to any particular pay regulation in force at any particular time as governing the scale for the pay of prisoners of war, and as no agreement had been concluded which excluded any change of the pay regulations as they existed at the conclusion of the Convention, the EWGG and its entry into force on September 1, 1939, as regards Poland was not an infringement of the Geneva Convention.

" The application of the EWGG did not constitute a discriminatory measure as defined in Article 1 of Chapter Ten of the Settlement Convention. The fact that it affected prisoners of war was due to the dependence of Article 23 of the Geneva Convention on the pay regulation in force for the German armed forces. Above all, all officer prisoners of war, regardless of nationality, had received combat pay only, and thus Polish officers were not treated differently from officer prisoners of war of other nations.

" In conclusion, the *Bundesamt* observed that the provisions of § 3 of the EWGG (continued payment of peace-time rates to professional soldiers and other salaried officials in public service) and of § 9 of the EWGG (payment of family allowance to members of the armed forces who are not professional soldiers or other salaried officials), were not applicable to the complainant. The *Bundesamt* held that the payments provided for in these provisions are intended solely for the maintenance of the officers' families and that the pay which Article 23 of the Geneva Convention guarantees for officer prisoners of war does not include maintenance of their families.

" On November 27, 1957, the complainant appealed from the decision served upon him on November 2, 1957.

" The complainant contests the view of the *Bundesamt* that this is not a case of the restoration of a right as defined by Article 1 of Chapter Ten of the Settlement Convention. He had been deprived [he maintained] of his claim to peace-time pay by the EWGG, particularly as the defendant still holds that that Law had altered the pay claims of officer prisoners of war with legal effect from the outbreak of war.

" In view of Article 1 of Chapter Ten of the Settlement Convention and the principle of *clausula rebus sic stantibus* normally applicable to international agreements, the EWGG which, with effect from the outbreak of war, had reduced payments as compared with those previously in force, should not be applied to Polish prisoners of war. Article 23 of the Geneva Convention provided that officer prisoners of war were to receive from the Detaining Power the same pay as officers of corresponding rank serving in the army of that State. But one could not simply unilaterally change the effect of agreements on reciprocal obligations upon the outbreak of war. The amounts of the obligations of Polish officer prisoners of war had been established prior to the outbreak of war. They had been known to both parties and had been tacitly accepted. Upon the outbreak of war, Germany was not entitled to alter the pay of prisoners of war which had been fixed in relation to Poland. Furthermore, the complainant contends that, with effect from the date of his captivity, he had no longer been on special assignment as defined by the EWGG and that, therefore, the pay regulation of the EWGG was not applicable in his case.

" Even if the EWGG were to be accepted as a basis, he would still have been entitled to the full peace-time pay due to a German officer. Pursuant to Article 11 of the Implementing Ordinance to the EWGG of August 31, 1939, German officers captured by the enemy were entitled to full peace-time pay. Moreover, even German officers on special assignment had been in a more favourable position. Apart from officers' rations and accommodation, salaried officials (public officials and professional soldiers) had continued to receive peace-time rates pursuant to § 3 of the EWGG, and officers outside that category had received a ' family allowance ' pursuant to § 9 in addition to combat pay. Not only had the Polish officers not received officers' rations or accommodation, they had been paid only combat pay, that it to say, mere pocket money. He regards as immaterial the reference of the *Bundesamt* to the fact that officer prisoners of war of other nations had all been treated in the same way; since those States had entered the war with Germany only at a later date, [those prisoners] had been able to maintain their relations with their own State and had been able to return home after the war. Moreover, the reference was irrelevant because it only showed that prisoners of war of other nationalities had also been discriminated against."

The Arbitral Commission fixed the date for the oral proceedings for June 10, 1958, and at the session heard the parties.

" The complainant moved that the decision be set aside, that judgment be rendered in accordance with his petition to the *Bundesamt*, that the defendant be ordered to pay to the complainant the sum of 10,854 RM, and that the costs of the case be assessed against the defendant.

" The defendant moved that the appeal be rejected. It denied that the complainant is still a Polish national and on all other points relied upon the reasons stated in the contested decision.

" Upon questioning, the complainant stated that he had been a reserve officer and had practised as a lawyer prior to the war.

" In answer to the Commission's request to define the discriminatory measures on which he bases his claim, the complainant stated that he considered these to be as follows: (1) that on September 1, 1939, the German Reich had revoked the peace-time rates of pay and enforced a different pay regulation, namely, the EWGG; (2) that Article 11 of the Implementing Ordinance to the EWGG had not been applied to the complainant; and (3) that Polish prisoners of war had not been granted the family allowance provided for under § 9 of the EWGG.

" In other words, the complainant contends that the German Reich had no right to apply the EWGG to him at all, and alternatively, if it had such right, it applied the EWGG erroneously; and that, in either event, the action of the Reich constituted discriminatory treatment."

*Held:* that the appeal must be dismissed. The alleged annulment, prejudice to, or impairment of the conplainant's right resulted from measures which could not have been regarded as discriminatory treatment in the sense of Article 1 (4) of Chapter 10 of the Convention on the Settlement of Matters Arising out of the War and Occupation 1952–1954.

The Commission said: " The sole basis for the complainant's petition is Article 1 of Chapter Ten of the Settlement Convention. Pursuant to paragraph 3 of that Article, the persons entitled to claim are the United Nations and their nationals provided that the latter were United Nations nationals at the date of the discriminatory treatment. It is certain that at the time of his being taken prisoner, the complainant was a Polish national. In regard to the question whether he is still in possession of Polish nationality although he did not return to Poland upon the termination of the war and of his capitivity, the *Bundesamt* stated as follows:

' The complainant himself states that he has not acquired German nationality and has not lost his Polish nationality, and in particular, that he has not been expatriated by the Polish State (his passport has been marked " nationality unknown "). If he has not acquired German nationality—and this is not disputed—there is no question of a loss of Polish nationality pursuant to the Polish Nationality Law due to the acquirement of the nationality of another country. Since, under that Law, there is no possibility for the Polish State to order any mass expatriation, and since no evidence has been forthcoming as to any individual expatriation of the complainant, it is justifiable to proceed upon the basis that he has not lost his Polish nationality.'

" The Commission considers these reasons to be apposite and has nothing to add thereto. The complainant must be regarded, therefore, as entitled to assert a claim under Article 1 of Chapter Ten of the Settlement Convention.

" As a resident of the Federal Republic of Germany, and in accordance with Article 6, paragraph 4, of the Charter of the Commission in conjunction with Article 12, paragraph 1, sub-section (a), of Chapter Ten of the Settlement Convention, the complainant is entitled to appeal to the Arbitral Commission from the decision of the *Bundesamt*. The appeal, which was lodged in due time, is thus admissible.

" However, the appeal is not well-founded.

" Article 1 of Chapter Ten of the Settlement Convention grants an individual claim for the return of property and the restoration of rights and interests in the Federal territory to the extent to which such property, rights and interests suffered discriminatory treatment. Paragraph 4, sentence 1, of that Article defines the term ' discriminatory treatment ' as follows:

> " ' The term " discriminatory treatment " as used in this Article shall mean action of all kinds applied between September 1, 1939, and May 8, 1945, to any property, rights or interests, as a result of any exceptional measures which were not applicable generally to all non-German property, rights or interests, and giving rise to prejudice, deprivation or impairment without the free consent of the interested parties and without adequate compensation.'

[The Commissioner here quoted the German and French versions of the above provision.]

" The right, the restoration of which the complainant desires, is the claim in respect of pay to which he was entitled pursuant to Article 23 of the Geneva Convention. There is no doubt that a claim constitutes a right as defined by Article 1 of Chapter Ten of the Settlement Convention. According to paragraph 4 of that Article, prejudice, deprivation or impairment must exist (French: *préjudice*, *perte*, *dommage;* German: *Schädigung*, *Entziehung*, *Benachteiligung*). The term ' deprivation ', '*perte* ', ' *Entziehung* ', signifies the annihilation of a right. The *Bundesamt* has rightly stated that mere non-payment of a claim to pay does not annihilate the claim itself, but, although the complainant rightly qualified his claim as the difference between the amount which he says he ought to have received and the amount which he actually received, his claim is not to be treated as a mere claim for payment or for compensation. The complainant alleges that a claim to which he was entitled was annulled by a measure or measures adopted by the German Reich and the defendant relies upon the same measure or measures in order to show that the complainant had no right to the claim. It must also be remembered that the above-mentioned Article of the Settlement Convention speaks of prejudice and of impairment as well as of deprivation. If, as the complainant alleges, the German Reich, contrary to Article 23 of the Geneva Convention, wrongly purported to change the claim of the complainant to his disadvantage, either because it had no right to apply the EWGG at all or because, if it had that right, it exercised it in an erroneous manner, his claim in respect of pay was certainly prejudiced and impaired even if it was not annulled, and, if the action of the Reich constituted discriminatory treatment, the complainant, pursuant to Article 1, paragraph 1, of Chapter Ten of the Convention, would be entitled to claim the restoration of his right.

" There are, therefore, two prerequisites to the substantiation of the complainant's claim, namely,

" (a) that his claim to pay under Article 23 of the Geneva Convention had been annulled, prejudiced or impaired; and

" (b) that such annulment, prejudice or impairment resulted from an exceptional measure or measures not applicable generally to all non-German rights of the kind in question.

" The first of these prerequisites raises difficult questions of interpretation, which may depend upon matters which may not yet have been fully elucidated or sufficiently investigated in the present proceedings; and as, for the reasons hereafter stated, the second prerequisite cannot be fulfilled, it is not necessary for the Commission to express any opinion thereon.

" The Commission is of opinion that the second prerequisite cannot be fulfilled because, on the basis of the facts found by the *Bundesamt*, which were not disputed by the complainant, all the measures complained of by him were generally applied and treated as generally applicable to all non-German rights of the kind in question, namely, the rights of officer prisoners of war under Article 23 of the Geneva Convention, and no one of those measures, therefore, constituted discriminatory treatment within the meaning of paragraph 4 of Article 1 of Chapter Ten of the Settlement Convention.

" All the measures and omissions upon which the complainant relies, namely, the application of the EWGG in general and the failure to apply respectively Articles 3 and 9 thereof and Article 11 of the Implementing Ordinance of August 31, 1939, were applied generally and treated as generally applicable to all officer prisoners of war in German hands and therefore to all the non-German rights of such officers under Article 23 of the Geneva Convention and there was no discrimination in this respect as between Polish and other officer prisoners of war.

" At the oral hearing, and before the *Bundesamt*, the complainant sought to found a discriminatory treatment on the ground that German officer prisoners of war in enemy hands were treated by the German Reich more favourably than officer prisoners of war in German hands. Such treatment, however, does not fall within the definition of discriminatory treatment in paragraph 4 of Article 1 of Chapter Ten of the Settlement Convention because the rights of the German officer prisoners of war in enemy hands were not ' non-German rights.'

" The complainant also sought to found discriminatory treatment upon the fact that whereas in the case of Polish officers the EWGG was applied after the commencement of the war with Poland, it was in force in Germany before the commencement of war with the other States concerned. If, however, the German Reich had the right from time to time to alter the pay of its own officers and with such pay to alter also the entitlement to pay of officer prisoners of war in its hands, it is irrelevant whether such alteration took place before or after the commencement of war. If it had been intended by Article 23 of the Geneva Convention to confer upon officer prisoners of war a vested and unchangeable right to pay by reference to the pay of German officers of corresponding rank at a certain specific time—such as the peace-time pay immediately prior to the outbreak of war—that intention must have been expressly stated. Conditions are liable to change very considerably in time of war from those which are appropriate in time of peace, and such a possibility of change must have been present to the minds of the persons who framed the Geneva Convention and of those who represented the acceding States. The wording of Article 23 of that Convention is entirely consistent with an intention that the pay of the officer of corresponding rank of the detaining State, to which pay the officer prisoner of war was to be entitled, was the pay actually paid to the officer of the Detaining Power at the time and from time to time and, in the opinion of the Commission, that was its true meaning and effect.

" Finally, the complainant contends that the actual application of the EWGG to Polish officers was discriminatory in that, by the action of the German Reich in suppressing the Polish Government, the families of Polish officer prisoners of war were deprived of family allowances which the families of other officer prisoners of war were able to obtain from their own Governments. Whilst the Commission may well sympathise with the complainant and his compatriots in this respect, it does not think that the loss in this connection is one which relates to a right under Article 23 of the Geneva Convention or, indeed, to the deprivation, prejudice or impairment of any right within the circumstances envisaged in Article 1 of Chapter Ten of the Settlement Convention. The Geneva Convention was concerned with the treatment of prisoners of war as such, and not with the maintenance of their families; indeed, it would have been quite illogical, unreal and impracticable to have provided that the Detaining Power should be responsible for the maintenance of the family of a prisoner of war in his own country.

" For These Reasons the Arbitral Commission orders that: (1) the appeal be dismissed; (2) the complainant shall bear the Court fee of one hundred Deutsche Mark."

[Report: *Decisions of the Arbitral Commission*, I (1958) Case No. 22, p. 183.]

Treaties of peace—Analogous instruments—Convention with German Federal Republic on Settlement of Matters Arising out of the War and Occupation, 1952-1954—Chapter Ten—Restitution—Restoration of rights and interests—*Situs* of such rights and interests—Conditions laid down in Convention for restoration—Nationality of claimant—Choice-of-law system of the Arbitral Commission.

FÜRTH-PERL AND FÜRTH-STRASSER *v.* GERMAN FEDERAL REPUBLIC.

*Arbitral Commission on Property, Rights and Interests in Germany, Third Chamber.*

(Lagergren, Vice-President; Arndt, Phenix.)

*October* 15, 1958.

THE FACTS (as stated by the Commission).—" This is an appeal to the Arbitral Commission under Article 12, paragraph 1 (*a*), of Chapter Ten of the Settlement Convention from the decision of the Federal Restitution Office [*Bundesamt für die Prüfung ausländischer Rückgabe- und Wiederherstellungsansprüche*] dated September 30, 1957, rejecting complainants' claim for return of or compensation for property allegedly confiscated by the German authorities during the Second World War.

" Complainants, by letter received on April 30, 1956, by the Federal Restitution Office, asserted their claim for 40,250 Reichsmark corresponding to a balance of K. 402,500 in account No. 17481 at the head office of the Zivnostenska Banka in Prague, which balance had been taken by the German authorities on or about April 6, 1944, and transferred first to Vienna and thereafter to Berlin. The account had belonged to the complainant's father, a former national of Czechoslovakia, Dr. Ernst Jakob Fürth, who died on January 4, 1943, leaving the complainants as sole successors to his estate.

" In a letter dated April 22, 1957, also addressed to the Federal Restitution Office, Mrs. Eva Fürth-Perl submits that both complainants were Czechoslovakian nationals by birth, that they both married Hungarians, and subsequently emigrated to the United States [of America] in 1939, in which year they also received their so-called ' First Papers ' (Declaration of Intention to become United States citizens).

" In its decision the Federal Restitution Office recognized that the bank account had been seized by the German authorities in Prague and stated that the seizure took place on November 2, 1942, pursuant to the Ordinance of that day concerning the loss of Protectorate citizenship. Under the terms of that Ordinance the complainants' father, who was a Jew, lost his Protectorate citizenship with the result that, due to that loss, his property became forfeited to the German Reich with immediate effect. A declaration to this effect was published in the *Reichsanzeiger* of June 10. 1943.

" The Federal Restitution Office further held that since, at the time of confiscation of his property (November 2, 1942), Dr. Fürth had been a national of Czechoslovakia, *i.e.*, a national of one of the United Nations, the complainants, as his heirs, were therefore entitled to claim pursuant to Article 1, paragraph 3, of Chapter Ten of the Settlement Convention. The Federal Restitution Office also added that the complainants would equally be entitled to claim if the confiscation had become effective only by the publication of June 10, 1943. In that case the complainants, as their father's heirs, would have been the owners of the bank account at the time of its confiscation, and their right to claim would then follow from the (incorrect) assumption that they were nationals of the United States at that time as well as at the time of filing their claim.

" However, the Federal Restitution Office rejected the complainants' request on the following ground: ' According to Article 1, paragraph 2, of Chapter Ten of the Settlement Convention, the Federal Office shall only consider claims under paragraph 1 of that provision, *i.e.*, claims for return of property in its present condition and the restoration of rights and interests in the Federal territory to the extent to which such property, rights or interests suffered discriminatory treatment. But the undisputed facts in this case do not come within the scope of this provision, since the right of which the applicants have claimed restoration, *i.e.*, the bank account, did not at any time exist in the Federal territory, so that this is not a case of restoration of a right in Federal territory. By the forfeiture of Dr. Fürth's property under the Ordinance of November 2, 1942, his account had been taken from the owners. A claim for restoration of that account could thus aim only at restoration of same at the Prague Bank in Prague and not at restoration of a bank account in Federal territory. It is true that the balance of the account was transferred to Vienna and subsequently to Berlin, yet it was not transferred as the property of the former owner of the account, Dr. Fürth, or his heirs, but as the property of the German Reich, to which the Prague bank account had become forfeited. It was as such credited to the account of the *Oberfinanzpräsident* with the *Postscheckamt*, Vienna, and subsequently transferred to the *Reichshauptkasse* in Berlin.'

" On November 21, 1957, the complainants appealed from the decision of the Federal Restitution Office, served upon them on October 25, 1957."

" Before the Artibral Commission the complainants maintain their earlier arguments and submissions and, in addition, ask for interest, while the defendant asks for the appeal to be dismissed."

*Held:* that the appeal must be dismissed. Restoration of rights and interests in the Federal German territory pursuant to Chapter Ten of the Convention on the Settlement of Matters Arising out of the War and Occupation could be granted only with regard to such rights and interests which were situated in that territory at the time of the discriminatory treatment. The right or interest to be restored in this case had not had its *situs* in the said territory.

The Commission said: " The Arbitral Commission finds that the bank account was lost due to discriminatory treatment as defined in Article 1, paragraph 4, of Chapter Ten of the Settlement Convention. However, although the Ordinance of November 2, 1942 was directed, *inter alia*, at the confiscation of property of persons in the status of Dr. Fürth and his daughters, and the publication of June 10, 1943 makes express reference to Dr. Fürth (at that time no longer living), there is no proof of any actual acts of implementation with regard to the bank account prior to April 1944 when it was allegedly transferred from Prague to Vienna. The Arbitral Commission therefore holds April 1944 to be the time when discriminatory treatment took place.

" It is not contested that at that time the bank account belonged to the complainants. The admissibility of the complainants' claim before the Federal Restitution Office thus rests merely on the question of their own nationality at the date of confiscation and at the filing of their claim in April 1956. As the Arbitral Commission held previously in the case of *Mrs. Rosa Persitz-Keller* v. *German Federal Republic*[1] (Judgment AC/3/J [58] 1 of February 1, 1958) the possession of ' First Papers ' does not signify admission to citizenship of the United States, but is only proof of execution of a ' Declaration of Intention ' to become a United States citizen. But it is quite clear from the records before the Commission that the complainants became nationals of the United States in August 1944, and that they were nationals of the United States (*i.e.*, nationals of one of the ' United Nations ' as defined in Article 9 of Chapter Ten of the Settlement Convention) at the time of filing their claim with the Federal Restitution Office. Thus one important prerequisite of Article 1, paragraph 3, of Chapter Ten of the Settlement Convention has been met. It remains to consider the complainants' nationality at the time of the discriminatory treatment in April 1944, that is, shortly before they became nationals of the United States. They were at that time presumably either stateless as a result of some Nazi denationalization decree or—in accordance with their own statements—nationals of either Czechoslovakia or Hungary, or perhaps of both countries simultaneously. However, in view of the general policy of Chapter Ten of the Settlement Convention, the Arbitral Commission cannot recognize the validity of such denationalization

[1 Reported above, p. 234.]

decrees for the purpose of Article 1, paragraph 3, of that Chapter. In this case, the Arbitral Commission therefore holds that the complainants, at the time of seizure of their bank account, were nationals of either Czechoslovakia or Hungary, or of both countries. On the assumption that they were nationals of Czechoslovakia, they would have been nationals of one of the ' United Nations ' and their claim would have been admissible. If, however, the complainants are deemed to have possessed the nationality of Hungary only, their claim would be inadmissible as Hungary does not belong to the ' United Nations ' as defined in Article 9 of Chapter Ten of the Settlement Convention.

" However, any further investigation as to the nationality of the complainants would appear to be unnecessary as the Arbitral Commission is of the opinion that restoration of rights and interests (no other claim being possible in the present proceedings) in the Federal territory pursuant to Chapter Ten of the Settlement Convention may be granted only with regard to such rights and interests which were situated in that territory at the time of the discriminatory treatment. The right or interest to be restored in this case, however, that is, the credit balance in the bank account No. 17481 with the Zivnostenska Banka in Prague, obviously had its *situs* in Prague and not in the Federal territory. On this point the Arbitral Commission concurs with the above-quoted opinion of the Federal Restitution Office.

" For the foregoing reasons the Arbitral Commission can find no justification for the allowance of the appeal.

" For These Reasons the Arbitral Commission orders that: (1) the appeal from the decision of the Federal Restitution Office dated September 30, 1957, is dismissed; (2) the complainants shall bear the cost of the court fees."

[Report: *Decisions of the Arbitral Commission*, II (1959), Case No. 26, p. 137.]

Peace Treaties—Performance of—Restitution and reparation provisions—Placing of enemy-owned shares in " blocked account " —Whether a " special measure applied to property "—Failure of depositary of shares to take up option rights—Whether giving depositor right to compensation from Government.

SUDREAU CLAIM.

*Franco-Italian Conciliation Commission. September 15, 1955.*

(Perier de Feral, Sorrentino, Bolla.)

THE FACTS.—This was a reference under Article 83 of the Treaty of Peace of February 10, 1947, between the Allied and Associated Powers and Italy,[1] in connection with a claim under Article 78, paragraph 4, sub-paragraph (d),[2] of that Treaty, for compensation for loss caused to M. Sudreau, a French national, by the " blocking " during the war of certain shares belonging to him and deposited in a bank in Italy.

On June 10, 1940, the date of the declaration of war by Italy on France, the Bank of Italy had, in its Milan branch, 6,293 shares in the Snia Viscosa Company, of a nominal value of 250 lire each, held on an account headed " Banque Oustric in liquidation—Planque and Prévost trustees ". By a judgment dated January 20, 1947, duly notified to the Bank of Italy, Sudreau, the present claimant, was declared to be the owner of those shares. The Banque Oustric in liquidation also had an account with the Bank of Italy. On April 20, 1940, the trustees received a final notice from the Bank of Italy of a credit in favour of the Banque Oustric of some 633,547 lire. That credit was, in pursuance of the Italian Law No. 1994 of December 19, 1940, transferred to a blocked impersonal account with the National Institute for Foreign Exchange. It was into that account that dividends on the 6,293 Snia Viscosa shares were paid during the war. They were also constituted a special blocked account [*in deposito speciale vincolato*] with the Bank of Italy under Article 3 of Law No. 1994 above mentioned.

On June 14, 1941, the Snia Viscosa Company decided to increase its capital by, first, raising the nominal value of existing shares from 250 to 300 lire; secondly, issuing 560,000 new shares of 300 lire each, with a premium of 10 lire (payable on January 1, 1941),

---

[1] Article 83 of the Peace Treaty of 1947 provides in part that "Any disputes which may arise in giving effect to Articles . . . 78 . . . of the present Treaty shall be referred to a Conciliation Commission consisting of one representative of the Government of the United Nation concerned and one representative of the Government of Italy . . . [and] a third member selected by mutual agreement of the two Governments from nationals of a third country. . . ."

[2] Article 78, para. 4, sub-para. (d), of the Peace Treaty of 1947 provides:

" (d) The Italian Government shall grant United Nations nationals an indemnity in lire at the same rate as provided in sub-paragraph (a) above to compensate them for the loss or damage due to special measures applied to their property during the war, and which were not applicable to Italian property. This sub-paragraph does not apply to a loss of profit."

available only to former shareholders, at the rate of one new share for five old; thirdly, the issue of new shares the availability of which was not restricted to former shareholders.

The option rights attaching to the 6,293 shares of the Banque Oustric were sold for 548,438 lire, which was placed to the credit of the National Institute for Foreign Exchange.

After the end of the war attempts were made, without success, to reach agreement with either Snia Viscosa or the Bank of Italy, and in 1951 and 1952 Sudreau applied directly by letter to the Treasury of the Italian Republic for the return to him of the option rights attaching to his 6,293 Snia Viscosa shares. On August 18, 1952, the Delegation in Italy of the French Office of Private Property and Interests sent a letter of reminder to the Treasury on behalf of Sudreau. No reply having been received to these communications, the French Government on March 26, 1953, submitted to the Franco-Italian Conciliation Commission an application under Article 78, paragraph 3, of the Peace Treaty of 1947,[1] that Sudreau should be put into the position in which he would have been on the date when the Treaty came into force if he had exercised his rights of option in 1941; in addition, that the Italian Government should be ordered to pay Sudreau, under Article 78, paragraph 4, sub-paragraph (a), of the Treaty, compensation to the extent of the loss sustained by him as a result of his being prevented, in 1941, from taking up the new Snia Viscosa shares. On March 10, 1954, the French Government withdrew this claim.

On March 10, 1954, the French Government submitted a fresh application to the Commission asking that it should—

" 1.—order, by a decision given before formal judgment and with immediate effect, that there be produced both the papers drawn up in the interest of M. Sudreau and sent to the Treasury and the papers relating to any administrative enquiry which the Treasury may have set up;

" 2.—decide and hold:—

" (a) that the provisions of the Italian Law of December 19, 1940, No. 1994, which had been applied to the 6,293 shares in the Snia Viscosa Company belonging to M. Sudreau and held in Milan by the Bank of Italy in an account headed "*Banque Oustric en faillite*", and to the sums in respect of which the Bank of Italy was a debtor to the said account, were special measures taken during the war against United Nations property which did not apply to Italian property;

---

[1] Article 78, para. 3, of the Peace Treaty of 1947 provides as follows: " 3. The Italian Government shall invalidate transfers involving property, rights and interests of any description belonging to United Nations nationals, where such transfers resulted from force or duress exerted by Axis Governments or their agencies during the war."

" (b) that the application of the said provisions had, by depriving the French owner of the sums owing to him by the Bank of Italy, without assuring their management by appointing a sequestrator, had the effect also of depriving him of the opportunity to subscribe to the increase of capital decided on by the Snia Viscosa Company on June 14, 1941, even though the total of those sums was more than sufficient for that purpose; and by permitting only the alienation of the option rights attached to the 6,293 shares above-mentioned had removed the choice of alternatives which was essential to the exercise of the right of option in a case of increase of capital. The result of this had been a loss to M. Sudreau the measure of which was the difference, first, between the number of shares of which he remained owner and the number of shares of which he would have become owner if he had subscribed to the said increase of capital, and, secondly, between the income respectively produced by the said shares in either case;

" 3.—order, consequently, the Italian Government under Article 78, paragraph 4, sub-paragraph (d), of the Treaty of Peace, to pay to M. Sudreau compensation in lire equivalent to two-thirds of the sum necessary to make good the loss calculated as above;

" fix a time limit within which such compensation must be paid."

According to the French Government, the consequence of the non-availability of the sum of 750,000 lire standing to the credit of the impersonal blocked account opened with the National Institute for Foreign Exchange was that there remained only one of the alternative terms which were normally implied for the holder of original shares on an increase of capital (viz., sale of the option rights). Now, this non-availability resulted from the provisions of the Italian Law of December 19, 1940, No. 1994, which constituted speical measures applied during the war to the property of United Nations nationals and which were not applicable to Italian property. The normal alternative would have operated to the profit of the owner of the shares only if the sums for which the Bank of Italy was indebted to the owner had been placed under sequestration. In that case, the administrator-sequestrator would have made choice, in the place of the owner, between the two possibilities offered and would have had to elect, since the fact that the account was in credit permitted it, to subscribe to the increase in capital rather than to dispose of the option rights.

On behalf of the Italian Government, it was pointed out that the new claim alleged that the Italian Government had not put the shares under sequestration, while the first claim was based on the fact (which, it transpired, was inaccurate) that the shares had been sequestrated. The reason why the Snia Viscosa shares had not been placed under sequestration was because Snia Viscosa had reached an agreement with the Italian Government to the effect that—

" No use was made of sequestration or receivership in respect of the Company, and no sequestration took place of enemy-owned shares registered in the Share Register the share certificates of which were not in Italy. It was agreed that share certificates which were in Italy should be retained by the banks at which they had been lodged and the banks themselves authorized to exercise all rights pertaining thereto."

The Bank of Italy, to which the owner of the 6,293 Snia Viscosa shares had entrusted their administration, continued to manage them. If selling the option rights was an act of bad management, the Bank alone was responsible, in view of the civil law relationship between it and the owner. The provisions of Law No. 1994 of 1940 did not put the Bank of Italy under the necessity of selling the option rights, as a result of the non-availability of the money deposited. That Law provided, in effect, for the use, in case of *comprovata necessità* [proved necessity], of the money which was blocked by it. The authorization in question, had it been requested, would have been given without more, for it corresponded to the instruction given to the administrator-sequestrator to subscribe to increases of capital if money was available. Moreover, the intention of the owner of the shares to subscribe to the increase in capital had not been proved; regard must be had to the circumstances at the time: among the French shareholders of Snia Viscosa, some took up, others disposed of, their option rights and others again took up the option in part and sold the remainder of their rights.

On behalf of the French Government, application was made in a fresh *mémoire* to the Commission to:—

" 1. Invite the Agent for the Italian Government to produce the documents, on seeing which he had stated in several places in his *mémoire en réponse*—

" (a) that, before the commencement of hostilities between France and Italy, the Milan branch of the Bank of Italy had the mandate to carry out any act of administration with regard to the 6,293 shares of the Snia Viscosa Company deposited with it in the name of the Banque Oustric in liquidation, which had since then been recognized by the judgment of January 20, 1947, as being the property of M. Sudreau;

" (b) that the Bank of Italy had, in execution of the said mandate, decided, in consequence of the increase in capital resolved on June 14, 1941, by the Snia Viscosa Company, to surrender the option rights belonging to the said shares;

" 2. Order the production

" (a) of all acts or instructions of a general nature emanating from the Italian administrative authority and relating to the modalities of the application of the provisions of Law No. 1994 of December 19, 1940, especially Articles 3, 8 and 9 of that Law;

" (b) of all correspondence or documents relating to the application of the provisions of Articles 3, 8 and 9 of the said Law to property deposited with the Bank of Italy to the account of the Banque Oustric in liquidation, as regards both the sums of money due and the Snia Viscosa shares;

" (c) of the decision of the Italian Government summarized in the following passage, taken by the Agent of the Italian Government from the *mémoire en réponse* produced in the name of the said Government, in the *Société Anonyme de Filatures de Schappe* and *Société des Usines Chimiques Rhône-Poulenc* dispute:[1]

'. . . as far as share certificates in Italy were concerned [the Government] agreed that they should be retained by the banks at which they had been lodged and the banks themselves authorized to exercise all rights pertaining thereto . . .'

" 3. Invite the Agent of the Italian Government to produce all documents, whether general or particular in character, which would have the effect of establishing that, as he had declared in his *mémoire en réponse*, the intention to subscribe to the increase of the capital of a commercial company established under Italian law was among the grounds of proved necessity to which the Director of Finance could give effect by giving an enemy *ressortissant* the authorization provided by Article 15, paragraph 1, of the Law cited above."

In his observations on the foregoing, the Agent of the Italian Government commented:

1. It appeared from the two claims that the Bank of Italy had already, before June 10, 1940, received on deposit the 6,293 Snia Viscosa shares and was administering them.

2. It was not in dispute that Law No. 1994 of December 19, 1940, was applied to the shares and the cash belonging to the Banque Oustric in liquidation. As regards (c), the Agent referred to the file of the *Filatures de Schappe* case included among the records of the Commission.

3. The hypothetical proof that if a request had been put forward the Director of Finances would have given authority for the use of the blocked money for subscribing to the new capital, becomes meaningless as soon as it is shown that the request was never put forward; otherwise, it would be a *probatio diabolica*.

*Held:* that the application must fail. Compliance with the application made by the French Government was unnecessary to enable the Commission to arrive at a decision. The blocking of the account on which the shares were held did not prevent the Bank of Italy from applying for the new shares; the fact that the Bank did not

[1] See *Recueil des Décisions*, Part 2, p. 4; Part 3, p. 103.

do so did not engage the responsibility of the Italian Government, who were therefore not liable to pay compensation.

The Commission said: " 1.—It is not necessary for the present purpose to decide whether, in general, the fact that the Italian Government did not sequestrate shares belonging to nationals of the United or Associated Nations, the certificates of which were in Italy, was such as to engage the responsibility of the Italian Government in the sense of Article 78 of the Treaty of Peace.

" In this case, the fact that the Italian Government refrained from placing under sequestration the 6,293 Snia Viscosa shares which were held at the Bank of Italy to the account of the Banque Oustric in liquidation, can only have benefited the owner of the shares, which thus remained deposited in the financial institution to which they had been entrusted. The private law *nexus*, freely established by the Banque Oustric with the Bank of Italy, continued to have effect despite the war; the only difference consisted in the fact that the deposit was henceforth blocked [*vincolato*] within the meaning of the Italian war legislation, more particularly the Italian Law No. 1994 of December 19, 1940. But that ' blocking ' constituted no reason at all why the Banque Oustric in liquidation or its depositary, the Bank of Italy, acting on the account of the depositor, should not take up the option at the increase of capital effected by Snia Viscosa on June 14, 1941.

" 2.—The Bank of Italy, which held the 6,293 Snia Viscosa shares on deposit—as is recognized by the applicant—preferred to dispose of the option rights. It did so within the framework of the powers—as regards third parties—given to it by its contract with the Banque Oustric. It is not necessary for the Commission to enquire into the precise terms of the contract, because it is not entitled to decide the question whether, at the time of the increase of capital of Snia Viscosa, the Bank of Italy failed to fulfil its obligations to the Banque Oustric in liquidation which resulted from their internal private law relationship.

" 3.—The Agent of the French Government saw in the application of Article 3 of Italian Law No. 1994 of December 19, 1940, to the moneys owed to the Banque Oustric by the Bank of Italy a discriminatory measure of a kind which would engage the responsibility of the Italian Government under Article 78, paragraph 4, sub-paragraph (*d*), of the Treaty of Peace. Those moneys would have sufficed to pay for new shares on subscription; according to the Agent of the French Government, the fact that they were ' blocked ' caused the Bank of Italy to decide to realize the option rights.

" The chain of causation between the discriminatory measure constituted by the application of Law No. 1994 of 1940 to the account of the Banque Oustric and the failure to subscribe for [new] shares would require in any event that: *first*, the Bank of Italy, acting on the instructions of the trustees of the Oustric liquidation or, failing such instructions, of its own manager, should have intended to subscribe to the increase of capital; and *secondly*, the Bank of Italy, having asked the appropriate Director of Finances for an authority to use the blocked account for that purpose, should have met with a refusal, for Law No. 1994 of 1940 provided for such authorizations in case of ' proved need '.

" Now, it has not been proved either that the trustees of the Banque Oustric in liquidation had given the Bank of Italy the authority to subscribe for the new shares, or that the Bank of Italy, acting without instructions, but within its powers, had had any such intention. There was no compulsion at all to choose that alternative in June 1940, at which time the length and the outcome of the war, among other things, were unknown, as was also the ultimate fate of French property in Italy; the proof of that is that French shareholders who were in a position to act freely at that time sold their rights of option, as appears from the file of the case of *Filatures de Schappe—Rhône Poulenc* (Claim No. 37) heard by the Commission.

" On the other hand, the Agent of the French Government does not even allege that the Bank of Italy asked the competent Italian authority for authorization to employ the blocked account for subscribing to the new shares and that such a request would have been rejected. There is no way of telling what would have been the fate of such a request had it been made; in any event, as regards shares placed under sequestration the Italian Government permitted administrator-sequestrators to subscribe to increases of capital if they judged it opportune and if they had the necessary funds, which also appears from the case of *Filatures de Schappe—Rhône Poulenc* cited above.

" In these conditions, the order asked for by the Agent for the French Government appears to be unnecessary for the decision of this case."

[Report: *Recueil des Décisions*, Part 5, p. 243.]

Peace treaties—Restitution and compensation provisions—Meaning of " treated as enemy "—Allegation of obstruction of sale by Governmental authorities—Rejection of argument that delay constitutes hostile treatment—Critical dates for application of restitution provisions—Necessity for claimant to be national of claiming State when damage sustained.

See p. 91 (*Flegenheimer Claim*), at pp. 153–166.

Peace treaties—Performance of—Restitution provisions—Convention on the Settlement of Matters Arising out of the War and Occupation, 1952-1954—Claims for compensation—Distinguished from claims for restitution.

See p. 536 (*de Haan* v. *German Federal Republic*).

Treaties—Special kinds of—Peace Treaties—Analogous instruments—Agreement on German External Debts, 1953—Annex VII—Private law contracts—Regulation by Agreement—Claims with specific foreign character—Criteria for determining such character—Place of payment situated abroad—Meaning of—Whether to be ascertained in accordance with municipal law—Application of rule relating to interpretation of treaties—Natural meaning of term " place of payment " in contradistinction to other meanings—Corroborated by history of Agreement—Gold clause—Debts with—Conversion of such debts—Under Agreement on German External Debts—Foreign creditors.

See p. 33 (*Swiss Confederation* v. *German Federal Republic* (No. 1)).

Treaties—Special kinds of—Peace Treaties—Element of compulsion—Whether affecting contractual character of treaty.

See p. 313 (*Re Application to Swiss Nationals of the Italian Special Capital Levy Duty*).

## F—MISCELLANEOUS

Treaties—Modification of—Consent of all Parties—Need for.

See p. 540 (*Leupold-Praesent* v. *German Federal Republic*).

PART IX

# INTERNATIONAL ORGANIZATION AND ADMINISTRATION

## B—THE UNITED NATIONS

### II.—The General Assembly

**International organization—The United Nations—General Assembly—Resolutions of—Interpretation of—Relevance of statements made by representatives in *ad hoc* Political Committee—Resolution 388 (V) of December 15, 1950.**

See p. 2 (*Italy* v. *United Kingdom of Great Britain and Northern Ireland and United Kingdom of Libya. General List No. 1 (Merits)*).

## D—OTHER INTERNATIONAL ORGANIZATIONS AND ORGANS OF INTERNATIONAL ADMINISTRATION

**International organization—Whether an international organization has right to delegate its powers—Whether such right to be implied—Distinction between delegation of discretion and delegation of execution—European Coal and Steel Community Treaty, 1951—Period within which decision of High Authority can be annulled—Effect of challenge of that decision out of time—Right to challenge the validity of general decision when challenging validity of individual decision made in application of it—Duty to support decision by reasons.**

MERONIE & CIE, INDUSTRIE METALLURGICHE, S.U.A. *v.* THE HIGH AUTHORITY.

*Court of Justice of the European Coal and Steel Community.*

(Pilotti, President; Van Kleffens, Delvaux, Serrarens, Riese, Rueff and Hammes JJ.)

*June* 13, 1958.

THE FACTS.—In 1955, there was a shortage of iron and steel scrap within the Community. This shortage had existed for some eighteen months to two years previously, and the High Authority during that time had taken various decisions to deal with it. As these decisions, were however, due to expire on May 31, 1955, the High Authority in March 1955 passed Decision No. 14-55 which was entitled " a decision establishing a financial arrangement to ensure the regular supply of steel scrap to the common market." [1]

The difficulty which had to be met was, basically, that because there was not enough scrap within the Community some further scrap had to be imported, but the price of imported scrap was higher than the Community prices. If, therefore, scrap had been freely imported, there would have been a danger that the price of Community scrap would have risen to that of imported scrap. This was to be avoided by placing a subsidy upon imported scrap so that purchasers of it did not pay its full price. The money to pay this subsidy was to be provided out of a special Subsidy Fund. This Fund was to be created by the placing of a levy upon all consumption of scrap within the Community at a rate of so much per ton of scrap consumed. Further, in order to encourage a reduction in the consumption of scrap, a bonus was to be paid to every enterprise which reduced its consumption of scrap by using iron instead.

By decision No. 14-55, the carrying out of these arrangements was entrusted to two organizations: The *Office Commun* of Consumers of Iron and Steel Scrap and the *Caisse* for Subsidies upon Imported Iron and Steel Scrap. Both of these organizations had already been voluntarily set up by the steel industry itself and were centred in Brussels. There were also regional offices of these organizations, set up in each of the six member States.

The *Office Commun* was to negotiate the bulk purchase of scrap iron from countries outside the Community and to determine how much scrap should be imported and what prices should be paid for it. The actual contracts, however, were to be made between the suppliers and individual enterprises. [2] These enterprises were then to be told by the *Caisse* how much they would receive from it by way of subsidy.

The *Caisse* had two further important functions. First, it was to determine the formula to be used to determine what economies had been made in the consumption of scrap by the increased use of iron, and thus the amount of the consequent bonus payment. [3] Secondly, it was to fix the amount of the levy to the Subsidy Fund that was to be paid by all consumers of scrap and to decide the time within which that levy was to be paid. [4] If the payment were not made

---

[1] Decision No. 14-55 was taken under Article 53, para. 1 (b), of the Treaty. Article 53, para. 1, provides:

" (a) The High Authority may after consulting the Consultative Committee and the Council, authorize the creation, under conditions which it shall determine and under its control, of any financial arrangements common to several enterprises which are considered necessary for the accomplishment of the objectives defined in Article 3 and compatible with the provisions of this Treaty and particularly of Article 65;

" (b) the High Authority, with the unanimous agreement of the Council, may itself set up any financial arrangements answering the same purposes."

[2] Decision No. 14-55, Article 5.

[3] Ibid.

[4] Ibid., Article 3.

within the time specified, the *Caisse* could request the intervention of the High Authority, which could then by Article 92 of the European Coal and Steel Community Treaty, pass a decision demanding payment of the sum due. This decision had, by the Treaty, executory force.[1] The present case deals with one such decision of the High Authority.

The two organizations in Brussels were, however, not autonomous for, by the same Decision No. 14-55, the High Authority was to appoint a representative to each of them and these representatives could make the enforcement of any of the decisions of these organizations subject to the approval of the High Authority.[2] Further, if the unanimous agreement of the *Office Commun* or of the *Caisse* could not be obtained, the decision on any matter had to be taken by the High Authority.

In the present case, by a letter dated March 4, 1954,[3] the *Caisse*[4] requested from the plaintiffs the figures of all scrap bought by them so that it could determine the amount of their levy due to the Subsidy Fund. When it received no answer to this request, the *Caisse* sent a further letter and, after their continued silence, a registered letter was sent to the plaintiffs in May demanding these figures.

Thirteen months later, in June 1955, a further letter was sent stating that if no figures were supplied by the plaintiffs, these figures would be assessed by the *Caisse* itself and that the plaintiffs would then be charged upon that assessment. The following month a further letter was sent, this time demanding not figures but payment of a sum of just over 10 m. lire.

Nine months later, on April 12, 1956, the plaintiffs wrote to the High Authority suggesting a possible payment of 2 m. lire a month but without prejudice to their rights to deny the legality of the whole system of levies to the Subsidy Fund. This offer was rejected, and the *Caisse* requested the High Authority to take a decision demanding the money. This decision was passed on October 24, 1956, and claimed from the plaintiffs the sum of 59,819,656 lire.

---

[1] Article 92 of the Treaty states:

" The decisions of the High Authority imposing financial obligations on enterprises shall have executive force.

" They shall be put into forced execution on the territory of member States by means of the legal procedure in effect in each State, after the formula of execution in use in the State on whose territory the decision is to be carried out has been appended; this shall be done with no other formality than the verification of the authenticity of such decisions. The execution of these formalities shall be the responsibility of a Minister whom each Government shall designate for this purpose.

" The forced execution of such decisions can be suspended only by a decision of the Court."

[2] Decision No. 14-55, Articles 8 and 9.

[3] This letter was sent before the passing of Decision No. 14-55, under the authority of earlier similar decisions.

[4] The actual sender of the letter was CAMPSIDER (the abbreviated name of *Consorzio Approvvigionamenti Materie Prime Siderurgiche S. A. Milano*), which was the Italian regional office of the two Brussels organizations.

Under the Treaty, this decision had executory force and the plaintiffs' property was open to immediate seizure.

The plaintiffs appealed against this decision, alleging that it had not been adequately supported by reasons. They also sought to allege that the entire system of levies to the Subsidy Fund and of the working of the organizations in Brussels authorized by Decision No. 14–55 was void on the ground that the High Authority had delegated to these organizations powers which were wider than those which it possessed itself. The High Authority contended, however, that, as the one month period during which appeals could have been brought against Decision No. 14–55 had long previously expired, the plaintiffs could no longer challenge that decision, but were limited to challenging the decision which actually claimed the levy due.

*Held:* that the decision of October 24, 1956, should be annulled. It had not been adequately supported by reasons, as no breakdown of the sum claimed had been given. Further, as the decision of October 24, 1956, had been passed in application of Decision No. 14–55, the invalidity of that latter decision could be alleged even after the expiration of the specified time period. By Decision No. 14–55 the High Authority delegated to the *Caisse* and the *Office Commun* in Brussels powers wider than those originally conferred by the Treaty upon itself. Such delegation was therefore in violation of the Treaty. However, as the one month period for the annulment of Decision No. 14–55 had expired, the Court could not annul that decision, but its invalidity was a further ground for the annulment of the decision of October 24, 1956.

The Court said:

" . . . In this appeal against the decision of the High Authority dated October 24, 1956, which is of an executory nature within the meaning of Article 92 of the Treaty, the plaintiffs submit that Decision No. 14–55 of March 26, 1955, 'setting up a financial arrangement to ensure the regular supply of steel scrap to the common market', patently misconstrues the provisions of the Treaty and is vitiated by a *détournement de pouvoir*.

" By the terms of Article 33, appeals 'must be lodged within one month from the date of notification or publication, as the case may be, of the decision or recommendation '. Further, if the appeals are brought by an enterprise or association, as defined by Article 48, they are not admissible if they concern a general decision or recommendation unless the plaintiffs allege that these decisions or recommendations are vitiated by a *détournement de pouvoir* with respect to them.

" This appeal was brought on December 14, 1956, and, therefore, the time for bringing an appeal, as prescribed in the last paragraph of Article 33, has been complied with in regard to the decision of

October 24, 1956. It has expired in respect of Decision No. 14–55 of March 26, 1955.

" However, Decision No. 14–55 of March 26, 1955, has not been challenged directly, but by way of an appeal against the decision of October 24, 1956, which is of an executory nature.

" Whereas the decision of October 24, 1956, is an individual decision concerning the plaintiffs, Decision No. 14–55 of March 26, 1955, is a general decision upon which the decision of October 24, 1956, has been based.

" In order to determine the ability of the plaintiffs, in support of their appeal against the individual decision, to rely upon the irregularity of the general decision upon which it has been based, it is necessary to discover whether the plaintiffs are able to challenge that decision after the expiration of the period set out in the last paragraph of Article 33, and further, whether, in challenging that general decision, they may allege not only a *détournement de pouvoir* with respect to them but also the four grounds of annulment that are set out in the first paragraph of Article 33.

" In agreement with the conclusions of the Court Advocate, the Court holds that a general decision which has been taken irregularly cannot be applied to an enterprise, and that money payments cannot be deducted from that enterprise.

" Article 36 of the Treaty states that in support of an appeal against a decision of the High Authority imposing pecuniary sanctions or daily penalty payments:

'    . . . the petitioners may contest the legality of the decisions and recommendations which they are charged with violating.

" There is no occasion to hold this provision of Article 36 to be a special provision applicable only to the case of pecuniary sanctions and daily penalty payments, but as the application of a general principle, of which Article 36 is its application to the special case of an appeal *en pleine juridiction*.

" One cannot argue, from the express mention in Article 36, that the application of this principle is excluded in any case where it is not expressly mentioned, for the Court has decided in its judgment in Case No. 8–55[1] that such a mode of arguing is not admissible unless no other interpretation appears to be appropriate and compatible with the express wording of the provision, with its whole context, and with its underlying purpose.

" Any other interpretation would render the exercise of the right of appeal granted to enterprises and associations that comply with Article 48 difficult if not impossible, for they would be required to discover in every general decision as soon as it was published those provisions which possibly at some future time might damage them,

[1 *Fédération Charbonnière de Belgique* v. *The High Authority* (*Recueil de la Jurisprudence de la Cour*, vol. II (1955–1956)), reported below, p. 417.]

or which might be considered as vitiated by a *détournement de pouvoir* with respect to them.

" It would encourage enterprises and associations to allow those pecuniary sanctions or daily penalty payments prescribed in the Treaty to be imposed upon them in order to be able, by virtue of Article 36, to bring into issue the irregularity of those general decisions and recommendations which they would be accused of not having complied with.

" The ability of a plaintiff, after the expiration of the period set out in the last paragraph of Article 33, to rely, in support of his appeal against an individual decision, upon the irregularity of general decisions and recommendations upon which the individual decision has been based, cannot lead to the annulment of the general decision but only of the individual decision to which it gave rise.

" The Treaties establishing the European Economic Community and Euratom expressly adopt a similar interpretation when they set out in Articles 184 and 156 respectively that:

' notwithstanding the expiration of the time limit set out in Article 173, paragraph 3 (or, in the case of Euratom, Article 146, paragraph 3), any party in any action challenging a regulation of the Council or of the Commission may rely upon the grounds set out in Article 173, paragraph 1 (or, in the case of Euratom, Article 146, paragraph 1) when challenging that regulation before the Court of Justice.'

These particular Articles, without providing a conclusive argument, support the above reasoning by showing that it is also accepted by the draftsmen of these new Treaties.

" The annulment of an individual decision upon the ground of the irregularity of the general decision upon which it has been based does not alter the provisions of that general decision except to the extent to which those provisions have been made more specific by the individual decision which has been annulled.

" In challenging an individual decision that affects them, plaintiffs are entitled to allege the four grounds of annulment set out in the first paragraph of Article 33.

" Hence, nothing prevents a plaintiff when bringing an appeal against an individual decision from alleging the four grounds of annulment set out in the first paragraph of Article 33, so as to challenge the regularity of the general decisions or recommendations upon which that individual decision has been based.

" . . . The plaintiffs allege that the decision of October 24, 1956, ' clearly contains insufficient reasoning '. This particular decision only specifies two reasons, namely:

' that the *Société Anonyme Meronie & Cie, Industrie Metallurgiche, Stabilimento Elettrosiderurgico, Via della Cebrosa, Settimo Torinese,* being an enterprise within the meaning of Article 80 of the Treaty, omitted from April 1, 1954, to pay to the *Caisse de Péréquations des*

*Ferrailles importées* the contributions due from it in conformity with the decisions set out below;

'that the sums due for the period from April 1, 1954, to June 30, 1956, amount to the sum of 54,819,656 lire.'

In the opinion of the Court, these two paragraphs do not amount to a statement of those considerations both of law and of fact upon which the decision of October 24, 1956, was based. This decision is thus deprived of any statement of justification, which is indispensable to the exercise of any legal control.

" The decision of October 24, 1956, therefore, does not comply with the requirements of Article 15 of the Treaty, by the terms of which ' decisions . . . of the High Authority are to be supported by reasons.'

" . . . The plaintiffs allege against the High Authority the ' unchallengeable, not to say sanctified, character of the calculations made by the organizations in Brussels, which, if final, would be more rigid and certainly infinitely more important than actual decisions, which are always open to challenge before the Court of Justice '. Further, the plaintiffs accuse the High Authority of having delegated to the organizations in Brussels powers which by the Treaty were granted to itself, without subjecting their exercise to the conditions which the Treaty would have subjected them if those powers had been exercised by itself directly.

" . . . It is necessary to determine whether Decision No. 14–55 ' setting up a financial mechanism to ensure the regular supply of steel scrap to the common market ' constitutes an actual delegation to the organizations in Brussels of the powers which the Treaty had given to the High Authority, or whether it grants to those organizations only the power to issue ' findings ', the carrying out of which would rest with the High Authority which, thus, would retain full legal responsibility.

" . . . Of these two interpretations, the High Authority has chosen the first, by stating in its Defence that:

' The High Authority accepts the data supplied by the organizations in Brussels without having any power to question them. Any other attitude would have amounted to an unauthorized interference in the affairs of another organization by requiring it to explain the reasons by which it reached its decision.'

" . . . If the High Authority had itself exercised those powers which, by Decision No. 14–55, it conferred upon the organizations in Brussels, they would have been subject to the rules contained in the Treaty and particularly to those which impose upon the High Authority: the duty to support its decisions with reasons and to refer to the advice which it is required to obtain (Article 15); the duty to publish annually a general report upon the activities and administrative expenses of the Community (Article 17); the duty to publish data which may be useful to Governments or to any other interested parties (Article 47). Similarly, their decisions and recommendations would have been subject to the jurisdiction of the Court of Justice under the conditions set out in Article 33.

" Decision No. 14–55 has not subjected the exercise of the powers which it granted to the organizations in Brussels to any of the conditions to which that exercise would have been subject if the High Authority had itself acted directly. Even if this delegation consequent upon Decision No. 14–55 appeared to be in accordance with the Treaty, the High Authority could not grant powers to the entity concerned different from those which it has itself received by the Treaty.

" The ability of these organizations in Brussels to take decisions free from the conditions to which they would have been subject if they had been taken directly by the High Authority, in fact gives to the organizations in Brussels wider powers than those which the High Authority possessed by the Treaty. By not subjecting the decisions of the organizations in Brussels to the requirements to which the Treaty subjects decisions of the High Authority, the delegations consequent upon Decision No. 14–55 violate the Treaty. Therefore, the decision of October 24, 1956, giving executory force to an obligation imposed in application of the general Decision No. 14–55, which is itself irregular, must be annulled.

" . . . A delegation of powers can never be implied, and even when entitled to delegate its powers the authority delegating must take an explicit decision in order to delegate its powers. The *ex officio* fixing of the levy due and the notification of those provisional sums owing which had been calculated by the organizations in Brussels lack a legal basis, and for this reason, also, the decision of October 24, 1956, giving executory force to the obligations imposed by a procedure lacking legal validity, must be annulled.

" . . . The plaintiffs accuse the High Authority of having by its Decision No. 14–55 delegated to the organizations in Brussels powers which they were ill-qualified to carry out.

"Article 8 of the Treaty charges the High Authority

' to be responsible for assuring the achievement of the purposes stated in this Treaty within the terms thereof ';

but the Treaty does not contain a power to delegate.

" However, one cannot exclude the possibility that the carrying out of the ' financial arrangements common to several enterprises ' referred to in paragraph (*a*) of Article 53 may be entrusted to organizations in private law which have been endowed with a distinct legal personality and granted the appropriate powers. The financial arrangements set up by the High Authority itself in application of paragraph (*b*) of that Article must be directed towards the same ends as those which are authorized in application of paragraph (*a*). Therefore, the arrangements must be able to be of an analogous form and, in particular, they must be able to work through organizations possessing a distinct legal personality.

" Hence, the ability of the High Authority to authorize or to set up the financial arrangements mentioned in Article 53 of the Treaty gives that Authority the right to confer upon such organizations certain powers to be exercised under the conditions which it determines and under its own control. However, by the terms of Article 53 such delegations are not legal unless the High Authority

' considered [them] necessary for the accomplishment of the objectives defined in Article 3 and compatible with the provisions of this Treaty and particularly of Article 65.'

" Article 3 sets out no less than eight distinct and very general objectives, and it is not certain that they can all be pursued simultaneously in all circumstances and in their entirety. In the pursuit of the objectives set out in Article 3 of the Treaty, the High Authority must ensure the permanent reconciliation of the possible contradictions that exist among the objectives when they are considered individually. When such contradictions do arise, it must grant to some of the objectives of Article 3 such pre-eminence as may appear to it to be necessitated by the facts and economic circumstances in view of which it takes its decisions.

" The reconciliation of these diverse objectives of Article 3 implies the existence of a true discretionary power to make a difficult choice, based upon a consideration of the facts and economic circumstances in the light of which it must be made.

" The consequences resulting from a delegation of powers are very different according to whether that delegation concerns powers of execution which are clearly defined, the use of which, therefore, may be subjected to a strict control by reference to the objective criteria imposed by the delegating authority, or whether it concerns a discretionary power, involving extensive freedom to make assessments of situations, which is liable to develop in practice into what is in fact a true political decision.

" A delegation of the first type is not of a nature noticeably to alter the consequences which may result from the exercise of those powers which are involved, whereas a delegation of the second type, by substituting the discretion of the authority to which the power has been delegated for that of the delegating authority, acts as a complete transfer of responsibility.

" . . . By Article 9 of Decision No. 14–55, the High Authority has granted to its permanent representative to the organizations in Brussels the right to make any decision conditional upon the approval of the High Authority. Even by retaining this power to refuse its approval, the High Authority has not retained adequate powers in order that the delegation resulting from Decision No. 14–55 should be restricted within the limits set out above.

" The High Authority has admitted, in the paragraph that has been quoted from its Defence, that it ' accepted the data supplied by-the organizations in Brussels without being able to question it.'

" For these reasons the delegation of powers granted to the organizations in Brussels by Decision No. 14–55 gave them a right to make an assessment of the situation which involved a large discretionary power and which cannot be regarded as compatible with the requirements of the Treaty.

" The Decision of October 24, 1956, is based upon a general decision which according to the Treaty has been irregularly passed, and for that reason also it must be annulled.

[Report: *Recueil de la Jurisprudence de la Cour*, vol. IV (1958), p. 9 (in French).]

NOTE.—The above judgment is of importance both theoretically and in practice. By Article 33, para. 1, of the Treaty, member States of the Community can challenge decisions of the High Authority on the grounds of incompetence, violation of a substantial procedural requirement, violation of the Treaty, and *détournement de pouvoir*. An enterprise such as the plaintiffs in the present case can challenge on these same four grounds any decision of the High Authority which is individual to itself; and it can also challenge any general decision, but only on the grounds of a *détournement de pouvoir* with respect to itself. Furthermore, all these appeals must be brought within a period of one month from the notification or publication of the decision concerned.

The plaintiffs in the present action, therefore, could originally only have challenged the general Decision No. 14–55, which set up the system of subsidies, upon the ground of a *détournement de pouvoir* with respect to itself, and clearly no such *détournement* existed. When the plaintiffs challenged the decision of October 24, 1956, they could allege against that decision all the four grounds set out in Article 33, because that decision was an individual one. The Court, however, held that in their action the plaintiffs could allege against the general decision, under which the individual one had been passed, all the four grounds of invalidity in Article 33, although in the Treaty only member States are expressly granted the right to do this. Further, it was held that this challenge of the general decision could be made even after the expiration of the time-limit for the bringing of actions. Although the Court held that the general Decision No. 14–55 was invalid it had no power to annul it, because the period of time during which decisions could be annulled had expired. The invalidity of the general decision, however, caused the decision taken in application of its provisions to be open to annulment if challenged within the prescribed period of time.

International organization—European Coal and Steel Community
—Interpretation of Treaty establishing—Articles setting out
fundamental aims of Treaty to be read as a whole—Power of
international organization to give predominance to certain of these
aims—Interpretation of fundamental aims in light of subsequent
provision of Treaty—Whether failure to comply with fundamental
aims of Treaty amounts to *détournement de pouvoir*—Dominant
purpose of Treaty.

GROUPEMENT DES HAUTS FOURNEAUX ET ACIÉRIES BELGES *v.* THE
HIGH AUTHORITY.

*Court of Justice of the European Coal and Steel Community.*

(Pilotti, President; Van Kleffens, Delvaux, Serrarens, Riese, Rueff and
Hammes JJ.)

*June* 21, 1958.

THE FACTS.—In 1957, the shortage of iron and steel scrap within
the Community was as acute as it had been in 1955 and earlier, when
the High Authority had authorized the importation of scrap and
had given a subsidy to it in order to keep down its price.[1] To meet
this continued shortage, the High Authority passed Decision No.
2–57, which continued both the subsidy payments and the bonus
to enterprises which economized in the use of steel scrap by an
increased use of iron. It continued also what it called " the basic
tax " upon the consumption of scrap in order to provide revenue
for the Subsidy Fund, but it introduced a new tax, " the supplementary tax ", which was imposed upon any enterprises which were
increasing their consumption of scrap. To calculate this increased
consumption each enterprise was to select a " period of reference ",
that, is, a period of six calendar months out of seven consecutive
calendar months between January 1, 1953, and January 31, 1957.
An enterprise's "consumption of reference" was then, basically,
their average monthly consumption of scrap during that period.[2]

Decision No. 2–57 inaugurated accounting periods of three
months, starting from February 1, 1957,[3] and if in any of these
periods an enterprise's average consumption was in excess of its
" consumption of reference ", the supplementary tax had to be paid
upon that excess.[4] The amount of the supplementary tax was calculated as a percentage of the basic tax,[5] but a remission was granted
where the consumption of all types of scrap used by an enterprise

---

[1] See *Meronie & Co., Industrie Metallurgiche, S.P.A.* v. *The High Authority*, reported above, p. 369.
[2] Decision No. 2–57, Article 6 (1). Provision was made for the case where new
machinery or productive processes were introduced during the " period of reference ",
so that their consumption only related to part of the period.
[3] Decision No. 2–57, Article 3 (2).
[4] Decision No. 2–57, Article 3 (1) (b).
[5] Decision No. 2–57, Article 8.

was less than its "consumption of reference" or where the consumption was less than the average of the Community as a whole.

As with the earlier decisions of the High Authority, the running of this system was given over to the *Office Commun* and the *Caisse* in Brussels.[1] The *Office Commun* was given the power to propose to the *Caisse* such matters as the amount of the subsidy, the maximum price of importation, the amount of the basic tax, and the amount of the bonus payment for economies brought about by the increased use of iron.[2] The *Caisse* was given the final power to determine upon these matters.[3] As before, the High Authority appointed a representative to each of these organizations who had the power to make any decision of either of them conditional upon approval of the High Authority.[4] The *Caisse* was further empowered to inform enterprises of the amount of the tax due from them,[5] and if payment were not made as requested the High Authority could subsequently pass a Decision having executory force under Article 92 of the European Coal and Steel Community Treaty, 1951.[6]

The plaintiffs were a group of Belgian blast furnaces and steel works and they alleged that the system established by Decision No. 2–57 constituted a *détournement de pouvoir*. The system had been established under Article 53 (*b*) of the Treaty, whereby the High Authority can set up any financial arrangements "considered necessary for the accomplishment of the objectives defined in Article 3 and compatible with the provisions of this Treaty." The plaintiffs claimed that Decision No. 2–57 did not further the aims of the Community as set out in Articles 2, 3, 4 and 5 of the Treaty.[7] The High Authority, therefore, had imposed the system for a purpose other than the one authorized by the Treaty. The decision was thus alleged to be void as a *détournement de pouvoir*.

[1] As to these, see above, p. 370.
[2] Decision No. 2–57, Article 11 (1).
[3] *Ibid.*
[4] Decision No. 2–57, Articles 14 and 15.
[5] Decision No. 2–57, Article 12 (2).
[6] Decision No. 2–57, Article 12 (3). For the provisions of Article 92 of the Treaty see above, p. 371, n. 1.
[7] Article 2:
" The mission of the European Coal and Steel Community is to contribute to the expansion of the economy, the development of employment and the improvement of the standard of living in the participating countries through the creation, in harmony with the general economy of the member States, of a common market as defined in Article 4.
" The Community must progressively establish conditions which will in themselves assure the most rational distribution of production at the highest possible level of productivity, while safeguarding the continuity of employment and avoiding the creation of fundamental and persistent disturbances in the economies of the member States."
Article 3:
" Within the framework of their respective powers and responsibilities and in the common interest, the institutions of the Community shall:
(*a*) ensure that the common market is regularly supplied, while taking into account the needs of third countries;
(*b*) assure to all consumers in comparable positions within the common market equal access to the sources of production;

*Held:* that the action must fail. Any financial arrangement set up under Article 53 (*b*) of the Treaty must further the objects of the Community as set out not only in Article 3, but also in Articles 2, 4 and 5. Not all these objects could be pursued at one and the same time and the High Authority had power to choose one or more of these objects and seek their achievement rather than that of the other objects. The system set up by Decision 2–57 was justified by the situation existing at the time when that decision was taken, and that decision was in conformity with Article 3 (*a*) and (*d*), Article 2, para. 2, and Article 5, paras. 2 and 3.

The Court said: " . . . The High Authority has chosen Article 53 as the legal authority for the system of subsidising steel scrap which it has set up. This article places at its disposal a means of intervention to achieve those objectives which the Treaty, especially in Article 3, has granted to it.

" Article 53 comes within Chapter II, entitled ' Financial Provisions ', which in its other articles deals with the use that is to be made of the funds which are obtained by the High Authority by means of levies upon production or by means of borrowing. One may note that the financial arrangements contained in Article 53 are arrangements based upon the transfer of resources, especially by

(*c*) seek the establishment of the lowest possible prices without involving any corresponding rise either in the prices charged by the same enterprises in other transactions or in the price-level as a whole in another period, while at the same time permitting necessary amortization and providing the possibility of normal returns on invested capital;

(*d*) ensure that conditions are maintained which will encourage enterprises to expand and improve their ability to produce and to promote a policy of rational development of natural resources, while avoiding undue exhaustion of such resources;

(*e*) promote the improvement of the living and working conditions of the labour force in each of the industries under its jurisdiction so as to harmonize those conditions in an upward direction;

(*f*) foster the development of international trade and ensure that equitable limits are observed in prices charged in foreign markets;

(*g*) promote the regular expansion and the modernization of production as well as the improvement of quality, under conditions which preclude any protection against competing industries except where justified by illegitimate action on the part of such industries or in their favour."

Article 4:

" The following are recognized to be incompatible with the common market for coal and steel, and are, therefore, abolished and prohibited within the Community in the manner set forth in this Treaty;

(*a*) import and export duties, or taxes with an equivalent effect, and quantitative restrictions on the movement of coal and steel;

(*b*) measures or practices discriminating among producers, among buyers or among consumers, especially as concerns prices, delivery terms and transport rates, as well as measures or practices which hamper the buyer in the free choice of his supplier; . . ."

Article 5:

" The Community shall accomplish its mission, under the conditions provided for in this Treaty, with limited intervention.

" To this end, the Community shall assure the establishment, the maintenance and the observance of normal conditions of competition, and take direct action with respect to production and the operation of the market only when circumstances make it absolutely necessary; . . ."

means of subsidy payments or of compensation. This interpretation is confirmed by the last paragraph of Article 62, which states that ' certain compensation schemes may, in addition, be set up under the terms of Article 53 '.

" The subsidy payments do not directly affect prices but they do affect the factors which contribute to their formation. Hence, without interfering with the free determination of prices, these factors affect the level at which prices become fixed. It is by these modifications of the level of prices that the financial arrangements referred to in Article 53 have an influence upon the other characteristic elements in the state of the market, and especially upon the supply and demand of products affected. There exist therefore in the hands of the High Authority powerful and effective means of intervention, but these means are, by their nature, ' indirect ' within the meaning of Article 57 of the Treaty, in contrast to the means of direct action by the fixing of quotas of production (Article 58) or by the apportionment of resources (Article 59).

" The use of the financial arrangements referred to in Article 53 allows the High Authority to exercise a substantial influence upon the market for coal and steel, subject, however, to the reservation in Article 53 which limits the use of these arrangements to procedures ' necessary for the accomplishment of the objectives defined in Article 3 and compatible with the provisions of this Treaty, and particularly Article 65 '.

" The express mention of Article 3 does not release the High Authority from the obligation to respect the other articles of the Treaty, and in particular Articles 2, 4 and 5, which, with Article 3, must always be respected because they set out the fundamental aims of the Community. These provisions have equal binding force and must be read together if they are to be correctly applied. These provisions are self-contained and are immediately applicable unless they are referred to in any other provision of the Treaty. If they are referred to, or elaborated, in other provisions of the Treaty, the texts are to be regarded as a single provision which must be interpreted as a whole and jointly applied. One may note, however, that in practice one must undertake a certain reconciliation between the diverse objectives of Article 3, for it is clearly impossible to achieve them simultaneously, each one to its full extent, for these objectives are general principles and one must seek their realization and harmonization to the greatest extent possible. On the other hand, the financial arrangements must be established without prejudice to the provisions of Article 58 and of Chapter 5 of Title III of the Treaty.

" Decisions prior to Decision No. 2–57 had as their object the equilization of the prices of imported and home-produced scrap metal. Decision No. 2–57 continued this system but amended it and added to it new provisions having an effect both upon the price of scrap metal and upon the volume of purchases. This was done with the aim of encouraging enterprises to make economies in scrap metal in the interests of the regular provisioning of the market.

" The excess of the demand over the supply of scrap metal, if it had continued, could have created ' a serious shortage ' amenable to the procedures set out in Article 59. The High Authority, if it had wished to avoid adopting these procedures—and the provisions of Article 57 required them to seek as far as possible to avoid them —would not have been able to escape the necessity and the duty of applying the procedure set out in Article 53 (b), subject to the need to respect the conditions of its application.

" However, contrary to the plaintiffs' contention, one cannot admit that, in the examination of an allegation of a *détournement de pouvoir* in relation to the fundamental provisions of Articles 2, 3, 4 and 5, which specify the aims and purposes of the Community, it is enough to allege a contradiction between, or an incompatibility of, the measures challenged and one or more of these fundamental provisions, or that this allegation, in itself, removes the need for any examination of the basic aims of these measures, when such an examination is required in respect of a claim of a *détournement de pouvoir* relating to any of the other provisions of the Treaty.

" In fact, Article 33, para. 2, of the Treaty does not give to enterprises a right of appeal against the general decisions of the High Authority, unless the enterprises believe these decisions to be vitiated by a *détournement de pouvoir* with respect to them. The provision is clearly restrictive and limiting, and involves the prevention of any abuse of power. It involves, in essence, a control over aims being pursued, an examination of the basic purposes of the measure being challenged. In the establishment of the proof of a *détournement de pouvoir* there is no provision of the Treaty which justifies any derogation from this.

" . . . By the terms of Article 53 (b) of the Treaty, the High Authority, upon the unanimous advice of the Council, may itself set up any finanical arrangements which it believes necessary for the carrying out of the powers which are thus granted to it subject to the conditions set out in Articles 2 to 5, which provide for the establishment, administration and orientation of the common market.

" By the terms of Article 2 of the Treaty, the Community has as its mission to contribute to economic expansion, to the development of employment and to the improvement of the standard of living in the member States. The means set out to realize these objectives comprise the establishment of a common market under the conditions defined in Article 4 concerning the removal of all hindrances to free competition. It is incumbent upon the Community, by virtue of this Article 2, to bring about the progressive establishment of conditions which will in themselves assure the most rational distribution of production at the highest possible level of productivity, whilst safeguarding the continuity of employment and avoiding the creation of fundamental and persistent disturbances in the economies of member States.

" To these ends, the Community must ensure the establishment, the maintenance and the respect of normal conditions of competition within the market and, subject to conforming to the principle established by Article 57 of the Treaty that indirect rather than direct means of intervention are desirable, it is required, in compliance with the provisions of Article 5, 'not to exercise a direct action upon production and the market except when circumstances so require'.

" In the pursuit of the objective set out in Article 3 of the Treaty, the High Authority must ensure such permanent reconciliation which the possible contradictions between these objectives, considered individually, may require, and, when such reconciliations appear impossible, grant to one or other of these objectives that temporary predominance which may appear to the High Authority to be required by the facts or economic circumstances in view of which it passed its decisions with the object of carrying out the mission entrusted to it by Article 8 of the Treaty.

" By virtue of the provisions of Article 57 of the Treaty, the High Authority, in the realm of production, is to give preference to the indirect means of action which are available, especially as concerns interventions in matters of price. Among the means of action thus set out one must consider, as has already been said, the financial arrangements referred to in Article 53. These arrangements affect prices, particularly by means of subsidy payments and by means of a correction of the factors which influence the formation of those prices. These arrangements, by influencing the formation of prices, alter the level of these prices upon the market, and thereby affect the results which those levels have upon the orientation of production and, thus, upon the whole structure of the means of production, These arrangements thus give to the High Authority a means of altering the effects of ' normal conditions of competition ', while at the same time ensuring, in conformity with the requirements of Article 5 of the Treaty, the maintenance and respect of such conditions. By a judicious use of this powerful means of intervention, the High Authority can, in the accomplishment of the mission which has been given to it and provided circumstances require it, to a large extent ensure the necessary reconciliation of the objectives set out in Article 3 of the Treaty.

" The powers thus granted to the High Authority are, however, restricted by the specific provisions contained in Title III of the Treaty. These powers are, however, divorced from their legal objectives if it appears that the High Authority, in dealing with the circumstances with which it is faced, has used them with the sole purpose, or at any rate with a dominant purpose, of avoiding a special procedure provided by the Treaty.

" At the time when the challenged provisions were passed, the market in steel scrap was generally known to be suffering from an acute shortage of home-produced supplies as a result of the increasing difficulties of importation, and of the large and rapid increase in the price of steel scrap coming from other countries. From no standpoint could the situation created by these facts and economic circumstances be regarded as *prima facie* precluding the intervention of the High Authority when it sought to avoid those consequences contrary to the aims of Article 3 of the Treaty which this situation was liable to produce. Moreover, the assessment by the High Authority of the situation, in view of which these challenged provisions were taken, does not reveal, by itself, the existence of an illegal motive on the part of the authors of these measures.

" From this, the Court can only accept that the circumstances at that time did justify action by the High Authority in the market in steel scrap with the purpose of affecting indirectly the means of production, which rely upon this material.

" . . . Thus defined, the dominant aim of the challenged provisions falls, in law, within the scope of indirect action—within the meaning of Article 57—undertaken in the market in steel scrap in order to ensure the regular supply of the common market, account being taken of the facts and circumstances as they were then known. The above-mentioned aims are in conformity with the combined provisions of Article 3 (a) and (d), in its closing words, Article 2, para. 2, and Article 5, para. 2 (3), of the Treaty.

" There is need, however, to consider whether the measures taken are compatible with the rules in Article 3 (b), (d), in its opening words, and (g), objectives which the plaintiffs accuse the High Authority of having patently misconstrued in enacting these measures.

" By the terms of Article 3 (b) of the Treaty, the institutions of the Community must, within the scope of their respective functions and in the common interest, ensure to all consumers on the common market, who are placed in comparable conditions, equal access to the sources of production. This provision constitutes an objective governing the action of the High Authority in its use of the powers which are granted to it by the Treaty. The violation of the principle of the equality of consumers, qualified as above, if it occurred in any regulation of economic affairs, would establish the existence of a *détournement de pouvoir* with respect to the persons or group deliberately sacrificed.

" A general principle which is found in the law of member States, namely, the equality of all parties affected by economic regulations, does not prevent the establishment of different prices based upon the particular situation of users, or of categories of users, provided that the difference in treatment corresponds to a difference in the conditions in which they are placed. In default of an objectively determined basis, these differences of treatment would have an arbitrary and discriminatory character and would be illegal. The regulation of economic matters cannot be alleged to be unequal on the grounds that it leads to different consequences or to unequal sacrifices on the part of those affected, provided that this situation appears to be the result of the different conditions of operating in which they are placed.

"The supplementary charge imposed by Article 3, para. 1 (b), of the challenged decision applies in a general and absolute manner to all consumption of purchased steel scrap exceeding that obtained during a period of reference. The freedom given to the enterprises concerned themselves to choose, within the limits of time expressly fixed, the period which is the most favourable to them, does not, however, deprive the above-mentioned principle of differentiation of its objective character, without which it would become arbitrary. In effect, the factual differences resulting for enterprises from this situation are caused by their different conditions of operating and not by any inequality which may be inherent in the decision.

" . . . By the terms of Article 3 (d) and (g) of the Treaty, the institutions of the Community, and in particular the High Authority when it uses the powers granted to it by Article 53 (b), must seek to maintain those conditions which encourage enterprises to develop and to improve their productive potential and promote the regular expansion and modernization of production as well as the improvement of quality. The High Authority sets out these legal objectives at the head of the decision which has been taken, of which the expressed aim is to ensure the regular supply of steel scrap to the market and to encourage enterprises to reduce the use of this material without, however, rendering more difficult the creation of new capacities for the production of steel.

" . . . The realisation of the objectives specified in (d) and (g) of Article 3 of the Treaty may not be pursued separately from the other aims mentioned in that Article and achieved by ignoring those other aims. The regular expansion and modernization of production can legally be sought by means of integrated action based upon the reconciliation of the objectives of Article 3, giving to one or other of them, should the need arise, that predominance which the situation resulting from the facts or economic circumstances observed at the time of the intervention may justify.

" Moreover, the objectives set out in Article 3 of the Treaty must be considered as a whole and pursued for purposes exclusively within the common interest. Far from being limited to the sum total of the particular interests of those coal and steel enterprises under the jurisdiction of the Community, the concept of common interest referred to in that Article greatly exceeds the extent of these interests, and is defined by reference to the general aims clearly specified in Article 2.

" In consequence, the pursuit of the objectives set out in Article 3 does not hinder the adoption of particular measures, determined principally by the nature of the means of production which they are to develop or create, if it appears that the economic circumstances and the reasonably foreseeable development of the conditions of the market require such measures.

". . . If the High Authority wished at the same time ' to promote a policy of a rational development of the natural resources while avoiding their undue exhaustion '—an objective set out in Article 3 (d) of the Treaty—it should equally have taken account of the existing conditions of the various categories of consumers, and then differentiated in the application of the supplementary charge which was applied to them according to the variations in their consumption of steel scrap. This differentiation would have involved the progressive elimination of the effects of the subsidy payments and might have gone as far as their total disappearance in certain cases.

" The system which is being challenged thus attempted above all to safeguard the regular supply of the market and the promotion of a policy of rational use of resources. However, nothing justifies one in holding that by temporarily giving pre-eminence to certain of the aims set out in Article 3 and, as a result, only partially achieving a reconciliation of all the aims set out in that Article, the High Authority has used the powers which were given to it by the Treaty for purposes other than those for which they were granted.

" The *détournement de pouvoir* not having been substantiated, this ground of annulment must be rejected . . ."

[Report: *Recueil de la Jurisprudence de la Cour*, vol. IV (1958), p. 223 (in French).]

NOTE.—As the plaintiffs in this action were an enterprise, they could, by Article 33, para. 2, of the Treaty, challenge the validity of Decision No. 2–57, which was a general decision, only on the ground of a *détournement de pouvoir* with respect to them. By Article 3 (b) of the Treaty, enterprises are to be given equal access to the sources of production. The Court accepted that " the violation of the principle of the equality of the consumer, if it occurred in any regulation of economic affairs, would establish the existence of a *détournement de pouvoir* with respect to the persons or group deliberately sacrificed." The plaintiffs, therefore, had sought to show that they were persons who were being placed at a disadvantage and " deliberately sacrificed ".

The subsidy system here being considered was set up under Article 53 (b), by which the High Authority may set up financial arrangements " necessary for the accomplishment of the objectives defined in Article 3." To set up these arrangements for a purpose other than the accomplishment of these objectives would therefore be a *détournement de pouvoir*.[1] The Court in its judgment was forced, therefore, to undertake a fundamental analysis of the basic objectives of the whole Coal and Steel Community.

---

[1] Although not necessarily a *détournement de pouvoir* with respect to the plantiffs.

**International organization—European Coal and Steel Community —Article 60 of Treaty establishing—Meaning of " discrimination " —Publication of lists of steel prices—Decision of High Authority authorizing steel enterprises to deviate from their published selling prices—Whether decision in violation of Treaty—Meaning of phrase " price-lists applied by enterprises shall be made public " —Whether " price " means " exact price "—Whether publication must be before application of the lists—Whether authorization of existing breaches of a decision of the High Authority amounts to a *détournement de pouvoir*.**

THE FRENCH GOVERNMENT *v.* THE HIGH AUTHORITY.

*Court of Justice of the European Coal and Steel Community.*

(Pilotti, President; Serrarens, Hammes, Riese, Delvaux, Rueff, Van Kleffens JJ.)

*December* 20, 1954.

THE FACTS.—The background to this case, as one of a series arising under Article 60 of the Treaty establishing the European Coal and Steel Community, is set out in the Note printed at p. 403 below. In the present case, the plaintiffs challenged the validity of Decisions 1–54, 2–54 and 3–54 on the grounds of violation of the Treaty and of *détournement de pouvoir*. They contended that when Article 60 (2) required price-lists to be published it did so with the aim of preventing discriminations. Decision 1–54, however, allowed discriminations, by authorizing variations from price-lists. The provision that these variations must be the same for all " comparable transactions " was completely obscure because, strictly, only simultaneous transactions were comparable.

The High Authority replied that there was a complete distinction between a discrimination, which was prohibited by the Treaty, and the publication of prices. Although one of the objects of publishing prices was to prevent discrimination, a variation from those prices did not automatically amount to a discrimination.

The plaintiffs claimed, next, that both Decisions 2–54 and 3–54 also violated the Treaty. Article 60 (2) (*a*) required that " price-lists . . . applied by enterprises . . . shall be made public ". This meant, they alleged, that the publication must be made *before* the prices in the lists were applied by the enterprises. The power of the High Authority, therefore, when it was to prescribe the " extent and form " of the publication, could not detract from this principle of prior publication. Article 1 of Decision 2–54, however, was doing just that. Further, price-lists of enterprises were of no value to their competitors who wished to align their prices unless they specified the exact prices being charged, and not merely average prices. The High Authority was thus violating the Treaty in allowing enterprises to deviate from their lists.

The High Authority in reply declared that when Article 60 (2) (a) required that " price-lists . . . applied by enterprises . . . shall be made public ", it used the word " applied " and not " to be applied ", so that there was no requirement that the publication should precede the application. Further, the High Authority claimed that because it was allowed by the Treaty to prescribe both the extent and the form of the publication, it possessed, therefore, the widest possible powers. The High Authority also argued that the publication of exact prices was not necessary to enable alignment to occur because in a market as well organized as that of steel it was always possible to know the actual prices of one's competitors.

Finally, the plaintiffs alleged that the decisions were void for *détournement de pouvoir*. The High Authority, they declared, had been faced with the situation where many enterprises were violating the High Authority's earlier decision that no deviations were to occur. The correct action, therefore, would have been for the High Authority to fine the enterprises concerned. Instead of doing this, however, it had sought to authorize the very breaches themselves, which was an example of using its power in relation to the publication of price schedules for a purpose other than that for which it had been granted.

The High Authority replied that by Article 57[1] of the Treaty it was expressly required to give preference to indirect means of action at its disposal rather than to direct action. Fining enterprises would have been direct action, whereas the passing of the present decisions amounted to the indirect action there being referred to.

The submissions of the Advocate General were that the appeal should be dismissed.

*Held:* that Article 1 of Decision 2-54 must be annulled and the matter referred back to the High Authority. The appeal for the annulment of Decisions 1-54 and 3-54 and of Article 2 of Decision 2-54 must be rejected. The variations from an enterprise's price schedules which Decision 1-54 allowed was not void on the ground that, as alleged, it enabled discriminations to occur. Discriminations were expressly excluded by the provision that deviations were to be applied to all transactions which were comparable, and whether transactions were comparable or not could be determined objectively.

Article 60 (2) (b) of the Treaty, however, provided that " price-lists . . . shall be published to the extent and in the form prescribed by the High Authority . . ." As the object of such publication was to allow competitors to know an enterprise's exact prices, the term

---

[1] Article 57 provides:
" In the field of production, the High Authority shall give preference to the indirect means of action at its disposal, such as: co-operation with Governments to stabilize or influence general consumption, particularly that of the public services; intervention on prices and commercial policy as provided for in this Treaty."

" price-lists " must mean lists of exact prices. Further, and for the same reason, these lists must be published before any contracts of sale based upon them were entered into.

This being so, the power of the High Authority to prescribe the extent and form of these lists did not allow it to depart from the principle of the prior publication of exact prices. Article 1 of Decision 2–54, which sought to authorize just such a departure, had been passed in violation of Article 60 (2) (b).

Further, Article 1 of Decision 2–54 had been passed without the Council of Ministers having been consulted. By Article 60 (1), such consultation would have been required if the High Authority had been defining what practices were prohibited under that article. In default of such consultation the decision would have been open to annulment for violation of a substantial procedural requirement. Decision 2–54, however, was not defining such practices and, therefore, could not be challenged on this ground.

Decision 3–54, requiring deviation from price-lists to be reported twice in a month to the High Authority, had been issued in pursuance of Article 47 of the Treaty and was valid. It was nevertheless rendered of no practical application owing to the annulment of the provision authorizing deviation.

No *détournement de pouvoir* had been established, for even if an unjustified motive—such as the desire to avoid penalising defaulting enterprises—was present together with motives which did justify the action of the High Authority, the decisions would not thereby be vitiated by *détournement de pouvoir* provided that the justified motives predominated.

The Court said:

"The plaintiffs challenge Decisions 1–54, 2–54 and 3–54 on the grounds of violation of the Treaty and of *détournement de pouvoir*.

"A.—*The ground of violation of the Treaty*

"I. *As regards Decision No.* 1–54.—Decision 1–54 introduces a clear distinction between publication and discrimination, thus creating two kinds of contraventions, namely, the offence of discrimination, on the one hand, and contravention of the rules concerning the publication of prices, on the other. Yet, while recognizing that there exists a connection in the aims of the two paragraphs of Article 60, the Court does not see any violation of the Treaty in this distinction. Indeed, the Treaty nowhere provides that every breach of the rules concerning the publication of prices constitutes at the same time one of the practices prohibited by Article 60, para. 1. Particularly where the prohibition of discriminatory practices is concerned, it is undeniable that the fact of deviating, to whatever extent, from the prices or conditions provided for by an enterprise's price-list does not constitute a discrimination so long as the deviation concerns a unique transaction or provided that the same deviation is applied to all comparable transactions. Decision 1–54 is thus compatible with the Treaty on this point. One could, on the other hand, have claimed that Decision 30–53 was open to challenge, when, without expressly allowing any proof to the contrary, it declared certain transactions to be discriminations which, in fact, were not such at all.

" (1) The allegation is also ill-founded that the absence of any precise definition of unique transactions and comparable transactions opens the door to discriminations, and facilitates them instead of prohibiting them, and takes all meaning from the notion of discriminatory practices. It is true that the old system of the strict observance of the published prices seems to have aimed at the exclusion of all discrimination, except in the case where an enterprise deliberately violated its obligations. On the other hand, under the new system it is theoretically possible for an enterprise acting in good faith to commit a discrimination when it erroneously believes that it is undertaking a non-comparable transaction or a unique transaction. Indeed, the new system leaves it to the enterprise itself to assess the unique or non-comparable character of transactions. However, Decision 1–54 lays the burden of proof upon the enterprises; if they are not in a position to prove the unique or non-comparable character of the transaction they will be responsible for their error and will be liable to the sanctions provided for in Article 64.[1] Finally, it must be admitted that the notion of unique or non-comparable transactions does not easily lend itself to an abstract definition. It is, indeed, possible that transactions concluded within an interval of only one day could constitute non-comparable transactions, if in the meantime the market had completely changed. On the other hand, it is possible that two transactions are comparable, although concluded several weeks apart, if the market had remained stable during that time. Comparability can, therefore, only be assessed in relation to the market situation. Similarly, the uniqueness of a transaction can only be established in the light of the circumstances which characterize the transaction. The two characteristics—comparability and uniqueness—can be objectively assessed by the enterprises and by the High Authority, and, therefore, the system here challenged in no way deprives the notion of discrimination of its meaning. On the contrary, it makes it possible to act against every discriminatory practice. From the above it also follows that the plaintiffs' argument that only simultaneous transactions are still subject to be regulated by identical prices and conditions of sale is without foundation.

[1 Article 64 provides:
" The High Authority may impose upon enterprises which violate the provisions of this Chapter [Articles 60–64] or the decisions taken in application thereof, fines not to exceed twice the value of the unauthorized sales. In case of a second offence the above maximum may be doubled."]

" (2) Decision 1-54 does not abolish the obligation to publish prices: on the contrary, it expressly continues it. The objection that the decision violates the rules concerning the publication of prices and that it abandons the principle of publicity as a means of preventing prohibited practices, is, therefore, groundless. When considering Decision 2-54, the Court will examine whether the fact of allowing deviations within certain limits and exempting enterprises from publishing their new prices is consistent with the Treaty. In any event, this allowance and exemption cannot be used as an argument against Decision 1-54, which in no way affects the principle of publication.

" (3) Decision 1-54 by no means abolishes sanctions in cases of discrimination. If comparable transactions are concluded at different prices and under different conditions of sale, the sanctions provided for in Article 64 are always applicable.

" (4) Finally, the plaintiffs' argument that Decision 1-54, instead of defining prohibited practices, legalizes certain practices which were illegal under the old system, is ill-founded. It has been explained above that Decision 1-54 establishes a new definition of prohibited practices by separating the rules on non-discrimination from the provisions governing publicity. If, under the new definition, practices which were prohibited before, namely, deviations from the published prices, are now allowed, it nevertheless provides that these deviations must be uniformly applied to all comparable transactions, with the exception of unique transactions which cannot give rise to a discrimination. The principle of the prohibition of all discriminatory practices is, therefore, strictly respected. Decision 1-54, while it abandons the previous automatic system, remains within the framework of defining prohibited practices.

" For these reasons, Decision 1-54 does not violate the Treaty; consequently the appeal for annulment brought against this decision, in so far as it is based on violation of the Treaty, must be rejected.

" II. *As regards Decision No. 2-54.*—The Court holds that Article 1 of Decision 2-54 is incompatible with the Treaty to the extent to which it permits enterprises to apply an average upward or downward variation between the prices published and those actually charged, without prior publication of these modifications to the price-schedules. This violation of the Treaty results from the following:—

" (1) Before interpreting paragraph 2 of Article 60 of the Treaty in detail it is necessary to examine the objective which the High Authority is required to pursue when it defines the prohibited practices and when it regulates the publication of prices and conditions of sale.

(a) Articles 2, 3 and 4 of the Treaty, referred to at the beginning of paragraph 1 of Article 60, constitute fundamental provisions establishing the common market and the common objectives of the

Community.[1] Their importance is clearly seen from Article 95.[2] When empowering the High Authority to define prohibited practices, the Treaty requires it to take into account all the objectives set out in Articles 2, 3 and 4. This follows from the express reference to these articles that is made at the beginning of Article 60. When defining prohibited practices, the High Authority has therefore not

[1 Article 2 provides:
" The mission of the European Coal and Steel Community is to contribute to the expansion of the economy, the development of employment and the improvement of the standard of living in the participating countries through the creation, in harmony with the general economy of the member States, of a common market as defined in Article 4.

" The Community must progressively establish conditions which will in themselves ensure the most rational distribution of production at the highest possible level of productivity, while safeguarding the continuity of employment and avoiding the creation of fundamental and persistent disturbances in the economies of the member States."

Article 3 provides:
" Within the framework of their respective powers and responsibilities and in the common interest, the institutions of the Community shall:

(a) ensure that the market is regularly supplied, while taking into account the needs of third countries;

(b) assure to all consumers in comparable positions within the common market equal access to the sources of production;

(c) seek the establishment of the lowest possible prices without involving any corresponding rise either in the prices charged by the same enterprises in other transactions or in the price level as a whole in another period, while at the same time permitting necessary amortisation and providing the possiblity of normal returns on invested capital;

(d) ensure that conditions are maintained which will encourage enterprises to expand and improve their ability to produce and to promote a policy of rational development of natural resources, while avoiding undue exhaustion of such resources;

(e) promote the improvement of the living and working conditions of the labour force in each of the industries under its jurisdiction so as to harmonise those conditions in an upward direction;

(f) foster the development of international trade and ensure that equitable limits are observed in prices charged in foreign markets;

(g) promote the regular expansion and the modernisation of production as well as the improvement of quality, under conditions which preclude any protection against competing industries except where justified by illegitimate action on the part of such industries or in their favour."

Article 4 provides:
" The following are declared to be incompatible with the common market for coal and steel, and are therefore abolished and prohibited within the Community in the manner set out in the present Treaty:

(a) import and export duties, or taxes with an equivalent effect, and quantitative restrictions on the movement of coal and steel;

(b) measures or practices discriminating among producers, among buyers, or among consumers, especially as concerns prices, delivery terms and transport rates, as well as measures or practices which hamper the buyer in the free choice of supplier;

(c) subsidies or State assistance or special charges imposed by the State, in any form whatsoever;

(d) restrictive practices tending towards the division or exploitation of markets.

[2 Article 95 provides:
" In all cases not expressly provided for in the present Treaty in which a decision or a recommendation of the High Authority appears necessary to fulfil . . . one of the objectives of the Community as defined in Articles 2, 3 and 4, such a decision or recommendation may be taken with the unanimous agreement of the Council and after consulting the Consultative Committee. . . .

only the right but also the duty to bear in mind both the action to be taken against agreements among producers and the need to seek the establishment of the lowest possible prices under the conditions mentioned in Article 3 of the Treaty, and must also bear in mind the action to be taken against unfair competitive practices and discriminatory practices. For these reasons the Court cannot accept the plaintiffs' submission that Article 60 refers only to action against discriminations, wheras action against agreements is only dealt with by Article 65 and action encouraging the establishment of the lowest possible prices is dealt with by Article 61.[1] It is true that Articles 65 and 61 of the Treaty confer upon the High Authority means of direct action against agreements and against an increase of prices, but it follows from the Treaty (*inter alia*, from Article 57 which relates to production[2]) that the High Authority, before making use of direct means of action, must give preference to the use of "the indirect means of action at its disposal". Thus, the High Authority can also use its right to define prohibited practices, with regard to prices, in order to prevent practices which are contrary to one of the objectives specified in Article 60.

"On the other hand, it follows from the words ' in particular ' (in the first paragraph of Article 60) that Article 60 refers mainly to unfair competitive practices and discriminatory practices.

(*b*) As regards, more particularly, the rôle which the Treaty assigns to the publication of price-lists, the Court holds, in agreement with the Advocate General, that compulsory publication is provided for in the Treaty in order to achieve the following three aims:

(1) to prevent as far as possible prohibited practices;

(2) to enable buyers to acquaint themselves with ·the exact prices, and also to participate in the regulation of discriminations;

(3) to enable enterprises to know the exact prices of their competitors in order to give them the opportunity to align their prices.

"Although publicity has been provided for with the above-mentioned aims, the Treaty does not regard this as sufficient to guarantee that these aims are effectively attained—publicity is but one of the means provided for in the Treaty.

"If, after the transitional period . . ., unforeseen difficulties revealed by experience in the methods of executing the present Treaty . . . should require an amendment of the rules for the exercise by the High Authority of the powers conferred upon it, appropriate modifications may be made provided that they do not infringe the provision of Articles 2, 3 and 4, . . . "]

[1 Article 61 provides:

" . . . the High Authority may fix for one or more products subject to its jurisdiction:

(a) maximum prices within the common market, if it finds that such a decision is necessary to obtain the objectives defined in Article 3 and particularly in para. (c) thereof;

(b) minimum prices within the common market, if it finds that a manifest crisis exists or is imminent and that such a decision is necessary to obtain the objectives defined in Article 3 . . . "]

[2 For the text of Article 57 see above, p. 389, n. 1.]

" The publication of price-lists is governed by public law; their effects in private law have not been regulated by the Treaty. However, this public law character, as is correctly stressed by the Advocate General, does not conflict with the plaintiff Government's submission that the publication of price schedules must also have legal consequences with regard to third parties, particularly with regard to enterprises which wish to align their prices with those of their competitors. It is this result which is inherent in the publication of price-lists, which distinguishes this publication both from the simple information obtained by the High Authority in accordance with Article 47,[1] as well as from the publication in accordance with Article 46,[2] of statistical documents issued by the High Authority. If the publication were not intended to inform the general public, one could not explain why the Treaty does not confine itself to stating that ' the price-lists shall be communicated to the High Authority '.

" (2) In its first paragraph, Article 60 directly prohibits certain practices: the High Authority is empowered to define these, but it cannot depart from the principle of their prohibition.

" Paragraph 2 of Article 60 provides for the compulsory publication of price-lists ' for the above purposes '. These words clearly indicate that the nature of the provisions which follow concerning the publication of prices is that of implementation. This publication is imperatively provided for: it is considered as an appropriate means for achieving the ends specified in the first paragraph. Such publication is thus only a means, but a means imperatively prescribed and not a means which can be replaced by any other means whatsoever even if they are able to achieve the same results.

" This obligatory character of the publication of price-lists follows also from the words ' shall be made public '. The Court is thus led to interpret the obligation to publish price-lists and conditions of sale as being a strict rule of law, from which no derogations are permitted. The obligation is absolute, and must be complied with in its entirety.

" The Court does not accept the defendants' submission that the expression ' être rendus publics ' is less strong than if the Treaty had said ' être publiés '. Indeed, in the last two paragraphs of Article 46

[1 Article 47 provides:
" The High Authority may gather such information as may be necessary to the accomplishment of its mission. It may have the necessary verifications carried out. . . "
[2 Article 46 provides:
" . . . In order to provide guidance for the action of all interested parties . . . and in order to determine its own action within the conditions laid down by the Treaty, the High Authority shall, by means of the consultations mentioned above:
(1) . . . .
(2) periodically draw up programmes giving forecasts, for guidance, of production, consumption, exports and imports;
(3) periodically set out the general objectives with respect to modernization, the long term planning of production and the expansion of productive capacity; . . . "]

the Treaty uses those two expressions as being identical.[1] In any event, the publication has to be made in such a way that all who participate in the market (possible future buyers and competitors) may be able to know the prices: only such a publication is consistent with the purposes for which it was laid down.

" (3) Paragraph 2 (a) [of Article 60] does not expressly say at what moment the price-lists and conditions of sale must be published. One has only to read paragraph 2 (b), concerning the methods of quotation, to understand that the publication of price schedules is to be prior to any sales taking place on the common market.

" Indeed, letter (b) of paragraph 2 of Article 60 specifies that the methods of quotation applied must not have the result of introducing into the actual prices any increases over the prices 'indicated by the price-list'—which again confirms both that the price-lists contain a list of prices at which the products are offered, which permit the exact calculation of all legal transactions, and that these price schedules must be published prior to their application.

" Moreover, paragraph 30, No. 2, of the Convention containing the Transitional Provisions stipulates that the prices charged by enterprises for the sales of steel on the Italian market may not be lower than the prices specified in the price-lists for comparable transactions. This provision confirms that the price-list is solely a list of selling prices prior to any contract of sale.

" The Treaty is, furthermore, very clear in its language when it makes reference to 'the price-lists' and not 'price-lists'. The price-lists mentioned are, thus, not documents related merely to the Treaty and specially established for the purposes of the Treaty, but documents of a type accepted by established trade practices and which, in accordance with these practices, have always, although in a general or provisional way depending upon the case, the character of an offer to contract upon the basis of the prices which they set out.

" The price-lists do not lose this character of an offer to contract although the Treaty assigns to them those purposes of public interest which are specified by its provisions. There is therefore no doubt that the expression 'price-list' retains in the Treaty its usual meaning and refers to the prices on the basis of which the enterprises declare themselves ready to sell their products.

" This interpretation is further confirmed—and on this point the Court agrees with the opinion of the Advocate General—by the fact that the text of Article 60, paragraph 2, distinguishes between applied prices and practised prices, for this last expression, used under letter (b) of paragraph 2 of Article 60, denotes the prices at which the transactions are actually concluded. It appears, therefore, that the expression 'prices applied' refers to the prices of the sellers'

[1 Article 46, paras. 4 and 5, commence in French with the words: " *Elle publie les objectifs généraux:* ... " and " *Elle peut rendre publiques les études* ... "]

offer, although it would have been clearer if the Treaty had for this purpose used the words 'prices to be applied'.

"It is, moreover, in this sense that the High Authority, both in its previous decisions as well as in Decision 2–54, seems always to have interpreted the Treaty; for it is stated in Article 4 of Decision 31–53, as well as in Article 3 of Decision 2–54, that the price-lists and conditions of sale are to enter into force 'at the earliest, five clear days (one day, according to Article 3 of Decision 2–54) after having been forwarded, in print, to the High Authority'.

"It follows, also, from the preamble to Decision 2–54 that the High Authority itself starts from the idea of a prior publication of the price-lists. After stating in the second paragraph of the preamble that the price-lists must express the price-level clearly established by the market, the third paragraph refers to certain facilities which are intended to be granted to enterprises, and to those facilities the fourth paragraph adds an additional one which consists of a reduction to a minimum of the time-limit for the entering into force of the new price-lists. It would be difficult, however, to consider this as a facility if the price-lists were only to reflect 'ex post facto' the evolution of the market. One can only speak of a facility if one accepts the postulate of prior publication, because only then will the enterprises benefit, by not having to wait several days before being able to conclude contracts of sale on the basis of the new prices.

"It must therefore be admitted that the publication of the price-lists is required to be made before enterprises are enabled to apply the new prices.

"Furthermore, it follows from the foregoing considerations that the words 'price-list' always refer to published price-lists. On this point, also, the Court agrees with the opinion of the Advocate General. The defendant's submission that the words 'price-list' should be understood in a sense which has no bearing on this point is not accepted by the Court.

"(4) After having determined that the price-lists and conditions of sale must be published prior to their application on the Common Market, it remains to be decided whether the Treaty requires the publication of the exact prices or whether it is sufficient to publish average or approximate prices. However, there is no doubt that the Treaty requires a publication of exact prices in the form of price-lists. This follows from the purpose which the publication of prices is intended to achieve; information given by buyers only has value for them if it informs them of the exact prices at which they can make purchases. Likewise, publication must make alignment possible, and this alignment must be made with the exact prices of the competitor. Alignment is a right granted to the enterprises by the Treaty, and not merely a faculty which can be exercised only if enterprises are able by other more or less fortuitous means to acquaint themselves with the prices established by their competitors.

" If the Treaty for the above-mentioned reasons thus provides in an imperative manner for the prior publication of the exact prices, it follows that the competence granted to the High Authority to fix the extent and the form of the publication does not allow it to impair the principle of the compulsory publication of exact prices.

" In view of the strict legal character of paragraph 2 (a) of Article 60, and in the absence of any text to the contrary, the power granted to the High Authority by the phrase ' to the extent and in the form prescribed by the High Authority ', cannot be interpreted in a sense which would permit the High Authority not to require the publication of the price-lists. By the terms of this phrase one must conclude that the High Authority is empowered to determine the contents of the price-lists. However, these contents must satisfy the public interest, so that the High Authority is competent only to prescribe minimum requirements for the outline of the price-lists.

" In other words, the phrase ' to the extent and in the form prescribed by the High Authority ', does indeed empower the High Authority to prescribe the extent, that is to say, the scope, of the publication in so far as it concerns the regulation of its form. The High Authority can, for example, fix, as it has done, the time-limit for the entering into force of a new price-list; establish that certain rebates—such as the rebate for a further option to purchase, etc.—have to be mentioned in the price-lists; decide if on-costs have to be published or not. On the other hand, under the system imposed by the Treaty all that is indispensable for knowledge of the exact price must of necessity be mentioned in the price-lists. The fact that the publication of price-lists has to take into account the purposes which, according to the Treaty, this publication should pursue, does not allow acceptance of the High Authority's contention that it has the power to prescribe, at its own discretion, what must be published and what must not be published. According to this contention—which the Court rejects—there would be no limit to what could be exempted from the obligation to publish. The High Authority could then allow much greater deviation, and one does not see where this would end: it could authorize a simple publication of maximum and minimum prices (e.g.: prices 80 to 120) or even no publication at all for prices of whole categories of products; in a word, it could circumvent the principle of compulsory publication, which is a principle provided for in the Treaty.

" Finally, if it is true that the power of the High Authority in this matter is a power to regulate what are to be the minimum requirements with which the price-lists must comply, this is also true with regard to the scope of the publication itself. It is not enough, therefore, that the forwarding of the price-lists to the High Authority is ensured; if it were so, the Treaty would have been content to have specified this obligation and no more. The price-lists are required to be published and the power of the High Authority to prescribe ' the extent and the form ' implies the obligation upon it to ensure that the extent and form in which the price schedules are published and placed at the disposal of the public adequately meet the needs of the public interest.

" The text of Decision No. 31–53 has been drafted with very great care. Its first article declares that the enterprises of the steel industries must publish their price-lists and conditions of sale, as well as every subsequent modification of them, in accordance with the provisions of that decision; Article 2 then sets out the very precise information which the price-list must contain, thus interpreting in a reasonable way the words ' extent ' and ' form ' used in the Treaty; Article 4 declares that the price-lists shall enter into force not earlier than five clear days after they have been forwarded to the High Authority, and that they must be communicated by the sellers on demand to any person interested.

" On the other hand, the first article of Decision 2–54 does not establish the extent to which the price-lists must be published by enterprises, but only the extent to which the High Authority authorises the non-observance of these published price-lists. This is contrary to Article 60, para. 2, of the Treaty.

" It should, in addition, be mentioned that the interpretation adopted by the Court is supported by the fact that the High Authority may determine the extent of the publication merely after consultation with the Consultative Committee, whereas, in order to define prohibited practices, it must also consult the Council of Ministers. This is understandable if the High Authority, when it determines the extent of the publication, has to refrain from infringing the principle of the compulsory publication of the exact prices and conditions of sale. If the Treaty had wanted to grant it more freedom and accord to it the right to derogate from this principle, this power would logically also have been made dependent upon consultation with the Council.

" (5) It remains to examine whether the result to which a study of the text and of the *ratio legis* has brought the Court is not at variance with other objects of the Treaty or whether it is liable to be rendered invalid by other considerations. In the present case this is not so. It should first of all be repeated that the system of prior publication of exact prices constitutes the compulsory principle prescribed by paragraph 2 of Article 60. It follows that this principle cannot be evaded, even to give way to a system better adapted to the objects in view. It is not the task of the Court to give its opinion about the appropriateness of the system imposed by the Treaty or to suggest a revision of the Treaty; but it is required, by Article 31, to ensure the respect of law in the interpretation and application of the Treaty in the form in which it has been drawn up.

" (a) The contention that the control by buyers does not operate when prices fall is not relevant because the publicity is not intended only to permit this control, but also to place the buyers in a position to acquaint themselves with the exact prices and to permit alignment by enterprises. This contention, therefore, is not sufficient to justify abandonment of the principle of publication prescribed by the Treaty.

" (b) The defendant has insisted upon the danger of agreements among producers, a danger which was inherent in the previous system. However, it has not been proved that this danger is removed by the introduction of the average margin. Even if the new régime had certain advantages in diminishing this risk, that would not justify neglect of the other purposes which publicity must serve. Moreover, the Treaty permits the High Authority to intervene by other means when it finds that agreements have been made.

" (c) The situation of the market, particularly the tendency for prices to fall, cannot justify the abolition of the principle of price-publication either, since this publication is required by the Treaty. In the event of a crisis or of disturbances in the market, the Treaty confers different powers upon the High Authority—particularly in Article 60, at the end of paragraph 2 (b),[1] Article 61, Article 63,[2] Articles 58[3] and 59[4]—but at no time is abolition of the compulsory publication of price schedules provided for. Moreover, the principle of compulsory publication prescribed by the Treaty has a general character and is in no way dependent upon the immediate economic situation.

" (d) Protection of the free formation of prices has particularly occupied the Court. This, however, cannot justify a different decision. The Treaty starts from the assumption that the free formation of

[1 The final words of Article 60 (2) (b) read as follows:
" These decisions [fixing the limits below which price reductions from an enterprise's price-lists may not occur] shall be taken when they appear necessary to avoid disturbances in all or any part of the common market, or disequilibria resulting from a difference between the methods of quotation used for a product and those used for its raw materials. . . . "]

[2 Article 63 (1) provides:
" If the High Authority finds that discrimination is being systematically practised by buyers, in particular discrimination resulting from clauses in contracts concluded by public services, it shall address the necessary recommendations to the Governments concerned ".]

[3 Article 58 (1) provides:
" In case of a decline in demand, if the High Authority considers that the Community is faced with a period of manifest crisis and that the means of action provided for in Article 57 are not sufficient to cope with this situation, it must, after consulting the Consultative Committee and with the agreement of the Council, establish a system of production quotas, . . . "]

[4 Article 59 (1) provides:
" If, after consulting the Consultative Committee, the High Authority finds that the Community is faced with a serious shortage of certain or of all of the products subject to its jurisdiction, and that the means of action provided for in Article 57 do not enable it to cope with this situation, it shall bring it to the attention of the Council, and shall propose the necessary measures, unless the Council decides to the contrary by a unanimous vote . . . "]

prices is guaranteed by the freedom given to enterprises to fix their prices themselves and to publish new price-lists when they wish to modify them. If the economic situation changes, the producers are forced to modify their price-lists, and it is in this way that ' the market makes the price '. But, although the Treaty starts from the assumption of a free formation of prices, it should not be forgotten that the Treaty forbids all discriminations and that it provides for the right of alignment. For these reasons, the Treaty has established the principle of the compulsory prior publication of price-lists and conditions of sale. The Court has to abstain from giving its opinion about the suitability of this system; it can only declare that it has been provided for by the Treaty which—rightly or wrongly—does not contain a provision permitting a certain flexibility of the price-lists in the case of minor or passing fluctuations.

" On all these grounds, the Court holds that Article 1 of Decision 2–54 violates the Treaty. This article must therefore be annulled.

" Moreover, the Court of its own motion has examined the question whether Article 1 of Decision 2–54 constitutes a violation of a substantial procedural requirement. According to its wording, this article only defines the new conditions under which the new price schedules have to be published. It can be asked, however, whether this article, read in connection with Decision 1–54, does not, in fact, in a disguised way, add to the definition of prohibited practices. If this were the case, if this were an indirect and complementary definition of prohibited practices, the Council should have been consulted, by virtue of Article 60, para. 1. However, such an official consultation has not taken place, and the unofficial informing of the Council by the High Authority could not be considered as an observance of this requirement. However, it is the opinion of the Court that Article 1 of Decision 2–54 does not contain a definition of prohibited practices but that it is limited to regulating the system of the publication of price-lists.

" The reference, made in Article 2 of Decision 2–54, to Article 1, does not justify annulment of Article 2, as this reference loses its meaning following the annulment of Article 1.

" The other articles of Decision 2—54 have not been challenged by the plaintiffs and the Court is of the opinion that there are no grounds for their annulment.

" III. *As regards Decision No. 3–54.*—Decision 3–54, whose purpose is to introduce a system for obtaining information and for exercising control, is based on Article 47 of the Treaty.[1] This article permits the High Authority to obtain the information necessary for the accomplishment of its mission; Decision 3–54 is,

[1 Article 47 provides, in part, as follows:
" The High Authority may collect such information as may be necessary for the accomplishment of its mission. It may take the necessary steps to verify such information."]

therefore, consistent with the Treaty. The fact that the High Authority has combined this system for obtaining information with exercise of control over publicity which is provided for in Article 60, does not justify any challenge.

" Although Decision 3–54 is apparently intended to complete the system of deviations introduced by Article 1 of Decision 2–54 and declared above to be incompatible with the Treaty, it is not, however, by itself contrary to the Treaty. Consequently, there are no grounds for its annulment, although it obviously becomes inoperative and without effect following the annulment of the first article of Decision 2–54.

" B.—*The ground of* détournement de pouvoir

" In agreement with the findings of the Advocate General, the Court is of the opinion that the ground of *détournement de pouvoir* cannot be invoked against the defendant in respect of the decisions challenged.

" It has been stated above that the High Authority, when performing its duty to act principally against unfair competitive practices and against discriminatory practices, has the right to take into account the prohibitions resulting from Articles 2, 3 and 4 so that it cannot be held accountable for having considered them.

" Even if the decisions in question have been partially inspired by the desire to introduce a new system more likely to be observed by enterprises than the previous one, one cannot conclude from this that it was intended to legalize infractions previously committed. In any event, it is clear that the decisions were above all intended to achieve the objects referred to in the Treaty. Even if an unjustified motive, namely, the desire to avoid applying sanctions to defaulting enterprises, is present together with motives which, of themselves, justify the action of the High Authority, the decisions would not, on this account, be vitiated by a *détournement de pouvoir*, provided that they do not infringe upon the essential aim, which is the prohibition of unfair competitive practices and discriminations. The Court holds that such is not the case for the reasons mentioned under 1 above.

" *Costs and the reference back of the case to the High Authority.*—

" 1. By virtue of Article 60 of the Rules of the Court,[1] any party in a contentious matter which loses shall be condemned in costs. The Court may nevertheless, under paragraph 2 of that Article,[2] apportion costs either wholly or in part if the parties fail respectively on one or more heads.

[1 Article 60, para. 1, of the old Rules provided: " In contentious matters, any party which loses shall be condemned in costs." This provision is now contained in Article 69, para. 2, of the Rules.]

[2 Article 60, para. 2, of the old Rules provided: " The Court may apportion costs wholly or in part if the parties each lose on one or more heads of claim." This provision is now contained in Article 69, para. 3, of the Rules.]

" In the present case, the plaintiffs have succeeded as to part and on an important point, namely, the annulment of the first article of Decision 2–54 which introduced the system of average deviation from the prices published in the price schedule. Under these conditions, the Court holds that it would be equitable to grant to them the right to be reimbursed one-half of their expenses by the defendants. However, the plaintiffs having expressly renounced their right to be reimbursed costs, and not having presented any claim concerning costs, the Court gives effect to this declaration and decides that each party shall bear their own costs.

" 2. By Article 34 of the Treaty, to the extent to which an annulment has been declared the matter must be referred back to the High Authority, which is required to take the measures which comprise the execution of the decision of annulment.

" The Court, rejecting all further arguments or submissions to the contrary, adjudges and declares:

" Article 1 of Decision 2–54 is annulled and, in this respect, the matter is referred back to the High Authority;

" The appeal for the annulment of Decisions 1–54 and 3–54 and of Article 2 of Decision 2–54 is rejected.

" As the plaintiffs have refrained from claiming costs, the Court takes judicial notice of this:—each party to pay its own costs."

[Report: *Recueil de la Jurisprudence de la Cour*, I (1954–55), p. 9 (in French).]

NOTE.—The following is a note on the background of this and other cases relating to the publication and observance of price-lists under Article 60 of the Treaty establishing the European Coal and Steel Community, and establishing the invalidity of all variations therefrom.

Before the common market for steel came into force on May 1, 1953, the prices for steel in the countries of the Community were almost entirely determined by the steel cartels and by a very large number of price-fixing agreements. When the Coal and Steel Treaty came into effect, these cartels and price-fixing agreements became legal,[1] and as a result steel producers were free to fix their own prices in the price schedules which they published and issued to potential customers.

During the course of 1953, however, these steel producers, in the face of the competition from each other, tended to sell at prices which were below those stated in their price-lists. To meet this situation the High Authority at the end of 1953 issued a decision[2] stating that for the future it would be illegal for a steel producer to sell at a price other than the one set out in than producer's price-list.[3] A further

---

[1] This was achieved by Article 4 of the Treaty.
[2] Decision 30-53.
[3] This decision was issued under Article 60, para. 1, which reads as follows:
" Pricing practices contrary to the provisions of Articles 2, 3 and 4 are prohibited, and in particular:
—unfair competitive practices, in particular purely temporary or purely local price reductions the purpose of which is to acquire a monopoly within the common market;

decision[1] required all new price schedules to be published and submitted to the High Authority at least five clear days before they came into force, with the purpose thereby of preventing sudden alterations of prices.[2]

Following this, the prices of steel in Europe continued to fall, this time largely owing to the boom in industry occasioned by the hostilities in Korea. Steel producers, however, were reluctant continually to issue new price-lists, as they were required to do in respect of every alteration in price. Instead, they lowered their selling prices while retaining their old price-lists.

As this action was illegal by the terms of the recent decision, the High Authority would have been justified in imposing a fine upon the steel producers concerned.[3] Instead of doing so, however, the High Authority repealed the decision that no variations from price-lists were allowed, and substituted, in Decision 1–54, a provision that price deviations were henceforth to be lawful provided that these deviations did not constitute a discrimination, because all discriminations are forbidden by the Treaty.[4] It was declared in the decision that a price deviation would not amount to a discrimination if it was applied to what was called a unique or once-for-all transaction or if the price deviation, once made, was subsequently applied to all other transactions of a comparable nature.

By Article 1 of Decision 2–54, the previous requirement—that new price-lists were to be published before any alterations were allowed from the prices stated on the old lists—was abolished and, instead, producers of steel were allowed to vary their prices by up to 2.5 per cent. above or below those stated in their existing price-lists without being required to publish new lists. As soon as they exceeded this limit, however, producers were required to publish new price-lists, and any further price alterations were calculated with respect to this new price-list. By this decision, also, the provision that the lists must be submitted to the High Authority five days before coming into force was modified, and a period of one clear day's notice was substituted.

—discriminatory practices involving within the common market the application by a seller of unequal conditions to comparable transactions, especially according to the nationality of the buyer.

" After consulting the Consultative Committee and the Council, the High Authority may define the practices covered by this prohibition."

[1] Decision 31–53.

[2] This decision was issued under Article 60 (2), which provides as follows:

" For the above purposes:

(a) the price-lists and conditions of sale applied by enterprises within the common market must be made public to the extent and in the form prescribed by the High Authority . . .

(b) The methods of quotation applied must not have the effect of introducing into the prices charged by an enterprise in the common market, . . .

—increases over the price indicated by the price-list in question for a comparable transaction: or

—reductions below this price whose amount exceeds [a stated level]. . . "

[3] Article 65 provides:

" The High Authority may impose upon enterprises which violate the provisions of this Chapter or the decisions taken in application thereof, fines not to exceed twice the value of the unauthorized sales. In the case of a second offence, the above maximum may be doubled."

[4] Article 4 (b).

Despite this flexibility, however, enterprises were naturally still required not to discriminate among buyers, so that any deviation had to be applied uniformly to all comparable transactions. If deviations were not applied uniformly, the burden was upon the enterprises concerned to show that the transactions which had occurred at different prices were not comparable.

In order to keep a check on enterprises, Decision 3–54 was issued by which on 1st and 15th of each month all enterprises were required to inform the High Authority what deviations had occurred, and to justify them.

Further than this, the High Authority undertook certain spot checks upon enterprises, and, as two of the cases show, fined those enterprises which were not complying.

Decisions 1–54, 2–54 and 3–54 were the subject-matter of four of the cases. The main reason why these actions were brought was the desire of enterprises to know what were the exact prices of their competitors, and this they would not readily be able to discover if variations of 2.5 per cent. each way was allowed on every price published in those competitors' lists.

Other cases in which similar issues were involved were the following: *Italian Government* v. *The High Authority* (Case 2–54), *International Law Reports*, 1955, p. 737; *Associazione Industrie Sidérurgiche Italiane (Assider)* v. *The High Authority* (Case 3–54), reported below *Industrie Sidérurgiche Associate (I.S.A.)* v. *The High Authority* (Case 4–54), reported below, p. 411; and *Associazione Industrie Sidérurgiche Italiane (Assider)* v. *The High Authority* (Case 5–55), *International Law Reports*, 1955, p. 886.

**International organization—European Coal and Steel Community —Article 60 of Treaty establishing—Admissibility of appeals— Rights of associations—Allegation of *détournement de pouvoir*— Whether general decision may be disguised individual decision.**

Associazione Industrie Sidérurgiche Italiane (Assider) v. The High Authority.

*Court of Justice of the European Coal and Steel Community.*

(Pilotti, President; Serrarens, Hammes, Riese, Delvaux, Rueff, Van Kleffens JJ.)

*February 11, 1955.*

THE FACTS.—This was an appeal by an association of Italian steel enterprises with their head office in Milan against Decisions 1–54, 2–54 and 3–54 of the High Authority. The background to this case, which is one of several relating to the application of Article 60 of the Treaty establishing the European Coal and Steel Community, is set out in the Note printed at p. 403 above. The reason for the duplication of actions all challenging the same decisions was that until 1954 the Court did not make public the fact that an appeal had been lodged.[1]

The High Authority denied the admissibility of the present appeal. By Article 33, paragraph 2, of the Treaty, associations " may bring an appeal . . . against general decisions . . . which they believe to be vitiated by a *détournement de pouvoir* with respect to them ". This meant, it alleged, that the decision being challenged was general only in appearance, whereas in reality it affected individually the plaintiff association or its constituent enterprises, so that the High Authority would have used its powers to pass a general decision for a purpose other than that prescribed by the Treaty. Further, the High Authority alleged that a mere allegation of a *détournement de pouvoir* was not sufficient; the plaintiffs must show in their request that the *détournement* had in fact been committed.

The plaintiffs contended that by Article 33 they could challenge any general decision if they alleged in their request that in passing that decision the High Authority had committed a *détournement de pouvoir*, with respect to themselves or to one of the enterprises which formed their association.

As the decisions in question were general decisions, the plaintiffs were limited to alleging *détournement de pouvoir* with respect to themselves. They alleged, first, that by Articles 4 (*b*) and 60 (1) the High Authority was required to prevent all discrimination, whereas the 2.5 per cent. deviation from price schedules which was allowed by Article 1 of Decision 2–54 opened the way to discriminations, many of which had already occurred.

The High Authority replied that as the deviations were to be applied to all comparable transactions, discriminations were still illegal, and by the terms of Decision 3–54 all deviations had to be reported to the High Authority, which enabled a detailed check to be undertaken. Furthermore, it denied that any discriminations had already occurred.

The plaintiffs alleged that the failure of the High Authority under Article 64[2] to fine those enterprises which had infringed the previous regulations concerning prices, amounted to a manifest injustice and thus a *détournement de pouvoir* with respect to those enterprises which had observed the Treaty.

The High Authority pointed out that it was empowered, but not required, to fine enterprises. Further, it would only be equitable if it fined all the enterprises which had committed breaches, whereas it did not possess adequate co-operation to enable it to do this. The object of Decision 3–54 was precisely to give it this co-operation for the future.

---

[1] By an *Avis* of July 20, 1954, the Court decided that the fact of the introduction of an appeal was in future to be published in the *Journal Officiel*.

[2] For the text of Article 64 see above, p. 391, n. 1.

This system of reporting deviations, however, as required by Decision 3–54 was, the plaintiffs claimed, impracticable and thus illogical and in consequence a *détournement de pouvoir*. Enterprises were unable to specify the exact deviations in their prices, particularly when they sold through representatives.

The High Authority contended that even if a decision was illogical it was not thereby vitiated by a *détournement de pouvoir*. In any event, Decision 3–54 was not impracticable; enterprises must know what deviations their representatives allowed or they would have no control over them.

Finally, the plaintiffs referred to Section 30 (2) of the Convention containing the Transitional Provisions. By this provision, they alleged, all deviations from price lists, even if they did not amount to discriminations, were illegal in the Italian market. As this provision was inserted for the benefit of Italian enterprises, a violation of it amounted to a *détournement de pouvoir* with respect to those enterprises.

The High Authority replied that Section 30 prevented non-Italian enterprises aligning their prices with those of Italian steel enterprises. The new system had in no way altered this. Non-Italian enterprises would still be unable to sell at the same prices as Italian enterprises, particularly because the cost of transport would always prevent this.

The submissions of the Advocate General were that the appeal should be dismissed.

*Held:* that there was no occasion to rule upon the appeal for annulment of the first Article of Decision 2–54 and of Decision 3–54. The appeal for annulment of Decision 1–54 and of Articles 2 to 5 of Decision 2–54 must be rejected.

By Article 33, paragraph 2, of the Treaty, the only requirement for a plaintiff to challenge a general decision of the High Authority was that it should formally allege a *détournement de pouvoir* with respect to itself. Where, however, the plaintiff was an association, it sufficed if that association alleged the *détournement* with respect to one of its member enterprises.

As Article 1 of Decision 2–54 had already been annulled in the *French Government case* (reported above, p. 388), there was no occasion for a further ruling. Decision 3–54, which required all reports of deviations to be sent twice a month to the High Authority, had been repealed by the High Authority so that there was no further need to consider that part of the appeal.[1]

The appeal against Decision 1–54 and against the other articles of Decision 2–54 employed the same arguments as those already

[1] Judgment in the *French Government case* was delivered on December 20, 1954. Decision 3-54 was repealed on January 4, 1955 (see Decision 1-55: *Journal Officiel*, January 11, 1955, p. 542).

rejected by the Court in the *Italian Government's case* against the High Authority.[1]

The Court said: " The Court, in judging the present action, relies in law on the following:

" 1. *Concerning admissibility.*—

" (a) The Court holds that by clause 2 of their articles the plaintiffs are an association of enterprises which fulfil the conditions laid down in Articles 33, paragraph 2, and 48 of the Treaty.

" (b) The decisions being challenged have the character of general decisions. The Court rejects the defendant's submission that the admissibility of appeals submitted by enterprises or associations of enterprises against general decisions is dependent upon proof of the existence of a *détournement de pouvoir* committed with respect to them. Indeed, by the terms of Article 33, paragraph 2, of the Treaty, enterprises or associations of enterprises ' may bring an appeal . . . against general decisions . . . which they believe to be vitiated by a *détournement de pouvoir* with respect to them '. According to this provision, which is perfectly clear, it is sufficient for the admissibility of appeals that the plaintiffs formally allege a *détournement de pouvoir* with respect to them, in the same way that it is sufficient for the appeal of a State to be admissible that it alleges the existence of one of the four grounds of annulment set out in the first paragraph of Article 33 of the Treaty.

" This allegation must specify the reasons which, in the plaintiffs' opinion, give rise to the *détournement de pouvoir* with respect to them. However, these requirements have been fulfilled in the present instance. In the case of an appeal brought by an association of enterprises, it is sufficient if it alleges a *détournement de pouvoir* with respect to one or more of the enterprises which are members of the association. In the present action, the plaintiffs allege, with supporting arguments, a *détournement de pouvoir* with respect to the enterprises which they represent. This *détournement de pouvoir* is alleged to exist with respect to Section 30 of the Convention containing the Transitional Provisions, as well as with respect to Articles 4 (b), 60 and 64 of the Treaty and from the fact also of the illogical character of the decisions in question.

" The Court holds that the Treaty does not provide and does not require any further condition for the admissibility of appeals, such as, in particular, the proof that a *détournement de pouvoir* with respect to the plaintiffs has actually been committed. This proof will be necessary to establish that the case is well founded—but this matter belongs to the examination of the merits and does not affect admissibility.

---

[1] *International Law Reports*, 1955, p. 737.

" (c) The Court, in agreement with the advocate general on this point, accepts the possibility of one appeal challenging the three decisions here in question.

" 2. *Concerning the Merits.*—For the above reasons, the Court holds that the appeal has been rendered unnecessary to the extent that it concerns the request for the annulment of the first article of Decision No. 2–54 of the High Authority, as well as the request for the annulment of Decision No. 3–54. As for the request for the annulment of Decision No. 1–54 and of Articles 2 to 5 of Decision No. 2–54, it appears that it is ill-founded.

" There is, therefore, no occasion for the Court to pronounce upon the definition of *détournement de pouvoir* within the meaning of paragraph 2 of Article 33 of the Treaty, nor upon the interpretation of the words ' vitiated by a *détournement de pouvoir* with respect to them ' which are there used.

" (1) The first Article of Decision No. 2–54 of the High Authority having been annulled *erga omnes* by the judgment of December 21, 1954, in the case of *The French Government* v. *The High Authority*,[1] the present request for annulment has on this point been rendered unnecessary.

" It is not necessary, therefore, to examine whether, on this point, the appeal is well-founded or not or to state this expressly in the judgment, because a decision which has already been annulled or abrogated in the meantime cannot adversely affect the plaintiff's rights or interests. Consequently, the present judgment, in so far as it concerns the request for the annulment of the first article of Decision No. 2–54 of the High Authority, is limited to declaring that there is no occasion for a ruling by the Court.

" (2) The same conclusion applies as regards Decision No. 3–54, the High Authority having abrogated it by its Decision No. 1–55 of January 4, 1955 (*Journal Officiel de la Communauté* of January 11, 1955, p. 542). Consequently, there is no occasion for a ruling by the Court with regard to Decision No. 3–54 of the High Authority.

" (3) As regards Decision No. 1–54 of the High Authority, the plaintiffs have advanced the same arguments as the Government of the Italian Republic advanced against the High Authority (Case No. 2–54).[2] The Court has rejected these arguments in its judgment given in that case, by holding that the provisions in question do not violate the Treaty or the Convention containing the Transitional Provisions and that they do not constitute a *détournement de pouvoir*. No new argument has been produced which could lead the Court to another conclusion, whatever interpretation one wishes to give to the notion of '*détournement de pouvoir* with respect to them ' in Article 33 of the Treaty.

[1 Reported above, p. 388.]
[2 *International Law Reports*, 1955, p. 737.]

" Indeed, although Decision No. 1–54 of the High Authority declares not to amount to a discrimination any deviations from the prices stated in the price lists of an enterprise, when they concern a unique transaction or when the same deviation is applied to all comparable transactions, yet it expressly maintains the obligation to obey the rules concerning the publication of price lists. This provision does not infringe in any way upon the legal position of the Italian steel industry and does not seek to legalise previous breaches.

" (4) The judgment given on December 21, 1954, in the case of *The Italian Government* v. *The High Authority*, declared that Articles 2 and 3 of Decision No. 2–54 of the High Authority do not constitute a violation of the Treaty or of the Convention containing the Transitional Provisions, nor a *détournement de pouvoir*.

" As for the provisions of Article 3 of Decision No. 2–54 of the High Authority, which reduce to one day the time-limit specified for new price lists to come into force, although they compel the Italian enterprises to react more rapidly to alterations in the price schedules of their competitors they do not, however, seriously detract from the special protection provided for their benefit.

" Articles 4 and 5 of Decision No. 2–54 of the High Authority are of an entirely general nature and in no way constitute a threat to Italian steel enterprises or associations of enterprises. The aim of these articles is not relevant to the present action. Moreover, the plaintiffs, who have not advanced any argument on this matter, have not been affected by it. The said articles can therefore not be vitiated by the *détournement de pouvoir* which the plaintiffs allege.

" (5) From the above survey, it follows that none of the provisions challenged referred to under headings (3) and (4) violates the Treaty or the Convention containing the Transitional Provisions.

" There is, therefore, no occasion to consider the question whether, and under what conditions, enterprises and associations of enterprises can challenge a general decision of the High Authority on the ground of violation of the law.

" (6) The Court rejects the request for the production of all documents relevant to the case. Those which the defendants have produced suffice in the present case to inform the Court about the aims pursued by the High Authority.

"*Costs.*—As the defendants have lost as [far as] concerns their principal submission that the appeal should be declared inadmissible (*improponibile*), the Court, in accordance with paragraph 2 of Article 60 of its Rules, deems it just to apportion the costs.[1]

" The Court, rejecting all further arguments in favour or to the contrary, adjudges and declares:

[1 Article 60, para. 2, of the old Rules stated: " The Court may apportion costs wholly or in part if the parties each lose on one or more heads of claim". This provision is now contained in Article 69, para. 3, of the Rules.]

" There is no occasion for pronouncing judgment upon the appeal for annulment brought against the first article of Decision No. 2–54 of the High Authority and against Decision No. 3–54 of the High Authority.

" The appeal for annulment brought against Decision No. 1–54 of the High Authority and Articles 2 to 5 of Decision No. 2–54 of the High Authority is rejected.

" The costs are apportioned. Each party to pay its own costs."

[Report: *Recueil de la Jurisprudence de la Cour*, I (1954–55), p. 125 (in French).]

International organization—European Coal and Steel Community —Article 60 of Treaty establishing—Admissibility of appeals— Rights of associations—Allegation of *détournement de pouvoir*— Whether general decision may be disguised individual decision— Article 15 of Treaty—Requirement that reasons for decisions be given—Whether dissenting opinions in Council and Consultative Committee need be stated.

INDUSTRIE SIDÉRURGICHE ASSOCIATE (I.S.A.) *v.* THE HIGH AUTHORITY.

*Court of Justice of the European Coal and Steel Community.*

(Pilotti, President; Serrarens, Hammes, Riese, Delvaux, Rueff, Van Kleffens JJ.)

*February* 11, 1955.

THE FACTS.—The plaintiffs in this action were an association of Italian steel enterprises with their head office in Milan, who found themselves adversely affected by Decisions 1–54, 2–54 and 3–54 of the High Authority. Their appeal was filed on the same day as that in the *Assider case* (Case 3–54; reported above, p. 405). The background to the present action is set out in the Note which appears at p. 403 above.

The plaintiffs advanced the same arguments as had the plaintiffs in the *Assider case* and the replies of the High Authority were in substance the same as those already given in that case. The High Authority itself only contended that the present action was inadmissible by the terms of Article 33, paragraph 2, of the Treaty of 1951 establishing the Community.

The plaintiffs also claimed that on important matters both the Council of Ministers and the Consultative Committee had expressed views against the provisions subsequently incorporated in the three decisions in question. The High Authority, however, had failed to mention these, which, they alleged, amounted to a violation of the principles of proper administration. If this omission did not, of itself, constitute a *détournement de pouvoir* it was at least evidence of such a *détournement*.

The High Authority replied that the Council of Ministers had been unanimous and the Consultative Committee unanimous but for one vote in accepting the principle of allowing divergences from price schedule. The only division of opinion was upon the subsidiary matter of whether the deviation should be of a fixed or an average amount. Further, the High Authority maintained that by Article 15 of the Treaty[1] there was no obligation to set out dissenting opinions if any had been given.

The submissions of the Advocate General were that the appeal should be dismissed.

*Held:* that there was no occasion to rule upon the appeal for annulment of the first article of Decision 2-54 and of Decision 3-54. The appeal for annulment of Decision 1-54 and Articles 2 and 3 of Decision 2-54 must be rejected.

By Article 15 of the Treaty, the High Authority was required to give the reasons for its decisions and also to refer to the opinions which it was required to have obtained. This provision required the High Authority to set out the fact that it had received these opinions but it in no way required it to set out or refute dissenting opinions. The failure of the High Authority, therefore, to do this in the present instance had no bearing upon the validity of the decisions.

The greater part of the judgment of the Court in the present case was identical with that in the *Assider case* (reported above, p. 405). The Court, however, added the following considerations:

" The plaintiffs see a breach of the rules of good administration and, therefore, grounds establishing a *détournement de pouvoir* in the fact that the High Authority, in setting out the reasons for the decisions being challenged, has omitted to comment upon the dissenting opinions expressed in the consultative bodies.

" The Court does not accept this submission.

" By the terms of Article 15 of the Treaty, the High Authority is required to ' include the reasons ' for its decisions and to ' refer to ' the opinions which the High Authority is required to obtain. It follows from this that the High Authority must specify the reasons which have led it to issue the regulations in question and that it is required to state the fact that the views required by the Treaty have been given. On the other hand, the Treaty does not require it to set out—and even less that it should seek to refute—the dissenting opinions expressed by the consultative bodies or by certain of their members.

[1] Article 15, para. 1, provides: " The decisions, recommendations and opinions of the High Authority shall include the reasons therefor, and shall refer to the advice which the High Authority is required to obtain."

" Hence, the omission which is alleged cannot be considered as proof, or even as the mere beginning of proof, in support of a claim of a *détournement de pouvoir*.

" *Costs*.—As the defendants have lost as regards their principal submission that the appeal should be declared inadmissible (*improponibile*), the Court, in accordance with paragraph 2 of Article 60 [1] of its Rules, deems it just to apportion the costs.

" The Court, rejecting all further arguments or submissions to the contrary, adjudges and declares:

" There is no occasion for pronouncing judgment upon the appeal for annulment brought against the first article of Decision No. 2–54 of the High Authority and against Decision No. 3–54 of the High Authority.

" The appeal for annulment brought against Decision No. 1–54 of the High Authority and against Articles 2 and 3 of Decision No. 2–54 of the High Authority is rejected.

" The costs are apportioned. Each party to pay its own costs."

[Report: *Recueil de la Jurisprudence de la Cour*, I (1954–55), p. 179 (in French).]

---

**International organization—European Coal and Steel Community —Article 35 of Treaty establishing—Appeal to High Authority by consumers' association—Admissibility of—Meaning of " associations " in Article 35—Definition of " enterprise " in Article 80.**

ASSOCIATION DES UTILISATEURS DE CHARBON DU GRAND-DUCHÉ DE LUXEMBOURG *v.* THE HIGH AUTHORITY.

*Court of Justice of the European Coal and Steel Community.*

(Pilotti, President; Serrarens, Hammes, Riese, Delvaux, Rueff, Van Kleffens JJ.)

*April 23, 1956.*

THE FACTS.—These joint cases (8–54 and 10–54) were brought by an association of coal consumers in the Grand Duchy of Luxembourg. The background to these cases is the same as that to the case of *Groupement des Industries Sidérurgiques Luxembourgeoises* v. *The High Authority* (Joint Cases 7–54 and 9–54), reported in *International Law Reports*, 1956, p. 597. It is convenient, nevertheless, to reproduce the relevant facts in the present report.

Although Luxembourg is an important steel producing country, it possesses no coal mines of its own. All coal, therefore, which is consumed in the country has to be imported. By a Ministerial Decree of March 8, 1954, the Luxembourg Government established an

---

[1 Article 60, para. 2, of the old Rules provided: "The Court may apportion costs wholly or in part if the parties each fail on one or more heads of claim." This provision is now contained in Article 69, para. 3, of the Rules.]

Import Office[1] and granted to it the sole right to import solid fuel into the country.[2] More than this, the Decree initiated a compensation system.[3] A levy of 8 Belgian francs was to be imposed upon the sale of every metric ton of coal and coke purchased by Luxembourg industry. This levy was to be paid into a *Caisse de Compensation* which was set up as part of the Import Office. The levy when collected was to be used by the Government to subsidise the price of coal sold for household purposes, and thereby keep down the cost of living. The decree came into force on April 1, 1954.

In July 1954, the plaintiffs wrote to the High Authority requesting it, first, to issue a decision or recommendation declaring the Import Office to be illegal in so far as it possessed the monopoly to import coal, and secondly, to order the Luxembourg Government to abolish the *Caisse* and the whole compensation system.

During the two months following this request the High Authority did not take the action requested, so that at the end of those two months the High Authority was deemed to have issued a decision refusing to comply with the plaintiffs' request.[4] The association brought an action (Case 8–54) before the Court against this implied decision of refusal.

On November 27, 1954, the High Authority wrote to the association setting out its reasons for refusing to issue the decision or recommendation requested. The association thereupon brought a second action (Case 10–54), appealing against the decision contained in this letter. The Luxembourg Government intervened to support the High Authority.[5]

The Court joined the two actions for the purposes of trial and judgment.

The High Authority denied the standing of the plaintiffs to appeal to the Court. By Article 33 of the Treaty, the only associations

---

[1] *Office Commercial du Ravitaillement.*

[2] This office replaced others which had existed before the Treaty was signed.

[3] *La Compensation.* The High Authority's translation of this term is " compensation system "; a better translation would have been " subsidy system ".

[4] Under Article 35 of the Treaty establishing the Community, which reads as follows:

" In the cases where the High Authority is required by a provision of this Treaty or of the regulations for its execution to issue a decision or recommendation, and fails to fulfil this obligation, the omission may be brought to the attention of the High Authority by the States, the Council or the enterprises and associations, as the case may be.

" The same shall be true if the High Authority refrains from taking a decision or formulating a recommendation when it is empowered to do so by a provision of this Treaty or the regulations for its execution, where such failure to act constitutes an abuse of power.

" If at the end of a period of two months the High Authority has not taken any decision or formulated any recommendation, an appeal may be lodged before the Court, within a period of one month, against the tacit negative decision presumed to result from such failure to act."

[5] In an Ordinance dated November 24, 1955, the Court declared that the intervention of the Luxembourg Government was admissible.

entitled to appeal were those " referred to in Article 48 ",[1] whereas the plaintiffs, they alleged, were not a producers' association but, as their name showed, a consumers' association. Further, although the Treaty allowed certain associations engaged in distribution to appeal,[2] this right was limited to cases concerning agreements and concentrations.[3]

The plaintiffs replied that although they were not entitled to bring an appeal against an express decision under Article 33, yet the first of their present actions was being brought under Article 35, that is, against an implied decision. As Article 35 made no reference to the requirement that appeals could only be brought by associations referred to in Article 48, such a restrictive condition [they maintained] could not justifiably be read into the Treaty.

The remaining arguments were substantially the same as those advanced in the cases of *Groupement des Industries Sidérurgiques Luxembourgeoises* v. *The High Authority* (Cases 7–54 and 9–54), reported in *International Law Reports*, 1956, p. 597.

*Held:* that the appeal must be rejected. The only associations entitled to appeal to the Court were associations of those enterprises which were defined in Article 80,[4] because this definition was applicable to the entire Treaty. If this were not so, an association would be able to appeal where none of its constituent members could have done so themselves. The plaintiffs, by their articles, were clearly an association defending and representing the interests of its members in their capacity as consumers of coal.

The plaintiffs, therefore, had no standing before the Court, and their action was inadmissible.

The Court said: " The Court, in judging the present actions relies in law upon the following considerations:

*As to admissibility.*—As regards the plaintiffs' ability to appeal to the High Authority under Article 35 of the Treaty, Article 35 grants to 'enterprises and associations' the right to appeal to the High Authority. The associations referred to in that expression can only be associations of enterprises within the meaning of the term 'enterprise' as defined by Article 80 of the Treaty for the entire

---

[1] Article 33, para. 2, of the Treaty provides: " Enterprises or associations referred to in Article 48 may, under the same conditions, appeal . . . "

Article 48, para. 3, provides: " The High Authority shall normally call upon producers' associations to obtain information which it requires . . . provided that the associations in question either permit the properly chosen representatives of the workers and consumers to participate in the direction of these associations or in consultative committees attached to them, or in any other way give a satisfactory place in their organisation to the expression of the workers' and consumers' interests."

[2] For text of Article 80 see below n. 4.

[3] The present actions were brought under Articles 65 and 66.

[4] Article 80 provides: " The term 'enterprise', as used in this Treaty, refers to any enterprise engaged in production in the field of coal and steel, within the territories [of the member States] . . . "

Treaty. Indeed, if this were not so, an association would possess a right to bring an appeal which none of its constituent members separately and on their own behalf would have been able to exercise. In the absence of an express statement to the contrary, the Treaty cannot establish any such disparity of treatment between an association and its constituent members.

" It is necessary to examine whether the plaintiffs fulfil the conditions mentioned above.

" The Association des Utilisateurs de Charbon du Grand-Duché de Luxembourg is composed as follows:—Fédération des Industries Luxembourgeoises; Groupement des Industries Sidérurgiques Luxembourgeoises; Groupement des Négotiants de Combustibles en gros; Société Nationale des Chemins de Fer Luxembourgeois; M. Leon Brasseur, Engineer, representing the Usines à gaz du Grand-Duché de Luxembourg.

" By Article 1 of its articles of association, its objects are: (a) to defend and to represent the interests of the consumers of coal within the limits of the aims of the European Coal and Steel Community; (b) to give advice concerning questions which are of interest to consumers of coal and which are submitted to it either by an institution of the European Coal and Steel Community or by any other authority. It is also, as its title expressly indicates, an association of consumers of coal.

" The presence of the Groupement des Industries Sidérurgiques Luxembourgeoises among the members does not alter the character of the Association, and furthermore, the Groupement has already submitted an appeal on its own account, having the same objects as the present appeal.

" Article 1 of the articles of association leaves no doubt that its objects are to defend and to represent the interests of its members in their capacity as consumers of coal, and to give advice on questions of interest to consumers of coal.

" For these reasons, and without this decision prejudging the qualifications needed to bring an appeal under other articles of the Treaty, the Association des Utilisateurs de Charbon du Grand-Duché is not one of the associations empowered to appeal to the High Authority in application of the terms of Article 35.

" Therefore, Appeals 8–54 and 10–54 are inadmissible.

" The Court, rejecting all further arguments or submissions to the contrary, adjudges and declares: In the joint cases Nos. 8–54 and 10–54 the appeal is rejected. The plaintiffs are condemned in costs, including the costs of the intervening party."

[Report: *Recueil de la Jurisprudence de la Cour*, II (1955–56), p. 159 (in French).]

International organization—European Coal and Steel Community —Article 33 of Treaty establishing—Decisions of High Authority —Right of associations and enterprises to challenge decisions— Whether decisions general or individual—Whether a letter from High Authority to a Government constitutes a decision—Grounds of challenge.

FÉDÉRATION CHARBONNIÈRE DE BELGIQUE *v.* THE HIGH AUTHORITY. (INTERIM JUDGMENT.)

*Court of Justice of the European Coal and Steel Community.*

(Pilotti, President; Serrarens, Hammes, Riese, Delvaux, Rueff, Van Kleffens JJ.)

*July* 16, 1956.

THE FACTS.—In the present case, the background to which is set out in the Note which appears below, at p. 423, the plaintiff federation challenged the validity of Decision 22–55 of the High Authority and of a letter of May 28, 1955, from the Authority to the Belgian Government. The plaintiffs argued that Decision No. 22–55 was an individual decision because, by altering prices, it altered the amount of compensation payable. Three collieries of the Campine area received different rates of compensation and would thus be affected differently from other collieries. The High Authority declared that the fact that a decision might have different effects for different collieries was not relevant to determining the nature of the decision. A decision was general or individual because of the scope of its application.

The High Authority denied that the threat to withdraw compensation contained in the letter of May 28, 1955, constituted a decision and maintained, therefore, that no appeal under Article 33 could be brought against it. However, if it were a decision, the High Authority claimed that an appeal could only be brought against it on the sole ground of a *détournement de pouvoir*, and then only if the High Authority had disguised under what appeared to be a general decision what was in fact an individual decision with respect to the plaintiffs.

The plaintiffs denied this. They contended that in order to establish a *détournement de pouvoir* vitiating a general decision they might prove any of the other three grounds of appeal set out in Article 33.

The Court postponed consideration of the merits of the case until a later judgment.[1]

*Held:* that the appeal was admissible. Decision No. 22–55 was a general decision because it applied to all enterprises producing coal in Belgium, and if a new coal deposit were discovered its production

[1] Reported below, p. 425. The submissions of the parties on the merits appear at pp. 425-427.

also would be governed by the decision. The letter of May 28, 1955, in so far as it reduced compensation from three collieries, was an individual decision. The rest of the letter also constituted a decision because it specified what action the High Authority would take if certain events occurred. It thus constituted a rule capable of being applied. This part of the letter constituted a general decision.

Against the individual decision the plaintiff could appeal on all the four grounds set out in Article 33, but against the general decision it could appeal only on the ground of a *détournement de pouvoir* with respect to itself.

The Court adjourned the case to enable the approximate costs of production of each type and grade of coal at the end of the transitional period to be determined.

The Court said: " As regards the law

" A.    *Concerning the admissibility of the appeal.*—The appeal seeks the annulment of:

" (1) Decision No. 22–55 of the High Authority of May 28, 1955, and the scale of prices annexed hereto, published in the *Journal Officiel de la Communauté*, May 31, 1955, in so far as they fix reduced prices for certain types of coal:

" (2) The decisions contained in the letter addressed by the High Authority to the Belgian Government and dated May 28, 1955, and in the table of tariffs of compensation payments attached to this letter,

" (a) in so far as a discrimination is established between producers of identical grades of coal by the withdrawal or the reduction of compensation from certain collieries,

" (b) in so far as, by the terms of the said letter, the compensation payments will be, or may be, withdrawn from certain enterprises on the grounds that they have not achieved that re-equipment which is judged practicable and necessary or have refused to yield up or exchange deposits where this is deemed indispensable to more satisfactory arrangements for mining.

" As respects Decision No. 22–55, the plaintiffs submit that it is an individual decision. The defendants maintain, on the contrary, that it constitutes a general decision. According to the plaintiffs, the individual character of the decision is established by the fact that, because of the indissoluble link that exists between compensation and the fixing of prices, the effects of the price lists differ in the three collieries of the Campine from those in other Belgian mines in so far as the compensation granted to those three collieries is not the same as that received by the other mines.

" Without denying that the effects of the price lists will vary to the extent that the compensation itself will vary, the Court rejects the plaintiffs' contention that this variation in the effects of the scale of prices determines the nature of Decision No. 22–55. Indeed, this decision has been taken within the framework of the special system established by Section 26 of the Convention [containing Transitional Measures] to meet the situation in Belgium, and it is intended to last for the duration of the transitional period. This system is applicable, according to the particular circumstances, however detailed or varied they may be, to all the enterprises and to all the transactions falling within its scope.

" Within the framework of this system, this decision applies to enterprises by reason only of the fact that they are producers of coal, without any other requirement. In the case of a new coal deposit being discovered in Belgium, its products would be required to be sold at the prices fixed by this decision. On the other hand, the territorial delimitation contained in the decision does not imply any individual character of that decision and is justified by the fact that the Belgian industry is in need of compensation.

" The fact that Decision No. 22–55 consists of a detailed and concrete set of rules applicable to different situations, is not contrary to the general character of the decision. In effect, the Treaty in Article 50, paragraph 2, states that the method of assessing and collecting levies is to be fixed by a general decision of the High Authority, which shows that concrete, detailed and varied consequences of a general decision do not detract from that general character.

" The fact that the plaintiff association includes all the enterprises referred to in the decision—and only those—does not lead in any way to a different conclusion. If it did, one would be forced to deny the general character even of a decision applicable to all the enterprises of the Community in a situation where these had formed themselves into one and the same association. The individual or general nature of a decision must be established by reference to objective criteria, so that it becomes impossible to make a distinction according to whether the plaintiffs are an association or an enterprise.

" As for the decisions contained in the letter of May 28, 1955, the parties contend that the first, concerning the reduction and withdrawal of compensation, is of an individual character, and that the second, concerning the threat to withdraw compensation, is of a general character. On this, the Court accepts the view of the parties.

" In the course of the oral proceedings, the defendants posed the question whether it was possible to regard this second declaration as being a decision which is capable of being made the subject matter of an appeal for annulment under Article 33 of the Treaty. Now, in its letter of May 28, 1955, the High Authority has recognized that the grant of compensation must of necessity be accompanied by a series of measures to be carried out by the Belgian Government. The High Authority mentioned, moreover, that the Belgian Government must carry out four measures, specified as (a), (b), (c) and (d). The terms of (d) are, therefore, part of the series of measures that the Belgian Government would be required to take if the necessity arose. The High Authority has thus determined, in an unequivocal manner, the action that from now on it has decided to take in a case where the conditions specified under the heading 2 (d) of the letter are fulfilled. In other words, it has set out a rule capable of being applied if the need arises. It must, therefore be seen as a decision within the meaning of Article 14 of the Treaty.[1]

" The individual or general character of each of the decisions having been established, the plaintiffs are correct in requesting the annulment of the declaration concerning the reduction and withdrawal of compensation—the individual decision contained in the letter of May 28, 1955—by alleging all the grounds set out in Article 33 of the Treaty. They are correct in bringing an appeal for annulment of the two other decisions, which are general decisions, to the extent that they believe that they are vitiated by a *détournement de pouvoir* with respect to them.

" In order that an appeal for the annulment of a general decision may be admissible, it is sufficient if the plaintiffs formally allege a *détournement de pouvoir* affecting them by indicating the facts which, in their view, constitute this *détournement de pouvoir*.

" The above mentioned conditions are fulfilled in the present action, which is, therefore, admissible.

" However, the views of the parties differ upon what is the exact effect of Article 33 of the Treaty concerning the admissibility of certain grounds alleged by the plaintiffs against these general decisions.

" The defendants maintain that an enterprise can allege a *détournement de pouvoir* affecting them only if the High Authority has disguised, under what appears to be a general administrative act, an individual decision ' with respect to ' that enterprise.

" This contention must be rejected. Indeed, a disguised individual decision remains an individual decision. The nature of a decision does not depend upon its form, but upon its content. Moreover, such an interpretation of Article 33, and especially of the words ' with respect to them ', cannot be accepted, because the phrase ' with respect to them ' has no other meaning than that of the words which express it, namely that the decision affects that enterprise which is the object, or at any rate the victim, of the *détournement de pouvoir* which it alleges. The Court is of the opinion that Article 33 clearly states that associations and enterprises can challenge not only individual decisions, but also general decisions in the proper sense of that term.

" Alternatively, the defendants submit that the grounds which the plaintiffs may validly allege are limited to the sole ground of

[1 Article 14 provides:
" In the execution of the tasks entrusted to it by the present Treaty and in accordance with the provisions thereof, the High Authority shall take decisions, formulate recommendations and issue opinions.
" Decisions shall be binding in every respect . . . ".]

*détournement de pouvoir*, as all the other grounds have been excluded. The plaintiffs, on the other hand, maintain not only that they have the right to allege all the grounds for annulment, provided that with supporting reasons they have alleged a *détournement de pouvoir*, but, furthermore, that they may prove the other grounds as a means of establishing the *détournement de pouvoir*.    In their opinion, the Treaty creates a legal system in which private enterprises may only allege the ground of *détournement de pouvoir* affecting them; it would be wrong, therefore, to give this ground an exceptional and extended meaning.

" This contention must be rejected.  If the Treaty provides that private enterprises have a right to request the annulment of a general decision on the grounds of a *détournement de pouvoir* with respect to them, it is because the right to appeal on other grounds has not been granted to them.

" If the plaintiff's contention were correct, enterprises would have as extensive a right of appeal as that of the States and of the Council, and it would be inexplicable why Article 33, instead of simply equating the appeals of enterprises to those of States or of the Council, has introduced a very clear distinction between individual decisions and general decisions, and has limited, as far as enterprises are concerned, the annulment of general decisions to the ground of *détournement de pouvoir* with respect to these enterprises. The phrase ' under the same conditions ' cannot be interpreted as meaning that the enterprises, after having established a *détournement de pouvoir* with respect to them, have the right to allege the other grounds for annulment as well, because, when a *détournement de pouvoir* with respect to them has been established, the annulment of the decision in question must follow and does not have to be pronounced on other grounds.

" These considerations are clearly contrary to the plaintiffs' submission that one must subordinate the interpretation of the Treaty to the desire to allow private enterprises a right of appeal which is practically identical with that of the States and the Council. Such a desire is understandable, but there are no indications in the Treaty which allow one to conclude that such a right of challenge of the ' constitutionality ' of general decisions, that is to say, of their conformity with the Treaty, was granted to enterprises, since general decisions are quasi-legislative acts originating from a public authority and have a normative effect *'erga omnes'*.

" It is true that Article 33 grants a right of appeal for the annulment of a general decision on the ground of *détournement de pouvoir* with respect to an enterprise, but this is an exception and is explained by the fact that in this case it is still the individual element of that decision which is predominant.

" It is thus, only admissible for the plaintiffs to challenge decisions upon the sole ground of *détournement de pouvoir* with regard to them;

as concerns the individual decision—the parties having agreed that it is individual—it is admissible for the plaintiffs to allege all the grounds specified in paragraph 1 of Article 33.

" B. *Concerning the Merits.*—Before examining any questions relating to Decision No. 22–55, and in particular the question whether the High Authority is empowered to fix selling prices and is empowered to enact the provisions contained in its letter of May 28, 1955, it is first necessary to analyse the means whereby the level of the estimated costs of production have been fixed.

" Concerning the determination of this level, the plaintiffs maintained, first, that the High Authority was not empowered to alter the initial evaluation of the estimated costs of production, because this estimate constituted a 'stopping place', determined at the beginning of the transitional period, thereafter remaining unalterable unless modified by general agreement.

" This contention of the plaintiffs must be rejected because Section 26 of the Convention provides that the extent of the unavoidable lowering of Belgian prices is to be determined by the level of the estimated costs of production at the end of the transitional period. It follows that in the case of an alteration in the estimated level of the costs of production, it is necessary to make a new evaluation which takes this alteration into account.

" Secondly, the parties disagree as to the method to be adopted for evaluating the level of the estimated costs of production. The Court is of the opinion that, before taking a decision, the level which reasonably constitutes ' the approximate costs of production at the end of the transitional period ' must be determined on the basis of forecasts for each of the types and grades of coal—forecasts which have themselves taken into account the facts and circumstances known at the moment of evaluation.

" The answers given by the parties to the questions asked by the *juge rapporteur* are not adequate for this purpose.

" As the parties in their joint reply have declared that such a determination cannot be submitted to the Court within the time-limit granted, it is necessary to grant a new time-limit for this purpose.

" The Court, rejecting all further arguments or submissions to the contrary, adjudges and declares:

" 1. The appeal is admissible.

" 2. The oral proceedings are re-opened. They shall concern exclusively the level, per type and per grade, of the estimated costs of production of the Belgian coal at the end of the transitional period, and the position of these costs relative to the prices fixed by Decision No. 22–55.

" 3. The date by which the parties are required to file with the Registry of the Court the information and supplementary specifications indicated in the present judgment is fixed at September 1,

1956, and the oral proceedings will take place on September 20, 1956, at 10.30 a.m.

" 4. Costs are reserved."

[Report: *Recueil de la Jurisprudence de la Cour*, II (1955-56), p. 201 (in French).]

NOTE.—The following is a note on the background to this case and the case of *Société de Charbonnages de Beeringen* v. *The High Authority* (Case 9-55, reported below, p. 441].

After the Second World War, the costs of producing coal in Belgium rose steadily and by 1947 had become considerably higher than those of coal production in either the Netherlands or West Germany. In addition, an extensive programme of re-equipment and of mechanization was needed in the mines. If this programme were to be financed by the coal mines themselves out of their own profits, the price of Belgian coal would have had to have been raised even higher, and this in its turn would have raised the costs of the very large number of products which use coal in their manufacture. In 1947, therefore, the Belgian Government paid to collieries a grant-in-aid of 35-45 Belgian francs per ton of coal sold, and this grant was to be expressly earmarked for re-equipment. In 1949, certain of the marginal mines were closed down and others were amalgamated. Others received lump sums from the Government as short term subsidies, and the Government also granted several " contractual " subsidies to cover the estimated losses of particular collieries over the following five years.

When Belgium signed the Coal and Steel Community Treaty in 1951, it was realized that the Belgian coal industry would be unable to compete with production in the other Community countries, and particularly with production in the Ruhr. Special provisions were, therefore, included in the Treaty, the most important of which allowed the Belgian Government, if it so desired, to set up during the transitional period mechanisms under the control of the High Authority which would make possible the separation of the Belgian market from the Common Market.[1] This provision, however, was never invoked.

A further provision authorized a compensation system[2] to make it possible to bring the price of Belgian coal for all consumers within the Common Market as near as possible to prices in the Common Market generally, so as to reduce Belgian prices to a level near to that of the estimated costs of production at the end of the transitional period.[3] To

---

[1] Convention containing the Transitional Provisions, Section 26, (3), para. 1.

[2] *La péréquation*. All the official translations refer to this term as " compensation": a better term, however, would probably have been " subsidy ".

[3] Section 26 (2) (a) of the Convention. This reads:

" The compensation system is designed, starting from the beginning of the transitional period:

" (a) to make it possible to bring the price of Belgian coal to all consumers in the Common Market as close as possible to prices in the Common Market generally, so as to reduce Belgian prices to a level near that of the estimated costs of production at the end of the transitional period. The price lists established on these bases may not be changed without the agreement of the High Authority."

For some inexplicable reason the final sentence above has been omitted from the official English translation of the Treaty.

carry out this provision, the High Authority imposed a levy upon German and Dutch coal production at the rate of 1.1 per cent.[1] and, out of the money raised, payments were made to Belgian mines. The amount of the compensation to be paid was determined by reference to two schedules. One of these, an account schedule, showed the pre-Treaty prices of each type and grade of coal,[2] the other, a sales schedule, showed the actual prices obtained for the coal produced.[3] Where the actual price obtained was lower than the pre-Treaty price of the particular type of coal concerned, the difference between the two schedules represented the loss incurred by the colliery. The compensation payment was the amount of this loss—half being paid by the High Authority, and half by the Belgian Government.

Although there were occasional amendments of the sales schedules,[4] no major alteration in the compensation system occurred until 1955. In that year, the High Authority passed Decision No. 22–55. This again amended the sales schedules, but this time the decision no longer merely fixed maximum prices, but fixed the actual price for the sale of coal. For certain types of coal these new prices involved a reduction as compared with the previous prices.

Further, by a letter dated May 28, 1955, and sent to the Belgian Government, the High Authority replaced the accounts schedule altogether, and in its place substituted a " Table of Tariffs of Compensation Payments for Certain Types of Belgian Coal ". By this table, instead of the compensation payments being determined as the difference between the accounts schedule and the sales schedule, the compensation was fixed at so much per ton. This amount varied for different types of coal, and for some types compensation was ended altogether. This had the effect of substantially reducing the amount of compensation payable to many collieries, and particularly to three collieries situated in the Campine.[5]

Finally, whereas previously the compensation for all collieries had been given automatically, this letter now made these payments conditional. The letter stated:

" It is recognized . . . that the assistance granted to Belgian coal mines by way of compensation must be accompanied by a series of measures which the Belgian Government is required to take. The High Authority believes, especially, that the provision of compensation must be made conditional upon action by our Government in the manner set out below . . . ".

There then followed a list of four things under headings (a) to (d), which the Belgian Government was required to do. They included, under (a), the granting of special credit facilities by means of reduced interest rates and by the issuing of State guarantees of loans; under (b), the facilitating

---

[1] This meant a tax of about 0.55 DM and 0.42 Guilders per ton of merchantable production—see Second General Report on the Activities of the Community, para. 62. About one-fifth of the money raised, however, was allocated to subsidize Italian mines:

[2] Annex to the High Authority's letter to the Belgian Government dated March 8, 1953.

[3] Decision No. 24-53.

[4] Decisions No. 40-53, 41-53 and 45-54.

[5] For the action brought by these three collieries see *Société de Charbonnages de Beeringen and Others* v. *The High Authority*, reported below, p. 441.

of short-term credits; and under (c) the financing of constructional works in the mines. Sub-paragraph (d) referred to:

" The withdrawal in agreement with the High Authority of compensation payments from enterprises which do not achieve that amount of re-equipment judged practicable and necessary, as well as from those which have refused to yield up or exchange deposits deemed indispensable to a more satisfactory arrangement for mining."

The two cases reported above, p. 417, and below, p. 441, challenged the legal validity of this letter and of Decision No. 22-55.

International organization—European Coal and Steel Community —High Authority of—Competence of—Whether competent to fix selling price of Belgian coal—Absence of express power in Treaty —Whether competence may be implied—Convention containing Transitional Provisions, Section 26—*Détournement de pouvoir*— Relevance of wrong motives—Primary and subsidiary aims— Effect of error.

FÉDÉRATION CHARBONNIÈRE DE BELGIQUE *v*. THE HIGH AUTHORITY

(FINAL JUDGMENT).

*Court of Justice of the European Coal and Steel Community.*

(Pilotti, President; Serrarens, Hammes, Riese, Delvaux, Rueff, Van Kleffens JJ.)

*November 29, 1956.*

THE FACTS.—Interim proceedings in this case are reported above, at p. 417, and a Note on the factual background is printed at p. 423 above. The Court had adjourned the case after delivering the Interim Judgment to enable the approximate costs of production of each type and grade of coal at the end of the transitional period to be determined. The arguments of the parties were as follows:

The plaintiffs challenged the legal competence of the High Authority, as exercised in Decision 22-55, to fix the selling prices for Belgian coal. By Article 61 of the Treaty[1], the High Authority can fix maximum and minimum prices, but not selling prices in between these two levels. Further, Section 26 of the Convention containing the Transitional Provisions declares that " price lists . . . may not be changed without the agreement of the High Authority ". As the basic assumption of the Treaty was that enterprises were

[1] Article 61 provides; " . . . the High Authority may fix for one or more products subject to its jurisdiction:
(a) maximum prices within the Common Market, if it finds that such a decision is necessary to attain the objectives defined in Article 3 and particularly in para. (c) thereof;
(b) minimum prices within the Common Market, if it finds that a manifest crisis exists or is imminent and that such a decision is necessary to attain the objectives defined in Article 3 . . . "

to run their own affairs, it could not be assumed that this provision had taken away from enterprises their power to draw up their own price lists, or that it had conferred power on the High Authority to fix prices.

The High Authority replied that as by Section 26 Belgian prices were to be brought " as close as possible to prices in the Common Market generally ", this alignment could only be achieved if the prices were fixed by itself, and not by the enterprises, because the latter prices would be subject to the laws of supply and demand.

The plaintiffs also claimed that Decision 22–55 was vitiated by a *détournement de pouvoir*, because the High Authority in that decision had sought to achieve structural changes in the Belgian coal industry by causing certain mines to close, and that the Authority's aim was also to encourage the sale of Belgian coal by lowering its price. These aims, the plaintiffs contended, were different from those which the High Authority ought to have had, namely, of merely aligning Belgian prices with those of the Common Market.

The High Authority denied this, and referred to the many consultations with the Belgian Government and also to the Report of the mixed Commission on Mines to illustrate what its intention had been.

In determining what were " the prices in the Common Market generally ", to which Belgian prices must be equated, the High Authority had taken as a guide the prices in the Ruhr, because the Ruhr produced the greatest surplus of exportable coal and the Ruhr exercised what the High Authority claimed was a " price leadership ".

The plaintiffs objected to this because the prices of the Ruhr were being kept abnormally low by the High Authority itself. Further, they contended, Belgian prices ought to have been equated with those ruling in the Nord and Pas-de-Calais coal mines, and in Aix-la-Chappelle, all of which were higher than those in the Ruhr.

By Section 26, Belgian prices were to be reduced " to a level near that of the estimated costs of production at the end of the transitional period ". These costs had been estimated by the High Authority as 29 francs below the costs in 1952. The plaintiffs challenged this figure as being too low because the High Authority, when calculating it, had refused to include in the costs of production any possible increases in wages and salaries. The High Authority justified this refusal by contending that such increases were too speculative to have been included.

Finally, the plaintiffs alleged that the new system set up by the letter of May 28, 1955, written to the Belgian Government, by which compensation payments could be withdrawn from enterprises which did not carry out their programme of re-equipment, could lead to discrimination in the treatment of those enterprises *vis-à-vis* others which did carry out their programmes.

The High Authority denied any possibility of discrimination. Compensation payments were to assist enterprises to re-equip their mines. If this re-equipment was not being carried out, compensation payments were clearly not being justified, and could, therefore, be withheld.

*Held:* that the appeal must be rejected. The High Authority was competent to fix selling prices of Belgian coal, because only by such direct intervention could Belgian prices be equated with those of the Common Market.

The plaintiffs' evidence did not support their claim of a *détournement de pouvoir*, and in any event, even if the High Authority had pursued certain unjustified aims, this did not alter the fact that its primary aim was to implement Section 26.

The Court found that Ruhr prices did determine the prices of coal in the Common Market generally. This being so, it was irrelevant that these prices were to some extent artificial, because they nonetheless determined the prices of coal. Further, whether or not the High Authority's calculation of the foreseeable cost of production at the end of the transitional period was accurate, was not a matter which could in any way affect its aims in exercising its power under Section 26, and for the present action was, therefore, irrelevant.

Finally, the threat to withdraw compensation from enterprises which did not undertake re-equipment was held not to be able to lead to a discrimination, but to be an essential part of the whole system of compensation.

The Court said:

" A.  As regards Decision No. 22–55 of May 28, 1955

" I. *The Power of the High Authority to establish price lists and to fix these at a lower level.*—In conformity with Section 8 of the Convention [containing Transitional Provisions], the bringing into force of the mechanism of compensation specified in the third part of this Convention must precede the establishment of the Common Market.[1] It is, therefore, only in application of special measures, in particular by the introduction of a system of compensation, that the Convention from the beginning exposes the Belgian market in coal to the effects of the Common Market. These measures are justified by the existence of a difference between Belgium and the other countries of the Community which causes disadvantageous conditions of production.

" In the course of the oral proceedings, the defendants set out the causes of this disadvantage. These have not been disputed, and

[1 Section 8 provides, in part: " . . . The compensation schemes provided for coal in accordance with Part Three of this Convention shall be put into effect within six months from the date of the High Authority's assumption of its duties. . . . "]

they appear to the Court to be correct. In effect, there exists in Belgium:

" (1) Geological conditions of production less favourable, in general, than those of the countries determining the prices on the Common Market, which shows itself in the existence of a certain number of mines which are known as ' marginal '; (2) a technological backwardness owing to the impossibility for many years of undertaking the necessary investment; and (3) a level of wages higher than those of other producing countries.

" For these reasons, the costs of production in Belgium are higher than elsewhere, which causes a level of prices higher than those of other countries. With a view to integrating the Belgian market into the Common Market and to ensuring an approximation of prices, the Treaty, under the conditions set out in Section 26 of the Convention, sought to end the effects of this by reducing the differences in costs of production by means of compensation. This paragraph provides for a lowering of the price of Belgian coal for all consumers of this coal, with the aim of approximating these prices to those of the Common Market while specifying the requirements which enterprises must possess in order to benefit from the compensation, the date from which the above-mentioned approximation must take place, as well as the extent to which the lowering of prices must occur. The interests of consumers as thus recognized require, therefore, that lowering of Belgian prices to a level near to the foreseeable costs of production should have its full effects to the exclusion of fluctuations of the Belgian market. If the approximation of prices were achieved by a raising of the prices of the Common Market, and not by a lowering of Belgian prices as the plaintiffs have contended, it would transform the compensation into a subsidy deprived of any purpose or object.

" By the terms of Section 26 of the Convention, the situation justifying the compensation implies the necessity of lowering the level of Belgian prices to a level that is more or less fixed and which is the result of a general evaluation based upon forecasts concerning the costs of production in Belgium at the end of the transitional period. On the other hand, it is necessary to note that the text of Section 26 does not contain any precise indication enabling one to know how the approximation of prices within the prescribed limits is to come about: whether it is to be effected by the enterprises themselves, or by means of administrative action.

" However, the plaintiffs have contended that the Treaty provides a sales structure in which enterprises fix the prices, unless there is an express derogation from this, so that in the present case it is the enterprises themselves which fix the prices and which must determine the level of the foreseeable costs of production when they receive the benefit of compensation. The plaintiffs do not, however, entirely exclude the intervention of the High Authority in the fixing of prices, but limit it to the cases expressly provided for in the Treaty, particularly in Article 61 thereof.

" The lowering of Belgian prices required by the Convention is an operation of considerable importance, having as its object the preparation, under particularly difficult conditions, of the integration of Belgian coal into the Common Market, and is inspired by the general interest of the Community in progressively making normal the Common Market in coal.

" According to this contention, all these objectives should thus be subject to or related to the chief aim of unfettered determination by individual Belgian coal mines during the period of transition. This consequence cannot be accepted.

" Moreover, the normal interplay of the economy of the market would lead to the formation of market prices which were the result of supply and demand, and which would be subject to continual variations. However, the price of Belgian coal during the period of transition must establish itself and maintain itself at near the level of the foreseeable costs of production. This limit, the determination of which results from a general evaluation based, *inter alia*, upon the forecasts of improvement in yield of collieries and upon the effects of the programmes for closing marginal mines, avoids the influences of the market. If the prices of Belgian coal were left to the interplay of supply and demand upon the market their lowering would not be assured.

" Indeed, Article 61 of the Treaty is not here applicable. In effect this provision allows intervention only in case of necessity to prevent transitory ill effects from excessive increases which are the result of the normal interplay of the market economy. It would be to turn this article from its proper purpose to use it permanently to obtain the maintenance of prices at an artificial level resulting from the evaluation of foreseeable costs of production at the end of the transitional period. Moreover, the cumbersome nature of the procedure of Article 61[1] is securely applicable to a fixing of prices subject to revision on account of modifications in the evaluation of foreseeable costs of production which occur as one approaches the end of that period and as plans are already partly carried out.

" Moreover, what well shows that Article 61 has not been enacted for a case of this character, is that it requires prior consultation with the Consultative Committee and the Council ' concerning the advisability of these measures as well as concerning the price level which they determine ', that is to say, it depends upon considerations of

[1 Article 61 provides:
" On the basis of studies undertaken jointly with the enterprises and their associations . . . and after consulting the Consultative Committee and the Council as to the advisability of these measures as well as concerning the price level which they determine, the High Authority may fix . . .
(a) maximum prices . . .
(b) minimum prices . . . "]

economic advisability. In the present case the situation is entirely different, namely, to estimate the future costs of production taking account of the increase in production following upon the carrying out of plans for re-equipment and modernisation, which is of a purely technical nature. As to the extent of the reduction, this had not been discussed by the time the Convention had already been drawn up.

" However, the plaintiff observed in the course of the oral proceedings that to the extent to which enterprises do not comply with the obligation to lower their prices within the limits set out in the Convention, the High Authority may use indirect means to ensure the realization of the object of Section 26, that is to say, it has the means of withdrawing compensation from enterprises which have failed in their obligations. This means being sufficiently effective, there is no need to admit that the fixing of prices by administrative action would be indispensable.

" The Court cannot accept this argument, because, in application of a generally accepted rule of law, such indirect action of the High Authority in response to a wrongful act of enterprises must be proportionate to the gravity of that act. For this reason, the High Authority should be empowered to reduce the compensation only to an extent equivalent to that to which the enterprises had not lowered their prices within the prescribed limits. However, in this case, enterprises would always have a certain interest in risking such a reduction in the compensation and in preferring profits from relatively higher prices instead of benefiting from increased compensation which would correspond to the lowering of the prices if they had in fact lowered them. They would particularly have this interest because the available funds for compensation are limited.

" It follows from the above that indirect intervention by the High Authority such as a reduction of compensation is insufficient to ensure the attainment of the object which Section 26 (2) (a) of the Convention prescribes.

" Having regard to these considerations, it is necessary to note that only direct intervention of the High Authority is of a nature to guarantee the immediate realization of the lowering of prices which must of necessity accompany compensation.

" The plaintiffs contended in the course of the oral proceedings that the absence in the Treaty of an express grant of power to fix prices by administrative action prevents the recognition of such power by means of an interpretation which they believe to be extensive and inadmissible in law. The Court is not of that opinion, inasmuch as the present case concerns a power without which, as the Court has determined here, the compensation cannot function as Section 26 of the Convention intends, that is to say, upon the basis of an immediate and assured lowering of prices. In the opinion of the Court, it is permissible, without involving a wide interpretation, to allow a rule of interpretation that is generally admitted as much in international law as in municipal law, by which the norms established by an international treaty or by a law imply these norms without which the former would not make sense or would not permit of a reasonable and useful application. Moreover, the High Authority is charged by the terms of Article 8 of the Treaty to ensure the realization of the objects of the Treaty under the conditions set out therein. It is necessary to conclude from this provision, which is a principle governing the grant of power to the High Authority as defined in Chapter 1 of the Treaty, that it enjoys a certain autonomy in order to determine the measures of execution which are called for by the realization of the objectives set out in the Treaty or in the Convention which forms an integral part of it. As it is necessary in the present instance to realize the object of Section 26 of the Convention, the High Authority has the power, if not the duty, to take measures—within the limits set out in this provision —of a nature to ensure the lowering of the prices of Belgian coal.

" It follows from this that the accomplishment of this task requires, in the present case, the High Authority to have the power to fix prices. One must recognize, however, that the extent of this power is limited to the sole objective of ensuring for all consumers of Belgian coal a reduction of the price of this coal from the beginning of the transitional period and to the extent prescribed by the Convention in Section 26.

" The plaintiffs have also denied to the High Authority the power to fix prices by contending that the words in Section 26 (2) (a), ' the price lists established upon these bases may not be changed without the agreement of the High Authority', must be interpreted as prohibiting the High Authority from determining in a table the level to which prices of Belgian coal must be lowered in application of Section 26 of the Convention. However, such a prohibition is not contained in the text cited. It is deduced by the plaintiffs in an indirect fashion and as a converse. Such a means of arguing is only admissible, however, as a last resort and when no other interpretation would be adequate or compatible with the wording and context of the above-quoted provision, and its purpose. That is not the case in the present instance. The wording, as drafted, is explained by the need to subordinate every subsequent alteration to the approval of the High Authority, in any instance where the High Authority would not have been able to interfere, namely, where the enterprises have lowered their prices on their own initiative.

" Although it follows from the above considerations that in the present case the High Authority has acted within the apparent scope of its powers, it is still necessary to examine whether it has committed a *détournement de pouvoir* with respect to the plaintiffs in that, as the plaintiffs allege, it may have sought structural changes, and in that its action may have been inspired by the desire to lower prices, regard being had to certain difficulties in the sale of coal at the time when the challenged decision was taken.

" However, the lowering of prices as part of the compensation system is made obligatory by Section 26 of the Convention, as also is the extent of that lowering. Under these conditions, there could be no question of a *détournement de pouvoir* when the sole measure which the High Authority can take with a view to achieving the objective of Section 26 was precisely that which consisted in the lowering of the price of Belgian coal. In default of proof that the level of prices which the High Authority had fixed by means of its Decision 22-55 was different from the level resulting from a correct fixing of the prices by application of Section 26 (2) (*a*) of the Convention, the decision in question could not be vitiated by *détournement de pouvoir*. In effect, even if it were proved—which it has not been—that the High Authority was inspired by the desire either to bring about certain structural changes or to avoid difficulties in selling by means of a lowering of prices, it would have produced the effects which would have been inevitably, and in any event, the consequences of the pursuit of the lawful object of its action. Moreover, one cannot blame the defendant for having tried from 1952 to 1955 to perfect its approximations of the foreseeable costs of production in 1958, nor for having received for this purpose, as it has done, documents of a nature to throw light upon this matter. It appears from the report of the Mixed Commission charged with the study of the compensation of Belgian coal, as well as from the detailed calculations of the High Authority relating to the evaluation of the level of foreseeable costs of production, that the High Authority has followed, *inter alia*, the aim of lowering the prices of Belgian coal within the system set out in Section 26 of the Convention, and in particular in the measure prescribed by this provision. Even if an unjustified motive had been joined to motives which, in themselves, justified the action of the High Authority, the decision would not for this reason be vitiated by a *détournement de pouvoir* provided that it did not affect the essential aim of Section 26 of the Convention.

" For the reasons stated above, the first and second grounds set out in the request must be rejected.

" II. *Relation between the selling price and the foreseeable costs of production.*—The plaintiffs have alleged that the High Authority has committed a *détournement de pouvoir* by fixing prices without taking account of the foreseeable costs of production at the end of the transitional period in such a way that the Table which it has published for this purpose gives a price somewhat below the foreseeable costs of production.

" However, Section 26 of the Convention specified the means by which the approximation of Belgian prices to those of the Common Market is to be realized, taking account of the fact that if the prices of the Common Market have exceeded the level of the foreseeable costs of production in Belgium there would be no need to lower the Belgian prices to a level near to the foreseeable costs of production, because, if this occurred, the purpose of the equalization of prices would have been achieved.

" Before examining the question whether the High Authority has fixed the prices in the prescribed manner, it is necessary to consider whether it is true—as the plaintiffs allege—that the High Authority has substituted prices in the Ruhr for those in the Common Market and without having taken account of the artificially low level of the Ruhr prices as well as the higher level of prices of certain other basins.

" The defendants contend that they wished to reduce, within the above limits, the difference between Belgian prices and those of the Ruhr, the latter having the ' price leadership ' in the Common Market by reason of the fact that it possesses the greatest exportable surplus of the types of coal falling within the compensation system.

" In this dispute, the Court holds that the High Authority, by reducing the difference between Belgian prices and those of the Ruhr, and by basing itself upon the Ruhr prices as far as was practicable, that is to say, without taking account of the possibly artificial character of these prices, has left a certain margin existing between these two levels of prices. As regards the possibly artificial nature of the prices of the Ruhr, the High Authority was correct in not taking it into account because the question of knowing whether the prices of the Common Market are determined by the prices in the Ruhr is a question of fact, which does not depend upon the possibly artificial nature of these prices. It being accepted, therefore, that the High Authority has not fixed Belgian prices at the same level as the prices of the Ruhr, it is necessary to set out that the plaintiffs have shown that the prices fixed by the High Authority were, in some cases, appreciably below the prices existing in certain other basins, in particular those of Aix-la-Chappelle, as well as those of the Nord and of the Pas-de-Calais. In these cases only, it is alleged that the High Authority has exceeded the level of prices on the Common Market. However, the plaintiffs have not relied upon any fact or circumstance allowing one to hold that, in the above-mentioned cases, the level of prices of the basins in question determined those of the Common Market. Under these conditions, there is no occasion to admit that, in the present case, the prices fixed by the High Authority were below those of the Common Market.

" The first question which arises, therefore, is that of knowing whether the High Authority, in seeking the equalization of prices, by fixing Belgian prices at a level below those previously existing has or has not deviated from its aim of evaluating the foreseeable costs of production in 1958, towards which the High Authority was required to proceed, the level of these costs being, by the terms of

Section 26, the limit of the entire reduction of prices which the compensation system was likely to justify.

" In effect, the aim of achieving the complete and final integration of Belgian coal into the Common Market without doubt conformed to the general intention of the Treaty, but it exceeded that of the terms of Section 26 (2) (a) of the Convention, which prescribed integration only to the extent which the costs of production in Belgium at the end of the transitional period permitted. During this period, the terms of Section 26 (2) (a) provide a system of compensation which is limited as to time. The compensation is, therefore, tied to the alteration of the foreseeable costs of production with a view to ensuring a corresponding alteration of prices. It may be that, at the end of the transitional period, a more drastic reduction of the costs of production will become necessary in order to permit the final integration of Belgian coal into the Common Market. The realization of this new objective will depend upon factors existing at that time, but this question lies outside the application of Section 26 (2) (a) of the Convention and of the system which it authorizes. If, as the plaintiffs allege, the High Authority had fixed prices with the sole aim of equalizing them with the prices of the Common Market and had completely ignored the level of foreseeable costs of production at the end of the transitional period, this decision would be vitiated by a *détournement de pouvoir* and would have to be annulled. However, this is not so in the present case.

" The plaintiffs have not established proof, as is required of them, that the defendants, contrary to the provisions of the Treaty, to the objective facts and to the interests of the Belgian coal mines, had fixed selling prices and that they had estimated the foreseable costs of production of the coal in question in 1958, with the sole aim, or even more or less with the principal aim, of lowering prices without taking account of the limit imposed by Section 26 (2) (a) of the Convention.

" The differences in the calculations demonstrated by the parties in the course of the hearing, as to the evaluation of the costs of production of Belgian coal at the end of the transitional period turn solely upon matters of a statistical nature. An assessment of the mathematical correctness of these calculations does not affect the legality of the measure challenged, because this assessment does not reveal any evidence of a nature to establish that the High Authority in its evaluation had followed an aim other than that defined by Section 26 (2) (a) of the Convention.

" Even if the defendants have committed certain errors in the choice of factors in these calculations, as is the case as regards the year of reference, and, as equally appears with regard to amortisation and the grouping of categories of coal, yet it does not follow that these errors constitute *ipso facto* proof of a *détournement de pouvoir* if it is not also established that the High Authority in this particular case, by reason of a serious lack of foresight and of circumspection amounting to a misconstruction of the legal objective, has followed aims other than those in furtherance of which the powers contained in Section 26 (2) (a) have been granted.

" In effect, with regard to the establishment of the foreseeable costs of production in 1958, it seems evident—as regards the choice of the 1952 year of reference *caeteris paribus*, rather than the 1955 year, the year in which the decisions in question were taken—that factors which were not foreseeable in 1952 or earlier were, or ought to have been, foreseeable in 1955. Also, one must note that nevertheless the defendants have reduced, or at least tried to reduce, errors which increased either the selling prices of coal or the amount of the compensation, regard being had to the rise in salaries and to certain matters of lesser importance. One must also note that the defendants have taken account of forecasts made in 1955 concerning the reorganization of marginal mines (see the report of the Mixed Commission on Mines), as well as certain grants and certain expenses for the renewal of installations, paid under the head of amortization, without, however, considering the charges in respect of those paid out by enterprises themselves. These facts, whether considered together or taken individually, are characteristic of the legitimate desire and the wish of the defendants to reach an even closer approximation to the foreseeable costs of production at the end of the transitional period.

" As to the division or ' grouping ' of coal by types and grades, the parties are in agreement in recognizing that only a division by types is possible. After having, before the judgment of July 16, 1956, and despite certain reservations on one side and the other, proposed a common agreement upon figures representing the average of a grouping of all types combined, the parties, subject to their reservations, in their argument and in their pleading have made references to new groupings so different that it became difficult, if not impossible, to compare the figures. However, without deciding upon the respective intrinsic merits of these different methods of grouping, it is necessary to state that a detailed examination of them does not reveal that the defendants have been led by their choice of methods to a result which is incompatible with the approximation of the prices of Belgian coal and those of the Common Market at the level near to the foreseeable costs of production in 1958.

" For the reasons set out above, the ground of *détournement de pouvoir* has not been established as far as concerns both the level of selling prices and the relationship between that level and the level of the foreseeable costs of production at the end of the transitional period.

" III. *The Intervention of the Belgian Government.*—When the plaintiffs allege that Decision No. 22-55 has lowered selling prices with a view to serving the proper objectives of the economic policy of the Belgian Government, as well as in relation to the intervention of the latter, they have failed to set out upon what points these objectives are contrary to, and should have been substituted for, those which the High Authority was entitled to pursue. The plaintiffs have not established any proof that the High Authority by its Decision No. 22–55 has sacrificed the legitimate interests of Belgian producers for the benefit of the politics of their Government. It is, moreover, usual that discussions and consultations should be held on such a matter. The fact, which is not challenged, that the High Authority has fixed selling prices at a level above those proposed by the Belgian Government indicates, furthermore, that the High Authority has retained its freedom of action.

" In these circumstances, the present ground is not well-founded.

" IV. *The fixing of selling prices in certain cases without the granting of compensation.*—The defendants submit that the exclusion of unclassified types of caking coal of the Campine from benefiting from compensation in no way indicates that these types are already sufficiently integrated into the Common Market to be taken out of the compensation system. They are of the opinion that account must be taken of the case where it would again be necessary to bring about a certain reduction in Belgian prices and, in such a case, once more to grant compensation payments to the collieries of the Campine.

" In effect, the letter of May 28, 1955, retains these particular types of coal within the compensation system despite the modifications which it introduces into that system, by which, for certain enterprises, the payment of compensation is ended. From then on the system established by Section 26 (2) (a) of the Convention is applicable to these types of coal, especially that part which is concerned with the need to secure the full benefits of that system by means of having prices fixed.

" However, the fixing of prices appears, as has already been stated, to be a general measure and one which is indispensable to the application to the entire production of Belgian coal of the exceptional system referred to in Section 26 (2).

" The question whether this system is of a type to allow the reduction or even the withdrawal of compensation, depending upon the conditions of production of certain individual enterprises, raises the issue of the principle of selection in the application of Section 26. The legality of this selection will be examined below, in connection with all the terms of the letter of the High Authority to the Belgian Government of May 28, 1955. On the other hand, it can be stated here that, quite apart from the decision which will be taken on the matter of principle, it is as impossible to conceive of the existence of several scales of prices for the consumers of Belgian coal, as it is of the existence, for the same types of coal, of two prices, one free and the other fixed.

It follows, therefore, in the present case, that the reduction or even the withdrawal of compensation from certain types of coal and in certain individual cases only, does not imply that these have been taken out of the scale of prices for such types of coal. The scale of prices which results from the application of Section 26 (2) must be one and the same for all consumers of Belgian coal.

"Decision No. 22–55 is thus seen as the normal application of the system provided for by Section 26, and the normal exercise of a power necessary for the carrying out of that system. The ground of *détournement de pouvoir* is, therefore, not substantiated.

" B. Concerning the letter of May 28, 1955

" I. *The reduction or withdrawal of compensation from certain enterprises.*—The plaintiffs submit, first, that the introduction of a selective criterion into the system of compensation, that is to say, the adaptation of compensation payments to the particular situation of enterprises, constitutes a discrimination which is forbidden by the Treaty.

" This submission must be rejected. Consequent upon the decision contained in the letter of May 28, 1955, compensation payments were reduced, or even withdrawn, to the extent to which the handicap of unfavourable geological conditions—which is one of the very preconditions of the special treatment afforded to the Belgian coal-mining industry—has in fact been overcome. As a result, differences in the amounts of compensation, which are related to the conditions of actual production, tend to reflect the differences which exist in fact, so as to insure an equal benefit in comparable situations and thereby to avoid discrimination. The plaintiffs' contention would only be valid if the High Authority had not applied an objective and uniform criterion to determine whether the particular conditions of enterprises satisfied the requirements for the grant of compensation. However, the decision contained in the letter has defined such a criterion, and the conformity of the situation existing in the three collieries with this criterion has not been challenged.

" Secondly, the fact that Section 26 (2) speaks of ' Belgian coal ', and that the compensation payments referred to in paragraphs (b) and (c) are of a general nature, is, the plaintiffs claim, conclusive to prove that the compensation referred to in paragraph (a) is also general.

" This argument is not conclusive, because it is accepted that the compensation under (b) and (c) is clearly intended to enable the Belgian steel industry, as well as exporters of coal, to meet the competition of the Common Market in cases where the foreseeable costs of production would be too much above the prices of the Common Market. For these reasons the compensation under (b) and (c) is of a different nature from the compensation under (a). Furthermore, paragraphs (b) and (c) contain a number of provisions regulating the

expenditure of this compensation, whereas for compensation under
(a) such rules do not apply.  In view of these differences between
paragraphs (a), (b) and (c), and in view of the fact that the expression
' Belgian coal ' is explicable in each of these contentions, the terms
of Section 26 of themselves do not justify the conclusion that the
compensation under (a) must be held to be applicable generally.

" Moreover, on the assumption that the payments of compensation under (a) were uniform for all enterprises, regardless of the
differences in their conditions of production, the compensation
would become discriminatory and would lose its *raison d'être*, because
it would become a subsidy to the extent to which it was granted to
enterprises whose conditions of production were not exposed to
adverse conditions, whereas such exposure is the very precondition
for receiving compensation.  It follows, therefore, that the compensation must, of necessity, take into account the individual situation
of the enterprises as far as their conditions of production are concerned.

" To support their contention, the plaintiffs rely also upon the
existence of a guarantee that the receipts of enterprises will be
maintained.

" Despite the silence of the Convention upon the existence, if
the necessity should arise, of a relationship between compensation
and receipts, it being mentioned only in Section 25, in relation to the
assessment of levies, such an interpretation would only be admissible
if the compensation were necessarily, and in all circumstances, to
cover the whole of the difference between the reduced selling price
and receipts existing at the beginning of the transitional period.
However, this is not so.  The compensation is only a safeguarding
measure necessary in order to avoid the results caused by a sudden
and dangerous disturbance in production.  The special system set up
for this purpose must, in conformity with Section 24 of the Convention, take account of the situation existing at the time of the establishment of the Common Market.  It is not permissible, however, to
interpret this provision in a wide sense, that is to say, as a guarantee
that the then-existing level of gross incomes would be maintained.
The introduction of a special system, such as the compensation
system in question, is explained by the existence in Belgium of certain
conditions of production which are as it happens different from
those of the other countries of the Common Market.  The compensation must not, therefore, exceed the limits which are strictly necessary in order to neutralize to a certain extent the disadvantages
resulting from these differences.  This does not imply a guarantee of
the original receipts.  The question of deciding to what extent the
sum total of the selling price and the compensation—which total
determines the receipt of the enterprises—is to be varied during the
course of the transitional period, is a question which the High

Authority must examine in the light of the progress made in the re-equipment and re-organization of the Belgian coal mines.

" Moreover, if the compensation were intended to guarantee original receipts, it would infringe the principle of a gradual reduction which is contained in Section 25 of the Convention. Furthermore, the Convention provides, in Section 1, for the progressive adaptation of production to the new conditions resulting from the establishment of the Common Market, and not for the adaptation of the new conditions to the continuance of the situation existing at the beginning of the transitional period. Moreover, if, as the plaintiffs maintain, the compensation were to guarantee to collieries the financial assistance which is judged essential for the carrying out of their programmes of re-equipment, the object of the compensation would greatly exceed the grounds which justify it, and would transform it into a measure intended to contribute in an active and direct way towards the re-organization of the Belgian coal mines, which would be contrary to the essentially passive character of a safeguarding measure.

" The plaintiffs rely, finally, upon the contention that the compensation must be uniform for all collieries by reason of the fact that the Treaty and the Convention, in particular by Article 5, para. 4,[1] and Article 62 of the Treaty,[2] as well as Section 24 (b)[3] and Section 26 (4)[4] of the Convention, provide special measures intended to equalize any differences existing between collieries considered individually.

" This argument is not valid, for if the above-mentioned provisions provide measures, other than compensation, to remedy the differences existing between collieries, that is not in any way in conflict with the fact that, in the case of Belgium, the compensation must

[1 Article 5, para. 4, provides: " ... The Community shall: ... publish the reasons for the action and take the necessary measures to ensure observance of the rules set out in the present Treaty . . . "]

[2 Article 62 provides as follows:
" If the High Authority considers such an action the most appropriate for preventing the price of coal from being established at the level of the production costs of the most costly mines to operate and whose production is temporarily required to ensure the fulfilment of the objectives defined in Article 3, the High Authority, after consulting the Consultative Committee, may authorize compensation schemes:
—among enterprises of the same coalfield applying the same price list;
—after consulting the Council, among enterprises situated in different coalfields. . . "]

[3 Section 24 provides:
" . . . The High Authority shall, where necessary, authorize under its supervision . . . (b) the continuation or creation of national compensation funds or schemes, financed by a levy on national production, without prejudice to the exceptional expedients described below."]

[4 Section 26 (4) provides:
" . . . the Belgian Government may grant subsidies which correspond to the additional operating costs arising out of the nature of its coal deposits, and which take into account any expenses resulting from manifest disequilibria which increase operating costs. The procedures for granting such subsidies and their size shall be subject to approval of the High Authority . . . "]

likewise take into account the individual differences to the extent to which the system of compensation set up for this country requires.

" In consequence, therefore, the allegation set out above is not well-founded.

" II. *The threat to withdraw compensation.*—The compensation is a safeguarding measure permitting the incorporation of Belgian coal into the Common Market from the beginning of the transitional period, during which period the work of reorganization and re-equipment must be completed. It is not intended to assist that work in any active or direct way. It is clear that this compensation is granted on the assumption that the reorganization and re-equipment of the Belgian coal mines can be achieved to an extent sufficient to allow the final incorporation of Belgian coal into the Common Market at the end of the transitional period.

" This compensation is not intended to finance the re-equipment and reorganization of the collieries. On the other hand, if it should become clear that this work of reorganization and re-equipment has not been carried out by certain enterprises, and that they are responsible for this failure, it must be recognized that the compensation has then lost its whole purpose or *raison d'être*. These enterprises would, thus, by their own default, have deprived themselves of the right to be granted compensation.

" The High Authority must take account of such a possibility. It has done this in paragraph 2 (*d*) of its letter of May 28, 1955, by conditionally authorizing the Belgian Government in such a case to withdraw the compensation subject to the prior approval of the High Authority. The text of this letter, however, does not allow one to assume that the High Authority will base its approval upon non-objective criteria or criteria not justified by facts. The High Authority has thus not committed a *détournement de pouvoir*, and the appeal is not well-founded on this point.

" C. Costs

" By the terms of Article 60 of the Rules of the Court, any party which fails shall be condemned in costs. It is necessary, therefore, to condemn the plaintiffs in the costs of the action.

" The Court, rejecting all other submissions in favour or to the contrary, adjudges and declares:

" The appeal for the annulment of the decision of the High Authority No. 22-55 dated May 28, 1955, and of certain decisions of the High Authority contained in the letter addressed by it on May 28, 1955, to the Government of the Kingdom of Belgium concerning the management of the system of compensation is rejected.

" The plaintiffs are condemned in the costs of the action."

[Report: *Recueil de la Jurisprudence de la Cour*, II (1955-56), p. 291 (in French)].

International organization—European Coal and Steel Community —Treaty establishing the Community, Article 33—Decisions of High Authority—Whether general or individual—Letter from Authority specifying required action—Whether letter constitutes decision—Right of associations and enterprises to challenge general decisions—Grounds upon which challenge may be based.

SOCIÉTÉ DES CHARBONNAGES DE BEERINGEN AND OTHERS
v. THE HIGH AUTHORITY.

*Court of Justice of the European Coal and Steel Community.*

(Pilotti, President; Serrarens, Hammes, Riese, Delvaux, Rueff, Van Kleffens JJ.)

*November 29, 1956.*

THE FACTS.—The background to this case and to the case of *Fédération Charbonnière de Belgique* v. *The High Authority* (Case 8–55; reported above, at p. 425) is set out in the Note printed at p. 423 above. Both cases involved a challenge of the validity of Decision No. 22–55 of the High Authority and of a letter of May 28, 1955, from the Authority to the Belgian Government.

The plaintiffs in the present case were the three enterprises of the Campine coalfield in Belgium which were able to mine their coal under conditions that were more favourable than those existing in other Belgian collieries. As a result of this, the High Authority after its letter to the Belgian Government of May 28, 1955, withdrew all compensation to these three enterprises. They therefore challenged the validity of this withdrawal and also the validity of the fixing of the actual prices at which certain types of coal was to be sold.[1]

The plaintiffs advanced the same arguments as those of the Fédération Charbonnière de Belgique.[2] In addition, they claimed that the withdrawal of the compensation payments from them was arbitrary and inspired by considerations other than those contained in Section 26 of the Convention containing Transitional Measures. The plaintiffs contended that compensation payments were withdrawn from them owing to their solid financial position.

The High Authority replied that the criterion for the withdrawal was solely the plaintiffs' cost of production and their particularly favourable conditions for mining. The High Authority also requested the Court to strike out the plaintiffs' fourth head of claim, in which they alleged the incompetence of the High Authority to give the actual selling price of coal, as this head had not been set out in the plaintiffs' request: they had merely referred to the same head of claim in the action of the Fédération Charbonnière de Belgique.

The plaintiffs replied that this omission was justified owing to the close connection of their action and that of the Fédération.

[1] Decision 22-55.
[2] See above, p. 425-426.

The High Authority further requested that the plaintiffs' fifth head should also be struck out, on the ground that it merely alleged that Decision 22–55 was illegal, without specifying which of the four grounds of annulment under Article 33 were being alleged.

*Held:* that the appeal for annulment must be rejected. The fifth head of claim had been validly introduced, but the fourth head must be struck out as to this extent the plaintiffs' request did not satisfy the rules of the Court that it must contain a summary of the grounds on which the action was being brought.

The Court held that the withdrawal of compensation was not arbitrary, but was based upon the extent to which the enterprises concerned had achieved their plans for re-equipment and re-organization.

The Court said:

" A. *Concerning the admissibility of the appeal.*—The appeal seeks the annulment of:

" 1. Decision No. 22–55 of the High Authority of May 28, 1955, and the scale of prices annexed thereto, published in the *Journal Officiel de la Communauté,* No. 12 of May 31, 1955, in so far as they fix reduced prices for certain types of coal.

" 2. The decisions contained in the letter addressed by the High Authority to the Belgian Government and dated May 28, 1955, and in the table of tariffs of compensation payments attached to that letter:

(*a*) in so far as a discrimination is established between producers of identical grades of coal by the withdrawal or the reduction of compensation from certain collieries,

(*b*) in so far as, by the terms of the said letter, the compensation payments will be, or may be, withdrawn from certain enterprises on the grounds that they have not achieved that re-equipment which is judged practicable and necessary, or have refused to yield up or exchange deposits where this is deemed indispensable to more satisfactory arrangements for mining.

[The Court here repeated word for word that part of its interim judgment in *Fédération Charbonnière de Belgique* v. *The High Authority*[1] beginning with the paragraph " As respects Decision 22-55 . . . " (see above, p. 418), and continued:]

"As for the fourth and fifth grounds, the defendants have raised the question of whether the request introduced by the plaintiffs complies with the requirements of Article 22 of the Statute of the Court[2] as

[1 Reported above, p. 417.]
[2 Article 22 of the Statute reads, in part as follows:
" . . . The request shall contain the name and address of the party and the capacity of the signatory, the subject matter of the dispute, the argument, and a short summary of the grounds on which the action is based. . . . "]

well as with Article 29 of its Rules,[1] in particular as regards the mention of the grounds relied upon as well as a brief statement thereof.

" However, the submissions in the request specify the grounds relied upon in support of these claims, which suffices for compliance with the above-mentioned provisions. Indeed, it may be held that a brief statement of the grounds is incorporated into the request in support of the fifth head of claim. However, such is not the case as regards the fourth head. In effect, the fourth head consists only of a reference made to 'the statement contained in the request of *Fédéchar*[2] which declares the illegality of the decision of the High Authority in so far as, acting as a public authority, it fixes the scale of reduced prices for certain types of coal '. In spite of the indisputable connection between these two appeals, a general reference to what has been stated in another action is not sufficient in order that the request should comply with the above-mentioned provisions, and even less when the reference—as is the case of the fourth head of claim in the present action—has been made without at the same time a request for the joining of the actions, such a request having been made only at the beginning of the oral proceedings. The fourth head of claim is not admissible.

" Moreover, the grounds which the parties have raised for the first time in their reply, without having made any reference to them in the request, must be declared inadmissible. These concern the relation between the selling price and the foreseeable costs of production as well as to the intervention of the Belgian Government.

" Subject to the above, the appeal is admissible."

[The Court here repeated word for word that part of its interim judgment in *Fédération Charbonnière de Belgique* v. *the High Authority* beginning with the paragraph: " However, the views of the parties differ . . ." to the end of the section on admissibility (see above, pp. 420-422).]

" B. *Concerning the merits.—Head* 1. The reduction or withdrawal of compensation from certain enterprises.—[The Court here repeated word for word what it had stated under this heading in *Fédération Charbonnière de Belgique* v. *The High Authority (Final Judgment)*.[3]]

" *Head* 2. The forfeiting of the new compensation payments.— This head of claim alleges that the new system, which comprises a forfeiture of the new compensation payments without reference to the ' accounts ' schedule, appears arbitrary and is inspired by considerations other than those contained in Section 26 of the Convention.

[1 Article 29 of the old Rules stated:
" . . . The request must contain . . . the facts and grounds and the submission of the plaintiff, as well as the offers of proof presented in support of the appeal." The equivalent rule is now Article 38.]
[2 This refers to the request in *Fédération Charbonnière de Belgique* v. *The High Authority* (Case 8-55), reported above, p. 425.]
[3 Reported above, p. 425, at pp. 437-440.]

" It is relevant above all to note that the selling price fixed for each type of coal together with the appropriate compensation due, which was previously called the ' account ' price, is lower in four cases, but higher in fifty-two cases than the ' account ' price previously in force.  Before examining whether these new amounts of compensation when added to the new selling prices reveal anything of an arbitrary character, it is necessary to note that such arbitrariness of the compensation cannot be established from variations which result from ' the principle of selection ' which the High Authority had the right to apply.

" However, as regards the determining of the compensation for the particular types and categories of coal, the Court holds that the very nature of this compensation requires the High Authority to adapt it to the needs of the enterprises.  It must be considered that the High Authority must especially take into account the reduced amount of the funds available for compensation as well as the progress achieved or believed achievable towards the effort of re-equipment and reorganization of the Belgian coal mines.

" From the above considerations it follows that the amounts of compensation will of necessity vary according to the particular case, with the existence of these variations, of themselves, indicating that the High Authority has not fixed that compensation in an arbitrary manner and one alien to the aims that the Convention requires. The present claim, must therefore, be rejected.

" *Head* 3.  The threat to withdraw compensation.—[The Court here repeated word for word what it had stated under this heading in *Fédération Charbonnière de Belgique* v. *The High Authority* (*Final Judgment*).[1]].

" *Head* 5.  The fixing of selling prices in certain cases without the granting of compensation.—[The Court here repeated word for word what it had stated under this heading in *Fédération Charbonnière de Belgique* v. *The High Authority* (*Final Judgment*).[2]]

" C.  *Costs.*—In accordance with Article 60 of the Rules of the Court,[3] the losing party is condemned in costs.  It is necessary, therefore, to condemn the plaintiffs in the costs of the action.

" The Court, rejecting all further submissions in favour or against, adjudges and declares:

" The appeal for the annulment of certain decisions of the High Authority contained in the letter of May 28, 1955, addressed by it to the Government of the Kingdom of Belgium concerning the mode of operating the system of compensation, and of the decision of the High Authority No. 22–55, dated May 28, 1955, is rejected.

[1 Reported above, p. 425, at p. 437.]
[2 At p. 436.]
[3 Article 60 of the old Rules stated:
" In contentious matters, any party which fails shall be condemned in costs. The Court, however, may apportion the costs either in whole or in part if the parties fail respectively on one or more heads of claim." The equivalent rule is now Article 69.]

" The plaintiffs are condemned in the costs of the action."

[Report: *Recueil de la Jurisprudence de la Cour*, II (1955-56), p. 325 (in French).]

International organization—European Coal and Steel Community —Decisions of High Authority—*Détournement de pouvoir*— Relevance of aims of High Authority as published in Memoranda —Relevance of lack of foresight on part of Authority—Relevance of motive of avoiding administrative difficulties—Uniform subsidy tax—Whether constituting discrimination within Article 4 of Treaty establishing Community.

COMPAGNIE DES HAUTS FOURNEAUX DE CHASSE *v.* THE HIGH AUTHORITY (NO. 1).

*Court of Justice of the European Coal and Steel Community.*

(Pilotti, President; Van Kleffens, Delvaux, Serrarens, Riese, Rueff, Hammes JJ.)

*June* 13, 1958.

THE FACTS.—This case was one of a series brought by various enterprises challenging the validity of Decision 2–57 of the High Authority. That Decision amended an earlier system of subsidising imported steel scrap. The facts relating to the original subsidy system are set out in the case of *Meronie & Cie., Industrie Metallurgiche, S.P.A.* v. *The High Authority*, reported above, p. 369. For the background to the cases arising out of Decision 2–57 see the Note at the end of the present report.

The plaintiffs in the present case were the same company which appeared as plaintiffs in Case 15–57 (reported below, p. 457).

They objected to the tax imposed on scrap by Decision 2–57, for two reasons:

First, by this tax the plaintiffs were being asked to subsidise the price of imported scrap which they did not require and had never purchased. Secondly, because the tax was one placed uniformly upon every ton of scrap purchased, regardless of its price, the tax fell proportionately most heavily upon the cheapest types of scrap, such as that which the plaintiffs used. They therefore felt themselves to have been unfairly treated, and in February 1957 they brought an appeal against Decision No. 2–57.

As Decision 2–57 which the plaintiffs were challenging was a general decision, they were entitled to challenge its validity only on the ground that it constituted a *détournement de pouvoir* with respect to them.[1] The High Authority contended that the plaintiffs' arguments

---

[1] Article 33, para. 2, of the Treaty. Article 33 provides, in part:
" The Court shall have jurisdiction over appeals by a member State or by the Council for the annulment of decisions and recommendations of the High Authority

were tantamount to alleging what in fact amounted to a violation of the Treaty and not to a *détournement de pouvoir*. It maintained, therefore, that the appeal was inadmissible. Further, the High Authority held that many of the plaintiffs' arguments had not been stated in their request, and were thus inadmissible.[1] Finally it declared that the subsidy system had been first set up by decisions in 1954, and that the plaintiffs should have challenged it then if they wished to do so at all.

The plaintiffs replied that their arguments did relate to a *détournement de pouvoir*, but in any event if in fact they related to a violation of the Treaty a *détournement de pouvoir* could be proved by establishing the existence of such violation. They also replied that they had not introduced any new grounds of appeal, but merely enlarged upon those originally set out in their request.

In their challenge of Decision No. 2–57, the plaintiffs maintained that as a serious shortage of scrap existed within the Community, any action taken by the High Authority to deal with that shortage should have been taken under Article 59 of the Treaty, by which that Authority acting with the Council of Ministers could establish consumption priorities.[2] Instead of this, the plaintiffs declared, the High Authority had acted under Article 53, by which it could set up " financial arrangements common to several enterprises ". This

on the grounds of lack of legal competence, major violations of procedure, violation of the Treaty or of any rule of law relating to its application, or abuse of power [*détournement de pouvoir*] . . .

" The enterprises, or the associations referred to in Article 48, shall have the right of appeal on the same grounds against individual decisions and recommendations affecting them, or against general decisions and recommendations which they deem to involve an abuse of power affecting them."

[1] By Article 29, para. 3, of the old Rules it was provided that the request must set out the arguments and submissions of the plaintiffs. This provision is now Article 38, para. 1, of the Rules.

[2] Article 59, paras. 1 and 2, of the Treaty provides:

" 1. If, after consulting the Consultative Committee, the High Authority finds that the Community is faced with a serious shortage of certain or of all of the products subject to its jurisdiction, and that the means of action provided for in Article 57 do not enable it to cope with this situation, it shall bring it to the attention of the Council, and shall propose the necessary measures, unless the Council decides to the contrary by unanimous vote.

" If the High Authority fails to act, one of the member States may bring the matter before the Council, which by unanimous decision may recognise the existence of the above-mentioned situation.

" 2. The Council, acting by unanimous vote, shall on the basis of proposals made by the High Authority and in consultation with it, establish consumption priorities and determine the allocation of the coal and steel resources of the Community among the industries subject to its jurisdiction, exports, and other consumption.

" On the basis of the consumption priorities thus established, the High Authority shall, after consulting the enterprises concerned, draw up production programmes which the enterprises shall be obliged to carry out."

Article 57 of the Treaty provides:

" In the field of production, the High Authority shall give preference to the indirect means of action at its disposal, such as:

—co-operation with governments to stabilise or influence consumption, particularly that of the public services;

—intervention on prices and commercial policy as provided for in this Treaty."

wrongful use of one article of the Treaty in place of another amounted, they alleged, to a *détournement de pouvoir*.

The High Authority denied that it had acted under Article 53 with any wrongful intention, and contended that Decision 2–57 satisfied the requirement of that article that such action was " necessary for the accomplishment of the objectives " of the Treaty.

The plaintiffs then alleged that the High Authority had already declared in certain memoranda that it was seeking to obtain a balance between the markets for iron and those for steel,[1] whereas Decision 2–57 was seeking to obtain a regular supply of steel scrap to the common market regardless of the effects of this upon iron. This change of purpose, they alleged, amounted also to a *détournement de pouvoir*.

The High Authority denied that there was here any change of purpose, as both the memoranda referred to and Decision No. 2–57 were evidence of the same policy of meeting foreseeable economic expansion.

The plaintiffs next contended that although the High Authority had been faced with a shortage of scrap iron since 1955, it had failed to see the economic effects which subsidising scrap had upon the sale of pig-iron, and that to act without seeing the wider implications of their acts amounted to a wrongful use of its powers. The High Authority admitted that its system for the subsidising of scrap might affect the sale of pig-iron, yet it denied that this in any way invalidated Decision 2-57, which had been introduced with no other intention than to ensure the regular supply of scrap to the common market.

Finally, the plaintiffs claimed that Decision 2-57, which imposed a tax which was uniform upon every ton of purchased scrap regardless of its cost, had been passed merely to avoid administrative complications although such a tax was clearly unjust to those who, like the plaintiffs, merely bought the cheaper types of scrap, and that this again was a use of their powers for a wrong purpose. The High Authority replied that such a uniform tax was not unfair because nearly all types of scrap were interchangeable and no one enterprise purchased merely one type of scrap. Furthermore, it denied that it had imposed a uniform tax to avoid administrative difficulties.

The submissions of the Advocate General were that the appeal should be dismissed, and that costs should be borne by the Compagnie des Hauts Fourneaux de Chasse.

*Held:* (1) *As to admissibility*, that the appeal was admissible. The fact that the plaintiffs had made allegations of *détournement de pouvoir* which they might not be able to prove went to the merits of the case and did not affect its admissibility. During the proceedings the plaintiffs had not introduced new grounds of appeal which would

---

[1] Reference was made to the *Journal Officiel* of July 19, 1955, and August 20, 1957.

have been admissible, but had merely elaborated those already set out in their request. Further, the fact that the subsidy system had first been set up in 1954 did not affect the plaintiffs' ability to challenge a decision of 1957 continuing that system.

(2) *As to the merits:* that the appeal for annulment of Decision 2-57 must be rejected.

The High Authority had acted under Article 53 instead of under Article 59 because the latter article was applicable only to cases of " serious shortage ", and the shortage of scrap which existed was not " serious " within the meaning of that article.

The Court did not consider whether or not Decision 2-57 was in conformity with certain prior memoranda of the High Authority because lack of such conformity would in no way effect the validity of that decision.

The Court further held that the plaintiffs had not proved that the subsidy system had been introduced for any improper reason.

The uniformity of the tax to the subsidy fund regardless of the cost of the scrap did not vitiate that tax, because the grades of scrap were in practice interchangeable and there was a general tendency for the cost of all types of scrap to become the same.

As regards the desire to avoid administrative complications by means of a uniform tax, because such a tax was in conformity with the Treaty its existence could not affect the validity of the decision even if the tax had been made uniform in order to avoid administrative complications.

The Court said:

" A. *Concerning Admissibility.*—

" *(a)* The defendants maintain that the plaintiffs described as amounting to a *détournement de pouvoir* a series of allegations which, for various reasons, do not fall within this head of annulment but within that of violation of the Treaty. For this reason the defendants claim that Article 33 does not allow the plaintiffs to rely upon these allegations.

" The Court rejects this reasoning.

" In effect, in their request, the plaintiffs have alleged a *détournement de pouvoir* with respect to them, and they have set out a series of arguments which they believe to be of a nature to justify this allegation.

" It is possible that these arguments will not reveal a *détournement de pouvoir*, but to know whether this is the case the merits of the action must be examined. Hence, according to previous decisions of the Court, the objection upon which the defendants rely is no bar to the admissibility of this appeal.

" *(b)* The defendants are of opinion that the reply contains certain new grounds of action concerning " the extent of the powers of the High Authority, under Article 53 of the Treaty, with regard to the distinction between a normal situation and an exceptional situation ', as well as ' the use of Article 53 instead of Article 59 '.

" On this point, the Court is of the opinion that one must distinguish between the introduction of new heads of action in the course of the proceedings and, on the other hand, the introduction of certain new arguments. In the present instance, the Court finds that the plaintiffs have not introduced any new heads of action but that they have merely developed those which were contained in their Request by relying upon a certain number of arguments, some of which have been presented for the first time in the reply. Under these conditions, there is nothing to prevent the Court from examining them.

" (c) The defendants, without expressly declaring that the action is inadmissible, also ask whether the plaintiffs ought not to have challenged the system of payments to the subsidy fund at the time that the payments were made obligatory, that is to say, in 1954.

" This question must receive a negative answer, for, if the decision now being challenged once again sets up a system of payments to the subsidy fund, it is once again subject to the time periods for appeals set out in Article 33, notwithstanding the existence of an earlier decision having the same effect.

" For the above reasons the appeal is admissible.

" B. *Concerning the Merits.*—

" *First Head.*—Decision No. 2-57 places the producers of iron in the same position as the producers of steel and misconstrues the objectives specified in the Treaty, which constitutes a *détournement de pouvoir*.

" The plaintiffs allege in their Request that the payments to the subsidy fund do not comply with the general objectives of the Treaty, that they interfere with the normal interplay of competition, that they tend to favour the consumption of scrap at the expense of that of iron, that they impose exorbitant charges upon the plaintiffs without any counterbalancing advantage, and that they do not contain any measures adequate to prevent the consequences prohibited by Section 29 of the Convention. Measures of safeguard were required to be adopted in order to take account of the special situation of the plaintiffs, a situation which is not comparable with that of producers of steel. In these circumstances, and in view of the local supply conditions, the plaintiffs are the victims of a discrimination which amounts to the *détournement de pouvoir* alleged.

" Upon this basis, and in greater detail, the plaintiffs have set out how the alleged *détournement de pouvoir* arises from the following facts.

" In the first place, the plaintiffs maintain that by imposing payments to the subsidy fund under Article 53(b) of the Treaty, the High Authority has shown an intention of avoiding the guarantees contained in the provisions of the Treaty which govern exceptional situations, such as the guarantees contained in Article 59. On this point, it must be recognised that a *détournement de pouvoir* would have been possible if the High Authority, finding itself faced with a situation which necessitated the application of the procedure set out in Article 59, had nevertheless, in order to avoid the guarantees of Article 59, proceeded under Article 53(*b*) and the financial arrangements which it contains. However, it has not been established that at the time when this challenged decision was taken the High Authority was faced with such a situation. In these circumstances, proof that the system of payments to the subsidy fund, as a financial arrangement set up under Article 53(*b*), is vitiated by a *détournement de pouvoir*, has not been substantiated. The present claim is not well founded.

" In the second place, the plaintiffs rely upon the fact that, according to the text of this challenged decision, it had as its object the regular supply of scrap to the common market, but that this aim had been substituted for the objective which had been set out in the Memoranda of the High Authority in its declaration of general objectives of July 6, 1955, and of April 1957, published in the *Journal officiel* of July 19, 1955, and of May 20, 1956, namely, the search for a balance between the markets for iron and steel. The plaintiffs maintain that this substitution reveals a *détournement de pouvoir*. The defendants have replied that it is not possible either in the memoranda or in Decision No. 2-57 to discover a compromise between the conflicting interests of the producers of iron and of steel, but merely the introduction of a group of measures which the High Authority believed were necessary in order to take account of the foreseeable economic expansion. From this point of view, the decision of the High Authority had as its aim the establishment of reasonable prices for scrap in order to ensure the regular supply of this material, as well as that of increasing the capacities for producing iron.

" This ground of appeal must be rejected, because the legality of the decision challenged does not depend upon its conformity with the memoranda which the High Authority has published, but solely upon its conformity with the Treaty. In effect, the memoranda by no means contain the only definition possible of the legitimate aim which the High Authority is empowered to follow. In order to establish a *détournement de pouvoir* the plaintiffs would have needed to show that the decision itself was in fact seeking a purpose other than that which the High Authority was empowered to seek. The difference which the plaintiffs have shown between the wording of the memoranda and that of the decision challenged is not sufficient to amount to such a proof.

" In the third place, the plaintiffs see a lack of foresight or of any serious consideration, such as amounts to a misconception of its legal aim, in the fact that in taking Decision No. 2-57 the High Authority, despite the fact that it had been faced with this problem since 1955, failed to take account of the disturbances affecting iron which would follow from the system of subsidies.

" The defendants admit that the subsidy had a tendency to encourage an increased consumption of scrap, and that unfavourable repercussions for producers of iron were not ruled out. That was why, later, it sought to remedy these by the introduction of a bonus payment for an increased consumption of iron, and later still by the supplementary tax authorised by Decision No. 2-57.

" However, it is accepted that the High Authority has introduced bonus payments and the supplementary tax as a form of indirect action, with the aim of encouraging economies in the consumption of scrap. It is agreed also that these two measures favoured an increase in the consumption of iron. Neither in the course of the written proceedings nor at the time of the oral hearing was it established that the High Authority had taken the two measures specified for a purpose other than that for which the system of payments to the subsidy fund had been instituted and lawfully brought into force.

" It has likewise not been established that the alleged ineffectiveness of the system of bonus payments and of the supplementary tax implied a disregard of the legal aim of the decision.

" For these reasons, the *détournement de pouvoir* has not been established and the present claim must be rejected.

" *Second Head.*—Decision No. 2-57, for reasons alien to the aim of the subsidy system, subjects heavy scrap and light scrap to a uniform tax payable to the subsidy fund. This constitutes a *détournement de pouvoir*.

" The plaintiffs allege that the imposition of a uniform tax payable to the subsidy fund constitutes a case of *détournement de pouvoir*. They consider, in effect, that this uniformity was not necessary for the attainment of the prescribed purpose, but that it has been imposed in order to avoid the administrative difficulties which would have resulted from the application of a differentiated tax possessing an equitable relationship to the price of different qualities of scrap, and especially to those used exclusively by the unamalgamated producers of iron.

" Before determining upon this head, it is necessary to examine whether the imposition of a uniform tax is compatible with the provisions of the Treaty. Concerning this question, the plaintiffs allege that the imposition of such a tax creates a discrimination which is prohibited by the terms of Article 4(b) of the Treaty. They maintain that they are an exclusive user of light scrap which they obtain at a low price and upon which the incidence of the uniform tax payable to the subsidy fund is relatively greater than it is upon the heavy scrap used by steel foundries, La Compagnie de Chasse also finds itself in a situation which is not comparable to that of steel works, and the application of a uniform system would, in this case, constitute a prohibited discrimination.

" The defendants, on their side, assert that there exists among the different categories of scrap a factual similarity resulting from their interchangeable character and from their use in common by different consumers. A graded tax to the subsidy fund imposed upon the different categories of scrap would thus place the plaintiffs in a situation comparable to that of other users, so that there cannot be any question of a discriminatory system.

" It appears from the documents submitted by the parties at the Instruction, that no consumer of scrap—including the plaintiffs— solely uses one particular type of scrap. Thus the plaintiffs, in their consumption of scrap, use—according to the nomenclature established by the High Authority (Decision No. 28-53: *Journal Officiel de la Communauté*, No. 5 of March 15, 1953, pp. 98-99)—about 80 per cent. of ' *tournures* ' and 20 per cent. of packets falling within the category ' light scrap ', whereas the steel works of the same region use between 10 per cent. and about 25 per cent. of ' *tournures* ' and, for the rest, in varying proportions, ' heavy ' and ' light ' scrap.

" There exist, therefore, two types of purchasers using in part the same categories of scrap. However, to the extent to which steel works, in the case of 75 per cent. of their purchases, buy certain categories of scrap which the plaintiffs do not use, a difference in the incidence of a uniform tax is not impossible. However, the Instruction did not produce any clear evidence which would enable one to affirm the existence of such a difference. In view of the fact that a possible difference would occur only in respect of a part of the purchases, and, taking account of the general tendency towards an alignment of the actual prices of the various categories of scrap from within and from outside the Community, the plaintiffs have not satisfied the legal burden of proof that the imposition of a uniform tax amounted to discrimination against them.

" As regards the *détournement de pouvoir* alleged by the plaintiffs, the Court finds that the defendants, in their defence as well as during the course of the Instruction, have set out the difficulties and the administrative complications which would have resulted from the establishment of a system of differentiated tax. Nothing, however, justifies one in holding that the desire to avoid complications of this nature was the main consideration which led the High Authority to impose a uniform tax. This tax being in conformity with the provisions of the Treaty, the decision being challenged would remain one that had been properly passed even if it were proved that the choice of a uniform tax might, in addition, meet the desire to avoid administrative complications.

" The present claim must, therefore, be rejected.

" *Costs.*—By the terms of Article 60 of the Rules of the Court,[1] any party which loses is condemned in costs. It is necessary, therefore, to condemn the plaintiffs in the costs of this action.

" The Court, rejecting all other submissions in favour or to the contrary, adjudges and declares:

" The appeal for the annulment of the Decision of the High Authority No. 2–57 of January 26, 1957, is rejected.

" The plaintiffs are condemned in the costs of the action."

[Report: *Recueil de la Jurisprudence de la Cour*, IV (1958), p. 131 (in French).]

NOTE.—The following is a note on the background to this and other cases challenging the validity of Decision 2–57.

The subsidy system set up by Decision 14–55 which gave rise to the three cases of *Meronie & Co., Industrie Metallurgiche, S.P.A.* v. *The High Authority* (reported above, p. 369); *Meronie & Cie, Industrie Metallurgiche, Società in Accomandita Semplice* v. *The High Authority* (reported below, p. 454) and *Compagnie des Hauts Fourneaux de Chasse* v. *The High Authority* (*No.* 2) (reported below, p. 457), was extensively remodelled by the High Authority. This it did by passing Decision 2–57 which, while continuing in force the levy to the subsidy fund imposed upon every ton of scrap purchased by enterprises, which now became known as the " basic levy ",[2] imposed a supplementary tax upon any consumption of purchased scrap which during any three-month accounting period[3] was in excess of what was called an enterprise's " reference consumption ". This reference consumption was equal basically to half of the amount of purchased scrap consumed by an enterprise during any six months in any seven consecutive months between January 1, 1953, and January 31, 1957, selected by itself.[4]

Many enterprises challenged the validity of Decision 2–57[5] but because it was a general decision the plaintiffs were placed in the great difficulty of being enabled to allege only a *détournement de pouvoir* with respect to themselves. None of the plaintiffs was successful.

[1] The reference here is to the old Rules. This article has now been replaced by Article 69 of the Rules.

[2] Article 3, para. 1.

[3] Article 3, para. 2.

[4] Article 6, para. 1. For example, one plaintiff's reference consumption was 2,760 metric tons, when in the accounting period of February-March-April 1958 the actual consumption of purchased scrap amounted to 4,523 metric tons. The supplementary tax was imposed upon the excess consumption, namely, 1,763 metric tons: see *Société Métallurgique de Knutange* v. *The High Authority* (Joint cases 15-59 and 29-59).

[5] *Groupement des Hauts Fourneaux et Aciéries belges* v. *The High Authority* (Case 8-57; reported above, p. 379); *Chambre syndicale de la Sidérurgie française* v. *The High Authority* (Case 9-57; reported below, p. 490); *Société des anciens établissements Aubert et Duval* v. *The High Authority* (Case 10-57; reported below, p. 470); *Société d'électrochimie, d'électro-métallurgie et des aciéries électriques d'Ugire* v. *The High Authority* (Case 11-57; reported below, p. 475); *Syndicat de la Sidérurgie du Centre-Midi* v. *The High Authority* (Case 12-57; reported below, p. 478); *Wirtschaftsvereinigung Eisen- und Stahlindustrie* v. *The High Authority* (Case 13-57; reported below, p. 484).

**International organization—Whether an international organization has right to delegate its powers—Whether such right to be implied —Distinction between delegation of discretion and delegation of execution—European Coal and Steel Community Treaty, 1951— Period within which decision of High Authority can be annulled —Effect of challenge of that decision out of time—Right to challenge validity of general decision when challenging individual decision made in application of it—Duty to support decision by reasons.**

MERONIE & CO., INDUSTRIE METALLURGICHE, SOCIETÀ IN ACCOMANDITA SEMPLICE *v.* THE HIGH AUTHORITY.

*Court of Justice of the European Coal and Steel Community.*

(Pilotti, President; Van Kleffens, Delvaux, Serrarens, Riese, Rueff, Hammes JJ.)

*June* 13, 1958.

THE FACTS.—The background to this case, one of three arising out of the system established by decisions of the High Authority for subsidizing the prices of imported steel scrap, is set out in the Facts of the case of *Meronie & Cie, Industrie Metallurgiche, S.P.A.* v. *The High Authority*, reported above, p. 369).

The plaintiffs were a steel producing enterprise whose registered office was in Erba, in the Italian province of Como. Although they were a distinct legal entity, they were closely related to the Meronie Company who were the plaintiffs in the above-mentioned case.

Between October 22, 1954, and August 16, 1956, the *Caisse* in Brussels sent 26 letters to the plaintiffs[1] setting out the provisional amount which the plaintiffs were declared to owe to the *Caisse*. Further, during the period February 8, 1955, to September 18, 1956, circulars had periodically been sent to them setting out what was the then existing levy upon every ton of scrap purchased.

On April 13, 1956, the plaintiffs wrote to the High Authority suggesting a possible payment of 1 m. lire a month, but without prejudice to their rights to deny the legality of the whole system of levies to the subsidy fund. This offer was rejected, and the *Caisse* requested the High Authority to take a decision demanding the money. This decision was issued by the High Authority on October 24, 1956, and stated as the reason why it had been taken that the plaintiffs

" . . . have failed as from April 1, 1954, to pay to the *Caisse* the contributions due from them in conformity with the decision set out below;

"That the contributions due for the period from April 1, 1954, to June 30, 1956, amount to the sum of 23,174,181 lire ".[2]

---

[1] The actual sender of the letters was CAMPSIDER, the abbreviated name for Consorzio Approvvigionamenti Materie Prime Siderurgiche S. A. Milano, which was the *Caisse*'s Italian regional office.

[2] Just over £13,500, or about $3,800.

By Article 92[1] of the Treaty, this decision had executory force so that the plaintiffs' property became liable to distraint. The plaintiffs appealed against this decision in December 1956.

Both in relation to the decision of October 24, 1956, itself, and to the general Decision No. 14–55 which set up the *Caisse* in Brussels and empowered it to run a subsidy system, the plaintiffs alleged the same grounds of invalidity as had been alleged by the plaintiffs in the other *Meronie* case.[2] The present plaintiffs, however, omitted arguments concerning the invalidity of the *Caisse's* power to assess the amount of scrap purchased and to declare the amount of tax due. The replies of the High Authority were identical with those which it gave in the other *Meronie* case.

The submissions of the Advocate General were that the decision of the High Authority of November 9, 1956, concerning the company "Meronie & Co., Industrie Metallurgiche, Società in accomandita semplice", Erba, in the province of Como, and notified to them on November 14, 1956, should be annulled; and that the defendants, in conformity with Article 60, paragraph 1, of the Rules of the Court,[3] should be condemned in the costs of the action, and the matter should be referred back to the High Authority in accordance with Article 34 of the Treaty.

*Held:* that the appeal was admissible and that the decision of the High Authority of October 24, 1956, must be annulled.

In challenging the individual decision of October 24, 1956, demanding payment, the plaintiffs could allege the invalidity of general decision No. 14–55 under which the individual decision had been taken, but because the period for appeals against Decision No. 14–55 had expired the Court had no power to annul it.

The decision of October 24, 1956, had been issued without sufficient justification of the sum claimed and without any authority having been cited showing that the *Caisse* could proceed to an *ex officio* assessment to tax. The decision, therefore, was to be annulled for violating the substantial procedural requirements set out in Article 15 of the Treaty. The decision was also to be annulled because in the decision the High Authority had failed to publish the reasons for its action, as required by Article 5 of the Treaty, and had failed to publish data useful to the interested parties, as required by Article 47 of the Treaty.

[1] Article 92 provides:
"The decisions of the High Authority imposing financial obligations on enterprises shall have executive force.
"They shall be put into forced execution on the territory of member States by means of the legal procedure in effect in each State, after the formula of execution in use in the State on whose territory the decision is to be carried out has been appended; this shall be done with no other formality than the verification of the authenticity of such decisions . . ."
[2] See above, p. 369.
[3] This refers to the old Rules of the Court. The present equivalent provision is Article 69, para. 2.

The Court did not consider the legal effect of the alleged inaccuracy of the calculation of the organization in Brussels, or of the alleged violation of the unanimous recommendation of the Council of Ministers. The Court held, however, that the organizations in Brussels were by Decision No. 14–55 empowered to issue decisions free from the restrictions which would have been imposed upon them if they had been issued by the High Authority itself. The decision delegating such powers to those organizations therefore violated the Treaty. The decision of October 24, 1956, having been taken in application of the system wrongly established by Decision No. 14–55, must be annulled for this reason only.

The Court said:

"A. *Concerning admissibility.*—[The Court here repeated what it had stated under this head in *Meronie & Co., Industrie Metallurgiche, S.P.A.* v. *The High Authority* (Case 9–56; reported above, p. 369.]

"B. *Concerning the merits.—*

"*First Head: Violation of substantial procedural requirements*

"The plaintiffs see a violation of a substantial procedural requirement in the failure to give reasons which occurs in the decision which has been issued.

"The plaintiffs allege that the decision of October 24, 1956, 'clearly contains insufficient reasoning'. This decision specifies only the two following reasons:

"That the enterprise 'Meronie & Co., Industrie Metallurgiche', of Erba (in the province of Como), being an enterprise within the meaning of Article 80 of the Treaty, has failed after April 1, 1954, to pay to the *Caisse de Péréquation des Ferrailles importées* the contributions due from it in conformity with the decision set out below;

"that the contributions due for the period from April 1, 1954, to June 30, 1956, amount to the sum of 23,174,181 lire.

[With the omission of the paragraphs dealing with the *ex officio* power of the *Caisse* both to assess the amount of scrap purchased and to declare the amount of the levy, the Court repeated its judgment in Case 9–56, reported above, p. 369.]

"*Costs.*—The defendants have lost on each of their arguments.

"In conformity with Article 60, first paragraph, of the Rules of the Court,[1] any party which loses shall be condemned in costs.

"The Court, rejecting all further arguments in favour or to the contrary, adjudges and declares:

"1. The appeal is admissible.

"2. The decision of the High Authority of October 24, 1956, ratified to the plaintiffs by post on November 14, 1956, by which the plaintiffs were required to pay to the *Caisse de Péréquation des Ferrailles importées* the sum of 23,174,181 lire, which decision

[1 For text, see above, p. 444, n. 3.]

possesses executory force within the meaning of Article 92 of the Treaty, is annulled.

" The defendants are condemned in costs."

[Report: *Recueil de la Jurisprudence de la Cour*, IV (1958), p. 53 (in French).]

International organization—European Coal and Steel Community —Convention containing Transitional Provisions, Section 29— Scope of application of—Treaty establishing Community, Article 3 —Meaning of acts " in the common interest "—Article 59—Scope of application of—Article 4—Discrimination—Whether uniform subsidy system amounts to indirect grant prohibited by Article 4 —Relevance of interference with normal competition—Whether a violation of Treaty—Duty of High Authority to limit foreseeable injury to third parties—*Détournement de pouvoir*—Relevance of aims of High Authority as published in Memoranda—Relevance of motive of avoiding administrative difficulties.

COMPAGNIE DES HAUTS FOURNEAUX DE CHASSE *v.* THE HIGH AUTHORITY (No. 2).

*Court of Justice of the European Coal and Steel Community.*

(Pilotti, President; Van Kleffens, Delvaux, Serrarens, Riese, Rueff, Hammes JJ.)

*June* 13, 1958.

THE FACTS.—This was the third of the cases arising out of the system established by decisions of the High Authority for subsidizing the prices of imported steel scrap. The background to all three cases is set out in the Facts in the case of *Meronie & Co., Industrie Metallurgiche, S.P.A.* v. *The High Authority*, reported above, p. 369.

The plaintiffs in the present action were a French company with a registered office in Lyons. The sole product which the company made was hermatite iron, produced in blast furnaces. The only scrap which they purchased was comparatively small quantities of light, cheap scrap from local suppliers, which they used to enrich the fusion beds of the furnaces. As the plaintiffs did not employ any imported scrap in their manufactures they were particularly reluctant to pay the levy to the subsidy fund out of which their competitors were to be assisted. This failure to pay the levy was reported to the High Authority by the *Caisse de Péréquation*, and the High Authority in May 1956 issued a decision having executory force stating that the plaintiffs owed the sum of 45,133,691 francs as tax for the period April 1, 1954, to December 31, 1955, as well as a further sum of 482,258 francs and 144,158 francs as interest.[1]

[1] In all, about £32,000 or $90,000.

No part of this sum was paid, and on December 12, 1956, a second decision, also with executory force, was issued by the High Authority, this time demanding the payment of 84,582,316 francs.[1] The plaintiffs challenged the validity of this decision.

The plaintiffs contended that the decision of December 12, 1956, by which they were being fined, had been issued as part of the subsidy system set up by Decisions No. 22–54 and 14–55, and that the two latter decisions were themselves invalid. The High Authority replied that the plaintiffs were unable to challenge the validity of the two earlier decisions as the time-limit for such a challenge had already expired.

With regard to the validity of Decisions No. 22–54 and 14–55, the plaintiffs contended that Section 29 of the Convention containing the Transitional Provisions listed certain consultations which the High Authority was required to undertake as part of the special precautionary measures to prevent shifts in production arising out of the introduction of the Common Market.[2] Section 29, they argued, was of general application, and the High Authority, although acting under Article 53 of the Treaty, was still required to undertake these consultations. A failure to do so amounted to a violation of Section 29.

The High Authority replied that Article 53 of the Treaty was entirely distinct from Section 29 of the Convention, and in any event a failure to hold the consultations required would have amounted to a violation of the Treaty, which the plaintiffs could not allege against a general decision.

The plaintiffs alleged a further violation because the High Authority, they maintained, had subsidized the price of scrap to the detriment of the producers of pig-iron. The High Authority,

---

[1] About £60,000, or $170,000.

[2] Section 29 provides as follows: " It is recognized that special precautionary measures may be necessary for the steel industry during the transitional period to prevent shifts in production arising out of the introduction of the Common Market from creating difficulties for enterprises, which, after adaptation in accordance with Section 1 of the present Convention, would be in a position to meet competition, or leading to the displacement of more workers than can benefit from the provisions of Section 23 [which concerns readaptation]. If the High Authority finds that the provisions of the Treaty—in particular, the provisions of Articles 57, 58 and 59 and Article 60 (2) (b)—cannot be applied, it shall have power to resort to the procedures set out below in the order of preference in which they are listed:

(a) after consulting the Consultative Committee and the Council, the High Authority may limit directly or indirectly the net increases from one region to another in the Common Market;

(b) after consulting the Consultative Committee and with the agreement of the Council on both the appropriateness of these measures and as to their nature, the High Authority may make use of the means of intervention specified in Article 61, para. (b) [fixing minimum prices] . . .

(c) after consulting the Consultative Committee and with the agreement of the Council, the High Authority may set up a system of production quotas . . . ;

(d) after consulting the Consultative Committee and with the agreement of the Council, the High Authority may authorize a member State to apply the measures provided for in Section 15 (6) [concerning protection of indirect imports] . . . "

although admitting that some loss of trade might be suffered by producers of pig-iron, denied that this loss could affect the validity of the decision. It pointed also to the bonus to be paid for an increased use of pig-iron.

The plaintiffs alleged further that, by Article 2 of the Treaty, the High Authority was to act "in the common interest", and not merely in the interest of the majority; because by this decision the High Authority had not acted in the interest of some producers, these decisions violated Article 3.[1]

The High Authority denied that the term "in the common interest" could bear the meaning which the plaintiffs sought to put upon it: it declared that the phrase was, in fact, synonymous with "in the general interest".

The plaintiffs next alleged that a uniform tax upon purchased scrap constituted a discrimination prohibited by Article 4(b) of the Treaty.[2] The High Authority replied that such a uniform tax was not unfair because nearly all types of scrap were interchangeable and no one enterprise purchased merely one type of scrap.

The plaintiffs then claimed that the subsidy payment amounted to an aid or subsidy forbidden by Article 4(c) of the Treaty.[3]

Under the head of *détournement de pouvoir*, the plaintiffs maintained that as a serious shortage of scrap existed within the Community, any action taken by the High Authority to deal with that situation should have been taken under Article 59 of the Treaty, by which that Authority acting with the Council of Ministers could establish consumption priorities. Instead of this, the plaintiffs declared, the High Authority had acted under Article 53, by which it could set up "financial arrangements common to several enterprises". This wrongful use of one article of the Treaty in place of another amounted, they alleged, to a *détournement de pouvoir*.

The High Authority denied that it had acted under Article 53 with any wrongful intention and contended that the two general decisions satisfied the requirement of that article that its action was "necessary for the accomplishment of the objectives" of the Treaty.

The plaintiffs then alleged that the High Authority had already declared in certain memoranda that it was seeking to obtain a balance between the markets for iron and those for steel,[4] whereas

[1] For the text of Articles 2 and 3 see above, p. 393, n. 1.

[2] Article 4 of the Treaty provides:
"The following are recognized to be incompatible with the common market for coal and steel, and are, therefore, abolished and prohibited within the Community in the manner set out in the present Treaty . . . (b) measures or practices discriminating among producers, among buyers or among consumers, especially as regards prices . . ."

[3] Article 4 provides: "The following are recognized to be incompatible with the Common Market for coal and steel, and are, therefore, abolished and prohibited within the Community in the manner set out in the present Treaty . . . (c) subsidies or State assistance or special charges imposed by the State, in any form whatsoever."

[4] Reference was made to the *Journal Officiel* of July 19, 1955, and May 20, 1957.

Decisions No. 22–54 and 14–55 were seeking to obtain a regular supply of steel scrap to the Common Market regardless of the effects of this upon iron. This change of purpose, they alleged, amounted also to a *détournement de pouvoir*.

The High Authority denied that there was here any change of purpose, as both the memoranda referred to and Decisions No. 22–54 and 14–55 were evidence of the same policy of meeting foreseeable economic expansion. Finally, the plaintiffs argued that the uniform tax imposed upon scrap, regardless of the cost, had been imposed merely to avoid administrative difficulties. This the High Authority denied.

The submissions of the Advocate General were that the appeal should be dismissed, and that costs should be borne by the Compagnie des Hauts Fourneaux de Chasse.

*Held:* (1) *As to admissibility*, that the appeal was admissible. In challenging the individual decision of December 12, 1956, demanding payment, the plaintiffs could allege the invalidity of general decisions No. 22–54 and 14–55 under which the individual decision had been taken, but, because the time-limit for appeals against general decisions had expired, the Court had no power to annul them.

(2) *As to the merits*, that the appeal for the annulment of the decision of December 12, 1956, must be rejected. Section 29 of the Convention could be employed only to prevent sudden shifts in production being caused by the creation of the Common Market. The plaintiffs, however, had not shown that their difficulties were caused by the creation of the Common Market, so that this paragraph could not be invoked.

A decision of the High Authority was not illegal merely because it might injure a particular enterprise. However, the High Authority must limit as far as possible any foreseeable injury. In the present instance, the High Authority had sought to limit any injury which might be suffered by producers of pig-iron by granting a bonus for an increased consumption of pig-iron.

When by Article 3 of the Treaty the High Authority was to use its powers " in the common interest ", this did not prevent it using its powers to meet the needs of certain situations even if this use would injure certain interests.

The plaintiffs had failed to establish that they would not benefit from the subsidy payments and the Court held that the prices of their suppliers would have risen without such payments.

The uniformity of the tax to the subsidy fund did not constitute a discrimination prohibited by Article 3(*b*) of the Treaty, because the grades of scrap in practice were interchangeable and there was a general tendency for the cost of all types of scrap to become the same. Further, the subsidy itself did not violate Article 4(*c*) because that provision merely prohibited grants made by States and not those made by the High Authority.

The High Authority had not committed a *détournement de pouvoir* by acting under Article 53(*b*) instead of under Article 59, because the latter article was only applicable to cases of " serious shortage ", and the shortage of scrap which existed was not " serious " within the meaning of that article.

The Court did not consider whether Decision 2-57 was in conformity with certain prior memoranda of the High Authority or not because lack of such conformity would in no way affect the validity of that decision.

As regards the desire to avoid administrative complications by means of a uniform tax, because such a tax was in conformity with the Treaty its existence could not affect the validity of the decision, even if the tax had been made uniform to avoid administrative complications.

The Court said:

" A. *Concerning admissibility*. The plaintiffs challenge the individual decision demanding payment which was taken with respect to them by the High Authority on December 12, 1956. This decision has been taken in conformity with the system for subsidizing imported scrap which was established by Decision No. 22-54 of March 26, 1954, and by Decision No. 14-55 of March 26, 1955. In the plaintiffs' opinion these two decisions are vitiated by certain defects, and the resulting irregularity necessarily renders irregular the decision applying them with respect to the plaintiffs, and which is challenged by them.

" The defendants maintain that the regularity of these two decisions, which are general decisions, may not be challenged by the plaintiffs in their capacity of a private enterprise except under the conditions and within the time set out in Article 33 of the Treaty.

" By the terms of Article 33, appeals ' must be brought within a time period of one month reckoned, according to the case, from the notification or from the publication of the decision or recommendation ". Should these appeals be brought by an enterprise or association mentioned in Article 48 of the Treaty, and concern a general decision or recommendation, they are only admissible if the plaintiffs allege that these decisions or recommendations are vitiated by a *détournement de pouvoir* with respect to them.

" The present appeal was lodged on May 6, 1957, and, as a result, the time period set out in the last paragraph of Article 33 had been observed with regard to the decision of December 12, 1956. This decision has been given executory force by the appending to it of the executory formula by the competent authority on March 4, 1957. Notification of this was given by the High Authority by a certified copy of a letter of March 30, 1957. The time period has expired as regards Decision No. 22–54 of March 26, 1954, and Decision No. 14–55 of March 26, 1955. These latter decisions are not challenged directly but only as part of the appeal against the decision of December 12, 1956, which has executory force. Whereas the decision of December 12, 1956, is an individual decision with respect to the plaintiffs, Decisions No. 22–54 and 14–55 are general decisions, upon which the decision of December 12, 1956, has been based.

[The Court then repeated virtually word for word what it had stated concerning the admissibility of the case of *Meronie & Co., Industrie Metallurgiche, S.P.A.* v. *The High Authority* (reported above, p. 369), when it considered whether the invalidity of a general decision can be alleged in support of an action brought against an individual decision, where that individual decision was passed in furtherance of the general decision. The Court held that such invalidity could be alleged. It then held this action to be admissible and continued:]

" B.   *Concerning the merits*

" 1.   *Violation of the Treaty*

" (a) *Violation of Section 29 of the Convention.*—The contention of the plaintiffs consists in saying that Section 29 has been inspired by the desire to avoid any disturbance in production. The High Authority would, therefore, be required to take special measures of safeguard not only when difficulties arose at the time of the establishment of the Common Market, but also when an enterprise found itself adversely affected by the measures which the High Authority decided to take in application of the provisions of the Treaty, such as Article 53.

" However, Section 29 in no way contains such an obligation. It is limited to recognising that measures of safeguard may be necessary in order to prevent the establishment of the Common Market suddenly creating shifts in production which enterprises will only be in a position to overcome after a certain amount of adaptation. In the present case, the plaintiffs have not established that the difficulties of which they complain, and the displacements of production which they fear, are attributable to the establishment of the Common Market. The fact that these difficulties might have resulted from a particular action—the setting up of a subsidy system—which the High Authority has taken in the exercise of the powers which the Treaty has conferred upon it, without the exercise of those powers being directly linked to the establishment of the Common Market, would not justify the adoption of the measures of safeguard contained in Section 29 of the Convention.

" Section 29 of the Convention cannot be invoked and the present claim must be rejected.

" (b) *Interference with the normal conditions of competition.*— According to the plaintiffs, the normal interplay of competition has been interfered with by the subsidy system, which has the effect of encouraging the consumption of scrap at the expense of that of pig-iron.  The defendants do not deny that the lowering of prices of imported scrap as a result of the subsidy might encourage enterprises to increase their consumption of scrap.  Indeed, the defendants admit to a certain aggravation of the situation for the plaintiffs by their being an éxclusive producer of hematite iron.  However, they have remedied this by the grant to scrap-consuming enterprises of a bonus in respect of scrap saved by means of an increased use of iron (Decisions No. 26–55 and 3–56).

" The question which arises, therefore, is whether the High Authority, which was convinced of the supreme importance of preventing the price of scrap produced within the Community from rising to the level of the price of imported scrap, and which was for this reason led to introduce the subsidy system, was required in law to prevent all the repercussions of that system which were likely to affect adversely the interests of the producers of pig-iron, or of certain of them.  Accepting that by instituting the subsidy system the High Authority has taken indirect measures, e.g., the bonus for scrap saved as a result of an increased use of pig-iron, in order to some extent to relieve the situation of producers of pig-iron, one must ask whether this precaution was sufficient, or whether the maintenance of the competitive position of producers of pig-iron would not have been more completely safeguarded by, for example, a direct measure exempting scrap used in the production of pig-iron from contributing to the subsidy fund.

" On this point, the Court holds that the plaintiffs' contention that the High Authority in taking these measures was required to ensure that the competitive position of producers of pig-iron vis-à-vis the other consumers of scrap underwent no alteration, imposes an excessive requirement.  In effect, if one admitted the existence of such a strict requirement, it would have to be applied not only to the case of producers of pig-iron, but also to all cases where the competitive position of a producer falling within the jurisdiction of the Community was—even indirectly—affected.

" Every regulation in the economic field necessarily has repercussions even upon the interests of those to whom the measures are not directly addressed.  The application of the principle advocated by the plaintiffs would make illegal any intervention in the economic field which the public authority believed necessary for safeguarding important interests if, subsequently, it did not benefit all interests affected, however far removed that interest might be from those which were primarily affected.  A public authority is subject to the obligation to act with care, and to intervene only after having carefully considered the different interests involved, while limiting —as far as possible—any foreseeable injury to third parties.

" One must, therefore, consider whether, in this case, the High Authority has sufficiently taken into account the interests of the producers of pig-iron.  Thus, to this end, the Court requested the parties in the course of the Instruction to supply concrete evidence about the results of the measures taken by the High Authority with a view to encouraging purchasers of scrap to increase their consumption of pig-iron.

" In its reply, the High Authority supplied figures for the period from April 1, 1955, to July 31, 1957, from which it appears that the savings in scrap, for which the bonus has been paid, increased by 1,643,101 tons, or 21 per cent. of the scrap imported. These figures prove that a considerable quantity of scrap has been saved and replaced by pig-iron. The period under consideration included six months of the new system set up by Decision No. 2–57. However, this fact is not important because, under the new system, the bonuses previously paid in cases of the substitution of pig-iron for scrap were continued for these six months.

" The plaintiffs for their part have limited themselves to pointing to a certain reduction in the production of Martin steel (in comparison with electric steel), but they have not replied in a satisfactory way to the question posed and they no longer challenged the figures supplied by the High Authority. In their final written submissions, as well as in the course of argument, the plaintiffs declared that the High Authority figures did not prove anything because the Authority had not indicated to what extent enterprises producing hematite iron—and in particular the plaintiffs' enterprise—had benefited from the savings which had thus been made. The plaintiffs, however, have not challenged the conclusions which followed at the same time from the facts cited by the High Authority, and from the data based upon them, that the bonus in fact had had the effect of remedying the ill-effects for producers of pig-iron which had followed from the institution of the subsidy system.

" Similarly, the plaintiffs are unable to invoke in support of their case the fact that the High Authority had recognized, in the preamble to Decision No. 2–57, that Decision No. 26–55, concerning the means of applying the financial arrangements, did not appear plainly effective to achieve a saving in scrap by an increased use of pig-iron. In fact, even if the system of bonuses has not ensured complete protection to the producers of pig-iron, one cannot from that conclude that the system disregarded in any excessive or arbitrary way the interests of producers of pig-iron. Indeed, the fact—pointed out by the plaintiffs in reply to the questions asked during the Instruction—that the production of Martin steel may not have made the same advance as that of electric steel, does not rule out the possibility that scrap—as the High Authority has shown—may have been replaced to a considerable extent by pig-iron. The contention of the plaintiffs is not supported by facts.

" In taking these special measures with a view to limiting the consumption of scrap by the increased use of pig-iron, the High Authority has proved that it had taken account, in a reasonable and considered manner, of the interests of the producers of pig-iron. The Instruction has shown that these measures have not been without considerable effect. The legality of the actions of the High Authority is not to be determined by their effectiveness in maintaining the pre-existing relationship between scrap and pig-iron. Thus, the subsidy system does not violate the rules of the Treaty concerning the maintenance of normal conditions of competition.

" The claim that the subsidy system is illegal because it affects the competitive position of the plaintiffs has not been substantiated.

" (c) *Interference with the general aims of the Treaty.*—According to the plaintiffs, Article 3 of the Treaty requires the institutions of the Community to act ' in the common interest ', this expression signifying that the institutions must act in the interest of all the entities controlled by it without exception. The High Authority is, therefore, not empowered to take measures ' in the general interest ' —that is to say, measures which may be in the interest of the majority only of those affected—which may be liable adversely to affect the interests of certain among them, such as those of the plaintiffs in the present case. Moreover, Article 59, para. 4, confers upon the High Authority special powers in the cases there expressly set out. Even in these cases, the interests of the parties concerned are protected by a certain number of guarantees, set out as much by Article 59 as by Annex II of the Treaty. If follows that the High Authority is equally required to respect these guarantees when it acts under Article 53.

" The Court rejects the interpretation which the plaintiffs give to the expression " common interests '. As has been stated under (b) above, the rôle of the High Authority, acting as a public authority, in no way imposes the obligation not to use its regulating powers except on condition that no interest is adversely affected by them. This does not mean that the High Authority may disregard the particular interests of the parties affected and rigorously pursue its course of action so that these interests become more adversely affected than it was reasonable to expect. On the contrary, the High Authority is required to act with the utmost care and to give the consideration necessary to assess and weigh up the various interests in question, which may be in conflict one with another, and to avoid causing any greater damage than the nature of the decision to be taken reasonably requires. Although the High Authority is empowered to take measures ' in the common interest ', it may use its regulatory power according to the requirements of the circumstances, even where this is to the detriment of certain particular interests.

" The reference to Article 59 is similarly ill-founded. In effect, the precautions laid down by this article, as well as by Annex II of the Treaty, relate to the exercise of special powers that are granted to meet the situation there envisaged. However, such a situation did not exist at the time when these decisions were taken. The fact that the High Authority may not proceed to an equitable allocation of resources without a compulsory consultation with producers affected is explained by the gravity of the situation with which such allocation is required to deal. It is not possible to give to this special provision a general application to a case other than that mentioned in Article 59.

" (d) *Prohibited discrimination creating an indirect subsidy.*—

" (i) The first argument advanced by the plaintiffs under this head is based upon the fact that their position is not comparable to that of other consumers of scrap. They only use scrap supplied from the Lyons region, in respect of which the subsidy payments were in no way necessary. They deny that the price of scrap from this region would be aligned to that of imported scrap if the subsidy system had not been introduced, the allegation of the contrary being declared by the plaintiffs to be merely hypothetical and incapable of proof.

" The Court rejects this argument, for it is clear that as long as the supply of scrap produced within the Community was insufficient to meet the needs of the Common Market, the price of such scrap would tend to become aligned with the higher prices of imported scrap. There is no reason why the prices of scrap from the Lyons region should escape this general tendency, and the plaintiffs have failed to mention any special circumstances showing that this region would remain unaffected by the general trend in prices. Moreover, it appears from the figures produced in the course of the Instruction that the prices of scrap in the Lyons region have risen along with the prices of scrap in other regions and with the prices of imported scrap. Indeed, the plaintiffs have themselves observed that the prices of the scrap which they bought had somewhat increased by reason of purchases made by competing enterprises, particularly by foundries using hot air cubilots, which, to a greater or less extent, are not subject to the subsidy system.

" The plaintiffs' contention that there did not exist any possibility that competing enterprises would obtain their supplies of light scrap from the Lyons market is not well founded either. In the Lyons region, the plaintiffs are not the sole purchasers of scrap and there does not exist any reason to believe that other purchasers would not appear upon this market if the difference in prices noticeably exceeded the difference attributable to additional costs of transport.

" (ii) The plaintiffs allege, in the second place, that the imposition of a uniform subsidy tax on all categories of scrap creates a discrimination which is prohibited by the terms of Article 4(b) of the Treaty. They maintain that they are an exclusive user of light scrap which they obtain at a low price and upon which the incidence of the uniform tax payable to the subsidy fund is relatively greater than it is upon the heavy scrap used by steel foundries. The Compagnie de

Chasse also finds itself in a situation which is not comparable to that of steel works, and the application of a uniform system would, in this case, constitute a prohibited discrimination.

" The defendants, on their side, assert that there exists among the different categories of scrap a factual similarity resulting from their interchangeable character and from their use in common by different consumers. A graded tax to the subsidy fund imposed upon the different categories of scrap would thus place the plaintiffs in a situation comparable to that of other users, so that there cannot be any question of a discriminatory system.

" It appears from the documents submitted by the parties at the Instruction that no consumer of scrap—including the plaintiffs—solely uses one particular type of scrap. Thus the plaintiffs, in their consumption of scrap, use—according to the nomenclature established by the High Authority (Decision No. 28–53, *Journal Officiel de la Communauté* No. 5 of March 15, 1953, pp. 98–99)—about 80 per cent. of ' *tournures* ' and 20 per cent. of packets falling within the category ' light scrap ', whereas the steel works of the same region use between 10 per cent. and about 25 per cent. of ' *tournures* ' and, for the rest, in varying proportions, ' heavy ' and ' light ' scrap.

" There exist, therefore, two types of purchasers using in part the same categories of scrap. However, to the extent to which steel works, in the case of 75 per cent. of their purchases, buy certain categories of scrap which the plaintiffs do not use, a difference in the incidence of a uniform tax is not impossible. However, the Instruction did not produce any clear evidence which would enable one to affirm the existence of such a difference. In view of the fact that a possible difference would only occur in respect of a part of the purchases, and, taking account of the general tendency towards an alignment of the actual prices of the various categories of scrap from within and from outside the Community, the plaintiffs have not satisfied the legal burden of proof that the imposition of a uniform tax amounted to a discrimination against them.

" For these reasons, the validity of the present claim cannot be accepted.

" (iii) The third point raised by the plaintiffs concerns the violation of Article 4(c) of the Treaty by reason of the discriminatory effect—equivalent to an indirect grant—which the subsidy system has in favour of steel works to the detriment of producers of pig-iron. The defendants admit that the subsidy system tends to encourage the consumption of scrap. That is why they have wished to correct this tendency by the introduction of a bonus payment upon any increased consumption of pig-iron.

" This question has already been examined above under point (b), in order to determine whether one must conclude that an interference with the normal conditions of competition has occurred, a question which has been answered in the negative. For the same reasons, the effects caused by the decisions to the respective situations of producers of pig-iron and those of steel works cannot be held to constitute either discriminations or indirect grants, because the prohibition of the latter by Article 4(c) of the Treaty only extends to grants made by States. The present claim has, therefore, not been substantiated.

" 2. *Détournement de pouvoir*

" Both the parties declare that in order to show the existence of a *détournement de pouvoir* one must establish the existence of a power and then the use of that power with an aim other than that for which it has been granted.

" As to the existence of a power to set up a financial arrangement by virtue of Article 53(b) of the Treaty, that is to say, a subsidy system, the parties are in agreement. The Court likewise takes this point as accepted.

" It remains, therefore, solely to determine whether the use which the High Authority has made of this power can be held to amount to a *détournement de pouvoir*. However, the greater part of the plaintiffs' arguments has already been considered above from the point of view of the violation of the Treaty. There is no need in the circumstances of the present case to examine them again from the point of view of a *détournement de pouvoir*, as the plaintiffs have not specified what constitutes this *détournement de pouvoir*. Nevertheless, the grounds which the plaintiffs have added to those which have already been considered must be examined more particularly in relation to a *détournement de pouvoir*.

" In the first place, the plaintiffs maintain that by imposing payments to the subsidy fund under Article 53(b) of the Treaty, the High Authority has shown an intention of avoiding the guarantees contained in the provisions of the Treaty which govern exceptional situations, such as the guarantees contained in Article 59 of the Treaty.

" On this point, it must be recognized that a *détournement de pouvoir* would have been possible if the High Authority, finding itself faced with a situation which necessitated the application of the procedure set out in Article 59, had nevertheless, in order to avoid the guarantees of Article 59, proceeded under Article 53(b) and the financial arrangements which it contains. However, it has not been established that at the time when the challenged decision was taken the High Authority was faced with such a situation. In these circumstances, proof that the system of payments to the subsidy fund, as a financial arrangement set up under Article 53(b), is vitiated by a *détournement de pouvoir*, has not been substantiated. The present claim is not well founded.

" In the second place, the plaintiffs rely upon the fact that, according to the text of the challenged decision, it had as its object the regular supply of scrap to the Common Market, but that this aim had been substituted for the objective which had been set out in the Memoranda of the High Authority in its declaration of general objectives of July 6, 1955, and of April 1957, published in the *Journal officiel* of July 19, 1955, and May 20, 1956, namely, the search for a balance between the markets for iron and steel. The plaintiffs maintain that this substitution reveals a *détournement de pouvoir*. The defendants have replied that it is not possible either in the Memoranda or in Decision No. 2-57 to discover a compromise between the conflicting interests of the producers of iron and of steel, but simply the introduction of a group of measures which the High Authority believed were necessary in order to take account of the foreseeable economic expansion. From this point of view, the decision of the High Authority had as its aim the establishment of reasonable prices for scrap in order to ensure the regular supply of this material, as well as that of increasing the capacities for producing iron.

" This ground of appeal must be rejected, because the legality of the decision challenged does not depend upon its conformity with the Memoranda which the High Authority has published, but solely upon its conformity with the Treaty. In effect, the Memoranda by no means contain the only definition possible of the legitimate aim which the High Authority is empowered to follow. In order to establish a *détournement de pouvoir*, the plaintiffs would have needed to show that the decision itself was in fact seeking a purpose other than that which the High Authority was empowered to seek. The difference which the plaintiffs have shown between the wording of the Memoranda and that of the decision challenged is not sufficient to amount to such a proof.

" In the third place, the plaintiffs allege a *détournement de pouvoir* resulting from the imposition of a uniform subsidy tax not because this uniformity was required for the attainment of the prescribed purpose, but for the avoidance of the administrative difficulties which would have resulted from the application of a differentiated tax possessing an equitable relationship to the price of different qualities of scrap, and especially of those used exclusively by the unamalgamated producers of iron.

" It is true that the defendants, in their defence as well as during the course of the Instruction, have set out the difficulties and the administrative complications which would have resulted from the establishment of a system of differentiated tax. Nothing, however, justifies one in holding that the desire to avoid complications of this nature was the main consideration which led the High Authority to impose a uniform tax. This tax, being in conformity with the provisions of the Treaty, the decision being challenged would remain one that had been properly passed even if it were proved that the choice of a uniform tax might, in addition, meet the desire to avoid administrative difficulties.

" The present claims are, therefore, not substantiated.

" *Costs.*—By the terms of Article 60 of the Rules of the Court, any party which loses is condemned in costs, but the Court may nevertheless apportion the costs, in whole or in part, if the parties lose respectively on one or more heads.

" The defendants having lost as concerns the admissibility of this appeal, costs are apportioned so that one quarter of the total costs is borne by the defendants and three quarters by the plaintiffs.

" The Court, rejecting all further submissions in favour or to the contrary, adjudges and declares:

" The appeal for the annulment of the Decision of the High Authority of December 12, 1956, declaring the obligation of the Compagnie des Hauts Fourneaux de Chasse, Chasse-sur-Rhône, Isère, to pay to the *Caisse de Péréquation des Ferrailles importées* the sum due up to August 31, 1956, in execution of the provisions concerning the subsidy upon imported scrap, is rejected.

" The costs are apportioned: one quarter of the total costs is borne by the defendants and three quarters by the plaintiffs."

[Report: *Recueil de la Jurisprudence de la Cour*, IV (1958), p. 157 (in French).]

**International organization—European Coal and Steel Community —Interpretation of Treaty establishing—Articles setting out fundamental aims of Treaty to be read as a whole—Power of international organization to give predominance to certain of these aims—Interpretation of fundamental aims in light of subsequent provision of Treaty—Effect of failure to comply with fundamental aims—Whether a *détournement de pouvoir*—General decision challenged by enterprise—Necessity of showing *détournement de pouvoir* with respect to that enterprise—Relevance of alleged aim of Authority to penalise a particular enterprise.**

Société des anciens Établissements Aubert et Duval
*v.* The High Authority.

*Court of Justice of the European Coal and Steel Community.*

(Pilotti, President; Van Kleffens, Delvaux, Serrarens, Riese, Rueff, Hammes JJ.)

*June 26, 1958.*

The Facts.—A Note on the background to this and other cases in which enterprises and associations challenged the validity of Decision 2-57 of the High Authority appears above, at p. 453.

The plaintiffs in the present case were a steel works employing about 2,000 workers, which had been established at Ancizes, Puy-de-Dôme, France, in 1917. Their registered office was at Neuilly-sur-Seine. The plaintiffs produced high quality steel, and being well supplied with hydraulic and electric power they produced their steel mainly in electric furnaces. However, in these electric furnaces neither solid nor liquid pig-iron was able to be used in place of scrap, so that the plaintiffs were not able to qualify for any rebate of tax. Further, they had planned to replace one of their old inefficient furnaces by an electric furnace, but, as this replacement would occur after January 31, 1958, this furnace would not be granted any reference consumption[1] and any increase in production, by naturally involving an increased consumption of scrap, meant that the plaintiffs would be heavily taxed to the subsidy fund.

As a result of Decision 2-57, the plaintiffs had already been forced to limit their production to the level at which it was at the time of their reference period, and they were doing nothing to meet the increasing demands for steel.

The plaintiffs therefore challenged the validity of Decision 2-57, but, because that decision was a general one, they were limited to alleging its invalidity on the grounds of a *détournement de pouvoir* with respect to themselves.[2]

The High Authority contended that the appeal was inadmissible in that the plaintiffs, although contending that a *détournement de pouvoir* had occurred, had not shown that this *détournement de pouvoir* was specifically with respect to themselves, as they were required to show by Article 33, para. 2, of the Treaty.

The plaintiffs replied that they were challenging the unequal effect of Decision 2-57, because this effect varied according to whether an enterprise was or was not able to economize in the use of scrap. As the plaintiffs were, themselves, unable to economize, they were one of those adversely affected and thus had standing to appeal.

On the merits, the plaintiffs advanced three arguments which were substantially the same as those advanced by the plaintiffs in *Groupement des Hauts Fourneaux et Aciéries Belges* v. *The High Authority*,[3] namely, that the passing of Decision 2-57 constituted a *détournement de pouvoir* with respect to Articles 3 and 4 of the Treaty, *inter alia*, by not encouraging the regular expansion of production; and also a *détournement* with respect to Article 59 of the Treaty because the High Authority had in fact made an allocation of resources without complying with the procedural requirement for so doing which Article 59 contains; and, finally, because Decision 2-57 amounted to a control over enterprises' investment programmes without compliance with Article 54 of the Treaty.

The replies of the High Authority were also substantially the same as those set out above.

---

[1] Under Decision 2-57. For an explanation of " reference consumption " see the Note at p. 453 above.
[2] Article 33, para. 2, of the Treaty: for text, see above, p. 445, n. 1.
[3] Case 8-57, reported above, p. 379.

Further, the plaintiffs alleged a *détournement de pouvoir* with respect to Article 3(e) of the Treaty, in that the decision taken did not promote the improvement of the living and working conditions of the labour force.[1] This was so because the only means by which the plaintiffs could obtain a rebate from a use of pig-iron was by moving their enterprise elsewhere, and Decision 2-57 encouraged them so to do. This would result in unemployment and not in the improvement of working conditions.

The High Authority replied that its action to keep down the price of scrap throughout the Community most certainly did promote improvement of working conditions, which would have greatly suffered if a sharp rise in scrap prices had driven some steel enterprises out of business.

The plaintiffs then alleged that Decision 2–57 had knowingly been passed specifically to injure themselves. The decision, they declared, was quite unable to achieve its express aims and could not be explained as a mere error of judgment on the part of the High Authority, but only as the pursuit of an aim specifically directed to steel works possessing electric furnaces.

The High Authority denied this contention, and pointed out that the taxing of steel works possessing electric furnaces, far from being its sole aim, as alleged, produced only a very small amount of the total revenue to the subsidy fund, and in any event the contributions to be paid by such steel works were periodically adjusted.

The submissions of the Advocate General were that the appeal should be dismissed, and that the costs should be paid by the plaintiffs.

*Held*: (1) *as to admissibility*, that the action was admissible. The plaintiffs had alleged a *prima facie* case of a *détournement de pouvoir* adversely affecting them.

(2) *As to the merits*, that the appeal for the annulment of Decision 2–57 must be rejected. The Court repeated its judgment in *Groupement des Hauts Fourneaux et Aciéries Belges* v. *The High Authority*[2] with respect to the three arguments advanced which were in common with those in that case.

Because the plaintiffs had not developed their allegation that Decision 2–57 did not seek to improve living and working conditions, the Court rejected it. It also found that the allegation that the decision had been taken specifically to injure the plaintiffs had no justification in fact.

---

[1] Article 3 provides as follows:
" Within the framework of their respective powers and responsibilities and in the common interest the institutions of the Community shall:
" . . . (e) promote the improvement of the living and working conditions of the labour force in each of the industries under its jurisdiction so as to harmonise these conditions in an upward direction . . . "
[2] Case 8-57, reported above, p. 379.

As the High Authority had lost on its challenge of the admissibility of the action, it was condemned in one-fifth of the costs; the plaintiffs bore the other four-fifths.

The Court said:

"A. *On admissibility.*—By the terms of their articles, the plaintiffs are a private company in French law having as their object the carrying on of a productive activity in the field of steel within the territories mentioned in Article 79, first paragraph, of the Treaty. They, therefore, have standing within the meaning of the provisions of Articles 33 and 80 of the Treaty to appear before the Court to challenge the decisions and recommendations of the High Authority.

" In effect, by virtue of the provisions of Article 33, para. 2, of the Treaty, the enterprises mentioned in Article 80 are permitted to bring an appeal for the annulment of general decisions of the High Authority which they believe to be vitiated by a *détournement de pouvoir* with respect to them.

" Decision No. 2–57 is a general decision which establishes a normative principle imposing in a general fashion conditions for its application and specifying the legal consequences which it will bring about.

" The plaintiffs allege that they are adversely affected by the provisions challenged by reason of the very great difficulty which they are experiencing in making economies in scrap and consequently by reason of the necessity which is imposed upon them of paying the supplementary contribution if they increase their consumption of purchased scrap. The plaintiffs formally allege one or more *détournements de pouvoir* with respect to them, setting out in the required manner the reasons which, in their opinion, give rise to these *détournements de pouvoir.* In effect, the arguments advanced seek in particular to show that in enacting the challenged provisions the High Authority has used the powers which are granted to it by Article 53(b) of the Treaty for purposes other than those for which they were given. This it is alleged to have done as much by a serious misconstruction of certain of the objects set out in Article 3 as by the manifest desire to attain the objects specifically regulated by Articles 54 and 59 in order to avoid the special procedures provided in those articles.

" The plaintiffs' appeal is, therefore, admissible.

" B. *Concerning the merits.*—[The Court here repeated virtually word for word that part of its judgment in *Groupement des Hauts Fourneaux et Aciéries Belges* v. *The High Authority,* Case 8–57 (reported above, p. 379), where it had analysed the provisions of Article 3 and had discussed whether the High Authority in passing Decision 2–57 had committed a *détournement de pouvoir* with respect to Articles 3 and 4 of the Treaty; where it had considered whether the financial arrangements had been passed under Article 53(b) so as to avoid observance of the terms of Article 59; and where it had considered whether the High Authority had committed a *détourne-ment de pouvoir* by seeking to prohibit certain new installations or to favour certain investments without observing the requirements of Article 54. The Court then continued:]

" 4. As to the allegation of *détournement de pouvoir* with respect to Articles 2 and 3(*e*) of the Treaty and of Section 29 of the Convention containing the Transitional Provisions, whether the aims of the challenged decision appear contrary to those which are imposed upon the Community in relation to the continuity of the employment of workers and the improvement of living and working conditions:

" The plaintiffs in the course of the proceedings did not develop this allegation and they have not advanced any relevant evidence in support.

" The *détournement de pouvoir* with regard to Articles 2 and 3 and Section 29 of the Convention has not been proved.

" 5. As to the allegation of *détournement de pouvoir* resulting from the fact that the High Authority, by the provisions of Decision 2–57, has knowingly pursued an aim specifically to injure the plaintiffs:

" The allegation of having pursued aims which are strictly financial and fiscal to the detriment of enterprises such as the plaintiffs, which produce special high quality electric steels, and of having thereby camouflaged under the appearance of a general decision, a decision which has as its only reasonable and explicable aim to penalise one type of enterprises, has no foundation in fact.

" This ground, therefore, is not well founded.

" *Costs.*—By the terms of Article 60 of the Rules of the Court, any party which loses is condemned in costs. In the present action the plaintiffs have lost on the merits and the defendants upon the admissibility of the appeal. It is necessary, therefore, in accordance with paragraph 2[1] of that article, to condemn the plaintiffs in four-fifths of the costs of the action and the defendants in one-fifth.

" The Court, rejecting all further submissions in favour or to the contrary, adjudges and declares:

" The action is admissible but not well founded. In consequence, the appeal for the annulment of the provisions contained in [Articles] 3.1(*b*), 4.3, 5, 6, 7, 8 and 9 of Decision No. 2–57 of the High Authority of January 26, 1957, is rejected.

[Report: *Recueil de la Jurisprudence de la Cour*, IV (1958), p. 401 (in French).]

[1 Article 60, para. 2, of the Old Rules provided: " The Court may apportion costs wholly or in part if the parties each fail on one or more heads of claim." This provision is now contained in Article 69, para. 3, of the Rules.]

International organization—European Coal and Steel Community
—Interpretation of Treaty establishing—Articles setting out
fundamental aims of Treaty to be read as a whole—Power of
international organization to give predominance to certain of
these aims—Interpretation of fundamental aims in light of subsequent provision of Treaty—Effect of failure to comply with fundamental aims—Whether a *détournement de pouvoir*—General
decision challenged by enterprise—Necessity of showing *détournement de pouvoir* with respect to that enterprise.

Société d'Électro-Chimie, d'Électro-Métallurgie et des
Aciéries Électriques d'Ugire *v.* The High Authority.

*Court of Justice of the European Coal and Steel Community.*

(Pilotti, President; Van Kleffens, Delvaux, Serrarens, Riese, Rueff,
Hammes JJ.)

*June 26, 1958.*

The Facts.—A Note on the background to this and other cases
in which enterprises and associations challenged the validity of
Decision 2–57 of the High Authority appears at p. 453 above.

The plaintiffs in the present case were an enterprise producing
special steels at three foundries at Ugire, at Moustiers and at Ardoire,
all of which possessed solely electric furnaces, in which for technical
reasons it was impossible to employ solid pig-iron and, for geo-
graphical reasons, impossible to use liquid pig-iron. The plaintiffs
were therefore unable to benefit from the rebate given for an increased use of pig-iron.[1] Further, certain furnaces at Ardoire would
not be able to be brought into service before January 31, 1958, so
that they would not be granted a reference consumption.[2] For this
reason and because the plaintiffs planned a 30 per cent. increase in
production during the following few years, they would be heavily hit
by the supplementary tax to the subsidy fund. They therefore
brought the present action challenging the validity of Decision 2–57.
As this decision, however, was a general decision, they were able to
challenge it only on the ground of a *détournement de pouvoir* with
respect to themselves.[3]

The High Authority contended that the appeal was inadmissible
in that the plaintiffs, although contending that a *détournement de
pouvoir* had occurred, had not shown that this *détournement* was
specifically with respect to themselves, as they were required to do
by Article 33, paragraph 2, of the Treaty.

The plaintiffs replied that as they produced steel only in electric
furnaces, they were unable to make any economies in the use of scrap.
Further, as their installation at Ardoire would not benefit from any

[1] Under Decision 2-57.
[2] For an explanation of " reference consumption " see the Note at p. 453 above.
[3] Article 33, para. 2: for text, see above, p. 445, n. 1.

reference consumption, they would be required to pay the supplementary tax at the highest rate. This, they alleged, amounted to a *détournement* with respect to themselves.

On the merits, the plaintiffs advanced three arguments which were substantially the same as those advanced by the plaintiffs in *Groupement des Hauts Fourneaux et Aciéries Belges* v. *The High Authority*,[1] namely, that the passing of Decision 2–57 constituted a *détournement de pouvoir* with respect to Articles 3 and 4 of the Treaty, *inter alia*, by not encouraging the regular expansion of production, and also a *détournement* with respect to Article 59 of the Treaty because the High Authority had in fact made an allocation of resources without complying with the procedural requirements for so doing which Article 59 contains; and finally, because Decision 2–57 amounted to a control over enterprises' investment programmes without compliance with Article 54 of the Treaty.

The replies of the High Authority were also substantially the same as those set out in the above-mentioned case.

The submissions of the Advocate General were that the appeal should be dismissed, and that the costs should be paid by the plaintiffs.

*Held:* (1) *As to admissibility*, that the action was admissible. The plaintiffs had alleged a *prima facie* case of a *détournement de pouvoir* adversely affecting them, and the appeal was consequently admissible.

(2) *As to the merits*, that the appeal for the annulment of Decision 2–57 must be rejected.

The Court repeated its judgment in *Groupement des Hauts Fourneaux et Aciéries Belges* v. *The High Authority* with respect to the three arguments advanced which were in common with those in that case.

The Court said:

"A. *On admissibility*.—By the terms of their articles, the plaintiffs are a private company in French law having as their object the carrying on of a productive activity in the field of steel within the territories mentioned in Article 79, first paragraph, of the Treaty. They therefore have standing within the meaning of the terms of Articles 33 and 80 of the Treaty to appear before the Court to challenge the decisions and recommendations of the High Authority.

" In effect, by virtue of the provisions of Article 33, para. 2, of the Treaty, the enterprises mentioned in Article 80 are permitted to bring an appeal for the annulment of general decisions of the High Authority which they believe to be vitiated by a *détournement de pouvoir* with respect to them.

" Decision No. 2–57 is a general decision which establishes a normative principle, imposing in a general fashion conditions for its

---

[1] Case 8-57, reported above, p. 379.

application and specifying the legal consequences which it will bring about.

" The plaintiffs allege that they are adversely affected by the provisions challenged, by reasons of the very great difficulty which they are experiencing in making economies in scrap and consequently by reason of the necessity which is imposed upon them of paying the supplementary contribution if they increase their consumption of purchased scrap. They formally allege one or more *détournements de pouvoir* with respect to them, setting out in the required manner the reasons which, in their opinion, give rise to these *détournements de pouvoir*. In effect, the arguments advanced seek, in particular, to show that in enacting the challenged provisions the High Authority has used the powers which are granted to it by Article 53(*b*) of the Treaty for purposes other than those for which they were granted. This it is alleged to have done as much by a serious misconstruction of certain of the objects set out in Article 3 as by the manifest desire to attain the objects specifically regulated by Articles 54 and 59 in order to avoid the special procedures provided in those articles.

" The plaintiffs' appeal is therefore admissible.

" B. *Concerning the merits.*—[The Court here repeated virtually word for word that part of its judgment in *Groupement des Hauts Fourneaux et Aciéries Belges* v. *The High Authority* (Case 8–57, reported above, p. 379) where it had analysed the provisions of Article 3 of the Treaty and had discussed whether the High Authority in passing Decision 2–57 had committed a *détournement de pouvoir* with respect to Articles 3 and 4 of the Treaty; and where it had considered whether the financial arrangement had been passed under Article 53(*b*) so as to avoid observance of the provisions of Article 59, and where the Court had considered whether the High Authority had committed a *détournement de pouvoir* by seeking to prohibit certain new installations or to favour certain investments without observing the requirements of Article 54. The Court then continued:]

" *On costs.*—By the terms of Article 60 of the Rules of the Court, any party which loses is condemned in costs. In the present action the plaintiffs have lost on the merits and the defendants upon the admissibility. It is necessary, therefore, in accordance with paragraph 2 of that article,[1] to condemn the plaintiffs in four-fifths of the costs of the action and the defendant in one-fifth.

" The Court, rejecting all further submissions in favour or to the contrary, adjudges and declares:

" The action is admissible but not well founded. In consequence, the appeal for the annulment of the provisions contained in Articles 3.1, 4.3, 5, 6, 8 and 9 of Decision 2-57 of the High Authority of January 26, 1957, is rejected.

[1 Article 60, paras. 1 and 2, of the old Rules of the Court are now contained in Article 69, paras. 2 and 3, of the Rules.]

" The plaintiffs are condemned in four-fifths of the costs of the action and the defendants in one-fifth."

[Report: *Recueil de la Jurisprudence de la Cour*, IV (1958), p. 437 (in French).]

International organization—European Coal and Steel Community —Interpretation of Treaty establishing—Articles setting out fundamental aims of Treaty to be read as a whole—Power of international organization to give predominance to certain of these aims—Interpretation of fundamental aims in light of subsequent provision of Treaty—Effect of failure to comply with fundamental aims—Whether a *détournement de pouvoir*—Dominant purpose of Treaty—Meaning of concept of " common interest " in Article 3 —Article 4 (*b*) and (*c*)—Whether financial arrangement under Article 53 can be special charge within Article 4 (*c*)—Unequal imposition of charges—Article 65—Whether acts of High Authority more restrictive than necessary for their purpose.

SYNDICAT DE LA SIDÉRURGIE DU CENTRE-MIDI *v.* THE HIGH AUTHORITY.

*Court of Justice of the European Coal and Steel Community.*

(Pilotti, President; Van Kleffens, Delvaux, Serrarens, Riese, Rueff, Hammes JJ.)

*June 26, 1958.*

THE FACTS.—A Note on the background to this and other cases in which enterprises and associations challenged the validity of Decision 2–57 of the High Authority appears above, at p. 453.

The plaintiffs in the present case were a syndicate of steel producers of the Centre-Midi in France, with their registered office in Paris. Their constituent enterprises were adversely affected by the supplementary tax imposed by Decision 2–57 and, in addition, none of them was able to benefit from the rebate given for an increased use of pig-iron. This was due to three reasons: first, none of the enterprises could produce their own Thomas pig-iron owing to the lack of phosphorous; secondly, their blast furnaces required a very large amount of scrap in order to counteract the effect of manganese in the local iron ore; and thirdly, the steel factories used almost exclusively Martin furnaces or electric furnaces which could not reduce their import of scrap. The plaintiffs therefore brought the present action challenging the validity of Decision 2–57. As this decision, however, was a general decision, they were able to challenge it only on the ground of a *détournement de pouvoir* with respect to themselves.[1]

[1] Article 33, para. 2: for text, see above, p. 445, n. 1.

The High Authority contended that the appeal was inadmissible in that the plaintiffs, although contending that a *détournement de pouvoir* had occurred, had not shown that this *détournement* was specifically with respect to themselves, as they were required to show by Article 33, para. 2, of the Treaty.

The plaintiffs replied that they challenged the varying effects which Decision 2–57 would have upon enterprises according to their ability or inability to economise in the use of scrap. As the plaintiffs represented enterprises which were unable to economise in the use of scrap they were adversely affected by the supplementary tax and this, they alleged, rendered the *détournement* one with respect to themselves.

On the merits, the plaintiffs advanced three arguments which were substantially the same as those advanced by the plaintiffs in *Groupement des Hauts Fourneaux et Aciéries Belges* v. *The High Authority*,[1] namely, that the framing of Decision 2–57 constituted a *détournement de pouvoir* with respect to Articles 3 and 4 of the Treaty, *inter alia*, by not encouraging the regular expansion of production, and also a *détournement* with respect to Article 59 of the Treaty because the High Authority had in fact made an allocation of resources without complying with the procedural requirements for so doing which Article 59 contains, and finally, because Decision 2–57 amounted to a control over enterprises' investment programmes without compliance with Article 54 of the Treaty.

The rights of the High Authority were also substantially the same as those set out in the above-mentioned case.

The plaintiffs further contended that there had been a *détournement de pouvoir* with respect to Article 4(c) of the Treaty in that Decision 2–57 constituted a special charge prohibited by that article.[2] The High Authority pointed out, however, that Article 4(c) referred only to special charges imposed by a State and not to charges imposed by the Treaty.

The plaintiffs next argued that there was a *détournement de pouvoir* with regard to Article 4(b) of the Treaty[3] because Decision 2–57 did not affect all enterprises equally nor all machinery equally, and in particular it treated differently machinery brought into operation before and after January 31, 1958.

The High Authority replied that the decision had been based upon objective criteria, and that it was not necessary in order for it

---

[1] Case 8-57; reported above, p.379.
[2] Article 4 provides:
" The following are recognised to be incompatible with the Common Market for coal and steel and are, therefore, abolished and prohibited within the Community in the manner set out in the present Treaty. . . . (c) subsidies or assistance, or special charges imposed by the State, in any form whatsoever . . . "
[3] Article 4(b) provides:
" . . . (b) measures or practices discriminating among producers, among buyers or among consumers, . . . "

to be valid that all enterprises should be affected in an identical manner.

The plaintiffs further maintained that because Article 53 of the Treaty, under which this decision had been framed, made express reference to Article 65 of the Treaty, the provision in Article 65 that the action to be taken under that article was "not to be more restrictive than is necessary" applied also to action taken under Article 53. They then contended that Decision 2-57, by not granting a reference consumption to new installations brought into service after January 31, 1958, was more restrictive than was necessary.

The High Authority replied that if this contention were correct it would go to prove a violation of the Treaty and not a *détournement de pouvoir*, but that in any event the provisions of Article 65 applied only to trading agreements and not to financial arrangements such as a subsidy system.

Finally, the plaintiffs argued that there had been a *détournement de pouvoir* with respect to Article 3(e) of the Treaty because Decision 2-57 was bound to cause extensive social problems rather than an "improvement of living and working conditions".

The High Authority replied that its action did in fact improve such conditions, because they would have been very adversely affected if a sharp rise in the cost of scrap had been permitted.

The submissions of the Advocate General were that the appeal should be dismissed, and that the costs should be paid by the plaintiffs.

*Held:* (1) *As to admissibility*, that the action was admissible. The plaintiffs had alleged a *prima facie* case of a *détournement de pouvoir* adversely affecting some of the interests which they protected.

(2) *As to the merits*, that the appeal for the annulment of Decision 2-57 must be rejected. The Court repeated its judgment in *Groupment des Hauts Fourneaux et Aciéries Belges* v. *The High Authority*[1] with respect to the three arguments advanced which were in common with those in that case.

The supplementary tax imposed by the High Authority could not amount to a special charge within the meaning of Article 4(c) of the Treaty even if this provision applied to the High Authority, because it was based on objectively established criteria. Similarly, because the decision was based on such criteria it could not be held to create discriminations among enterprises within the meaning of Article 4(b). Further, even if the provisions of Article 65 applied to financial arrangements enacted under Article 53, the present decision was not more restrictive than was necessary, so that the requirements of Article 65 were satisfied. Finally, because the plaintiffs had not developed their allegation that Decision 2-57 did not seek to improve living and working conditions, the Court rejected it.

[1] Case 8-57, reported above, p. 379.

As the High Authority had lost on its challenge of the admissibility of the action, it was condemned in one-fifth of the costs: the plaintiffs bore the other four-fifths.

The Court said:

" A. *On admissibility.*—By the terms of their articles, the plaintiffs are a private association in French law having as their objects the promotion of the general interests of their members, who are producers of iron and steel, and of ensuring their protection. It has not been disputed that the provisions of general decision No. 2–57 here challenged are of a nature to affect certain interests, however divergent they may be, which the plaintiffs protect. They therefore have standing to appear before the Court in conformity with the provisions of Articles 33, 48 and 80 of the Treaty.

" The plaintiffs formally allege one or more *détournements de pouvoir* with respect to their members. They set out in the required manner the reasons which, in their opinion, give rise to the alleged *détournements de pouvoir*. The arguments advanced seek, in effect, to show that in enacting the challenged provisions the High Authority has used the powers which are granted to it by Article 53(b) of the Treaty for purposes other than those for which they were granted. This it is alleged to have done as much by a serious misconstruction of certain of the objects set out in Article 3 as by the manifest desire to attain the objects specifically regulated by Articles 54 and 59 in order to avoid the special procedures provided in those articles.

" The plaintiffs' appeal is therefore admissible.

" B. *Concerning the merits.*—[The Court here repeated virtually word for word that part of its judgment in *Groupement des Hauts Fourneaux et Aciéries Belges* v. *The High Authority* (Case 8–57, reported above, p. 379), where it had analysed the provisions of Article 3 of the Treaty and had discussed whether the High Authority in issuing Decision 2–57 had committed a *détournement de pouvoir* with regard to Articles 3 and 4 of the Treaty; and where it had considered whether the financial arrangements had been passed under Article 53(b) so as to avoid observance of the provisions of Article 59, and where the Court had considered whether the High Authority had committed a *détournement de pouvoir* by seeking to prohibit certain new installations or to favour certain investments without observing the requirements of Article 54. The Court also repeated what it had stated in *Chambre Syndicale de la Sidérurgie Française* v. *The High Authority* (Case 9–57, reported below, p. 490), concerning the meaning in Article 3 of the phrase ' in the common interest '. The Court then continued:—]

" 4. On the claim of the existence of a *détournement de pouvoir* with regard to Article 4(c) of the Treaty, a consideration is whether the High Authority has imposed upon certain enterprises a special charge prohibited by that article.

" The plaintiffs allege a breach of the provisions of sub-paragraph (c) of Article 4 of the Treaty which prohibit subsidies or State assistance or special charges imposed by the State in any form whatsoever.

" There is no occasion to consider in the present action the question whether the High Authority is equally forbidden to impose special charges. However, in any event, there cannot be a special charge within the meaning of the article when the High Authority, in setting up a financial arrangement of the type provided for by Article 53(b), imposes upon certain enterprises contributions which are greater than those upon others, when this unequal imposition of charges is based upon criteria objectively established and justified by the aims which that arrangement legally pursues.

" The ground of appeal based upon a *détournement de pouvoir* with regard to Article 4(c) of the Treaty must, therefore, be rejected.

" 5. Upon the claim of the existence of a *détournement de pouvoir* with regard to Article 4(b) of the Treaty, a consideration is whether the High Authority has set up a régime which is unequal to enterprises from the fact that the remissions are not equally obtainable by all of them or in respect of all types of machinery.

" It has been established that the provisions being challenged are based upon criteria that have been objectively adapted to the pursuit of the legitimate aim of the High Authority's action. One cannot, therefore, regard as illegal such a system and say that it tends to interfere with the interplay of competition by placing certain enterprises at a disadvantage in respect to others.

" In consequence, the ground concerning the creation of a system which is unequal to certain enterprises must be rejected.

" 6. Upon the claim of the existence of a *détournement de pouvoir* with regard to Article 65 of the Treaty, a consideration is whether the High Authority, by creating a quasi-prohibitive system for machinery and manufacturing processes brought into service after January 31, 1958, has taken measures having a more restrictive character than their objective required.

" It has already been established that the economic circumstances existing at the time of the High Authority's intervention in the scrap market justified the taking of the steps which have been challenged concerning the financial charge to the subsidy fund and that, in particular, these steps could lawfully comprise the bringing into existence of a progressive tax and the imposition of the financial charge varying not only with the tonnages consumed but with the periods of consumption and with the nature of the machinery.

" These steps are thus not more restrictive than the object of the financial arrangements required, so that even if Article 65, para. 2(b), were applicable to them, the condition which it imposes would have been satisfied.

" The contention based upon the misconstruction of Article 65 is, thus, without foundation.

" 7. Upon the claim of the existence of a *détournement de pouvoir* with regard to Article 3(*e*) of the Treaty, a consideration is whether the challenged provisions have the effect of creating social problems as grave and acute as they are widespread, and which by being unexpected cannot be avoided by the application of these provisions.

" The plaintiffs in the course of the proceedings did not develop this allegation and they have not advanced any relevant evidence in its support.

" Hence the ground based upon the *détournement de pouvoir* with regard to Article 3(*e*) of the Treaty must be rejected.

" *Costs.*—By the terms of Article 60 of the Rules of the Court, any party which loses is condemned in costs. In the present action the plaintiffs have lost on the merits and the defendants upon the admissibility. It is necessary, therefore, in accordance with paragraph 2 of that article, to condemn the plaintiffs in four-fifths of the costs of the action and the defendants in one-fifth.

" The Court, rejecting all further submissions in favour or to the contrary, adjudges and declares:

" The action is admissible but not well founded. In consequence, the appeal for the annulment of the provisions contained in articles 3.1(*b*), 4.3, 5, 6, 8 and 9 of Decision 2/57 of the High Authority of January 26, 1957, is rejected.

" The plaintiffs are condemned in four-fifths of the costs of the action and the defendants in one-fifth."

[Report: *Recueil de la Jurisprudence de la Cour*, IV (1958), p. 473 (in French).]

International organization—European Coal and Steel Community
—Interpretation of Treaty establishing—Articles setting out
fundamental aims of Treaty to be read as a whole—Power of
international organization to give predominance to certain of
these aims—Interpretation of fundamental aims in light of subsequent provision of Treaty—Effect of failure to comply with fundamental aims—Whether a *détournement de pouvoir*—Article 65—
Whether acts of High Authority more restrictive than necessary
for their purpose—Application of Article 65 to financial arrangements—Whether general decision can be challenged on ground of
violation of Treaty.

WIRTSCHAFTSVEREINIGUNG EISEN- UND STAHLINDUSTRIE AND
OTHERS *v.* THE HIGH AUTHORITY.

*Court of Justice of the European Coal and Steel Community.*

(Pilotti, President; Van Kleffens, Delvaux, Serrarens, Riese, Rueff,
Hammes JJ.)

*June 21, 1958.*

THE FACTS.—A Note on the background to this and other cases
in which enterprises and associations challenged the validity of
Decision 2–57 of the High Authority appears above, at p. 453.

There were five plaintiffs in the present action:—

1. Wirtschaftsvereinigung Eisen- und Stahlindustrie—a syndicate open to all iron and steel enterprises carrying on business
within Western Germany. Its aims were to protect the collective
interests of its members, and its registered office was in Düsseldorf.

2. Gussstahlwerk Carl Bonnhoff—a steel works with its registered
office at Wetter in the Ruhr. This plaintiff did not itself produce any
supplies of pig-iron, so that it could not benefit from the provision of
Decision 2-57 which granted a rebate for any increased use of pig-
iron. Further, this plaintiff intended to instal electric furnaces
during 1958 and under the terms of this decision these furnaces
would not possess any reference consumption.[1] As a result of both
these factors, the plaintiffs calculated that on every metric ton of
ingots produced it would be paying about 43.40 marks[2] tax to the
subsidy fund.

3. Gussstahlwerk Witten—an enterprise with its registered office
in Witten, producing special steels in Martin and electric furnaces.
Because technical reasons prevented any reduction being made in
the amount of scrap used in producing these special steels, this
plaintiff also found itself hard hit by the increased tax on scrap.

4. Ruhrstahl. This plaintiff had its registered office at Hattingen,
and was installing electric furnaces which would not be in service
before January 31, 1958, so that they also would not qualify for a

---

[1] For an explanation of "reference consumption" see the Note at p. 453 above.
[2] Just under £4, or about $11.

reference consumption. As a result, every metric ton produced in these furnaces would by Decision 2–57 carry a supplementary tax of about 13.85 E.P.Us.[1]

5. Eisenwerk Annahütte Alfred Zeller, with registered office in Hammerau. This plaintiff had recently installed two Martin furnaces which, owing to the date of their installation, possessed a very low reference consumption. It was calculated that for every metric ton of steel produced 842 kg. of scrap was required. With the new supplementary tax, the tax on this scrap would amount to 35.40 marks,[2] or 9.8 per cent. of the selling price.

If Decision 2–57 was a general decision, these plaintiffs would be able to challenge it only on the ground of a *détournement de pouvoir* with respect to themselves.[3] They alleged, however, that it amounted to a series of individual decisions so that they were entitled to challenge it on all of the four grounds set out in Article 33.

The plaintiffs alleged that Decision 2–57, although framed in general terms, in fact constituted a series of individual decisions: (i) because certain enterprises were carefully particularized, such as those referred to in Article 6, who brought new installations into service between February 1, 1957, and January 31, 1958; (ii) because the provisions concerning the supplementary tax were penal; and (iii) because, by Article 13, the *Caisse* and the *Office* were specifically referred to by name and were required to alter their statutes.

The High Authority replied that the decision laid down a general principle and specified the legal consequences which it entailed. The High Authority then referred to the Court's ruling on the nature of a general decision in *Fédération Charbonnière de Belgique* v. *The High Authority*.[4]

The High Authority also challenged the admissibility of the present joint action because, it alleged, the plaintiffs were each affected differently by the decision in question. There was, therefore, no common basis for a joint action.

The plaintiffs replied that if their five actions could not properly be brought together this would not affect admissibility, but would only require the actions to be separated. Further, they declared that a claim of *détournement de pouvoir* places in issue the aims behind the administrative act, and is thus independent of the personality of the plaintiffs.

Next, the High Authority argued that an appeal could be brought by an association on the ground of *détournement de pouvoir* only if the alleged *détournement* affected all of the enterprises which it represented. In the case of the first plaintiff, the interests of its

---

[1] About £5, or $13.85.
[2] Just over £3, or about $8.5.
[3] See Article 33, para. 2, for the text of which see above, p. 445, n. 1.
[4] Case 8–55, reported above, p. 417.

constituent enterprises diverged and thus no appeal could be brought by it because its members as a whole were not affected.

The plaintiffs replied that this argument sought to impose a limitation upon the right of appeal of associations which was not to be found either in the Treaty or in any Court decision. Further, even if the High Authority were correct, all the constituent enterprises of the first plaintiff had a common interest that the High Authority should not act illegally and that the guarantees contained in the Treaty should not be set aside.

The plaintiffs then advanced three arguments which were substantially the same as those advanced by the plaintiffs in *Groupement des Hauts Fourneaux et Aciéries Belges* v. *The High Authority*[1], namely, that the passing of Decision 2–57 constituted a *détournement de pouvoir* with respect to Articles 3 and 4 of the Treaty; that the aims actually being pursued differed from those stated in the preamble to the decision; and thirdly, that the decision had been issued so as to avoid observance of the provisions of Article 59.

Finally, the plaintiffs claimed that because Article 53 of the Treaty, under which this decision has been issued, made express reference to Article 65 of the Treaty, the provision in Article 65 that the action to be taken under that article was "not to be more restrictive than is necessary"[2] applied also to action taken under Article 53. They then contended that Decision 2–57, by not granting a reference consumption to new installations brought into service after January 31, 1958, was more restrictive than was necessary.

The High Authority replied that if this contention were correct it would go to prove a violation of the Treaty and not a *détournement de pouvoir*, but in any event the provisions of Article 65 applied only to trading agreements and not to financial arrangements such as a subsidy system.

The submissions of the Advocate General were that effect should be given to the withdrawal of Ruhrstahl (Hattingen); that the appeals should be dismissed; and that each of the plaintiffs should pay its share of the costs.

*Held*: (1) *As to admissibility*, that the action was admissible. Decision 2–57 was a general decision because it established a normative principle and imposed in a general fashion the condition for its application and specified the legal consequences which it would bring about. The first plaintiff had standing to appear before the Court because some of the interests which it protected, however divergent they might be, were adversely affected by the decision.

---

[1] Case 8-57, reported above, p. 379.

[2] Article 65 (2) provides: " . . . The High Authority shall authorize agreements to specialize in the production of, or be engaged in the joint buying or selling of, specified products, if the High Authority finds: . . . (b) that the agreement in question is essential to achieve these results [substantial improvement in production or distribution] and is not more restrictive than is necessary for that purpose . . . "

(2) *As to the merits*, that the appeal for the annulment of Decision 2–57 must be rejected. The Court repeated its judgment in *Groupement des Hauts Fourneaux et Aciéries Belges* v. *The High Authority*[1] with respect to the three arguments advanced which were in common with those in that case. It then held that, even if the provision of Article 65 applied to financial arrangements enacted under Article 53, the present decision was not more restrictive than was necessary, so that the requirements of Article 65 were satisfied.

As the High Authority had lost in part on its challenge of the admissibility of the action, it was condemned in one-tenth of the costs, the plaintiffs bearing the remaining nine-tenths.

The Court said:

" A. *On admissibility.*—By the terms of their articles plaintiffs No. 1 (Wirtschaftsvereinigung Eisen- und Stahlindustrie) are a private association in German law having as their objects the promotion of the general interests of their members, who are producers of iron and steel, and of ensuring their protection. It is not disputed that the provisions of the general decision No. 2–57 here challenged, are of a nature to affect certain interests, however divergent they may be, which the plaintiffs protect. They therefore have standing to appear before the Court in conformity with the provisions of Articles 33, 48 and 80 of the Treaty.

" Plaintiffs No. 2, 3, 4 and 5, by the terms of their articles, are private companies in German law. They have for their object the carrying on of a productive activity in the field of steel within the territories mentioned in Article 79, first paragraph, of the Treaty. They therefore have standing within the meaning of the provisions of Articles 33 and 80 of the Treaty to appear before the Court to challenge the decisions and recommendations of the High Authority.

" By virtue of the provisions of Article 33, paragraph 2, of the Treaty, the enterprises mentioned in Article 80 are permitted to bring an appeal for the annulment of general decisions of the High Authority which they believe to be vitiated by a *détournement de pouvoir* with respect to them.

" Plaintiffs No. 2, 3, 4 and 5 allege that they are adversely affected by the provisions challenged by reason of the very great difficulty which they are experiencing in making economies in scrap and consequently by reason of the necessity which is imposed upon them of paying the supplementary contribution if they increase their consumption of purchased scrap.

" Decision No. 2–57 affects all the enterprises specified in Article 80 of the Treaty to the extent to which they use scrap, and not only those which exist at present but also those which will come into existence during the time that the decision is in force. This is a general decision; it establishes a normative principle, it imposes in

[1] Case 8-57, reported above, p. 379.

a general fashion the conditions for its application and it specifies the legal consequences which it will bring about. The allegation of plaintiffs No. 2, 3, 4 and 5 that this general decision constitutes also an individual decision or collection of individual decisions with respect to them cannot be accepted.

" Plaintiffs No. 1 formally allege one or more *détournements de pouvoir* with respect to their members. Plaintiffs No. 2, 3, 4 and 5 formally allege one or more *détournements de pouvoir* with respect to them, and all the plaintiffs set out in the required manner the reasons which, in their opinion, give rise to the alleged *détournements de pouvoir*. The arguments advanced seek, in effect, to show that in enacting the challenged provisions the High Authority has used the powers which are granted to it by Article 53(*b*) of the Treaty for purposes other than those for which they were granted. This it is alleged to have done as much by serious miscontruction of certain of the objects set out in Article 3 as by the manifest desire to attain the objects specifically regulated by Articles 54 and 59 in order to avoid the special procedures provided for in those articles.

" By the terms of Article 33, paragraph 2, of the Treaty, enterprises or associations mentioned in Article 48 can bring an appeal against general decisions only if they believe them to be vitiated by a *détournement de pouvoir* with respect to them. In this action, the grounds based upon violation of the Treaty cannot be accepted.

" If one rejects the allegation made by certain of the plaintiffs concerning the individual character with respect to them of the decision which has been taken, the plaintiffs all challenge this decision upon the same grounds and advance the same arguments. The bringing of appeals in the form of a joint action is valid in the present action.

" The plaintiffs' appeal is admissible but only to the extent that they allege the ground of *détournement de pouvoir* either with respect to themselves or with respect to their members.

" B. *Concerning the merits.*—[The Court here repeated virtually word for word that part of the judgment in *Groupement des Hauts Fourneaux et Aciéries Belges* v. *The High Authority* (Case 8–57, reported above, p. 379), where it had analysed the provisions of Article 3 of the Treaty and had discussed whether the High Authority in passing Decision 2–57 had committed a *détournement de pouvoir* with respect to Articles 3 and 4 of the Treaty; and whether a *détournement de pouvoir* existed because it was alleged that the aims stated in Decision 2–57 differed from those actually being pursued and it had considered whether the financial arrangement had been passed under Article 53(*b*) so as to avoid observing the provisions of Article 59. The Court then continued:]

" 4. Upon the claim of the existence of a *détournement de pouvoir* with regard to Article 65 of the Treaty, a consideration is whether the High Authority, by refusing to grant a reference consumption for machinery and manufacturing processes brought into service after January 31, 1958, and by subjecting any excess consumption to a supplementary tax, has taken measures having a more restrictive character than the fulfilment of their object required.

" It has already been established that the economic circumstances existing at the time of the High Authority's intervention in the scrap market justified the taking of the steps which have been challenged concerning the financial charge to the subsidy fund and that, in particular, these steps could legally comprise the bringing into existence of a progressive tax and the imposition of the financial charge varying not only with the tonnages consumed but with the periods of consumption and with the nature of the machinery. These steps are thus not more restrictive than the object of the financial arrangements required, so that even if Article 65, paragraph 2(b), were applicable to them, the condition which it imposes would have been satisfied.

" The contention based upon the misconstruction of Article 65 is without foundation.

" 5. Upon the ground of violation of Articles 2, 3, 4, 5, 53, 54, 58, 59 and Annex 11 and of Article 65 of the Treaty:

" Decision No. 2–57, being a general decision, cannot be challenged except by alleging the ground of *détournement de pouvoir*.

" The grounds alleging violation of the Treaty must be rejected.

" 6. Upon the withdrawal of the plaintiffs Ruhrstahl, of Hattingen:

" Plaintiffs No. 4, Ruhrstahl, of Hattingen, withdrew at the public hearing of February 20, 1958.

" The present action being an appeal for annulment, the consent of the defendants to this withdrawal is therefore not required.

" *Costs.*—By the terms of Article 60 of the Rules of the Court, any party which loses is condemned in costs. In the present action the plaintiffs have lost on the merits and the defendants in part upon the admissibility. It is necessary, therefore, in accordance with paragraph 2[2] of that article, to condemn the plaintiffs in nine-tenths of the costs of the action and the defendants in one-tenth.

" As regards plaintiff No. 4, Ruhrstahl, of Hattingen, which was withdrawn, it must bear together with the other plaintiffs that part of the costs arising out of its intervention. This part is determined as half that of each of the four other plaintiffs.

" The Court, rejecting all further submissions in favour or to the contrary, adjudges and declares:

" The action is admissible but not well founded. In consequence, the appeal for the annulment of the provisions contained in Article

[1 Article 60, para. 2, of the old Rules provided: " The Court may apportion costs wholly or in part if the parties each fail on one or more heads of claim." This provision is now contained in Article 69, para. 3, of the Rules.]

3.1(*b*), 4, 5, 6, 7, 8, 9, 11.1(*f*) and (*g*), 16.1, and 17 of Decision No. 2–57 of the High Authority of January 26, 1957, is rejected.

" The plaintiffs are jointly condemned in nine-tenths of the costs of the action and the defendants in one-tenth.

" The plaintiffs Ruhrstahl withdrew. They will pay the costs jointly with the four other plaintiffs to the extent of one half of the amount of one of them."

[Report: *Recueil de la Jurisprudence de la Cour*, IV (1958), p. 263 (in French).]

**International organization—European Coal and Steel Community —Interpretation of Treaty establishing—Articles setting out fundamental aims of Treaty to be read as a whole—Power of international organization to give predominance to certain of these aims— Interpretation of fundamental aims in light of subseuqent provision of Treaty—Effect of failure to comply with fundamental aims— Whether a *détournement de pouvoir*—Dominant purpose of Treaty —Meaning of concept of " common interest " in Article 3.**

CHAMBRE SYNDICALE DE LA SIDÉRURGIE FRANÇAISE *v*. THE HIGH AUTHORITY.

*Court of Justice of the European Coal and Steel Community.*

(Pilotti, President; Van Kleffens, Delvaux, Serrarens, Riese, Rueff, Hammes JJ.)

*June 26, 1958.*

THE FACTS.—A Note on the background to this and other cases, in which various enterprises and associations challenged the validity of Decision 2–57 of the High Authority, appears above, at p. 453.

The plaintiffs in the present case were a syndicate of French iron and steel producers with their registered office in Paris. Several of these producers found themselves adversely affected by the financial arrangements set up by Decision 2–57, and particularly by the supplementary tax on increased consumption of scrap. The syndicate therefore brought this action on behalf of its members.

As, however, Decision 2–57 was a general decision, the plaintiffs were able to challenge it only on the ground of a *détournement de pouvoir* with respect to themselves.[1]

The High Authority challenged the standing of the plaintiffs to bring the present action because, it alleged, they could do so only if all their members were affected by the decision in question. The plaintiffs replied that Decision 2–57 affected all their members, although it affected some members more severely than others.

On the merits, the plaintiffs advanced three arguments, which were substantially the same as those advanced by the plaintiffs in *Groupement des Hauts Fourneaux et Aciéries Belges* v. *The High*

---

[1] See Article 33, para. 2, of the Treaty, reproduced above, p. 445, n. 1.

*Authority*,[1] namely, that the passing of Decision 2–57 constituted a *détournement de pouvoir* with respect to Articles 3 and 4 of the Treaty, *inter alia*, by not encouraging the regular expansion of production, and also a *détournement* with respect to Article 59 of the Treaty, because the High Authority had in fact made an allocation of resources without complying with the production requirements for so doing which Article 59 contains, and finally, because Decision 2–57 amounted to control over enterprises' investment programmes without compliance with Article 54 of the Treaty.

The replies of the High Authority were also substantially the same as those set out in the above-mentioned case.

The submissions of the Advocate General were that the appeal should be dismissed, and that the costs should be paid by the plaintiffs.

*Held:* (1) *As to admissibility*, that the action was admissible. The plaintiffs did possess standing to appeal to the Court regardless of how diverse the interests of their constituent member enterprises might be, provided that some of their interests had been adversely affected by the decision.

(2) *As to the merits*, that the appeal for annulment of Decision 2–57 must be rejected.

The Court repeated its judgment in *Groupement des Hauts Fourneaux et Aciéries Belges* v. *The High Authority* with respect to the three arguments advanced which were in common with those in that case.

The Court said:

" A. *On admissibility.*—By the terms of their articles, the plaintiffs are a private association in French law having as their objects the promotion of the general interests of their members, who are producers of iron or steel, and of ensuring their protection. It is not disputed that the provisions of general Decision No. 2–57 here challenged are of a nature to affect certain interests, however divergent they may be, which are the concern of the plaintiffs. They therefore have standing to appear before the Court in conformity with the provisions of Articles 33, 48 and 80 of the Treaty.

" The plaintiffs formally allege one or more *détournements de pouvoir* with respect to their members. They set out in the required manner the reasons which, in their opinion, give rise to the alleged *détournements de pouvoir*. In affect, the arguments advanced seek to show that in enacting the challenged provisions the High Authority has used the powers which are granted to it by Article 53(*b*) of the Treaty for purposes other than those for which they have been granted, as much by the serious misconstruction of certain of the objects set out in Article 3 as by the manifest desire to attain the

[1] Case 8-57, reported above, at p. 379.

objectives specifically regulated by Articles 54 and 59 in order to avoid the special procedures provided for in those articles.

" It follows, therefore, that the plaintiffs' appeal is admissible.

" B. *Concerning the merits.*—[The Court here repeated virtually word for word that part of its judgment in *Groupement des Hauts Fourneaux et Aciéries Belges* v. *The High Authority* (Case 8–57, reported above, p. 379), where it had analysed the provisions of Article 3 of the Treaty and had discussed whether the High Authority in issuing Decision 2–57 had committed a *détournement de pouvoir* with respect to Articles 3 and 4 of the Treaty. In the course of its judgment the Court added:]

" By the terms of Article 3, first paragraph, of the Treaty, the institutions of the Community in the execution of the missions defined in that Article are required to act in the common interest. Far from being limited to the sum total of the particular interests of the coal and steel interests which are placed under the jurisdiction of the Community, the concept of common interest referred to in that article greatly exceeds the extent of these interests, and is defined by reference to the general aims clearly specified in Article 2.

" The safeguarding of the common interest does not prevent, if the situation so requires, action combining the pursuit of the diverse objects set out in Article 3 of the Treaty and comprising all those measures with selective and graduated effects which are compatible with the principle of equality and which are necessary for the execution of the missions prescribed by that article. In consequence, a mode of indirect action upon production cannot be regarded as incompatible with the safeguarding of the common interest on the ground that it comprises means involving non-uniform treatment.

[The Court then repeated what it had stated in the above-mentioned case concerning whether the financial arrangement set up by Decision 2–57 had been passed under Article 53(*b*) so as to avoid observance of the provisions of Article 59, and concerning whether the High Authority had committed a *détournement de pouvoir* by seeking to prohibit certain new installations or to favour certain investments without observing the requirements of Article 54. The Court then continued:]

" *On costs.*—By the terms of Article 60 of the Rules of the Court, any party which loses is condemned in costs. In the present action the plaintiffs have lost on the merits and the defendants upon the admissibility. It is necessary, therefore, in accordance with paragraph 2 of that article,[1] to condemn the plaintiffs in four-fifths of the costs of the action and the defendants in one-fifth.

[1 Article 60, paras. 1 and 2, of the old Rules of the Court are now contained in Article 69, paras. 2 and 3, of the Rules.]

" The Court, rejecting all further submissions in favour or to the contrary, adjudges and declares:

" The action is admissible but not well founded. In consequence, the appeal for the annulment of the provisions contained in Articles 3.1(b), 4.3, 5, 6, 7, 8 and 9 of Decision No. 2–57 of the High Authority of January 26, 1957, is rejected.

" The plaintiffs are condemned in four-fifths of the costs of the action and the defendants in one-fifth."

[Report: *Recueil de la Jurisprudence de la Cour*, IV (1958), p. 365 (in French).]

**International organization—In general—Powers—Use of—*Détournement de pouvoir*—Relevance of unjustified motives—Importance of " essential aim ".**

See p. 388 (*French Government* v. *The High Authority*).

**International organization—European Coal and Steel Community—Compensation payments to Belgian mines—Whether threat to reduce or withdraw compensation amounts to discrimination forbidden by Treaty.**

See p. 425 (*Fédération Charbonnière de Belgique* v. *The High Authority* (*Final Judgment*)).

**International organization—European Coal and Steel Community—Compensation payments to Belgian mines—Whether threat to reduce or withdraw compensation amounts to discrimination forbidden by Treaty—Discretion of High Authority to determine compensation for different types of coal.**

See p. 441 (*Société des Charbonnages de Beeringen and Others* v. *The High Authority*).

**International organization—European Coal and Steel Community—Decisions of High Authority—Appeals against—Admissibility of—Allegation of *détournement de pouvoir*—Relevance to admissibility—Periods of limitation—Decision amending earlier decision—Whether time runs again from second decision.**

See p. 445 (*Compagnie des Hauts Fourneaux de Chasse* v. *The High Authority* (*No.* 1)).

**International organization—European Coal and Steel Community —High Authority—General decisions of—Period within which decision can be annulled—Right to challenge validity of general decision when challenging individual decision made in application thereof.**

See p. 457 (*Compagnie des Hauts Fourneaux de Chasse* v. *The High Authority* (*No.* 2)).

# PART X

# DISPUTES

## A—ARBITRATION

### I.—In General

#### i.—Conception and Function of Arbitration

**Arbitration—In general—Conception and function of arbitration —Appeal to Arbitral Commission from decision of municipal court—Selection of applicable law—Arbitral Commission on Property, Rights and Interests in Germany—Competence to fix royalties for exploitation of patent and other terms.**

PURFÜRST *v.* ETABLISSEMENTS VITOUX

(MERITS).

*Arbitral Commission on Property, Rights and Interests in Germany, Second Chamber.*

(Sauser-Hall, Vice-President; Schwandt, Marion.)

*March* 29, 1958.

THE FACTS (as stated by the Commission).—" By decision of February 14, 1958,[1] the Arbitral Commission has declared admissible the application dated August 16, 1955, filed on August 19, 1955, at *Rathaus* Herford (Westphalia) by the complainant Purfürst against the decision of the Grand Senate of the German Patent Office of February 21, 1955, and served on April 19, 1955, by which the terms of a non-exclusive licence under patent 537 631 owned by the firm S. A..Établissements Vitoux and exploited by the defendant were fixed.

" At the hearing of February 14, 1958, the two parties approved of the judgment of admissibility, thus dispensing with their right to appeal under Article 66 of the Rules of Procedure of the Commission so that it became possible to open the oral hearing immediately.

" From the pleadings exchanged between the parties and the oral arguments presented by them before the Commission, the following facts appear to be underlying the case:

" The firm S. A. Établissements Vitoux, a company established under French law, is the owner of the German patent 537 631 concerning a ' Device for the Repair of Ladders in Woven Articles and Hosiery ' and of the additional patent 652 269 concerning the same object. The duration of the main patent commenced on October 31, 1928, and ended on October 30, 1946. [The period of validity of

---

[1 Reported below, p. 530 (*sub nom. Purfürst* v. *Établissements Vitoux* (*Admissibility of Appeal*)).]

the main patent was subsequently extended until November 26, 1956.] The patent covers a compressor and a needleholder guide which, for the first time, permitted the use of compressed air as propelling force for the needle so that the compressed air operates directly on the part bearing the needle in the interior of the needleholder guide.

" In view of the events during the Second World War, the Patent Administrative Department, by Order of February 12, 1951, has restored to the owner of the main patent 537 631 its former rights and has extended the period of validity of the latter pursuant to Article 5 of Allied High Commission Law No. 8 concerning Industrial, Literary and Artistic Property Rights of Foreign Nations and Nationals (as amended by Laws Nos. 30, 39, 41 and 66) with the effect that the twelfth year of duration of the patent commenced on November 29, 1949. The patent in question was thus protected in Germany until November 28, 1956, the normal duration of patents under German law being 18 years. The additional patent 652 269 of the firm [of] Vitoux is of no immediate relevance for the present case since no licence for this patent has been applied for.

" The complainant, a resident of the Federal Republic of Germany, is the owner of a German patent 758 173 concerning a ' Support for a Device for the Repair of Ladders ' for which a period of protection of 18 years was granted on March 16, 1941. This so-called *Kraucher Patent* also concerns an apparatus operated by compressed air in which, however, the needleholder has been arranged differently, the advantage being that no oil can flow from the needle. The complainant started to manufacture and sell these machines for the repair of ladders prior to September 30, 1949, and has continued to do so without interruption.

" The firm [of] Vitoux has brought an action against the complainant Purfürst for infringement of patent which was dismissed in the first instance by the *Landgericht*, Dusseldorf, by its decision of December 12, 1951, subsequently by the *Oberlandesgericht*, Düsseldorf, by decision of December 29, 1952, and in the last instance by decision of the *Bundesgerichtshof* of October 6, 1953, on the ground that the complainant Purfürst had acted in good faith in manufacturing and selling the object of the patent and that he was entitled to an interim use of the patent by virtue of Article 7 of Allied High Commission Law No. 8. The complainant Purfürst, on his part, brought an action for nullity against the firm [of] Vitoux concerning patent 537 631, which was also dismissed in the last instance by the *Bundesgerichtshof*, by its decision of January 7, 1955. All these decisions are final and definite. It has been established therein that patent 758 173, being the cinematic inversion of the construction of the needleholder designed by the firm [of] Vitoux, undoubtedly comes within the scope of protection of patent 537 631 and that it is dependent on the latter. It has, therefore, been recognized in the decision that the complainant is permitted under Allied High Commission Law No. 8, without liability for infringement, to continue to exploit patent 537 631 by virtue of a non-exclusive licence but on terms to be mutually agreed between the patent holder restored to its patent rights and the holder of a non-exclusive licence. In the absence of an agreement, the above Law provides that each party may request the Grand Senate of the Patent Office to fix such terms.

"Upon complainant's application, the Grand Senate fixed the terms of the licence granted to him by decision of February 21, 1955. The complainant Purfürst lodged an appeal against this decision with the Arbitral Commission asserting that, in fact, he only exploits his own patent 758 173, the so-called *Kraucher Patent*, and that patent 537 631 should not have been restored for two reasons: (1) because the actual invention of the defendant forms only the subject matter of the additional patent 652 269 since the main patent 537 631 covered merely technical processes known in the art, and (2) because the firm [of] Vitoux which was able to exploit its patent in Germany during the war had not suffered any damage to justify the restoration of its patent since it had not been subject to any war-time discriminatory measures in Germany. While the complainant does not intend to oppose an extension of patent 537 631, he is of the opinion, however, that these facts have to be taken into consideration when the terms of the non-exclusive licence to which he is entitled are fixed, particularly with a view to the royalties which might be imposed on him.

"In this connection, the complainant states that he only used his own patent 758 173 for manufacturing his machine for the repair of ladders which, although also operated by compressed air as in the case of patent 537 631, was not simply a cinematic inversion of the process covered by the latter since the true innovation of the process invented by the firm Vitoux formed the subject-matter of the additional patent 652 269 of which the complainant makes no use. From this he concludes that even if it was admitted that he had impaired patent 537 631, the progress achieved by the invention protected by this patent was so slight that non-imposition of royalties was justified in the case of a non-exclusive licence. Finally he mentions the fact that in non-exclusive licence agreements concluded during the war the defendant had demanded of the licensees royalties to the amount of only 1.— or 1.50 Deutsche Mark per machine, *i.e.*, for the exploitation of patent 537 631 including additional patent 652 269 (which is said to cover the actual invention) so that the defendant could only demand an even smaller amount for a non-exclusive licence granted pursuant to Article 7 of Allied High Commission Law No. 8 since such licence was based on a right to interim use acquired in good faith."

The complainant moved (1) that the Commission set aside the decision of the Grand Senate of the German Patent Office of February 21, 1955, and declare that the complainant be exempted from paying royalties; or (2) alternatively, that the Commission stipulate royalties at an appropriate amount; and (3) as a precautionary measure, the Arbitral Commission refer the case to the Commission in plenary session, pursuant to Rule 21 (*b*) of its Rules of Procedure.

On the other hand, the defendant Company submitted to the Commission several new motions as to royalties to be paid by the complainant.

*Held:* that the appeal must be rejected, and the defendant's motions allowed in the manner indicated below.

The Commission said: " It is beyond any doubt that the Convention on the Settlement of Matters Arising out of the War and the Occupation of October 23, 1954, did not abrogate or modify the material provisions of Law No. 8. This is clearly shown by Article 8 (1) of Chapter Ten of the Settlement Convention, which stipulates:

' (1) Allied High Commission Law No. 8 on Industrial, Literary and Artistic Property Rights of Foreign Nations and Nationals, as amended by Allied High Commission Laws Nos. 30, 39, 41 and 66 together with the First and Second Implementing Ordinances under Allied High Commission Law No. 8 of May, 1950, and November 9, 1950 . . . shall be maintained in force.'

" The Settlement Convention has modified Law No. 8 only with regard to the bodies competent to decide on disputes arising out of its application, as provided in Article 8 (2 [*a*] and [*b*]) of Chapter Ten, which stipulates:

' (*a*) An appeal may be taken to the Arbitral Commission on Property, Rights and Interests in Germany referred to in Article 12 of this Chapter from any decision of last instance of the Patent Office or of its Grand Senate or from any decision in the first instance of the regular courts, in accordance with the provisions of Article 12 of this Chapter and the Charter of the Arbitral Commission.

' (*b*) The powers of the Occupation Authorities under the last sentence of Article 2 and paragraph 3 of Article 7 of Law No. 8 shall lapse.'

" From the provisions quoted above it is obvious that the Arbitral Commission shall not decide whether patent 537 631 has been infringed by the complainant, whether it is void, whether patent 758 173 owned by the complainant is dependent on the patent of the firm [of] Vitoux, whether an extension of patent 537 631 is justified or not, and whether the right to the patent was acquired *bona fide* or whether a patent the duration of which has been extended by virtue of Law No. 8 has been used *bona fide*. All these questions were dealt with in the final decisions and judgments of the competent German authorities or ordinary courts, and the Commission is bound by these decisions and judgments. In the present case it is competent only to decide on the amount of royalties to be paid by the complainant and on the terms under which he shall meet his obligations.

" The complainant recognizes the correctness of this view but asserts that these different points should be re-examined by the Arbitral Commission in connection with the obligations which may be imposed on him. However, the Arbitral Commission cannot enter into considerations of that kind but has to accept as established the factual observations and legal appreciations made in the judgments and decisions mentioned above. Moreover, the Arbitral Commission shall estop the complainant and shall contest the complainant's right to infer any arguments in his favour from the fact that his patent 758 173, covering a machine for the repair of stockings operated by compressed air, did not interfere with patent 537 631, since he has made diametrically opposed observations on this subject in the course of the action for infringement brought against him by the firm [of] Vitoux, and since he escaped an unfavourable decision only by assuming that he was entitled to interim exploitation of patent 537 631, by virtue of Article 7 of Law No. 8, as finally confirmed by the *Bundesgerichtshof* in its decision of October 6, 1953, page 5, section 3, by establishing that the complainant had met the prerequisites for the right of use. One cannot hold two differing views at the same time.

" It must be emphasized that the defendant firm has moved before the German courts that it should be allowed royalties of 50.— Deutsche Mark per complete machine sold which corresponds to about 8½ per cent. of the price of their machine ' Vitos Desmo ' (patents 537 631 and 652 269) which it sells at 592.50 Deutsche Mark. In its contested decision the Grand Senate reduced the royalties by more than half and fixed them at 4 per cent. of the net sales price. The Arbitral Commission concludes, therefore, that the Grand Senate has taken into consideration to a certain extent the arguments presented by the complainant Purfürst in order to arrive at a reduction of the royalties, but the Senate was unable to comply with the complainant's request to exempt him entirely from payment of royalties because, in the exploitation of his patent 758 173, he uses a needleholder which does not run within the guide and was thus a new invention. This opinion has already been finally refuted by the decisions of the *Bundesgerichtshof* in which it has been established that this alleged invention is a simple cinematic inversion of the principle governing the construction of the needleholder protected by patent 537 631 of the firm Vitoux and that, for this reason, it encroaches on the scope of protection of the latter because it also combines its two characteristics.

" Moreover, the Arbitral Commission is of the opinion that the perfection of an idea which provides a new solution to a technical problem depends under Patent Law on the original idea. It cannot admit, therefore, that a difference should be made in patent 537 631 between the use of compressed air as propelling force, on the one hand—a method of application known prior to the existence of this patent—and the immediate operation of the compressed air on the part bearing the needle in the interior of the needleholder guide, on the other, in order to conclude that the royalties should be computed only according to the value of the latter part of the machine and not of the compressor. This particular point might be taken into consideration, if at all, for reasons of equity accepted by the Grand Senate, in order that the royalties applied for by the patent holder at the commencement of the proceedings be reduced.

"The Arbitral Commission further holds that in answering the question of whether the royalties have to be fixed on the basis of the price of the complete machine or only part thereof, one cannot rely merely on the scope of protection of the patented objects, but that it is the economic value of the patent which must be regarded as decisive. Even if it were assumed that only part of the machine was protected by patent and that this part represented only a fraction of the entire value of the machine the royalties would still have to be computed on the basis of the complete machine if the part in question is of vital importance for the functioning of the machine or for improving its efficiency or facilitating its sale. In the present case it would be unnecessary to examine whether or not the patent covers the construction of the compressor since the decisive factor for the stipulation of the royalties is that the use of compressed air is covered by patent 537 631. Each enterprise engaging in the repair of stockings needs for its installation a compressor adapted to the needleholder, and, in fact, the needleholder was always purchased together with the compressor; separate needleholders were sold only as spare parts; the compressor constitutes the main value of a machine for the repair of ladders and the technical progress achieved by the firm Vitoux consists just in the use of compressed air for operating a needleholder of special construction, a combination which meant the creation of a new stocking repair machine. This new machine was launched on the market and its sales price must be considered the determinant in fixing the royalties.

"Even if the machine of the firm [of] Vitoux is one of the most expensive offered on the market, this does not permit any conclusion with regard to the fixing of royalties since the price of such a machine depends on its quality and on the customers' demands.

"Nor can the Arbitral Commission allow the complainant's claim to be treated as the most favoured licensee. The agreements which the defendant concluded with third parties are for the complainant Purfürst *res inter alios actae* on which he cannot rely. Like all other agreements they are governed by considerations of expediency, interest and personal relations which may vary in different agreements. It is entirely at the discretion of the defendant firm to choose what special conditions it would grant to the licensee in an amicable arrangement which has the advantage, among other things, of avoiding high court fees on the part of the defendant. Such an arrangement cannot serve as basis for the stipulation of adequate royalties which should, as far as possible, correspond to normal royalties and to those fixed by courts in parallel cases.

" In the opinion of the Arbitral Commission, the Grand Senate set out from a just and reasonable point of view when it described the *Reichsgericht* as having followed the principles of justice when, as a court of appeal in a forced licence proceeding in 1942 concerning the same patent holder, it had laid down in its decision royalties of 5 per cent. of the net sales price per machine. However, taking into consideration the fact that the complainant had fitted the machine with a needleholder of his own construction, the Grand Senate considered it right and just to lower the royalties imposed on the complainant Purfürst to 4 per cent. of the net sales price of the complete machine. As regards the sale of the needleholder with or without needle, it fixed the royalties at 8 per cent., on the ground that this part of the machine constituted a major proportion of the invention. These royalties were accepted by the defendant although they were considerably below the amount applied for. The complainant disputes the fact that these royalties were in accordance with the principles of equity, without having been able to convince the Arbitral Commission by his arguments. The Commission finds, therefore, that there is no sufficient reason to justify any alteration in the royalties laid down by the Grand Senate.

" In view of the fact, however, that patent 537 631 became extinct on November 27, 1956, as on that date the time-limit for extension laid down by Order of the Patent Administrative Department dated February 12, 1951 had expired and that consequently the dates of payment laid down by the Grand Senate in its decision of February 21, 1955 became invalid, the Arbitral Commission deems it appropriate to take into consideration the defendant's new motions as far as mere implementation is concerned, in the manner formulated under I and II of its rejoinder of October 23, 1957, and during the oral hearing on February 18, 1958, by the submission of a supplement application concerning the manner of the rendering of accounts by the complainant and the payment of royalties. The Arbitral Commission rejects the motions under II as far as the buyers are concerned, and the motions under III and IV concerning the employment of an auditor and the payment of interest on the hitherto unpaid royalties partly because they are unfounded and partly because they have not been presented to the Grand Senate.

" The Arbitral Commission considers it unnecessary to declare its decision enforceable, as has been submitted by the defendant, since pursuant to Article 13 (2) of its Charter ' judgments and orders of the Commission shall be binding on all parties and shall not be subject to appeal' subject to the other provisions of this Article and to paragraph 2 of Article 9 and Article 10 of the Charter of the Arbitration Tribunal.

" No decision will be made on costs as in the present proceeding no costs were incurred by the Arbitral Commission, and since Rule 70 of the Rules of Procedure states that, in general, each party shall pay its own costs with the exception of special cases which do not arise here.

" The application by the complainant, which the defendant opposes, to submit the case to the Commission in plenary session is rejected since this application had been made only as a precautionary measure and submitted after the main and alternative motions of the complainant."

" For these reasons the Arbitral Commission decides: (1) to reject the complainant's appeal; (2) to allow the defendant's motions in the following manner:

" I. The complainant Purfürst shall pay to the firm [of] Vitoux the following royalties for exploiting German patent 537 631:

" (1) for the manufacture or delivery of the complete machine, including compressor, foot starter, lamp, stretching device (*Strumpfbecher*), needleholder with needle, 4% (four per cent.) of the total net sales price;

" (2) for the manufacture or delivery of the needleholder with needle or the needleholder alone 8% (eight per cent.) of the net sales price of the needleholder;

" (3) the net sales price is the sales price entered in the invoice, less packing charges, freight, insurance, discount and commission.

" II. The complainant Purfürst shall render accounts to the defendant on the number of machines and parts thereof described under I which have been manufactured and delivered during the period from October 1, 1949, to November 27, 1956, and, for this purpose, he shall compile a list of quantities delivered, prices and dates of delivery, which may be verified. The obligation to render accounts also applies to those objects which were manufactured before the expiry of the period of protection but delivered after November 27, 1956.

" III. Payment of the royalties resulting from the presentation of the accounts shall be effected within a time-limit of three months after service of this decision."

[Report: *Decisions of the Arbitral Commission*, I (1958), Case No. 16, p. 154.]

**Arbitration—In general—Conception and function of arbitration —Decision on interpretation and application of international Agreement—In contradistinction to decision on claim.**

See p. 33 (*Swiss Confederation* v. *German Federal Republic* (*No. 1*)).

## ii—The Law Applied by Arbitral Tribunals

**Arbitration—In general—Law applied by arbitral tribunals— Arbitral Commission on Property, Rights and Interests in Germany—Application of principles of equity.**

N. V. Philips' Gloeilampenfabrieken *v.* German Federal
Republic (No. 1).

*Arbitral Commission on Property, Rights and Interests in Germany,
First Chamber.*

(Wickström, President; Euler, Bodenhausen.)

*October* 30, 1958.

THE FACTS (as stated by the Commission).—" By decision of July 29, 1955, served on August 6, 1955, on N. V. Philips' Gloeilampenfabrieken (hereinafter called ' Philips–Eindhoven ') and on Philips Patentverwaltung G.m.b.H. (hereinafter called ' P.V.'), the Appeal Senate 1a of the German Patent Office (*Beschwerdesenat 1a des Deutschen Patentamts*) rejected the appeals lodged by the two Companies against the decision of the *Patentverwaltungsabteilung* of June 9, 1952, by which their claims for the restoration of patent 473 141 and for the extension of its duration had been dismissed.

" By applications submitted to the Commission on September 2, 1955, the two Companies appealed separately against the decision of July 29, 1955. P.V. requested that so far as its appeal was concerned the proceedings should be stayed and the judgment reserved until a decision had been delivered on the appeal of Philips–Eindhoven.

" In its answer, the defendant requested that the two appeals should be examined simultaneously and that they should be referred to the Commission in plenary session (*cf.* Rule 21 [*b*] of the Rules of Procedure of the Commission).

" In their replies, the two Companies objected to the latter application.

" The Commission decided: ' (1) by Order of April 19, 1958, that the proceedings in the appeal of P.V. should be stayed until further order or until a final judgment has been delivered in the matter of Philips–Eindhoven; (2) by Order of April 28, 1958, that the application for the appeal of Philips–Eindhoven to be referred to the Commission in plenary session be rejected.'

" During the oral hearing . . . Philips–Eindhoven moved that it should be ordered that patent 473 141 be restored under Allied High Commission Law No. 8 on Industrial, Literary and Artistic Property Rights of Foreign Nations and Nationals, and its duration extended under Article 5 of that Law.

" The defendant moved that the application should be rejected as being unfounded. . . .

[The Commission, after quoting Articles 1, 4, 5 and part of Article 14 of Law No. 8, continued:]

" It is established: ' (1) that in 1925 the patent in question was granted and entered in the Patent Register in the name of Philips–Eindhoven; (2) that in 1935 the patent was transferred in the said Register into the name of P.V. as a result of (a) an application dated June 4, 1935, filed with the *Reichspatentamt* by Philips–Eindhoven which therein stated that it assigned its rights to the patent to P.V., and (b) a statement of the same date made by P.V., by which it accepted the assignment and the transfer of the patent into its name; and (3) that Philips–Eindhoven has always owned the whole capital of P.V., and that according to paragraph 2 of its statutes the object of P.V. is the administration, exploitation and acquisition of patents, utility models and industrial designs of Philips–Eindhoven and its affiliated companies as well as the safeguarding of all rights arising thereunder.

" Philips–Eindhoven has contended that, under the agreement concluded between it and P.V. in 1934, it has remained the true owner of the patent, and that the formal transfer of its rights to P.V. and the transfer of the patent in the Patent Register into the name of P.V. had been effected only in order to give to P.V. the authority necessary to enable it to act in its name *vis-à-vis* third parties.

" The defendant has contested not only that the alleged agreement was concluded but also that the meaning of the word ' owned ' in Article 5 of Law No. 8 might extend to any rights over the patent that Philips–Eindhoven could have. [After examining the evidence, the Commission arrived at the conclusion that the two companies had concluded an agreement (*Treuhand* Agreement), Clause 4 of which read as follows:]

' Either party may terminate this agreement at the end of each year by giving six months' notice. In the case of such denunciation, Philips Patentverwaltung Gesellschaft m.b.H. shall re-transfer to N.V. Philips' Gloeilampenfabrieken, Eindhoven, all rights transferred to them by virtue of this agreement.'

[The assertions of the parties regarding the question of ownership of the patent involved are omitted here.]

" Finally, Philips–Eindhoven maintained that even if one considered that, as the result of the transfer of the patent in question to P.V., it was no longer entitled to demand application of the provisions of Article 5 of Law No. 8, it had again become qualified to act in 1941. In support of this assertion it stated the following: In 1941 it agreed with P.V. that the patent in question, as well as all the other industrial property rights which it had formerly transferred to P.V., should be re-transferred. If this had been done, Philips–Eindhoven would again have become the nominal owner of the patent and as such would have been entitled to claim restoration of the patent and extension of its duration. However, the custodians appointed by the German authorities for the property of Philips–Eindhoven and of P.V. did not consent to such re-transfer although it had been envisaged in the *Treuhand* Agreement. It would be contrary to the principles of good faith for the defendant now to rely on the lack of qualification of Philips–Eindhoven, since it was due to the arbitrary refusal of the custodians appointed by the German authorities and acting under their influence that Philips–Eindhoven had been prevented from acquiring such qualification. According to the wording of Article 162 of the German Civil Code, no party may rely on the fulfilment or non-fulfilment of a condition if that party has in bad faith caused or prevented the fulfilment of such condition. This Article was not directly applicable to the present case but it defined precisely the principle of good faith which applies generally whenever the circumstances essential for the creation or existence of a legal relationship have been caused or prevented in bad faith by a party.

" The following answer was given by the defendant: that Law No. 8 accords an extension only in cases where certain definite facts exist; that an extension for reasons other than those fixed by the Law could not be granted even if the defendant had incurred an obligation to pay damages; and that, moreover, the custodians could not have acted contrary to the principles of good faith even if they had declined re-transfer, a fact which has been contested by the defendant. In their capacity of *Treuhänder* [trustee administrators] of P.V., they were obliged to safeguard the property of that Company by preventing transfer of such property to another, independent, juristic entity. . . ."

*Held:* that the proceedings must be re-opened " concerning the question whether the re-transfer of the patent in question to Philips–Eindhoven was demanded and declined in 1941 " and " concerning the question of the applicability of Article 8 of the Charter of the Commission and the effect of its possible application."

The Commission said (with reference to the problem of the law to be applied[11]): "Article 8 of the Charter of the Commission stipulates that:

'In arriving at its decisions, the Commission shall apply the provisions of the Convention and of legislation made applicable thereby. Where necessary to supplement or interpret such provisions, or in the absence of any relevant provisions, it shall apply the general principles of international law and of justice and equity.'

"The Commission is of the opinion that in the present case there might be a lacuna which should be filled by the application of principles of equity since, if Philips–Eindhoven demanded re-transfer to which they were entitled according to clause 4 of the *Treuhand* Agreement, and if the custodians declined such re-transfer, equity might require that Philips–Eindhoven be treated as if it had obtained such re-transfer.

[The Commission then considered a submission by the defendant regarding the interpretation of Articles 1, 4 and 5 of Law No. 8. No issues of international law were raised in this part of the judgment.]

"For these reasons, the Arbitral Commission orders the re-opening of the proceedings concerning: (1) the question whether the re-transfer of the patent in question to Philips–Eindhoven was demanded and declined in 1941; (2) the question of the applicability of Article 8 of the Charter of the Commission and the effect of its possible application."

[Report: *Decisions of the Arbitral Commission*, II (1959), Case No. 27, p. 141.]

NOTE.—In the decision on the merits in the above case the Commission also applied the general principles of justice and equity in accordance with Article 8 of its Charter (*ibid.*, Case No. 45, p. 183).

The final judgment of the First Chamber in this case was given on April 13, 1959 (*ibid.*). This judgment ordered that the decisions of the *Patentverwaltungsabteilung* of the German Patent Office and of the Appeal Senate 1a of that Office (referred to in the statement of facts above, at p. 503) should be set aside and that Patent No. 473 141 should be restored and its duration extended by virtue of Article 5 of Allied High Commission Law No. 8. The final judgment will be reported in a later volume of the *International Law Reports*.

In *S.A. Violatomiki and Kingdom of Greece* v. *German Federal Republic* (*ibid.*, Case No. 33, p. 151), the Commission "in accordance with the principles of equity and good faith" declared admissible applications which were filed with the Commission one day after the expiry of the time-limit allowed for appeals. The Commission arrived at the conclusion that the delay was not caused by the complainant's fault.

[1 The remaining part of the judgment does not deal with any points of public international law.]

Arbitration—In general—Law applied by arbitral tribunals—Generally recognized principle—Application in matters of intervention.

See p. 544 (*Greek Powder & Cartridge Co.* v. *German Federal Republic.*)

Arbitration—In general—Law applied by arbitral tribunals—Municipal case-law—Application of—By Arbitral Commission.

See p. 552 (*La Mont Corporation* v. *German Federal Republic*).

Arbitration—In general—Law applied by arbitral tribunals—Principles of equity.

See p. 495 (*Purfürst* v. *Établissements Vitoux (Merits)*.

Arbitration—In general—Law applied by arbitral tribunals—General principles of international law, of justice and of equity—Application by Arbitral Commission.

See p. 527 (*Scheidt* v. *German Federal Republic (Jurisdiction)*).

Arbitration—In general—Law applied by arbitral tribunals—Private international law—Problem of *lex fori*—Choice of law in contract cases.

See p. 33 (*Swiss Confederation* v. *German Federal Republic (No. 1)*).

### iii.—The Arbitration Treaty. Appointment and Withdrawal of Arbitrators

Arbitration—In general—Arbitration treaty—Establishment of Arbitral Commission—Date of—Whether identical with date of appointment of members of Commission—Importance for time-limits—Applicant's ignorance of establishment of Commission—Effect on time-limits for bringing appeal.

WESTERN MACHINERY COMPANY *v.* GERMAN FEDERAL REPUBLIC.

*Arbitral Commission on Property, Rights and Interests in Germany, Third Chamber.*

(Lagergren, Vice-President; Arndt, Edelman.)

*December* 13, 1957.

*Plenary Session. June* 30, 1958.

(Wickström, President; Sauser-Hall, Lagergren, Vice-Presidents; Schwandt, Euler, Bennett, Arndt, Marion, Phenix.)

THE FACTS (as stated by the Third Chamber).—" The complainant appeals from a decision of the First Appeal Senate of the German Patent Office rendered November 17, 1955, which rejected its application for restitution of the *status quo ante* in regard to its alleged patent priority rights. It was late in filing its priority rights for a German patent but contends that it was refused a reinstatement of the *status quo ante* which would have been granted to a German national. Complainant makes its claim under Articles 10 and 13 of Allied High Commission Law No. 8, contending that it is entitled thereunder to the same kind of relief as German law affords to German nationals in like circumstances (*viz.*, German Ordinance of November 9, 1940). The appeal is brought here under Articles 8 and 12 of Chapter Ten of the Settlement Convention, which confers a right of appeal from any decision of the last instance of the Patent Office in respect of Law No. 8 proceedings.

" The defendant has raised a preliminary objection in bar of the proceedings, asserting that the appeal to this Commission was not filed within 30 days after the decision appealed from was served upon the complainant, as provided in Article 12 of Chapter Ten, and hence that the appeal should be dismissed. On October 2, 1957, we ordered a separate and prior trial of this issue and an oral hearing was held before the Commission on December 7, 1957."

*Held* (by the Third Chamber): that the preliminary objection filed by the German Federal Republic must be sustained, and the appeal must be dismissed. The complainant's ignorance about the change-over from the Occupation Laws to the Bonn Settlement Convention, 1954, did not constitute adequate grounds for restoring the complainant to its *status quo ante* before the running of the thirty-day period. The Arbitral Commission was established upon the entry into force of the Settlement Convention on May 5, 1955, and the fact that its members were not sworn in until November 9, 1956, does not alter this, nor does it suspend the running of time-limits for appeal.

The Commission said: "Article 12, paragraph 1, of Chapter Ten of the Settlement Convention provides:

> 'The following decisions may be appealed to the Arbitral Commission on Property, Rights and Interests in Germany, referred to in Article 7 of Chapter Five of the present Convention, in accordance with the provisions of its Charter, upon application to the Commission by the party concerned within thirty days after the service thereof'

. . . . . . . . . . .

> '(f) decisions of the last instance of the German Patent Office or its Grand Senate under Allied High Commission Law No. 8 or decisions of the regular courts of first instance under that Law pursuant to Article 8.'

"The final decision of the German Patent Senate was concededly served upon complainant on November 30, 1955. The appeal to this Commission was dated March 21, 1956, and was not filed until April 11, 1956.

"Complainant asks relief from a stringent application of the 30 day limit largely on the ground that its representative was not adequately informed of the changes in the governing Occupation law and the change-over wrought by the effectuation of the Settlement Convention on May 5, 1955. Even as late as April 11, 1956, when complainant's appeal was finally filed, its representative was apparently still without knowledge of the creation of this Commission or the particulars regarding dissolution of the old and establishment of the new appellate machinery. Its notice of appeal was addressed to: 'The Allied High Commission Office of the Secretary General—Board of Appeal in Patent Matters—Bad Godesberg, or the office competent after dissolution of the AHC.' The complainant's notice of appeal reads in part as follows:

> 'It is known to me that the Allied High Commission was dissolved on May 5, 1955, its last official act having been the abrogation of a number of laws. At present it is, however, not yet known whether Law No. 8 concerned here as well as its implementing regulations are affected, too, and whether the invoked Board of Appeal for patent matters was dissolved accordingly or whether its functions were transferred to a German authority. Therefore, for reasons of precaution, an appeal is lodged pursuant to Section 8 of the decision of the AHC concerning Rules of Procedure of the Board of Appeal for patent affairs (*Official Gazette* of the Allied High Commission No. 117 of July 18, 1954, page 3020).'

"While we are quite convinced of the *bona fides* of complainant's claimed ignorance and confusion over the change-over from the Occupation Laws to the Settlement Convention, we do not deem such ignorance to constitute adequate grounds for restoring complainant to its *status quo ante* before the running of the 30 day period.

"Nor can the running of complainant's time to file his appeal be deemed stayed only because the Commission was not in fact sworn until November 9, 1956. The Commission was, however, established from the entry into force of the Settlement Convention, *i.e.*, May 5, 1955 (see Articles 1 and 17 of the Charter of the Commission), and an express notice was published in the *Bundesanzeiger* on May 18, 1955, jointly issued by the Three Powers and the Federal Republic of Germany to the effect that all papers to be filed with the Commission are to be filed at the *Rathaus, Herford*.

"For these reasons the Arbitral Commission orders that: (1) The preliminary objection filed by the Federal Republic of Germany is sustained. (2) The appeal is dismissed."

Mr. Edelman gave the following dissenting opinion:

"My two brethren and I are in agreement on that portion of the Commission's opinion which deals with discussion of the issues and the arguments of the parties, but I do not concur with the decision reached. I would dismiss the defendant's objection and sustain the admissibility of the appeal.

"I would strike the final paragraph of the Commission's opinion appearing at the bottom of page four of the decision, and would substitute, in lieu thereof, the following conclusions:

'We are, however, aware of another and more compelling reason for accepting the appeal as timely. While the Convention was by its terms to come into force on May 5, 1955, and while it provided for the immediate establishment of the Arbitral Commission, the Commission was not in fact organized and sworn until November 9, 1956. It is quite true, as defendant's counsel pointed out in oral argument, that Article 1 and Article 17 of the Charter of the Commission, which is annexed to the Convention, state that:

"The Commission is established for a period of ten years to run from the entry into force of the present Charter" (Art. 1) and
"The present Charter shall enter into force on the entry into force of the Convention" (Art. 17)."

'But neither of those statements alters the fact that no Arbitral Commission existed until its members were appointed and were sworn and organized themselves into a court in being. This did not occur until November 21, 1956—seven months after this complainant lodged his appeal. And it is to be noted that the Charter just as clearly provided that the Governments of the Three Powers and the Federal Government shall make known their first appointments (of members of the Commission) not later than 30 days after the entry into force of the present Charter. That was not done until very long after the 30 days period. If that has been treated as flexible—then complainant is entitled to have us treat the thirty days limit of [Article] 12 as operative only from and after the date of establishment of the Commission.

'It is all very well to say that complainant could have filed his appeal despite the non-existence of the Commission and that an express notice was published in the *Bundesanzeiger*, jointly issued by the Three Powers and the Federal Republic, to the effect that all papers to be filed with the Commission are to be filed at the *Rathaus Herford* until further notice

—but these are not answers to the non-existence of the appeal court itself. The *Rathaus Herford* was a mail-box, not a tribunal.

' In our view, no litigant's time to file his appeal should be held to run while the Court to which his appeal will be taken does not yet exist. The fundamental conception of an appeal is to bring before a higher magistrate or authority a claim that error has been committed below and justice has been denied. The appellate magistrate or authority must be established as a court before a litigant's right of appeal becomes a reality.

' Cases decided after the Convention became effective (*i.e.*, after May 5, 1955), as this one was, were clearly intended to be embraced within its appeal provisions. And no time could be said to have been lost by reason of the delay in filing, prior to the establishment of the Commission as a court in being.

' The foregoing considerations are particularly compelling where litigants must find their way through a succession of unusual and unprecedented Occupation and war settlement statutes, with the uncertainties inherent in the successive changes regarding the scope of the appellate power and the repository of the appellate function.' "

The complainant appealed.

*Held* (by the Plenary Session): that the judgment of the Third Chamber must be confirmed. The fact that on May 5, 1955 (*i.e.*, the day of the entry into force of the Convention establishing the Commission) members of the Commission had not yet been appointed, did not operate to prevent the establishment of the Commission on that day.

The Commission said: " Pursuant to the provisions of Article 12, paragraph 1, of Chapter Ten of the Settlement Convention, an appeal against a decision of the last instance of the German Patent Office must be lodged within 30 days after the service thereof.

" It is not disputed that the contested decision was served upon the complainant on November 30, 1955, and that the complainant submitted its notice of appeal only on April 11, 1956. However, the complainant contends that its notice of appeal was not too late because on April 11, 1956, the Arbitral Commission was not in existence and that the time for the filing of the appeal could not begin to run prior to the establishment of the Arbitral Commission.

" Article 7, paragraph 1, of Chapter Five of the Settlement Convention provides:

' The Signatory States hereby establish an Arbitral Commission on Property, Rights and Interests in Germany, which shall function in accordance with the provisions of its Charter annexed to the present Convention.'

Pursuant to Article 17, paragraph 1, of the Charter, the Commission is established upon the entry into force of the Convention.

" The fact that at that time the members of the Commission had not been nominated does not operate to prevent the establishment of the Commission on May 5, 1955.

" The public was notified by a publication in the Federal Gazette (*Bundesanzeiger*) of May 18, 1955, published by the Signatory States to the effect that any documents intended for the Arbitral Commission should be addressed to the *Rathaus Herford*, and it is obvious that this order became binding upon any parties intending to apply to the Commission.

" The Third Chamber was right, therefore, in finding that the notice of appeal was lodged too late.

" As an alternative motion, the complainant applied for reinstatement, basing itself on its ignorance of the establishment of the Commission, of the time-limit for appeals and of the office with which the appeal should have been lodged.

" Even if the Commission had the power to order such a measure, it would not be justified in the present case since the complainant lodged its notice of appeal more than four months after service of the contested decision, although it could have acquired the necessary information with little effort by studying the *Bundesgesetzblatt* and the *Bundesanzeiger* and in any case by inquiry at the German Patent Office, the German Foreign Office or at any of the Embassies of the three other Signatory States.

" The contested decisions must therefore be confirmed.

" For These Reasons the Arbitral Commission (1) confirms the judgment of the Third Chamber; (2) orders that the complainant bear the court fee of one hundred Deutsche Mark."

[Report: *Decisions of the Arbitral Commission*, I (1958), Case No. 21, p. 181.]

NOTE.—A similar decision was given on December 17, 1958, in *Singer Nähmaschinen A.G.* v. *German Federal Republic* (*ibid.*, II, Case No. 36, p. 159), where the Commission cited the above decision in the *Western Machinery* Company case.

## II.—Procedure

### i.—Procedure before the Tribunal (Oral and Written Arguments)

Arbitration—Procedure—Procedure before arbitral tribunal—Arbitral Commission on Property, Rights and Interests in Germany—Article 6 of Charter of Commission—Right of recourse to Commission—Whether possessed by nationals or residents of non-contracting States.

JÜRGENSEN v. GERMAN FEDERAL REPUBLIC.

*Arbitral Commission on Property, Rights and Interests in Germany, First Chamber.*

(Wickström, President; Euler, Bennett.)

*January 15, 1958.*

THE FACTS (as stated by the Commission).—" By its decision of November 30, 1956, which was served on the complainant on January 11, 1957, the *Bundesamt für die Prüfung ausländischer Rückgabe- und Wiederherstellungsansprüche* [Federal Restitution Office] dismissed the complainant's claim for payment of the price of three lorries sold by him in 1942 to the German army.

" In his complaint lodged with the Commission on February 8, 1957, the complainant gave notice of appeal against this decision.

" On April 12, 1957, the complainant submitted an application for the grant of legal aid.

" By its Order of May 6, 1957, the Commission rejected this application.

" The complainant subsequently paid the DM 100 fixed by Rule 69 of the Rules of Procedure and thereupon his notice of appeal was served on the defendant.

" By its answer, the defendant contended that no appeal lay on the ground that, as a Danish national, the complainant had no right of recourse to the Commission.

" The complainant, who in his notice of appeal had already admitted that, following the cession of North Schleswig to Denmark in 1920, he had automatically become a Danish national, replied that he belonged to the group of persons of German ethnical origin and that, as an ex-member of the *Waffen-SS* and in accordance with the law then in force, he had been deemed to be a German national.

" The defendant rejoined that the fact that the complainant was of German ethnical origin did not operate to confer German nationality upon him and that service in the *Waffen-SS* would not have operated to confer such nationality upon him unless he had obtained a *Feststellungsbescheid* [certificate of entitlement] before the entry into force of the Federal Nationality Law of February 22, 1955."

*Held:* that the appeal must be dismissed. The complainant possessed Danish nationality, and as Denmark was not a party to the Commission's Charter he was precluded by Article 6 of the Charter from enjoying the right of recourse to the Commission.

The Commission said: " It is clear that in accordance with the provisions of Article 116 of the Basic Law [of 1949] of the German Federal Republic and of the Federal Law of February 22, 1955, (BGBl. I, p. 65), the fact that the complainant, who became a Danish subject in 1920 and resides in Denmark, is of German ethnical origin does not confer German nationality upon him nor entitle him to be treated as ' a German ' within the meaning of the said Article. Further, it is also clear that in accordance with the provisions of Article 10 of the latter Law, the fact that the complainant served in the *Waffen-SS* does not confer German nationality upon him, unless a *Feststellungsbescheid* was served upon him before the entry into force of that Law. The complainant admitted that no such *Feststellungsbescheid* was ever delivered to him.

" The Commission, therefore, finds that the complainant possesses only Danish nationality.

" Paragraph 4 of Article 6 of the Charter of the Commission provides:

' Disputes within the jurisdiction of the Commission may be submitted by any of the Signatory States or any State which has acceded to the present Charter, by a national or resident of any such State or of any territorial entity which is administered or controlled by any such State or for whose international relations such State is responsible, or by a juristic person established under the laws of any such State or territorial entity.'

" Denmark is not a Signatory State and has not acceded to the Charter. In consequence, the complainant has no right of recourse to the Commission and his appeal, therefore, does not lie and must be rejected.

" On the question of costs, the only order that is necessary is that the complainant should bear the Court fee of DM 100 already paid by him.

" For These Reasons the Arbitral Commission (1) dismisses the appeal on the ground that it does not lie; (2) orders that the complainant shall bear the Court fee of one hundred Deutsche Mark."

[Report: *Decisions of the Arbitral Commission*, I (1958), Case No. 9, p. 137.]

Arbitration—Procedure—Procedure before arbitral tribunal—
Arbitral Commission on Property, Rights and Interests in Germany—Written arguments—Time-limits for filing appeals—
Claims—Requirement of clear definition of rights and interests
to be restored.

DRACOULIS (HEIRS) *v.* GERMAN FEDERAL REPUBLIC.

*Arbitral Commission on Property, Rights and Interests in Germany,
First Chamber.*

(Wickström, President; Euler, Kokinopoulos.)

*December* 10, 1958.

THE FACTS (as stated by the Commission).—" By a decision of
June 21, 1957, served upon Mr. Hector C. Dracoulis on July 25,
1957, the *Bundesamt für die Prüfung ausländischer Rückgabe- und
Wiederherstellungsansprüche* [Federal Restitution Office] rejected
his claim based on the provisions of Article 1 of Chapter Ten of the
Convention on the Settlement of Matters Arising out of the War and
Occupation [1952–1954].

" Mr. Hector C. Dracoulis has lodged an appeal against this
decision requesting that his claim be allowed.

" In its answer, the defendant requested that the appeal be
rejected.

" Mr. Hector Dracoulis died on February 4, 1958, leaving as his
heirs his widow Calliope, his three sons Constantine, George and
Spyros and his daughter Mary, wife of Mr. P. Verykios. The widow
Calliope Dracoulis is Spyros' guardian.

" The above heirs intervened in the proceedings on behalf of the
late Hector C. Dracoulis . . .."

*Held:* that the appeal must be rejected. The appeal had not
been filed with the Commission within the prescribed time-limit.
Besides, the complainant failed to define clearly the rights and
interests in respect of which he demanded restoration.

The Commission said: " Pursuant to paragraph 1 of Article 12
of Chapter Ten of the Settlement Convention, appeal shall be lodged
with the Commission within thirty days after service of the decision.
In the present case, the time-limit for appeal expired on August 24,
1957, and the appeal was filed with the Registry of the Commission
only on August 26, 1957. The appeal is thus inadmissible.

" Moreover, the appeal is not well-founded as will be shown by
the following considerations:

" It is uncontested that the late Hector C. Dracoulis was the
owner of the ship *Ithakos* which was lying at anchor in the harbour
of Antwerp when German troops occupied Belgium in 1940; that
the German authorities prevented the departure of the ship, which,
upon the outbreak of hostilities between Germany and Greece, was

confiscated on behalf of the German Reich; and that, after the end of the war, the ship was restored to the late Hector C. Dracoulis.

" The claim as phrased by the late Hector C. Dracoulis before the *Bundesamt* was very vague. He contended that the preventing of the ship from leaving the harbour of Antwerp at a time when Greece was still a neutral country constituted a discriminatory measure which gave rise to prejudice, deprivation and impairment being suffered by him, and that the provisions of paragraph I of Article I of Chapter Ten of the Settlement Convention were applicable to the extent to which they provided for the restoration of his rights and interests. However, he has at no time clearly defined the rights and interests in respect of which he demands restoration.

" The late Hector C. Dracoulis has not been any more explicit before the Commission, where he referred to his previous statements before the *Bundesamt*; nor have his heirs defined the claim any more precisely.

" In these circumstances, it is found that the claim is unjustified.

" For These Reasons the Arbitral Commission decides: Oral proceedings will be dispensed with. The appeal is rejected. The complainants will bear the court costs of one hundred Deutsche Mark."

[Report: *Decisions of the Arbitral Commission*, II (1959), Case No. 35, p. 157.]

Arbitration—Procedure before arbitral tribunal—Written arguments—Parties restricted under Rules of Procedure of Tribunal to arguments contained in memorials and counter-memorials—Whether restriction may be modified in the event of major change in factual situation occurring after filing of pleadings—Request for interim measures of protection—United Nations Tribunal for Libya, Rules of Procedure, Article 11.

See p. 517 (*Italy* v. *United Kingdom of Great Britain and Northern Ireland and United Kingdom of Libya. General List No. 1 (Interim Measures*)).

Arbitration—Procedure—Procedure before Tribunal—Principle of estoppel.

See p. 495 (*Purfürst* v. *Établissements Vitoux (Merits)*).

Arbitration—Procedure—Procedure before tribunal—Arbitral Commission on Property, Rights and Interests in Germany—Appeals to Commission—Admission of—In matters involving patents.

See p. 335 (*Spanier* v. *German Federal Republic*).

**ii.—Competence.  Competence to Determine Jurisdiction**

Arbitration—Procedure—Competence—Requirement of existence of a dispute—Whether existence affected by continuing negotiations between the parties—Interim measures of protection —Principle upon which relief to be granted—United Nations Tribunal for Libya, Rules of Procedure, Articles 25 and 26.

ITALY *v*. UNITED KINGDOM OF GREAT BRITAIN AND NORTHERN IRELAND AND UNITED KINGDOM OF LIBYA.

GENERAL LIST NO. 1 (INTERIM MEASURES).

*United Nations Tribunal for Libya.  February* 18, 1952.

(Yörükóglu, President; Wickström, Sanchez-Gavito, Judges.)

THE FACTS.—This Tribunal was set up under Resolution 388 (V) of December 15, 1950, of the General Assembly of the United Nations.[1] The Resolution is entitled " Economic and Financial Provisions Relating to Libya ", and the preamble refers to the desirability that such provisions should be determined before the transfer of power in Libya took place. Article X of the Resolution, providing for the establishment of the Tribunal, reads as follows:

" *Article X*
1. A United Nations Tribunal shall be set up, composed of three persons selected by the Secretary General for their legal qualifications from the nationals of three different States not directly interested. The Tribunal, whose decisions shall be based on law, shall have the following two functions:
(a) It shall give to the administering Powers, the Libyan Government after its establishment, and the Italian Government, on request by any of those authorities, such instructions as may be required for the purpose of giving effect to the present resolution;
(b) It shall decide all disputes arising between the said authorities concerning the interpretation and application of the present resolution. The Tribunal shall be seised of any such dispute on the unilateral request of one of those authorities.
2. The administering Powers, the Libyan Government after its establishment and the Italian Government shall supply the Tribunal as soon as possible with all the information and assistance it may need for the performance of its functions.
3. The seat of the Tribunal shall be in Libya. The Tribunal shall determine its own procedure.  It shall afford to the interested parties an opportunity to present their views, and shall be entitled to request information and evidence which it may require from any authority or person whom it considers to be in a position to furnish it.  In the absence of unanimity, the Tribunal shall take decisions by a majority vote.  Its decisions shall be final and binding.'

[1] *Official Records*, Fifth Session, Supplement No. 20 (A/1775).

The present case concerned the transfer of the administration of properties comprised in the categories specified in Article I, paragraphs 3 (*a*) and 5, of the Resolution. The relevant paragraphs of Article I provide as follows:

" 1. Libya shall receive, without payment, the movable and immovable property located in Libya owned by the Italian State, either in its own name or in the name of the Italian administration of Libya.

" 2. The following property shall be transferred immediately:

(a) The public property of the State (*demanio pubblico*) and the inalienable property of the State (*patriomonio indisponibile*) in Libya, as well as the relevant archives and documents of an administrative character or technical value concerning Libya or relating to property the transfer of which is provided for by the present resolution;

(b) The property in Libya of the Fascist Party and its organizations.

" 3. In addition, the following shall be transferred on conditions to be established by special agreement between Italy and Libya:

(a) The alienable property (*patrimonio disponibile*) of the State in Libya and the property in Libya belonging to the autonomous agencies (*aziende autonome*) of the State.

   .      .      .      .      .      .      .

" 5. Italy shall retain the ownership of immovable property necessary for the functioning of its diplomatic and consular services and, when the conditions so require, of the schools necessary for the present Italian community whether such property is owned by the Italian State in its own name or in the name of the Italian administration in Libya. Such immovable property shall be determined by special agreements concluded between Italy and Libya."

On December 22, 1951, the Agent of the Italian Government filed with the Tribunal a Memorial against the British Government and a Request for Interim Measures. In the Memorial, the Agent asked that his Government be reinstated in the administration of (*a*) its alienable patrimony in Tripolitania and Cyrenaica; (*b*) the buildings which it would like to use for its diplomatic and consular establishments in Libya; and (*c*) the buildings that it desired to dedicate to the educational needs of the Italian community in the said country. These properties were listed specifically in the annexes to the Memorial.

The Request for Interim Measures contained the petition that the Tribunal should take such steps as it might deem appropriate in order to ensure the administration of the properties concerned.

On December 24, 1951, the independence of Libya was proclaimed. The Tribunal decided, on December 29, 1951, that in view of the fact that the Libyan Government as well as the British Government had an interest in the pleadings presented by the Government of Italy, the Memorial and the Request for Interim Measures should be communicated to both the British and the Libyan Governments.

In an Answer of January 7, 1952, and in a Reply of January 31, 1952, the Libyan and Italian Agents, respectively, referred to the Tribunal's ruling on the subject. The British Answer of January 9, 1952, and Counter-Memorial of January 31, 1952, did not refer to the matter. The Tribunal considered that the Libyan and Italian Agents' remarks on this point did not constitute an exception to its ruling. Therefore, the Tribunal formally confirmed the implication of its ruling, *i.e.*, that the Libyan Government was to be considered as a co-defendant.

The Answer of the Libyan Government questioned the Tribunal's jurisdiction to entertain the action and the related Request for Interim Measures. The Libyan Agent contended that the Italian Government's claim was in essence a petition for equitable arrangements and that there was no dispute with respect to the listed properties either between the Italian and the Libyan Governments or, so far as he was aware, between the Italian and the British Governments. The Agent informed the Tribunal that negotiations had been proceeding between the Governments of Libya and Italy, with a view to carrying out the terms of General Assembly Resolution 388 (V), and concluded that the Tribunal was without jurisdiction either to order an equitable arrangement or to decide the Italian Government's claim under the terms of Article X, paragraphs 1 (*a*) and (*b*), of the Resolution, because the existence of such negotiations made it impossible to contend that there was a dispute between the parties.

On the matter of competence, the British Answer of January 9, 1952, and the Counter-Memorial of January 31, 1952, raised no exceptions.

*Held:* that the exception of lack of jurisdiction raised by the Libyan Answer of January 7, 1952, must be rejected, and that the Request for Interim Measures by the Italian Government must also be rejected.

The Tribunal said:

" The Tribunal considers that the Libyan Agent has not established the validity of his contention to the effect that the Italian Government's claim is essentially a petition for amicable settlement. The Tribunal also considers that the circumstance that negotiations are being carried on by the parties does not impede them from bringing before it one or several of the questions being discussed in such negotiations. Therefore, it believes that the action introduced by the Italian Government by means of its Memorial of December 22, 1951, falls within the scope of its jurisdiction, in view of the fact that its subject-matter is the transfer of the administration of properties comprised in the categories specified in Article 1, paragraphs 3 (*a*) and 5 of Resolution 388 (V) and that the said Government has based its action on Article X, paragraph 1 (*b*), of Resolution

388 (V). Consequently, the Request for Interim Measures has been properly brought before the Tribunal, the said Request being incidental to the action introduced by means of the Memorial.

" Having disposed of the exception of lack of jurisdiction and confirmed its ruling on the status of the Libyan Government, the Tribunal will examine the said Request for Interim Measures in the following paragraphs:

" 1. As has been stated above, the Italian Government, in its Request dated December 22, 1951, asks the Tribunal to take such measures as it may consider appropriate to ensure the administration of the properties listed in the annexes to the Memorial presented by that Government on the same date.

" 2. In the Request, the Italian Government proposes, as specific measures of protection, either that it be entrusted provisionally with the administration of the listed properties or that the said administration be given to a Government not involved in the case. Italy bases its Request on Article 26 of the Tribunal's Rules of Procedure.

" 3. Now, both Articles 25 and 26 of the Rules of Procedure were adopted in order to empower the Tribunal to protect jeopardized rights of the parties. The Tribunal's thoughts on the subject were that a possibility existed that the parties would legitimately fear that, unless certain of their rights were afforded judicial protection within a reasonably short period of time, the ultimate recognition by the Tribunal of such rights would lose, in practice, part if not all of its value. Interim measures, therefore, will be taken only in those cases in which the Tribunal is convinced that a right not as yet established by it, but susceptible of being so established, is actually in jeopardy.

" 4. The Agent of the Libyan Government has properly understood the nature of the procedure in question. In his Answer, he states that ' a Court will only grant interim protection if this is necessary to preserve the property, the subject of the claim, i.e., if failure to grant it may result in the claimant losing the fruits of his action if he is successful '.

" 5. The procedure is not foreign to the legal system of Italy. In fact, the *Nuovo Digesto Italiano* contains the following definition of *Atti Conservativi*, which adequately describes the procedure the Tribunal had in mind when it adopted Articles 25 and 26 of its Rules, to wit:

> ' Atti conservativi sono le misure dirette ad evitare il pericolo da cui è minacciato il soddisfacimento di un diritto, non ancora definitivamente accertato, ed a garantirne l'eventuale futuro soddisfacimento per il caso che se ne riconosca giudiziariamente l'esistenza.' [1]

[1 Interim measures (*atti conservativi*) are measures directed to avoiding the danger with which the satisfaction of a right, as yet not definitely ascertained, is threatened, and to guaranteeing the eventual future satisfaction of such right in the event that its existence is judicially recognized.]

" 6. In the present case, the Request of the Italian Agent, with regard to the question of the danger it seeks to remedy, merely stated that, upon the termination of the British administration of Tripolitania and Cyrenaica, the listed properties were to be deprived of an administering agency. In this connection, the Libyan Government does not limit itself to stating that the properties had been placed under its own administration, but goes on to say that the Custodians of Property in Cyrenaica and Tripolitania, under the British Administration, have been retained in their posts, together with their staffs, and that the said officers will exercise their functions in accordance with the Control of Property legislation, under the direction of the Financial and Economic Adviser of the Libyan Government.

" 7. Although the Italian Agent objects to this arrangement, on the grounds that it constitutes a form of unilateral control (Reply of January 31, 1952), in the Tribunal's estimation it solves in a satisfactory manner the problem which the said Agent posed in his Request.

" 8. But in his Reply the Italian Agent sets forth an entirely new basis for his petition for interim measures. This runs counter to the underlying principle of Article 11, paragraph 3 of the Tribunal's Rules of Procedure according to which the parties in the replies and rejoinders may develop only the arguments set out in their memorials and counter-memorials. The Tribunal is willing to entertain it, nevertheless, in view of the special situation confronting the Italian Agent when he produced his Reply. He was, in fact, pleading a case which had substantially changed only two days after the presentation of the Request, i.e., when Libya achieved its independence and the administration of the listed properties was transferred to its Government by the British authorities.

" 9. The Italian Agent contends, in his Reply, that this action on the part of the British authorities has restricted the right of his Government to have the transfer regulated by the agreements referred to in Article 1, paragraphs 3 (a) and 5 of Resolution 388 (V) and to choose the buildings which it would like to dedicate both to its diplomatic and consular establishments and to the educational services of the Italian community. He further contends that the Request for Interim Measures was meant to avoid a modification of the factual and legal status existing before the transfer of administration and that such a modification is detrimental to Italy's position in the negotiation of the agreements under reference (Reply, paragraph 7). On this basis the Italian Agent asks that his Government's rights be restored to the situation obtaining prior to the transfer of administration.

" 10. It is the Tribunal's opinion that this alleged restriction of or damage to the rights of the Italian Government is not a matter which can be remedied by means of the procedure established by Article 26 of the Tribunal's Rules, the characteristics of which have been set forth above. The Tribunal believes, consequently, that the Request for Interim Measures presented by the Italian Government on December 22, 1951, should be rejected.

" For these reasons, the Tribunal decides:

"I. the exception of lack of jurisdiction which the Libyan Agent raised in his Answer of January 7, 1952, is rejected;

"II. the request for Interim Measures, presented by the Italian Government on December 22, 1951, is likewise rejected.

" The present decision has been drawn up in the English and French languages, the English text being authoritative."

[Report: Unpublished.]

**Arbitration—Procedure—Competence—Power to order interim protection—Lack of express provision giving such power to Arbitral Commission—Inherent character of such power.**

VEERMAN v. GERMAN FEDERAL REPUBLIC.

(INTERIM PROTECTION.)

*Arbitral Commission on Property, Rights and Interests in Germany, Third Chamber.*

Lagergren, Vice-President; Arndt, Edelman.)

*October 28, 1957.*

THE FACTS.—Coenraad J. Veerman, complainant, who was engaged in litigation against the German Federal Republic for compensation on account of the alleged removal of property from Holland by the German occupying authorities, filed an application with the Commission for interim protection. The complainant asserted that the defendant State had engaged " in threats and acts of intimidation against the complainant's German attorney by reason of the allegations of violation of due process by the *Land-gericht* contained in paragraph Sixth of the complaint filed with this tribunal." In particular, the complainant maintained that by reason of threats of prosecution before the Disciplinary Court of the German Bar Association, the complainant's attorney was intimidated and induced to file with the Arbitral Commission two letters of retraction, dated June 26 and July 10, 1957, respectively, relative to the allegations contained in the aforesaid paragraph Sixth of the complaint. He also asserted that the letters of retraction were filed without his knowledge or consent.

The complainant further alleged that the aforesaid threats against his attorney constituted " a violation of the immunity conferred upon the agents, counsel and representatives of parties before this tribunal under Article 11, paragraph 5, of its Charter." He asked the Commission to issue an order "directing the defendant, and especially its referee in the *Bundesfinanzministerium* [Federal Ministry of Finance], to cease and desist from intimidating and prosecuting complainant's attorney both before criminal and disciplinary German courts."

*Held:* that the application for an order of interim protection must be refused for lack of satisfactory proof as to the existence of facts justifying such an order. However, the Commission had no doubt as to its " inherent power to issue such orders ".

The Commission said: " The defendant answers that no power rests in this tribunal to grant the relief sought; that the interim protection provisions of Article 7 of the Charter relate only to rights which are the subject of proceedings before this tribunal, namely, compensation claims; that Article 7 can never be invoked in an application relating to the immunity provisions of Article 11; that those provisions can only be advanced, if at all, by the Three Powers which are Parties to the Settlement Convention, and never by a party to proceedings before this tribunal. At the same time the defendant submits an absolute denial of the alleged acts of intimidation by its agents.

" We reject the defendant's contention that the tribunal is powerless to act upon an application of this character. We have no doubt of our inherent power to issue such orders as may be necessary to conserve the respective rights of the parties, including their freedom from interference in the prosecution of their claims before us, and thereby to assure that this Tribunal's jurisdiction and authority are made fully effective.

" There is, however, no satisfactory proof before us that the defendant or its agent did in fact engage in threats or acts of intimidation against the complainant's attorney. The complainant's bare assertion, apparently based upon hearsay, cannot be taken as proof of a charge of coercion or intimidation in the face of unqualified denial of the defendant's agent. Nor does it appear that any such acts are now threatened or imminent. The complainant's application for interim protection, by way of an order directed to the defendant, must therefore be denied.

" No question regarding the alleged interference by the Judges of the *Landgericht* is before us under the applicant's prayer for relief, and we therefore make no finding in respect thereto.

" For These Reasons the Arbitral Commission orders that the application of the complainant for an order of interim protection is denied."

[Report: *Decisions of the Arbitral Commission*, I (1958), Case No. 1 p. 119.]

Arbitration—Procedure—Competence—Right to submit case pending in municipal court to Arbitral Commission—Contemptuous or obstructive conduct of submitting party as bar to such submission—Chapter Five, Article 7 (3), sentence 2, of Convention on the Settlement of Matters Arising out of the War and Occupation, 1952–1954—Reference of case to municipal court—Fixing of conditions of such reference.

LEVIS AND LEVIS *v.* GERMAN FEDERAL REPUBLIC.

(JURISDICTION.)

*Arbitral Commission on Property, Rights and Interests in Germany, Third Chamber.*

(Lagergren, Vice-President; Arndt, Edelman.)

*December* 13, 1957.

THE FACTS (as stated by the Commission).—" On May 3, 1956, the complainants brought suit against the Federal Republic of Germany in the *Landgericht* at Bonn, pursuant to Articles 3 and 4 of Chapter Five of the Convention on the Settlement of Matters Arising out of the War and the Occupation.

" On June 3, 1957, the complainants brought their claim directly to the Arbitral Commission, asserting that the *Landgericht* at Bonn had failed to render a decision within one year after submission of the claim, and invoking Article 7, paragraph 3, of Chapter Five of the Settlement Convention as authority for their right of direct submission to the Commission.

" The defendant concedes that complainants' case has been pending undetermined in the *Landgericht* for more than a year, but contends that Article 7, paragraph 3, is not applicable because the delay in the proceedings below is not attributable to any failure to act on the part of the *Landgericht*, but rather to the complainants' own fault. The fault lies, the defendant asserts, in the complainants' failure and refusal to comply with an order of the Court directing the deposit of security for costs. We have heretofore directed the separate and prior trial of the issue raised by this objection in bar (decision of October 2, 1957).

" It appears that the defendant moved in the *Landgericht* on July 26, 1956, for an order directing complainants to post security for costs pursuant to § 110 of the German Code of Civil Procedure. On August 2, 1956, the *Landgericht* entered an order directing complainants to deposit the sum of DM 17,000 as security for costs that might be incurred by the defence in the *Landgericht* itself as well as in the intermediate appellate Court [*Oberlandesgericht*] and in the highest appellate Court [*Bundesgerichtshof*].

" The complainants immediately took exception to the Court's ruling, claiming error in the fixing of security without an oral hearing, error in requiring security at all, and error in the formulation of the amount thereof. The Court acceded to the complainants' demand for an oral hearing, which was held more than five weeks after the submission of complainants' exceptions. Thereafter, a period of six months elapsed while inquiries were addressed by the Court to the German Ministry of Foreign Affairs concerning New York procedural law on security for costs, and while opposing counsel sought to reply to the opinion submitted. Finally, on April 2, 1957, the Court entered a new order fixing security for costs in the sum of DM 5,050. The order directed compliance by the complainants not later than May 10, 1957. On June 3, which was within the 30-day period after the expiration of one year from the date of submission of their claim to the *Landgericht* (June 2 being a Sunday), the complainants filed their case here."

*Held:* that the Commission possessed jurisdiction in the case. The complainants' non-compliance with the municipal court orders relative to costs resulting in the expiration of the time-limit fixed by Chapter Five, Article 7 (3), sentence 2, of the Convention on the Settlement of Matters Arising out of the War and Occupation, 1952–1954, did not bar their right of appeal to the Commission unless it constituted contemptuous or obstructive conduct. The Commission, in now sending the case back to the municipal court for a hearing and decision on the merits, did so only on the understanding that the complainants were assured of no less favourable conditions for the prosecution of their case in that municipal court than they would now enjoy before this Commission.

The Commission said: " Defendant's objection that complainant was at fault for failure to comply with the Court's order, and that the time limit fixed by Article 7, paragraph 3, was tolled by such non-compliance, cannot be sustained. The language of the statute is clearly couched in terms of expiration of time, not in terms of relative or comparative fault. It provides:

' If the German agency or the German court does not render a decision within one year after submission of the claim, the claimant may submit his claim directly to the Commission within thirty days following the expiration of the one year period.'

" Needless to say, contemptuous or obstructive tactics on the part of a complainant would estop him from asserting his right of direct access under the statute. But there is no such conduct in the record here. The complainants were assiduous in the prosecution of their claim. Their refusal to comply with the Court's decree ordering security for costs was based upon substantial legal objections, which they submitted to the Court upon oral argument and in written memoranda.

" The complainants acted precisely in the manner that a litigant should act who considers the ruling of the Court to be erroneous and wishes to take an appeal therefrom. The German Code of Civil

Procedure, § 113, provides that a plaintiff's complaint may be dismissed for failure to post security ordered by the Court; and such a final decision is subject to appeal. The next step was not up to the complainants, but to the defendant and the Court. While we ascribe no fault to the defendant in not moving more quickly for a dismissal of the complaint, following entry of—and non-compliance with—the security order, the absence of fault on its part is not determinative of the complainants' right of direct submission.

" There was no unwillingness on complainants' part to proceed in the *Landgericht*, but an unwillingness to post security.

" We find that complainants were *bona fide* resisting an order they deemed erroneous. Article 7 affords a complainant two alternative avenues of access to this Commission, one by way of an appeal from a final decision of a German court, the other by way of a direct submission of his claim to the Commission upon the mere pendency of his case before the German court for more than one year without decision. It is by way of the latter alternative that complainants now submit their claim to this Court [Commission]. It is quite immaterial that perhaps in a short time the defendant would have moved for a dismissal of the case and that the *Landgericht* might thereupon have granted such a motion, in which event complainants would come before us by the avenue of an appeal. They are within their rights to come to us now upon the running of the one year period of limitation provided in the Convention.

" We therefore hold that the complainants are properly before the Commission and that the Commission has full jurisdiction now to try the case upon the merits, or to send the case back in whole or in part with instructions.

" We concur in the view of the defendant that it is generally appropriate for the court of first instance to try first the issues of fact and law. However, if the Commission now refers the case to the *Landgericht* for a hearing and decision on the merits, it will do so only if the complainants are assured of no less favourable conditions for the prosecution of their case in the *Landgericht* than they would now enjoy before this Commission. No security for costs would be imposed here, and consequently reference back will be conditional upon a withdrawal of the demand for security in the *Landgericht*. Moreover, since time is of the essence in the right of direct access provided under Article 7, paragraph 3, of the Convention, our order of remand will fix a time-limit within which a final decision must be reached in the *Landgericht*, failing which the case is to be re-submitted to the Commission for trial.

" For These Reasons the Arbitral Commission orders that: (1) the direct submission of the complainants' case to the Commission lies; (2) the Commission accepts jurisdiction of the complainants' case for all purposes; (3) the case is remanded to the *Landgericht* at Bonn for hearing and final decision within four months from the date of issue of this order, failing which the case shall be restored to the Commission for further proceedings; (4) the *Landgericht* is further instructed to restore the case to the Commission if the defendant does not within thirty days from the date of issue of this order withdraw its demand for security for costs, so that the *Landgericht* may vacate its prior order of April 2, 1957, requiring the deposit of security."

[Report: *Decisions of the Arbitral Commission*, I (1958), Case No. 4, p. 124.]

Arbitration—Procedure—Competence—Right of parties to direct access to the Commission—Depending on expiration of time—Understanding between the parties on suspension of further proceedings before municipal court until other cases decided by such court—Whether such understanding restricts right to proceed before Arbitral Commission—Jurisdiction of arbitral commission —Chapter Five, Article 7 (3), sentence 2, of Convention on the Settlement of Matters Arising out of the War and Occupation, 1952-1954.

SCHEIDT *v.* GERMAN FEDERAL REPUBLIC.

(JURISDICTION.)

*Arbitral Commission on Property, Rights and Interests in Germany, Third Chamber.*

(Lagergren, Vice-President; Arndt, Edelman.)

*December* 13, 1957.

THE FACTS (as stated by the Commission).—" The defendant here pleads a stipulation between the parties, made in the proceedings before the *Landgericht*, as a bar to the present submission of the case to the Commission. The stipulation was in the form of an understanding not in writing, between counsel, that further proceedings in this case (as well as in other parallel cases in which the same attorney represented the complainants) would be suspended until the two leading cases selected by counsel, namely, *Levis*[1] and *Veerman*[2], should be heard and decided.

" At a hearing before the *Landgericht* held on June 19, 1956, the understanding previously reached between counsel was presented to the Court, and upon motion of the attorney for the complainants an order was entered by the Court suspending further proceedings in the instant case.

[1 *Levis and Levis* v. *German Federal Republic* (*Jurisdiction*): reported above, p. 524.]
[2 *Veerman* v. *German Federal Republic* (*Interim Protection*): reported above, p. 522.]

" The instant case had been commenced in the *Landgericht* on May 5, 1956. The stipulation of suspension of proceedings was finalized on June 19, 1956. Thereafter the *Landgericht* entered orders in the leading cases (*Levis* and *Veerman*) directing the complainants to deposit security for costs. These orders were resisted by the complainants Levis and Veerman, and objections were filed thereto before the *Landgericht*.

" The period from June 19, 1956, until April 2, 1957, was consumed with submissions regarding security for costs and with orders and revised orders entered by the Court in the test cases. Finally, by its revised orders of April 2, 1957, the *Landgericht* directed complainants Levis and Veerman to deposit sums of DM 5,050 and DM 8,500, respectively. The latter orders were by their terms to be complied with not later than May 10, 1957.

" Since the instant action had been instituted in the *Landgericht* on May 5, 1956, the period of one year expired on May 5, 1947. On June 3, 1957, the complainants filed their claim here, at the same time that the claim in the so-called leading case *Levis* was filed here."

*Held:* that a stipulation made by the parties in litigation before a German court that further proceedings would be suspended, does not bar the complainant from appealing to the Arbitral Commission pursuant to Chapter Five, Article 7 (3), sentence 2, of the Convention on the Settlement of Matters Arising out of the War and Occupation. " The stipulation of the parties should certainly not be construed to restrict or limit complainants' right of appeal or of access to the Arbitral Commission, unless such an intention is plainly evidenced."

The Commission said: " In the instant case, as in *Levis* v. *German Federal Republic*, No. 251, also decided this day, there is the threshold objection by the defendant that submission of the case to the Commission is premature. We have heretofore directed the separate and prior trial of the issue raised by the objection in bar (decision of October 23, 1957).

" As in *Levis*, the complainants here invoke Article 7, paragraph 3, of Chapter Five of the Settlement Convention, and now bring their case directly to the Commission on the ground that the *Landgericht* failed to render a decision within one year. We have held in our decision in *Levis* that the language of the statute is plainly couched in terms of expiration of time, not in terms of relative fault of the parties, and that barring any contemptuous or obstructive tactics on the part of a complainant sufficient to estop him, the right of direct access ripens upon the lapse of the one-year time limit.

" In the instant case we are confronted with a somewhat different issue from that presented in *Levis*. [The Commission here stated the facts of the case as reported above.]

" The defendant asserts that the stipulation of the parties binds them before the German courts, and should likewise be binding before the Commission in the light of Part II, Article 8, of the Charter of this Commission, which provides that it ' shall apply the general principles of international law and of justice and equity '. The defendant further argues that the complainants knew of defendant's intention to demand security for costs before the stipulation was agreed to, pointing to its agent's minutes (not controverted) of the hearing of June 19, 1956, in the *Landgericht*, where reference is made to the matter of security for costs, and at which hearing the stipulation of suspension of proceedings was finalized.

" We note that the *Landgericht*'s order of suspension was entered upon the offer and application of complainant's counsel to suspend in this and other parallel cases while the test cases proceeded. We find nothing in the aforesaid minutes of the hearing of June 19, 1956, or in the formal Court order of the same date, or in the conduct of the parties, evidencing an intention to restrict complainants' right to proceed before this Commission. Whatever construction might be placed upon the stipulation with respect to initial proceedings before the *Landgericht*, we hold that it is clearly no bar to complainants' submission of their case to this Commission pursuant to Article 7, paragraph 2 or paragraph 3. The stipulation of the parties should certainly not be construed to restrict or limit complainants' right of appeal or of access to the Arbitral Commission, unless such an intention is plainly evidenced.

" While our disposition would be to remand to the *Landgericht* a case that is ready for trial, with appropriate instructions and time limitations (see *Levis* v. *[German] Federal Republic*, decision of this date [reported above, p. 524]), we consider such a remand in the instant case at this time to be inappropriate and perhaps futile. In view of the remand of the *Levis* case in our decision of even date, and the likelihood that the parties in the instant case would hold further proceedings below in abeyance to await the event in the *Levis* case, we deem it proper to retain the case before the Commission at this time. The case is retained subject to the further order of the Commission in regard to trial here or remand for designated purposes, in the light of the course of the *Levis* case.

" For these reasons the Arbitral Commission orders that: (1) The direct submission of the complainants' case to the Commission lies; (2) the Commission accepts jurisdiction of the case for all purposes; (3) the case is retained by the Commission at this time, subject to the further orders of the Commission regarding submission of pleadings and trial of the issues."

[Report: *Decisions of the Arbitral Commission*, I (1958), Case No. 3, p. 122.]

Arbitration—Procedure—Competence to determine jurisdiction—
*Ex officio* exercise of such competence—Principle of *forum prorogatum*—Whether applicable to Arbitral Commission on Property,
Rights and Interests in Germany—Time-limits—Change of—New
time-limits—Whether applicable with retroactive effect—Inter-
temporal conflict of procedural law—Whether solved by Charter
of Arbitral Commission.

PURFÜRST *v.* ÉTABLISSEMENTS VITOUX.

(ADMISSIBILITY OF APPEAL.)

*Arbitral Commission on Property, Rights and Interests in Germany,
Second Chamber.*

(Sauser-Hall, Vice-President; Schwandt, Marion.)

*February* 14, 1958.

THE FACTS.—By a decision of February 21, 1955, the Grand
Senate of the German Patent Office fixed the terms of a non-exclusive
licence under patent No. 537631 owned by Établissements Vitoux
S.A. This decision, which was served upon the complainant on April
19, 1955, had been rendered pursuant to Article 7, section 1, of
Law No. 8 of the Allied High Commission on Industrial, Literary
and Artistic Property Rights of Foreign Nations and Nationals of
October 20, 1949, as amended by Law No. 66 of November 15, 1951.
The complainant appealed to the Arbitral Commission, by application dated August 16, 1955, and filed at the Rathaus, Herford,
Westphalia, on August 19, 1955. His application was thus lodged
within the prescribed time-limit of six months under Law No. 8.
However, it was not lodged within the new time-limit of thirty days
stipulated in the Convention creating the Commission. During a
public hearing the defendant contended that the appeal was inadmissible because it was not lodged within the prescribed time-limit.

*Held:* that the appeal was admissible. The new time-limits
set for lodging appeals with the Arbitral Commission were not to be
applied retroactively, *i.e.*, to cases where the old time-limits, more
advantageous than the new ones, had not yet expired.

The Commission said: " On account of the special and exclusive
jurisdiction vested in it by virtue of the Convention on the Settlement
of Matters Arising out of the War and the Occupation of October 23,
1954, which came into force on May 5, 1955, and of Article 6 of its
Charter annexed to the Convention, the Arbitral Commission—
like any other international tribunal—must examine *ex officio*
questions concerning its own jurisdiction and the admissibility of
claims submitted to it, as the principle of *forum prorogatum* does
not apply to organs of international jurisdiction charged with the
performance of special functions as defined in the above-mentioned
Convention, with the sole reservation that the Commission has

also jurisdiction to deal with any other matter which may be referred to it from time to time by agreement between the Signatory States (Charter, Article 6, section 3).

" The Arbitral Commission states that, pursuant to Article 12 of Chapter Ten of the Convention on the Settlement of Matters Arising out of the War and the Occupation, appeals against final decisions of the German Patent Office or its Grand Senate under Allied High Commission Law No. 8 must be submitted to it within thirty days after service of the decision, applications received by the Commission at the *Rathaus*, Herford, up to May 1, 1957, being considered as received in the Registry of the Commission.

" If this provision is applied, the complainant's appeal would have been filed too late and he would be barred from proceeding with his action, since the decision had been served on April 19, 1955, and the appeal was lodged on August 19, 1955.

" However, on the date of service of the decision of the Grand Senate upon the complainant on April 19, 1955, he was entitled by virtue of Allied High Commission Law No. 8 and Article 8 of Regulation No. 1 of April 3, 1954, to a six months' time-limit for an appeal, which would expire on August 21, 1955. In Article 7, section 3, Law No. 8 provides that decisions of the Grand Senate may be subject to appeal to the Occupation Authorities in such manner as may be prescribed in regulations issued by them. If these provisions are applied, the complainant's appeal to the Arbitral Commission at the *Rathaus*, Herford, which was received there on August 19, 1955, was lodged within the prescribed time-limit of six months.

" As the objection that the complainant's appeal had been lodged too late was not raised by the defendant, the Arbitral Commission, in the course of the *ex officio* examination of its jurisdiction and the admissibility of the claim, invited the parties to present their motions concerning this question. The motions were presented verbally at the public hearing on January 17, 1958, and in writing in the pleadings of January 27 and 28, 1958.

" The complainant moved that the appeal be declared admissible on the grounds that on the day of the rendering of the decision he was entitled to a time-limit of six months for lodging his appeal and that the entry into force of the Settlement Convention could not have abridged this time-limit since it had not yet expired on that date. The complainant, therefore, is of the opinion that the appeal filed at the *Rathaus*, Herford, was lodged in due time. Alternatively, he moves that re-instatement be granted to him for reasons of equity.

" The defendant moved that the appeal be declared inadmissible since the time-limits for an appeal were of a preclusive nature under *jus cogens* and therefore immediately applicable—unless a different regulation was expressly made in the new provisions—irrespective of the date on which the disputed decision was rendered or of the time-limits for an appeal prescribed in the legislation in force at that time.

" In its decision concerning these questions the Commission does not disregard the principle that all provisions under procedural law and, in particular, all time-limits for an appeal, non-observance of which leads to preclusion, are of imperative force as from their effective date. However, the immediate application of the new time-limit cannot generally be given retroactive effect.

" The Arbitral Commission is thus faced with an inter-temporal conflict of procedural law inasmuch as the previous law accords to the parties a longer time-limit for an appeal than the new law, *i.e.*, the Settlement Convention, without this new law expressly providing a solution to this question. The Settlement Convention contains only two provisions on this subject, the exact meaning of which may be defined as follows:

" Article 8, section 2 (*a*), of Chapter Ten of the Settlement Convention has modified Allied High Commission Law No. 8 (as amended) as follows:

' An appeal may be taken to the Arbitral Commission on Property, Rights and Interests in Germany referred to in Article 12 of this Chapter from any decision of last instance of the Patent Office or its Grand Senate or from any decision in the first instance of the regular courts, in accordance with the provisions of Article 12 of this Chapter and the Charter of the Arbitral Commission.'

" This provision concerns only decisions of the German courts mentioned therein which have been rendered after May 5, 1955, as is apparent from the formulation ' may be taken to the Arbitral Commission ', ' *pourra faire l'objet d'un appel* '. It is thus not applicable to the fixing of a time-limit for an appeal in the present case.

" The second provision to be taken into consideration is Article 12, section 1, paragraph 2, of Chapter Ten of the Settlement Convention which runs:

' Appeals under the last sentence of Article 2 and paragraph 3 of Article 7 of Allied High Commission Law No. 8, pending the entry into force of the present Convention, before the Patent Appeal Board established by Regulation No. 1 under Law No. 8 (amended) are hereby transferred to the Arbitral Commission and shall be dealt with by it in the same manner as appeals under this Article.'

" This provision, which concerns appeals already pending, cannot have the effect that the time-limit of thirty days for an appeal prescribed in Article 12, section 1, is applied to them as, otherwise, the Arbitral Commission would have to reject as being too late all appeals duly filed within the time-limit of six months prescribed in the previous Law but not within the time-limit of thirty days stipulated in the Settlement Convention. This can hardly be considered to correspond to the intention of the Signatory States to transfer to the Arbitral Commission for decision all such appeals.

" There is no stipulation in the Settlement Convention which would provide a solution to the (inter-temporal) conflict of procedural law existing between the previous Law and the new Law in respect of the time-limit for an appeal. It thus lies with the Arbitral Commission where necessary to fill the gap existing in the Convention in this respect, by interpreting the provisions in compliance with Article 8 of its Charter, which provides:

' In arriving at its decisions, the Commission shall apply the provisions of the Convention and of legislation made applicable thereby. Where necessary to supplement or interpret such provisions, it shall apply the general principles of international law and of justice and equity.'

" The time-limit for an appeal accorded to the parties on the day of service of the decision must, therefore, continue to be effective after May 5, 1955. This method was also suggested and communicated to the defendant by the German Patent Office [in] Munich in its decision of April 25, 1956, attached to the records of the present case. It must be applied to all decisions rendered prior to May 5, 1955, against which no appeal was lodged but which could be made the subject of an appeal, as the time-limit of six months from the date of the decision provided in Law No. 8, Article 7, section 3, of the Allied High Commission had not expired on that date.

" In the present case, the decision of the Grand Senate was rendered on February 21, 1955; the six-months' time-limit for an appeal expired on August 21, 1955, and has thus been observed by the complainant, who filed his appeal at the *Rathaus*, Herford, on August 19, 1955.

" For These Reasons the Arbitral Commission orders that the appeal lodged on August 19, 1955, is admissible. An appeal lies against this decision according to Article 66 of the Rules of Procedure."

[Report: *Decisions of the Arbitral Commission*, I (1958), Case No. 11, p. 142.]

Arbitration—Procedure—Competence—Dependence upon nationality of claimants—Arbitral Commission on Property, Rights and Interests in Germany.

GEYER v. GERMAN FEDERAL REPUBLIC.

*Arbitral Commission on Property, Rights and Interests in Germany, Second Chamber.*

(Sauser-Hall, Vice-President; Schwandt, Marion.)

*March 20, 1958.*

THE FACTS (as stated by the Commission).—" By his application of May 20, 1957, the complainant, Ernst Geyer, appealed against a decision of the *Bundesamt für die Prüfung ausländischer Rückgabe- und Wiederherstellungsansprüche* [Federal Restitution Office] of January 14, 1957, served upon the complainant on January 16, 1957, and rejecting his claim for restitution of securities confiscated in the United States of America. This decision was based on the following facts which, according to the complainant's submissions, have not been contested:

" The complainant's uncle, Johann Georg Geyer, an American national, owned two gold bonds No. M 2972 and 2973 of the Botany Consolidated Mills Inc., New York, New Jersey, U.S.A., of 1,000 dollars each, which had been deposited with the Chase Manhattan Bank at New York. These gold bonds, which were payable on April 1, 1934, were not redeemed but were replaced by two certificates which were transferred by inheritance, first to Johann Nikolaus Geyer, the complainant's father, a German national, after the death in 1931 of Johann Georg Geyer, and subsequently, upon the demise of Johann Nikolaus Geyer on February 23, 1955, at Plauen/Vogtland in the Eastern Zone of Germany, to the complainant himself, Ernst Geyer, also a German national.

" During the War these gold bonds were confiscated as foreign property by the Administration of Enemy Property in the United States, thus becoming the property of the United States.

" The complainant made inquiries of the Chase Manhattan Bank, which informed him that the said gold bonds had been transferred by them to the Attorney General of the United States under Nos. 28-29813. They recommended that he should address himself to the Office of Foreign Property of the American Department of Justice in Washington. However, the request addressed to this Office was rejected on the ground that the time-limit for the submission of restitution claims had already expired on February 9, 1955.

" The complainant applied to the Arbitral Commission for reinstatement into the situation in which he had been placed prior to the expiry of the time-limit, relying on the fact that his father, being a resident of the Eastern Zone of Germany, had not been in a position to apply in due time to the competent American authorities, that it had been impossible on account of the political situation prevailing in the said Zone to submit such an application, and that at that time the further settlement of inheritance affairs of persons deceased in that Zone whose heirs were resident in the Western Zone of Germany was so difficult and complicated that it was impossible for the claimant to submit his claim in due time."

*Held:* that the complaint was inadmissible. The Arbitral Commission had no jurisdiction in cases in which neither the complainant's father nor the complainant as his heir were nationals of one of the United Nations during the period from September 1, 1939, to May 8, 1945.

The Commission said: " In view of these circumstances, the Arbitral Commission finds that the complainant does not fulfil the basic requirement of Article 1, paragraphs 3 and 4, of Chapter Ten of the Convention on the Settlement of Matters Arising out of the War and the Occupation of October 23, 1954, and Article 6 of the Charter of the Commission, according to which only the United Nations and their nationals as well as the successors of such nationals are entitled to submit claims to the Arbitral Commission, provided that, at the date of the discriminatory treatment on which they rely for the substantiation of their restitution claim, they had in fact been nationals of the United Nations.

" Since the complainant is and always has been a German national, he does not at present possess the nationality of any State belonging to the United Nations, nor has he ever possessed such nationality previously. The same applies to his father, to whose rights he has succeeded by inheritance. During the whole period of September 1, 1939, to May 8, 1945, neither the complainant nor his father were nationals of a State belonging to the United Nations. It is thus a matter involving persons who throughout the period covered by the Settlement Convention have possessed only German nationality, and it is their property rights exclusively which were affected by the measures of the American Administration since the complainant's uncle, an American national and former owner of the said gold bonds, had died already in 1931, long before the confiscation of these securities by the American Administration so that his American nationality can be disregarded here. Furthermore, no discriminatory measure by the German authorities has been alleged by the complainant.

" The Arbitral Commission is not competent, therefore, to release the complainant from the observance of the time-limit laid down under American law concerning a matter which is covered exclusively by American jurisdiction.

" As both parties have dispensed with an oral hearing pursuant to Rule 37 of the Rules of Procedure, the Commission decides on the basis of the files.

" For These Reasons the Arbitral Commission orders that the complaint submitted on February 5, 1957 is inadmissible."

[Report: *Decisions of the Arbitral Commission*, I (1958), Case No. 15, p. 152.]

Arbitration—Procedure—Competence—Limitation of—Arbitral Commission on Property, Rights and Interests in Germany—Effect of Convention on the Settlement of Matters Arising Out of the War and Occupation, 1952–1954—Chapter Ten, Article 12, paragraph 1 (a)—Claims against German Federal Republic—Distinction between claims for restitution and claims for compensation—Absence of jurisdiction over latter.

DE HAAN *v.* GERMAN FEDERAL REPUBLIC.

*Arbitral Commission on Property, Rights and Interests in Germany, Third Chamber.*

(Lagergren, Vice-President; Arndt, Phenix.)

*August* 11, 1958.

THE FACTS (as stated by the Commission).—" This is an appeal under Article 12, paragraph 1 (a), of Chapter Ten of the Bonn Settlement Convention against a decision of the *Bundesamt für die Prüfung ausländischer Rückgabe- und Wiederherstellungsansprüche* [Federal Restitution Office] dated September 12, 1957, which denied appellant's request for compensation for four cases of skin cream allegedly confiscated by German authorities between the beginning of 1943 and May 8, 1945.

" Before the Commission, the appellant maintains his earlier arguments and submissions with a view to obtaining compensation from the Federal Republic of Germany, but he also submits a request to the effect that the liquidator of the Rohstoff-Gesellschaft m.b.H. [hereinafter referred to as " Roges "], which company had apparently disposed of the goods, be adjudged to pay to the appellant the equivalent value of the goods, that is, 1,387.20 Dutch Florins plus interest from 1943. The appellant further presents three documents in support of his claim, the first being a receipt from Roges (Enclosure B of the appellant's pleading of November 9, 1957), the second being a letter of February 22, 1957, from the Industriebeteiligungsgesellschaft m.b.H. (the liquidator of Roges) to the appellant (Enclosure E of the same pleading), and the third being a letter of February 27, 1957, from the same sender to the *Bundesamt* (page 12 in the files of the *Bundesamt*)."

*Held:* that the appeal must be dismissed. An appellant under Article 12, [paragraph] 1 (*a*), of Chapter Ten of the Convention on the Settlement of Matters Arising out of the War and Occupation could not ask for relief other than against the Federal Republic of Germany. If the property that had been subject to discriminatory treatment was no longer capable of being restored, the only claim which could arise was a claim for compensation. The Commission had no jurisdiction to adjudicate on such a claim.

The Commission said: " As the present appeal comes under Article 12, paragraph 1 (*a*), of Chapter Ten of the Settlement Convention, the appellant cannot ask for relief other than against the Federal Republic. Therefore no appeal lies in as far as his claims are directed against Roges.

" After considering the circumstances of the case, the Commission has come to the conclusion that the appellant was the owner of the four cases of skin cream and that his loss of them was due to discriminatory treatment as defined in Article 1, paragraph 4, of Chapter Ten of the Settlement Convention.

" However, this places the appellant's request for compensation, whether based on some sort of acknowledgment or not, under the provisions of paragraph 6 of the same Article, which denies jurisdiction to the *Bundesamt* and to the Commission. In this respect the Commission quotes, with approval, the following paragraphs of the decision of the *Bundesamt:*

' [The Federal Restitution Office] is competent only to deal with claims for return of property removed from the owner and restoration of rights and interests on Federal territory in so far as these goods, rights and interests were subject to discriminatory treatment. No other claims may be submitted to the *Bundesamt.* The applicant's claims, however, do not aim at restitution but at compensation since, as the applicant states, Roges, "have disposed of their property without any justification". Nor do the investigations made by the *Bundesamt* in any way disclose what happened to the four cases after their removal to Berlin. Roges, who lost their business records as a result of war events, are unable to give any explanation in this connection. They merely assume that in the performance of the duties incumbent upon them at the time, they sold the goods delivered to them by order of the German Reich. The assumption that the skin cream confiscated in 1943 was sold and used also appears likely in view of past experience. As it cannot thus be ascertained that the merchandise is still in existence and traceable on Federal territory, return cannot possibly be effected on Federal territory, so that a compensation claim results.

' According to the foregoing observations, the competence of the *Bundesamt* is restricted to claims for return and restoration and does not extend to compensation claims. This also follows from Article 1, paragraph 6, which expressly stipulates that the provisions made therein shall not be applicable to claims for compensation of property, rights and interests which were subject to discriminatory treatment or arising out of the war by any other means, whether directly or indirectly. . . . '

" For the foregoing reasons the Commission can find no justification for the allowance of the appeal.

" For These Reasons the Arbitral Commission orders that: (1) the appeal from the decision of the *Bundesamt für die Prüfung ausländischer Rückgabe- und Wiederherstellungsansprüche* dated September 12, 1957, is dismissed; (2) the appellant shall bear the court fee of one hundred Deutsche Mark."

[Report: *Decisions of the Arbitral Commission*, I (1958), Case No. 23, p. 190.]

---

**Arbitration — Procedure — Competence — Competence to decide question of interim protection—Claim for costs—Interim protection for purpose of immediate satisfaction of such claim— Whether admissible.**

HERRMANN *v.* GERMAN FEDERAL REPUBLIC.
(INTERIM PROTECTION.)

*Arbitral Commission on Property, Rights and Interests in Germany, Third Chamber.*

(Lagergren, Vice-President; Arndt, Phenix.)

*September 30, 1958.*

THE FACTS (as stated by the Commission).—" The complainant claims from the defendant dollar bonds in the face amount of $740,000 of which he was allegedly deprived during the war owing to discriminatory treatment. On March 15, 1957, the *Bundesamt für die Prüfung ausländischer Rückgabe- und Wiederherstellungsansprüche* [Federal Restitution Office] rejected his claim. According to the Certificate of Acknowledgment of Service issued by the German Consulate-General in New York, that decision was served upon the complainant on March 29, 1957. The complainant appealed from the decision by telegram received in the Registry of the Commission on May 3, 1957.

" By pleadings dated May 24, 1958, June 19, 1958, July 8, 1958 and August 27, 1958, complainant applied for interim protection, under Rule 53 of the Rules of Procedure of the Commission, in the form of an Order directing the defendant to pay immediately the amount of $3,000 as an advance payment for costs incurred in the appeal proceedings. The advance payment was to cover the complainant's travel expenses to and from Europe as well as other relevant cash expenses.

" By pleading dated June 23, 1958, the defendant moved for the rejection of the application for interim protection stating that while Rule 70 of the Commission's Rules of Procedure contemplates special orders as to costs in exceptional cases where the Commission finds the proceedings to have been malicious or vexatious, no right to reimbursement of costs exists until the Commission has made the necessary finding, and that under Rule 53 of the Commission's Rules of Procedure the Commission cannot grant interim protection in respect of not yet existing rights.

" As to the merits, the defendant has submitted that the complainant's appeal was lodged too late and has therefore requested that, pursuant to Rule 58 (*b*), the objection of inadmissibility be made the subject of a separate decision and that the appeal be rejected as inadmissible.

" In an Order dated July 28, 1958, the President of the Third Chamber held that no case of urgency existed as defined by Rule 53 (*e*) of the Rules of Procedure, and ordered as follows:

'(1) The application of the provisions of Rule 53 (*e*) of the Rules of Procedure of the Commission to the petition for interim protection submitted by the complainant in his letter of May 24, 1958, is denied;

'(2) The complainant's petition for interim protection is referred to the Chamber, meeting again after the termination of the judicial vacation, on September 1, 1958.' "

The present decision was the one given by the Arbitral Commission upon the above-mentioned petition.

*Held:* that the application for interim protection must be rejected. The complainant did not ask for the conservation of a right to reimbursement of costs, but for immediate satisfaction of his claim for costs. The Commission was competent to decide the question of interim protection although an objection on the admissibility of the appeal had been raised and no decision had yet been reached.

The Commission said: " The Commission deems it appropriate to decide the question of interim protection although an objection on the admissibility of the appeal has been raised and no decision has yet been reached (see in this connection Guggenheim, *Zeitschrift für ausländisches öffentliches Recht und Völkerrecht*, 1958, pp. 139 *et seq.*).

" It is not necessary to decide at this time whether Rule 70 in conjunction with Rule 69 (*b*) of the Commission's Rules of Procedure makes it impossible in any circumstances for the Commission to order interim protection in respect of costs. In the present case the order applied for by the complainant is not one for the *conservation* of a right to reimbursement of costs; it is one for the immediate satisfaction of his claim for costs. Even if it were a claim for conservation, there can be no question that the defendant Federal Republic would comply with any judgment of the Commission requiring it to reimburse the complainant for his costs. No conservation of a possible future right is therefore necessary, since no such possible future right is in any jeopardy whatsoever, and measures under Rule 53 of the Commission's Rules of Procedure are inadmissible if only for that reason.

" For These Reasons the Arbitral Commission orders that the application for interim protection is rejected."

[Report: *Decisions of the Arbitral Commission*, II (1959), Case No. 24, p. 133.]

**Arbitration—Procedure—Jurisdiction—Jurisdiction of Arbitral Commission on Property, Rights and Interests in Germany— Conferred only in relation to rights of United Nations nationals —Extension of that jurisdiction—Conditions of such extension— Capacity to appear as party before Arbitral Commission—Effect of entitlement to " most-favoured-nation " treatment.**

LEUPOLD-PRAESENT *v.* GERMAN FEDERAL REPUBLIC.

*Arbitral Commission on Property, Rights and Interests in Germany, First Chamber.*

(Wickström, President; Euler, Bennett.)

*November 27, 1958.*

THE FACTS (as stated by the Commission).—" By decision rendered on April 24, 1956, and served upon the complainant on May 17, 1956, the *Finanzgericht* of Hamburg rejected the appeal lodged by the complainant against the decision dated June 14, 1955, of the *Finanzamt* of Hamburg-Dammtor concerning a levy imposed under the Equalization of Burdens Law of August 14, 1952, on profits resulting from the conversion under the currency reform of two mortgages on property owned by the complainant.

" By application filed with the Commission on June 16, 1956, the complainant appealed against the decision of the *Finanzgericht*.

" In its answer, the defendant raised the objection that the Commission had no jurisdiction to entertain the appeal."

*Held:* that the complainant was entitled to appear before the Commission. The Commission, however, was incompetent to decide on the complainant's appeal, since it had jurisdiction only with respect to the rights of nationals of one of the United Nations. The jurisdiction of the Commission could have been extended to cover also a right of a Swiss national (*i.e.*, someone who was not a national of one of the United Nations) only through the agreement of all the States parties to the Convention establishing the Commission.

The Commission said: " It will be convenient at the outset to make it clear that the claim directed to the exemption of the complainant from the payment of the above-mentioned levy is based: (1) on the provisions of Article 6 of Chapter Ten of the Convention on the Settlement of Matters Arising out of the War and the Occupation, [1952–1954] which provides that nationals of any of the United Nations shall be exempted from the payment of certain taxes, levies and imposts; and (2) on the provisions of Article 1 of the Agreement as to the Equalization of Burdens in Germany, concluded on August 26, 1952, between the Swiss Confederation and the Federal Republic of Germany, pursuant to which Swiss nationals enjoy the same benefits in relation to the Equalization of Burdens as are accorded in this field to nationals of the most-favoured-nation.

" *The right of the complainant to submit the dispute to the Commission.*—Pursuant to paragraph 4 of Article 6 of the Charter of the Commission, disputes within the jurisdiction of the Commission may be submitted by any of the Signatory States or any State which has acceded to the Charter or by a national or resident of any such State.

" The complainant is a national of the Swiss Confederation, which is not a Signatory State and which has not acceded to the Charter. The argument of the complainant that the fact that the Swiss Confederation concluded the [above-mentioned] Agreement with the Federal Republic in 1952, that is to say, at a time when the Settlement Convention had not yet entered into force but when its contents were already known, should be considered as an accession in advance to the Convention and to the Charter annexed thereto, and that it should therefore have the same effect as a subsequent accession, is unfounded because Article 16 of the Charter provides that any State desiring to accede to the Charter of the Commission shall communicate its decision so to do by written notification addressed to each of the Signatory States through diplomatic channels and shall deposit with the Federal Government an instrument of accession to the Charter. This, however, has not been done by the Swiss Confederation.

" It is now uncontested, however, that the complainant is a resident of the Federal Republic of Germany, which is a Signatory State. As such, she is entitled to appear before the Commission.

" *Jurisdiction of the Commission.*—The defendant contended that the jurisdiction of the Commission cannot be extended by an agreement concluded between the Federal Republic of Germany and another State without the consent of the States which concluded the Settlement Convention (Signatory States), and that, moreover, the Agreement of August 26, 1952, expressly denied jurisdiction to the Commission. With regard to the latter point, the defendant referred to: (1) Article 3 of the above Agreement which stipulates that ' the administration and courts competent under the Equalization of Burdens Law shall decide on the interpretation of the provisions applicable under this Agreement, and (2) the protocol of negotiations on the above Agreement bearing the same date as the Agreement, which contains the following paragraph:

'Concerning Article 3: It was the agreed view of the parties that an appeal to the "Arbitral Commission" provided for in Article 12 of Chapter Ten of the "Settlement Convention" would not lie and that it would not be opportune to establish an Arbitral Commission for the purposes of the present agreement. In view of this position, the Federal Ministry of Finance will formulate an appropriate administrative measure to meet any cases of special importance in which the Federal Finance Court (*Bundesfinanzhof*) should differ from a decision of the "Arbitral Commission".'

"Paragraph 1 of Article 6 of the Charter provides that the Commission shall have jurisdiction in all disputes envisaged under Article 7 of Chapter Five and Article 12 of Chapter Ten of the Convention, and this means that the claim of one of the parties must be based upon some provision of these Chapters. Article 6 of Chapter Ten, which is the provision relied upon by the complainant, is concerned only with the right of exemption granted to persons who were nationals of one of the United Nations on a certain date, and it is only in relation to the rights of such a national that jurisdiction is conferred upon the Commission.

"It is true that, by agreement with a country which, like the Swiss Confederation, is not a member of the United Nations, the Federal Republic of Germany could grant the nationals of such a country the same concessions as those granted under Article 6 of Chapter Ten, but it has no power to extend the jurisdiction of the Commission to disputes with such nationals without the consent of the other Signatory States. The Commission was established by the Convention and its jurisidiction is defined therein and in the Charter annexed thereto. Any extension of that jurisdiction would constitute a modification of the Convention and of the Charter and, as in the case of any modification of an agreement, may be made only with the consent of all the Parties thereto. This principle, moreover, has been expressly recognized in paragraph 3 of Article 6 of the Charter, which provides that the Commission shall also have jurisdiction in any other matter which may be referred to it from time to time by agreement between the Signatory States and that, if any acceding State is directly concerned in the matter, the consent of its Government shall also be necessary.

"It was not disputed before us that the other Signatory States have not given their consent to an extension of the jurisdiction of the Commission.

"It was clearly because the Federal Republic of Germany was unable to extend the jurisdiction of the Commission to nationals of the Swiss Confederation that it caused the provisions of Article 3 to be inserted in the Agreement, and those provisions can only be interpreted as expressing the intention of the two States to exclude any recourse to the Commission by conferring sole jurisdiction on the German authorities and courts with regard to litigation arising from the interpretation of the Laws governing the subject-matter in question. The interpretation is confirmed, moreover, by the fact that the protocol signed on the same day as the Agreement contains a formal declaration excluding the jurisdiction of the Commission. Contrary to the contention of the complainant, the fact that this protocol was not published or ratified does not diminish its significance in relation to the interpretation of the Agreement in a dispute between the two States which signed it or their nationals.

" In these circumstances, it follows that the Commission has no jurisdiction to entertain the appeal here in question. It is unnecessary, therefore, to consider the other legal grounds, and in particular those based on an interpretation of the provisions of Article 10 of Chapter Ten of the Convention, on which the complainant sought to establish the jurisdiction of the Commission.

" For These Reasons the Arbitral Commission declares that the complainant is entitled to appear before it; finds that it is incompetent to decide on the appeal and consequently rejects it; orders that the complainant shall bear the court costs of one hundred Deutsche Mark."

[Report: *Decisions of the Arbitral Commission*, II (1959), Case No. 34, p. 153.]

**Arbitration—Procedure—Competence to determine jurisdiction —United Nations Tribunal for Libya—Preliminary exception— Admissibility of—General Assembly Resolution 388 (V), Article X, 1 (b).**

See p. 13 (*Italy* v. *Libya* (*General List No.* 2)).

**Arbitration—Procedure—Right of recourse to Arbitral Commission—Nationality as criterion—Nationality of claimant.**

See p. 234 (*Persitz-Keller* v. *German Federal Republic*).

Arbitration—Procedure—Competence—Jurisdiction—Of Arbitral Tribunal for Agreement on German External Debts—Exclusive jurisdiction regarding interpretation or application of Agreement —Attempt to settle dispute by negotiation prior to submission to Arbitral Tribunal—Competence of other arbitral body yet not established—*Litispendence*—Principle of *perpetuatio fori*—Dispute between Governments distinguished from dispute between private individuals—Request for decision distinguished from request for advisory opinion.

See p. 33 (*Swiss Confederation* v. *German Federal Republic* (No. 1)).

Arbitration — Procedure — Competence — Jurisdiction — Arbitral Commission on Property, Rights and Interests in Germany— Extension of jurisdiction—Whether permissible—Request for declaratory judgment.

See p. 341 (*Heidsieck & Cie* v. *German Federal Republic*).

### iii.—Intervention

Arbitration—Procedure—Intervention—Rules of procedure of arbitral commission—Absence of rules on conditions of intervention —Admissibility under generally recognized principle—Legitimate interest as basis of intervention—Whether such interest existing.

GREEK POWDER & CARTRIDGE CO. (KINGDOM OF THE HELLENES, INTERVENOR) *v.* GERMAN FEDERAL REPUBLIC.

*Arbitral Commission on Property, Rights and Interests in Germany, First Chamber.*

(Wickström, President; Euler, Kokinopoulos.)

*January* 10, 1958.

THE FACTS (as stated by the Commission).—" The *Bundesamt für äussere Restitutionen* [Federal Office for External Restitution), by a decision dated May 7, 1957, rejected the complaint submitted by the Royal Hellenic Government demanding restitution of certain property previously owned by the Greek Powder & Cartridge Co.; alternatively, compensation in respect of this property.

" On May 31, 1957, the complainant [the Greek Powder & Cartridge Co.] submitted to the Commission an application for reversion of this decision.

" In its answer, the defendant raised the objection of inadmissibility of the complaint on the grounds that the complainant was not entitled to claim since it could not be considered as a 'party concerned ' within the meaning of Article 7, paragraph 2, of Chapter Five of the Convention on the Settlement of Matters Arising out of the War and the Occupation [1952–1954] and that the Royal Hellenic Government alone, having previously brought this complaint before the *Bundesamt*, could have submitted such a complaint.

" On December 30, 1957, the firm [of] Apostolides filed an application asking to be admitted as an intervening party in the present case. The complainant declared that it would raise no objection against this intervention, but the defendant opposed it.

" Finally, on January 4, 1958, the Royal Hellenic Government submitted a pleading by which they intervened in the matter in order to support the claims submitted by the complainant and by the firm [of] Apostolides, both being Greek nationals."

*Held:* that the intervention by the firm of Apostolides was not admissible. " Anyone desiring to intervene must prove to have a legitimate interest which might be affected by the decision to be taken." The fact that in an action instituted by the would-be intervenor against the same defendant, a similar plea had been raised by the latter, did not suffice to establish such a legitimate interest.

The Commission said: " In order to substantiate their intervention the firm [of] Apostolides contended that in Case No. 215 pending before the Commission and instituted by them against the defendant, a similar objection had been raised by the latter. The decision to be rendered in the present case on this objection would constitute a precedent and would thus be of considerable importance to the firm [of] Apostolides.

" In its Rules of Procedure, the Commission has not laid down any conditions for intervention, but the Commission intends to apply the generally recognized principle according to which anyone desiring to intervene in a case must prove that he has a legitimate interest which might be affected by the decision to be taken.

" In the present case the firm [of] Apostolides did not prove such a legitimate interest, since it is not bound by the Commission's decision in the present case; and in their own case, it may use all arguments available.

" The intervention is thus rejected on the ground of inadmissibility.

" It is unnecessary to render a decision on costs as neither party has submitted an application to this effect.

" For these reasons the Arbitral Commission (1) agrees to decide on the admissibility of the intervention of the firm [of] Apostolides by a separate judgment; (2) declares that this intervention is inadmissible."

[Report: *Decisions of the Arbitral Commission*, I (1958), Case No. 7, p. 135.]

**Arbitration—Procedure—Intervention—Rules of procedure of Arbitral Commission—Absence of rules on conditions of intervention—Admissibility under generally recognized principle—Legitimate interest as basis of intervention—Intervening Party—Not allowed to make submissions differing from main application.**

KINGDOM OF THE HELLENES *v.* GERMAN FEDERAL REPUBLIC.

*Arbitral Commission on Property, Rights and Interests in Germany, Third Chamber.*

(Lagergren, Vice-President; Arndt, Kokinopoulos.)

*May* 16, 1958.

THE FACTS.—In this case D. S. Theodoropoulos and E. D. Kyvelos applied to be admitted as intervening party. The case involved a compensation claim presented by the Greek Government on the ground of the non-restitution of property owned by the dissolved firm [of] Theodoropoulos & Kyvelos. The applicants proved that they were legal successors of the said firm. The Greek Government supported the application for intervention, while the defendant Government contested its admissibility.

*Held:* that the intervention in favour of the Greek Government must be allowed in so far as it purported to support the main submission. An intervening party was " not entitled to submit new submissions or submissions differing from the main application." Although the Rules of Procedure of the Arbitral Commission did not clearly define the conditions for intervention, admissibility of intervention was " dependent upon the legitimate interest of the applicants in the result of the litigation."

The Commission said: " Since Rule 52 of the Rules of Procedure of the Arbitral Commission does not clearly define the conditions for intervention, it is deemed expedient in this case to apply the generally recognized principle according to which admissibility of intervention is dependent upon the legitimate interest of the applicants in the result of the ligitation, as was set forth in a Judgment by the First Chamber of the Arbitral Commission of January 10, 1958, in Case No. 247 (*Greek Powder & Cartridge Co.* v. *German Federal Republic*[1]).

" In cases of this kind, moreover, the principle of admissibility of intervention does not contravene the provisions of the [Bonn] Settlement Convention [1952–1954], which contains neither in Chapter Five nor in the Annex thereto, nor in particular in Section 5 of the latter, any provision prohibiting intervention.

" There is no doubt that the applicants for intervention hold a legitimate interest which justifies intervention since they appear in their capacity as legal successors of the Company which was the

[1 Reported above, p. 544.]

owner of the property which had allegedly been removed by the German authorities from Greek territory.

" It is appropriate, in the last analysis, to examine the objection raised by the defendant Government to the effect that the application for intervention in the proceedings was inadmissible on the ground that the submissions of the intervening parties differ from the main application.  It is a principle that a party intervening on behalf of one of the litigants must restrict itself to supporting the litigant's submissions, and is not entitled to submit new submissions or submissions which differ from the main application.

" However, in the present case, the main request of the intervenors' submissions is that the Arbitral Commission grant the compensation claim of the Greek Government.  In so far as the purpose of the intervention is that the Arbitral Commission shall grant the main submission, the intervention must be allowed.

" For These Reasons the Arbitral Commission orders that: (1) the intervention in favour of the Greek Government is allowed in so far as it purports to support the main submission.  All other submissions of the interveners are rejected. . . ."

[Report: *Decisions of the Arbitral Commission*, I (1958), Case No. 19, p. 171.]

### iv.—Procedure

**Arbitration—Procedure—Time-limits fixed in Charter establishing Arbitral Commission—Impossibility of changing such time-limits on basis of Commission's Rules of Procedure—Convention on the Settlement of Matters Arising Out of the War and Occupation, 1952–1954—Appeals to Arbitral Commission under Chapter Ten, Article 12, paragraph 2, second sentence, of Convention—Retroactive application of appeal provisions—Whether permissible—Change of law on appeals—Admissibility of certain appeals under new law—Inadmissibility of other appeals—Whether constituting discriminatory or unequal treatment.**

MERCEDES BÜROMASCHINEN-WERKE A.G. *v.* GERMAN FEDERAL REPUBLIC.

*Arbitral Commission on Property, Rights and Interests in Germany, Third Chamber.*

(Lagergren, Vice-President; Arndt, Edelman.)

*December* 13, 1957.

THE FACTS.—The complainant in this case, a German subsidiary company wholly owned by a United States parent corporation, sought extension of the protection period of its patent No. 509656 and 144 other patents. Both the German Patent Office and its Appeal Senate 1a rejected the complainant's claim. The final decision of the Appeal Senate was rendered on March 23, 1953. The Company then appealed to the Allied High Commission, and that organ transferred the appeal to the Patent Appeal Board. On April 29, 1955, the Board held that it was without jurisdiction. On May 5, 1955, the Convention on the Settlement of Matters Arising out of the War and Occupation became effective, and on June 3, 1955, the Company filed its appeal with the Arbitral Commission set up under that Convention. The complainant's appeal was lodged under Chapter Ten, Article 8, paragraph 2, of the Convention, read in conjunction with Article 12. The latter Article provided that decisions therein defined might be appealed against " upon application to the Commission by the party concerned within thirty days after the service thereof." This time-limit was prescribed, *inter alia*, for any appeal from a final decision of the German Patent Office or its Senate under Law No. 8 of the Allied High Commission, *i.e.*, the kind of appeal pending in the present case. The Arbitral Commission stated the remaining facts relevant to the case in the following terms:

" Complainant asks the Commission to give it relief, despite the clear time prescription of the Convention, on any one of three theories: (1) through a liberal application of Rule 23 (*d*) of the Commission's Rules of Procedure; (2) through the application of what complainant's counsel terms the 'mysterious' provisions of the second sentence of Article 12 (2) of Chapter Ten of the Convention, but which he believes can be moulded to fit complainant's situation; or (3) through the application of 'constitutional' protections against discriminatory or unequal treatment as between litigants in identical circumstances.

" On July 9, 1957, the Government of the Federal Republic filed an answer in which it asserted the inadmissibility of the appeal as filed too late, and presented this contention as a preliminary objection under Article 58 of the Commission's Rules of Procedure. The defendant points out that the challenged decision had already become final on service upon the complainant in April 1953, and that there is thus no legal possibility now of review by the Arbitral Commission. To allow an appeal in cases which have long since become final, argues the defendant, would constitute so far-reaching a measure that the Signatory States would surely have stipulated expressly for the allowance of such appeals. Any retroactive change in the legal situation as it existed until the entry into force of the Convention has been ruled out, the defendant asserts, by the express limitation of the time for lodging an appeal to a period of thirty days after service of the decision below. As the Settlement Convention came into force on May 5, 1955, appeals against decisions of the German Patent Office served before that date are possible, at most, in cases where the time-limit of thirty days for lodging an appeal had not yet expired on May 5, 1955."

*Held:* that the preliminary objection raised by the defendant must be sustained and the appeal of the complainant dismissed. The Commission had no right to extend the time-limits fixed in the Settlement Convention. In this case there was no ground for appealing to the Commission under Chapter Ten, Article 12, paragraph 2, second sentence, of that Convention. The clear language of the Convention ruled out a general retroactive application of its appeal provisions. Non-admission of the complainant's appeal did not constitute unequal or discriminatory treatment.

The Commission said: " We first take up the question of whether the present appeal embraces only complainant's patent No. 509656 or all the patents listed in its enclosure annexed to the complaint. In the course of oral argument, the defendant took the position that the appeal must be deemed to have been taken solely from the decision on patent No. 509656. This is so, it argues, because separate appeals were not filed in respect to each of the more than one hundred companion patent claims which were rejected by the Patent Senate.

" The Commission finds that each of the 144 companion patents appeared on a list entitled ' Schedule A ', which was referred to in the complainant's notice of appeal to this Commission, and were made a part thereof by reference. The Commission rules that the present appeal embraces all decisions of the Patent Senate of March

23, 1953, pertaining to all the patents listed in the aforesaid 'Schedule A'.

" We now turn to the three alternative grounds which complainant suggests might support the allowance of the appeal. The wording of Rule 23 (d) of the Commission's Rules of Procedure does afford a certain flexibility in the enforcement of the Commission's procedural rules. The discretion that rests in the Rule does not extend, however, to time-limits which are fixed in the Settlement Convention or by the Charter of the Arbitral Commission.

" Nor can the Commission find any source of relief for the complainant under Article 12, paragraph 2, second sentence, of Chapter Ten. That sentence must be read in conjunction with the first sentence of the same paragraph. It covers a case where an appeal to this Commission from the German court of first instance was not possible because no rulings relating to Articles 1 through 8 of Chapter Ten of the Convention were involved, but where the higher German Court renders a decision which, in the opinion of the party concerned, violates some provision of the aforesaid Articles of the Convention. There is no connection between the circumstances just described and the situation of this complainant.

" Finally, we come to complainant's plea that unless the appeal provisions of Article 8 [of] Chapter Ten are given retroactive effect, they will work an unjust discrimination against those claimants whose cases happen to be decided by the Patent Office or the Patent Appeal Board before the effective date of the Convention. This will mean, argues the complainant, the exclusion of those claimants by ' mere chance ' from the benefits of an appeal to the Commission, while others, subject to identical judgments entered one day after the effective date of the Convention, will be afforded a full review of the decisions of the German Patent Office.

" The language of Articles 8 and 12 of Chapter Ten of the Convention, which define the reach of our powers in patent cases, is plainly expressed in prospective, and not retroactive, terms. Article 12 defines the decisions which are appealable to the Commission, and contains the following internal time-limitation: ' upon application to the Commission within thirty days of the service thereof ', i.e., service of the decision from which the appeal is taken.

" The clear language of the Treaty in our view rules out a general retroactive application of its appeal provisions. As if to confirm this express intention, the Signatory Powers added a special provision to allow a limited retroactivity in the case of certain appeals pending before the Patent Appeal Board at the effective date of the Convention. Provision is made for the transfer to the Commission by Article 2 and Article 7 (of Law No. 8) of appeals pending before the Patent Appeal Board on May 5, 1955.

" In applying the provisions of Articles 8 and 12, the Commission recognizes that an appeal would seem to be allowable from Patent

Office decisions rendered before the entry into force of the Convention, *i.e.*, May 5, 1955, but where the time-limit of thirty days for lodging an appeal had not expired by that date. An appeal might also be admissible where the time-limit for appeal under the provisions in force before May 5, 1955 (for instance, under Regulation No. 1 of Law No. 8), had not yet expired at that date. But in the case at bar, the Commission can find no justification in the language of the Convention for the allowance of an appeal.

" The Commission further observes that the reserved power of broad discretion which has been vested in the Patent Appeal Board under the Occupation Statutes (Allied High Commission Law No. 13) was not transferred to the Commission. Therefore, notwithstanding the fact that the Patent Appeal Board might have been able to exercise such discretion until May 5, 1955, the Commission is not vested with that power. Nor is review of decisions of the Patent Appeal Board within the jurisdiction of the Commission.

" The mere fact that laws or statutes are changed, making certain cases appealable after the change which may not have been before, does not of itself constitute an unconstitutional inequality or discrimination. Complainant's argument also ignores the considerations of fairness and equality of treatment due [to] those who on their part relied upon the finality of decisions under the applicable law.

" Much as we deplore the fact that this complainant cannot now obtain a review by this Commission, we find that no other course is properly open to us but to apply the clear language and intention of the governing Treaty.

" For these reasons the Arbitral Commission orders that: (1) The preliminary objection filed by the Federal Republic of Germany is sustained; (2) the appeal from the decisions of the Appeal Senate 1a of the German Patent Office entered March 23, 1953, relating to patent No. 509656 and 144 other patents of the complainant, is dismissed."

[Report: *Decisions of the Arbitral Commission,* I (1958), Case No. 6, p. 130.]

NOTE.—See also *Ambi-Budd Presswerk* v. *German Federal Republic* (*ibid.,* Case No. 13, p. 146), decided along similar lines and in which the Commission referred to the above decision in the *Mercedes* case.

In *Hall Laboratories, Inc.* v. *German Federal Republic* (*ibid.,* II (1958), Case No. 25, p. 135), the Commission cited its judgment in the *Mercedes* case and maintained the view that its jurisdiction to hear appeals from decisions of the German Patent Office or the Senate of that Office extended only to appeals filed with it within thirty days after the service of the decision on the complainant.

However, in *S.A. Violatomiki and Kingdom of Greece* v. *German Federal Republic* (*ibid.,* Case No. 33, p. 151), the Commission decided to admit applications which were filed with it one day after the expiry of the thirty-days' limit. The applications in question were late owing to the overburdening of the postal services in Germany with mail during the Christmas season. The Commission held that "in accordance with the principles of equity and good faith, no prejudice should result to the complainants from that delay" (at p. 153).

In *Dracoulis (Heirs)* v. *German Federal Republic* (reported above, at p. 515), the Commission found the appeal to be inadmissible because of a two-days' delay in filing the appeal.

*Cf.* also the decisions in *United States Radium Corporation* v. *German Federal Republic* (*ibid.*, II (1958), Case No. 40, p. 166), and *Du Pont de Nemours & Co.* v. *German Federal Republic* (*ibid.*, Case No. 43, p. 171).

Arbitration—Procedure—Time-limits—Reinstatement—Requirements of—Not examined by municipal court—Whether question of reinstatement to be decided by Arbitral Commission.

LA MONT CORPORATION *v.* GERMAN FEDERAL REPUBLIC.

*Arbitral Commission on Property, Rights and Interests in Germany, Third Chamber.*

(Lagergren, Vice-President; Arndt, Phenix.)

*March 11, 1958.*

THE FACTS (as stated by the Commission).—" On October 18, 1950, the complainant firm applied belatedly under Article 5 of Law No. 8 of the Allied High Commission for an extension of the protection period of the patents described in the first of the two contested decisions by the German Patent Office of April 8, 1957—file number Patent 608782. At the same time complainant requested revival of its claim notwithstanding the expiry of the time-limit for filing an application, basing its request on the ground that the premises of the German company 'La Mont-Kessel Herpen & Co. K.G.' situated in East Berlin had been closed down in the middle of September 1950 by the People's Police of the German Democratic Republic. This Company was complainant's licensee and the data necessary to support an application under Law No. 8 had again to be procured from the United States on account of the said seizure.

" The Patent Administrative Department allowed the revival of the claim but rejected the application for extension.

" By the first of the two contested decisions the Appeal Senate 1a of the German Patent Office rejected the complaint on April 8, 1957. In giving the reasons for its decision, the Appeal Senate points out:

' With regard to the present decision the Senate had to examine first the admissibility of the application for extension. In this connection it had to be re-examined whether the requirements for revival of the claim notwithstanding the expiry of the time-limit for filing an application had been fulfilled.'

" The Senate arrived at the following result which was substantiated in detail:

' According to the facts which have so far been adduced, the requirements for revival have been insufficiently proved.'

" At the end of their discussion of the revival question, the Senate said with regard thereto:

' It is unnecessary, however, to attempt further investigation and to go into the question whether, notwithstanding the time-limits set by § 43 of the Patent Law, it is legally admissible to correct the deficiency in the submission, since in examining the factual requirements for an extension claim the Senate has not reached any conclusion on the question of ownership other than that in the contested decision.'

" The latter opinion is then substantiated in detail.

" Also on April 8, 1957, the Appeal Senate 1a of the German Patent Office rendered the second of the two contested decisions— file number N 550 Ia/13a. It rejected an appeal by the complainant against the decision of the Examining Office for Category 13a, given on September 27, 1952. In these proceedings, too, the complainant had applied for revival of the claim notwithstanding the expiry of the time-limit (here the time-limit for lodging an appeal under Article 30, paragraph 1, of the First Regulation under Law No. 8). Referring to the decision concerning patent No. 608782, the Appeal Senate left undecided the question whether revival was legally possible or factually justified and rejected the complaint on substantive grounds.

" By a pleading of May 29, 1957, received by the Arbitral Commission on June 1, 1957, the complainant lodged an appeal against the decisions served upon the complainant on May 3, 1957, giving detailed reasons in support thereof."

*Held:* that the case must be referred to the Appeal Senate of the German Patent Office for decision as to the admissibility of the application notwithstanding the expiration of the prescribed time-limit for the filing thereof. The Arbitral Commission, as an international court, had deemed it appropriate not to decide at that time on the question of revival of the claim but to refer the case to the municipal tribunal.

The Commission said: " In the proceedings concerning patent No. 608782 and others, the Arbitral Commission further had to examine whether revival of the application notwithstanding the expiry of the time-limit for its filing was properly granted by the Patent Administrative Department. This question should already have been decided by the Appeal Senate 1a. Only if the requirements for revival of the application notwithstanding the expiry of the time-limit for its filing had actually been fulfilled could the Court of higher instance concern itself with the proceedings. The question of a timely filing of the application involves a preliminary procedural requirement which must be officially examined by any court. The highest German courts have invariably decided that a court of revision, too, is obliged officially to examine whether revival of the claim by a lower court, notwithstanding the expiry of the time-limit, corresponds to the statutory requirements, as the admissibility of further proceedings is dependent upon this fact (see recent decisions of the Federal Supreme Court, vol. 6, p. 370, and vol. 12, p. 165).

" A similar procedural error exists also in the proceedings M 550 Ia/13a, because here the preliminary question as to legally effective revival was erroneously left undecided.

" The Arbitral Commission, as an international court, has deemed it appropriate not at this time to decide on the question of revival of the claim but to refer the case to the Appeal Senate 1a of the German Patent Office pursuant to Article 7, paragraph 4, of Chapter Five of the Settlement Convention.

" For these reasons the Arbitral Commission orders that: (1) The proceedings concerning the patents No. 608782 and others are joined to the proceedings in the case of patent application M 550; (2) the case is remanded to the *Beschwerdesenat* 1a of the German Patent Office for decision as to the admissibility of the application notwithstanding the expiration of the prescribed time-limit for the filing thereof; (3) if the reinstatement is finally allowed the Arbitral Commission will proceed with the consideration of the merits of the case and render its decision."

[Report: *Decisions of the Arbitral Commission*, I (1958), Case No. 14, p. 149.]

## Arbitration—Procedure—Time-limits—Application of.

See p. 508 (*Western Machinery Company* v. *German Federal Republic*).

## Arbitration—Procedure—Competence to determine rules of procedure.

See p. 190 (*Re Application No.* 235/56 (*Mr. X. and Mrs. X.* v. *German Federal Republic*)).

## Arbitration—Procedure—Application for order of interim protection.

See p. 555 (*Scheidt* v. *German Federal Republic* (*Interim Protection*)).

## III.—Evidence

**Arbitration—Evidence—Offer of proof in regard to facts and allegations pertaining to another case—Whether admissible.**

SCHEIDT *v.* GERMAN FEDERAL REPUBLIC.
(INTERIM PROTECTION.)

*Arbitral Commission on Property, Rights and Interests in Germany, Third Chamber.*

(Lagergren, Vice-President; Arndt, Edelman.)

*November 27, 1957.*

THE FACTS.—The complainants, in a submission dated October 22, 1957, asked for an order of interim protection directing " the defendant, and especially its referee in the Federal Ministry of Finance, to cease and desist from intimidating and prosecuting Dr. S. (complainants' attorney here), both before criminal and disciplinary German courts."

*Held:* that the application for an order of interim protection must be refused. The Commission could not " entertain an offer of proof by a litigant in regard to facts and allegations pertaining to another case pending before " the Commission.

The Commission said: " The submission is based entirely upon the statements and contentions heretofore submitted to us by the complainant Veerman in a parallel case pending before us (*Veerman v. German Federal Republic,*[1] No. 243). The complainants herein merely incorporate by reference Mr. Veerman's submission of August 9, 1957. The same attorney represents the complainants in both actions, and the application for interim protection relates to alleged acts of intimidation against him.

" The Commission has already rendered its decision upon the application for interim protection in the *Veerman* case, upon which the instant application wholly rests. (See *Veerman v. German Federal Republic,* No. 243, Decision of October 28, 1957.)

" In response to the complainants' application for interim protection here, the defendant filed its answer dated November 6, 1957. In reply thereto complainants have filed two further submissions dated November 8, 1957, and November 14, 1957, respectively. In the latter submission the complainants take note of the Commission's decision of October 28, 1957, in *Veerman v. Federal Republic;* and suggest that their most recent submission ' should have dispelled the doubts entertained by the Third Chamber of the Arbitral Commission as to the insufficiency of the evidence adduced in the *Veerman* case '. They then address themselves to lines of

[1 Reported above, p. 522.]

proof that might be adduced through certain witnesses designated in their papers to substantiate the allegations of intimidation asserted in the *Veerman* case regarding matters of fact that relate to the *Veerman* case. We cannot entertain an offer of proof by a litigant in regard to facts and allegations pertaining to another case pending before us.

" For these reasons the Arbitral Commission orders that the complainants' application for an order of inter improtection is denied."

[Report: *Decisions of the Arbitral Commission*, I (1958), Case No. 2, p. 121.]

# B—INTERNATIONAL COURT OF JUSTICE

## II.—Contentious Jurisdiction

### ii.—Procedure

**Disputes—International Court of Justice—Contentious jurisdiction —Procedure—Conclusions of parties—Legal effect of—Hague Convention of 1902 on Guardianship of Infants.**

See p. 242 (*Case concerning the Application of the Convention of 1902 Governing the Guardianship of Infants*), at pp. 259, 266, 276, 287.

### iii.—The Law Applicable

**Disputes—International Court of Justice—Contentious jurisdiction —Law applicable—Municipal law as determining content of public policy—Right of Court to examine—Hague Convention of 1902 on Guardianship of Infants.**

See p. 242 (*Case concerning the Application of the Convention of 1902 Governing the Guardianship of Infants*), at pp. 258, 268.

## C—CONCILIATION

**Conciliation—Conciliation Commissions—**

—Evidence before—Examination of certificate of nationality—Probative value of certificate in international law—Need for caution in absence of previous doubts as to nationality invoked—Review of validity of naturalization of ancestor on which claim to nationality *jus sanguinis* based—Refusal to examine circumstances and subsequent conduct of ancestor—Relevance of fact that ancestor not a party to proceedings—Review of statements made by claimant to passport or other authorities—Principle of " estoppel " or "*non concedit venire contra factum proprium*"—Rejection of doctrine—Rejection of evidence conflicting with public documents.

—Law applied by—Question of legal system applicable—Provisions of Peace Treaty as *lex fori*—Ouster of national law—Nationality—Claims—Examination of laws of naturalizing State —Examination of treaties—Question of supremacy of municipal law subsequent to treaty—Duty of Commission to give priority to international law.

—Right of investigation in questions of nationality.

See p. 91 (*Flegenheimer Claim*), at pp. 98–100, and 112 *et seq.*, 151.

Disputes—Conciliation—Procedure—Legal and factual elements in a dispute—Separation of these elements in pleadings, oral arguments and report of Conciliation Commission—Use of factual data from negotiations prior to conciliation—Italian-Swiss Permanent Conciliation Commission, 1956.

See p. 313 (*Re Application to Swiss Nationals of the Italian Special Capital Levy Duty*).

## F—MISCELLANEOUS

Disputes—International courts—Court of European Coal and Steel Community—Procedure—Withdrawal of plaintiff during proceedings—Whether consent of defendant required—Appeal for annulment—Costs of party withdrawing.

See p. 484 (*Wirtschaftsvereinigung Eisen- und Stahlindustrie and Others* v. *The High Authority*).

Disputes—International courts—Court of European Coal and Steel Community—Procedure—Power of Court to call for further information—Re-opening of oral proceedings.

See p. 417 (*Fédération Charbonnière de Belgique* v. *The High Authority* (*Interim Judgment*)).

**Disputes—International courts—Court of European Coal and Steel Community—Parties—Joinder of actions—Action by producers of iron and steel appealing against a general decision—Decision affecting each party differently—Whether common basis for joint action.**

See p. 484 (*Wirtschaftsvereinigung Eisen- und Stahlindustrie and Others* v. *The High Authority*).

**Disputes—International courts—Court of European Coal and Steel Community—Parties—Capacity to appear before Court—Associations of producers of iron or steel—European Coal and Steel Community Treaty, 1951, Articles 53, 48 and 80.**

See p. 490 (*Chambre Syndicale de la Sidérurgie Française* v. *The High Authority*) and p. 475 (*Société d'Électro-Chimie, d'Électro-Métallurgie et des Aciéries Électriques d'Ugire* v. *The High Authority*).

**Disputes—International courts—Court of European Coal and Steel Community—Pleadings—Introduction of new head of action in reply—Distinction between new head of action and new argument—Rules of Procedure, Article 38 (1).**

See p. 445 (*Compagnie des Hauts Fourneaux de Chasse* v. *The High Authority (No. 1)*).

**Disputes—International courts—Court of European Coal and Steel Community—Pleadings—Request—Form and content of—Whether reference to statement in request in similar action sufficient—Admissibility of grounds raised in reply but not in request.**

See p. 441 (*Société des Charbonnages de Beeringen and Others* v. *The High Authority*).

**Disputes—International courts—Court of European Coal and Steel Community—Costs.**

See p. 388 (*French Government* v. *The High Authority*).

**Disputes—International courts—Court of European Coal and Steel Community—Costs—Apportionment of.**

See p. 490 (*Chambre Syndicale de la Sidérurgie Française* v. *The High Authority*) and p. 475 (*Société d'Électro-Chimie, d'Électro-Métallurgie et des Aciéries Électriques d'Ugire* v. *The High Authority*).

## PART XI

# WAR AND NEUTRALITY

## A—WAR IN GENERAL

## V.—Effects of Outbreak of War

### iv.—On Enemy Subjects with regard to—

(b) THEIR PROPERTY AND OTHER RIGHTS

War—Effects of outbreak of—On enemy property—Placing of enemy property under custodianship—Whether admissible in international law.

See p. 341 (*Heidsieck & Cie* v. *German Federal Republic*).

War—Effects of outbreak of—On enemy property—German measures of 1940—Property of one's own subjects resident in enemy country—Treatment of such property by Germany—Discrimination against Jewish property.

See p. 335 (*Spanier* v. *German Federal Republic*).

## IX.—Prisoners of War

Prisoners of War—Geneva Convention of 1929—Article 23—Meaning and effect of—Modification by Detaining Power of pay of its own officers—Whether such modification applicable to prisoners of war—Family allowances—Whether covered by Article 23.

See p. 349 (*Zgainski* v. *German Federal Republic*), at pp. 355–356.

## XIII.—Effects of Treaties of Peace

### iv.—Miscellaneous

War—In general—Effects of treaties of peace—Analogous instruments—Convention on the Settlement of Matters Arising Out of the War and Occupation, 1952–1954—Restitution—Nationality of claimant.

See p. 534 (*Geyer* v. *German Federal Republic*).

# INDEX